UNDAUNTED ZEAL

To Ginny —
my companion in peace —

Womens Speaking

Juſtified, Proved and Allowed of by the SCRIPTURES,

All ſuch as ſpeak by the Spirit and Power of the Lord JESUS.

And how WOMEN were the firſt that preached the Tidings of the Reſurrection of *JESUS*, and were ſent by CHRIST's Own Command, before He aſcended to the Father, *John* 20.17.

And it ſhall come to paſs, in the laſt dayes, ſaith the Lord, I will pour out of my Spirit upon all Fleſh; your Sons and Daughters ſhall Propheſie, Acts 2.27. Joel 2.28.

It is written in the Prophets, They ſhall be all taught of God, ſaith Chriſt, John 6.45.

And all thy Children ſhall be taught of the Lord, and great ſhall be the Peace of thy Children. Iſa. 54.13.

And they ſhall teach no more every man his Neighbour, and every man his Brother, ſaying, Know the Lord; for they ſhall all know me, from the leaſt to the greateſt of them, ſaith the Lord. Jer. 31.34.

London, Printed in the Year, 1666.

Title Page of Margaret Fell's tract, Womens Speaking Justified, *written in 1666.*
(Reproduced with permission of the Religious Society of Friends in Britain.)

Undaunted Zeal

The Letters of Margaret Fell

Edited and Introduced by Elsa F. Glines

Foreword by Rosemary Moore

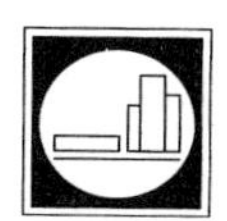

Friends United Press
Richmond, Indiana
www.fum.org

© Copyright 2003 Elsa F. Glines

All rights reserved

Printed in the United States of America
Published by Friends United Press
Richmond, Indiana 47374

Printed on acid-free paper by Cushing-Malloy, Inc.
Ann Arbor, Michigan

Cover and book design by Shari Pickett Veach

Cover photograph: Swarthmoor Hall. *Watercolor of exterior by Charlotte D. Pearson. Original in Friends House, London. (Reproduced with permission of the Religious Society of Friends in Britain.) Swarthmoor Hall is now owned by Britain Yearly Meeting of the Religious Society of Friends, and is used for Quaker retreats and workshops.*

Library of Congress Cataloging-in-Publication Data

Fox, Margaret Askew Fell, 1614–1702.
Undaunted zeal: the letters of Margaret Fell / edited and introduced by Elsa F. Glines; foreword by Rosemary Moore.
p. cm.
Includes bibliographical references and index.
ISBN 0-944350-64-X (alk. paper)
1. Fox, Margaret Askew Fell, 1614–1702-Correspondence. 2. Quakers-Great Britain-Correspondence. I. Glines, Elsa F., 1930– II. Title.

BX7795.F75A4 2003
289.6'092-dc21
[B]

2003051376

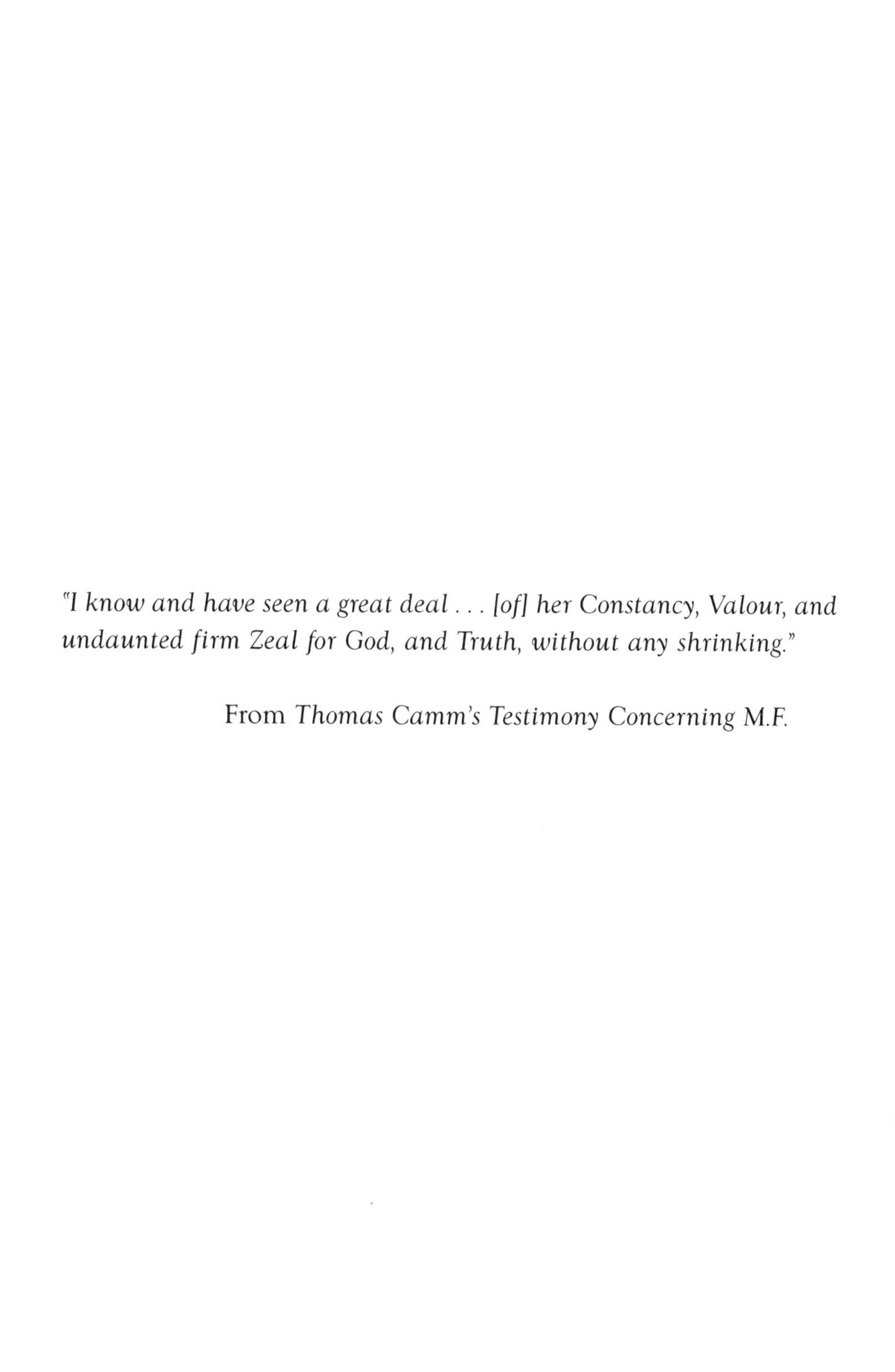

"I know and have seen a great deal . . . [of] her Constancy, Valour, and undaunted firm Zeal for God, and Truth, without any shrinking."

From *Thomas Camm's Testimony Concerning* M.F.

Contents

Foreword

The arrival of *Undaunted Zeal: The Letters of Margaret Fell* marks the first publication of a complete corpus of early Quaker letters. Much of the recent work in the field of early Quaker studies has been based on the pamphlet literature of the time, a vast field in itself, but the huge mass of early Quaker manuscripts has never been fully explored. The first Quakers were great letter-writers, and a surprising amount of their correspondence has survived, but it is not readily accessible. Most of the collections have been listed, and some have been partly or wholly transcribed, but only by hand or typewriter, so that they are not conveniently available to enquirers. Some of Isaac Penington's letters are reproduced in the new edition of his works, and there are a few letters included in Hugh Barbour's and Arthur Roberts's *Early Quaker Writings.* Old Meetinghouse libraries may have a copy of the nineteenth-century *Letters of Early Friends,* edited by A. R. Barclay, and the Friends Historical Society has from time to time published other letters in its journal and supplements. All these merely serve to whet the appetite. To investigate further, the Quaker letters must be accessed by microfilm, where available, or by visiting the libraries where they are preserved, most of them being in Friends House, London. *Undaunted Zeal* moves Quaker studies into a new dimension appropriate for the new millennium.
Therefore I was delighted, and flattered, to be asked to write a foreword for this volume. It was August 1993 when I first heard of the project. I received a letter from Elsa Glines, then unknown to me, asking for a copy of a recent paper of mine on the reliability of the sources available for the study of early Quakerism. She thought that it might be useful in connection with her own plan, which was to produce an edition of the letters of Margaret Fell, "making it as complete and faithful to the original as possible." She wrote to me that, "transcribing from microfilm is very hard on the eyes, but it seems worth doing. I *like* Margaret Fell, even if she was cantankerous. The Biblical language is wonderful."

Afterwards, I got to know Elsa when she was in London, checking the original manuscripts in Friends House Library. When I needed to refer to Margaret Fell's letters in connection with my own work on early Quakers, she very generously sent me copies of several of her own transcriptions. From time to time we made enquiries of each other as to the progress of our work. My book eventually found a publisher, and, not having heard from Elsa for a while, I hoped that she was having equal good fortune.

Now, thanks to the good sense of the Friends United Press, we see the result of this long labour of love. This is a mighty work of scholarship, much more than just a compendium of letters. The informative introductory essays set the scene for each historical period, while every letter is preceded by a summary elucidating difficulties, giving full biographical details about the individuals addressed or mentioned, and cross-referencing to secondary material. If readers who are not seventeenth-century experts find the letters alarming at first glance, because of Elsa's scholarly decision to retain the original spelling of Margaret Fell's amanuenses, they should not be put off. With a little practice and persistence the style becomes familiar, and the volume is certainly more valuable to serious scholars in this form.

There is material here for anyone interested in women's history, Quaker history, or the history of the seventeenth century in any aspect. And there is Margaret Fell herself, cantankerous indeed on occasion, a great family matriarch, the power behind George Fox and James Nayler in the first days of Quakerism, obstinate and defiant in her trial and imprisonment, exemplar and supporter of women's part in the Quaker Meetings, and a voice of authority among Quakers to the end of the century. It is good that her authentic voice is now being heard.

Rosemary Moore

Acknowledgments

I wish to thank the many people who have helped in the writing of this book. I owe thanks for the Henry J. Cadbury Scholarship, which permitted a year of study at Pendle Hill in Wallingford, Pennsylvania. The staffs at numerous libraries have generously provided guidance and access to their collections, particularly the Friends House Library, London; Friends Historical Library, Swarthmore College; Haverford College Quaker Collection; and California State University Library, Hayward. Thanks also to the Historical Society of Pennsylvania; the Henry Ransom Humanities Research Center; the University of Texas at Austin; the Public Record Office, London; the Nottinghamshire Archives; and the Lancashire County Record Office, Preston.

I can mention only a few of the many friends who have encouraged me in various ways, some by lending rare books: Susan V. Hartshorne, Bruce Folsom, and Robert Levering; Larry Ingle who lent microfilm as well as giving advice; Steve Wolgast, who patiently helped a technophobic writer; Carol Mosher, who regularly asked how the work was progressing; and other friends who kindly listened to me expound on Margaret Fell and seventeenth-century Quakers. Thanks to all of them, and special thanks to the Friends of Strawberry Creek Meeting, Berkeley, California, and to my daughter, Melinda Glines, for years of interest and expectation.

Terry Wallace, author of *A Sincere and Constant Love, An Introduction to the Work of Margaret Fell*, and Thomas Hamm, Archivist and Professor of History, Earlham College, have carefully read and commented on the manuscript, and their help has been invaluable. I feel fortunate that Barbara Mays, editor of the Friends United Press, was brave enough to undertake the massive task of producing this volume. She gently and graciously saw me through the process, and I am grateful to her.

Introduction

"As to Margaret Fell, it is certain that her contributions to the movement have not been adequately evaluated. Her endowments as an organizer and as inspired spiritual leader should be reassessed and more widely recognized."

Raymond Ayoub and David Roeltgen
Quaker History, v. 87, no. 2, p. 49 (1998)

"Quaker historiography is, of course, replete with women figures, but it is also clear that male Friends found ways to maintain their control of instruments of power despite resourceful women. Unfortunately the tendency to celebrate women's achievements has not been matched by the kind of critical study that would reveal the concrete reach of these advances, or more significant, continuing male control."

Larry Ingle, *JFHS*, v. 58, no. 1, p. 8 (1997)

Margaret Fell's Place in History

Margaret Fell was one of the most important of these Quaker women figures, and it is important to let her voice be heard as it was, in all of its various tones: pastoral, consoling, angry, disputatious, explaining, explicating, pleading for justice, and rejoicing in her faith.

Margaret Fell was an extraordinary and attractive woman who played a major role in the development of Quakerism in the seventeenth century. Bonnelyn Young Kunze, one of her biographers, describes her as "an authoritative female public minister in a radical religious movement" (p. 1) whose "way of life was, in part, similar to many religiously motivated landed women of her era. At the same time her experiences as a literate, independent, wealthy, and widely traveled religious leader place her among a tiny minority of women who may claim some degree of historical influence" (p. 3).

Her accomplishments include: being a most important, if not the principal, organizer of the loose movement that became Quakerism, the Religious Society of Friends; promoting and establishing Women's Meetings; asserting the validity of women's right to preach; writing the first declaration of the Quaker peace principle; writing numerous letters to Friends and to non-Friends explaining Quaker principles; and being the first among Quaker leaders to write to the Jews. Kunze writes: "She not only wrote prophetic tracts and important pastoral epistles to Friends throughout England and beyond the seas, she was also one of the chief controversialists for early Quakerism" (p. 7).

There are several biographies of Margaret Fell, but little of her own writings are available. Most of the pamphlets that were published in her lifetime have long been out of print, and there has never been an edition of her letters.

Recent historians acknowledge that Margaret Fell's role, like that of women in general, has been underplayed, and they are attempting to rectify the error. Sara Heller Mendelson writes, "Those who advocate the historical reconstruction of past communities confess that the sources permit them to reconstruct only the male half of the population" (*Mental World of Stuart Women*, p. 3). And Rosemary Radford Ruether points out that "seventeenth-century England is notable for the large number of writings by women and men who challenge women's subordination in religion. Both Christian religious historians and English social historians have, as yet, paid insufficient attention to the enormous number of women's writings in this period. . . . There is still much work to be done to make the broad range of seventeenth-century English women's religious writings accessible and especially to study the relationship of religion and feminism in their thought" (pp. 1–2).

THE LETTERS

More than five hundred letters to Margaret Fell exist (Nuttall, Greaves, 1:273), and much of the history of the beginning of the Quaker movement is based on these letters. Until now, however, her letters have not been published, except for a few in her *Works*, published in 1710, some in the *Journal of the Friends Historical Society*, and a few in the biographies. Of these letters some are complete, but more have been excerpted to fit the needs of the writer. Frequently they have been heavily edited.

This collection is the first to include all of her known letters, one hundred sixty-four of them; two additional letters by her daughters are included. The fact that there are so many more written to her is an indication that many others have been lost. Nevertheless this is an unusually large body of work by a women to have survived and would be a treasure even if Margaret Fell were not such an influential figure. The collection will, I hope, be of use to students of history and religion, for women's studies, and for the understanding of early Quakerism. They may also be enjoyed as a gateway to understanding the life and faith of a person who could use words and ideas with great facility.

CONTENT OF THE LETTERS

Margaret Fell was unusually intelligent, educated, and capable of commitment to a cause, all characteristics that are evident in her correspondence. Margaret J. Ezell, in her provocative study *The Patriarch's Wife, Literary Evidence and the History of the Family*, points out that "There is an obvious distinction between domestic letters concerned with a family's health and happiness and an 'epistle' or essay in letter form on an intellectual or literary topic which was directed outside the immediate family circle. . . . An interesting feature of this period's correspondence is the quantity that has been preserved, not only in the original letters, but also in letter books and transcribed copies. Such practices argue that correspondence of a certain type was viewed not as a discreet communication between two people only, but a formal composition to be preserved and perused by others as well" (p. 73). Many of Margaret Fell's letters meet this definition of "epistle," including their being carefully copied before being posted, as well as the occasional postscript reading, "Let this be copied over & sent."

The letters are arranged chronologically. It might have been useful to arrange them by subject, but unfortunately too many of them cover several topics.

They can be loosely divided into four categories: 1. Letters to family and friends; 2. Letters of petition to those in authority; 3. Polemics, in which she argues or tries to persuade non-Quakers or anti-Quakers of the truth of Quakerism; and 4. Pastoral epistles, either to an individual or to Friends Meetings.

Letters to family and friends include numerous letters to her daughters, particularly while she was in London; to George Fox, William Penn, Will Caton, and other traveling Friends; to her son and sons-in-law; and others with whom she had a personal relationship. She relayed information from correspondence that she received from all parts of England to those who were traveling or lived in different places.

The letters of petition include five to Oliver Cromwell; nineteen to King Charles II; two early letters (1653) to John Sawrey, a local justice; one to the lord mayor of London; and numerous others. They usually concerned Quakers in prison or unjustly fined (including herself).

The polemics are explanations of Quaker principles and theological beliefs. They are frequently written to ministers or "hireling priests" who have preached or written against Quakers. Some are answers to particular charges and arguments.

The pastoral letters or epistles are sometimes addressed to individuals and sometimes to Friends in a particular area. As in the polemics, she explains

Quaker principles and doctrines, often using biblical references, but the tone to Friends or to those who might become Friends is noticeably warmer. They are letters of encouragement and comfort, and there are many testimonies to the importance that these letters played in the lives of the recipients.

LANGUAGE

The language of the 1600s at first seems awkward and strange in the twenty-first century. The vocabulary, syntax, long, convoluted clauses, and the sentences running on for many lines are so different. But with familiarity the language becomes rich and expressive.

Margaret Fell wrote like her contemporaries. The King James version of the Bible was published three years before her birth, and it, and language like it, is reflected in all that she wrote. The letters are full of rhetorical flourishes, like this to Jeffrey Elletson: "Therefore repent & turne to the Lord, for a day of Lamentation & howling & woe & misery is coming upon thee & all thy gospell ministers as thou calls them" (Letter 50).

Although her expressions and her style are her own, still she fits clearly into the mode of seventeenth-century correspondents. More particularly, her writing is like that of Puritan and sectarian writers, with some expressions that are peculiar to Quakers.

The strong bonds of affection among this first generation of Friends are reflected in their language. Margaret writes: "Deare heart, my deare love in the lord Jesus Christ is to thee" and "My dearely beloved" (Letter 4); "And veryly my love to thee is inexpressable Neither can pen write. . . . Truly my love runs forth to thee exceedingly" (Letter 41).

Similarly John Stubbs, in a letter of 20 September 1656 writes, "oh, oh, dear Margaret, I and thousands are refreshed in thy bowels, and truly under thy shadow there is delight" (Nuttall, p. 201).

Walter Summers writes. "Deare deare dearly beloved . . . who art . . . the blessed of the lord . . . with thy travell [travail] I have Found deliverance & have as it were sate on thy knee & been suckled at thy breast." Norman Penney comments on this passage: "for extravagance of language, [this letter] can hardly be beaten, even in a time of freeness in the use of terms of endearment" (*CJ*, 2:480).

This language is significant as an indication of the warmth and feelings for each other that these often beleagured co-religionists had for each other. The emotional bonds would have been a strengthening factor that enabled them to endure the hardships they suffered.

There are also instances in vocabulary where usage has changed over the centuries. The use of the word *bowels*, for example, is somewhat of a shock until one realizes that it means "the seat of the tender and compassionate emotions, pity, compassion, feeling, heart" (*OED*). I will attempt to explain some of these words as they appear.

There have been useful studies of Quaker rhetoric, particularly Richard Bauman's *Let Your Words Be Few, Symbolism of Speaking and Silence Among Seventeenth-Century Quakers.* He discusses Margaret Fell's writings as an example, pointing out, among other things, that the repetition in her prose indicates the oral nature of her writing. In making a speech or a sermon, repetition of phrases and ideas enhances and may be necessary to convey meaning. Many of her letters were probably dictated to scribes, her daughters and others. The epistles to Friends particularly have a quality that is more effective if they are read aloud.

Her letters are replete with biblical quotations. It was still considered a way to godliness to be able to read scripture. Members of both establishment and sectarian churches, clergy and laymen alike, read, studied, quoted, and analyzed biblical passages. Margaret Fell, like George Fox, seems to have known the Bible by heart, and it was so much a part of her normal thinking and speaking that most of her writing is sprinkled with biblical phrases. When quoting, she was probably relying on her memory, rather than checking the Bible, because the quotations are often paraphrases or slightly different from the actual words. I have attempted to identify biblical references.

Her use of biblical quotations demonstrates a thorough knowledge of the context of the passage. Knowing this context, as many of her contemporaries did, adds depth to the meaning of her statements.

SOURCES OF LETTERS

The source of most of Margaret Fell's letters is the magnificent collection of manuscripts held at the Friends House Library, London, many of which have been microfilmed. One particular manuscript, "Spence Manuscript, volume 3," has over one hundred of her letters. Many of these are copies made at the same time the original was dispatched to the recipient.

Someone decided which of her letters to retain. It may have been Margaret herself, or George Fox, or other persons. Many of the letters are "endorsed," that is to say, someone has identified, often on the verso of the letter, the writer, the recipient, and the date. George Fox's handwriting is unique and easily recognized, and I have noted his endorsements.

Some letters are included in other manuscripts at the Friends House Library, Thirnbeck, Gibson, etc. Some are inserted in "Boxes" or "Portfolios." Other institutions that hold one or more of her letters include the London Public Record Office, the Pennsylvania Historical Society, Haverford College, Swarthmore College, and the University of Texas at Austin.

A number of letters, particularly the pastoral epistles to Friends, are available only in her *Works.* These were edited according to seventeenth-century standards. Most likely any passages considered personal were deleted.

Another source has been the very careful transcriptions published in the *Journal of the Friends Historical Society.*

For each letter I have noted the source that I used and the endorsements, if any. When two copies exist, my assumption has been that the manuscript at the Friends House Library contains the earlier version and thus is closer to Margaret Fell's original words. This may not always be the case. It seems likely that sometimes that copy is a draft, and a later version was the one that was actually sent. In a number of instances, there are several copies of a given letter that seem to be contemporary, and it is remarkable how similar they are. Most scribes were evidently careful when they made their copies.

It is also possible that there are other unknown letters in people's attics or in institutions that I did not contact. I would be grateful to be notified of such.

EDITORIAL POLICY

I have given a great deal of thought to the best method of presenting the letters. My goal is twofold: firstly, to publish the letters so accurately and carefully that scholars will know that they have Margaret Fell's exact and complete words (subject to any errors I have made); and secondly, to make the letters available to the general reader with an interest in going to the source and a willingness to do so. These goals are incompatible to the extent that the scholar may wish to preserve every y (y=th) and abbreviation, whereas these will be obstacles to the general reader.

A printed letter can never exactly duplicate the handwritten version, and compromise is inevitable. For these letters, the compromise has been made somewhat easier because of knowing that very few of them are actually in Margaret Fell's hand. Most of them are copies, probably made before the original was sent, written by her secretaries, her daughters, and others acting as amanuenses. The letters, therefore, include numerous individuals' versions of how to write particular words and do not necessarily represent Margaret Fell's way of writing.

Craig Horle, the editor of the *Records of the Courts of Sussex County of Delaware 1677–1710* writes: "Any editor of early colonial records is immediately struck with the problem of retaining the integrity of the original while promoting readability. The task is made more difficult by the fact that the shortage and high cost of paper and ink, combined with the need to save time for letterbook copies . . . had resulted in the use of tildes [˜], thorns [y] . . . and abbreviations. In addition, the seventeenth century was an evolutionary period for spelling, punctuation, and capitalization. There was very little consistency, even in the work of the same clerk" (p. 25).

With the goals of accuracy and clarity, I have used the following procedure: The thorn (y) is written as *th*. For example, *ye* = the; *yt* = that; *ym* = them.

u and *v*, which were interchangeable, are written as they would be in modern English, e.g. *loue* = love; *liueing* = liveing.

i and *j*, also interchangeable at that time, are written as our contemporaries do. Examples are: *iust* = just; *ioy* = joy.

Words that include the *p*, which can represent *par, per, por, pre, pur, pro,* are spelled out; e.g., *pish* = perish or parish, *psecutor* = persecutor.

The most common abbreviations are spelled out. This includes:

agt = against
con = tion (as in condition, foundation)
or = our (as in our, your)
mt = ment (as in judgment, testament)
r = er
wch = which
wt = what
ye = the, they, thy
ym = them
yt = that
yu = you

When a tilde (˜) is used to indicate a double letter, I have simply written the double letter.

All other words are spelled according to the source, with the modern spelling following in brackets when it seems necessary. It is not unusual for the same word to be spelled two or three ways, even within the same letter. Multiple spellings may occasionally cause confusion, but part of the joy of reading original documents is to see how words were written at the time. In cases of doubt as to the meaning of a word, it is helpful to pronounce it out loud; this often resolves the doubt.

Capitalization follows the original, and thus is very different from modern prose. Words that we capitalize, like *God*, *Jesus Christ*, and other proper nouns, may not be capitalized; and alternatively, ordinary nouns and occasionally adjectives, may be capitalized, as the scribe sees fit. The page thus looks different from a modern text but is not, I believe, difficult to read. My aim has been to keep to the original when it is not misleading.

How to handle punctuation is a major problem. In these letters, periods are seldom used; commas and semicolons are used with great abandon; and sentences run on and on, often connected by *and* and *but*. In the interest of accuracy I have retained marks of punctuation and suggest to readers that they not take these marks too seriously. I have also added punctuation in brackets.

In the manuscripts, there are sometimes words or phrases, indicated by a caret [^], written above the line. Since these seem to be a copyist's corrections, rather than the author's afterthought, I have not indicated that they are superscriptions.

When I could not decipher a word or words, this is indicated by a blank space. If I felt confident enough to guess at a word, it is enclosed in brackets.

In some cases words have been crossed out. These seem to be scribal errors that do not affect the meaning of the sentence. I have omitted these, except in the rare case where it seems to indicate the correction of a thought.

Another difficulty is the question of the date of a letter. Very often the only visible date is not on the letter itself but is an "endorsement" on the verso. Many of these endorsements are by George Fox. Others may be by the scribe of the particular copy or by some other person. Craig Horle's work on the "Spence Manuscript Index" has been an invaluable help with those letters. Sometimes the contents can be used to date a letter.

In the seventeenth century, England still used the Julian calendar, which begins the new year on March 25. Most dates are therefore two months off, according to current usage. In the heading of each letter I have given the date in modern terms, but in the body of the letter the date remains as written.

At the end of each letter I have indicated the source; and any endorsement is given, exactly as written, within quotation marks. In the annotations preceding each letter, I have identified most of the individuals to whom Margaret Fell wrote or whom she mentions. I was unable to identify a few individuals.

There may be errors in reading particular words. Fading ink, browning paper, and even tears make this all too possible. I would appreciate hearing from readers who question particular words or phrases.

ABBREVIATIONS OF FREQUENTLY CITED WORKS

Besse—Joseph Besse. A *Collection of the Sufferings of the People Called Quakers . . . from 1650–1689*. 2 vols. London: Luke Hinde, 1753.

BQ—William C. Braithwaite. *The Beginnings of Quakerism*. 2nd ed. Revised by Henry J. Cadbury. York: William Sessions Ltd., 1981.

Braithwaite—William C. Braithwaite. *The Second Period of Quakerism*. 2nd ed. Prepared by Henry J. Cadbury. York: William Sessions Ltd., 1979.

CJ—George Fox. *The Journal of George Fox*. Edited by Norman Penney. 2 vols. Cambridge: Cambridge University Press, 1911.

Crosfield—Helen G. Crosfield. *Margaret Fox of Swarthmoor Hall*. London: Headley Brothers, 1913.

DAB—*Dictionary of American Biography*.

DNB—*Dictionary of National Biography*.

EQW—Hugh Barbour and Arthur Roberts, eds. *Early Quaker Writings, 1650–1700*. Grand Rapids, Mich.: William B. Eerdmans, 1973.

Fox.Short.—George Fox. *The Short Journal and Itinerary Journals of George Fox*. Edited by Norman Penney. Cambridge: Cambridge University Press, 1925.

FPT—Norman Penney, ed. *The First Publishers of Truth*. London: Headley Brothers, 1907.

Greaves—Richard L. Greaves and Robert Zaller, eds. *Biographical Dictionary of British Radicals in the Seventeenth Century*. 3 vols. Brighton: Harvester Press, 1982–84.

Horle—Craig Horle. "Index to Spence MSS, vol. 3." (unpublished typescript) London: Friends House Library.

Horle, *Q.&EngLegalSys*—Craig Horle. *The Quakers and the English Legal System, 1660–1688*. Philadelphia: University of Pennsylvania Press, 1988.

JFHS— *Journal of the Friends Historical Society*.

Kunze—Bonnelyn Young Kunze. *Margaret Fell and the Rise of Quakerism*. Stanford: Stanford University Press, 1994.

PWP—Penn, William. *The Papers of William Penn*, Edited by Mary Dunn and Richard S. Dunn (and others). 5 vols. Philadelphia: University of Pennsylvania Press, 1981–1986.

Ross—Isabel Ross. *Margaret Fell, Mother of Quakerism*. 2nd ed. York: William Sessions Book Trust, 1984.

Spence—"Spence MSS, vol. 3." London: Friends House Library.

Webb—Maria Webb. *The Fells of Swarthmoor Hall and Their Friends*. 2nd ed. London: F. Bowyer Kitto, 1867.

Works—Margaret Fell. A *Brief Collection of Remarkable Passages and Occurrences Relating to the Birth, Education, Life, Conversion, Travels, Services and Deep Sufferings of that Ancient and Faithful Servant of the Lord, Margaret Fell, but by Her Second Marriage, M. Fox*. London: J. Soule, 1710.

Part I

Margaret Fell and the Birth of a Movement, 1652–1658

Deare Husband

my deare love and tender desires to the lord runs forth for thee I have received a letter this day from you I am very glad that ye lord carry[ed] you ... your journey soe prosperously ...

[illegible]

Swarthmore the ... ffeb: 1652

To Judge Thomas Fell, February 18, 1653. See page 17.
(Reproduced with permission of the Religious Society of Friends in Britain.)

Chronology Through 1658

1598	Birth of (Judge) Thomas Fell
1603	Death of Queen Elizabeth I; Accession of King James I
1614	Birth of Margaret Askew at Marsh Grange
1616	Death of William Shakespeare
1624	Birth of George Fox
1625	Accession of King Charles I
1632	Marriage of Thomas Fell and Margaret Askew
ca. 1633	Birth of Margaret Fell, Jr.
ca. 1635	Birth of Bridget Fell
ca. 1637	Birth of Isabel Fell
ca. 1638	Birth of George Fell
1642–1651	Civil Wars
1642	Birth of Sarah Fell
1647	Birth of Mary Fell
1649	Execution of King Charles I
1659	Birth of Susannah Fell
1652	George Fox first comes to Swarthmoor
	Margaret Fell's conversion to Quakerism
1653–1658	Oliver Cromwell Lord Protector of England
1653	Birth of Rachel Fell
1654	Margaret Fell, with the help of George Taylor and Thomas Willan, establishes the Kendal Fund to aid traveling ministers and their families
1656	Margaret Fell writes *To Manasseh-ben-Israel*
1657	Margaret Fell writes *A Loving Salutation*
Sept. 1658	Death of Oliver Cromwell
Oct. 1658	Death of Thomas Fell

Brief Biography and Convincement by George Fox

Margaret Fell Fox was born Margaret Askew (1614) at Marsh Grange, Dalton-in-Furness, Lancashire, the daughter of John Askew, a gentleman. We know nothing of her education except that she was highly literate and articulate. She married Thomas Fell of Swarthmoor Hall, Ulverston, before she was eighteen. He was lord of the manor of Ulverston and held many offices during his lifetime, including that of vice-chancellor of the duchy of Lancashire and judge of Assize for the Chester and North Wales District. He was elected to Parliament in 1645 and "was a prominent Commonwealth political and legal figure in Lancashire" (Greaves, 1:273). They had eight children who lived to adulthood, one son and seven daughters, an unusual record in a century with high mortality rates.

As the mistress of a large household, which not only included a husband and children, but also secretaries, tutors, servants, and managers of the farms and related industries, Margaret Fell had large scope for her intelligence and administrative ability. Her husband, Judge Fell, was often away from home for weeks at a time on the Welsh circuit, and she was responsible for the household. Seventeenth-century women of the gentry, unlike Victorians, were busy providing food and clothing, dispensing medicine, and keeping household accounts. Especially in the rural areas, remote from London, families had to be self-sufficient. It was good training for the leadership that she later provided in Friends' activities.

In religion the Fells were Independents (Puritans) and attended the parish church in Ulverston. They were known for their hospitality, and traveling ministers were welcome at their home. In 1652, when Margaret was thirty-eight, George Fox, the charismatic preacher, came to Swarthmoor Hall, expounding his radical message.

The following are the important principles of the early Quaker message.

It was based on the belief that the spirit of God and Christ is available to all men, women, and children. "We are all one in Christ." This was an egalitarian message that was threatening to the established order, a hierarchical society.

The experience of God was not to be mediated by priests but was available by looking inward. The true church was not buildings and institutions but the people living under the guidance of the spirit of Christ.

The attitude to sin was significantly different from that of the Puritans. Quakers did not emphasize sin and evil, although they recognized that one function of the Light is to illuminate one's sins and faults. The experience of the Light could be painful as well as nurturing. Right action was best discerned through the inward conscience by attention to the Presence of God and through the wisdom of a community gathered in the Light. The latter distinguished Quakers from Ranters, a contemporary sect which went to extreme measures in allowing all behavior that felt right to the individual.

Quakers were thoroughly versed in and used the Bible, but they believed in continuing revelation, that scripture must be interpreted according to changing context and with spiritual insight.

In her *Works*, Margaret Fell writes that she had been a "seeker after truth" for twenty years. She was immediately convinced by the doctrine that George Fox preached and knew that she had finally found the right way. For the rest of her long life she devoted herself to living and furthering the cause of that doctrine.

Kunze writes: "Margaret Fell's home was a haven for George Fox, a clearing house for Quaker correspondence, and an important center for the organizational activities of men and women in the rise of Quakerism" (p. 143). Swarthmoor Hall was an invigorating and warm environment. There are numerous testimonies to the hospitality the Fell family provided to visitors and friends. The seven daughters all became enthusiastic followers of George Fox and Quaker principles.

Judge Fell never became a Quaker, but he allowed Swarthmoor Hall to be used for religious silent Meetings every Sunday from the first week that he met George Fox. At Meeting there was no prepared sermon, and men and women spoke only when they felt impelled to do so. Judge Fell was the friend of numerous Friends, giving legal advice and support. As long as he lived his status and political connections protected Margaret from the persecution many Quakers endured. Judge Fell died in 1658, and after that Margaret was liable to the same pressures other dissenters experienced.

The Cromwellian Era: Politics and Religion

The 1640s were the period of the English Civil Wars, struggles that had many political, economic, and religious elements. On one side of the conflict were the monarchy and the church, with a king who claimed to rule by divine right and with a church governed by an episcopal hierarchy. On the other was Parliament, which controlled the right to tax, and whose members were largely Puritan in religion, either Presbyterian or Independent. After a series of battles in England and Scotland, Parliament and the New Model Army under Oliver Cromwell's leadership won the Civil Wars, which ended in 1651 with the battle of Worcester. The king, Charles I, was executed in 1649.

A Commonwealth was set up by Parliament, without a king or House of Lords, and in 1653, a Protectorate, with Cromwell as Lord Protector. He ruled like a monarch until his death in 1658. The beheading of Charles I was seen by Oliver Cromwell and his followers as the ending of tyranny, but to others, particularly the wealthy, it was seen as anarchy and the end of good order in society. Anglican clergy were removed from office and replaced by those with a Puritan, Calvinist theology, opposed to the rituals and institutions of the established church.

This change created a climate of freedom for dissenters of all varieties. Nonconformists could preach and write and publish as never before, and they did. Religion was a burning concern. Small groups formed: Ranters, Levellers, Diggers, Quakers, and others. Each sect had its own philosophy and customs. The Ranters were particularly disturbing to those in authority, both for their outrageous personal behavior and for their egalitarianism, which challenged the social structure.

The Quaker movement grew from a small number of men and women in the north of England. George Fox, James Nayler, John Stubbs, and other gifted preachers traveled and found groups of seekers who eagerly welcomed the Quaker message. Meetings were set up, with frequent contact between them; and between 1650 and 1660 the movement grew to an estimated thirty or forty thousand (*BQ*, p. 512; Greaves, *Deliver*, p. 11).

As Quakers increased in numbers they aroused fear. Two pillars of society had been attacked: the monarchy was gone and the Anglican Church, as it had been since the Tudors, was endangered. Quakers and other dissenting sects protested against the injustices of society. They also protested against tithes and abuses of the church. They questioned the need for elaborate "steeplehouses" and for "hireling priests," as Quakers derisively called church buildings and their ministers. People were forced by law to pay tithes, and some of the anger of the anti-Quaker ministry was very likely due to fear of loss of income and employment should Quaker views prevail.

Although Cromwell initially had considerable sympathy for Quakers, some local officials continued to persecute nonconformists, enforcing and interpreting laws as it suited them. Many Quaker men and women spent time in prisons.

Quakers questioned many of the tenets of the church: the doctrine of the Trinity and sacraments, like baptism. It was an age of pamphleteering, and Quakers and non-Quakers alike wrote passionate defenses of their beliefs. There is an entire literature of anti-Quaker writing, with strong and violent protests. An example is: "The Quakers, that Spawn of Antichrist, & bain of all Religion, whose naturall tendence is to Subvert all religion, & to turn men into mere bruits. These Cry down all Sacraments as Carnall things, & so depice the Lords Supper . . . " (Tayler, E. 2:804).

By 1658, the year of the deaths of Cromwell and of Judge Fell, the scattered group of nonconformist preachers and seekers, coalescing around George Fox, and other "Publishers of Truth," had grown to a strong movement, with a center of communication at Swarthmoor Hall.

Margaret Fell's Letters

Margaret Fell's letters of this period include letters to friends and Friends, those with family connections, and to gatherings of Friends. She wrote to those in prison and to those who requested her help. She organized a fund to give aid to itinerant Friends and their families, the beginning of an important tradition. Her mission of petitioning for the rights of Quakers and for liberty of conscience began with letters to a local justice and to Oliver Cromwell. She wrote to explain Quaker principles and, if she was answering strong anti-Quaker charges, she used equally strong rhetoric.

List of Letters 1–76, 1652–1658 — Page

1 TO GEORGE FOX 1652

"We hope thou wilt not leave us Comfortlesse,
but wilt come againe, though that sorrow be for A time,
yet joy comes in the morning."

This first and most extravagant letter written to George Fox demonstrates several characteristic traits of the Margaret Fell correspondence, but it is also an anomaly. The characteristics include the biblical quotations and the fulsome praise. The term "nursing father" is illustrative of the Quaker's use of male and female imagery in nonconventional ways. It reflects the belief that in relation to God or Christ all men and women are the "weaker vessel" and can equally play the nurturing role.

The letter is a clear demonstration of the effect that George Fox had on Margaret Fell's family. It places him on a pedestal, close to a level with the divinity. It is to George Fox's credit that he did not encourage this adulation; he was the messenger and not the message itself. Though Margaret Fell was his disciple, as well as a friend, advisor, and later, his wife, she did not address him in this manner again.

Terry S. Wallace's analysis of the letter concludes that the enthusiastic exclamations are Margaret's direct transcription of her young daughters' reactions. The more measured latter portion is Margaret's own response (pp. 97–100).

The four children who wrote individual notes are age 3(?) (Susannah), 10 (Sarah), 12(?) (Isabel), and 5 (Mary). Thomas Salthouse was Judge Fell's steward; Will Caton was the companion of George Fell, the only son; Ann Clayton and Mary Askew were also members of the Swarthmoor household.

We do not know who the man was "who would not receive thee." There is speculation that it referred to Judge Fell, but George Fox's note saying that he "was not long after convinced" contradicts that notion, since Judge Fell never became a Friend. More likely it is Thomas Ayrey; see Letter 2.

for g f
Our dear Father in the Lord, for though wee have ten thousand Instructers in Christ, yet have we not many fathers for in Christ Jesus thou hast begotten us thorrow the Gospell [1 Cor. 4:15], eternall praises be to our father, wee thy babes with one consent being gathered together in the power of the spirit, thou being present with us[,] our souls doth thirst & languish after thee, & doth challenge that right that wee have in thee, oh thou bread of life, without which bread our soulls will starve, oh for ever more give us this bread & take pitty on us, whom thou hast nursed up with the brests [breasts] of consolation, oh our life our desires is to see thee againe that wee may be refreshed & established & soe have life more abundantly [John 10:10], & let not that beastly power which keepes us in bondage seperate thy bodyly presence from us, who reignes as King Above it, & would rejoyce to see thy kingly power here triumph over it, oh our dear nursing father [Num. 11:12], wee hope thou wilt not leave us Comfortlesse, but wilt come againe, though that sorrow be for A time, yet joy comes in the morning [Ps. 30:5], oh our life we hope to see thee againe, that our joy may be full, for in thy presence is fullnesse of joy, & where thou dwells is pleasures for evermore [Ps. 16:11], oh thou fountaine of eternall life our soulls thursts after thee [Ps. 63:1], for in thee alone is our life & peace, & without thee have we no peace, for our soulls is much refreshed by seeing thee, & our lifes is preserved by thee, O thou father of eternall felicytie,

O my dear Father when wilt thou come Susan Fell,
Dear Father pray for us Sarah Fell

oh my dear hart shall wee not see thee
once more againe Issabell Fell
Thou art the fountaine of life [Ps. 36:9] Mary Fell
Margrett Fell
Tho. Salthouse
Ann Cleaton
Mary Askew
Margrett Fell
Bridgett Fell
Will. Caton

My owne dear hart, though thou hast shaked the dust of thy foot, at him who would not receive thee, nor is not worthy of thee, which shalt be A testimony against him for ever, yet thou knowest that we have received thee into our harts, & shall live with thee eternally, & it is our life & joy to be with thee, And soe my dear hart [,] let not the power of darknesse separate thy bodyly presence from us, which will be A griefe and trouble to us, and especially thorrow him, whom thou knowes can call nothing his owne but the plagues & woes. My soull thirsts to have thee to come over, if it be but for two or three dayes[,] to strike downe the deceit in him for the truths sake./

And if thou doe not come, it will add abundantly to our sorrow, & strengthen the beastly power. I know it is A burden and suffering to thee, but thou hast borne our burdens & suffered for us & and with us, & now dear hart, doe not leave us nor forsake us, for life & peace is in thee./

M.F.

1652
[In George Fox's hand:]
this was sent to gF & he came back againe to thes that sent for him & he, that he shakd the dost [dust] of his feet against[,] was not long after convinsed

Spence 3/24–26. The three copies in Spence are evidently the original, p. 25, and two early photocopies. Addressed: "To G.F. Swarthmore." Endorsed: "MF & her childern to GF, 1652" by George Fox.

2 TO THOMAS AYREY 1652

"Therefore in love to thy soull I doe thee exhort."

Margaret felt confident of her ability to recognize right action or the lack of it, and this early letter, like many others, clearly demonstrates her forthrightness.

It is most likely that it was George Fox who sent for Thomas Ayrey. The Annual Catalogue *(Cadbury, pp. 210, 155H) quotes Fox, "Thomas Ayrey, I received thy paper in answer to mine, written to thee in which thou stands out in thy rebellion and disobedience." The* FPT *(pp. 266–267) has a full page about Thomas Ayrey who was evidently not like the numerous Friends who spent months and years of imprisonment for their beliefs: "Thomas Ayrey . . . Husbandman, & of a Considrable Estate in the world, was also Called to the worke of the Ministry, & had an Exelent gift given him of God, and was of great service for a time. And in the yeare 1654 . . . John Audland and the s[ai]d Tho: Ayrey [went] west wards through the edge of Walles . . . and to Plemouth, where this Tho: Ayrey begun to Fainte, and turned homeward, and left John Audland alone . . . And allthough he mostly held the profession of Truth in frequenting Freinds Meettings, yett a very weake & faithless man all his days after. Could suffer nothing for truth, for not sweareing, he truckled under, and tooke an oath."*

Tho: Ayrey I warn thee from the Lord God, beware as thou tendes thy owne soull & eternall peace, here thou disobeyes the Command of the lord in not goeing to him who sent for thee, which was the word of the lord to thee, & from the terrour of it, if thou doe not obey it[,] thou shalt never fly; therefore in love to thy soull I doe thee exhort, to bee obeydient to the lord god, & to that of him in thy conscience, by which thou shalt bee eternally saved or condemned, soe in obeydience to the Lord & his Command I doe thee againe exhort to goe over; to him, who sent for thee, least hee cast thee of [off] as an emptie vessell, which will not hold the pretious Liquor[;] and this the word of the lord to thee, whether thou wilt hear or forbear, which thou shalt eternally wittnesse.

Margret Fell

Spence 3/23. Addressed: "To Tho.Ayrey". Endorsed: "M.F. to T,Ayre, 1652,4".

3 To Justice John Sawrey 1652

"My father [i.e., God] hath made me willing to lye under any reproach, or scandle, for the truthes sake, and to make it my joy and crowne, that I should be found worthy to be partakere of his sufferinge, and I doe committ all unto him."

John Sawrey was a Puritan justice of the peace from Ulverston and a member of Parliament in 1653 (EQW, p. 609). He was present at George Fox's first appearance at the church in Ulverston and tried to prevent his speaking to the congregation (Nickalls, p. 115). Sawrey was one of several neighbors who were offended by the radical preachers who, in their view, departed from rational, acceptable behavior, and even worse, who led a leading citizen, like Margaret Fell, into perilous ways. He tried to persuade Judge Fell to prevent his wife from associating with the Quakers but to no avail. George Fox writes: "And then that envious Justice Sawrey he came to Swarthmore also . . . And Judge Fell for all their opposition, let the Meeting be kept at his house" (Nickalls, p. 119).

Margaret Fell was a woman of strong feeling who, once she was convinced of the truth of the Quaker message, threw herself heart and soul into the movement. With the protection of Judge Fell she did not face the legal consequences of her beliefs at this period of her life; but at a later time she proved that her willingness to "partake of suffering" was genuine.

We do not know how she was educated, but her writings show that she was well versed in the theological controversies of the day. The terminology and the biblical quotations are common to the tracts and sermons of the period. The language is strong, and she seems to take pleasure in exercising her gift for invective. There is, for example, the play on words, "the seed of the woman shall bruise the serpents head, examine and try whether the serpent be not head in thee."

One note that is repeated throughout her works is the difference between what is within and what is without. The stress is on the importance of the inward life, not on the outward profession of religion or on status. She has no respect for "professors" of religion or those who quote the scriptures without understanding or living the meaning of those scriptures.

To Justice Sawrey: a persecutor from M F: 1653

O Thou seeming professor, but rayally [really] A parsecutor of the truth of god, & A peearcer [piercer] of Jesus Christ which will be to thy utter Trying and destruction, except thou repent. it is hard for thee to kicke against the prickes; Thou hast bene A professor long of god and

Christ, and the letter without thee, but it is plainly manifested in thy life and practise, both in thy generall & particular calling, that there is no rayall possession of them within, examine thine actions truly in generall & thou shall find it soe. soe if thou can witnes one word of the scriptures, that thou hast talkt soe long on without thee, to be fullfilled within thee, the first word of the Gospell is; the seed of the woman shall bruise the serpents head [Gen. 3:15], examine and try whether the serpent be not head in thee, if thou wilt deal truly with thy owne heart, thou shalt find that thou art full of serpentine witt, serpentine suttilty, serpentine malicse, pride and revenge which is of the devill and that all thy pharisekel profession, and thy looking without thee, for other mens workes and experiences, speaking without thee, therein thou eats of the tree of knowledge, of good & evill, which the lord did forbide, thou shall find it soe, if ever thou came to know the truth to thy everlasting comfort, that thy teacher is within thee, and there is nothing thine, but what is fulfilled and witnesed in thee, and that thy looking out, to have it without thee drawes thee from thy teacher within, thou hase made many long prayers and great profession of the scripture without thee, but if ever thou come to know the truth, thou shalt find, that they were Caines sacrifieces, and that thou offered them up in the Carnish [carnal] nature, which never was nor never shall be accepted, but is an abomination to the lord, examine truly and Se [see] what fruits they have brought forth, looke into thy famely, and thou shall find them to be A famaly of lyers, tatlers, tale bearers, false accusers[,] incontinent, lovers of pleasures more then lovers of god, and if thou wilt deale truly in thy examination, thou shalt find that you are of the same profession that those jewes were, that Jesus Christ spoke too, which said they had Abraham for their father, and that they never were in bondage, but his answer was to them that they were of their father the devill, and the workes of their father they did doe. The devill is the father of lyes, and thy famyly practices much in that trade, lye away your profession for shame, for you have out runne it, it is manifested to the world what monster you serve, doe not accuse me falsely, as that I should write this to thee, in revenge of your executinge of your malice towards my childe, my friends and famyly, neither in revenge of your lyes, and scandles which you have raised of me[.] I deny any such occasion, my father hath made me willing to lye under any reproach, or scandle, for the truthes sake, and to make it my joy and crowne, that I should be found worthy to be partakere of his sufferinge, and I doe committ all unto him, who hath said vengence is mine and I will repay it [Rom 12:19]; I am moved of the lord to bid you repent and turne to the lord, and see what you possesse of him in your hearte, and if ever any of you come to know the truth of god in the power of it, yee shall wittnesse with me every word above written and say the same words, I charge thee keep this and if ever thou know the truth thou will owne it every word.

M F

Spence 3/144. "M:F:s Epistle to John Sawrey; caled a Just[ice] whoe was dronned [drowned] in a pudle soone after 1652"; " written over but uncompared".

4 To Colonel William West 1652

"If thou owned us, thou might suffer, which is greater riches then all the treasures of Egipt."

Colonel William West (1612–1670) was a friend of Thomas Fell and his family and, like Judge Fell and Anthony Pearson, was sympathetic to Quakers and had the power to help them. He was an attorney, had been a colonel in Cromwell's army, served in Parliament in 1653, 1659, and 1660, and became mayor of Lancaster in 1668–1669. In 1656 he proposed marriage to Margaret Fell, Jr. but was rejected (Letter 54).

He was arrested in 1661 at the rising of the Fifth Monarchy rebellion and then released. Although an Independent in religion and a republican politically in the 1650s, he later conformed to the Church of England and supported the Cavaliers (Kunze, p. 35; Henning, p. 691). Margaret Fell continued to count on his support even after Judge Fell's death and Col. West's changing politics (see Letter 132).

At the beginning of the movement, Margaret is trying to persuade Col. West to wholeheartedly join it. She is enthusiastic and hopeful, "the Exaltation of the lambe in this his day shall prosper." She begins the letter with "if thou owned us," i.e., if he acknowledged himself to be a Quaker, he might suffer but the reward would be great. She ends the letter saying that God "whom thou hath owned may owne & honour thee with his grace."

Deare heart my deare love in the lord Jesus Christ is to thee, which changes not but Indures forevermore, and as I tould thee before, if thou owned us, thou might suffer, which is greater riches then all the treasures of Egipt. And blessed bee of the lord for this his day of seperation [Heb. 11:26], & let thy soule and all that is within thee prayse the lord, that thou art sett on the right hand amongst his lambs, Tho: [though] nombered amongst transgressers, And counted as sheep for the slaughter, yet here is our glory and our crowne. that for the lambes testimony wee suffer, not for any evill they have against us, but our King shall reigne. And of his dominyon (and Government) there shall bee noe end, but the end of the wicked is destruction, and the beast & the false profett shall bee taken alive (and cast into the lake) [Rev. 19:20]

My dearely beloved waite in thy measur (but awhile) and thou shalt see what wilbe the end of there plotting and [confounding], who diggs deep to hide there counsell from the lord, but the day starr is riseing which makes them manifest, and the day is comming on which to them wilbee blackness and darkness, & the Exaltation of the lambe in this his day shall prosper and there covenant with hell & death shalbee broken [Isa. 28:18]; Lett patience posses thy soule and in thy measure waite which makes the seperation from them, and there Abominations, And the blessing of god thou wilt see upon thee for hee that confesseth mee before men, him will I confese before my father which is in heaven saith Christ [Matt. 10:32], soe the lord god of power & life, keepe thee Faithfull and true to thy measure, of him untill the end, and in the end, This I was moved of the lord to write to thee, soe god=all=mighty of life and power keepe thee, and preserve thee, that whom thou hath owned, may owne & honour thee with his grace./

Thy deare Friend
Mar: Fell

Gibson, MSS 1:109. Addressed: "To Collonell West". Endorsed: "M F to W West [George Fox] 1652"; "when G F was brought to tryall for his life to prests combined Against him at Lancst 1652".

5 To Judge Thomas Fell February 18, 1653

"Now I besech thee let them be printed
[that they] may openly appear to the world
what we live in and be not ashamed [of the] truth."

This letter to her husband is thought to be one of only two surviving letters in Margaret Fell's handwriting (see Letter 123). Thomas Fell (1598–1658), "a gentleman of ancient Lancashire family" was the owner of Swarthmoor Hall, a barrister, judge for the Chester and North Wales circuit, member of Parliament, vice-chancellor of the duchy of Lancaster, and holder of numerous other offices. He married Margaret Askew in 1632 when he was thirty-five and she not quite eighteen (DNB). In her memoir Margaret describes him: "He was much esteem'd in his Day by all sorts of people, for his Justice, Wisdom, Moderation, and Mercy, being a Terror to Evil-doers, and an Encourager of such as did well, and his many and great Services made his Death much lamented. We liv'd together twenty-six years, in which time, we had nine children. He was a tender loving Husband to me, and a tender Father to his Children, and one that sought after God in the best things." (Works, pp. 1–2)

Thomas Fell never became a Quaker, but he played a major role in protecting the growing movement. He allowed Friends to hold Meetings at Swarthmoor Hall, and it became a center for the zealous men and women who were spreading the message. Margaret Fell was not personally persecuted during his lifetime, and even after his death, as the widow of Thomas Fell she was accorded entrance to many in high places.

Judge Fell gave legal advice to George Fox and others. Like his peers, Gervase Benson, William West, and Anthony Pearson, who also served as justices in the district, he gave all possible latitude to the Quakers. This may be one reason why the movement was able to flourish in this part of England.

In the writings about Thomas and Margaret Fell there is considerable speculation about the degree of his interest in Quakerism. Was he truly a believer who did not join out of expediency? Was he trying to protect his wife by retaining his offices and positions? Or was he of a skeptical disposition who was not easily moved to extreme positions? As a leading Puritan in the district he may have leaned more toward reform of the existing church. Since he left no writings on the subject we may never know, but various incidental references show that he associated closely with numerous Quakers. William G. Bittle writes: "Fox and Nayler held a large Meeting with 'many precious Friends' among whom was Judge Fell, who attended in the company of Giles Calvert, one the principal publishers of Friends' books during the Commonwealth" (p. 78); and "Thomas Rawlinson, a north Lancashire Quaker who had . . . narrowly escaped arrest at Taunton when he and Judge Fell were traveling to Launceston" (p. 89).

Margaret sends news to her husband in London of happenings in the north. James Nayler was imprisoned at Appleby in January 1653 (Greaves, 2:257), and she notes that he has no fire and little to eat. George Fox is in danger of arrest. She sends a copy of a letter of Col. Benson's, another justice and a leading man of affairs in the north of England, who was sympathetic to Quakers (BQ, p. 92). The purpose of the letter, however, is to urge Judge Fell to aid Friends by presenting their case "to them that are in authority" and by getting various documents printed: "deare hart I pray thee doe not neglect" and "It is very hard that the priss should bee open for all pamflets and ballats [ballads] and must be shut against the truth." It is an indication of Judge Fell's involvement with Quakers.

18 xii 1652
Deare Husband

My deare love and tender desires to the lord runs forth for thee[.] I have receved a letter this day from you and ame very glad that the lord caryed you on your Jurney soe prosperously[.] thou wrot to me that those which professeth to worship god which profeshon wee doe deny without possesing the raile [real] substans[,] and if wee inJoy the Liveing power of the Lord and walke humbly with our god [Mic. 6:8] and be taught of him alone[,] there will be noe offense given unto man in whom the Lord ruleth[,] but the ofence will bee to that which must die and be crucifide and we are not to be in obedines to man that lives in [sin?]. deare harte[,] minde the lord above all with whom there is noe variablness nor shadow of turning [James 1:17] and who will overturne all powers that stands against him[; they?] shall be as chafe before him[.] therefore be faithful: unto death and he will give thee [the] Crowne of life [Rev. 2:10], and stand firme and close to the lord and bee not afraid of man[.] greater is hee that is in you then hee that is in the world: minde that which is of [life] in thy own perticular to keepe thee pure and cleare and single before him without [any?] end whatsoever, and that will stand before the fire of his wrath which burns up [all] but what is of himselfe[.] we sent to my deare Brother James Nailer and hee is kept very close and cannot be sufered to have any fire; hee is not free to eat of the Jelors [jailor's] meat, so they eat very littel but bread and water[.] hee wret to us that they are Ploting againe to get more false witnessis to sweare against him things that he never spoke. I sent him 20s [shillings] but hee took but 5[.] they are mighty violent in westmerland and all parts over everywhere towards us[.] they bid 15 [£] to any man that w[ould] take George [Fox] anywhere that they can find him within westmorland[.] I sent [thee] orders that cam from Coll [Colonel] Benson which should have beene at London ________ as sone [soon] as you but I am afraid they have miscaried[.] I send with them a c[opy] of a letter concerning some passages at the sesshons houlden at [Lanc]kester where Judge Thorpe was, and hee was very faverable to our fr[iends] there and did take notis of the priests tiranny: I shod [should] have beene glad you had received them[.] heare is a coppy of Corll Benson['s] letter that I have sent thee[, and] heare is a declaration that Corll. Benson and other frends drew[,] if the lord move any to present it to them that are in athoryty[;] and heare is a note that Georg was moved to rise out of bed and writ that should bee shewed to any in Parlament that is a frend to the truth[.] deare harte I pray thee doe not let it lay [at] thy dore but shew it to any that is anything loveing to the truth[.] it will stir up the pure in them which is one with that which it came fr[om.] heare is likewise a declaration of these things that we live in and a note concerning faith and the 2 seeds[,] the seed of the serpent and the seed of the w[oman,?] which should be put in print. now I beseche thee let them be printed [that they] may openly apeare to the world what we live in and be not ashamed [of the] truth[,] for it will stand when all other things shall be as stuble[,] so hopeing that thou will be faithfull to me and to the lord, farewell. [May] the everlasting god of power and love keepe thee up to himself ______ to his everlasting prayse and glory[.] The Children are all in health, praysed be the lord[.] George is not with us now but he remembere his deare love to thee[.] Heare is a note James Nailers hath put forth, I [pray] thee lett this and the other that concerns him which you had along with you be put in print in a booke[,] and the query and ansers that was put to George be printed and the prists petishon and John Lawsons be printed in another Booke. I much desire to have them printed[.] It is very hard that the priss should bee open for all pamflets and ballats [ballads] and must be shut against the truth. deare hert I pray thee doe not neglect[,] for I am sure if they be published they will worke for the glory of my father[,] to whom [be] prays and glory for evermore.

Thy dutiful wife till death,
Margaret Fell.

Swartmore this
Feb: 1652

I pray thee sweethart doe not slight these things for they are of great concernment, but let them be maid known, as they have beene acted openly, soe let them be published and [page cut]

Abraham MSS 1. Also in Ross, pp. 119–121. Endorsed: "M:F to thomas fell her husband 1652"; "Margt Fell to Tho Fell in 1652"; "These are written & Compared".

6 To Justice Anthony Pearson 1653

"My dear hart, waite upon the Lord in the light of god in thee."

Anthony Pearson (ca. 1626–1666) became an influential Quaker. He was the holder of many offices, including Judge advocate at Newcastle, clerk to Sir Arthur Haselrig, sequestration commissioner for county Durham, and justice of the peace for Cumberland and Westmorland. He was on the bench at James Nayler's trial in 1652, and it was there that he was attracted to Quakerism, having previously been an enemy. Shortly after he went to Swarthmoor Hall, and a letter of his says: "Oh! how gracious was the Lord to me in carrying me to judge Fell's, to see the wonder of His power and wisdom . . . I was so confounded, all my knowledge and wisdom became folly . . . I have been at Judge Fell's, and have been informed from that precious soul his consort, in some measure what those things mean, which before I counted the overflowinge of giddy brains . . . " [Fr. Lib. 11:327–328].

In this letter Margaret is encouraging him and expressing some of the basic themes of Quakerism, such as the light of God within each person and the seed as a metaphor for the potential of growing in a life with God. Pearson became an active Quaker, writing tracts, ministering, and using his considerable influence with Oliver Cromwell, Sir Henry Vane, and other prominent persons. Toward the end of his life he gradually moved away from Quakers and returned to the Anglican church.

As usual in her correspondence, along with the pastoral message Margaret also mentions some immediate, practical details. She encloses a copy of a letter from John Lawson (1615/16–1689), who was "cruelly beaten and stoned & set in the stocks," being careful to enclose the mittimus, *the warrant of committal, so that Pearson might aid him. Her considerable knowledge of the requirements of the law, undoubtedly learned from discussions with Judge Fell, frequently proved useful to Friends. Lawson was a shopkeeper of Lancaster who preached in Lancashire, Cheshire, Derby, and Wales. He was imprisoned numerous times (*EQW, *p. 600; Besse, 1:99–100, 302, 307).*

Dorothy Benson (?–February 1660?) was the first wife of Gervase Benson, a colonel, Justice, mayor of Kendal, and devoted Quaker. Dorothy Benson was an enthusiastic supporter of George Fox. She preached in the churches at York, was imprisoned in York Castle, and gave birth to a son, Immanual, while in prison in 1654 (Letter of Gervase Benson in Caton MSS 2:116; CJ, 1:403–404; Nickalls, p. 162).

Thomas Aldam (ca. 1660–1666) was a Separatist leader before being converted by George Fox in 1651. He became a leading Quaker, preached, wrote tracts, and he was the first to use the term "Friends." He was imprisoned in York Castle from May 1652 until December 7, 1654 for disrupting church services. Pearson secured his release by obtaining Cromwell's intervention (Greaves, 1:4).

Dear brother and friend of the truth, my dear love in the Lord Jesus salutes thee, dear hart, mind the liveing God which is unchangable, who is the Father of spirits, with whom there is no variablenesse nor shaddow of turning [James 1:17], And see what thou can wittnesse of him made manifest in thee, for there thou must find him, and see him if ever thou know him for thy comfort, And see if that which is of him in thee bee not in bondage in Egipt, in darknesse under pharoh which is A taskemaster [Exod. 1:11], the fleshly man, which keepes the seed of god in bondage, but my dear hart, waite upon the Lord in the light of god in thee, which is moses [Moses,] and it will bring the seed of god out of prison if thou harken to it and be obeydient to it, and the Lord will poure the plagues upon Pharoh and his host, and bring forth his owne seed that it may serve him in the Land of the liveing For our god is not the god of the dead but of the liveing [Matt. 22:32], and it is the liveing sacrifice that he Accepts [Rom. 12:1], And it is the liveing that prayses the Lord, this may be strange Language to thee, and to the highest profession in the world, but if thou waite in the light of god in thee and be obeydient to it, when it checks and calls and crosse thy owne fleshly will, which is an enemie to it, and be low and watchfull, and mind that which keep[s] thy peace, and it will show thee what brings trouble, and it will let thee see the truth of these things which thou never saw, and it will come near to thee in Judgement, and raise up the wittnesse in thee, which shall testifie against all the world and all the profession in the world, and all the worshipps in the world and the god of the world, and it will lead thee to another kingdome which is not of this world, which is righteousnesse and peace and joy in the holy Ghost [Rom. 14:17], and then thou wilt see the vanytie, & emptienesse of these vanishing things, which all the world is buisseing [busying] themselves about, for the very fashion of this world shall passe away, at the voyce of the Lord, who hath promissed[,] saying I shake not the earth only but the heavens alsoe[,] signyfieing the removeing of these things that are shaken, as of things that are made; that those things which cannot be shaken may remaine, but we have received A kingdome that cannot be moved [Heb. 12:26–28] eternall prayses be to our Father for evermore, of which kingdome thou may be A subiect of, if thou turne not thy selfe out by disobeydience, and with Esua [Esau] sell thy birthright [Heb. 12:16], Therefore dear hart[,] mind thy Assurance, and in trust in the lord, and let all other things stand without thee and let the lord alone who is workeing for his owne glory & will set up his owne kingdome; which shall be to the confusion of all the plottings and inventings of man and which shall be crosse to all their wills and crosse to all their wayes, and purposses, and he will breake to peeces at his appointed time all their powers, that is irrected [erected] against him and his truth, and to him doe we commend all [,] in whom wee live, move, and have our being. Here is A Letter that John Lawson write to me, and A coppy of the Mittimus, Thou may doe as the lord orders and moves thee, the lord hath made thee very serviceable for poore saints[.] he was cruelly beaten and stoned & set in the stocks four houres before he was set in prison, Collonell Benson wife & Tho. Aldam, is in prison yet, and four more was set in prison at Kendal since the other was released.

This is the time of Jacobs trouble [Jer. 30:7], and these times are suffering times[,] but the day of our rejoyceing as at hand, and the world is deceived in parsecuteing of the saints[,] for their life & comfort is not in theise outward things[,] no not in outward Lyberty[,] for our life is hid with Christ [Col. 3:3] in god from all eyes liveing[,] which none of the princes of the world shall ever know, soe fare thee well, and the eternall and everliveing and Infinite wise God direct[,] guide & keepe thee in his fear, which is the begining of pure wisdome [Ps. 111:10], and to whom alone be everlasting prayses

Spence 3/28. Endorsed: "M F to Anth pearson 1653 when he was newly convinced".

7 TO JAMES NAYLER AND FRANCIS HOWGILL 1653

"Now god hath raised up his glorious light
and brought the immortall to light in your understandings,
therefore waite on the lord alone."

James Nayler and Francis Howgill were imprisoned at Appleby when Margaret wrote this letter of encouragement. She praises them for their faithfulness and expresses her confidence that "the lord hath sett you forth to do his work." The image of the seed of god appears and is opposed to "earthly notions and earthly wisdom." The images of the ploughman, weather, and sowing remind us that the Swarthmoor estate included farms.

James Nayler (ca. 1618–1660) was a highly respected soldier and preacher before he met George Fox in 1651 and was convinced by Fox's teachings. Nayler "brought great gifts of conviction and eloquence to the embryonic movement" (Greaves, 2:257) and many considered him the leader of the Quakers. He wrote over sixty tracts (EQW, pp. 602–603), some with Fox; was a keen disputant with clergy, both orally and in writing; and attracted many people to Quakerism. It was James Nayler who, along with Richard Farnsworth, spoke to Judge Fell the day he met George Fox and convinced Judge Fell that intelligent, respectable men were involved in the movement. There is no foreshadowing here of the later scandal in Bristol and its tragic consequences (Letter 49).

Francis Howgill (1618–1669) was also an eloquent preacher, and he wrote forty-four works. He was educated to be an Anglican minister, but his search for truth led him to the Independents, Baptists, and Seekers. He met George Fox in June 1652 at Sedbergh, where many were converted, and he became one of the principal leaders among the early Friends (CJ, 1:404). Greaves comments: "Howgill's writings exhibit a polemical bitterness toward opponents which contrasts strikingly with the tenderness and sensitivity of his letters to other Friends." The same comment could be made of Margaret Fell. Later, in 1663, Howgill was again imprisoned at Appleby and kept there until he died in 1669. The suffering that he witnessed and experienced makes bitterness understandable.

This letter was printed in the Works, *pp. 51–53, but does not include the more personal remarks about Judge Fell or the "man out of darby" who was rebuked for not being "serviceable." More tellingly, the name of James Nayler was omitted in the printed version, an example of Quaker censorship of one who had been in disgrace.*

Deare Brethren James & Francis[,] prisoners of the Lord [Eph. 4:1] Called faithful & Chosen[,] abideing faithfull in the will of god, &

there stand[,] you have peace, you have joy[,] you have boldnes and you stand over all the worlds standing, over it in the particuler, stand over it all in the generall [,] in purity, in love[,] glory, in righteousnes[;] and there is a pure discerning springing which is refreshed by you, I do se [see] the secret work of god going on in peoples minds, look not at the work[,] nor look not at Bryars [briars] nor look not at all the thorns[,] nor at the mountains, nor the Coldnes[;] for well it may be so for there hath been no vinedresser nor no plough man there; none to dresse the grund [ground,] no seeds man to saw [sow] the seed, and therfore the lord hath sett you forth to do his work, & the plough man shall not plough in vaine nor the seeds man shall not saw [sow] in vaine, the seeds man must not regarde the weather[,] the winds that blow, hee saws [sows] the seed before the winter; there is a winter and there is a sommer; there is a time to saw [sow] the seed, there is a time to reap it; so thou son of man understand, the lord give thee an understanding in all things [2 Tim. 2:7], and the glorious god keep thee in his glory; and both of you in his love[,] keep you wholy in his power up to himselfe for there is never no fainting[.] but to that minde which goes from that which is pure within that will feint [faint]; which runs for a while, and hath a joy in the earth[.] the earthly mind is in the earth & so it faynts but I know there is that in you which is eternell [;] [Several of the following sentences have words crossed out and are unclear.] & stand in the will of god being guided by that which [is] eternell unto god, who is eternall [,] out of your own wills, which is Carnall, & externall[,] and you wil se [see] how all the plotting of there [their] minds which are earthly and with there earthly notions and earthly wisdom, wilbe [will be] broken peices, for that which is earthly houlds[;] for it is abve [above] the seed of god & that which prisons the seed of god in the selfe perticuler; that makes the band to prison them, where it is risen[;] but no earthly band can hould, but where it is eternall, but wilbe [will be] broken to peices, & therefore wate [wait;] for the lord is doing now great things, for long this darknes & this heathenish ministry hath reigned & dark powers of the earth, now god hath raised up his glorious light and brought the immortall to light in your understandings, therefore waite on the lord alone and rejoyce that you are made worthy to suffer for his sake and be faithfull in what yee know, treading and tramplling over the deceit[.] and the lord god of power keepe you faithfull bould, and pure every way in his power, to his everlasting praise[.] I ame well [,] praised be the lord[,] and am at Judg

Fells[,] yett only somtime I go into the Country, not fare of the place; and Judge Fell desired me to remember his lov unto thee[,] James. there came a man out of darby [Derby] towne which had been a frind and he had been at york [York] amoung our frends there[,] & they writt somthing unto me concerning him which was in that note I sent over to thee[;] & I did let him se [see] & shew him his Condition plainly[;] & he did owne the Judgment & was brought to say I had power over it, and he had thoughts to have Comed to Kendell and over to thee[;] but I saw he was not serviceable among weak ones & did speake to him plainly and then I saw he had no mind to come to the lord[;] keep all frends that way in savory to disown the voice of a stranger from the voice of our Lord Jesus xt [Christ;] that they may be kept cleane from the polutions of the world [2 Pet. 2:20] & out of the myre, durt[,] myre & clay[,] up to god, who is pure, for all must be accounted so in respect of him[,] the god and father of our lord Jesus xt to whome be all praise & glory honour forever and ever, so with my lov, and prayers to god for you all I rest[.] blessed be the god & father of our Lord and saviour Jesus Christ who keeps you, and perserves you in his powre for his owne work, therefore look not at your liberty outwardly nor at men nor at time, but at the lord who wilbe your portion eternally, your reward is in the lord[.] the lord hath a secret work there amongst you, there must be a great deale of plucking up; & calling downe & the wilde beasts driven out of the feild, therfore look at the lord alone, which is ever, therfore look to see, see the lord present with you, with his power & with his suporting[,] nor lifteing up your hads [heads], above all your enimies[;] to whom be praises praises honour and glory for ever whose mercy endures for ever/

Spence 3/27. Also in Works, *pp. 51–53. Endorsed: "M F to [initials crossed out] & f h [George Fox]"; "Ja Nall 1653".*

8 TO COLONEL WILLIAM WEST 1653

"There was comand given to the Jelor [jailer] that he [George Fox] shoud be put in the common Goall [jail] amongst theeves and murderers, & in the most odious place that ever man was putt into, and there he is now."

This is a plea to Colonel William West (see Letter 4) to aid George Fox who was in prison at Carlisle for seven weeks (Nickalls, p. 159). The letter expresses Margaret's concern for George Fox and describes the lamentable condition of the jail where he was kept. She rails against the cruelty and unjustness of the enemies of Friends, their "filthy deceites" and "idolatrous worshipes . . . which is abominable to the lord."

She includes a copy of the warrant by which George Fox was apprehended and ends with a question: has Col. West received earlier letters that she and James Taylor wrote to him? She offers to send additional copies if he has not received them, which is an indication of the careful records she kept. It lies "upon our conscience till we know that thou hast received them." This is a theme that is frequently heard in these letters: Having faith in the will of God, Friends can rest easy after they have fulfilled a charge upon them, regardless of the success of the action.

*Gervase Benson and Anthony Pearson were both justices of the peace and supporters of the Quakers. Robert Widders (or Widder or Withers, 1618–1686?) was a preaching companion of George Fox and a devoted friend of Margaret Fell's (CJ, 1:395). Nightingale writes that Widders "became one of the most vigorous missionaries of the new movement . . . A warrant issued against him led to his appearance at the Lancaster Assizes, but the case was dismissed, probably through the influence of Judge Fell" (*Q. Movement in Lancaster, *p. 24).*

The name of James Taylor (?–1687) of Cartmell appears in George Fox's Journal *as early as 1652. He was a supporter of Margaret in a legal battle in 1670 (Kunze, p. 118), and shortly before his death Taylor wrote a "Testimony" for Robert Widders (CJ, l:406). His wife, Mary, was active in the support of Quaker women (Kunze, pp. 92, 95). Together with Margaret Fell and Thomas Atkinson he wrote* The standard of the Lord lifted up against the Beast which is pushing with his iron horns against the family of the Lamb, 1653, *a manuscript in the British Library, London (Kunze, p. 292).*

Sheriff Lawson is not the same person as the Quaker, John Lawson.

The reference to Queen Mary is to "Bloody Mary," or Mary I (1516–1558), the Catholic daughter of Henry VIII who tried to return England to Roman Catholicism. More than three hundred persons were burned at the stake during her reign, and she revived severe laws against heresy. Margaret likens the seventeenth-century persecution to that earlier period.

Dear brother my dear and tender love unto thee in the Lord Jesus presents it selfe unto thee hopeing in the lord that thou abide in the truth, & in the love of it, and those that are sufferors for it, as thou hast shewed thy self heretofore, and I am sure thou needs not be ashamed of it, for it shall stand when all the deceitfull devices of man shall fall, though all the powers of the earth combine themselves & gather together against the lord and his Anoynted [Ps. 2:2], yet will he be glorified in his saints [2 Thess. 1:10], & in the distruction of his enemies, as they shall find and see when it will be to late, I sent thee up A note from my dear brother George [Fox] & Robert Withers, and likewise the warrant by which the persecutone of the truth did apprehend him, and I did expect to have herd something from thee concerning him before this, The Judges at the Assizes would not suffer him to come before them, but did reville him and scofe towards him behind his backe, and did give what incorragement they could to the Justices to excersise their cruelty upon him, he was then in the Jaylers house; but kept closse up in the Assize weeke, & no friend suffered to goe to him, both Collonell Benson and Justice pearson (Pearson) was denyed, but all drunkards and lude parsons was suffered to goe in, the next day after the judges went forth there was comand given to the Jelor [jailer] that he shoud be put in the common Goall [jail] amongst theeves and murderers, & in the most odious place that ever man was putt into, and there he is now, Lawson that is the sheriffe of the county is his greatest enemy, and was one of them that was the greatest cause of his commitment though he had no power to Act then, he being the sheriffe of the county, but all such unjust actions is suffered, & all such tyrants is upheld by those that are in Authority, & the truth only suffers & is imprisoned by them[.] never was the like horrible blasphemeing of God & dissembleing with him as is in these days by those that professe A god in words and in all their actions fighte against him and his truth and the spreading aboad of it[,] which is blasphemie indeed which they soe much speake on[.] O let all profession and great words, and bostings of light and high formes, let them all blush and be ashamed before the lord who will not be mocked with them, though they falsely pretend that they stand for liberty of conscience, and propigation of the Gospell, and keepes these men in Authority under them, who watches & lyes in waite for an opportunity to destroy those whom the lord sends forth to preach the everlasting gospell [.] & some they Stone, and some they beate & shamefull use, and ever when they can have any collour caste them into prison, most part of the Godly in the north part of England hath some freinds of the truth in[,] as Yorke; Carelile [Carlisle,] Apulby [Appleby], Lancaster, now be yee judges your selves[,] yee pretenders of liberty of conscience, and consider what liberty you give to tender consci[ence,] which never committed any offense to any man but for conscience sake, O how dare you professe reformation when cruelty and tyrany rulles in the land, O looke backe & see if ever there was the like in all the kings or Bishops time since Queen Mary dayes that slew the marters, that soe many Goalls was furnished with prisoners meeerly for conscience sake, or was ther ever any that suffered for conscience, that was put among theeves and murderers, or scarse ever was there any except it was papish preiste or Jesuites that ever was kept in prison but they either spoke treason againe King or State, or gave some other offense more than meerly conscience, which no man can ever rigtly accusse any of these with, bu[t] meerly they suffer for the truthes sake, and by the Imediate moveing of the lord doe Speake against the abominations of the times, and the filthy deceites, and the Idolatrous worshipes which is holden up, which is abominable to the lord, but he is comeing to confound & throw downe that filth[y] Idoll which they call their worshipe[,] which is odious in his sight, he will destroy it by the spirit of his mouth & the brightnesse of his coming, the decree is gone out from the Lord[.] distruction is comeing upon it & all the upholders of it, there let the powers of the earth stand out as long as they can[.] the woe & the curse is upon them that strives with their maker [Isa. 45:9] and he will overturne them[;] roott & branch [Mal. 4:1], they shall not escape the Judgement of God for he is the same god that ever he was, & he will not give his glory to another, & now his glory suffers by the persecuters of the power of truth, but he is comeing who rulles with A rod of iron [Rev. 2:27], which sh[all] dash to peeces all his enemies [Exod. 15:6], but who may abide the day of his comeing or who can stan[d] when he appeares [Mal. 3:2], for terrible will he be to his enemies. Dear hart[,] I cannot but let thee know the cruelty of these tyrants, & O these Acts and pretences that they have to act by is odious, to all that have but common honesty, that the state should pretend love to the truth, & yet suffer such things to be of force that all bloody persecutors may have their will soe fare [far] as the Lord gives them power upon those that lives in the truth, they intend banishment to George, or else to the takeing away of his life if it be in their powers now at their Sessions[;] for the Judges left him to them to proceed against him According to the Act, And Lawson was in hopes to have gotten away[,] his life now taken away at the Assizes, and gave it out that he would come to be tried for his life, though that they had nothing against him at all, but what they had gotten their false wittnesses to swear, & there is nothing that they swore that is within the Acte; yet they thirst soe for his blood, that their wills will be their lawes if the Lord doe not prevent them by some meanes or Instruements that he will raise up; doe what the lord moves thee; and what he makes way for thee, For it is no mans strength nor power that wee looke at, but the Lord alone who is the same to us that he was to Daniell in the midst of the lions [Dan. 6:22], and the three children in the firy furnas [Dan. 3:17] the same power doe we dwell & stand in, and the same power will deliver out of the hands of all bloody persecutors[;] and it is but to make up their iniquity and to fatt them for distruction[;] for that is their portion, that that he spoke there be[fore] them A thousand will wittnesse the same thing with him[,] & subscribe their names[,] & would ley do[wn] their lifes[,] And is not afraid of any man whatsoever, everlasting prayses be to our father for ever, Here is some hints of the passages that Justice Pearson & Justice Benson tooke, of the proceedings of those they call Judges, but it may be they will hereafter send them more at large[;] he that runes [runs] may reed their Injustice[.] their baisenesse was observed in all the countrys where they came, which is little credite for them that set them A worke, now I have let thee know how things is, I am discharged, & let my heavenly father worke how he will, & by whom he will, and as thou arte for the truth thou shalt be preserved by the lord of truth, and if thou neglect any opportunity that is offered to thee[,] the lord will require it at thy hands[;] for he takes strict notice of you, though you may take liberty to your selves[.] yet never any pretended such high things for God as you do, which is the highest dissembling with the lord[,] which he will be Avenged of, let your high formes and great professions consider now, who is persecuted for the truth, who it is that persecutes them, they have long stooden in their formes[,] but never was there any persecution till now, that the power of truth is made manifest, which will confound & breake to peeces all their formes, now doth the lord of glory suffer indeed in his saints by those that professe him in words & deny his power[.] but their power is limitted & he will recover his glory out of their hands, which shall be to the confussion of all his enemies and to the exultation of his great name upon the earth, they shall find that the lord of the vinyard is comeing to looke for fruites, and will reward every man according to his deeds[;] for the keeper of Israell neither slumbers nor sleepes [Ps. 121:4], but takes notice of all the Actions[,] words[,] thoughtes & intentions of his enemies, soe let them act what they can, their compasse is knowne[.] their time is but short.

I was moved to write A letter to thee A good while agoe[,] and James Tayler was moved to write another the next weeke after, but we never heard whether thou received them or noe. I desire thee to let us know in two words whether thou did receive them or noe[.] if thou did not receive them we shall send thee coppies of them, for though thou may looke lightly upon them, yet will they lye upon our conscience till wee know that thou hast received them[,] & then it will returne to thee, and we shall be discharged, if ever thou know what the moveing of the power of the lord is, thou wilt know the punishment of disobeying him, but soe long as he is unknowne[,] he is lightly looked on, soe faretheewell & the lord God of power of heaven & earth direct & keep thee in his fear & in the love of his truth[,] & soe thou shalt escape the plagues of his enemies, doe not neglect in sending us word whether thou received these Letters or noe.

Thy Dear sister
Margrett Fell

Spence 3/29–30. Also in Works, *pp. 40–45 and* CJ, *1:116–120. Address: "Deliver this to Collonell West" Endorsed: "M F to Wilem Collonell West [by George Fox]"; "when he was a member of parlament when G F was a prisoner in Carlisle in Olevers days 1653".*

9 To Colonel William West 1653

I "am willinge when ever called to it, to seale this Testimony with my blood . . . and if thou owne us, thou must suffer with us . . . my soules desire is that thou . . . might come to partake with us, and be made one with us in life & power, and in Joy."

Margaret is replying to a letter of Col. West (see Letter 4) in which he confessed his inability to see the "expedience" of Quaker teachings. She urges him to mind the light and "that of God in thee" and to join Friends even if they must suffer. She expresses her willingness to suffer and says that she will not attempt to restrain other Friends.

Margaret uses the image of the Lamb's War, an important theme in Quaker writings, "The war is begun . . . But the lamb shall overcome." Lambs are a frequent biblical symbol for meekness and sacrifice, but it is also an "expression of the final victory promised by God to the elect despite their weakness—the lamb is occasionally a conquering figure that is to overcome all the evil beasts that symbolize sin and revolt against God" (Oxf. Comp. to Bible, *p. 418).*

She accuses Col. West of yielding and complying with the "deceivers and idolators" who complain of Friends and says that they would not have dared to approach her husband with their complaints. She commends him for his "service for the truth [which] hath been much." It is a warm letter, written to a friend, with great enthusiasm for her arguments.

Thomas Atkinson of Cartmel (ca. 1604–168?) wrote several pamphlets, including one with Margaret (CJ, *2:390) (see Letter 8).*

Deare Heart

I have received thyne, wherin thou Confesseth that thou cannot see any eXpedience in the things of that nature[.] The light of Jesus is the eye, by which all sees, whose eyes is opened, which eye the God of the world hath blinded of all whose minds are turned from it, who have eyes but see not, and this light is the Condemnation of the world, though they know it not, nor will not turne too it, nor mind it[.] yet it Shall purSue them, and find them out one day, & be their Condemnation forever. And the light Shines in thy face _______, and would let thee See[,] if thou would mind it, and know what is expediente in things of that nature which is hidd from all the world whose minds are turned from the light, Thou saith thou dost beleeve that the Testimony that hath beene borne, against the hyrlinge Preists hath something of god in it The Testimony is one, and thou hast that in thee, which if thou did keepe thy mind to it, and be obeydient to that measure which thou hath reced [received] from God[,] thou would beare the same Testimony, And if thou did beleeve soe as to be Baptized into his death, and to be buried with him in Baptisme, then would thou know, & waite for a great thinge, brought forth in thy owne particular, and not looke for it abroad only: but at home alsoe, And soe Longe as thou lookes from the measure within thee, thou wilt never know the depth of the mistery nor the season of it. My Soules desire is that thou would mind that of God in thee, Soe as it might carry thee above the feare of a man that Shall dye, which would bringe thee into the feare of the lord, Then would thou know what it is to limitt the holy one, which is not to be offended nor limitted in Jew, nor in Gentile, Thou may read the Apostle in those words, he Spoke concerninge that of God in the Conscience, to those who exercised that of God in the Conscience, which that in thy Conscience knowes of, these deceivers and Idolators doth not: But doth eate that, which is offered unto Idolls, which doth offend that in the Conscience [1 Cor. 8:7], Contrary to the Apostles Command: and therfore doth that in the Conscience which is offended crye against them, and Cannot eate of that which they eate of which is offered to Idolls for Conscince sake[,] which is for the glory of God, read & understand. And them who are sent of God to beare his witnesse & testimony, doe become anything X [?? Indicates an omission.] you, to offer their backes to the Smiter [Isa. 50:6], or to be hayled to the stockes, beaten & reproached as all these can witnesse, for the good of their soules to whom they were sent. Doe but seriosly & honestly consider, & weigh with that which is Just & equall in thee[,] what their end can bee in goinge amongst such a rude multitude who are ready to pull them to peeces, if that of god in their Conscience to which they are obeydient, were not offended. And in obeydience to the pure meening of the Lord, whose Indignation burnes against their Abomination & Idolatry. And wheras thou desires me to restrayne them[,] The wisdome of God, & his power moves to it, and I beare Testimony to the same and am a witnesse for the liveinge God and stands a witnesse against them for ever. And am willinge when ever I am called to it, to seale this Testimony with my blood. And those that are offended at this, are such as the lord hath a Contraversie with, and there is noe reconciliation betwixt xt [Christ] and Beliall, light and darknes. The warr is begun[.] Michall and his Angells, and the Dragon & his Angells: is feightinge [fighting;] [Rev. 12:7] But the lamb shall overcome [Rev. 17:14]. And I know thy Suffering for us[;] and if thou owne us, thou must suffer with us[,] for [thy portion ?] is suffering for these presently[,] but my soules desire is that thou would limit that which would carry thee above sufferinge, that thou might come to partake with us, and be made one with us in life & in power, and in Joy: which the world knowes not, nor never shall[.] And that thou would be more Seperated from them, for that of God in thee cryes & calls thee to come out of from amongst them and be not partaker of there sins[,] least thou be partaker of there plagues[.] And thy Familiarity with them opens a gapp unto them, to runn upon thee, and make these complaints, which if thou kept of them, they would not dare to doe. This old Serpent which brought thee these, Though they had boyled [boiled] in his bosome, hee would not have come to my husband with them. But it is thy yeelldinge, and Complyinge with them that makes way for them and brings thee into Sufferinge. This I speake in love to thee, and not for any revenge (God is my witnesse) For when I heard of thy Complyinge with them, I was troubled for thy sake. For I know eternally that the Cursssed vengence of god hanges over their head, and waites for them till they have made up their messure of their iniquity. The same God that moves any of his Children to beare witnesse for his name __________ against deceipt, and Deceivers will carry them out in whatsoever he calls them too. And deare heart, for thy Sufferinge, thou wilt not loose thy reward, if thou Suffer patiently. And those, who are bought with a price [1 Cor. 6:20], must not be servants of men. But he that is called of the lord beinge free, is Christs Servant, and every man[,] wherin he is called[,] is to abide with god, but this the world knows not. And this is our Joy and our peace to follow the Lambe where ever he goes [Rev. 14:4], throrow [through] reprouches, whippings[,] stockings [being placed in stocks], Imprisonement. Through good report and evill report, Glory and prayses be to our god for evermore, And the witnesse of god which is our witnesse against them lives for ever. And though thou might promisse to write to me or Thomas Atkinson, yet he who was dead is alive[,] who was slaine since the foundation of the world, for in that he dyed he dyed unto Sin once, but in that he lives, he lives unto God [Rom. 6:10]. whose name is called the word of god[,] who lives forever more. And this witnesse, and testimony shall never dye but beare witnesse against thee forever and take the beast & the false prophett alive and cast them into the lake [Rev. 19:20]. And soe in much love and tendernesse, I have answeared thee, And oh that thou would be true to thy owne measure, that thou would not betray him into the hands of Sinners, and have noe fellowshipp with the unfruitfull workes of darknes [Eph. 5:11]. and really, in much pitty I Speake it to thee. thou must be Seperated from them, or thou will suffer by them. Eternally thou shalt witnesse me.

From one who desires thy owne good more than all, though thy service for the truth hath beene much

M:F:

Spence 3/31. Endorsed: "To Willm Westte frm M.F 1653".

10 To Isabel Gardner and Peter Moser 1653

"I have stretched out my hand, and you have not regarded, but yee have set at nought all my Counsell, & would none of my reproofe."

There are many examples of the high esteem in which Margaret Fell was held, but this letter clearly shows that not all of her neighbors accepted her authority. Evidently Isabel Gardner, Peter Moser, and Thomas Wilson spoke against her and accused her of "departing from the living God." Margaret indignantly denies this and vehemently accuses them of being Judas.

There are few references to Peter Moser; he was in jail at Appleby in 1660 (Besse, 2:10) and fined £1 15s. 2 1/2p. in 1678 (Besse, 2:24). Thomas Wilson is noted as "exalted" in a letter of John Camm, 1655 (Nuttall, #156). The term "exalted" carried negative connotations to Quakers, meaning those with wild imagination. Wilson was taken to prison in Lancaster Castle from Swarthmoor in 1661 (Besse, 1:308). Phyllis Mack notes: "Isabel Garnet and Thomas Wilson organized a Separatist movement in Westmoreland" (p. 203).

Isabell Gardner & Peter, that Day that you came to me with that lyinge false message, which the livinge god abhorres for ever, after you were gone I walked into the Garden, and it was Revealed unto me from the lord god, that it was the Betrayinge Spirit that brought you, and when thou came with Tho:[Thomas] Wilson I tould thee of it, and badd thee tell Isabell, and thou called me by from Thomas Wilson, and tould me, that when thou came backe from me with Tho: Robertsons wife[,] That Tho: Wilson called thee forth one night, and showed thee a starr, and asked thee if it was not over Swarthmore, and he asked thee how I did[,] and thou said I was well, or as I used to bee or such like words. And he Said that I was departed from the livinge God. And thou said that something in thee rise against him when he said soe, this thou said he said to thee before you came[,] but after this thou entered into the Temptation, & came of his message and soe betrayed the Just in thy selfe: but could not have power to betray mee[,] who deserned the spirit, prayses be to my heavenly Father, And Isabell Gardner & thou did make it more manifest: who did joyne [join] together againe in bearinge witnesse against mee, and accusinge of me behinde my backe[,] openly in your meetinge, and here you prooved your selves to be Judas indeed[,] who did not only Smite me secretly [Deut. 27:24], but openly, you said that I laughed at you, truly the lord god is my witnesse, and many witnesses of god I have how I have borne with you, and with the Deceipt that I saw in you both[,] least that I should hurt the pure of god. But now that you have betrayed the Just in you[,] and would have betrayed me alsoe[,] and hates to be reformed, because I have called & yee refused, I have stretched out my hand, and you have not regarded, but yee have set at nought all my Counsell, & would none of my reproofe. I alsoe will laugh at your destruction, and will mocke when your feare cometh, & when your desolation & calamity cometh, and anguish & distresse cometh upon you as a whirlwind, in the day of your callamitie [Prov. 1:24–27], then shall yee remember me: and then shall I have a witnesse in you for mee, which shall witnesse me to be of god, and my testimony to be true. though now you will have none of my Counsell and dispises all my reproofe. Therfore shall yee eate of the fruite of your owne way and be filled with your owne desires, which will be sorrow, and anguish, and woe & misery in the end. And this yee shall eternally witnesse to be truth. And for other passages I shall speake more at large hereafter

M:F

Spence 3/22. Endorsed: "M. F. to E. Garnar [George Fox] & Peter Moser, being betrayed, 1653"; "To Isabell Garner and Peter."

11 To Oliver Cromwell 1653

"To the Light of Christ in thy conscience I Speak, which is pure and tender, which if thou harken to it & come downe and be low, it will lead thee into the obedience of the Lord."

Oliver Cromwell (1599–1658), who ruled England from 1649 to 1658 during the Commonwealth and Protectorate, began life as a gentleman from Huntingdon, became a member of Parliament in 1628, and did not come to prominence until the age of forty-four when he showed genius as a military leader and led the Parliamentary Army in the Civil Wars against King Charles I. In 1649, the king was beheaded, with Cromwell being one of the signers of the death warrant. The Commonwealth was established, and Cromwell became lord protector. He was offered the crown, but refused, though he ruled like a monarch until his death.

He was a man of great complexity, and he has been described as "ambiguous, pragmatic, intuitive, vacillatory, ambivalent, opportunistic, eclectic, even flatly self-contradictory" (Greaves, 1:197). In religion he was a Puritan and favored the Independents rather than the Presbyterians who ruled in Scotland. He supported religious toleration, and "he told the 1654 Parliament that liberty of conscience was fundamental" (Greaves, 1:199), which was important for the newly developing Quaker movement.

There are numerous instances of Quakers appealing to Cromwell in person as well as in writing, and Margaret Fell is one of those who tried to persuade him to have a "tender conscience" and to understand the principles of Quakerism. This is the first of five letters to Cromwell. She expresses such themes as: God or Christ "teaching his people himself" in the individual conscience, rather than needing a mediating priesthood; "harken to [thy conscience] and come downe and be low," by which she means the necessity for humility, recognizing one's own unworthiness; and both Jews and Gentiles have consciences that are "of God" and can be "pure and tender."

In this primarily pastoral letter she charges him not to "give way to the men of the world" who would "make Lawes over consciences," a view that Cromwell supported as long as it did not interfere with political needs.

To O: Crumwell: from MF: 1653

Friend Above words I am moved of the Lord to write & A warning to thee from the Lord God of heaven & Earth that thou harken to the light of god in thy Conscience, which is the Light of Chr[ist]: who doth enlighten everyone that comes into the world, that by it thou may be guided[,] lead & taught, And now is the mighty day of the Lord come & comeing, wherein he is teaching his people himselfe, by his owne Imediate light and power which is eternall, therefore beware[,] I charge thee[,] that thou be not found amongst them that heapes up teachers to themselves, haveing icthing [itching] eares which cannot abide sound doctrines [2 Tim. 4:3] for now is the time come & comeing, wherein the Lord is fullfilling his promisse, and makeing manifest the new Covenant in his people, writting his Law in their harts, & putting it in their Inward parts, and now is he fullfilling his promisse, which he hath made to the righteous seed which is Christ the mistery, And if the Lord had not left us this seed[,] wee had bene like unto Sodom and

Gomorrah [Isa. 1:9), but of this all the world and all the Teachers of the world, and all the worshipes in the world and all professions and formes, and the highest notioner Imitation, are all ignorant of him which is the substance, and is without Forme beauty or Comelyness[.] to them who lives in these [Tymes which] is now made manifest by his owne Imediate teaching and leading of the eternall Light where it is obeyed and followed, prayses, praises eternall prayses be unto the holy God; And by this Light are all these high formes and high Notions and all outside professions, all the teaching of man, and all worshipp which is without[,] seen & knowne and discerned to be without God, by the eternall light which is of god, & now is the spirit of the Living god made manifest, by which hee is worshiped in spirit & in truth, & puritie & holyness without which none shall see the Lord [John 4:24], and now is the Lord seperateing betwixt the pretious & the vile, and he is making A seperation betwixt those that serve him and they that serve him not [Jer. 15:19], the mighty god of power is arisseing[,] the glittering sword of the Lord is drawne to cutt downe all fruitelesse trees which hath soe long Cumbred the ground[.] And the day of the Lord of hoasts is Comeing upon every one that is proud and lofty[,] & upon every one that is lifted up[,] he shall be brought low[.] upon all the Cedars of Lebanon, and that is high and lifted up, & upon all the Oakes of Bashon, and upon all the high mountaines, and upon all the hills that are lifted up and upon every high Tower, & upon every fenced wall [Isa. 2:12–15], all shall be as stuble before him, nothinge can stand before the fire of the Lords Jayllesie [jealousy], and now thou may read the acting of the Lord in the 2 of Isaiah; all shall be as A plaine before him, and terrible and dreadfull is hee when he shall appear to shake terribley the Earth [Isa. 2:21], & he will be avenged of his enemies. Therefore to the Light of Christ in thy conscience I Speak, which is pure and tender, which if thou harken to it & come downe and be low, it will lead thee into the obedience of the Lord, and it will let thee see the terrour of the Lord when he is disobeyed, which all the world is ignorant of, and by the obedience of the leading of it, thou wilt come to wittnesse A tender Conscience, and then thou wilt know what it is to offend that in the Conscience which is of god, which is pure & tender, & is not to be offended in Jew nor in Gentile, nor to be Limitted by the will of man, nor any Carnall Law which stands in the will of man, which is acted & executed according to the will of man, for to that in the Conscience which is pure & eternall is the living God made manifest, & by that is he served & obeyed, and by the obedience of that is he knowne. Therefore from the liveing god[,] I warne thee and charge thee as thou wilt Answer it before him at the dreadfull day, when the booke of Conscience shall be opened and all judged out of it[,] that thou beware how thou stands against the mighty dreadfull god that is now made manifest in his people, for by that shalt thou & all that stands up against the Lords Anoynted and prophetts which he sends forth into the rude world to make manifest his great name & power, and by that same power will he overturne all the oppessors & ganesayers of the eternall truth[.] the mouth of the lord of host hath spoken it; For to the first nature that all the world lives in[,] God is unknowne, & they are ignorant of that in the Conscience, Soe I charge thee in the presence of the living god to beware how thou gives way to the men of the world, who live in the flesh[,] which cannot please God, to make Lawes over the consciences of the servants of the most high God, and that thou beware of harkening to evill Councellers, which would make A prey upon the people for their owne ends, and make A man an offender for A word, for therein thou wilt bring guilt[,] plagues & woe upon thy owne head for the living God of life and power is made manifest, and his kingdome is come and his will is done[.] Therefore if thou goe against his will and act contrary to the will of God and uphold and protect the enemies of God, thou wilt partake of the woe & plagues which shall come upon them, Not for any favour or protection from thee as thou art A governour outwardly doe I write this[,] for I utterly deny protection as from man, and in the eternall power of the living God wee stand, and are preserved and kept, the same that preserved Daniel, and Shadrach, Meshach, & Abednego [Dan. 3], and the same liveing God is warring with his enemies, and preserves his owne righteous seed now, as then, & for the good of thy soull which is dear unto mee, have I written these lines unto thee, that thou be not found among evill doers, and have thy percon [person] with hypocrites & unbeleievers, & to that of god in thee have I cleared my Conscience, which will wittnesse for mee eternally & Condemne thee if thou disobey it, Soe to the directing of thy mind to the first principle which is the Light, that soe thou may come to the baptizme of repentance, and the wasting away the filth of the flesh which is the messenger which goes before him to prepare the way for him that baptizeth with the holy Ghost, and with fire, & for the seeds sake in thee with which I have unitie, have I writte these things to thee, to the Informing of thy mind, the Lord God of power enlighten thy understandings that thou may be guided by that of god in thee which cannot erre.

M F

Spence 3/90. Addressed to: "Olever Crumwell". Endorsed: "M. F. to Olever Comvell [George Fox]."

12 TO JUSTICE JOHN SAWREY 1653

"Thou hast shutt thy selfe out from the knowledge of god & of the scriptures & from the simplycitie that is in Christ."

It is not clear if this is a letter that was sent to John Sawrey (Letter 3), or is a paper, or a draft of a paper, prepared in answer to a charge he made that the Quakers were "simple harts that were driving on a design for the devill." The manuscript is unusually difficult to read, with faded pale brown ink and tiny writing. I have had to omit numerous words and even entire lines.

The opening argument is a series of scriptural references concerning simplicity. The accusation of being simple evidently rankled, and Margaret Fell takes joy in proving by scripture that Justice Sawrey is a "painted serpent" and an enemy to the saints ("saints" being a term frequently used by Friends and other sects for their own members.) Her invective flows freely: "such fillthy feigning outside profession as thou live in, but within is filthynesse & rottennesse and dissimulation & hypocrisie." She emphasizes that simplicity or being simple is a virtue and should not be considered a term of opprobium.

John Sawrey said that hee was confident there was A company of simple harts that were driving on a dessigne for the devill. Psal 19.7[:] The Testimony of the Lord is sure makeing wise the simple. Psal:116.6 [:] The lord preserveth the simple, Psal 119:30[:] the entrance of thy words gives light, it gives understanding to the simple: Prov. 4:1[:] he gives subtilty to the simple, Prov 8:5[:] & yee simple ones understand wisdome, Prov 9:4[:] wisdome saith who is simple,let him turne in hither Rom 16:19[:] the apostle exhorts to bee wise unto that which is good and simple concerning evill; Rom 12:8[:] he that giveth let him doe it with simplycitie; 2 Cor.1.12. For our rejoycing is in this the testimony of our Conscience that in simplicity & godly sinceritie, not with fleshly wisdome but by the grace of the lord wee h[ave] had our conversation [in] the world, And from this conversation thou hast shutt thy selfe, ____________ that the devill drives A dessigne by it, and here let the scripture judge thee, and try thee what spirit thou art of. Let all people love justise, & ever the scripture ________ the devil driveing A dessigne by simple harts, but indeed the scripture makes mention that the people have been betrayed by ____ subtle servents as thou art for thou make it manifest that thou art of the seed of the serpent and in that _________ which called Chr:[Christ] A devill, and by such as thee the simple passe on and are punished Prov.22.3. And thou art hee that the Apostle was afraid of that beguiled eve [Eve] through subtiltie and would corrupt other minds from the simplycietie that is in Chr: [2 Cor. 11:3] thou may read thy selfe in 2.Corrin:11: who saith thou art confident there are A company [of] simple harts that are driveing on A dessigne for the devill; And here thou tempting serpent hath laid open thy self who art tempting from the simp[licity] which is in Chr: And saith that simple harts are driveing

[Several lines are illegible.]

of the true & living god, will the devill be served with A company of simple harts, for is not hee the devill the god of all the world, & doth not all the world lye in wickednesse, and are not these they that are without god in the world, and yet thou sayest that A company of simple harts are driveing A dessigne for the devill, here is thy ignorance of god made manifest, who, nether knowe god nor the devill, but speacks evill of things thou know[es] not, And what thou knowes, thou knowes naturally, as A bruit beast, and in these things thou hast corrupted thy selfe as thou hast made it manifest [read] thy ______ Jude 10.11 [Jude 1:10]. And so thou hast shutt thy selfe out from the knowledge of god & of the scriptures & from the simplycitie that is in Christ and art tempting into thy ___________, but thou art knowne & discovered, by the eternall Light of god, which light thou denyes and art an enemie to the good of the ___________, There it is made manifest and here be thou A wittnesse against thy selfe, that thou art an enemie to the simplycitie which was in these saints, that these scriptures speakes on, And thou may as well say that they were driveing A dessigne for the devill, but by the same eternall light & life thou art seen & knowne & thy owne place, eternall praises be unto the liveing god for evermore, but to the world, thou art A painted serpent, painted with others conditions, which thou never came to know but by hearsay and knowes thy selfe ever with A profession of that which is Anothers & not thine, that thy conscience will tell thee that the woe is to thee that is covered & not with the spirit of the liveing God, which spirit is truth & is no lye & wittnesses against such fillthy feigning outside profession as thou live in, but within is filthynesse & rottennesse and dissimulation & hypocrisie [.] the light of Christ in thy conscience if thou hearken to it could show thee soe, and to that I am made manifest, but to thy blind fleshly carnall knowlege thou that never know mee nor see mee. Simplycitie wee owne where it appeares, but such subtill servents as thou that _______ from it, wee deny, and for the simple ones sake have wee wreitten this, & to make known thy secrett subtiltie, that the simplicytie bee not _________ by thee!

To thee John Sawrey who saith that those that has the spirit of god, spoke no such Languidge as wee doe. Here thou dost _________ David not to have the spirit of god, who in the _____ Psal: saith the wicked are estranged from the womb, they go astray as soon as they be born, speakeing lyes; their poyson is like the poyson of A serpent, they are like the deaf adder that stoppeth her ear [Ps. 58:3–4]

[Eight lines are illegible.]

he that beleeves not shall be damned, Rom:14:3: [Rom. 14:23:] he that doubtes is doomed, 2 Thess.12 [:] that they all might be damned [2 Thess. 2:12] 2 Thess.1:8 [:] when the lord Jesus shall be revealed from heaven in flames of fire takeing vengance on them that knew not god & that obey not the Gospell of our Lord Jesus Chr: who shall be punished with everlasting distruction from the presence of the lord, & from the glory of his power [2 Thess. 1:8–9] and here thou hast set thy selfe who doth not know the gospell, nor the lett[er] of it, as thou hast made it manifest by thy ignorance of the letter, & art one of them that the scripture speakes on, stifenecked & uncircumsised in hart & eares, which doth alwayes resist the holy Ghost [Acts 7:51.] for shame[,] give over thy profession of the scripture, who saith, thou dost not doe that _________ ______ had the spirit of god spoke such Languadge as wee doe[.] there thou denyes them that spoke forth the scripture to have the spirit of god[.] And that nature that thou lives in cannot read the scripture, nor thy eye cannot see it, for that [to?] read the scripture is another & not thou, And thou that art in the first nature would have nature that all these scriptures speakes too is in thee, & thou must owne thy [percon?] in these scriptures, and by the same spirit that gave forth these scriptures art thou seen & knowne & _______ _______ _____ _______ thee, & condemnes thee in thy conscience, that I have unity with, & that will wittnesse for mee that I speake the truth.

M: F:

Spence 3/145. Endorsed: "An Answer to John Saurah from M F: 1653"; "In Answer to what John Sawrey said"; "M: F: Ansers to severall opposers".

13 To Justice John Sawrey 1653

"If thou had not putt me upon it [to give examples of his injustice] I would not have instanced any particular, Besides it is ordinary with thee to give out comands for people to come before thee, which thou hast noe color [i.e. reason] for, which my husband would never doe such injustice."

The following paragraph, probably by Margaret (Horle, p. 076), is appended to the letter. It is in the same handwriting as the letter. "Steeplehouse" was the derogatory term that Friends used for church buildings. They derogated them since the spirit of God could be anywhere.

This afores[ai]d pap[er] was writte to Jo[hn] Sawrey Called a Justice a great persecutor[,] one of the first in the north, that set the Rude Multitude to beat Friends[,] who set many in the stocks, & put in prison; and M F was moved to goe to the steplehouse to speak to the priest of the parish, where she, & he Lived, & when she was in the steeplehouse he [John Sawrey] Came to her, & said good M:s fell goe into your own pew, or else goe your way, & he took her by the Arme & offered to pull her away, but she said[,] hold thy hands off me, & she spoak to the priest, what she had to speak, & afterward she spoak to him [Sawrey], & she charged him to doe Justice, & not to wrong nor oppress the poor people, wherupon he was vexed, & writ a lettr to her & sent it to her Husband, & Charg[ed] her to prove what Injustice he had done; so this Lettr is an Answe[r] to his, & within a few years after [he] was drowned in a [little crossed out] water upon the Rode co[m]ing from York.

In her letter Margaret rebukes Justice Sawrey (Letters 3, 12) for abusing his office, taking advantage of poor people, and persecuting Quakers. She warns him: "thou art but A catterpiller, which shall bee swept out of the way." He had written and asked her to prove her charge of injustice. She does, with some reluctance, mention particular instances, such as his failure to prosecute cases brought by Arthur Longe and Richard Waller. Richard Waller was a Lancashire man, a Quaker, who preached in Westmorland and Ireland. He was imprisoned at Waterford in 1657 and died that same year (CJ, 2:472–3). The description of Sawrey's dealings with Richard Waller is confusing, but her feelings are made clear. It ends with the indignant statement, "Now if this bee faire dealinge, let any man judge."

She accuses Sawrey of "Ale house hauntinge," of "tendringe the oathes to pore ignorant people," and she asserts that her husband "would never doe such injustice." She urges him to repent.

Sawrey had accused her of being "puffed up with malice & pride, & that people saw it so." She rejects the charge, but it seems possible that her enthusiasm and certainty may have appeared that way to unsympathetic persons.

Sawrey did "indeed drown as he was crossing the treacherous sands of Morecambe Bay" (Ross, p. 40). Swarthmoor Hall and Plumpton Hall (Justice Sawrey's home) are on a peninsula separated from the mainland and Lancaster by Morecambe Bay, a dangerous water that could be crossed safely only at particular times.

To Justice Sawrey

O thou Persecuter and Enemie of the Lord[,] how darest thou professe him or take his name in thy mouth; since thou hatest to be reformed and letts the lyeinge Spiritt bee head in thee; which hardens thee against the truthe with a false Cover and forme of profession; which is hipocrise before the Lord, and acts contrary to the Commands of the Lord; And doth not the Lord say Touch not myne annointed nor doe my prophetts noe harme [1 Chron. 16:22]; and that it were better that a Milstone were hanged abbout their neckes, and they cast into the sea, then offend one of these little Ones [Matt. 18:6]; yet still thou goes on in opresinge the power of truth, what in th[ee lies.] thou art but A catterpiller, which shall bee swept out of the way. And the Lord wilbee avenged of all such enimies as thou art[,] for if thou goe on in that course thou art in the Vengeance and plauges [plagues] will bee upon thee, therfor repent and turne to the Lord, as thou lovest thyne owne Soule minde that of God which hee hath manifested within thee, and checks thee for thy vile deeds, and for these abominations thou walkest in, for if thou wilt hearken to it, it will shewe thee that thy life is death;

search search [sic] within thee; for it lies low, and is little in thee, and the filthie high pharisaicall nature is gott abbove it, and keepes it under, But if thou wilt lett it rise up and checke thee, and keepe downe the lustfull jearinge heardened nature which is in thee; it will lett thee see that all thy offringe which thou hast offerred up to the Lord is strange for & abhomination before the Lord, and if ever thou owne the Lord with comfort thou shalt owne us. Thou hast written a lre [letter] to mee, but it came to my husband first, and I did but heare a part of it wherein thou hast forged many a lye, as the Lord knowes and sees; Thou chargest mee with lyeinge in it, but if ever thou knowe the truth, which yet thou art ignorant of, thou shalt owne it to bee truthe, thou sais [says] that I was puffed up with malice & pride, & that the people saw it soe, & that I did not see my selfe soe, thy sight & the peoples is all one, you could but see mee without with a carnall eye, which is the eye that offends the Lord, and must be putt out before ever thou can see mee or that condition I was in, thou must have annother eye opened, and that eye must bee pluckt out [Matt. 5:29], for thou judges accordinge to outward appeareance, which Jesus Christ forbids, and thou art that Hypocrite, that hath the Beame in thy owne eye [Matt. 7:3], and hath not judged thy selfe, therefore thou shalt bee judged of the Lord, and therefore once more I bid thee, leave of[f] thy Alehouse hauntinge, and thy tendringe the oathes to pore ignorant people like thy selfe, which have the first nature standinge in them, which is Caine, who lives in envie, wrathe[,] malice & revenge and against annother, and comes to thee to sweare an oath against his NeighboR, it may bee, when he hast done his Neighbour wronge, yet if hee got to thee before the other partie & sweare an oath and give 2 or three shillings, thou gives him a warrant, and byndes the other party over; is this thy Justice, thou Enemy of righteousnesse tremble before the Lord of heaven & Earth; how darest thou professe Jesus christ who hath comanded not to sweare at all, and yet it is thy trade to get money, to tender oathes to pore ignorant people, stand in the feare of the Lord, and beware how thou tenders oathes, and takes money for them; Thou art soe impudent and grosse, that thou chardgest mee in thy Lre [letter] to instance in one particular; which I should have beene loathe to have done, but that I see it would bee a couleR [color] for thy filthynesse, if I did not, Therefore I shall instance in some that have beene with my husband and mee within these 4 or 5 daies [days], I shall take noe longer tyme; One Dodgson of the Lawecorte, who tooke a peece of land of Arthure Longe, and paid him for it in his life tyme, and some came by force and tooke it from him, and came to thee & got a warrt [warrant], and bound him over, [Binding over. "The act by which a court or magistrate requires a person to enter into a recognizance or furnish bail to appear for trial, to keep the peace, to attend as a witness, etc." *Black's Law Dictionary*] Likewise Richard Waller of Cartmell, hee had a warrt of thee, I cannott say how longe it is since, but hee paid thee for it, and bound the man over, But whether the man came to thee underhand or noe, hee cannott tell, but thou never prosecuted nor brought the man to any tryall, but let it fall downe; soe thats twoe of thy Actions, But since that tyme Richard Waller hath beene bound over by some that came to thee for a warrt against him, And bound him[,] his wife & his Mother & his Brother all over to answere at LancR [Lancaster] Sessions, soe hee came to my husband, and desired him that he would write to thee, in respect his wife had a younge Childe, and his Mother was an old woman that hee could not tell how to get her thither, and hee averred that the oathe taken against him was false, but my husband would not write, and hee told us, thou had done the like before and instanced in this abbove written; Soe I wished him to come to thee and tell thee, how thou had done with him before Soe hee came to thee as hee told mee the last tyme I saw him and told thee hee had given thee money for a warrt, and thou never brought the party to his tryall, whereupon hee desired thee to lett the other bussines cease, till my husband was at home, which was lesse then thou had done to him before, and hee said thou hange downe the head and soe farre as I remember bid him bee at LancR, and as longe as hee was there thou said nothinge to him, but promised thou would speake to one to stay it, and after he was come away made that man prosecute against him; Now if this bee faire dealinge, let any man judge[.] here are three of thy Actions instanced which will make thee appeare what thou art; Multitudes might be added; All the Countrey over complaines against thee, but I cease to accuse thee, and doe forwarne and informe thee; And if thou had not putt mee upon it, I would not have instanced any particular, Besides it is ordinary with thee to give out comands for people to come before thee, which thou hast noe color for, which my husband would never doe such injustice though hee never made such a profession as thou dost [A mark in the manuscript may mean that something has been omitted.] and Soe drawes people together to meete thee at the Alehouse day after day, there to make pore people pay for thy drinke, And it is reported that when drinke is new at one place yee goe to annother, and soe feeds and satisfies your lusts, and this is your order, And whereas thou hast accused handmaides which are laden with divers lusts, which is to mee a reproache, and a scandall, wherein thou hast shewed thy selfe to bee an Accuser, and a Reproacher; I desire thee in love to tell mee, in what lusts they followe, as divers lusts is many, soe mention them, as they are many in particular, for theise things wee doe abhorre and detest, and all the courses of the world; And whereas thou speakest of grace in words, which teacheth us and is our Teacher to deny ungodlynesse & worldly lusts, and if thou owne that as thou pretends it, thou woudst keepe at home, at thyne owne house and not seeke to a Teacher without thee, For the grace of god was and is the Saints Teacher; but thou art the woman that goes abbroade and dost not abbide in thy owne house, and if thou could wittnesse the parrable, the woman that sought for the groate, and when the Candle was lighted and the house swept, shee found it in her owne house and shee rejoyced with her Neighbors [Luke 15: 8–9], but thou art ignorant of the parables; And wherein thou accusest mee of raileinge and passion and a lyeinge spirit, but if ever thou wittnesse the truthe, thou wilt wittnesse mee, for it is for your souls good I came amonge you, and that which must dy in thee judges it to bee raileinge and passion and a lyeinge spirit, And whereas thou speakest of Saintes not beinge carryed away with theise delutions [delusions], pore heart[,] looke within thee and examine & Search, and thou shalt find thyselfe a Divele before thou knowe any of the Saintes conditions, and that god thou saith teacheth thee, is the god of the world, and the prince of the ayre [air] which rules in the children of dissobedience [Eph. 2:2], which leads thee into the lusts of the world, and the Waes [ways] of the World, and the unity with their Customes and fashons, and this is hee which in the latter End of thy lre [letter], thou bids rebuke the lyeinge spirit, which is gone out into the World, Soe hee will faile thee, for his power & thyne is lymitted, and thou shalt knowe to the destroyeinge of thee, and thy god what god wee Serve, and whom wee worshipp, Thou speakes of publishinge in the Markett, Now if thou bee free of theise things, publishe it in the markett, and lett mee bee found the Lyar, Now I have discharged my Conscience[,] Farewell, And if ever thou know the Lord of power thou shalt wittnesse mee/

M F

Spence 3/146–147. Endorsed: "M F to justes Sora [George Fox] 1653".

14 To Sir Richard Newdigate 1653

"As thou loveth thy owne soule beware how thou proceeds in Acting against the Lord God, But let things be fairely tryed and heard, and let truth be made manifest."

Sir Richard Newdigate (1602–1678), son of Sir John Newdigate and later baronet, was an eminent jurist (DNB) who, according to this letter, was guilty of persecuting Quakers. It was not Cromwell's policy, but at the local level, judges and magistrates had considerable discretion in how they implemented laws. There was a practice of paying informers, which frequently led to abuses.

Margaret addresses Judge Newdigate as "Friend," which does not necessarily imply an acquaintanceship, but the letter is strongly admonitory. It is interesting to note that Judge Fell was admitted as a student at Gray's Inn in 1623 and was called to the bar in 1631, while Judge Newdigate entered Gray's Inn in 1620 and was called to the bar in 1628. Many years later, in 1661, Newdigate then a "former judge," represented Quaker defendants in an important trial concerning the legality of Quaker marriages (Horle, Q.&EngLegalSys, *p. 235).*

To Judge Nudigate
Friend

In the presence of the Lord thou art, and from his all seeinge eye thou cannot fly, And to him thou must give an Accompt [account] of thy actinge, in this place that thou hast undertaken[.] if thou Judgest for the Lord, thou Judgest the people with just Judgment. And thou shalt not wrest judgment, thou shalt not respect persons read Deutrin: 16: 18: 19: [Deut. 16:18–19] unto the end. Consider and looke backe what thou hast done the last Assizes, how thou didest strengthen the hands of the wicked, against the Lord God of power by whom thou must be Judged: And did Cast his servants in prison, when thou hadst nothinge against them but what false witnesses Sweare, and was proved to be false and lyes before thy face in the open Court. And yet thou didst lye fynes upon their heads, and Cast them into prison, where they have layd ever since, and if thou and others should act as thou did then, there they may lye all the dayes of their lives, And this is thy act, and it lyes at thy dore; Therfore from the Lord, I warne thee, and Charge thee: as thou loveth thy owne soule beware how thou proceedes in Acting against the Lord God, But let things be fairely tryed and heard, and let truth be made manifest, Let the offenders be punished least the harmlesse and the innocent suffer; through thy default, & soe thou bringe woe, and Judgment upon thy owne head; And this in love to thy soule I am moved of the Lord, And remember that thou art warned, which if thou do not reed [read] thy portion, in the 2: Amos and the 7: of Micah: God is the same now as he was then, for he Changeth not, See whether thy Justice, will punish the false Swearer, or them whom they Sweare falsly against.

M F

Spence 3/130. Endorsed: "M F 1653 [George Fox]"; "These are to the Judges"; "Read over and Laid in order for writeing These are written & compared"; "M: F: letters to Magistrates".

15 TO JUDGE JOHN ARCHER 1653

"Oh repent & looke for the plagues of god to be powered [poured] upon you for that is your portion. And know that . . . thou hast exercissed thy cruelty upon A harmlesse people, that will offer violence to no man."

This is a harsh, accusatory letter to a judge who caused Quakers to go prison for speaking their beliefs. Margaret likens him to Pharisees and rebukes his "sottishness & Dishonesty and injustice." The last sentence is an interesting personal note: "I doe beleieeve if I were within thy liberty & power I should partake of thy cruelty as well as they, but I am not afraid of thee nor of no man whatsoever & Soe subscibe my name—Margrett Fell."

Characterizing Quakers as "A harmlesse people, that will offer violence to no man" is a very early statement of the peace principle which was not generally established among Quakers until 1660 at the time of the Restoration.

John Archer (1598–1682) was called to the bar in 1620 and served in Parliament in the 1650s. He did not support the Commonwealth and had an undistinguished career after the Restoration, though he was knighted in 1663. "Archer is characterized . . . as one 'of whose abilities time hath kept no record unless in the sinister way,' as uncertain in his law and afraid of a long and intricate cause" (DNB).

To John Archer of Kendal a persecutor from M F 53
Freind

Thou makes it manifest to the world what God thou serves, which is the God of the world, and the prince of the Ayre which rulles in the childr[en] of disobeydience, & his servant thou art whom thou obeyes, and thou hast made it manifest to the world that thou art A bloody persecutor of the servants of the most high god, & thou hast shewed forth thy sottishness & Dishonesty and injustice, if thou have but common honesty in the[e] thou would Scorne to bee A judge in thy owne cause, but it is like thy Justice to imprison Soe many people for speaking to thy particular, and to that filthy deceite that thou lives in, thou makes it appear to all the world what thou art, & thou filthy Sott, hast thou any president [precedent] that ever any man putt any in prison for speaking to themselves if they had spoken that the law could take hold on, but he that leads and teaches thee leads into distruction as thou shalt find it; but they spoke the truth to thee; as thou makes it manifest to the world by thy cruelty & actions, & thou dissembleing hypocrite, thou shewes that thou art, of the same generation that those pharesies were that Christ cried woe against [Matt. 23:13], that called Christ A devill, and soe doth thou, thou said the devill spoke in them when they Spoke to thee, but thou hast stolen that word as A theefe for it is but a late [of late] since the voyce of the divill was knowne, and thou that lives under the power of darkenesse calls God the devill, as they ever did that was where thou art, but thou shalt know that he whom thou calls the devill, shall confound thee & thy god and all such bloody persecutors as thou art, but goe on in thy way[,] for thy time & thy power is limitted by the liveing god whom thou knowes not but is an enemy too & he is comeing to be avenged of all such enemyes as thou art, & to powre [pour] downe his fury upon such heathens as thou art that knowes him not, but it is no wonder when he that is thy guide and leader which thou followes for thy ministrey for teaching after thou hast put them in prison, sayith it was no murder in him if he murder them, as bloody Caines[.] will not the Lord be avenged upon you as he was upon Caine, oh repent & looke for the plagues of god to be powered [poured] upon you for that is your portion[.] And know that though thou hast exercissed thy cruelty upon A harmlesse people, that will offer violence to no man, nor wrong any man[,] but when they are moved of the Lord to Speake to such filthy beasts as thee, thou would have them to be unfaithfull to the Lord as thou art who serves not the Lord Jesus Christ but thy owne belly, and thy filthy pride & deceite which thou would have to live in thee which is for the fier [fire] & the curse of god is upon it & upon thee that lives in it, that of God that is in thee is in prison, & that is by that filthy pride & high mind which imprisons them, but thou lets drunkards & swearers goe at liberty which is like thy Selfe, but god will smite thee thou whited wall [Acts 23:3] & thou shalt not escape the damnation of hell, Soe if thou love thy owne soul repent thee of the evill of thy deeds & be ashamed for soe thou may for thy actions shames all profession in the world [*& soe fare thee well* crossed out] & thou kickes against the prickes [Acts 9:5] & strives with thy maker therefore is thy portion[.]

Thou may call this A libell or a pamflett as thou did the booke that thou tooke which was other mens goods[,] but thou dissemble[r] pamfletts & baletts [ballads], & rimes, & libells may be sould & sung upp & down in the streets for thee long enough before thou would ceze [seize] upon them for they feed that nature thou lives in [.] thou & thy blind preists would suffer them long enough, but the truth which lyes open your filthynes ye will not endure, but seekes to smother it, & murder it where its made manifest[;] but the time is come that your coveringe is to [too] narrow for you, [Several lines are illegible.] and the [curse?] is Lying upon your abomination, and _______ _______ whoredomes ____ it were better that A milstone were hanged about thy neck [Matt. 18:6] thou art not knowne to mee outwardly but by thy unfruitfull workes of darkenesse I know thee, and therefore doe I reprove thee And I doe beleieeve if I were within thy liberty & power I should partake of thy cruelty as well as they, but I am not afraid of thee nor of no man whatsoever & Soe I subscribe my name

Margrett Fell

There are many that have bene moved of the lord to speake both to judges & Justices both publickely & privately & yet never any Set any in prison for speaking to their owne particular but thou hast shewed thy basenesse in avengeing of thy owne quarell but it is like thy pedleling Justice

[Another hand]

he which leads thee leads into the pit: & he whome thou sarves [serves] will leave thee in the pitt:

Spence 3/148. Endorsed: "from M F to John Archer 1653 [George Fox] of Kendal who was then a Justice in the towne & a Cruell persecutor of the Friends in the beginning, & caused many to suffer very much"; "A Coppy of the letter sent to John Archer".

16 AN EPISTLE TO FRIENDS 1653

"If you love your Souls, which is Immortal, abide in the Light, and love the Light, and walk in the Light, where the Fellowship and the Unity is."

The source for this Epistle to Friends is Margaret Fell's Works *published in 1710. It may have been edited; certainly the spelling and punctuation have been modernized to the standard of the day. The biblical phrases show her familiarity with both the Old and New Testaments. It was so much a part of her that the terms flow as natural expressions.*

It is a comforting, pastoral letter, like those of other respected Friends, and is made for reading aloud. There is emphasis on Light, that God is light, that there is light in each individual, and that by being "still and low . . . you may receive the teachings of the Lord . . . so that your Souls may live." It carries the Quaker message that "the Teacher" is within, not an outward priest or even the scriptures. She urges the reader to "examine and try your own selves," but without the Puritan sense of the hopeless sinfulness of mankind, except for the "elect."

Friends, whose Minds are turn'd to the Light, which comes from Jesus Christ, which never changeth, whose Light enlightens every one coming into the World; in it abide, and in it walk, and to it be faithful and obedient in your Measures, that with it your Minds may be guided up to God, who is the Father of Lights, that you may bring your Deeds to the Light, to try whether they are wrought in God.

My Dear Hearts, God is Light, and in him is no Darkness at all [1 John 1:5], the work that he works, is in the Light, which is pure, and leads to purity; which Light testifies against all Sin, and all the deeds of Darkness, and all Earthliness, Lust, Pride, and Covetousness, which is Idolatry; whose Minds turns from the Light, turns into the Idolatry, and into the Sorcery, under the dark Power, and into the Witchery, where the Devil hath Power.

Therefore if you love your Souls, which is Immortal, abide in the Light, and love the Light, and walk in the Light, where the Fellowship and the Unity is.—For if you walk in the Light, and abide in the Light, which is Low and Meek, and wait in Silence and Faithfulness, and Obedience, wait Patiently, and you shall have the Light of Life. Who hath Life, hath the Son, and who hath not the Son, hath not Life. And be still and low, that you may receive the teachings of the Lord; and learn of him, who is Low and Meek, and hearken diligently, and keep your Minds to the Light, that so your Souls may live. And the Light which comes from Jesus Christ, which is the Messenger of the Living God, sent from God, may bring your Souls out of Egypt, and out of the Fall, from under the Curse, which Disobedience hath brought upon all Men. Dear hearts, this is the Day of your Visitation, and Salvation, if you be faithful and obedient, for the everlasting God, which is the Life, Light and Substance of Life, is risen, and arising, and raising up the Dead to hear the voice of the Son of God, and they that hear do live. And the dead Bones is coming together, and standing up; yea, the Earth is giving up her Dead, if you be faithful to the measure of God's Spirit, by which he hath quickned you, this ye shall see, and witness; therefore go not forth, nor look out to them, that say lo here is Christ, or loe there is Christ, for no other Name under Heaven, but by this Name Christ Jesus, who is the Light which John bears witness to, which is come a Light into the World, and lighteth every Man that cometh into the World [John 1:6–9]; this is the Light that shines in a dark place, which you may do well to take heed unto, until the day dawn, and the day star arise in your hearts [2 Pet. 1:19]; and this you will witness if you be faithful to the Light; but if you turn from the Light, and hate the Light, then the Light makes you manifest that your deeds are evil, and that is your Condemnation, the Light that is come into the world, which you can never flee from, but wherever you go, the Light, that is the condemnation of the World will pursue you, and that of God in your Consciences will be your Condemnation. And this is your Teacher, and is always present with you, if you keep down to it, and close to it, it will keep your Minds low, and humble, and tender, and it will quicken you; and so you will come to know the pure Law, the righteous Law of God, which is the School-Master until Christ. And this is not the Letter without you, but this is the faithful Promise of God, which he hath promised to those who are taught of him, which is the substance of the New Covenant which he hath made; who hath said, I will put my Laws in their hearts, and write them in their inward parts [Jer. 31:33]. Therefore with the Light in you, which lighteth the Candle of the Lord in you, with which Candle he searcheth Jerusalem [Zeph. 1:12], let this Light search you, and try you, and mind whether you have receiv'd the New Covenant, which is everlasting, which never shall be broken, which is the Law written in the Heart; which Law is pure, which Law is Spiritual, Just, and Good. So examine and try your own selves, for if you know not that Christ is in you, you are Reprobates [2 Cor. 13:5].

So dear hearts, mind your Eternal Teacher, which is the Preacher of Righteousness, which speaks to the Spirits in Prison, for you cannot hear without this Preacher, nor any can speak to the Spirits in prison, but he who is sent of the living God, which is now made manifest, he that is anointed to preach glad tidings to the Poor, is come; he that gives liberty to the Captives [Isa. 61:1] is come, he that sets the Oppressed free is come; they who are faithful and obedient shall witness Redemption, and Zion is arising, for her Light is come; *Arise Zion, for thy Light is come*—So here is your Teacher, and your Preacher, and your Redeemer, and your Saviour, if you be obedient and faithful to the measure of this gift of God [Eph. 4:7], as it ariseth, and as it teaches, and as it makes the will of God manifest, and as it moves; if you be faithful and obedient to this, you shall eat the good of the Land. So the Lord God Almighty of Life and Power, keep you faithful and obedient to your measure made manifest, and preserve you in that of him, which is arising and quickning you, to his everlasting Praise; and so you will come to witness for the Lord in your measure, and by the invisible eye (which is the Light) and if you standing single in the Light, and if your eye be single in it, you will see the whole Body full of Light [Matt. 6:22], and this leads to the invisible God; and by your measure of this is the invisible God made manifest; and this is the invisible eye which sees God, that no mortal eye can behold or reach unto; and here is your Teacher if you never hear Man speak; and here is your Teacher, if you be faithful to the measure of God, and to the leading and guiding and moving of it, you will come to witness Christ Shepherd of your Souls, and the fat Pastures; and it will lead you to God, the Father of Lights, which all the World, and all the Ministry, and all the Worships of the World, which are out of the Light, are ignorant of; nor any that ever took upon them to teach from the Letter without them, or from an outward Call, can ever say they saw God, or knew him, or ever heard his Voice. So Life and Death is set before you; and if you be obedient to the Light, which never changeth, it will lead you out of death, and out of the fall from under the Curse, into the Covenant of Life, if you be faithful and obedient unto the Death: And the everlasting God of Life and Power, strengthen, nourish and refresh you, to his everlasting Praise and Glory; and so wait for the living Food, to come from the living God,

M. Fell.

Works, *pp.* 47–51.

17 To Prisoners in Lancaster Castle 1653

"If these tithes were not held up by the law, you had not bene empresoned."

This letter of praise and encouragement to prisoners at Lancaster Castle shows Margaret's ability to appreciate others' devotion and willingness to sacrifice. She expresses her admiration and her feeling of unity with them. The Friends mentioned in this letter were all from the northwest part of the country, and the sense of community was strong.

Margaret is concerned about the prisoners' physical needs, and she expresses her conviction that they should be given whatever monetary support they need, that they "ought not to lye at their owne charges." She had sent money to other prisoners and is willing to do the same for them. This seems to be the beginning of the Kendal Fund to assist Friends in need, the accounts of which begin in June 1654 (Ross, p. 62). She had sent money to Robert Widders (see Letter 8) and Thomas Lawson to distribute to Thomas Choron, Walter Miers, and Mary Howgill.

There is a play on the word deceit, *the deceit of the Quakers' enemies and the deceit within each person, including Quakers, and a similar contrast of physical imprisonment and imprisonment of the soul.*

Thomas Lawson (1630–1691) was educated at Cambridge and then became the rector at Rampside in Lancashire. He was convinced by George Fox in 1652 and "soon after became convinced of the unlawfulness of preaching for hire, and at twenty-three gave up his living to join the Quakers" (DNB). *He preached and wrote, was imprisoned and fined. He also was a distinguished botanist and a teacher.*

Walter Miers (1633?–1723/24) was another active lifelong Friend who traveled *in the ministry and spent periods in prison. In later years he was a respected businessman and a prominent Quaker in London (*CJ*, 2:475).*

*Mary Howgill was probably the sister of Francis Howgill of Grayrigg. There are records of her being imprisoned several times and of her letters to George Fox and Margaret Fell (*FPT*, pp. 200–201; Nuttall, p. 328).*

dear bretheren[,] in the eternall everlasting truth which never changeth doe I Reach you and mete you & am present with you who are faithfull[,] who are obedient[,] who are constant to the one eternall wittnesse which wittness against all deceit & deceits & against all sine and workes of darknes & thoughts of darknes in your particulers[.] to that which is pure of god in you, which lives for ever more am I made manifest[.] I charge you in the name & power of our lord Jesus christ to be faithfull & obedient unto your particuler mesurs commited to you[,] that when your lord & master Comes yee may be found faithfull shirds [shepherds] to give an account to him[,] the wittnes of a good conscience[.] my deere hearts[,] in the eternall one light which leads into the unitie & to the power of the lord god be subject[,] in which power you shall ever come & be made conquers [conquerors] & tread upon the nekes [necks] of your enimies[,] & dweling in it you shall be made free from sin and death which all the powers of the earth are under[,] the same wittnesse for which you stand to testifie for the truth against deceite, & thought [though] you are cast into preson by the deceite which yee witnesse against without yee[,] the same witnesse doth testifie against deceite within you which did call your soules into preson, & soe being faithfull to the wittness, yee shall wittness freedome to your soules, & then your outward bonds will be easy[.] theirfore in his feare stand which after hee hath kiled the bodie can cast the soule into hell [Matt. 10:28], the lord god all mightie of life & power keepe you faithfull to stand single & cleare before him who is pure & cannot behould Iniquitie,

I sent about a quarter of a yeare sense some money to our frinds which were cast into preson for speaking to the prists, I sent it to Robert widers [Robert Widders] by Thomas Lason [Thomas Lawson] and a noat [note] how it should be given, which was to Thomas Choron, waters mires [Walter Miers] and mary hugall [Mary Howgill], which was moved by the lord to goe to speake against the deceite, and soune after they were cast into presen I saw in the eternall light that they ought not to lye upon theire own charge, who went in the ware [the

Lamb's War], moved of the power of the lord, & soe they ought not to lye at their owne charges, now you that lye in for tythes, that is for your perticuler interests as to the outward thought [though] it be one in the substance, yet acording to the outward, it is a perticuler thing & there is abatement for your Impresentment, and the anchent [ancient] law of the nation would give him noe tithes soe long as you lye in preson if it were not by sherrifs writs and others under offisse[;] but you whoe went in obedence to the moving of the lord yee went in the servis of the lord, and whom hee sends forth frely neither takes gould nor silver, for the laborer is wordy [worthy] of his hire[,] saith Christ [Luke 10:7], soe a litle to informe your minds in this thing, that there is a diferance in these 2 Conditions and that their be noe morning [mourning] amonge you for I see in the eternall light that noe man that goes in the servis of the lord and soe be cast into preson & be taken from his outward being & famely ought not to mentaine him selfe in preson at his owne charge, it is Contrary to all saints practise in scriptur for the aposteles sayd noe man goeth a warfare at his owne charge[.] soe that your minds may be informed in this thing[,] they that goe a warefare acordinge to the moving of the lord are in the lords worke, that stand still & confese Christ come in the flesh; & if these tithes were not held up by the law, you had not bene impresoned, now they [who are] goeing acording to the moveing of the lord, theirfore are in the ware, soe let all your minds be turned to the light and yee will see the truth of this & the equity & the Justnes of this thing; & I write to them that had it, & Judge that in them that did not let you know of it, for I did that only by the eternall moving of the lord[,] & soe likewise when ye are in want, ye may let mee know that ye may be suplyed againe[,] for I see that which never changes that ye ought to be mentened [maintained] by the hole [whole] body, for hee that is the lords freman is christs servant to the light in all your consciences which drawes & unites & knites [knits] together & enlightens your understandings[.] to that all be faithfull & obedient, and the lord god all mightie of life & power keepe you and preserve you by his mighty power to his everlasting praise and glory

Margret Fell

for my deare bretheren presoners of the lord at lancaster Castell.

Dix Z.1, FHL MSS Vol. 294. Endorsed: "To Frends att Lankaster"; "a pesell [epistle] of M F [George Fox]"; "to Friends at Lancaster 1653".

18 To Jeffrey Elletson 1654

"Verily, I love that of God in thee, and thou hast beene often presented to me in the Invisible, and I know there is something of God in thee, which thou canst not fly from."

There are four letters to Jeffrey Elletson written over a period of four years, pastoral in tone, in which Margaret explains various principles of Quaker belief. This letter seems very personal: the endorsement is to "one of the same profession with mee whom I loved dearly."

She speaks of God being "in them that spoke forth the Scripture, before the Scripture was written," and if he does not know that, then he has "nothinge but the outside which is but paper, & incke."

She is probably referring to her own earlier searching for a true faith when she says "I know where thou art; and further in that profession I was I am sure, then ever thou was."

There is a reference to the Apostle Paul's forbidding "a woman to speake in the Church," which became the subject of her most famous pamphlet, Womens Speaking Justified.

She urges him to look inward, to "turne thy minde to the measure of God in thee," not to other authority. Then he will see that "that which was a barren wilderness is become a faithfull hill, and the knowledge of God covers the Earth, as the waters cover the Sea."

Jeffrey Elletson

To the light of Christ Jesus who is the light of the world, and enlightens every one that comes into the world [John 1:9], to the measure of which light in thee, I speak: which beares testimony for God, against sin & uncleanesse, and against pride & covetousnesse; and against the Deeds of Darknes, and all unrighteousnes. Something in thee testifies against all these things and Checkes, when any of these are Acted; or any Sin Committed. If thou hearken to it it will let thee see how thou hast spent thy tyme, and what assurance thou hast of the Love of God, who is righteous & just and cannot behould iniquity, nor cannot by no meanes cleare that which is guilty: for whosoever names the name of Christ must depart from iniquity. Now that thou may let the tyme past of thy life Suffice, which hath beene Spent in thy profession of God, & Christ; let that of God now search thee, & try thee what thou knowes of the true, & livinge God, if thou hadst never seene the scripture, for God was in them that spoke forth the Scripture, before the Scripture was written, Soe if thou doe not know that which gave forth the Scripture, how canst thou know that God which was in them which gave it forth; Seeing thou hast nothinge but the outside which is but paper, & incke; and why may not any that hath the outside, know God as well as thee. Now honestly with that of God in thy Conscience, Examine and see what thou possesseth, of that which is not paper & Incke, but the Spirit of the living God; for what would it avayle thee, or how couldst thou have lived with thy wife and children, if thou hadst had nothinge to have lived on, but the Covenannts or writings of an inheritance, and never have come to enjoyed the things they Speake of. I speake after the manner of men: Now doe but seriously Consider, how thou canst stand in the presence of the livinge God, because thou hast gotten the words which thy spoke forth which had the Spirit of the livinge God and yet thou lives in thy Sin, and in thy pride, and in thy lust; havinge an outside profession of the letter, without the Substance, & the life that Spoke it: all this is abomination to God; and that in thy Conscience which is of God, will answeare mee, that this is truth; Soe in love to thy Soule which lyes in the Death, which hath past over all men, which raignes from Addam till moses [Moses]; the light which Christ Jesus hath enlightened thee with, will let thee see, if thou turne thy mind to within to it; that thou art yet in Egipt, & utter darknes, and Moses which is sent of God, to bringe the seed out of the house of Darknes, & Bondage, thou Didst yet never know, nor never Shall, Soe longe as thou followes the way thou art in, yea, Eternally thou Shalt witnesse mee, for I know where thou art; and further in that profession I was I am sure, then ever thou was; though thou went away, for more knowledge of God (as wee Called it) and left this Country for want of that, yet the Eternall God Stayd; and that which was a barren wildernes is become a faithfull hill, and the knowledge of God covers the Earth, as the waters covers the Sea. Prayses eternall be to the glorious God: which is, and was, and is to come to thee, if ever thou witness him come, thou shalt witnesse, that he is not yet come. Soe beware how thou makest an Image, or liknes of truth, for god forbidds all Images, & Liknesses, in heaven above, or in Earth beneath: Soe a measure of the Substance, & of the life of all the types & figures, thou hast in thee, if thou be faithfull, & obeydient, when it Checkes and calls thee to repentance, for the Baptisme of repentance, which washeth away the filth of the flesh, thou art not yet come too: no nor the first principle that leads to it, which is the messenger that goes before him, to prepare the way for him, which Baptized with the holy ghost & with fire [Matt. 3:11]: Now minde honestly what thou hast, or can witnesse made manifest in thee, which Shall enter into the holy Citty; for nothinge that is uncleane shall enter: See whether thy Callinge & Election before, which none can lye anything to the Charge of gods elect which the Lord God justifyes. If thou will but seriously Consider thou wilt see thy blindnes, & Ignorance of God, & of his truth; for verily the living God thou art Ignorant of: and yet thou takes the Apostles words, and saith, that he forbidds a woman to speake in the Church [1 Cor. 14:34], but thou knowes not the life & Substance which was in him: for he knew the woman Clothed with the sonne [Rev. 12:1], & the woman that sitts upon the many waters [Rev. 17:1], which thou dost not, nor cannot put a difference be[twixt?] the pretious & the vile[.] Therfore let thy mouth be stopt, and beware (as thou lovest thy owne soule, & thy eternall peace) how thou speakes evill of the things that thou knowes not; and calls that common [?] & uncleane, which god hath Cleansed [Acts 10:14–15], as Some of thy Sect, & profession hath done, which is growne into high persecution & tyranny, for which there is a treasure laid up, in the wrath of the livinge God, which if thou live, thou Shalt See fullfild: verily, I love that of God in thee, and thou hast beene often presented to me in the Invisible, and I know there is something of God in thee, which thou canst not fly from, therfore to fly to it to be searched, & tryed is thy Safty. And if thou turne thy minde to the measure of God in thee, which beares witnesse for truth, & purity against sin and uncleanesse, thou wilt see this that I have written to be the truth, & that which I have written too, Shall be my witnesse Eternally, and to that of god in thee which my love is too, with which I have unity, I have cleared my Conscience, which thou shalt eternally witnesse and the lord god enlighten thy understandinge. Thou art affrayd to be deceived and thou that hast nothinge to trye the Spiritts with, whether they bee of God, thou art deceived, and art apt to beleeve every Spirit. But wee know the Spirits, And have that which tryes the Spirits, for the sonne of God is come; and hath given us an understanding, prayses be to the Eternall God forever. And if ever thou know the true & livinge God, thou must owne us, for god is but one, and the way one, the faith but one, & the Baptisme one by one Spirit into one body [1 Cor. 12:13], and the hope one, which hope purifies, and thy hope which Doth not purify, wee deny and thy faith which Doth not purifie the heart, wee deny: and thy Spirit which doth not Baptize into one body wee deny, Now try, & see where thou art, for he that is not with us, is against us, and the hipocrite & disembler, hath his portion with unbeleevers, and this thou shalt eternally witnesse, whether thou wilt heare or forbeare.

M: F:

Spence 3/155. Endorsed: "To Jeffrey Ellettson 1654 one of the same pffcion [profession] with mee whom I loved dearly"; "Several papers given forth by M: F: 1654".

19 TO JEFFREY ELLETSON 1654

"Oh, consider while thou hast tyme! of the livinge God I am moved to warne thee once more; for my Soule mournes over thee: thy Soule is deare unto me as my life."

This is the second letter (see Letter 18) in which Margaret pleads with Jeffrey Elletson to "turne to the light."

She explicates the meaning of "a pure conscience," and says, "this is all that you have of god." It is "the light of Jesus christ by which the Conscience is purged from dead workes, to serve the livinge God. But thou that denyes the light Shall never know what a Cleane conScience is."

Twice she uses the expression "hear or forbear," which appears four times in Ezekiel (2:5, 2:7, 3:11, and 3:27), when that prophet hears the message to be given to those that are "rebellious." She uses it appropriately, knowing that Elletson also will be familiar with that book.

It is interesting that at this early stage of her life as a Friend, Margaret felt able to write this pastoral letter, explaining Quaker principles. It indicates that she was well versed in scriptures and religion before she met George Fox and was able to grasp immediately the difference in what he was saying.

Jeffery Elletson

In much love, and tendernes to thy Soule doe I write to thee, and to the witness of God in thy Conscience doe I desire to be manifest. Oh man! what is become of thy Conscience? yee have a word in your profession of makinge a Conscience of your wayes; and that you must not goe against your Conscience. And all profession of what sort soever, yea, the very Papists will say they cannot Change their Religion for their Conscience? Now it is tryed how neare your Religion comes to the Conscience: when yee deny the light which Shines in the Conscience, which is the witnesse of god in the Conscience: which testifyes to your _______ when you doe amisse, which Checkes you when you act contrary to it, when you lye, this checkes you; when you Sweare, this checkes you; when you beare false witnesse against your neighbour, this Checkes you; this is all that you have of god. Oh miserable Creatures! what accot [account] will you give, to the lord when he comes & sayth, thou foole this night is thy Soule required of thee [Luke 12:20]? where wilt thou say thy Soule is? oh, consider while thou hast tyme! of the livinge God I am moved to warne thee once more: for my Soule mournes over thee; thy Soule is deare unto me as my life (god is my witnesse) oh stand still, and see where thy foundation is! Search and try with the light which shines in thy Conscience, which reprooves thee in Secrett: and shewes thee thy evill deeds. This will let thee see that thy foundation is on the sand. And the lord God shakes the pillars of the earth that it reeles to and fro like a Drunken man [Ps. 107:27]. where will thy profession be then? Thou professeth a god and a Christ in words (and Soe thou doest a Conscience) but in workes denyes all; who denyes the light of Jesus xt [Christ] by which the Conscience is purged from dead workes, to serve the livinge God. But thou that denyes the light Shall never know what a Cleane conScience is. Eternally thou Shalt witnesse mee. the light would guide thee, and lead thee out of Darknes and dead workes, and dead profession: to Serve the livinge God. But all who is out of the light, and denyes the light to be their guide, and teacher, Shall never know the livinge God. For that which may be knowne of god is made manifest in them, for god is light [1 John 1:5], and the light is of God: he is the Fath[er]: of light. The light comes From god, and witnesseth for god & leades to god. And this thou shalt eternally witnesse to be truth; whether thou heare, or forbeare [Ezek. 2:5]. And if ever thou know the livinge god, and the truth, as it is in Jesus thou must turne to the light. And if ever thou know thy owne Soule; (where it is, or what it is) thou must turne to the light. And if ever thou knowes the redemption of thy Soule from the death to the life: thou must turne to the light. and if ever thou know the Saviour (who saves his people from their sins) thou must turne to the light[.] And if ever thou knowes thy redeemer lives: thou must turne to the light. Thou may Say thou knowes he lives, but I aske thee where he lives in thee who denyes the light to be thy teacher. In much tendernes I have written; I find that love which I had to thee, was not faigned, neither doth it dye. For that witnesse of god in thy Conscience (to which I write) shall eternally witnesse it to be true love to thy Soule whether thou heare or forbeare [Ezek. 2:7]. Consider the Pharisies was convicted in their owne Conscience and went out one by one when christ Jesus (who Sayd I am the light) Spoke to them. And the Gentiles which had not the law, did the things conteyned in the law, which Shewed they had the law written in their hearts and their Conscience allsoe bearing witnesse [Rom. 2:14–15]. And the Apostle (who walked in the light) Sayd that that way which yee call heresie doe I worshipp the God of our Fathers [Acts 24:14] therin doe I exercise myselfe to have all ways a Conscience voyd of offense towards god, and towards men [Acts 24:16]. And the Apostle Sayd our rejoycing is this, the testimony of our conscience, that in simplicity, and godly Sincerity we have had our conversation amongst you [2 Cor. 1:12] in tyme past. And the Apostles walked by the manifestation of truth commendinge themselves to every mans conscience, in the sight of god. And the Apostle Spoke of houldinge the mistery of Faith in a pure conscience, & againe he saith, I thanke god whom I Serve with a pure conscience [1 Tim. 3:9]. Read the 9: Chapt. 10: Chapt: to the Hebrewes and there thou may See (if thou would turne to the light) thou may see the offeringe of christ the Substance, the everlastinge preisthood differinge from the first preisthood, which could not make the comers thereunto perfect as pertayninge to the Conscience. And soe now to thy conscience I have written and directed thy mind to that of god in thy conscience; that Soe thou might come to have thy heart sprinkled from an evill Conscience: and Soe might come to know the end of the Commandement which is Charity out of a pure heart, and a good conscience; and faith unfained. The Apostle Charged Tymothy to hould faith & a good conscience, which some had put away, who had made Shipwracke of their faith [1 Tim. 1:19]. And the Apostle Peter exhorted to Sanctify the love in their hearts, and be ready alwayes to give an answeare to everyman that asketh you a reason of your hope that is in you with meeknes and feare: havinge a good conscience, that wheras they Speake evill of you as evill doers, they maybe ashamed that falsly accuse your good conversation in xt. And when he spoke of Noahs preachinge to the Spiritts in prison, to them which were sometymes disobeydient he tould them they had the like figure wherunto even Baptisme doth allsoe Save us, not puttinge away the filth of the flesh; but the answeare of a good conscience towards god by the resurection of Jesus xt [1 Pet. 3:15–21]. Now See if thou have this answeare in thy conscience; who hath beene long professinge of Christ and his resurection: but the answeare of his witnesse in thy conscience Sees him not rissen yet. For death rainges in thee which hath passed over all men: and when hee is rissen; he redeemes from death to life. And soe now, as thou loves thy soule Search, and try: and remember thou art warned in thy life tyme, And when the day of thy callamity comes; then thou wilt remember me, and witnesse (when the booke of conscience is opened, and all Judged out of it) that this is love to thy Soule. Soe the lord god of power inlighten thy understanding and make thee Subject, that thou may not be high minded but feare. from a friend of thy Soule, & thy Eternall good

Margret Fell

Spence 3:156. Endorsed: "M F to jefery elleskin [George Fox] 1654"

20 To Gabriel Camelford, a Minister 1654

"I charge thee to proove thy wordes, or else confesse thy selfe to be a lyar & of thy Father the Devill who was a lyar from the beginninge."

This is a long denunciation of Gabriel Camelford, a minister at Staveley, not far fom Swarthmoor Hall. She calls him "a merchant of Babylon" with black and filthy wares; a "Child of Darknes & enemy of all righteousness"; "an Enemy of the first principle that leads to God"; and "a messenger of Sathen" among other things. The harsh language is not unusual for that era, though it may seem severe to twenty-first century ears.

She accuses Camelford of having no understanding of the living God, of Christ, and of the Light. On the contrary, his God is the "god of the world, & the prince of the ayre [air] which rules in the Children of Disobeydience." Camelford had evidently called Quakers "deluded," and she refutes this claim with invective and by quoting scripture. There are only rare touches of humor in Margaret's letters, and there is one bit of sarcasm here: "thou Blaspheamer and Antichrist who cannot confesse Christ come in the flesh, nor knows not of him but that thou hast heard he was Crucified at Jerusalem Sixteene hundred years agoe."

Although Camelford was detested by the Quakers, he was a respected minister with his own followers. Nightingale writes: "Camelford's character is above suspicion. The 'Commonwealth Survey' for 1650 speaks of him as 'a godly and painful man in his calling'; and Calamy refers to him as 'an useful Preacher in this remote Corner.' He clung to the neighborhood after his Ejection; suffered much for his steadfastness . . . " (Early Stages of the Quaker Movement in Lancashire, *p. 17). Camelford was "ejected" from his parish in 1662 after the Restoration, as were many Puritan and Independent ministers.*

Margaret refers to George Fox's enmity with Camelford: "And wheras thou saith Geo. Fox begune with thee, & thou made it good to his face[,] when was that, that thou stood to make any thinge good to his face . . . " George Fox writes: "I went to one preist Camelfords chapell & after hee had donne I began to speake the words of life to them & Camelford was in such a rage & such a fret & soe peevish that hee had noe patiens to heare but stirred uppe the rude multitude & they rudely haled mee out & strucke mee & punched mee & tooke mee & threw mee headlonge over a stone wall . . . " (CJ, *1:46). Fox was exercising his legal right, and Camelford's response was both illegal and cruel.*

Margaret challenges Camelford to prove that Friends "act or Speake or walke contrary to scripture." She berates him for preaching "in a pulpitt of wood"; for singing David's Psalms, as was the custom in some churches; and that "for a pretence [he] made longe prayers."

There is a reference to "going naked," which was a behavior of a few early Friends. It was intended as a visible sign to shock people into seeing their own sinfulness. Although the biblical sign was understood by people in the seventeenth century, as it would not be today, it offended their religious views, as well as scandalizing them. Margaret writes, "thou goes about by all meanes thou canst to make the truth odeous, & bringes in the going naked, who is[,] as the profett Is[aiah] saith[,] was set for signes & wonders amongst the generation of despisers." Isaiah 20:3 reads: "And the Lord said, Like as my servant Isaiah hath walked naked and barefoot three years for a sign and wonder upon Egypt and upon Ethiopia."

Her last word in this letter is simply a citation of a text: 2 Peter 2:1, which reads "But there were false prophets also among the people, even as there shall be false teachers among you, who privily shall bring in damnable heresies." Camelford would know whom she meant.

Camellford[,] thou hath shewed forth thy poyson & enmity, that Lodgeth in thee as no other can proceed from thee who art a marchant of Babilon, and now that the light is rissen which makes thee maniffest[,] soe that now thy wares which thou hast Soe longe Sould [sold] doth appeare blacke & filthy, and with the light of Jesus Christ which is now rissen, art thou & they condemned to the fire[.] But thou stands up for thy Kingdome of Sin, & Darknes & thy God who is the god of the world (which ha[th] blinded thy eye) thou pleads for; against the eye which is the light of the body which makes thee manifest to be of the Serpents brood, and of the seed of the Serpent whose head is to be bruised, with the seed of the woman [Gen. 3:15.] Christ Jesus the light, which Thou (Child of Darknes & enemy of all righteousnes) pleads against with thy filthy darke faigned imaginations, who knowes not the livinge God at all, but art an Enemy to the first principle that leads to him, who is the Father of light, For God is light & in him is no darknes at all [1 John 1:5]; and thou Enemy of God denyes this light. therefore blush thou messenger of Darknes & be ashamed & stopp thy mouth for ever speakinge of God or Christ[,] who denyes the first principle that leads to him, and the Doctrine of Christ thou denyes: and the words from Xts owne mouth thou denyes 8 John 12 [John 8:12] 3: John 19:20:21: [John 3:19–21] And the 12: John 46 [John 12:46]: & 1: John 9 [John 9:5]: now thou Blaspheamer and Antichrist[,] who cannot confesse Christ come in the flesh [1 John 4:2–3], nor knowes not of him but that thou hast heard he was Crucified at Jerusalem Sixteene hundred yeares agoe. Read thy selfe heare [here] to be a messenger of Sathan, and thy God the god of the world, & the prince of the ayre [air] which rules in the Children of Disobeydience [Eph. 2:2], and thy God is come to be Judged and now is he cominge to be cast out, and he is lifted up from the Earth that will draw all men after him, and soe thy torment & sorrow is begunne which shall never have an end[,] & soe the more thou stirrs & acts against him the more is thy torment & sorrow, and this thou shalt Eternally witnesse, strive as longe as thou can, and as longe as thy power will give thee leave, for thou art under the Chayne. And this that thou saith is the finest garment of Sathan Shall bind & Chayne thee & thy God and his power, and cast him into the pitt & sett the seale upon him[;] And Christ Jesus the sonne of the livinge god was ever Counted a devill with thee & thy Generation, who talked of him, but never knew him[,] but when he could, crucified him, as thou (Enemy of God) doth, who would keepe his witnesses Slayne, & in the grave, least they Should rise and witnesse against thee who art a murtherer, & a devourer. And thou Speakes of poore deluided Creatures, thou blind sott[,] who can be more deluided then thou art, who art a Child of Darknes yet, and a pleader for Sinne & the Divells

Kingdome, and an opposer of the light of Christ & perfection, what can they be deluded in, that turnes from thee, except thou call that Delusion, that turnes from Sin, & the Divell & Darknes[;] this is all that thy Kingdome is made of. And thou speakes of the devill transfforming himself into an angell of light: But thou art not come soe farr, for thou art a Child of Darkenes[,] & thy God is the prince of Darknes[;] and thou never knew what it was to be in the light yet, & the Divells knowes more of the true God then thou doest eternally, thou shalt witnesse this to be truth for the devills beleve & tremble and if ever thou know the livinge God thou shalt confesse it. And thou comes with a Charge in the presence of God & his holy Angells, & then afterwards thou saith att the great day when both you & I Shall appeare before God to give an accompt of what we have done in the flesh[.] Oh thou abominable blinde beast thou hast layd the shame of thy nakednes open, doth thou come with a Charge from God & the presence of his holy Angells with a lye in thy mouth, doth thou say thou art in the presence of God & hast not yet appeared before him, nor hast not yet given an accompt of thy deeds done in the flesh nor hath not yet seene the great day of the lord, canst thou stand in his presence which never saw his day yet[?] oh thou abominable lyar[,] stopp thy mouth, they are very blinde that cannot see thy blindnesse & darknes & confusion, let all who reeds thy words marke thy abominable grosse Ignorance & darknes, and presumption that dare talke of the presence of God & his holy Angells and never saw his day yet, but though thou be blind & doth not see it, the day of the lord is come & hath made thee manifest and from the presence of the lord & his holy angells thou art shutt Eternally[,] and before him thou cannot stand[,] who is a consuminge fire to thee, & all thy filthy blacke Darke stuffe, which thou conjures up in the blacke art of thy Imagination with thy mind turned from the light. Therfore doth the light condemne thee from God & all who is of him. And thou speakes of false Christs, & false prophetts [Mark 13:22]. oh. thou Enemy of all truth[,] whether art thou the false Christ & the false prophett, who denyes the light, which christ Jesus saith he hath enlightened every one withall or those who witnesse Christ to be the light who sayth I am the light of the world & doth enlighten everyone that cometh into the world [John 1:9]. Now let all people reed Christs words in the Scripture & trye thee whether thou be not the false prophet which denyes christ Jesus the light, or wee which witnesse him to be the light. And let the Scripture trye thee whether thou be the Antichrist which denyes christ come in the flesh [2 John 1:7], or we who witnesse him come in the flesh. And thou saith if you say it is the Doctrine of Christ that they bringe, & the power of Religion, Know that the Scripture will contradict you. Therfore I charge thee to proove thy wordes, or else confesse thy selfe to be a lyar & of thy Father the Devill who was a lyar from the beginninge, wherin doe wee act or Speake or walke contrary to Scripture, Charge us if thou canst by playne Scripture, or stopp thy mouth, And againe I charge thee to be an actor contrary to the Scriptures, and will proove thee by Scripture to be an adder, and a deminisher from the Scripture for which the plagues of god is added to thee (& that in the matter & forme of that thou calls thy worshipp,) in all that thou acts contrary to the script[ure]: did ever minister of the Gospell, preach in a pulpitt of wood, thou deceiver[,] & yet thou saith thou art one, did ever minister of the Gospell take a text and preach a Quarter of a yeare upon it as thou doest? did ever minister of the Gospell Singe Davids conditions in rime as thou doest? David was before the Apostles[.] which of them sings Davids conditions as thou doth? A day of vengence waites for thee[,] thou hippocrite, did not Christ Crye against those that devoured widdowes houses & for a pretence made longe prayers as thou doest [Matt. 23:14]. See now what Scriptures thou hath for any of thy practices[,] & yet thou chargeth us with contradictinge the Scriptures. oh that thou art not ashamed to open thy mouth with the Scripture. And when thou saith thou hath it under our owne hands that we deny the righteousnesse of Christ through faith[,] produce that I Charge thee, & bringe it to light or else confesse thy Father that setts thee a worke. And wheras thou saith Geo. Fox begune with thee, & thou made it good to his face[,] when was that, that thou stood to make any thinge good to his face, or any other (the least boye or girle that comes before thee) when did thou stand to vindicate thy god, or thy doctrine to their face, but the best way that thou hast is to turne thy backe & run thy way, or get thy hearers to hayle them out, or sett them in the stocks, or if it be in the markett thou gets among thy hearers that they may rayle [rail] against them, for thy god will not defend thee against them, this thy owne hearers will witnesse against thee, and yet thou art not ashamed to lye, although there be hundreds to witnesse against thee. And wheras thou saith their light, doctrine & practice is very dishonest, proove thy words I charge thee wherin, & how or else confesse thy selfe to be a lyar & a false accuser[,] and thus thou goes on lyinge and falsly accusinge the Innocent[,] for which the Lord god will plead with thee, who pleades the cause of the inocent, and thou goes about by all meanes thou canst to make the truth odeous, & bringes in the going naked, who is[,] as the profett Is[aiah] saith[,] was set for signes & wonders [Isa. 20:3] amongst the generation of dispisers and wonderers which shall perish, and as Ezekiell was who cut of[f] the one side of his haire of his head, & of his beard [Ezek. 5:1], and to lay seidge [siege] against a bricke which to thee would bee madnesse, & odious who art dead in thy sins & trespasses[,] who knowes no command of the Lord nor teaching of his Spirit in the least measure, but what thou knowes, thou knowes naturally as a brute beast, and soe in these things thou hast corrupted thy selfe, and lays open thyne abomination, and thou hast drunken deepe of thy mothers cupp of fornication [Rev. 17:4] & soe thou shalt drinke deepe of the wrath of the Almighty even to the dreggs. And for all thy hard speeches that ever thou hast spoken[,] and for all thy lyes & slanders which thou hast layd upon the truth of god[,] will the Lord god plead with thee by sword & by fire, at thy great day of appearance which thou confesseth is not yet come unto thee, and therefore thou knowes not thy doome; and yet thou Speakes of the presence of god, & his holy angells. oh thou disemblinge hippocrite, at that day thou shalt give an accompt for these words, and before his presence thou shalt fly, for thy damnation slumbereth not, nor thy Judgment of a longe tyme lingereth not 2:Pet 2:3

M: F:

Spence 3/125–126. Endorsed: "to Camellford from M: F: 1654".

21 To John Ravell 1654

"The scripteurs is Printed & I have them,
& doe read them & I do owne them to be as they speake,
& doth beare testemony to the truth of them.
by the same spirit as spoke them."

No biographical information is available about John Ravell. Internal evidence indicates that he may have been a minister; that he wrote controversial papers, like

Margaret Fell; and that he had criticized her writings, accusing her of not knowing the scriptures.

She refutes this contention, filling her paper with even more than the usual number of biblical references.

She asserts that Ravell's use of scripture is in error: "thou hast not wreten them as they were spoken, but sume [some] thou hast corrupted, to sum thou hast added, to sume deminished." The Quakers, including George Fox and Margaret Fell, believed that there had been centuries of misinterpretation of the Bible, and the Friends were going back to the original meaning. She writes of Ravell: "Thou art of the same Jeneration, & of the same spirit & of the same seed which Crusified him [Christ] & put him to deth," and that he "hath not his word abiding in thee."

She urges him to repent and gives a list of quotations concerning heaven and hell. There are a few softer notes: "In love to thy soule I did bid thee repent, & soe I doe yet" and "thou wilt find that the purest love to thy soule is to deale plainly and truly with thee." She must have realized that her letter is stern, for near the end she acknowledges that he may count her "worse then caine [Cain] becase I tell thee the truth."

An Answer to John Ravell. 1654.

A paper to hand receved from a troubled, tossed & unstabell spirit which is not founded upon the Rocke xt [Christ] Jesus, which is unmovable, & who is bulte upon him canot be moved, but thou art tossed to & frow in thy froththy immagannations and as the troubled seas; the Prophet speaketh of. the wicked is as the troubled sea casting up mier & derte [dirt] [Isa. 57:20]. thou art tormented. & thy tormenter is neare thee; thou will not git rede [rid] of it tho [though] thou thinkes to git ease by thy much babeling. thou Brings that scripteuer; where its said they make wise unto salvation [2 Tim. 3:15], but thee they have not made wise unto salvation, for thou art under condemnation, & where salvation is[,] it is given for wals [walls] & Bulworkes [Isa. 26:1], but this thou art an enemy to[,] whose folish hart is darkned; thou hath written downe many scripteurs in thy paper, but thou art soe blind & Ignorant, that thou hast not wreten them as they weare spoken, but sume thou hast corrupted, to sum thou hast added, to sume deminished[,] in sume thou hast set other words then they stand in the Scripteurs, as thou can doe noe other whoe art of another Spirit & of another Nateur then spoke them forth: thou confesseth they were given forth by Inspiration of the holy gost, which thou never knew but art an enemy to[.] soe lett thy mouth be stopped: for the scripteurs is Printed

& I have them, & doe read them & I doe owne them to be as they speake, & doth beare testemony to the truth of them. by the same spirit as spoke them, but thy Black darke spirit I doe deny. for thou brings the scripteurs but as the devill did, when he temted [tempted] christ[.] the divell knowes the scripturs[,] as thou doth whoe art an enemy to the light, hee is the Prince of darknes, & thou art one of his Children who contems the light[,] which xt Jesus who is the light hath lited every one with all; by which light hee teacheth his people, & the minesters of xt turned people from darknes to the light, & from the power of sathen [Satan], which power thou art under who art an enemy to the light[.] a child of darknes thou art; & a lyer: & all lying is of the Divell, & he is the father of all lyes [John 8:44]; in that thou chargeth me in thy paper that I will not be tryed by the scripturs; & that there should be sumthing in that I wrett, contrary to and against scriptur: I Charg thee hear [here] to be a lyer. & let my papers which I wret be my testemony, & let any that hath but any honnesty Reed them & try them, what ther is there wreten but there is scriptur for it & thou Let the scripurs Try thee & thy spirit to be of thy father the devell. And soe, I charge thee in the presence of the living god as thou wilt answer it at that dreadfull day of thy account[,] that thou let christs words & the Appoestels words, & the prophets words alone: for [they?] are now of him but as thou taketh them as a theefe, & soe as the appostle did, I say let him that stole heare now[.] I am against him[,] saith the Lord[,] that steals my word from his nebur [neighbor]; & [use?] there tongues, and say he saith it [Jer. 23:30–31], when saith the lord, I never spoke to him. Therefore beware of this[,] least the lord feed thee with worm wood, and make thee drinke the water of gale [gall] [Jer. 9:15]; thou saith that in this I bid thee doe that. which is Contrary to that which xt bad thee doe; hee bad thee search the scriptur [John 5:39]; I say, thou art of the same Jeneration, & of the same spirit & of the same seed which Crusified him & put him to deth, tho they had the scriptures that did testefy of him & they did search them, & xt tould them that they did thinke to have eternall life in them as such blind hipocrets as thou doth, but saith christ[,] yee will not come to mee that yee may have life; soe in this scripture that thou has brought[,] reed thyselfe to be one of the hipocrets, which xt cried woe Against which sought to kill xt, because hee made himselfe eaquell with god [John 5:18], as thou may reed verce [18th?] these weare [were] they that hee spoke too which had the scripturs, but did not know his testemony, noe more doth thou; thou naither knoweth xt nor the father; tho thou hast longe searched the scripturs yet thou hast naither hard [heard] his voyce at any tyme, nor seen his shape noe more then they did [,] verce the 37[,] & yee have not his word abbiding in you[.] for him whome he hath sent him yee beleivd not [John 5:37–38] saith xt, yet they had the scripturs, which did testefy one [on] him, but they did not beleive that the father had sent him, & soe here thou art; Amongst those that did persecute Jesus, & sought to slay him, & with them thou shalt have thy porshtion, And soe I bid thee againe, Let xts words & the Prophets & appostls words alone for thou art here found by thy owne testemony, amongst the unbeleivers, parsecuters of christ, which hath not his word abiding in thee [John 5:38,] which hath naither hard [heard] his voyce at anny tym nor seene his shape & this is the scripteur that thou hast owned for thy selfe, & soe herd[.] thou hast shut thy selves out from amongst the saints and servants of god, & hath owned thy selfe to be one of those to whome christ saith[,] I know you that you have not the love of god in you. I am com in my fathers name & yee Receve me not, if another shall com in his owne name[,] him yee will Receive; how can yee beleve, which receve honor one from another, & seek not the honour that coms from god only [John 5:42–44], Hard thou hast set & owned thy selfe, and hard I owne thee to be. soe thou stand, untill thou Receve thy Portion, for thou doth Err, & doth not know the Scripture nor the Power of god, But art an enemy to his Light & to his Power, And hast placed thy selfe amongst those that put him to Death: And thou has made answer for Keane [Cain] and saith hee kildd but his Brother[s] Body, but thou lookes upon mee to be worse, then Kaine: becase I bid thee Repent And told thee thou & thy spirit is condemned into the pit[,] which words I doe owne & say the same yet, But thou saith both soule and Body which I did not, as my Paper shall testefy for mee & in love to thy soule I did bid thee repent, & soe I doe yet, & I bid thee give over persecuting of Jesus, it is hard for thee to kick against the Pricks [Acts 9:5]; Lest sudden distruction Com upon thee, And remember that thou art warned, thou saith that the scripteure tels thee that them that is in hell, Canot com to heaven, & these that is in heaven Cannot com to hell, here thou shalt be tryed by the scripteurs; for a fier is kinled [kindled] in my anger and shall burne to the lowest hell [,] saith the lord Deu:32:22: the sorrowes of hell have compassed mee about, saith Divid [David] 2Sam:22:6: thou wilt not leave my soule in hell, Psalm:16:10: for great is thy mercy towards mee, and thou hast delivered my soule out of the lowest hell Psalm: 86:13: if I made my bed in hell behould thou art there[,] saith david Psalm 139:8: thou shalt beat him with the rod and shalt deliver his soule from hell saith Salomon provbes the 23 & 14: [Prov. 23:14] The strong among the mighty shalt speake to him out of the midest of hell eze: 32:21 [Ezek. 32:21] & they shall not lye with the mighty which are gone downe into hell verss, the 27 [Ezek. 32:27] Though they dig into hell Thence shall my hand take them though they clime up to heaven[.] thence will I bring them downe saith the lord Amos the 9:2 then Jonah prayed unto the lord his god and said[,] I cryed by reason of my Affliction unto the ld [Lord] & hee heard me[;] out of the belly of hell cryed I & thou heard my voyce Jonah 2:2 heare lest theis scripts [scriptures] try thy light & thy spiritt to bee a lying spirit contrary to the Scripts which makes thee manifest that Thy soule is in hell & Thy spiritt a spiritt of darkness which ariseth out of the bottomless pitt, & thether the light condems it [,] and from thence thou cannot git for thou art under the cheane [chain]: [Rev. 20:1] And thou saith that thou wret in thy leter for some of ous to com to thee[,] which I doe not remember that any such thing was in thy letter, Nether did I minde what had past betweene thee & others[.] But what was there wretten in the Paper, under thy one [own] hand, I answered, & that was as much as any honest man would have required but th[ou] art soe drouned in Envy that thou art past shame; it may bee ther may som com to thee, & stop thy mouth of that where in thou saith I am a lier, But it will be thou that will be found the lier for thou art soe full of confusion and darknes. And soe Drunk with passion, that noe body Knows what to make of thy writings, for thers nothing appears in thee but a black Confused Spirit, ignorant of god And of all Truth, and of the Scriptures; And thou That saith that thou art not in egipt, and that Phara [Pharoah] is dead, thou art the lyer, for Phara is alive in thee, which keeps the seed of god in Bondage, And thou art in the house of darknes and Bondage: and the witnes of god lise [lies] slaine in thee, as the scriptur saith, there dead Bodis [bodies] shall ly in the street of the great sety [city] which spiratelly [spiritually] is called Soddom & egipt, [Rev. 11:8] But thou who art the darke spirit which assendeth out of the Bottomles pit, looks upon it carnally. And soe art Blynd & yet have Eyes, and Deafe and yett have Ears[.] if thou have an Eare thou may hear what the spirit saith. Soe take thy ly home into thy owne Bosom, thou saith it is true that thou lives among sorcerers & south-sayers, if I could see my selfe and my generation; I answer I cannot see thee amongst us, neither cann thou see thy selfe amongst us, for thou knowes that thou and thy spiritt is condempned [condemned] into the pitt from amongst us, and soe thou may stay amongst the wiserds and deviners where thou confeseth thou art, for thou art heaping up teachers, thou cannot abide sound doctrine, thou thinkest it is hard to bee delt plainly with[.] thou seekes to kill him that would tell thee the truth, thou is one of them that saith prophesy smoth [smooth] things [Isa. 30:10], thou would bee dabed [daubed] with untempered morter, [Ezek. 13:10] the beast would have his wound healed [Rev. 13:12] but that will not stand forever, thou wilt find that the purest love to thy soule is to deale plainly and truly with thee & thou shalt etternally wittness that which hath beene written to thee to bee truth and love to thy soule[,] whether thou heare or forbeare [Ezek. 2:5], tho thou may shake it of[f] for the present[,] yet when thou comes to bee tryed by the sworde & by fire [Isa. 66:16] thou then wilt see that noe hipocricie nor deceipte can stand, when the dead[,] small and great[,] stands before god, and are Judged out of the things written in the booke according to thiere works [Rev. 20:12] then thou wilt wittness what I have written to bee truth and at that day thou wilt remember mee[,] though now thou countest mee worse then caine[,] because I tell thee the truth which thou shalt one day wittness, Thou saith the Apostle sett there hands to there letters but soe doth not I; An:[swer] the Apostles letters was writt to the saints and bretheren which was in the unyty of the spiritt, & in the bond of love sanctified in xt Jesus[;] but thou art none of these, to thee I am [as?] unknown & yet well knowne if thou had an eye to see;

M:F:

MSS at Swarthmore College Library. Endorsed: "by M: F 1654 [George Fox]".

22 To George Fox and Justice Anthony Pearson and his Wife 1654

To George Fox: "My deare brother who art in the power of the livinge god whose powerfull living presents [presence] is with you & doth manifest himselfe through thee."

To Anthony Pearson: "Deare brother Anthony thou hast bene servicable to the lord since thou wast caled [called], thou shalt not louse [lose] thy reward."

This letter was written to Anthony Pearson and his wife and to George Fox who was staying with them (Ross, p. 58). The first part of the letter is addressed to George Fox. It expresses her conviction that God has chosen him to "communicate to others" God's love and power and that they are living in a special time when "the lord is coming to visit his owne . . . now is the day: the deafe shall heare the words of the booke & the eye of the blind shall see out of obscuritie & darknese."

There was a tremendous sense of hope and joy among early Friends, the conviction that the entire world could be changed by people hearing and receiving directly the spirit and presence of God. This conviction gave them the strength and courage to change their own lives in spite of difficulties and hardships.

The last part of the letter is addressed to Anthony Pearson (Letter 6): "My deare & tender love in the bowels of love to my deare brother Antony Pearson & his wife[.] my deare harts waite upon the lord & be faithfull." It is kind and encouraging, "the lord [is] present, & neare for he is not a god afar off." She praises Pearson's being "servicable." Because of his knowledge and position as a judge he was able to assist Friends with their legal battles as well as writing for the movement.

There is a striking difference in the way Margaret addresses the two men. George Fox is considered to be on a much higher level in his relation to performing God's work in the world.

My deare eternale brother in the eternale love & ________ of my father, & heare my love meets thee & saluts thee, & therein am I present with thee, & have communion with thee, my deare hart whome the lord hath chosen out of the world & seperated thee out from the world, for his owne worke & service [Acts 13:2], to comunicate to others what thou hast receved from him[,] the fountain of infinit & eternale life, that others may p[artake] of the same with you, the lord god of power is arising & the glory of his majestie, & the livinge fountaine of life is opening[,] the streames of his everlastinge love is coming forth, into the harts of his people, & he is raising up his owne seed, that it may serve him in the land of the livinge, & now is he bringinge to pase [pass] & fulfilinge his many & great promises in the day of the deliverance of sion[.] now is he setinge his king[dom] upon the holy hill of Sion, & he is breakinge down his enimies under his feet[.] my deare brother who art in the power of the livinge god whose powerfull living presents [presence] is with you & doth make manifest himselfe through thee, to strike through the earthly vaile in others, to that which is pure of himselfe in them & now is the time that the lord is cominge to visit his owne. which is of him & soe many as receves him he gives power to becom the suns [sons] of god [John 1:12], the lord hath given thee [the] tongue of the learned [Isa. 50:4] to know: how to speake a word in due season,: to: him [that is] weary, [that hath laid] longe in the [grave] the house of darknesse & he is neare that Justifies: thee, & will stand up witnesse in all conciences for thee, there shall thou be knowne: for now the lord is makinge bare his holy arme: in the eyes: of all nations & all the ends of the earth shall see the salvation of our god[.] now is the day: the deafe shall heare the words of the booke[,] & the eye of the blind shall see out of obscuritie & darknese, the lord god of life[,] light & power direct thee to the guidinge[,] leadinge & raisinge up of that which is of him pure in every ones concience, that there thou maist [mayest] be cleared & Justified before him, who is the pure eternale Judge, & that in his power & life thou may dwell & stand, & tryumph over all the powers of darknese of hell death to raigne over all in him who is kinge of kings & lord of lords[.] my deare brother[,] I rejoyce to hear from thee. my life is with thee[,] & he shall keepe & preserve thee who is the life of all[,] the vertue of all things[,] & who uphoulds all things by the word of his power [Heb. 1:3] which word he hath given thee in thy hand which hath tow [two] edges which cuts downe all his enimies, & raises up his owne seed to the gathering together that which is scatred [scattered] & to the bringinge & againe that which is driven away[,] that his great name may be mad[e] manifest & be a praise upon the earth[.] to him be eternale praise & glory forever,

my deare & tender love in the bowels of love to my deare brother Antony Pearson & his wife[.] my deare harts[,] waite upon the lord & be faithfull to him in that which is mad[e] manifest in you: & be not troubled about many: things: but: be constant & faithfull to that one thing which is nesecary [necessary] & you shall see the lord present, & neare[;] for he is not a god afar of[f,] but where he is a god it is where he is neare at hand & where sumthinge of him is witnes[sed] & posest [possessed] there he is a god, but to them that looke at him afar of & without them, there he is not knowne and so they ignorantly worship the unknowne god [Acts 17:23]: & deare brother Anthony[,] thou hast bene servicable to the lord since thou wast caled [called], thou shalt not louse [lose] thy reward [Matt. 10:42], if thou wait thou shalt see the treasure of infinit riches open to thee[,] & the inheritance which never fades away [1 Pet. 1:4] but runs & streames out afresh, the lord god of power preserve you and keepe you faithfull waiting in the pure: which will lead you up to god who is pure: & eternale[,] & to him be eternale glory & praise for ever,

Swm MSS 3:100. Endorsed: "M F to G F 1654".

23 & 24 TO THOMAS SHAW, A MINISTER 1654

"Query: Whether thou be not
he that is the hyerlinge, and not the Shepheard,
whose owne the Sheepe are not . . .
and whether thou be not the hyerlinge . . . & careth not
for the Sheepe but thy care is for thy gaine?"

Letter 23 is a brief warning to Thomas Shaw, written on a page by itself. It may have been a preface to Letter 24, which is made up of two series of queries. The first twenty-one are Margaret's answers to queries that Thomas Shaw put to her, or possibly to Quakers in general, that she feels obliged to answer. The second series is made up of seventeen queries that she in turn puts to him. This format was often used in controversial tracts (BQ, pp. 194–195, 300–301).

Thomas Shaw was a priest at Aldingham, near Ulverston. The endorsement describes him as "that great persecutor . . . one of the first in England, that put friends in prison for tithes." One of the men he sent to Lancaster prison for non-payment of tithes remained there until he died in 1655 (CJ, 2:475). Shaw held the living at Aldingham from 1625 to 1667. Nightingale notes that Shaw cast Leonard Fell into prison in 1667, so Shaw was consistent in his persecution of Quakers. Nightingale also comments, "During the Commonwealth, and at the Restoration, [Shaw] adapted his principles to the changing times" (Nightingale, Early, *p. 33).*

The required payment of tithes to the established church was a major source of conflict for Quakers and for other nonconformist sectarians. They protested against being forced to pay for a minister and a teaching that they did not accept. To the Quakers "hireling priest" was an epithet that described a hypocritical parasite, living off poor people's money, totally removed from the teachings of Christ and the early message of the gospels. Some years later, in 1659, seven thousand women signed a petition to Parliament against oppression for non-payment of tithes, and "at the head of the list are the signatures of Margaret Fell and her seven daughters" (Ross, p. 42).

The questions Shaw puts to Margaret Fell concern theological beliefs and interpretations, and she answers with numerous scriptural references and with warnings that "the cupp of fury & Indignation of the Lord is coming towards thee . . . and a Day of vengence of the Lord waites for thee." The controversy particularly concerns the symbolism of the Book of Revelation, Isaiah, and Ezekiel. She refers to his church as "a heape of lyme & Stones" and insists that he does "not know the true church." She ends the series with "soe remember that thou art warned in thy life tyme."

The seventeen queries Margaret Fell puts to Shaw include accusations that he is a "blynde watchman" and a "greedy Dogg." By his preaching he "causes the people to Erre." Her indignation is aroused because he has not been a good shepherd of his flock. He has not strengthened the diseased, "neither healed the Sicke, neither bound up that which was broken. . . . But with force & Cruelty hast thou ruled." Is he not "one of the preists that teacheth for hyre, and that divineth for money: which Micha [Micah] was sent of the Lord to cry against?"

Letter 23.

Thomas Shawe the Indignation of the Lord is kindled against thee, and the fire of his jealosie is burninge, yea, that is kindled, which all the powers of Darknes Shall never quench, And thou art given a thorne in the flesh, and a Messenger of Sathan to buffett withall [2 Cor.12:7], which is good for those, whom the grace of the Lord is sufficient for./

Letter 24.

An answeare to some Queries which came from Preist Shaw or his Clerke, which Queries proceeds out of the mouth of the Dragon and out of the mouth of the Beast, and out of the mouth of the false prophet; as ye may read 16 Revel:13: [Rev. 16:13]

1:Q: First thou asketh when began the Christian Jewish Church?

Answ: When Christ their spirituall Kinge came, then Heathen, which never knew Christ nor none of his Church: for thou[,] preist Shaw[,] art Shutt out from him, & all who are of him Eternally.

2: Thou asketh when began the Christian Catholique Church?

Answ: that which the pope called Catholick When thy Father the pope Set up his Supramacy[,] from whom thou preist Shaw & thy Breth: [brethren] hath your Authority and ordination, and thy Christ, is Antichrist; for from Christ Jesus who is the Sonne of God, thou Shaw, & the pope, & all your Catholicke Church (as thou calls it) is Shutt ________ eternally

Q:3:4:5:6: Thou asketh what do you understand by the Dragon? 4: what by his heads? 5: what by his hornes? 6: what by his 7: Crownes?

Answ: Wee doe understand & knowe assuredly & affirme, that the pope ___ ___ ______ (who houlds your Catholique Church and thou, and all you who have your ground & ordination from the pope, are the Dragon: And with your Seven heads & 10: hornes and 7: Crownes (which thou speakes of) are you Standing before the woman, who is ready to be delivered, for to devoure her Child as Soone as he is borne [Rev. 12:3–5], as thou Shaw hath made it manifest Sufficiently, by thy pushing with thy 7: heads, & 10: hornes & thy 7: Crownes: But thy Crownes is falling and thy power is Limitte[d], and thy 10: hornes is a Falling; and the Dragon is coming to be Chayned, and the man Child is brought forth, and is caught up unto god, & to his throwne; who doth rule the nations with a rodd of Iron, and doth dash to peeces thee and all thy power, And by him Shalt thou (Shaw) be confounded & overturned, and thy 7: heads, & thy 7 Crownes:

7:8: What do you understand by the flood of waters? & who Drunk up the flood of waters?

Answ: We doe understand & know that thou[,] Shaw[,] who art of the Dragon, & the ould Serpent; that thy poyson & enmity which thou casts out of thy mouth is the water & the flood of poyson and persecution & tyranney which thou cast after the woman that thou might cause her to be carried away of the Flood of persecution[,] but the Earth helpeth the woman, and Swalloweth up the flood, which thou who is the dragon hast cast out of thy mouth [Rev. 12:15–16].

Q:9;10:11:12: Thou asketh what doe you understand by the first beast? & tenthly what by the Second[?] Eleventhly what manner did this beast arise? Twelfthly what is the two hornes of the beast?

Answ: Thou art of the Beast that riseth up out of the Sea: and the Beast riseth in that maner as thou riseth in persecution & tyranny for the Beast is like unto a Leapard and his feet are as the feet of a Bear, and his mouth is as the mouth of a Lion, and the Dragon gives him his power, & his Soule & great Authority [Rev. 13:1–2]. Now Shaw heal thy Selfe, and thou wilt See, thou art of the Beast who hath thy power & Authority from the Dragon, and thou art one of them that openeth thy mouth in the Blasphemy, against god to Blaspheame his name, & his Tabernacle [Rev. 13:6] & thou art one which makes warr with the Sts [saints] and thou must first See thy Selfe to be of the first Beast, with his 10: hornes pushinge, and who is full of the names of Blaspheamy, before thou know what the Second Beast is (which riseth out of the Earth) which hath but two hornes [Rev. 13:11], And what we doe understand, thou Shalt never know till thou knowest thy self for we know thee to be of the first Beast, and we know the Second Beast; but the Second Beast from thee is hidd, who art of the first Beast & doth the works both of the First & second.

13:Q: Thou asketh what is the whore of Bibilon?

Answ: The whore of Babilon is the mother of Harlotts, And thou Shaw art one of her Children, who would make thy Selfe Drunke with the blood of the Sts [saints] & of the Martyres of Jesus, as thy practice makes this manifest. Read thy Bible & thou wilt See that thou art of the whore of Babilon, and thou drinkes deepe of her abomination & filthynes & fornication (as thy fruits makes thee manifest) Therfore of the cupp of the fury of the Lord thou Shalt drinke even to the dreggs; the mouth of the Lord of hoasts hath Spoken it [Rev. 17:4 and 18:3].

Q:14: Thou asketh what doe you understand by the Angell?

Answ: we understand The Angell Michael & god fought against the dragon [Rev. 12:7] ______ _____ ____ _______ _________ manifest the mistery of Babilon: but this to thee is a mistery, who art of the Beast & of the whore.

Q:15: Thou asketh what is the end of the prophecy of this Church?

Answ: The end of the prophecy of the Church (as thou calls it) thou hast no Scripture for thy words but the end of the prophecy which knowes & Sees the Church thou shalt never know for thou doth not know the true Church, but art Ignorante of the first principle that leads to know it. Therfore Stopp thy mouth, for thou knowes no Church but a heape of lyme, & Stones, (which thou calls a Dreadfull house) except that thou know the popish Catholique Church (which is thy mother) but thou art Such a darke beast, that thou knowes not thy mother yett.

Q:16: Thou asketh what is the end of the prophecy of the world?

Answ: That is thy prophecy who is of the world which prophecyes for Baal, & divines for money, and the Lord god Saith he is against thee, and thy end is destruction, and thou art nigh unto cursinge whose end is to be burnt. And Soe thou Shaw read thy end, & the answeure to thy Querie.

Q:17: Thou asketh what is meant by the 7: Spiritts?

Answ: That thou (Shaw) Shalt never know, who art perfect in the mistery of Iniquity.

Q:18:19: What is meant by the waters which Ezekiell Saw issue from the Temple? And what is meant by the risinge of the waters?

Answ: The meaninge (as thou calls it) to thee Shalt never be knowne, that which Ezek: Spoke & knew (who was a true prophett of the Lord) from thee is hidd; for thou art curst: And the waters of Ezeck: and their risinge is a mistery to thee, who art the false prophett. And thou who would have a meaninge to them, the plagues of God is thy portion: and they are as they Speake, and knowne they are to all the true prophetts of the Lord, who are Sent of god as Ezeck: was.

Q:20:21: Thou asketh what is meant by the Lions whelpes? and what is meant by the Severall waters in the Sea?

Answ: Thou that knowes not the meaninge of this, art in the Sea, and thy waters is Babilons Confusion, and thou acts in the Darke, & in Iniquity; and thy iniquity to thee is a mistery, and thy Babilon is cominge unto heapes: and thy Dwelling [Jer. 51:37] is a place for dragons, & an astonishment and an hissinge it is cominge to bee and thy roaring like Lions is cominge on: and thy yelling like Lions whelpes is hasteninge. And Soe (Shaw) if thou canst read thy Selfe, thou mayst read the meaninge of thy Queries. But thou art blynde & the Queries thou hast asked is a mistery to thee, and the meaninge of them thou knowes not. But they are cominge on to be fulfilled (and that Shalbe for thy destruction, & for thy Sorrow, and misery) Thy Bibilon is fallinge, & her abomination is come up into the remembrance of the Lord: and the cupp of fury & Indignation of the Lord is cominge towards thee, which thou Shall be sure to Drinke deeply of. Therefore prepare for it, for thy Iniquity is allmost full, and a Day of vengence of the Lord waites for thee, till thou have filled up the measure of thy iniquity. Soe remember thou art warned in thy life tyme. Soe thy queries are answered and thou (foole), art never the wiser.

And now wee have answered thy Queries
a few Queries to thee preist Shaw

Queries

1 First Whether thou (Shaw) be not one of those blynde watchmen which queries after the meaning of the prophecy that are Ignorant, and one of those dumbe doggs that cannot barke, Sleepinge lyinge downe, loving to Slumber and whether thou be not one of those that Isaiah cryd against Such? [Isa. 56:10]

2: Whether thou Shaw be not one of the greedy Doggs, which can never have enough, and one of the Shepheards that cannot understand, which lookes for thy gaine from thy Quarter and whether thou be one of these, or Isaiah that cryed agt such? [Isa. 56:11]

3: Whether thou be not one of the prophetts that Comitts Adultery, and houlds up the horrible filthy [things?], and walkes in Lyes and strengthens the hands of evill doers: that none doth [turne?] from his wickednes, Soe that they are all of them as Sodome, and the inhabitants therof as Gomorah, whether thou be not one of these, or the prophett that cryed against Such?

4: Whether thou (Shaw) that Steales the word from thy neighbour and useth thy tongue & Saith, he Saith, when the Lord Saith he never sent thee? And whether thou doth not cause the people to Erre, by thy Lyes, & by thy lightnes: and therfore thou dost not profitt the people at all? And whether thou be one of these, or Jerem: [Jeremiah] that cryed against them? [Jer. 23:32]

5: And whether thou (Shaw) be not one of them that hath seene vanity & lying divinations[,] Sayinge The Lord Saith, & the Lord hath not sent thee? And whether thou be not one of those prophetts that prophecyes out of thy owne heart? And whether thou be one of these, or Ezeck: [Ezekiel] that Cryed against such? [Ezek. 13:6]

6: Whether thou be not he which Jerem: Speakes of, which is as a Cage full of birds, Soe art thou full of Deceipt; therfore art thou become great, & waxen rich, and for these things will the Lord visit thee? And whether thou be one those, or Jerem: that Spoke against those? [Jer. 5:27]

7: And whether thou be not one of those Shepheards that feeds with the fatt, and cloathes with the wooll: which the Lord Sent Ezeck: to cry woe against? And whether thou bee not hee which the Diseased hath not Strengthened, neither healed the Sicke, neither bound up that which was broken, neither hast thou brought that againe which was driven away, neither hast Sought that which was lost: But with force & Cruelty hast thou ruled? But now whether thou be not one of these, or Ezeck: that cryed against such? [Ezek. 34:2–4]

8: And whether thou be not one of those which causeth the people to Erre, and byteth with thy teeth, and he that putteth not into thy mouth, thou even prepareth warr against him? Now let thy practice Judge thee whether thou be not one of these or Micha [Micah] that cryd against such? [Mic. 3:5]

9 And whether thou be not one of the preists that teacheth for hyre, and that divineth for money: which Micha was sent of the Lord to

cry against? Now whether thou be the false prophett or Micha let thy practice Speak? [Mic. 3:11]

10 And whether thou be not the theefe which cometh not but for to steale, & to kill, & to destroy[,] which cometh not in at the Doore, but Clymbeth up another way; which all thee [the] Sheepe of Christ did ever deny: and doth deny thee? [John 10:1]

11 And whether thou be not he that is the hyerlinge, and not the Shepheard, whose owne the Sheepe are not; (which Christ Jesus Speakes of) and whether thou be not the hyerlinge; which flyeth because thou art an hyerlinge, & careth not for the Sheepe but thy care is for thy gaine? [John 10:12–13]

12: Whether thou be not of this sort which creepth into houses & calleth them Churches (and saith how Dreadfull is this house, which is nothing but lyme & stone) and soe leadeth captive Silly women laden with Sin, & ledd away with diverse lusts; ever learning & never able to come to the knowledge of the truth (the fruites of thy hearers makes thee manifest) let that Chapt: trye thee whether thou be Soe or Timothy that Spoke against Such? [2 Tim. 3:6–7]

Query 13 And whether thou be not he which through Coreteousnes [courteousness] & fayned words maketh marchandize of the people; but thy Damnation Slumbers not, nor thy Judgment of longe tyme lingreth not, for it is hastening & comeing upon thee; & will finde thee out?

14 And whether thou be not hee which the woe is too, which runs greedily after the Errour of Baalam for rewards: and in the way of Cain thou art; and perish thou shalt in the gain Sayinge of Care?

15 And whether thou be not one of those which Serves not our Lord Jesus christ but thy owne belly, and by good words & faire Speeches Deceive the hearts of the Simple? and whether thou be not one of these let thy practice Speake?

16 And whether thou art not one of those who are enemies to the Crosse of christ. whose end is destruction, whose god is their belly, and whose glory is their Shame, who mind earthly things[.] now let this Scripture and thy owne practice trye thee whether thou be not one of these, or the Apostle paul that Spoke against such?

17 And whether thou (Shaw) be not one of those whose mouthes must be stoppt, who Subverts whole houses, teachinge things which thou ought not for filthy lucres sake and whether thou be one of those or the Apostle who Spoke against these let all who knowes thy practice Judge.

Now answeare these Queries by plaine Scripture & thy owne practice, or also Stopp thy mouth & confesse thy Selfe to be a theefe, & a robber & a murtherer of Soules.

Spence 3/137. Endorsed: "to prest Shaw from M: F [George Fox]".

Spence 3/138–139. Endorsed: "M F to prest shaw 1654 [George Fox]"; "That great persecutor at the parish of aldingam in fornace [Furness] in Lancashire & one of the first in England, that put friends in prison for tithes & so Continued a Great persecutor till he dyed." ; "The Answeare to Shawes Queryes".

25 To Friends, Concerning Tithes 1654

"So every one to the light as you are moved . . .
it will let you pay no tythes, nor let you Joyne to them
that doth demand them, nor them that pay them."

"Tithes were due on wages, which did not endear the established church to poverty-stricken labourers. Levellers and other radicals won support . . . for their demand that tithes be abolished: so did Quakers." (Hill, Liberty, *p. 63)*

This paper may have been written in 1654 or later. Paying tithes continued to be a source of Friends' difference with society until well into the 1680s (Horle, Q.&EngLegalSys, *p. 144). The paper, or epistle, is a thoughtful consideration of the spiritual basis for refusing to pay tithes. Margaret contrasts the "changeable" of the outward world, which includes tithes and offerings, with the "unchangeable" that "with the light sees the ministry of Life, which is glorious." She writes: "they that prison you for tythes, prison the light of god in themselves."*

She urges Friends to "Bee bould [,] bee vallient [,] bee Courageous for the truth upon earth." She uses imagery from the book of Revelation: "fire . . . coming down from god;" and "the third Angell . . . which powers [pours] the vialls upon the waters which doth becom blood." It is remarkable how many Quakers were willing to go to prison, sometimes to remain and die there, for refusing to pay tithes.

Another theme is the necessity for repentance. "Be yee seperate, & touch no unclean thing, for God is making a seperation betwixt the pretious & the vile." The light will enable them to know the truth, to "discover unto you all your former ways." Quakers generally did not emphasize the sinful nature of man as much as the Puritans did, but repentance was seen as one element of being able to experience the grace of God.

The end of the epistle is like a benediction: "The Comfort & refreshment of the Lord, is in the Inward man, & that is spirituall & Eternall, which the world knowes not, so to the Eternall keping [keeping] & guiding, . . . of the Lord god Allmighty, I leave you." Her final reference to Joel 2 points to an Old Testament description of how "the day of the Lord cometh." [Joel 2:1]

Concerning tythes

All freinds who be in the Eternall Light, that sees the figures, the shadowes, the tipes, the begining & the ending of them, with the light which never Changith, & seeth that which Changeth, the Changable things, with which light you Come to see the sum, the substance of the things, which as figured and shadowed forth, so all you in the light dwell that with it you may come to know the ministry of Life, & the ministry of Condemnation; with the light that sees before that ministry was, and the end of it, and with the light sees the ministry of Life, which is glorious, which exceeds in glory the ministry of Condemnation, which is Condemnation with the light, which leads to the glory, the ministry of the spirit, so now all you, that now with the light witness the substance Christ Jesus, give a reason of your hope to every one that doth aske you of it, & with the light see what the Apostle spoake, when he spoake of tythes and offrings, & of the priesthood, & when hee spoake the sum of those things he had spoken, so with the light denyes the first priesthood, & the tythes & offrings that are Changable, those was to bee ministered that was Changable, now with the light Changable is Condemned, & the unchangable ministry of Life witnessed, & with the light that Law is denyed that gave the tythes, & the law & command with the light is denyed & Condemned, with which light god is seen before the things was, & the tyme & end of those things, Christ Jesus the sum the substance; to all you that bee Called with writs which Come from above, to answer because you will not pay tythes, to that light in you all I speake, which light comes from Jesus; that with the light you may all Com to see Jesus, the sum the substance; the end of the afore mentioned tythes and offrings, & so to the light in you all I speake, that with it your minds may bee guided, to answer & declare that truth, to the light in every ones Conscience, to witnesse the [sunne], & to shew to all, & to declare to the highest bentch in the Nation, when yee suffer for the sum [son], to trample upon all that is Contrary to the light the powers of the earth; and to witnesse the sum [son] who hath assended farr above all principallities

& powers, and to witnesse the ministry of life, & the ministry of Condemnation, & to shew forth the sum [son] & substance, and to give a reason of your hope to all principallities & powers, that ever then you may stand, in the light which Comprehends them all, you may see the sum [son] which sits above them all, & so then over all the world you stand, & all the workes are brought to the light, & you bring all mens workes to the light, & being guided with the light, it will not let you feyne to none of their Inventions, that is made in that nature that actes Contrary to the light, but it will bring you to witness the sum [son], & keep you from all the spirits of the world, and hear [here] the royall spirit in all begins to grow, which will bring you to witness the sum [son] over ______ world, & so if they will take goods let it go, & if he will have thy Cloak, let him have thy Coate alsoe, and still yee alone keep all to the light above which Comes from Jesus, to every ones Conscience I speake, to keep Clean the Conscience, that with it all that is Contrary to it may be Condemned, so every one to the light as you are moved, for it will let you pay no tythes, nor let you Joyne to them that doth demand them, nor them that pay them, but it will bring you to witness the sum [son], and it is the Condemnation of the Changable ministry, for the tythes & offrings was ministered in the first priesthood, & it was glorious in its place, with the light it was & is seen & Condemned, the begining the tyme & ending of it, & with the light the sum [son] is witnessed of those things the ministry of life, & all in the light dwells to guide you that to the light in all Conscience you may bee made manifest of Jesus, that they that prison you for tythes, prison the light of god in themselves in the parteculer, that over all yee may stand, & the light which is pure to lead you to act that, that no condemnation uppon your actions afterward may Come with the light[;] for who Contrary to the light doth act upon him & his actions Condemnation doth Come, & soe over all the world yee may stand in the light which doth it Comprehend & Condemne & that with it you may witness the sum [son], the end of the things, and to you this is the word of the Lord god; and none to act nothing in your owne wills, but who act Contrary to the light and pay tythes, goes to the Changable, and so with the unchangable is Cast out from the Children of the light and Condemned, and so the Children of light are one in the light and with the light seas [sees] the body, & the head and are all one. where did Christians sue one another for tythes in the first priesthood, but with the light they witnessed the Condemnation upon the first priesthood, & with it they witnessed the sum [son] Christ Jesus of the things in the first priesthood, to the light in your Consciences which comes from Jesus I speake, that with it you may all see what you act[.]

All from every where bee bould[,] bee vallient[,] bee Couragious for the truth upon earth, now shew your selves to bee valiant souldiers for the Lord, this is the day of the Lords battle, & this is the day of the deceivers of the nations, which are in the foure Corners of the earth, Gog and Magog are gathering together to battle [Rev. 20:8], to Compass the saints and the beloved City, but fire is coming down from god to devoure them, and the divell that deceives them is to bee Cast into the Lake, & the beast and the false prophet; now is the trumpet of the Lord sounding to battle, the alarum is beating[,] the flying angell is gone forth in the midst of heaven, having the Everlasting Gospell to preach to them that dwell on the earth, saying with a loud voice, fear god & give glory to him for the houre of his Judgment is Come [Rev. 14:7], now is the vialls pouring fourth, and the lord Comes as a theife in the night [2 Pet. 3:10.] he that watcheth is blessed and keepeth his garments least hee walk naked and see his shame, the third Angell is gone forth, which powers [pours] the vialls upon the waters which doth becom blood, and the righteousness of the Lord is appearing because he hath Judged that, for they have sheed [shed] the blood of saints, and of the prophets, and hee will give them blood to drinke, for they are worthy [Rev. 16:4–6], therefore all freinds stand up for the Lord, and bee valient souldiers in his battle, & bee not afraid of man whose breath is in his nostrills [Isa. 2:22], nor what man Can doe, for all his workes shall perish, and the mooth [Behemoth?] shall eate them, but fear the Lord god Allmighty, which is and which was and is to Come, and give glory to his name, for hee is worthy, and terrable is hee to his Enimies; and therefore take heed of siding with any man whatsoever, but with the Lord alone, and Come out from among them, and be yee seperate, & touch no unclean thing and I will receive you saith the lord god allmighty [2 Cor. 6:17], least you be partakers of the plauges, which is reserved for the wicked, for who may abide the day of his Coming, or who shall stand when he appeares, for he is as the refiners fire [Mal. 3:2] and dwells in the Everlasting burning, and wilbe avenged of all his Enimies, and soe deare freinds[,] as you tender your owne Eternall salvation, bee faithfull & bold in the tyme of tryall, for hee is making a seperation betwixt the pretious & the vile [Jer. 15:19], betwene theise that serve him and theise that serve him not, remember that you have weryed [wearied] the Lord with your words, but hee is sending his messengers to prepare the way before him, & the Lord whom yee seeke shall suddainly Come to his temple, even the messenger of the Covinent, behold hee will Come saith the Lord of hoasts [Mal. 3:1], therfore waite uppon the Lord that hee may purge you and refine you as gould and silver, that you may offer an offring unnto the Lord, an offring in righteousnesse [Mal. 3:3], which wilbee pleasant unto the Lord, for all your former offrings, and your sacrifice and your prayers, which yee offred up in the first nature (which is Cain) which all the world Lives in, & all the ministry of the world, and all the profession in the world, & the highest formes in the world whatsoever is beeloe the sonne of god, for he is without forme, yea all the best performance that ever you offred up in a forme is Cains sacrifice an abomination unto the Lord[.] neither did he ever except [accept] it, neither will he except you, but abell [Abel] & his offring he accepted, soe mind what generation you are on, & take heed of slighting or looking at the love of god lightly, or doing the worke of the Lord negligently, for the Curse is to that nature, therefore turne in & waite upon the Lord within you, & that Light of god will discover unto you all your former wayes, & it will let you see that all this while you have been making Clean the outside of the Cup & plates, as the pharisees did which Christ Cryed wo [woe] against [Matt. 23:25], and within all filthiness & rottennesse, therefore repent & turne unto the Lord & hast [haste] hast to meete the Lord, for the day of slaughter is at hand, as you tender your owne salvation, be not slothfull, nor hide not your talent in the earth [Matt. 25:25], for the Lord will require it at your hand, and you shall not escape the Judgement of god, all freinds who deare [dare?] owne the Lord to bee your freind, remember Moses, who Chused rather to suffer affection [affliction] with the people of god, then to Indure the pleasure of sin for a season for the wickednesse of the wicked shall Come to an end, and the Lord hath reserved the wicked for the day of trouble. I am blacke but Comly a daughter of Herusalem, looke not upon mee because I am blacke, because the son [sun] hath shined upon mee [Song 1:5–6]. persecution ever was & is the portion of the saints, if ever you owne god or the truth of god, you must owne persecution, but bee not discourraged, nor faint in the way, nether bee you of a doubtfull mind, for the scripture is now fulfilling, as you may read in Luke the 24th wher Jesus Christ saith, they shall lay there hands on you & persecute you and deliver you up to the sinagogues, and in to prison [Luke 21:12], and it shall turne to you for a testimony & hee saith when these things begin to Come to passe, then look up and lift up your heads for your redemption drawes nigh [Luke 21:28]. and so deare harts[,] the Lord is proving you, and trying you how you will stand for him now in the day of persecution & tryall, therefore bee strong in the Lord & in the power of his might, and bee faithfull in obedience of his truth in yourselves, though in never so little measure made manifest, if you harken to the Lord in you, your soules shall Live, & you shall eate the good of the Land, & bee kept in perfect peace whose mindes are stayed on the Lord [Isa.1:19], so waite to be made worthy to pertake of the blessing, which Jesus Christ spoake to his desciples, blessed are you when men shall hate you, & shall seperate you from there Company, & shall reproach you, & Cast out your name as evil for the son of mans sake, rejoice in that day and Leap for joy, for behold your reward is great in heaven [Luke 6:22–23.] now waite in obedience upon the Lord, and there will rise the swift witnesse in you, which will witnesse for the Lord against all the world, and the worlds wayes & worships and fachions & Customes & which will Carry you on above all the worlds persecutions, for it is but outward & Carnall, but the Comfort & refreshment of the Lord, is in the Inward man, & that is spirituall & Eternall, which the world knowes not, so to the Eternall keping [keeping] & guiding, leading & searching of the Lord god Allmighty, I leave you, and the Everlasting god of power bee with you[.] farewell, read the second of Joell & the second of the Corrinthians & the sixt, the Lord is fulfilling theise scriptures amongst you, send Coppies of this note to freinds in Cumberland/

Your dear freind in the truth of God
Margret Fell

Tapper MSS Box C:4:23, pp. 52–54.

26 TO FRIENDS IN THE NORTH 1654

"That there may be some money in a stocke,
for disbursing according to necessitie as the lord requires . . .
to prisoners necessitie."

Isabel Ross writes of Margaret Fell's contributions to the movement: "Another piece of work she did was to start a fund, known as the Kendal Fund, which functioned from 1654 to 1658, and led in a few years to the foundation of similar funds in other parts of the country. These were for the purpose of helping the missionaries with some of the necessaries of life. . . . The gifts included clothing, relief to the prisoners, books, and money for the expenses of travel" (JFHS *Suppl.*, *24:7). "Money collected was dispensed to itinerant Quakers in England, but beginning in 1655 modest amounts were channeled to support Friends witnessing in Scotland, Ireland, Venice, the Netherlands and Germany" (Greaves, 3:227). Braithwaite writes: "She took a leading part in the establishment, development, and administration of the fund collected at Kendal . . . the accounts of which were regularly rendered to her from 1654 to 1657, and are still preserved.* (BQ, *p. 135).*

Margaret's epistle to Friends is a carefully constructed plea for funds. The argument moves from her address to the "children of the Light," to "the Light which is the whole body," to an emphasis on the unity of the body of which they are members: "So my dear hearts, in that which is the Light of the whole body, that eye which leads into the unitie, to that be subject, and obedient, to be serviceable to the whole body." She reminds them that "where one member suffers all the members may suffer with itt" and speaks of the "bonds and imprisonment and hard persecution and tirany" suffered by some.

Then she points out that Friends in Westmorland have borne most of the financial burden, "the heate of the day," and that help is needed from the wider community. Margaret was the leading spirit of the Kendal Fund, and the two men who collected and disbursed monies were Thomas Willan of Underbarrow, near Kendal (EQW, *p. 616), and George Taylor. There are over seventy letters written by the two men to Margaret between 1654 and 1659* (CJ, *2:470). George Taylor (d. 1696) was an ironmonger of Kendal. In 1658 he was imprisoned for not paying a fine but was pardoned by a committee of the Council of State. He provided information to Parliament in 1659 on Friends and moderates who were qualified to serve as justices of the peace (Greaves, 3:227). In 1663 Will Caton addressed Thomas Willan as "my dear and ancient Friend"* (CJ, *2:471).*

To all my deare brethren and Sisters who be in the Light, children of the Light, who is obedient to the Light, which is the eye of the whole body[;] in which Light, everie particular dwell and stand single, and you shall see the whole Bodie full of Light: for this leads into the unitie and oneness, which is in the body, though many members; So my dear hearts, in that which is the Light of the whole body, that eye which leads into the unitie, to that be subject, and obedient, to be serviceable to the whole body; and give freely up to the service of the bodie which is one, and but one in all; and who is faithful, the one spirit makes subject: even soe yee are called in one hope of your callinge, where there is one lord, one faith, one baptism, one God and father of all, who is above all, and through and in you all. Soe all my deare brethren and sisters[,] in this which is etarnall, and leads into the etarnall unitie and oneness, be faithfull and obedient; be of one minde, and live in peace, for the promise is but to one seed, and you are all one in Christ Jesus, are faithfull in him, to whom all the promises are[.] Yea and Amen. & now is the lords day maid manifest, wherein he requires of you[,] in your particuler mesures[,] to be serviceable to the body in your particuler places, for there is many members, and but one body; and the head cannot say to the feet, I have noe need of you, for every one, in their measures, may be serviceable to the whole bodie, in what is called and required, and who dwels in the light, it makes subject, to be serviceable to the bodie, And now, that nothingg may be kept backe, but as you have received freely, soe freely you may administer, in obedience to the one Etarnal light, you may be serviceable to the whole bodie. And as the lord hath loved you, with his everlasting Love, and visited you, and hath made manifest his etarnall light in you, which is the way that leads to the father, and hath raised up the etarnall witnesse in you, of his everlastinge love, Soe let that love constreane you to love one another, and be serviceable to one another, and that evrie one may be made willinge to suffer for the bodies sake, and that there may be noe rent in the bodie, but that the members have the same care one over another, and where one member suffers[,] all the members may suffer with itt[.] & here is the unitie of the Spirit, and the bond of peace: And that you cannot be unmindful, nor is not ignorant of the present suffering, and service of many members of the bodie in this our day, who is in bonds and imprisonment and hard persecution and tirany, which is acted in the will of man, upon the righteous seed, which is of the body. And others there are that are sent forth into the service of the most high god[,] as Lambs amonge wolves[,] who is made willinge and subject to give their backes to the smiter [Isa. 50:6], yea to lay downe their Lives for the bodies sake, & great and hard persecutions hath been suffered for the testimony of lord Jesus. Now that everie particuler member of the body may be sensible of the hardship and sufferings of others and be willinge and serviceable in their places, in what the Lord requires, and to remember those that are in bonds, as bound with them, and them that suffer adversitie, as you beinge your selves also in the bodie, and that you may beare one anothers burdens and be equally yooked in the sufferings; our friends in Westmoreland haith borne the heate of the day, and many have bine sent forth into the [Lord's] service from thence, and that haith caused the burden to lie heavie upon the rest of the friends there about[.] and most of all on our friends att Kendal [.] our deare brethren, George Taylor & Tho[mas] Willan[,] who have bine verie servicable in their places to the truth to the whole bodie, to those that have been sent forth into the ministry, and to them that have suffered Imprisment, and for bookes, and severa[l] other things, that have bine needful, wherein they have bine serviceable to the truth[,] I beare them record, and have disbursed of their own moneys, when it haith bine needfull, untill it was contributed amonge friends thereabouts, soe I, knowinge at this time that they are out of purse, I see in the eternall unchangeable light of god, that all and everie member who are of the bodie, ought to be serviceable in their places, and to administer freely accordinge to their abilitie, as they have receaved of the lord freely, for Jerasalem [Jerusalem] which is above is free, which is the mother of us all, and who is here, is one; Therefore, that there may be some money in a stocke, for disbursing according to necessitie as the lord requires, either to friends that goe forth into service, or to prisoners necessitie, I see it convenient and necessarie in that which never changeth, and am moved of the lord to acquaint you with it, that in your severall meetings in this part of lancasshire, and westmoerland (exceptinge the towne of Kendal) & at the severall meetings in Cumberland[,] and soe to be gathered, and sent to Tho[mas] Willan and George Taylor to be disburst accordinge as the lord requires, and that the burden may not lie upon them more then others, who have bine verie servicable in that thinge. Soe my dear brethren and sisters[,] let brotherly love continue, that everie one[,] as the lord moves you and opens your hart, you may administer, that you may come into the oneness in all things, and in that abide which dwells in love and unitie, which is one for evermore. and soe you come to the fulfillinge of the scriptures in your mesures, and the pracktice of all the s[ain]ts in the light that ever went before./

Soe god almightie of life and power[,] preserve and keepe you in his everlastinge love and unitie./ Your deare sister in the everlasting unchangable truth,

Margret Fell

Thirnbeck MSS 1. Also in Works, *pp. 56–59. Endorsed: "To Friends Consering A Collection"; "to Frinds Consarninge Colecshon from M F 1654".*

27 To Ambrose Appleby 1654

"I have written in tendernes to thy soule, that thou would come Downe to the light which is all the sainst [saints] teacher to be guided & ledd by that where the unity is, where there is noe difference noe Division."

Ambrose Appleby was a scrupulous Friend who objected to collecting money for Friends who needed aid (as described in Letter 26) on the basis that it was "contrary to the Institution of Xt." Presumably this is the same objection that Friends had toward "hireling priests." There are references to a "paper" of Appleby's and Margaret's previous "note," and she affirms her concern for him: "truly that note which was written to thee was in love to thy soule & that of god in thee."

Margaret points out the inconsistency of Appleby's position, for he did contribute to the Kendal Fund. She argues: "if it be contrary to the Institution of Xt then it is Contrary to truth" and he "speakes & affirms one thinge & vindicates another." Her main argument is that the light and truth and Christ are all one, and this is a mystery not easy to fathom. She refers to scripture (though not quoting it), "For it is written in the law of Moses, Thou shalt not muzzle the mouth of the ox that treadeth out the corn (1 Cor. 9:9)" to strengthen her argument that it is appropriate to support those Friends who work in the ministry, i.e. they "reape Carnall things where they have sowne Spirituall things." Later in the letter she refers to the Key of David (Isa. 22:22) to indicate the need to understand the mysteries.

Ambrose Appleby of Stratford, Yorkshire, was converted to Quakerism by James Nayler in 1653 at a Meeting in Appleby's house. Nayler "publickly declar'd the messenger of the glad tidings of Truth, & hee & his message were gladly received by the said Ambrose Appelby" (FPT, *p. 88). Margaret is writing to a person who is a part of the movement, and she tries to persuade him to share her point of view. This letter, and others like it to early Friends, shows their need to gain clarity and work out their differences on issues where there is confusion.*

Ambrose Apleby I have recevd thy paper in answer to mine in which thou doth acknowledge that thou said a Collection for the ministers was contrary to the Institution of Xt. [Christ] truly that note which was written to thee was in love to thy soule & that of God in thee if thou wilt come downe to it, the light of Christ Jesus in thy Conscience which never Changes it will let thee see what it is that speakes in thee, and the light of the body which is the eye which is single which sees the whole body full of light [Matt. 6:22], this will passe Condemnation upon thy words: for if it be contrary to the Institution of Xt then it is Contrary to truth for there is no truth but what is in the Doctrine & Institution & order of Xt. & thou sayth that Labour might have beene spared in Citinge soe many Scripts [Scriptures] for the ministers of Xt. to reape Carnall things where they have sowne Spirituall things [1 Cor. 9:11], & thou Saith thou hast beene ready to contribute which I doe beleeve thou hast done, all which thyne or others Contribution, (if thy first words stand which thou saith thou will affirme) if it be contrary to the institution of Christ, then it is for Condemnation with the light which is Eternall, for Christ is but one, & his way & institution but one, now see where thou art who speakes & affirmes one thinge & vindicates another, for thou saith it is contrary to the Institution & yet thou Confesseth thou Acts in it. Now to the light of Chr: Jesus in thy Conscience I doe speake in love to thy soule that with it thou may see that which is yet a mistery to thee; though thou saith thou sawe as much as I but let that passe. And as I said to thee before, those whom Xt sends forth hath a treasury which thou knowes not, & the vinyard was not there planted. And for that thou sayes, I might have had thee & the Informer together, truly yee are both one in the thinge for thou sayth the very same as he sd [said] And though thou makes light of it, thou litle knowes what these words might have brought forth if they had gone abroad amongst friends, and for the note which was given forth to goe amongst friends the Liveing God of heaven & Earth will beare witnesse to it, And then wilt thou be found a false witnesse who saith it is Contrary to the Institution of Xt[;] but as for thy words I am willinge to beare them, but in love and tendernes to thy soule I exhort thee to turne to the light which leads to the Day which makes all things manifest, and though thou looke upon it to be plaine in the letter yet to thee it is sealed. Therfore to the key of David which opens & none shutts & shutts & none opens [Isa. 22:22] turne to this, for without this thou shalt never know, & thou then will see with what eye thou now sees, & this I have written in tendernes to thy soule, that thou would come Downe to the light which is all the sainst [saints] teacher to be guided & ledd by that where the unity is, where there is noe difference noe Division. And whatsoever thou Doth or acts for truth if it be not done in the light & from the pure principle of God in thee, it is out of the unity & out of the freedome of the Sts [saints] __________ who Dwells in the Eternall Light, And soe I have cleared my Conscience to thee & am willinge to Lye under any Censure Soe that I might gaine thy Soule[.] Soe I ame cleare of the blood of the Inocent in thee, & if thou come Downe to be guided by the pure & the Just in thee, which is of God, that will witnesse mee & condemne thee, & the same that condemes thee justi[fies the] elect.

all this is love to thy soule which thou shall Eternally witnesse, & that word contrary to the institution of Christ which thou saith thou wilt affirme if that be truth in thee, then it overturnes all that thou hast contributed & all that I have written & this thou makes litle of[;] soe let any wh[ich is] in the Eternall unity Judge with what eye thou sees

FHL MSS Box 10(7)1. (This is a photostat with a transcript.) Endorsed: "To Ambros Apleby". No signature or date on the photostat, but the folder cover says: "Margaret Fox to Ambrose Appleby 1654".

28 AN EPISTLE TO FRIENDS 1654

"My deare hearts, bee faithfull every one in your partecular measure of god, which hee hath given you, and in the Invisable waite in silence, and patience, and obedience, in that which opens the mistery of god."

This is a pastoral letter to Friends in which Margaret expounds some basic principles of Quakerism. She emphasizes the "measure of god," "the Light of Christ Jesus in every one of you," and the importance of waiting in silence in Meeting, as the Quakers did, in order to be guided to the right way. She urges them to "keepe in the fear of the Lord god, and be Loe [low]: that the plant of the Lord may take deepe roote downeward in you." To her, the Light is glorious, but it also is dreadful in bringing to light things that a person might rather not see.

The words "Imaginations, or images or formes" have different meanings than they do today. Imagination is suspect, for it turns people away from "pure worship"

and the "Eternal and Invisable." Genesis 8:21 says "The imagination of man's heart is evil from his youth." Forms and images are not the real thing.

Margaret gives direction for the requirements of speaking in the silent Meeting: "beware of hastiness, or frowardness, in speaking many words, except it bee from a Cleare Discerning, of a pure moving, and that you discern what you speake from, and what you speake to" for "soe to speake . . . is a minister." It is clear that the sex of the minister is not an issue.

A postscript requests that "this bee Coppied over & sent amongst freinds to be read at their meetings." Her epistles, like those of George Fox, Francis Howgill, and others, were distributed and read in this way.

> To all my dear bretheren and sisters who bee in the Light, which Christ Jesus hath Enlightned you with all, I warne you and Charge you from the Lord God, that you be faithfull and obedient unto the measure of god, which hee hath given to every one of you to profit withall, and that the Light of Christ Jesus in every one of you, Lead you, and guide you, that with it you may see all that which would lead you forth from it, and that with it you may see the theife, and the betrayer, which draws backe from it, and beware that you are not to [too] hasty in going before the light, and acting those things which are to bee Condemned by the Light, but bring all to the Light, to bee proved and tryed that their bee noe workes of darkness amongst you: but that you may bee keept in the fear of the Lord, and abide in that which keepes in his presence, the Light, for dreadfull and terrable is the Lord god to the disobedient, and those that will not that hee should raign over them, must bee bound in Chaines, and cast into utter Darkness, Theirfore my deare hearts[,] bee faithfull every one in your parteculer measure of god, which hee hath given you, and in the Invisable waite in silence, and patience, and obedience, in that which opens the mistery of god, and Leads to the Invisable god, which noe mortall eye Can reach unto or behold, therefore as you tender the good of your owne soules, and their Eternall good, keepe in the fear of the Lord god, and be Loe [low]: that the plant of the Lord may take deepe roote downeward in you, and that none of you fly above your measure, and soe the airey spirit get into the Imagination, and their [there] rest, and make an Image Like Truth, and soe yee eate from flesh and break the Command of the Lord, and so betrays the simplicity, and lead [?] out of the pollutions of the world, & the filthines of the flesh and in that which is pure worship god, in spirit & in truth, and now is the Lord seeking for such

worshipers in this his day, which day makes manifest, who turns out of the Eternal and Invisable, into the Imaginations, or Images or formes, though it bee of the Everlasting truth; if it bee a Form, or a Cover, it Cannot stand, but it is seen, and discovered, and knowne, wher the Eternall rules, therefore let the Eternall search and try every particuler, and see what you are covered withall; yea[,] let the living principle of god in you all, examene what you Injoy and possesse of him which is Eternall, and what is of him will stand in his presence, who is a Consuming fire unto all that is not of him, and what you doe Injoy of that, which is Eternall of god[,] begotten of him by the Immortall word; abiding, and being faithfull in that, yee shall witness a growth in that which is Eternall, in the Inward man, according to your measures, hee that is in the Light, if hee walke in the Light, and bee faithfull to it, hee shall have the Light of Life; and those that can witness this, waite to be made free with the son, for who the son makes free is their [there] free indeed, soe to the measure of god in every one of you I speake, that with it you may search and try wher you are, and what you Can really and truly witness in the presence of god, borne in you, that you do not deceive your selves, and worship the workes of your owne hands, for god is not worshiped, but in that which is spirit and truth; and I warne you, and Charge you[,] in the presence of the living god, that beware of strife amongst you, and of the spirit which exalts it selfe. for, hee that exalts him self shalbee brought Low, the Lord hath said, and your Lord and master, Jesus Christ knows that spirit, and will bring it down to the dust; therfore, in the fear of the Lord god stand and bee Lowe and humble, for hee that brings downe, and humbles that nature, which would bee up; hee shalbee exalted, soe Learne of him, that is Lowe and meeke, & that makes Cleane the house in Every parteculer, and beware of hastiness, or frowardness, in speaking many words, except it bee from a Cleare Discerning, of a pure moving, and that you discern what you speake from, and what you speake to, and soe to speake hear [here] is a minister, for your speaking words at random, when you are in the power, under pretence of a burthen, which burthen is the earthly part in your selves, and the words that you speake belonging to your owne parteculer, this being spoaken out to others, and not from a Clear discerning what it is to, then others take it and Judge it; Soe I warne you to bee silent, and to waite Lowe in the silence, untill the word bee Committed to you to menister, and never to strive for maistery [mastery], but Chuse to esteem others better then themselves, and that their bee noe deadness nor drousenes [drowsiness] among you; and Likewise I warne you from the Lord, who are soe forward and rash in Judging your bretheren and sisters, to beware of it, lest you bee found the hypocrite, and that you bee shure, that that which you Judge in another, bee Cast out in your selves, for whosoever Judgeth another, and hath not the beam Cast out [Matt. 7:4], is a hypocrite, and shall not Esscape the Judgment of god, it is that which Christ Jesus abhores, who is the Judge of the world, and the Apostle Likewise[.] and it is speaking in the Imagination of truth, both in your speaking and Judging, that Causeth divisions and strife amongst you, and all this is Cursed from god, and shut out of the kingdom for Ever, therfore in that which is pure and Eternall, which is one in all, which Leads into love and unity, dwell and abide faithfull, and Constantly obedient, and ye shall eate the good of the Land, and hear is noe striffe nor wrangling; yea[,] this leads to purity and holines, without which none shall see the Lord, and to the Church of the first borne, which is in god, wher he is one and his name one; soe my deare harts[,] you are in the way to this, if you keepe in the strait and narrowe way which Leads to Life, and bee faithfull to the Lord god in your measures, & to the end, and you shall Come heither, soe to you I have Cleared my Conscience & the burthen that Laid upon mee, and the Lord God Allmighty, of Life and power, keepe and preserve you all faithfull, in your parteculer measures to the Lord god, and I warne you, and Charge you, in the presence of the Living god, that all flesh bee silent before the Lord, untill the Eternall arise in you and speake.

Your Deare sister in the truth of God,
Margret Fell

Let this bee Coppied over & sent amongst freinds,
to bee read at their meetings, in Westmoreland
Cumberland & Bishupwricke

FHL Box C4/2, pp. 43–44. Also in Works, *pp. 53–56.*

29 TO PRISONERS IN LANCASTER CASTLE 1654

"Be subject and patient and do not look out, nor be weary, neither be of a doubtful Mind: for the . . . God you Suffer for . . . by the same you are Preserved."

This is a comforting letter to Friends in the prison where Margaret was to spend four years a decade later. She addresses the prisoners in tender terms: "my Love salutes you in the Heavenly Union: I am present with you"; "my Love flow[s] freely to you"; "My dear Hearts." It is not clear whether these are Friends whom she knew "in the body," as these Friends might say, or whether she had only heard about them. The message is that the Spirit will preserve them and they will have safety, strength and victory in the Eternal.

"The calm and serene courage with which the Quakers faced persecution was simply astonishing. Drums might be beaten to stop the Meetings of other dissenters at worship, but could do nothing against the silence of the Friends. The driving of coaches into their midst could part them, but utterly failed to disperse them. Violence could clap them in prison, but not make them lose their composure" (Davies, Worship & Theology, *2:492). They encouraged and supported each other.*

Dear Brethren, in the unchangeable, everlasting, powerful Truth of God; my Love salutes you in the Heavenly Union: I am present with you, who are obedient to the measure of the Eternal Light, which never changes, and who abides in the Oneness of the Spirit, and in the Bond of Peace, which never can be broken, nor taken from you: Here is Freedom, which the World knows not; to the Measure of God in every particular made manifest, and obeyed, and lived in, doth my Love flow freely to you. My dear Hearts, be faithful in every Particular to your own Measure of Grace, made manifest and enjoyed; and in that which is Eternal, wait continually, I charge you in the Presence of the Living God, that you do not neglect your several Measures, which the Lord God of Life and Power hath given you to profit withal; that so you may come to receive Living Vertue from the Living God, and be fed with the Living Bread [John 6:51], and drink of the Living Water of the Spiritual Rock [1 Cor. 10:4], which they drank of in the Wilderness. And be subject and patient and do not look out, nor be weary, neither be of a doubtful Mind: for the same God you Suffer for, and by the same you are Preserved, which Daniel, Shadrach, Meshach, and Abednego was [Dan. 3]; and by the same Spirit ye are preserved, which they were preserved by; therefore stand faithful and bold for the Truth upon the Earth, which strikes at the Foundation of all Deceit and Idolatry. And in the pure Eternal Light of God abide: which is the Stone cut out of the Mountain without hands [Dan. 2:45]; which strikes at the feet of the Image: which the Disobedient part, which look'd out from the Eternal, and is shut out from God, the Will of Man hath set up; and in that which is Eternal and Invisible, which overturns and brings down all Foundations, doth your Strength, and Victory, and Conquest stand, which is the Condemmnation of the World; and this is that which must sanctifie you, and justifie you, and present you pure and holy in his Sight; and here is your Safety, and here is your Peace and Joy, and Eternal Inheritance which never fades away: And the Lord God of Power keep you, and preserve you Faithful and Bold to his Eternal Glory, to whom be Eternal Praises for evermore.

M. F.

Works, *pp*. 59–60.

30 TO THE WORLD, PRIESTS AND PEOPLE 1654

"Now try your Teachers
(who draw you from the Light) by the Scriptures . . .
examine them honestly,
and see whether ye are not deceived by them."

This epistle is an exhortation to test the teachers of religion, the priests and ministers of all the churches, to see if they are indeed teaching a correct understanding of Christ, the Light, and other principles of the Truth. The priests are to be tested (tried) by seeing if they teach the scriptures correctly and if they live by them. Other ministers preached against Quakers for holding non-orthodox views, and Margaret is here defending Quaker beliefs and challenging the clergy at the same time.

It was an age when Bible reading was prevalant, and interpretations were frequently and hotly debated. Christopher Hill writes: "Bibles were not expensive as book prices went. . . . The Geneva Bible was published in pocketable editions, so that men could study it in the privacy of their homes, or could produce it in a church or *an ale-house to knock down an argument with a text" (*World, *p. 75). Margaret's use of scripture indicates that she understood the context of a particular passage. Often ministers were not so conscientious. She urges her readers to read and see for themselves who is preaching the truth.*

There are numerous references to the Gospels of John and Matthew's warnings against the "False Prophets, and Antichrists, and Deceivers" and the "Ravening Wolves," of their time, with direct comparisons to her contemporaries. She assures her readers that "those whose Minds are turned to the Light, and abide in the Light, they cannot deceive."

*Usually Margaret does not cite her biblical sources, but in this epistle she tells the reader: "Read 2 Pet 3:3,4;" "read Jude;" and numerous other citations. Jude has been described as "a letter of exhortation written to a community disturbed by false teachers" (*Women's Bible Commentary, *p. 376). It strongly reinforces Margaret's message. The "gainsaying of Core" is a reference to Khoreh or Korah in Num. 16:1–35 who denied Moses' authority and thus is like the false teachers of her day.*

Margaret discusses the principle of perfection, a doctrine that caused much confusion. It was not a claim of being perfect but of the possibility of living right and doing right with the help of the grace and power of God. It was an argument against the concept of the irredeemable sinfulness of man emphasized by the Puritans.

> *I Am the Light of the World, saith Christ, who lighteth every Man that cometh into the World* (John 8:12). And the Prophet Isaiah, who prophesied of Christ, saith *I the Lord have called thee in Righteousness[,] and will hold thine hand, and will keep thee, and give thee for a Covenant to the People, and a Light unto the Gentiles* (Isa. 42). Now all People, see where you are, and try your Teachers, what they lead you into, who draw you from the Light, which Christ Jesus hath enlightned you withal, who saith, *He that walks in the Light, shall have the Light of Life:* And John saith, *that in him was Life, and the Life was the Light of Men* (John 1). Now try your Teachers (who draw you from the Light) by the Scriptures, which they take to speak unto you, and (as they say) is their Rule: Let it likewise be your Rule to try them with; and search the Scriptures, examine them honestly, and see whether ye are not deceived by them, who draw you from the Light, which is, and ever was, the Saints Teacher, and ever shall be.
>
> And John saith, *that he was not that Light, but he was sent to bear witness of that Light, which is the true Light, which lighteth every Man that cometh into the World* [John 1:8–9]. Now all People, try and see your

Teachers, whether all your Priests of England are not Witnesses contrary to John: He bears witness to the *Light, that lighteth every Man that cometh into the World;* and they bear witness against the Light, and saith, *He doth not lighten every one that cometh into the World;* and tell People, *that they must look after them for Means and Ordinances;* and so blind poor People, and keep them in Darkness and Ignorance. But all People, as you love your own Souls, search into the Scriptures, and try them by the Scriptures, which you call the Word, and the Rule you pretend to walk by, and you shall find them the Deceivers, and the Antichrists, and false Prophets, which they tell you so much of, that should come in the latter Days. John saith, *Many false Prophets are gone out into the World* [1 John 4:1]: Now try your Teachers by this, and see whether they are not in the World, not separated from the World; but draw from the Light, that separates from the World, and leads out of the World; but they witness against the Light, and plead for Sin, and for the Kingdom of Antichrist, which is of the World.

And Christ saith, *This is the Condemnation, that Light is come into the World, and Men love Darkness rather than Light, because their Deeds are Evil. For every one that doth Evil, hateth the Light, neither cometh to the Light, lest his Deeds should be reproved: But he that doth Truth, cometh to the Light, that his Deeds may be made manifest, that they are wrought in God* [John 3:19–21]. Now, let all People see whether these are not the false Prophets, which are entred into the World, who draw from the Light, which is the World's Condemnation; and whether these are not the Deceivers and Antichrists, which John speaks of, who are entred into the World, who do not confess Jesus Christ to be come in the Flesh [1 John 4:2], and deny the Light; and do persecute and call them Deceivers, and false Prophets, who do witness him come in the Flesh, and walk in the Light, which he hath enlighted them withal; these they stock and imprison, and cause to be beat in their Synagogues, as all did that went before them, who ever persecuted the Righteous Seed, and denied the Light. The same John, who said, *False Prophets, and Antichrists, and Deceivers are gone into the World,* saith also, *These things have I written unto you, concerning them that seduce you: But the Anointing, which you have received of him, abideth in you; and you need not that any Man teach you, but as the same Anointing teacheth you of all things, which is Truth, and is no Lye, and even as it hath taught you, ye shall abide in him* (1 John 2:26,27).

Now all People, see who are the false Prophets, whether John, and they who witness the Anointing; or your Teachers, who draw from the Anointing.

Christ Jesus saith, *I am come a Light into the world, that whosoever believeth on me, should not abide in Darkness*; this same Christ saith, in the 7th of Matthew, *Beware of false Prophets, which come to you in Sheeps Clothing, but inwardly they are Ravening Wolves. By their Fruits ye shall know them* [Matt. 7:15]. Now try your Teachers by this Scripture, and see whether they have not been Cloathed all this while with the Sheeps Cloathing, the Saints Cloathing, the words and profession of Christ; but now when the Sheep come who know his voice, and will not follow Strangers (such as they) now see if they do not appear outwardly to be ravening Wolves; what they were before inwardly, their Fruits do make them manifest, therefore let that Scripture try them.

The same Christ Jesus saith unto his Disciples, who came unto him privately on the Mount of Oives. *And Jesus answered and said unto them, take heed that no man decieve you, for many shall come in my Name, saying, I am Christ, and shall deceive many* (Matt. 24:5). Now try your Teachers, and see if they have any thing but a Name, and a Profession of Christ, who draw from the Light; whereas Christ Jesus saith, *I am the Light*; and Christ saith, *Then shall they deliver you up, and kill you, and ye shall be hated of all Nations for my Names sake* [Matt. 24:9]. Now see whether those Priests of yours are hated and killed, which draw from the Light, or those who witness Christ Jesus, which is the Light, which saith, *many false Prophets shall arise, which shall deceive many*; and try if they are not them, which say, *loe here is Christ, and loe there*, but Christ's Command is, *believe them not, for there shall arise false Christs, and false Prophets, and shall shew great signs and wonders, insomuch that if it were possible, they would deceive the very Elect* [Matt. 24:24]. But the Elect who dwell in the Light which comes from Christ Jesus, they cannot deceive; in it they are seen and known, and tried, and made manifest to be the Deceivers, to be the False Prophets, and Antichrist; and with the Light that comes from Jesus they are Condemned, with the World, and turned from, by all the Children of the Light. Therefore Poor People who are out of the Light, you they do deceive; but those whose Minds are turned to the Light, and abide in the Light, they cannot deceive.

And Christ Jesus saith, *Woe unto you, when all men shall speak well of you, for so did their Fathers of the false Prophets* [Luke 6:26]. Now try them by this Scripture, and see whether this Scripture be not fulfilled upon them, and whether they are not of the False Prophets. And in 2 Pet.2.1. Peter said, *but there were false Prophets among the People.* Now try them by this Chapter, and see whether they are not these false Prophets which deny the Light which comes from Christ Jesus their *Lord that bought them; and through Covetousness, shall they with feigned words make Merchandize of you* [2 Pet. 2:3]. Let that in your Consciences now try and search them by this Scripture. And the same Apostle saith, in 2 Pet.1. *Ye have a more sure word of Prophesie, whereunto ye do well, that ye take heed, as unto a Light that shineth in a dark place, until the Day dawn, and the Day-star arise in your hearts: knowing this first, that no Prophesie of the Scriptures is of any private interpretation. For the Prophecy came not in old time by the will of man: but holy men of God spake as they were moved by the Holy Ghost* [2 Pet. 1:19–21]. Now see whether Peter, and those that draw to the Light, are the False Prophets, or them that deny the Light, and hate it, 2 Tim.3. Try them by this Scripture, and see if they are not found them that the Apostle speaks of there, *having a form of Godliness, but denying the power;* and he saith, *from such turn away.* And see if they are not of this sort, which creep into Houses, and call them Churches, (when as the Apostle saith the Church is in God) and *lead captive silly women, laden with sin, and led away with divers lusts; ever learning, and never able to come to the knowledge of the Truth* [2 Tim. 3:5–7].

Now see and try your Teachers by these Scriptures, and see what ye have learned of them all your days, that you have followed them; or what you can witness of God, or of Christ made manifest in you; nay, that in your Consciences will confess that you do not truly know the Holy Scriptures; which makes them manifest to be the False Prophets, and Deceivers, which draw from the Light, that gave forth the Scriptures: Even in the Knowledge of the outward Letter you are blinded. Read 2Pet 3:3,4 and see if you and they, *are not found those Scoffers, walking after your Lusts, saying, where is the promise of his coming.* And read Jude, and try them, and see whether they be not found there, under the woe that he speaks of, *whether they run not greedily for Gifts and Rewards, and so perish in the gainsaying of Core* [Jude 1:11, Num. 16:1–35]; And let that in your Consciences (which is of God) which respects no Person, Read and Examine those Scriptures, and try them, and see whether they are not erred from the Light, and so draw others from the Light, which is, and ever was the Saints Teacher, and ever shall be; from which all the Holy Men of God ever spake, as they were moved by the Holy Ghost; and from which Light all the Scriptures were given forth, which these Deceivers take into their mouths, and draw People from the Light that gave forth the Scripture, and so betrays their Souls.

And therefore all People, to the Light in your Consciences, which Christ Jesus hath enlightned you withal, turn within, keep to it, and go not forth, nor look not outward, and it will let you see the Deceivers and Betrayers of your Souls; and if you be faithful and obedient to it, it will let you see your Saviour, for false Prophets and Antichrists are in the world, and the Deceivers are of the world; but those that dwells in the Light, which Christ hath enlightned them withal, this leads out of the world, out of the worlds ways, fashions, and customs, and this makes a separation from the world, and this leads up to God, and this Light is the condemnation of the world, and the condemnation of all the Deceivers, False Prophets, and Antichrists which are in the world; and who are faithful and obedient to the Light, witnes Christ made manifest and come in the flesh, and these are no Antichrists; and these are they that go forth to bear witness against the false Prophets and Antichrists which are in the world; and these are they that are Stock'd, and Beat, and Imprisoned, and Persecuted by those who are of the first Nature, which is Cains, who slew his Brother, and this is of the world, and by this Generation all that will live godly in Christ Jesus, must suffer Persecution. And it is our Joy and Rejoycing, not only to believe on him, but also to suffer for his sake.

All poor People who are in the dark World, Blind, led with the Blind Guides, beware and look where you are, lest both you and they fall into the Ditch [Matt. 15:14]; and try your Leaders by the Scriptures, who plead for Sin and Transgression; and are telling you that you shall not be free from Sin, nor perfect while you are upon Earth.

Now is that fulfilling which the Apostle Paul spoke of, in 2 Tim. 3. *And the perilous Times are come,* and woe unto you if you do not hearken to the warning of the Lord God, who calls unto you for Repentance, and to turn to the Light of Christ in your Consciences; and to turn from that sort which the Apostle speaks of, *having a form of Godliness, but denying the Power,* of this sort is your Teachers, which are to be turned away from, *which creep into Houses, and lead silly Women Captive* [2 Tim. 3:6], and so keep you ever Learning, and tell you *That none can be perfect while they are here upon Earth.* And so they plead for Sin, and against Christ Jesus, and against the Apostles and Prophets, and all the

Holy Men of God; for Christ saith, *Be ye perfect, as your Heavenly Father is perfect* [Matt. 5:48]. And again, Christ said unto the young Man, (who asked Christ what he yet laked [lacked]) *If thou wilt be perfect, sell all that thou hast, and give to the Poor* [Matt. 19:21]. And again, the Apostle said, *He preached wisdom amongst them that are perfect* [1 Cor. 2:6]. And when he parted with the Brethren, *he bid them be perfect, be of good comfort, be of one mind,* 1Cor. 2.6 [2 Cor. 13:11].

And your Teachers tells you, That you must never be perfect, but that you must sin so long as you are upon the Earth, and so they are Ministers of Antichrist, and Upholders of Sin, and the Devils Kingdom. Try them by the Scriptures, and you shall find them contrary to the Doctrine of Christ, and of the Apostles, and not to have received the Gifts, which he gave to the Prophets, Apostles, and Evangelists, for the perfecting of the Saints, as you may read in Eph.4.11, 12, 13. *And the Apostle went about warning every Man in all wisdom, that he might present every man perfect in Christ Jesus.*

Now see your Leaders, and Teachers, if they have not another Spirit than Christ and the Apostles had, who makes it their Trade to plead for Sin, and against Perfection, which all that ever were sent of God, prayed and preach'd for, as the Apostle did night and day, *praying exceedingly that he might see their face, and might perfect that which was lacking in their Faith,* 1Thes.3.10. And the Apostle Peter prayed, *that they might be perfect, when they had suffered a while.* And the Apostle said (who was a Minister of Christ) *that the Scripture was given forth by Inspiration of God, that the Men of God might be perfect.* And here your Teachers are found to be deniers of the Scriptures, and not so much as Ministers of the Letter, who plead against it, and the ends that it was given forth for, and so are found to be Ministers of Antichrist, and out of the practice of all that ever taught for God. Noah was a Preacher of Righteousness, and he was a perfect Man. Abraham was a Friend of God, and God said unto him, *walk before me, and be thou perfect* [Gen. 17:1]. And Lot was a Just Man, and the Lord delivered him. And Job was a Perfect and Just Man and the Lord preserv'd him. And David saith, *Mark the perfect man, and behold the upright, for the end of that man is peace,* Psal. 37 [37:37].

And Solomon saith, *that the upright shall dwell in the Land, and the perfect shall remain in it,* Prov 2,21. And again he saith, *that the righteousness of the perfect shall direct his way,* Prov. 11:5. Now all People search the Scriptures, and try these Deceivers and Betrayers of your

Souls, and let them be witness against their selves, that they neither teach, nor you receive nothing of God from them: *for whatsoever is of God in the least measure is perfect,* the first principle that comes from God is perfect; *every perfect gift is from above* [James 1:17]. And the Apostle said, *as many as be perfect, be thus minded;* and the Apostle saith, *we are glad when we are weak, and ye are strong;* and this also we wish, *even your perfection.* And again he saith, *let us go on unto perfection.* Now you see your Blind Guides, whether they be not the Ministers of the Mystery of Iniquity, and under the Dark Power, who plead for Sin, and against Perfection, which all that ever were sent of God Preached for, and Pray'd for, and Labour'd for of the Lord, 2Cor. 7.1. Eph. 4.12.

M. Fell

Works, *pp.* 60–68.

31 TO JUDGE HUGH WYNDHAM 1654

"The said Judge, that stumbles, at the Light, & said it led into all sin; knows not the mariage that is honorab[l]e."

*Sir Hugh Wyndham (1603?–1684) was the eighth son of Sir John Wyndham of Orchard-Wyndham in Somerset, attended Oxford, then Lincoln's Inn, was called to the bar in 1629, and was knighted in 1670 (*DNB*). The endorsement on this letter reads 1653, but the trial of Cuthbert Hunter which Margaret refers to took place in August 1654 (Horle, "Index," p. 70). In the Swarthmore Manuscript there is a letter from William Dewsbury to M. F. dated 2 May 1654 in which he describes his own trial, with Wyndham as the judge, and his subsequent imprisonment (Nuttall, p. 109).*

The letter deals with two issues of importance to Quakers, the doctrine of the Light and the legality of Quaker marriages. Cuthbert Hunter had been married "before wittnesses" in the simple manner developed by nonconformists and was not married by a minister. He was accused of "Adultery; & fornication . . . because he was not marryed with the priests; of the world, which marry people for money; & for giveing of them a forme of words." In his charge, Margaret Fell reports that Judge

Wyndham had said "that the Light, the principle which wee hold, in every one, doth Lead into all manner of sin." Thus this principle had caused Hunter's crime.

Margaret disputes Wyndham's charge and asserts that the Light "is the Condemnation of all sin, wickedness[,] uncleanes & ungodlines." She accuses him of blasphemy in not accepting the principle of the Light and quotes John extensively in her analysis. She writes: "And thou who should be a Judge; upon the evill, art found to be a Judge upon the good, (the Light) Lett the Light in all Consciences beare wittness against thee . . . "

The question of the legality of Quaker marriages continued to be a problem for many years. Horle writes: "Potentially the Quaker crime with the most serious ramifications was their marriage within their own Meeting. Canon law stressed that marriages were legal only if they took place in the parish church or chapel before a minister . . . If Quaker marriages were illegal, the children of such unions were illegitimate." Horle refers to the Cuthbert Hunter case as "one of the earliest recorded cases involving Quaker marriages." Hunter was imprisoned but his "imprisonment, while unfortunate for him, did not signal the loss of freedom for all Quaker husbands and wives, and the bastardization of Quaker children" (Horle, Q.&EngLegalSys, *p. 234).*

Cuthbert Hunter was fined for attending Meetings as late as 1678 (Besse, 1:179 and 1:182).

> The herecy Judge Windham did say in his Charge; that the Light, the principle which wee hold, in every one, doth Lead into all manner of sin; the Light which Comes from Jesus Xt [Christ]; which he doth enlighten every one, that Cometh into the world; withall; is the Condemnation of all sin, wickedness[,] uncleanes & ungodlines, & the Light which is our principle, as hee Calls it; in every man, will wittnes against the said windham who is Called a Judge, & doth wittnes against sin; & the same Light will wittnes Christ, & make every tongue to Confesse, & is the Condemnation of all that hate it; whose deeds be evill; oh that ever such should be sett up; to be a Judge, who utters forth Blasphemy; that to say the Light, which he doth enlighten every man, that Comes into the world; withall; John 1:9: to it in every man; which we speake of; which is the Light of Xt, which is the Condemnation; of all sin & unrighteousnes; of all them that hate it: should Lead to Comit all manner of sin, as Judge Windham said in his Charge, here thou art manifest to be noe Judge, for god; but Judged with the Just; And of Light in every mans Conscience, which Comes from xt; will & doth wittnesse against thee; that thy Judgment is false; & speakes a ly.

who is out of the truth; & speakes of thy selfe; & the Light in thy owne Conscience which Comes from Christ: wittnesses against thee; for to the Light in every ones Conscience, Judge Windham, with it shall then be proved, whether it Leads into all manner of sin, or whether it testifie against all manner of sin; Lett it in all Consciences the[e] Judge; whether thou be a Judge for god yea or nay; that in thy Conscience, shall be a wittnes against thee, & wittnes mee, & be a wittnes for god, against thee; That which shewes ungodliness & sin; & manifests it, is Light, & the Light, doth not Lead into the sin; but Leads out of the sin; & testifies against itt; And this am I moved to give forth, who am a wittnes to the Light, in all tender Consciences, which is a wittnes against all sin; whose myndes are turned with the Light, towards Xt; And thou who should be a Judge; upon the evill, art found to be a Judge upon the good, (the Light) Lett the Light in all Consciences beare wittnes; against thee, which wittnesses against evill; and Leads not into it, who here hast manifested thyselfe, that thou art darknes, & doth not Comprehend Light, but at it stumbles; & the scripture is fulfilled upon thee, the saying of John, Light shines in darknes & darknes doth not Comprehend it [John 1:5]; & if you walke in the Light, yee have Fellowshippe one with another, & the blood of Jesus Cleanseth from all sin; & here againe thou may see, how Contrary takes hold upon them who acts Contrary to the Light; the Light wittnesses the Law; & the Law, wittnesses the Light; & the Law is a Judge upon them, who walke Contrary to the Light; & it is not a Judge upon them; that walke in the Light; here Lett the Light in all Consciences be a wittnes against thee; which Light wittnesses against all sin; & findes thee in the sin; & the Blasphemy who sayes the Light Leads into all sin; which Light is thy Condemnation; the Light; of him that doth evill; & hates the Light, as you may read John:3: And for the false accusation, of the said Judge windham; which did accuse Cuthbert Hunter, for Adultry; & fornication, because he tooke a wife; before wittnesses; & was not marryed with the priests; of the world, which marry people for money; & for giveing of them a forme of words; for money; but tooke a wife according to the mannour as he found in scripture; (wittnesses;) the holy men of god, & did not goe to the priests to give them money; but tooke before wittnesses; & denyes the priests for giveing them money: for marrying, for there is noe such example in scripture, that the priests were to have soe much for marrying people; & this Judge windham sayes, it is Contrary to the Law of god, & Contrary to the Law of man; which all may see it is a false accusation; for the Law of god wittnesses the same; the holy men of god wittnesses the same; that which Judge windham Calls Adultry, soe whome the Lord Joyneth together, Lett noe man put assunder [Mark 10:9]; the marriage that is honorable; Contrary to the Light, god doth not Joyne together; that marriage is not honorable; that bed is defiled; all that is Joyned there; in that Nature; Contrary to the Light, together with that which is Contrary to the Light; all this is with the Light, to be Condemned; & not honorable; for there the bed is defiled; All Covetousnes, & the whoremongers, & the Adulterers; such marriages Contrary to the Light; god doth not Joyne together; but is with the Light seene & Condemned; the bed that is defiled, is not honorable; & there is hardnes of heart; & putting assunder; but whome god Joynes together; Lett noe man put assunder; & such whome god doth Joyne, together with his Light (for god is Light) And the Children of Light, which be in his Light doth wittnes; his Joyning; as the scripture declares, & such doth the world Call adultry; as for example; Judge windham because they are not marryed with a priest; or Joyned together with a Carnall Law; but takes one another before wittnesses; as the manner of the holy men of god was;

And though the said Cuthbert hunter did take his wife after the example of the saints in scripture[,] he was not then brought into the truth; for it was halfe a year before; he owned the truth; & as for saying to the Judge; that the Lord maried him; that was another false accusation;

And all the Children of Light which sees god, & are of god, doth the marriages see, that be honorable; & doth them see whome god Joynes together; Lett noe man put assunder; & the marriage that is not honorable; is with the Lig[ht] seene, & Judged, & all the whoremongers & Adulterers; which is Contrary to the Light; Comprehendd & Condem[ned;] in which Light, all the Children of the Light dwell; & have unity; prayses prayses to the Lord god forever & the said Judge, that stumbles, at the Light, & said it led into all sin; knowes not the mariage that is honorab[le] whose Condemnation is with the Light; The Light in thy Conscience, is my wittnes; & all who are not together; with god, are not moved of the Lord; & a Condemnation must goe upon all; the marriag[es] are not moved of the Lord; & Joyned together by the Lord; for they are not honorable, & them men or women Joyne together Contrary to the Light; are with the Light Condemned, & sundred from honorable mariage, in the defiled bed;

M: F:

Spence 3/131. Also in Works, *pp. 39–40. Endorsed: "a leter to judge windom [George Fox] by M F 1653"; another hand crossed out "leter" and put "An Answer to judge".*

32 TO FRANCIS HOWGILL 1654?

"Deare bro. [brother] Francis[,] I receaved thy Letter & I rejoyce to hear of the Largenes of the love of God, the Praises be to the Lord God for evermore, & let us heare as often as you can conveniently."

Because of the reference to Oliver Cromwell this letter must have been written between 1654 and 1658. The enthusiastic language suggests an early date. Another of her letters in the same manuscript to Jeffrey Elletson is dated 1654.

The warmth and unity that she feels for her friends is notable, as is also the high expectations that they shared. The bonds of friendship between Margaret and those who traveled were maintained and strengthened by their active correspondence. She also played an active role in passing along information: John Camm and Edward Burrough may have reached London where Howgill is; she sends "Deare, & tender Love" to them and to John Audland, though she "know[s] not where he is;" George Fox has recently arrived at Swarthmoor Hall.

The Friends at this time were not modest in their goals. They wanted to change the world and were confident that they were in the "service of the liveing God." They were "Laborers in the vineyard of God[,] whom the Lord hath sent forth to be Manifested to the Consciences of Men." She writes, "You are the Condemnation of the world, you shall overturne all but what is pure & Eternall."

With her letter she encloses another to Oliver Cromwell. This is an example of "clearing her conscience" by doing what she feels compelled to do and then being willing to leave to others the fate of the action.

Francis Howgill (1618–1669) of Grayrigg, Westmorland, was educated for the Anglican ministry, but his religious search led him to the Independents, the Baptists, the Seekers, and then to the Quakers. He was convinced by George Fox at a famous

Meeting at Sedbergh in June 1652. and "he became one of the key leaders in the early expansion of the Quaker movement." (Greaves, 2:117)

He was imprisoned several times and spent the last five years of his life in Appleby Gaol. He wrote many works, even while in prison. The following lines are from a letter dated September 29, 1661: "Dear Margaret . . . I [do] most dearly salute thee. The former days are not forgotten by me, nor the years past, when we were all made to drink of one cup . . . And though it was irksome and grievous unto us, when our strength was but small; yet God, out of his infinite love and mercy, strengthened us to bear, and to suffer . . . like as we suffered one for another & one with another, so we might be made to rejoice one with another & for one another . . . And let me tell thee, I am no more weary then the first day the sickle was put into the harvest" (Hayes, pp. 49–50).

John Camm (1605–1657), John Audland (1630–1664), and Edward Burrough (1632–1663) were all converted to Quakerism by George Fox in 1652 (Greaves). They became active traveling ministers, having great influence in London, Bristol, Ireland, and other parts of England and Wales. Burrough was particularly brilliant, both in writing and in debate, and his early death in Newgate prison was a great loss.

To Francis Howgill & the rest at London

My deare Bretheren in the everlastinge Life & love doth my soule salute you & meet you, & am present with you who are the Elect of God & chosen before the foundation of the world, & now are seperated from the world for the service of the liveing God, & to testyfie against the world that the deeds thereof are evell, therefore hated by the world, & persecuted by the world[.] my owne heart & Life[,] all in every particular in the mighty power & dread of the Lord stand, & dwell in the Eternall Light & power of God[.] you shall overturne Nations[,] yea kings shalbe reproved for your sakes, for you are the Host of the Liveing God, whom he is Lord off [of] & whom he ownes, I see you dayly & am _______ abroad amongst you, & you all meet in my Heart & Soule together, soe my Deare heartes[,] abide in that which is pure & Eternall begotten of the Liveing God, & in that you shall see me present, & in the Eternall Life of God is our unity, & thus doe we all meet & there shall we all Joy & rejoyce[,] beholding our order Liveing in the Lord God, My owne deare[,] my bowells, reaches to you, & I know the power of the Mighty God is with you, who are Laborers in the vineyard of God[,] whom the Lord hath sent forth to be Manifested to the Consciences of Men, & to the raiseing of the dead out of the Grave that He may receave praises, & Glory of all [,] who is Lord of all, & over all blessed for evermore who is the Dread of all Nations & to whose Power shall all Nations bow & bend, soe my Deare Bretheren[,] in the Eternall Life of God, & in his power tread the Winepresse without the City [Rev. 14:20,] Trample downe the Desert, & by the Eternall word & Judgment, cut downe all fruitles trees that cumbers the ground, tread upon the deceit, which is above, & come under to the pure which is Eternall of God in every ones Conscience, & there you tread the Winepresse & there you shut out all deceit & Deceivers, & here you are unknowne & a mistery to the world & here you are the Condemnation of the world, you shall overturne all but what is pure & Eternall, & unto the liveing God of Glory doe I commend my Deare ones./ My deare Love to John Camme [?] and Edward Burrough[,] if they be come to London they pertake of this, you are all Deare unto me, & you are all present with me and are all met togather in my heart & I see you all in one power & in one Life, soe in that dwell & abide & stand to comprehend and reach over all the world[.] Deare bro. [brother] Francis[,] I receaved thy Letter & I rejoyce to hear of the Largenes of the love of God, the Praises be to the Lord God for evermore, & let us heare as often as you can conveniently, my Deare Love breaths & reaches unto John Audland, I know not where he is, but when you write to him remember my Deare, & tender Love to them, Deare Brother Francis, I was moved of the Lord to write a few word[s] to Oliver Cromwell, which I have here inclosed, if the Lord give you an opertunity thou may deliver it to some of his Family[,] open as it is[,] to try if he will suffer them to give him it, or read it to him, I see there about him a spirit that would drau [draw] him into Persecution, I have cleared my Conscience of him & leaves him to the Lord, when I began to write this Letter my deare brother George [Fox] was not here outwardly, but praised be to God he is now here, Let us heare from you my Bretheren[.] the Lord God Almighty of Power and Love preserve & keepe you by his Infinite wisdome & strength to his Eternall praises for evermore

Your deare Sister in the Eternall truth.

Margarett Fell

from Swarthmore in Lancashire

Markey MSS pp. 3–4.

33 To Oliver Cromwell 1654

"Gerves Benson wife, being moved of the Lord . . . [and] being great with child, goeing to speake against the deceite of the priest . . . hath bene imprisoned this quarter of A year, and is delivered of the child in the prison."

The dates on Margaret Fell's letters and the script of the letter itself are often written in different hands. The dates may have been added at a considerably later time. When a day and month is included that is a good indication that the date is correct. In this case the date of "1657" at the head of the letter is contradicted by Margaret's relation of a particular incident.

Dorothy Benson (Letter 6), the wife of Colonel Gervase Benson, was an enthusiastic supporter of George Fox. He writes in his Journal *that when he was in prison in 1653 "Justice Benson's wife was moved of the Lord to come and visit me and to eat no meat but what she ate with me at the bars of the dungeon window" (Nickalls, p. 162). She later went to York and preached in the streets. She was arrested and sent to prison in York Castle and was kept there although she was "great with child." The child, named Immanuel, was born February 2, 1654, in the prison (Webb, p. 70).*

Margaret indignantly writes of Dorothy Benson's having been in prison "this quarter of A year . . . contrary to all humanytie." Gervase Benson had been a colonel in the Commonwealth army, which made the treatment of his wife seem particularly unjust.

Margaret reminds Cromwell of his power and that "now hath the Lord putt an opportunity into thy hand." She appeals to his conscience to end persecution that is putting many men and women in prison. Some are charged with not paying tithes; others for "popery." A law passed in the time of Queen Mary Tudor aimed at Roman Catholics had been revived to use against Quakers who were accused of being secret Jesuits.

Cromwell had been installed as Lord Protector on December 16, 1653, and Margaret warns him "mind what it is that thou dost protect, For if thou protect, what is contrary to god . . . the same woe and Judgement shall persue thee," a reference not only to those then in prison but also to previous rulers who were overthrown.

To O: Crumwell From M:F: 1657

I am moved of the lord by the eternall spirit of life, to speak to that in thy Conscience, which is eternall, which is of god, which will be an eternall wittnesse for mee against all the pollutions that thou lives in, the burden of the word of the Lord lyes upon mee, to declare against thy hypocrisie, that thou hast lived in, all thy dayes, which profession stinkes in the nostrills of god, who is holy, who is pure, who is righteous, who is gloryous, whose power is made manifest in thousands in these northren parts, glory and prayses be to him, who respects no mans parson, but of his free will hath hee begotten many unto A lively hope, which shall live eternally, which hope purifies, which hope is christ within, which is wittnessed with thousands to be made manifest, to the overturning of all profession, and talkeing of such words. Thou hast bene a preacher, and a speaker, and an expounder of the Letter outwardly, which is hypocrisie before God, For the scriptures saith, that it is of no private Interpritation, but holy men spoke it forth as they was moved by the holy Ghost, And what meaning can thou give to that, which shutts out all expounding, & all takeing text and preaching of the outward Letter, which is shutt out from god, and where the life of the scripture is made manifest, it cryes against all these outward formes and worships which is without, which saith[,] low [lo,] here is christ, and low there, but Jesus xt [Christ] said goe not forth, And he saith the Kingdome of heaven cometh not with observations, but the kingdome of heaven is within you, For Eve that ______ ______ by disobeydience brought transgression upon all mankind, And death passed over all man, and reignes from Adam till Moses, see if the Light in thee can expound that, to that in thy Conscience I speak, which if thou waite in the Light, it will let thee see the state of Moses, which is the Light of Christ, which is moses[,] which brings out of Egipt, thou shalt see it & wittnesse it as it speakes, And thou shalt see all thy outward formes & worshipes to be without god in the broad way, and keepes in darkenesse and in Egipt still, And thou shalt never know the liveing God of truth, till thou harken to that in thy conscience to be guided by it, which is pure of god, and which leads up to god & to purity, but if thou disobey it, it shall eternally Condemne thee, and justifie the liveing god to be righteous, and A holy and just god, which if thou harken to it, thou shalt bear wittnesse with mee, for to that I speak, and to that I clear my Conscience, which burden lyes heavy upon mee, and which if thou obey it, that I shall bee knowne to, and that I speake to be of the truth, but if thou disobey it, it shall bee to thy eternall condemnation, and thou shalt be shutt out from god eternally, And see if thou can expound that scripture, where Jesus christ saith, I am the light of the world [John 8:12], and enlightens every one that comes into the world, the one he loves the light and brings his deeds to the light, and they are proved [reproved] by the light, the other he hates the light and goes from the light, because his deeds are evill, and will not bring them to the Light to be proved [John 3:19–20], now see if Jesus xt did not speake plaine truth to any single hart or mind, that loves him, For these that loves him, loves that in their conscience and these that hate it, it shall bee their eternall Condemnation, but all the preists in England denyes this doctrine of christ, the light to bee in every one, which makes manifest that they are haters of Christ, and doth not abide in his doctrine, And Christ is made A stumbleing stone and A rocke of offense, and stumbles at the Light of christ.

And Friend[,] the Lord hath made thee serviceable, and prospered thee wonderfully against the open enimeie without thee, And now thou art called to a high calling outwardly[;] but friend[,] to that in thy conscience I speake, mind what it is that thou dost protect, For if thou protect, what is contrary to god and the truth of god made manifest in the power of it, the same woe and Judgement shall persue thee, and overturne thee, that hath done these that were before thee, to that in thy conscience I speake, which I shall eternally wittnesse for god & mee, when the booke of conscience is opened, and all judged out of it, then thou shalt see who speakes the truth, (and lives in it,) as it is in Jesus[.] now hath the Lord putt an opportunity into thy hand, and he is trying of thee whether thou wilt stand for him or against him, and hee is trying thee, what all thy profession of truth, and the propigateing of the Gospell, which thou hast severall times declared for, whether it be in truth & reallytie yea, or nay. For there is nothing can Judge of truth, but that in thy Conscience, which is eternall of god, which is the worme which never dyes [Mark 9:44] but lyes eternally to torment, and condemne those that hate it, And if thou wilt harken to that, thou shalt see all the Lawes of this nation to be corrupt, And all the priests of this nation to be changeable, and leading to Teachers without, and denyes the one preist, which is unchangeable, eternall and forever, which if thou wilt harken to that in thy Conscience[,] it will let thee see, that they are all in one Generation, without god in the world, And their foundation to be sandy, and not built upon the rocke Chr[ist] which is the light within every mans conscience by which he is seen, they are leading forth from that within, giveing expossitions upon the Letter with their carnall minds, which holy men spoke forth as they were moved by the holy Ghost, which none of them can wittnesse the holy ghost, nor the annoynting which is Jesus christ, which is anoynted to preach glad tydings to the poore[,] which is A preacher of righteousnesse, who speakes to the spirits in prison, which many can wittnesse in these Northren parts, their spirits raised up out of prison, and speakes to that which is prison, eternall prayses be to the liveing god for evermore, which is moved of the Lord to cry against the preists of the world which worshipes Baall[,] by the eternall power of god[,] and to speak against their divination, and their giveing meanings upon the scripture with their carnall minds, whose spirit is in prison, & who lyes under the death, that hath passed over all men, who never came to moses [Moses'] state, nor never harkened to the light in their conscience, to lead them out of Egipt, which is all the world spiritually, And if thou hold up A Law to guard and protect Antichrist against the power of christ, which speakes in his servants, as many here can wittnesse, who suffers by that Law, which was made in Maryes dayes, though they spake against popery, but that is all they have to guard their ministry withall, and to protect them in their pullpitts, which was an Act made by her in her dayes[,] which makes them manifest they are Antichrist, and not of Christ, And severall prisoners have suffered in these northern parts, and doth suffer Imprisonment, both at Carlile[,] Kendal[,] Lancaster and Yorke, which is at this time imprisoned by that Act, others because they cannot pay tythes, contrary to that in their conscience, which if they doe, they must deny christ come in the flesh, And whosoever doth that is an Antichrist.

And Gerves Benson wife, being moved of the Lord to goe to the great steeplehouse, called the minster in yorke, being great with child, goeing to speake against the deceite of the priest, and their she was abussed [abused] by the rude multitude, and throne [thrown] downe under their Feet, the magistrate looking on, and afterward brought before the magistrate, and hath bene imprisoned this quarter of A year, and is delivered of the child in the prison, contrary to all humanytie or any appearance of god in the least measure, theeves and murderers might have had as much favour as she had there, her husband was A Collonell in the army, and suffered much by the enemie, and is A friend to the Commonwealth[,] but is brought into the truth, and is made willing to suffer for the truthes sake, And here I have cleared my conscience in letting thee know the cruell oppression and the tyranny that now rulls [rules] in the Land, And mind what thou protects, and beware of fighting against the lord, for no weapon formed against him shall prosper, but shall turne backe into the bowells of him that feights against him, And it is for no protection from thee, as thou art man, for wee utterly deny and abhore all the protection of man whatsoever[,] for our protector is the liveing god, and our deliver from all our enemies is the Lord[.] but for the good of thy soull that thou be not overturned with them that went before thee, A warning to thee, to that in thy Conscience I speake, and as thou hast often declared for the libertie of conscience, and the propigateing of the Gospell, mind what Libertie that in the conscience hath, which is limitted by A Carnall Law, which is of god, which cannot be limitted, but limitts, and testifies against all the workes of darkenesse, which leads up out of all uncleannesse to god, which is pure and holy, now thou that expounds the scripture, see if thou can expound that, that every one that names the name of the Lord Jesus xt should depart from iniquitie, see if all the preists in England can owne that scripture as it speakes, but rather that scripture is fullfilled, that the prophett Isa [Isaiah] speakes of, that all that departs from iniquity, becomes A prey to them, And to the magistrates of this nation, And I charge thee by the lord God of power & life, that there be A search made therron this nation, who it is that departs from Iniquitie, And what it is, that they can charge on us, whom they call quakers, anymore, but that we declare against the deceite, & if we be found guiltie, let us suffer, for it is justice that we try for, & equitie, & not daubing with untempred mortor with the priests of the world, which cryes peace, when their is no peace, and we have declared openly why we deny the priests of the world, & not in A corner, For we would have it published to open view, which wee hear is intercepted, and will not be suffered to be published, which we charge upon this Commonwealth to be deceite, for if they can justifie themselves in these things that we declare against them[,] wee are willing to suffer, or if we have transgresed any Law let us suffer by the Law, And see what it is that must be upheld by A carnall Law, and not to Intercept that which declares for the truth, and against the deceite, that all the priests lives in, And here I charge thee againe to that in thy Conscience I speake, that thou beware of protecting that, which is cursed from god, for the decree is gone out from the Lord, which is their rueing & distruction, for they have run all this while, and they were nower [nowhere] sent of the lord, which if thou wilt harken to that in thy conscience, thou wilt see them to be blind guides, leaders of the blind, and wittnesse the same against them as we have declared, And the Lord god of power awaken that in thy Conscience to lead thee out of dark formes & Customes which thou hast lived in, which thou wilt see if thou doe waite in that which is of god in thee, to be nothing but shaddows and for the fire and distruction, Jesus Chr: where he is made manifest, is without forme[,] beauty[,] or comelynesse to the carnall eye, for your highest formes is but A false cover[,] A shaddow without the substance, soe waite that thou may be hid in the day of the lords fearce wrath and vengance, that is comeing upon all flesh, and all formes and outside worshipes, and all which is not pure and eternall shall be done away, that, that [sic] which cannot be shaken may be set up.

A warning to thee for propigateing Baall, that light in thy conscience will let thee see him, and know him, as the prophetts did, which cryed against him, and them that set him up[;] and if thou doe Act contrary to that in thy Conscience, and set up Baall, & soe deny Christ, the light of christ in all consciences will cry against thee for vengance from god, soe faretheewell, And the Lord god of power enlighten thy understandings, and let thee see where thou art set, for assuredly from the mouth of the Lord I speake it, if thou do not harken to that light of god in thy Conscience, to be led by it up to god the Father of light, thou shalt be confounded & overturned, as all hath bene before thee, who have acted contrary to the light of god, the mouth of the Lord of hoasts hath spoken it.

M: F:

Spence 3/93–94. Summary dated 1654 in Works, *pp. 15–16. Addressed: "To Oliver Crumvell". Endorsed: "M F to Olefer Crumwell [George Fox]".*

34 To Oliver Cromwell 1655

"The Lord hath honoured thee thus farre[,] therfore beware thou doe not dishonour him with that which he hath committed unto thee."

This pastoral letter reminds Cromwell that his "victories over [his] enimies" were given by God. She warns him that God is testing him: what will he do for the sick and the hungry? The appeal to conscience and concern for the underprivileged appealed strongly to some people but also brought the Friends ridicule and fear. Men of property and those in positions of power feared the loss of their estates if there were more equality of people and of wealth. Some were concerned that the diminishment of the established church would cause disorder.

Margaret's mood is optimistic, "Now is the day in which the Lord alone wilbe exalted," and she is confident that God will preserve his people, "now hath he a dear & precious people in this nation which he will owne forever." But if Cromwell allows them to "suffer . . . oppression & tyranny . . . the judgment of God" will fall upon him.

She addresses the ruler of the nation in the same terms as any other individual. In a society with strong prescriptions about proper deference to class and authority this was remarkable. It did not make Quakers popular with those in high places. The fact that Cromwell had a certain tolerance for what could be regarded as impudence, thought of by some as "forthrightness," shows more understanding than many had. Cromwell was visited by other Quakers, such as George Fox and Anthony Pearson, and he was willing to listen and to talk with them (BQ, pp. 180, 161).

To the protector Oliver Cromwell
Friend

Of the living God I am moved before whom thou stands & to whom thou must give an account of that which thou hast undertaken[.] the outward power is now in thy hand from the Lord[.] I doe warn thee as thou tenders the eternall peace of thy soule that thou rule for the Lord & that thou mind that of him in thy conscience which shows thee what is evill and testifies against sin & works of darknes[,] which is the light which comes from christ Jesus in whom is life & he is the light of men & that is it which beares witnes for him against all the deeds thoughts & words of darknes & by that will he be justified to be the true the living the just the righteous God[,] & every tounge shall confesse that he is righteous & just & every mouth shalbe stopped & at the name of Jesus every knee shall bow [Rom. 14:11] & who is faithfull & obedient unto the light and walkes in the light shall have the light of life & who is disobedient & will not be guided by the light but turnes from the light it is their condemnation for ever[,] & now is the living God made manifest in this his day & consider that the Lord God hath been true & faithfull to thee & hath given thee many victories over thine enimies without thee & hath preserved thee from the jaws of death by his mighty power & hath brought thee & set to be a ruler & a govenour over the people[.] now as thou tenders thy owne soule which is eternall beware that thou doe not requite him evill for good

[1 Sam. 25:21] for now is he trying what thou will doe for him[.] he is sick & in prison[.] he is trying if thou wilt visit him[.] he is naked & he is trying if thou wilt clothe him[.] hungrey trying if thou wilt feed him[.] these are words of christ Jesus [Matt. 25:36–37] whom thou professes which never changes & they shall not fall to the ground[.] now see what fruits thou bringes forth of thy profession for he saith he that denies me before men him will I deny before my father which is in heaven [Matt. 10:33] & this stands forever[,] it is eternall [,] it never changes[,] therfore to the light of christ Jesus in thy conscience doe I speake which witnesses for God for ever against all deceit [,] that with it thou may be guided & led into uprightnes & singlenes[,] being subject to the Lord alone who is able to preserve thee[,] for verily thou hast many enimies & if thou turne thy hand against the Lord & his anointed for whose sake he will reprove kings it is just with him to cut thee of [off,] but if thou be obedient to the measure of God in thy owne conscience he is able to preserve thee above the heads of all thine enimies if thou be faithfull unto him to the measure of him made manifest in thee[,] that thou act according to what thou knows for the Lord, thou shalt rule above all the powers of darknes[,] for verily now is the day in which the Lord alone wilbe exalted therfore if thou wilt not exalt him in this his day thou wilbe puld downe[,] for noe weapon formed against him shall prosper for this is the day wherin all nations shall bow & tremble before him[,] therfore hear him who is the dread of all nations & fear not man nor what man can doe[,] for he is bringing all the haughtines of man under his feet & he will have the glory & honour himselfe [Isa. 2:11] whose right it is[,] for the king is set upon the holy hill of sion which reignes over the house of Jacob & sitts upon the throne of david of whose kingdom there is noe end & for him thou hast acted & been servicable in thy place & now is he coming to visit thee & try thee if thou wilt not owne him to be ruler over thy house[,] therfore now beware that thou turne not thy sword against him least he cut thee of[,] for now is he comming neer to judgment soe let him be judge & leader & guider in thee that soe thou may rule & guid for him[,] for now hath he a dear & precious people in this nation which he will owne forever[,] which if thou suffer the oppression & tyranny that is & hath been exercised upon them thou wilt find the judgment of God upon thee for it into whose power he hath committed the sword of justice[.] the Lord hath honoured thee thus farre[,] therfore beware thou doe not dishonour him with that which he hath committed unto thee now when he is comming to rule & soe thou be as a branch out of the Lord [He?] hath noe need of thy help but for thy eternall good[,] for by his mighty power & outstretched arme will get himselfe the victory & he alone will rule & be king & Lord & law-giver[,] & the time is come that the law shall goe forth of Sion [Mic. 4:2] & this thou hast professed to stand for[;] consider the foundation thou stands on for if thou be not built upon that rock on which all the prophets & apostles & holy men of God now are & ever more were built upon thou cannot stand [.] soe into thy soule from the Lord I have cleared my conscience[,] & remember that thou art warned in thy lifetime which shalbe eternall witnes for me & against thee if thou disobey it

A freind of thy soule &
a lover of thy etenall good
Margerett Fell

FHL Portfolio 33:154–155.

35 To John Garnet 1655

"Soe remember when the day of Calamitie comes that thou was warned in thy life time, which shall bee an eternall wittnesse against thee."

This is a strong denunciation of a person who evidently had been a Friend but now, according to Margaret, had a "backsliding treacherous Spirit" and wallowed in "lust and Coveteousness." She warns him that his conscience "shall arisse & find thee out, and pursue thee to the death." She urges him "as thou loves thy soull and thy eternall good turn to the light of Jesus Chr: which checkes thee for sin and evill."

The only reference to John Garnet in Lancashire in Besse 2:26 reports that he was fined for attending Meeting in 1678. If it is the same person, he returned to the fold.

J.G.

Thou who art turned with the dogs to the vomitt [Prov. 26:11], into thy drunkennesse and filthynesse, from the light of christ-Jesus which hee hath enlightened thee withall, which if thou were obeydient to it, it would show thee thy deceitefull hart [Jer. 17:9], and thy back-sliding treacherous Spirit, who hast turned from the measure of god which hee hath given thee to profitt withall, and turnes his grace into wantonnesse. Thou may goe on and wallow and take thy fill of the earth and of the lust, and Coveteousness, but know assuredly that the light of god in thy Conscience, which the liveing god hath placed in thee, which once thou did see shineing wittnesseing to thy face against thy fillthynes, which caused thy Torment; though now thou hast buryed it for the present, but it shall arisse & find thee out, and pursue thee to the death, from it thou shalt never fly, but the terrour & wrath of the Almighty shall overtake thee whither [?] ever thou goes, though thou may put the evill day afare of [off], and make A Covenant with hell and death; but hee is come & made manifest which is thy Condemnation, and now there is no cloake for thy sin and this thou shalt eternally wittnesse. Therefore as thou loves thy soull and thy eternall good [,] turne to the light of Jesus Chr: which checkes thee for sin and evill; and harken and bee obeydient to it, and if thou bee faithfull to the light by which the lord God teaches his people then thou may Come to wittness the promisse of the lord; who hath said I will heale the backesliding and love them freely [Hos. 14:4]; And by no other way nor name under heaven but Jesus Xt who is given A Covenant of light shalt thou ever know the liveing God, and this thou shalt eternally wittnesse to bee love to thy soull, soe remember when the day of Calamitie [Deut. 32:35] comes that thou was warned in thy life time, which shall bee an eternall wittnesse against thee

M.F.

Spence 3/4. Endorsed: "M F to J garnot [George Fox]"; "For John Garnet 1655".

36 To All Friends, Brethren and Sisters 1655?

"And truly deare Bretheren we would not have troubled you, at this tyme[,] having troubled you before so lately[,] but that the necesity is soe great, the worke soe large, and the Bretheren beinge gone into soe farr & remote places."

This pastoral letter begins and ends with the importance of the unity among Friends:

the "onenesse of the Spirit;" "the bond of peace;" "the unity [which] is our Strength;" "We all sitt at one table, & feeds & Drinkes all at one fountayne." It is the Light, the Quakers' "first principle," derived from God and Christ, which she describes with many quotations from John, Ephesians and Galatians, that is the source of their unity.

The epistle would be effective if read aloud, as it most likely was, in expressing the strong hopes and desires for a new revelation and a new world. "Now is this brought to passe, & fulfilled, and fulfillinge glory & prayses be unto the Lord forever."

It then segues into the part each person might play: "Now is the Lord tryinge you what you will doe toward the worke and what you will bringe in towards the building of the temple." There are those who travel in the ministry to "minister to the seed" and others who minister to these Friends' "Carnall" needs by giving money, but they all are "like minded, haveinge the same love, beinge of one accord." She apologizes for asking again, but "the necesity is soe great . . . and the Bretheren beinge gone into soe farr and so remote places," including North America.

Tolles describes this extraordinary time in Quaker history:

> *The number of Friends who crossed the Atlantic [between 1655 to 1662] is so large as to suggest that the Publishing of Truth in America was a major enterprise of the infant Society of Friends. No less than sixty men and women . . . carried the Quaker message to the New World in that brief span of years. . . . That such a large-scale missionary operation could have been initiated and carried on by a society so recently founded is an extraordinary testimony to the power of religious faith. . . . No executive body planned it, no consultative committee coordinated it, for the Children of the Light had no such central organs. If there was any planning and guidance, it came from Swarthmore Hall. (Tolles, p. 19)*

Margaret ends the letter with the request that funds be sent to George Taylor and Thomas Willan of Kendal and that her letter be "Coppied over and sent abroad."

> To all friends Bretheren & Sisters which be in the Eternall unity, and onenesse of the Spirit, and in the bond of peace which never can be broken: which unity is our Strength and is the walls, & bulwarkes of our safty and is our habitation & Dwelling where our separation is from the world, and where the world knows us not[,] where the mistery of the Fellowshipp is, where noe vullenous eyes nor venemous beasts can come, neither anythinge enter that defileth, nethr [neither] whatsoever worketh abomination or maketh a lye, but they which are writ-

ten in the Lambs booke of life [Rev. 21:27.] My Deare Bretheren, in the light which is the first principle, which is every particulers teacher, and which Leades and guides every particular into the way of life[,] which light shines, & proceeds from the father who is Light, and in him is no Darkness at all [1 John 1:5], which light Drawes to the sonne, for there is none comes to the sonne except the father Drawe him [John 6:44]: and there is none knowes the sonne but the father[.] nether knowes any man the father save the sonne & he to whom the sonne reveales him, Now he who Dwells in the light, and abides in the light; sees this mistery opened, and sees the unity & ___ in the father & the sonne. None knowes the father but the only begotten sonne [John 1:18] of the father, in this Light which leads to the Sonne which is the way to the father of Light; in this is our unity, and this gatheres together into one all hearts who are faithfull & obeydient to it, where all is one in Christ Jesus, who is the Seed to which the promisse is too [Gal. 3:16], and all who ever comes to obteyne the faithfull promisse of the father, it is by Dwellinge in the Light which comes from Jesus; [He ?] who walkes in it, comes to witnesse the light of life, to whom all the promisses are [an X in the margin may indicate an omission here] you, and amen, and who makes of twaine one new man in Christ Jesus [Eph. 2:15] and upon this rocke is the whole Church built, and the foundation of it stands in the light, wherein is the unity, where no eevl [evil] is, where no Division is [,] where no sect, nor schisme is [,] where no strife is, nor no particular propriety[,] but all one in Christ Jesus[,] the substance of all life, who comes to take upon him the seed of Abraham, and to gather together, & to make all one; I in them & thou in mee, that they may be made perfect in one; and if yee be Christs, then are yee Abrahams seed, & heires accordinge to promisse [Gal. 3:29], and the everlasting rich love of the everlasting God wherin he hath abounded towards us, in all wisdome & prudence; havinge made knowne unto us the mistery of his will accordinge to his good pleasure which he hath purposed in himselfe, that in the Dispensations of the fullnes of tymes, he might gather together all things in Christ, both things which are in heaven, and things which are on earth, even in him 1: Ephes: 10 [Eph. 1:10]: Now is this brought to passe, & fullfilled, and fulfillinge glory & prayses be unto the Lord forever; And now is he trying what his saints, & people will doe for him in this his Day & tyme[,] workinge in his harvest wherin hee is sendinge forth his laboures into his harvest [Matt. 9:38] which he calls forth to worke whilest tis

Day, least the night come when no man can worke [John 9:4]. Now Deare Brethr: as you tend to the glory of God, the prosperity of Sion, and the resurection of the Dead, the raysinge of the eternall witnesse of god, which lyes slaine in the streets of this great Citty Soddom & Egipt where our Lord Jesus Christ is also Crusified [Rev. 11:8]. Now is the Lord tryinge you what you will doe toward the worke and what you will bringe in towards the building of the temple of the livinge God [2 Cor. 6:16], and what you will offer towards the resurection of the Body of Jesus[;] for we beinge many, are one bread; and one Body[,] for we are all partakers of that one bread [1 Cor. 10:17]. Therfore as we all sitt at one table, & feeds & Drinkes all at one fountayne, which streames unto every particular, and are all guided & ledd by one light, which shines from the living god, into the Consciences of men, and are all knitt & united together by one Spirit of life which makes free from sin & Death, and free from the Earth, and free from the Creature, soe in the freenes of the Spirit in which all who are in [?] the Spirit is established[,] freely give to the Lord, and to his service, and offer freely of the Earth to his worke which is now great, and Deare Bretheren doe not looke out, at any want, for the fountayne is full & large wherein we drinke, and there is nothinge offered up to the Lord but shall bee restored an hundred fould. Now Concerninge the Collection for the saints, and for the ministringe to the Bretheren of the Carnall things[,] who ministers to the seed, which is of the body, spirituall things, you need, ___ [?] that I write unto you nether concerninge them which are in bondes, for who are faithfull & obeydient to the Lord, doth remember them that are in bonds as bound with them, and them which suffer adversity as being yourselves also in the body 13 Hebr: 3 [Heb. 13:3] and in him who is the head of the body the Church who is the beginninge, the first borne from the the Dead[,] you may remember the sufferings of the ministers of Christ who suffers in the flesh for the bodyes sake; and gives up their bodyes unto the service of the most high God, to smitings, to buffettings[,] Scourgings, prisonings, whippings, stocking[,] reproachinge you, all manner of persecution, Now Deare friends that you may all be fellow members in his sufferings and have a feelinge of the ministry[,] the Lord requires & calls for you to minister of the outward to them who ministers that which is eternall and for ever[,] to that which is eternall. And truly Deare Bretheren[,] this is great & weighty for the prise [price] of it is the blood of the only begotten of the father who values one soule more than the whole world, Soe let this sinke Downe into your pure minds, for none knowes the weight of this, but who are in the pure obeydience, soe as yee tender the resurection of soules which lyes in the Death[,] offer freely of the Creature to the ministers of the livinge god, which he hath sent forth in his power and anoynted to preach gladd tydings to the poore, liberty to the Captive and prisoner [Isa. 61:1], unto which now the Day of redemption is hasteninge on apace, glory, prayses be to the livinge God for ever. And truly deare Bretheren we would not have troubled you at this tyme[,] having troubled you before so lately[,] but that the necesity is soe great, the worke soe large, and the Bretheren beinge gone into soe farr & remote places, and now is even the heale of the Lords harvest, and the burthen lyes heavy upon friends in the North now at the present; but the Lord God is raysinge up his owne seed to which he will give the inheritance, yea the Earth which is the Lords & the fulnesse thereof [Ps. 24:1], and the Creatur which groanes and under the bondage of Corruption he is recoveringe, and the wooll, and the oyle [oil] & the flax the Lord is recoveringe from under the hand of oppressers. And the tyme is cominge wherin the Kingdome shall be given to the saints of the most high, and then shall the Earth yeeld her Increase. Soe now for the present Deare Bretheren offer freely to the necessityes of the saints, and to the worke of the Lord, and what yee doe, in this, yee doe it unto the Lord, and the lord will give you a reward for what ye doe, & what yee have done, eternall & everlasting[.] and the Lord god of power open your hearts, that yee may be like minded, haveinge the same love, beinge of one accord, of one mind, and in this worke you follow the practice of all the saints in light 1 Cor:16:1: 2 Chroni:24:6–9 / Exod. 30:12–13–14: That which the Lord menes you to give, you may gather it and let it be sent to Geo: Taylor, & Tho: Willan of Kendal, to be ministred forth accordinge to the Necessityes of the saints, and the lord god of life and power keepe you faithfull in that which keepes in love, & in unity and in lowlynesse of minde, all to be servicable one to another, in the worke of the Lord, to his everlastinge prayse & glory.

Let this be Coppied over and sent abroad
unto the Northerne Countyes and the
North parts of Lancashire

your Deare Sister in that which redeems
Israell out of Bondage, and setts the
Creature free from under Corruptions

Margt. Fell

Spence 3/8.

37 To Friends of Grayrigg 1655

"Looke not forth, from your owne measures
at others Condition, and soe neglect your owne.
I warne you & charge you to beware of that."

This letter is a combination of two pages in the Spence Manuscript, Sp.3/9 and Sp.3/166. C. Horle pointed out that they are probably connected ("Index," pp. 18, 86). The first page is a general epistle to the Friends at Grayrigg, and the second is directed to two individuals there, very pointedly on the same theme. The handwriting is the same. The pages are difficult to read, and I have filled in some words from the Works, in brackets.

This epistle does not have the upbeat tone with which Margaret usually addresses Friends. It is a strong statement of the importance of being "low" or humble, "faithfull to your owne measures," and paying attention to each particular person's own gifts. She uses the parable from Matthew 20:2–16, about the laborers who worked one hour being paid as much as those who worked all day, to show that everyone will be judged, "to be tryed sooner or later." They should not "Question or Judge the power of the liveing God," and she ends with "Keepe your minds in that that is low, & each esteem others better than yourselves."

The second page is addressed to individuals, Peter Moseley and "Widdow Gardner & her sister." There is the same warning to "keepe lowe in the feare of the lord" and "keepe Downe all that would be exalted above the pure."

It seems likely that this letter is related to Letter 10 though the names are not spelled the same. There were evidently differences among the Friends at Grayrigg and at Swarthmoor.

Friends of Grayrigge

Bretheren & Sisters in your measures of the livinge light & life of the living God, waite low and in the feare of the Lord god, Stand faithfull to your owne measures, & be obeydient to that which every particuler hath received of the livinge God which he hath given you to profitt withall and with your measures of that which is Eternall which beares wittnesse for the livinge God, which he hath placed in every particuler of you which if you keepe to it & mind it, and come to it to be tryed, & searched this will be swift to lett you see all that is contray to it, and this will come neare to you in Judgment [Mal. 3:5] therefore in this abide in your measures where the pure Judgment is sett up in your particulers and in your measures of the livinge word which is nigh in the heart which cutts downe all that is contrary to it by which the world [was made.] In this abide and Dwell, and in this Dwell in your owne particuler [measures within] you[.] I charge you and warne you as you will answare it before the [Lord, before whom you must] give an accounpt [account] that you be faithfull to your owne masters to which [you must stand or fall;] that as good stewards, you may give a good acounpt, and be found [faithful workers] in the Lords vinyard who is now at work, and will have none to [be idle, but calls] into the vinyard at every hower [hour;] and yee that was called at the first [hour of the day if yee be not faithfull & obeydient to improove your talents[,] hee that [cometh at the] eleventh houre will receive as much as you, and then he that hath been negligent will murmer & counts it hard. This parable you may read [Matt. 20:2–16]—with the Eternall light which never changes[,] come to be examined & tryss [every particular] of you and see where you are at present & how you stand in the presence of the livinge God whose purity cannot behould Iniquity, before whom you must appeare to bee tryed sooner or later, for that is made manifest that prooves all, & tryes all, the day makes all workes manifest of what sort it is. And looke not forth, from your owne measures at others Condition, and soe neglect your owne. I warne you & charge you to beware of that and thinke it not strange concerninge the firy tryall which is to try you and though some strange thing had happened unto you [1 Pet. 4:12] but in the feare of the lorde god keepe downe your minds that Questions & Stumbles at the power of the Lord which is made manifest for the working downe of the Deceipt; and beware how you Question or Judge the power of the livinge God, to which all the powers of Darkness shall bend & bow, but lett it alone and Dwell in your owne measures, & though you may see & discerne deceipt in those in whom it is manifested it can be no otherwise, the deceipt being unwrought [out] and it will act while it is there, but let it alone, the power of the lord is given for workinge it downe, and if they Dwell and abide in the power, the power of the lord will worke Downe, and bringe the fleshly man under, and bynd him that is stronge & spoyle his goods, and this you must not lymitt with your reason and wisdome for this is unlimitted, and this is various in its working and opperation accordinge to the necessity of the particuler on which it is manifested[.] and this is ordered by the wisdome of the livinge God which is foolishnes to the wisdome of man [1 Cor. 1:25], and soe be still and silent as you love your soules, And beware how you medle with that by which all shall fall which is contrary to it. Soe in the name and power of the Lord Jesus Christ, at whose name every knee shall bow [Phil. 2:10], be yee obeydient and faithfull to your owne measures in your owne particulers, and in the pure Eternall of God keepe your minds in that that is low, & each esteem others better than yourselves, and be Jealous over your owne hearts with a godly jealousie least the serpent beguile you as he did Evah through his subtillty, betray you from the simplicity which is in Christ [2 Cor. 11:3], soe the Lord God allmighty of life & power keepe you faithfull and obeydient to your own measures

M. Fell

And peeter Mosesley keepe lowe in the feare of the lord, and in the power keepe thy mind, & to the power be obeydient, and let it worke accordinge to the good pleasure of the Lord, and as the Deceipt is made manifest in thee, soe Judge it out & keepe it downe and keepe thy mind to the power & it will worke the deceipt out, & Downe. Soe be obeydient, & keepe the power which the lord God hath made manifest in thee for the workinge down of his Enemies, and be subject to the power which is ordeyned of God, for the bringing downe the powers of hell & Death, and looke not out at others words, but keepe thy mind low & still I warne thee, & charge thee, that in the feare of the lord, & in obeydience thou keepe low, low, and looke not out at others words, soe the lord god of power preserve that of him in thee.

M: F:

And widdow Gardner & her sister keepe in the pure feare of the Lord and dwell low in the power, and keepe Downe all that would be exalted above the pure in the low & in the humble waite and in the pure obeydience to your measures of the Lord God be faithfull, and there you will read the love of God, and be low & subject and willing to cast your [c]rowns at the feet of Jesus soe the lord God Allmighty of life and power preserve you faithfull and obeydient, and looke not out at others words, but in the pure power of the lord god Dwell.

M: F:

Spence 3/9 and 3/166. Also in Works, *pp. 68–70. Endorsed: (Spence 3/166)* "to Frinds at Grarige from M: F: 1655".

38 To Francis Benson 1655

"If you turne your mind never soe little
to thc holy within you[,] you will see them blinde
who is out of the light . . . then will the witnesse of God
rise in you . . . [that] which hath been slayne
Soe many years as you have followed them."

This pastoral letter explicates some principles of Quaker beliefs and warmly urges "turning to the light within." It was written to counter the influence of Gabriel Camelford (Letter 20), and Margaret confesses that at one time she had "a greater love & interest" in Camelford than the recipient of her letter.

It is addressed primarily to Francis Benson (?–1672) of Loughrigge in Westmorland who was in the process of being convinced by Quakerism (CJ, 2:390). It probably influenced him, for he did become a Friend, according to several records. George Fox stayed at his home in 1663 (Nickalls, p. 455); and in 1665 "for being at a Meeting, he had his Coat & Hat taken from him, & his Daughter her Petticoat" (Besse, 1:316).

Margaret speaks of the Light, the effect it has bringing "deeds . . . to be prooved & tryed, whether they be wrought in god." She contrasts the Quakers' understanding from within with other teachers who are "Deceivers & betrayers of your soules: for they deny the Cornerstone Christ Jesus, who is the light." She had once followed such ministers because she "did not know the true & living god." Camelford is an enemy of God and "a minister of Antichrist," because "the first principle he never knew, nor never owned yet." It is "a mistery which Chamellford nor none of his Bretheren ever know." She speaks out of her own experience and with "love to your soules, and your eternall good, wee havinge knowne ourselves to be in the same way."

She uses the image of Christ as the good shepherd, with quotations from John, and compares this with the "false shepheard & hyerlings . . . whose god is their belly." With a little sarcasm she adds, "who would keepe Christ without them[,] still as farr as Jerusalem, or in heaven, or they know not where."

To Francis Benson & his Familie or any else where this may come:

To the light of Xt. Jesus in your Consciences which he hath enlightened you withall [,] who is the light of the world, and doth enlighten every one that cometh into the world [John 1:9], and if you love the light[,] you bring your deeds to the light to be prooved & tryed, whether they be wrought in god[;] and this is the condemnation, that light is come into the world, & men love darknes rather than light because their deeds are evill, for every one that doth evill hateth the light, neither cometh to the light[,] least his deeds should bee reprooved: 3: John 18:19:20:21 [John 3:18–21] verses 1:J 4: & 9 [John 1:4 & 9] verses: 8: John 12:8 [John 8:12]. Now deare people[,] as you love your soules, search the scriptures and see whether Christ Jesus the sonne of God did not speake these words and leave this upon record, and every one who will owne the scriptures must owne this light for the Scriptures were given forth from the light, and the spirit of God was in them who spoke forth the scriptures[;] for they are of no private interpretation[,] but holy men speake them forth as they were mooved of the holy ghost [2 Pet. 1:20–21], and Christ Jesus who is the light, and doth enlighten every one that cometh into the world, in him is life, & this life is the light of men [John 1:4] and this same Jesus Baptized with the holy=ghost & with fire [Matt. 3:11]. Therefore now all people try those who calls themselves ministers of the Gospell by the scriptu[res;] and you shall find them the Deceivers & betrayers of your soules: for they deny the Cornerstone Christ Jesus, who is the light, & the rocke on which the whole Church is built[.] of these buillders of Babell hee is disalowed, & disanuled [?] [;] but to us, he is become the head of the Corner, glory & prayses be to the living god for ever: For the grace of God which hath appeared to all men teacheth us to deny ungodlines & all worldly lusts, and to live godly & soberly in this present evill world[,] prayses be to the livinge god for ever; But this we never learned of Camellford, nor of no such deceivers as he is, nether shall ever any who followeth them learne this of them, nor the livinge God of heaven & Earth[;] they shall never come to know who followes them: eternally you shall witnesse me[;] and further I was in a profession of a god & of a Christ then any of ye are, and yet I did not know the true & living God while I followed them[;] and a greater love & interest I had in Camellford (I beleeve) then any of you have, but then I did not know him; but now I know him, and his Spirit, and I doe utterly deny him & his ministry[,] which is out of the Darknes of Christ & all that ever taught for him, and the livinge God he is an enemy too [to], and a minister of Antichrist, and a witnesse I stand against him forevermore; And for no other cause but that he is an enemy to God & to his truth[;] and he laboures by all meanes to disapoynt the livinge god of his end and of his promisse, who hath promissed that he will teach his people himselfe and hath said they shall not say, know the Lord[,] but they shall all know him from the least to the greatest [Heb. 8:11]. But

Camellford would have them to come to him to know him who never knew him himselfe, for the first principle he never knew, nor never owned yet. But now is the lord God cominge to redeeme from the mouthes of these wolves which devoures the flock [Acts 20:29], and through fayned [feigned] words & Coveteousnesse makes marchandize [merchandise] of the people [2 Pet. 2:3]. But now the free [?] love of the livinge god is rissen & breaking forth, and his free grace [?] is appearinge by which the lord god teacheth to deny ungodlynes [2 Titus 2:12] which all these dumbe shepheards never did, and they themselves lives in all ungodlynes and worldly lusts[,] as their fruits maketh them manifest, and yet they would leane upon the Lord [Mic. 3:11], but the lord God is lying their abominations open, and a contrivarsie the Lord hath with them[,] which shall never be reconsiled, the decree of the Allmighty is gone out against them[;] their destruction is determened by the lord of hostes 2:Mal:1:2:3 [Mal. 2:1–3] and this they shall all witnesse fullfilled upon them, for the lord God cannot lye nor deny, and all them who are out of the light of Christ Jesus (who is the Cornerstone) the curse of God remaynes upon them for ever. And therefor waite but a while[,] and you shall see what will become of them and their Doctrine which they have upholden soe longe, and you shall see whether the livinge God be not against them or not, I am against them[,] saith the lord[,] who use their tongues and saith[,] the lord saith, when[,] saith the lord[,] I never spoke to them 23:Jerem:31:32:33:34 [Jer. 23:31–32]: Therfore a warnninge to you from the lord god[,] that you beware how you follow the blind leaders[,] who can lead none but those that are blind, and soe they both fall into the ditch [Matt. 15:14]: for if you turne your mind never soe litle to the holy within you[,] you will see them blinde who is out of the light, and if you keepe your minds to the light then will the witnesse of God rise in you & witnesse against them[,] which hath beene slayne by them, and laid slaine Soe many yeares as you have followed them, yea, Eternally yee shall witnesse me heare, for this I speake by experience. Soe if you keepe yor minds to the light then will you know the witnesse of God in you, which is better then a thousand false accusers without you, and that witnesse, which witnesseth for the livinge god, witnesses against them all to be without god in the world, whose minds are turned from the light[,] their deeds are evill, and soe the light is the Condemnation of the whole world; And this is a mistery which Chamellford nor none of his Bretheren ever know nor never shall, soe longe as they appose [oppose] & stand against it. And soe[,] friends[,] to that of god in your Consciences I speake which will witnesse for me for ever; and this to be love to your soules. That you would but consider what our end can bee anymore then love to your soules, and your eternall good, wee havinge knowne ourselves to be in the same way in blindnes and Ignorance of god, professinge a god but not knowing him at all as you are[.] And therfor to the directing of your minds to the light of Christ Jesus in you which is one in all[,] which is our teacher, & by which the lord god teaches, all that ever is taught of him[,] who is the good shepheard who hath given his life for his sheepe [John 10:11], for in him is life and his life is the light of men [John 1:4], and by this light he teacheth. But this the false shepheards & hyerlings cannot endure to heere [hear] of, whose end is destruction[,] whose god is their belly, who mind earthly things [Phil. 3:19]: who would keepe Christ without them[,] still as farr as Jerusalem, or in heaven, or they know not where, but he is rissen, who is the stone cutt out of the mountaine without hands [Dan. 2:45] and strikes at the feet of their Image which they have set up, and Sion is become a burthensome stone to the nations: and he is rissen who rules with a rodd of Iron, & of him shall they all bee dashed to peeces [Ps. 2:9]. Therfore all people[,] as you love your soules, turn to the light which showes you sin, & evill and lets you see the deceipt of your hearts, and all your hard thoughts & hard speeches & brings to remembrance what ever hath beene wrought in darknes, this is the light which shines in darknes, and darknesse comprehends it not [John 1:5], but it makes manifest darknes, and soe if you can be deluded by this now, this will let you see the deluders & betrayers of your soules, and it will let you see the deceivers of your soules[,] which would draw you from it, and if you be obeydient to it, it will let you see your Saviour[;] and if you turne from it & be disobeydient to it, it will be your eternall condemnation for ever, and no other way nor name under heaven[,] but by Jesus who is the light[,] shall yee ever come to be saved, or to know the livinge god. And soe in love to your soules have I written this[,] that yee might come to partake of the free grace of god[,] which is now appearinge in this his day. And soe to you I have cleared my Conscience[,] whether you will heare or forbeare. And if ever yee come to know the livinge god or to witnesse true peace in him[,] yee shall owne us, and our testimony to be true. And all false hyrelings and theeves and robbers which climbes up another way to be lyars. And all that ever calls themselves ministers of the gospell [,] let them professe what they will [,] though they seeme never soe zealous or godly[,] yet if they come not in at this doore which is Jesus christ the light but climbes up another way & denyes the light[,] let them be never soe high[,] they are theeves & robbers & no ministers of Jesus Christ: and this yee shall eternally witnesse[,] whether ever yee owne us or not. And consider what you have gayned [gained] or what yee know of god by followinge of them: nay[,] that in your consciences will witnesse to your faces that yee have not learned to know the first principle that leads to god by following of them. But in as much as yee owne the light in you & hearken to it, & be obeydient to it[,] soe will yee come to know god & soe will the witnesse of god in you arise[,] which witnesseth for god. And soe the Lord god of power rayse [raise] up his owne witnesse in you that yee may come to see the deceivers & betrayers of yourselves; and that will show you the deluders & enemies of your soules; and to that I am made manifest, which condemnes all the false prophetts and Antichrists which is in the world[,] the light which is the worlds condemnation[.] From one who loves & desires the good of all peoples and desires that all should be saved, & come to the knowledge of god, and one who knowes Camellford to the Bottome

Margret Fell

And for this note of Camellfords which is to goe to Camellford[,] let it not trouble you, for if ever yee owne the livinge God or his people, yee must deny Camellford, and if ever yee come to owne that of god in your Consciences, that will deny him[;] and if yee owne Camellford then yee deny God & that of him in your Consciences. And this yee shall eternally witnesse to be truth & love to your soules.

Spence 3/33–34. Endorsed: "to Francies Benson from M F 1655": "To Francis Benson".

39 To Christopher Fell 1655

"Thou that calls it reason that judgeth out sinne, & lust, knowes not what thou speakest, for that that judgeth out sinne is beyond thy reason."

Fell was a common name in northwest England, and Christopher Fell was not related to Margaret. His parents and their four sons all became Quakers in 1653. Since Christopher's name is omitted in later documents it "may point to his having fallen away from Truth" (CJ, 1:450–451).

Historian and Earlham College Archivist Thomas Hamm writes, "This may be the Christopher Fell who, according to Smith's Catalogue, *was coauthor with Francis Howgill and Thomas Woodrow of* A Few Words to the People of England. *If he is, then he was born in Lancashire in 1625 and died at Cartmel in 1706. He apparently made his peace with Friends, as his children married in Meeting and he died a Friend."*

The occasion for this letter was Christopher Fell's writing a note addressed to Margaret, disputing something that she had written. She points out that the note she wrote was "given forth generally to all friends, which are of the body" and that he attributes words to her that she did not write.

His fault is that his "broken language . . . cometh not from the eternall light" but is the notion that reason is sufficient to judge sin. He is in error in separating the eternal from the Light and in mixing things that do not belong together. She writes, "thy Judgment and thy Language is mixt," and she quotes Leviticus, which, in a series of "thou shalt nots" says: "Thou shalt not sow thy field with mingled seed: neither shall a garment mingled of linen and woollen come upon thee."

He needs to "come to [the light] to bee searched and tryed" so that he will more clearly discern what is beyond reason. She addresses him as "Friend" and asks him to "honestly consider" his actions.

Friend

I received a note from thee, which I know nothinge of, or the occation of writing it but by what thou mentioneth in thy paper, the note that I writt I was eternally moved of the Lord, and it was given forth generally to all friends, which are of the body: And likewise the end of it was, for the receiving of friends genrally of the same body. And not any perticular one had it relation unto. But I finde in thy note, words mentioned which were not at all in it (as it shall testifie where it is to be shewed) And broken Language I find in thine, which cometh not from the eternall light. where thou speakes for reasoninge and Judging, who were in the body and who were out of the body, and in our reason to Judge out sinn, as lust and Covetousnesse; all this is out of the truth, for there is not one word of this in my note, nether had I any thought of any persecuter when it was written; But to all that are of the body it is directed; And wheras thou sayes thou judges, And saith take heed of mixinge; these words thou must owne, for they are thy owne, thy Judgment and thy Language is mixt. Thou saith thou art a member of the same body, and subject to the same infirmity[;] now thou that art subject to infirmity, art not a pure Judge; And thy Garment is of linnen and woolen [Lev. 19:19], and this thou art a witnesse of. And thou warnes us to read this with the light, or rather (thou sayest) let the eternall in us read it, where thou makest two, of the Light, and of the eternall; which words are for Condemnation with the light which is eternall. And wheras thou saith, that it is the Eternall God of life (who is a Consuminge fire) [Heb. 12:29] that destroyes lust & Covetousnesse, In this thou hast made it manifest that thou canst not witnesse that in thee it is destroyed, and any without, will say, it is the Lord, as well as thou. Friend[,] when I writt the other note, I did not know thee, but now I know thee, and have tryed thee[.] And in the pure discerninge of what thou speakes, thou art not; and to the light thou must come to bee searched and tryed: and thou wilt find that thy suffering is not for well doinge. And thou that calls it reason that judgeth out sinne, & lust, knowes not what thou speakest, for that that judgeth out sinne is beyond thy reason: And thou that pleads for infirmity, art in thy reason, and soe lives in the infirmity and in the sinne, and lust; And this the light in thy Conscience will let thee see, and witnesse, if thou wilt be judged by it. Therfore honestly consider, and let the light search thee, And thou wilt see, that thou hast acted in darknesse; And this that thou Judgest with (in thy paper) is for Judgment and will not be owned for true Judgment, of him who is the eternall Judge. And of those words mentioned in thy paper, I am cleare, for they were never spoken by mee, yet when I sawe [saw] thy paper, I was moved of the Lord to write this to thee, (and of that of God in thy Conscience it wilbe owned, and in the eternall light thy note was read,) And the other I sent to Antho: Pearson as thou directed

Thy sister to all that which is obeydient
to the Eternall light
Margret Fell

Spence 3/35. Endorsed: "M F [George Fox] To Christopher Fell that sent a pap[er] amongst Friends against a pap of M.F.'s, 1655."

40 TO FRIENDS IN CUMBERLAND 1655

"He that is the Judge & the light is the eye, by which all is seen & made manifest."

This letter is confusing in several ways. The first paragraph ends in the middle of a sentence; it concerns Christopher Fell's paper (Letter 39) but does not say so. Although addressed to Friends in Cumberland it sometimes addresses Christopher Fell directly. This copy may be either a rough draft or a very poor copy. Another letter in a different hand, which seems to be addressed to Margaret Fell, is written upside down on the same page.

Margaret's concern is to clarify the meaning of judgment to Friends who may have been misled by Christopher Fell's paper. Judgment and condemnation of sin, which the Light discloses, come from Jesus. She says to Christopher Fell, "Thou speakes Confussion who exhorts . . . to waite in the light . . . And then afterwards Comes with a Comand to Judge." That is wrong, because "the light is the Judge & the condemnation of all unjust." She includes numerous permutations on the themes of judgment, condemnation, on the relationship of judgment and condemnation, and on the light.

To all my deare brethren & sisters, who bee in the light which xt [Christ] Jesus hath enlightened you with all; I warne you and charg you from the Lord God that yee bee faithfull and obedient: unto the measure of God which hee hath given you[,] to every one of you[,] to profitt with all and that the light of Christ Jesus which in every

That spirit which gave forth this paper [Christopher Fell's] is for Judgemt & Condemnation with the Light, which comes from Jesus who is the light of the world, who for Judgement is Come into the world; who is the Judge of the world [John 9:39] unto him is all Judgement Committed; And thou speakes Confussion[,] who exhorts and besceeches [beseeches] to waite in the light, and abide in the light, And then afterwards Comes with A Comand not to Judge, when as the light of the Judge & Condemnation of all[,] that is for Judgemt, here thou hast made it manifest that thy Comand & Authoryty is for condemnation with the light, which gives the Authoryty power to Command[.] And thou art afraid of Judgement, and that is the cause of thy writing, for where the light is dwelt in & lived in & obeyed[,] there is the pure Judgemt set up; and there can nothing passe but is Judged, and thou Comands not to Judge & yet exhorts to the light, here with the light see thy Confussion, and owne thy Condemnation & Judgement upon it, And whereas thou sayest that hee doth not Judge by the light of his eye nor by the hearing of his eare [Job 42:5], who Judges righteously; there thou art in the Confussion againe and knowes not what thou speakes[,] for hee that is the Judge & the light is the eye, by which all is seen & made manifest, and hee that makes the eare hee heares, & here hee is thy Judge & Condemnation of these words; Soe to the light of Christ Jesus[,] which is the searcher and tryer[,] turne; And let that Judge thee & try thee and thou wilt see that the rise & ground, why this paper [i.e., C. Fell's] was given forth was for fear of Judgement, for hee that st[ands?] cleare[,] Judged & tryed before the righteous Judge passes not for mans Judgement; And if they doe dwell & abide in the light as thou exhorts them & besceeches them; then must they Judge & passe Condemnation[,] for the light is the Judge & the condemnation of all unjust; and then they breake thy Command; And soe here thou speakes not as one that hath Authoryty [Matt. 7:29] ___ but is for Judgement & Condemnation with him that hath Autho[rit]y; And this is over & Comands thy Comand[,] which thou shalt eternally wittnesse

And all friends in the light dwell
which is the judge & Condemnation '
of all Uncleane spirits

Let this goe among Friends in
Cumberland where the other hath bene

Spence 3/36. Endorsed: "friends in Cumberland concerning Chris Fells paper against mine 1655"; "The Answer to Chr: Fells Note"; "That which wrote this paper is for Judgment, & condem."

41 To William Dewsbury August 14, 1655

"Veryly my love to thee is inexpressable
Neither can pen write, but where the Spirritt
of the liveing God unites . . . there is noe seperation,
but presence one with Another."

William Dewsbury (1621–1688) was "perhaps the sweetest and wisest of the early Friends" (BQ, *p.* 63). *Like George Fox he had a history of searching for truth from boyhood days. He was in the Puritan army, but "feeling conscious of a command to put away his sword, he left the army. . . . He heard George Fox preach at Balby in Yorkshire, and at once was in accord with him . . . "* (DNB). *He joined in spreading the Quaker message. He traveled widely, preaching eloquently, writing many epistles and tracts, forming* Meetings, *and spending many years in various prisons* (DNB, EQW, *p.* 590).

Henry J. Cadbury, *who transcribed this letter* (JFHS, Suppl. *22*), *notes that there were nine Friends in Northhampton Gaol at that time. Margaret writes: "*My deare love is to all thy fellowe prisoners: My deare Brethren stand fast in the liberty wherewith Christ hath made you free.*" In a postscript she enquires as to their "outward needs," and Cadbury notes that Dewsbury replied, "here is not the want of anything."*

My deare brother,

My deare everlastinge love & life in the everlastinge fountain is to thee, whom my heavenly Father hath called elect & chosen forth of the world for his owne service & worke & to suffer for the Testimony of Jesus. Oh my Deare brother, Thy faithfulness & service & sufferinge for the Lord makes thee smell sweete; oh blessed art thou & happy shal thou bee, Thy reward is with thee, Thy worke is before thee. In the everlastinge Fountaine of life, where the Covenant stands I am one with thee, where there is fullness of joy & peace for evermore, And veryly my love to thee is inexpressable Neither can pen write, but where the Spirritt of the liveing God unites, where there is noe separation, but presence one with Another, there tread my dear brother, where noe persecution touches, where no vulterous eye nor venomous beast shall ever come, oh here, here dwells my owne deare heart, where the Redemption is; And the assention above all the earthly wills of man: where the sitting together is in heavenly places, in Christ Jesus, where the perfect freedome & liberty is, which noe man can take from us, purchased by the Sonne of God, glory, glory to the Liveing God for ever. My deare love is to all thy fellowe prisoners: My deare Brethren stand fast in the liberty wherewith Christ hath made you free, Nott onely to beeleeve on him but alsoe to suffer for his sake, And doe not bend nor bow to the yoake of bondage of man's will: But a fast unto the Lord God keepe, which yee are now called unto; which is to loose the bonds of wickedness, to undoe the heavy burden & to lett the oppressed goe free & to breake every yoake [Isa. 58:6], which the Lord God of power is doeing in this his day. Soe my deare brethren bee faithfull to the worke of the Lord, for by him is all the power of Darkness limitted. And now is the time that the man of sin & the sonne of perdition is revealled [2 Thess. 2:3]; which hath soe long betrayed & crucyfied the Lord of glory: butt he is risen, who rules with a rodd of Iron, who dashes to peices [Ps. 2:9] all his enemyes, whose scepter is a scepter of Righteousness [Heb. 1:8], of whose Kingdome there is no end, to whom bee everlastinge glory & praise forevermore. My deare brother let me heare from thee. Truly my love runs forth to thee exceedingly. The presence of my heavenly Father is with thee. Oh stand bold & faithful unto the end; And in his Armes lye downe my deare one, Thee everlastinge strength & power of the everlastinge God bee with you all & keep you firme & sure, in obedience to his will, & faithfull to his everlastinge praise & glory.

Your deare sister in the unchangable Truth

M: F:

Deare brother lett me Know how yee are provided for in the outward.
Swarthmore 14th day of the 6 moneth

York, 14, from JFHS Suppl. 22 *(1948) pp. 34–35. Endorsed: "For My deare brother William Dewsberrye prisoner of the Lord att Northampton theise deliver".*

42 TO OLIVER CROMWELL 1655

"Consider honestly with the Just in thee, what thou hast done for god, sinse hee put thee in power and Authority, what unJust Lawes hast thou changed."

Margaret appeals to the "measure of god in thee" and reminds Cromwell that he was preserved "marrucullously many A time" in order "to Execute Justice" and "bee A terrour to the Evill doere." It is also a strong rebuke for continued persecution of those who are innocent.

The emphasis is on the need for liberty of conscience, which he had promised, and for the need to abolish tithes. The existing law caused a person with "a tender conscience" to be fined "in treble damage" and suffer "destrainte of his goods." She argues that "them that were free to pay priest tithes and to hear them, might pay tithes, and they that are not free to pay neither to hear them" should be free of the requirement.

To O: Crumwell from M. F. 1655
Freind

To that measure of god in thee, which searcheth thy heart, that with it thou may read in meekenesse and moderation, without prejudize, According unto the truth of god in thee which cannot beare false wittness, which testifies for god, who carried thee in his arme & power, & gave thee dominion over his enemies, and sett thee in their place, to try thee if thou would now rule for him, And execute Justice & true Judgement and performe thy vows and Covenant made with him, And that thou would performe FaithFully the End, which the light of god in thy Conscience tels thee caried thee on, for which end thou was reserved marruculllously many A time[,] which end was liberty of Conscience, which now the lord hath put freely into thy power, to Execute Justice, And that thou might bee A terrour to the Evill doere, And for the prayse of them that doe well, and here stands as it were and lookes on, to see how thou will performe with him, who hath beene A Faithfull god to thee, whose Long suffering hath Abundantly been Exersised toward thee, who hath preserved thee from many cruell plots, and bloody designes, which hath beene against thee, by murderous spirits, But oh man[,] Consider, how thou hast requited the lord, when Instead of humbleing thy selfe, In bending & boweing before him[,] that thou might know his will and mind what to doe, to requite his Fatherly and tender care over thee, that soe thou might returne true Honour and prayses to his name[;] but instead of this thou feasted, And fed the Lust of uncleane persons & had musicke And vaine Gesting and sporting, by uncleane and riatous spirits, which things is Abominable unto god, And his soule hates them. This is not A sacrifice Acceptable to god, nor is it becomeing of those that should walke According to the gospell of Jesus xt. who is to walke sircumspectly, not as fooles, but as wise, redeemeing the time because the dayes were evill, & when the lord did Frustrate thine enemies, and gave thee space to repent, And disCovered the plott by his owne true wittnesse in the Conscience, which wittnesse would not suffer it to bee hid, but forced the man to discover it, though not by any outward power, but by the __________ of the wittnesse of god in his Conscience, this might have reached that in thy Conscience if that thou had stoden [stood] in the feare of god, it would have lett thee serve what it is that reveales the secrets of all hearts, which is the righteous Judge in the Conscience, And reveales the righteousnesse of god against all the unrighteousnesse and ungodlinesse of men, If thou had minded this, this would have brought thee downe and have humbled thee, that thou would have Abhored those things Aforementioned; Againe Consider honestly with the Just in thee, what thou hast done for god, sinse hee put thee in power and Authority, what unJust Lawes hast thou changed, by which the Innocent is opressed[,] what unJust men hath thou turned out, onely for there cruelty exersised upon the Innocent, nay[,] have not they beene turned out that would have done Justice, which would have beene A terour to the evill doore [doer], And they taken in which are enemies to god and his truth, And hath beene Actuall enemies against the state, And yet these men comes to bee lords over tender Consciences, and to exersise there cruelty upon them under thy name who hath formerly ventured thy life and blood for liberty of Conscience, now let the truth in all hearts Judge, how thou Answers and performes thy promises[.]

Againe with the Just of god in thee, search honestly what Liberty of Conscience this is, when one who out of Conscience cannot pay a preist tithes, neither in Conscience cann hee partake of the preists ministry, for which tithes is paid, now what Justice or Equity is there in that Law or Magistrate, Ruler, or Governor that would give A priest tithes of that man, whose Conscience will not suffer him to partake of that ministry, which receives tithes, being that the end why tithes is given unto preists, is because they minister unto people, And this man, which out of tendernesse of Conscience, cannot pertake of his ministry, neither receive any from him as A minister, yet by Constrainte must hee pay tithes, And by A Law bee cast in treble damage, and after that pay by destrainte of his goods, may bee nay treble of that, And whether this bee not the greatest oppression and InJustice that ever A time brought forth, under A gospell dispensation, Lett the honest harted Judge, And whether this bee liberty of Conscience, which is under such Cruell sufferings for Conscience sake, even to the Impondrageing [impounding?] of peoples outward Livelyhoods, And whether this bee not A cruell bondage to the Tender Conscience, and opression of the Just[,] where there is breathings and desires after god and his truth, but seeing such Cruell sufferings Infflicted upon others for denyeing of the preist, that it is ever A torment to them and keepes them in bondage, And whether this bee liberty of Conscience, let the honest hearted Judge, when there is A priesthood set up out of the doctrine of christ. A changeable priesthood takeing tithes, A thing contrary to that in the Conscience, where the unchangable priest ministers, & who is come to know the unchangable priest, and doe wittnesse him minister life to them. And soe out of Conscience denies the changable, And yet by Constrainte of Law must pay the hireling wages or suffer the spoileing of Their goods[.] if this bee Justice let the Just Judge now[.] if there were but any signe or Couler [color] of Justice According to Liberty of Conscience, it were requissite that such lawes should bee Established, as were According to liberty of Conscience, that is, them that were free to pay priest tithes and to heare them, might pay them tithes, and they that are not free to pay them tithes neither to hear them, that they might bee freed from payeng them tithes. And soe have liberty of their Conscience, and this there cann none that pretends liberty of Conscience that hath either Justice or Equity in them deny, was there ever people that pretended liberty of Conscience, that would sett up A ministry, and hold them up by A Law Contrary to that in the Conscience, which ministry tender Consciences cannot owne, but doth utterly deny them, and there doctrine, and yet must be forced by A Law to maintaine them, and yet under pretence of Liberty of Conscience, now let the Just of god in thee weigh these things, for nothing els cann, and soe A time to take of [off] sume of the oppressions, yokes, and burthens, that is of the Innocent, that soe the Lord may blesse thee, and prolong thy dayes, and if thou doe not[,] Assuredly the cry of the Innocent will arise up onto him that will plead there cause, and woe unto the oppressor[.]

Spence 3/91. Also a summary in Works, *p. 16. Endorsed: "M F to Olefer Crumwell [George Fox]".*

43 To Gabriel Camelford, a Minister 1655

"Oh thou Serves an evill Master[.]
he Causes thee to ly thy nakednes & filthynes open[;]
And the shame of thy Abomination appears."

This is a denunciation of Gabriel Camelford (Letters 20, 38) and a refutation of his arguments against the Quakers. Margaret had written to him previously, rebutting his charge, in a letter to Francis Benson, that "wee did denie the righteousnes of faith." Camelford wrote again, charging Quakers with five errors, and Margaret is replying.

Before she begins her five arguments, she warns him of the consequences of his ways, with many references to Isaiah. Many of the polemical writings of the time use a format of question and answer, often numbering them. Margaret does not do this here, although she summarizes the charges near the end of her letter. I have inserted the corresponding numbers in the text. In her summary she asserts that it is Camelford, rather than the Quakers, who are guilty of these charges, i.e., he is:

1. "a pleader for sinn." Camelford evidently held the Calvinist position on the fallen state of man and on predestination.

2. "an enemy of god" and of the truth that Jesus purges and washes.

3. "an enemy to the light which is the first principle" and which reveals truth now as did to Nicodemus and Paul.

4. "antichrist & a denyer of Christ come in the flesh." She finds that in denying the Light he is a persecuter like the Apostle Paul before he "wittnessed the Sonn revealed."

5. "a devourer of widdowes houses."

She ends the paper by denying his charge that "wee did denie the righteousnes of faith." The Quakers believe that the "rightenes of faith speaketh on this wise: the word is nigh in the heart," whereas he preaches the "imputation of faith," a theological concept concerning righteousness and guilt.

The tone of the letter is harsh, not unusual for polemical writings of the day. She denounces Camelford, speaks of his "nakednes & filthynes," "the shame of thy Abomination," "thou Enimie of God," etc. Francis Benson had asked Margaret to reply to Camelford. She accepted the task for "the Cause of our writing to thee was for the simple & the Innocents sake."

Camelford thou art torm[en]ted[;] the power is over you[;] And under the Chaine thou art which Chaines the draggon [Rev. 20:1], which gives yee thy power[,] but he is Cominge to be Cast out into the Earth[.] thy tyme is short & therefore doth thou rage[.] the stone lyes upon thee & from under it thy god Cannot defend thee[;] And by that which Thou calls a sathanicall spirit art thou bound & Chained & thy God Judged[.] Therefore stopp thy mouth And be Silent for thou art to be broken in peices & thy Counsell to Come to nought[;] And thy Confederacye cannot make afraid[,] for he is risen who is the sanctuary

& A stone of stumbling [Isa. 8:9–14] And a hart of offense to thee And the pitt that thou hast denyed thou art fallen into and thy sword is broken & thy End thou shalt now acomplish[.] therefore see whatt God thou serves[,] for thou art amongst the familyer spirits And seekeing unto the wizzards that peepe And mutter & thou may goe on where thou art & frett till thou come to Curse thy king & thy God And looke upward & looke unto the Earth & behold Trouble & darknes & anguish & hither thy God drives thee into the darknes [Isa. 8:19–22] but Cannot delud thee and this thou shalt Eternally wittnes to be truth[;] & the Cause of our writing to thee was for the simple & the Innocents sake which thou roaringe lyon went about to destroye[;] but thy power is short & thy end is frustrated[,] And thou[,] foulor [fowler,] art taken in the Snare And the Innocent deluded[.] Glory And prayses be to the liveing powerful God forev[er]more which binds & Chaines thee And thy God[;] & for the paper that thou hast written it is nothing but the mire And dirt which thou Casts up out of thy troubled Sea[,] which hath laid tossinge in thee [Isa. 57:20] Almost this three yeares[.] it is nothinge to us[.] wee trample upon it as myre in the streets[,] for none of thy weapons that thou formes against us Can prosper[;] & thy tongue that riseth up in Judgment against us wee do Condemne[;] & that is our heritage ever to trample upon thee who art to be ground to powder[;] & Blessed be the ld [lord] God who hath delivered the poore & the needy[;] & the Innocent hath the ld delivered out of thy wolvish mouth And made thee manifest who art the devourer & the destroyer[;] & thou art So blinde And Impudent thy God that thou serves leads thee even to befoole thy Selfe[.] he leads thee into the pitt And there he leaves thee. [1.] And whereas thou puts me upon to proove wherein thou pleads for Sinn[,] lett all thy owne flanke which hath heard thee So often Say that there should none be free from Sinn[,] let them all witnes against thee & thou hath brought scripture to maynetayne it with[.] dost thou not Continue in all thy speaking And writing to say that none can be free from Sinn And to plead against perfection: oh thou Impudent wretch[,] doth not thy owne words And writinge wittnes against thee and prove thee to be a pleader for sinn & yet Thou puts us upon it to proove it[.] oh let shame strike thee in the face and stopp thy mouth And let thy practice proove thee [2.] And secondly whereas thou sayth thou art not an enemye of righteousnes here againe lett thy practice trye thee And lett thy hearers beare wittnes Against thy lyinge tounge[,] who heares the dayly pleading for Sinn And against perfection[;] but thou Sayes thou is not an Enimie of all righteousnes[;] but thy righteousnes[,] who sayth none Can be free from Sinn & as filthy raggs[,] And all thy prayers Shall be spread as dung upon thy face[,] for thy blessing the ld hath Curst alreadie[,] And thy God is Corrupt & Even the dung of thy Solemne feasts is spread upon your Faces [Mal. 2:3] ____ _____ _____ And the ld abhors thy Righteousnes[,] & the righteousnes of xt [Christ] Jesus which is puritie thou art an enimye too[,] & where Christ is made manifest his blood washes and Cleanses & purges from all Sinn[,] but this thou uncleane wretch knowes nothinge of [3.] And whether thou be not an Enemye to the light of christ Jesus which is the first principle that leads into the Eternall Truth lett thy darknes & thy practice Judge thee And try thee And let all that ever knowes thee & heares thee beare wittnes against thee. oh thou Serves an evill Master[.] he Causes thee to ly thy nakednes & filthynes open[;] And the shame of thy Abomination appeares[.] Oh thou Enimie of God And of all truth[,] was Nicodemus in the light who was ignorant of the new birth[,] or did that light lead Paul to persecute And Cause him to Err[,] as thou saith it doth[?] let all who reads thy words try thee whether thou be not an Enimie to the light which is the first principle[;] And let thy owne words stopp thy mouth which hath found thee out & made thee manifest to be an open lyer [4.] And for thy fourth[,] thou saith that wee Say that thou denies Christ Come in the flesh: I Answer[,] this wee doe afirme And doe Charge thee who denies the light & Cals it naturall & Saith that it ledd the Apostel to persecute & Caused him to ere[.] thou that saith this I Charge thee to be an antechrist & to denie christ Come in the flesh for, when the Apostle wittnessed the Sonn revealed in him[,] he did not then persecute as thou and thy generation doth now[,] but then he came to be persecuted & to be Called a pestilent fellow And a moover of sedicion [Acts 24:5] & his doctrine to be heresie And a Setter up of Strange Gods[.] now See if thou be not found amongst this generation who art Calling the truth a Sattanicall Spirit and poyson [poison,] delusion & temptation, now See if thou be not found in the persecutinge generacion. And for the Confession that thou makes of christ come in thy flesh[,] in that thou art a lyer & denied thou art of christ And all who is of him eternally[,] for thy flesh is filthye[,] polluted and uncleane who denies the light which makes Sinn And Uncleaness manifest & wher Christ is come in the flesh he washes & Cleanses from all Sinn And the Pope can confess xt come in the flesh as much as thou for he hath the Scripture that testifies of him as well as thou & thou knowes no more of him then the Apostle when he persecuted the Saints & So thy Confesion is false And thy faith is vayne who art yet in thy Sinn[,] & thy body is dead in Sins & trespasses And the dead in thee is not raised yet nor thou never heard the voyce of the Son of God yet[;] therefore Stopp thy mouth[.] thou who denies the light of Jesus to be sufficient to lead out of Sinn And call it naturall[,] thou art he that denies christ Jesus before men & thou & thy Confession doth he deny & condemne eternally [5.] And for thy fifth[,] that we say that thou devoures Widdowes houses[,] this againe wee afirm And charge thee with[,] that thou art one of them that xt Jesus Said that devoured widdowes houses [Mark 12:40] but did Say that they wronged them of farthings as thou Saith with thy darke Carnall minde: oh thou blind Sott[,] thy owne words makes thee manifest to be a grave Indeed which hath nothing in but rottenness And dead mens bones[.] Oh if ever peopel Should follow Such a blind Pharisee as thou[,] there Blood of thee Shall be required who art the devourer of their Soules[.] are they not all widdowes[?] bring me one that thou Can Say thou hast espoused to one husband as in the presence of the ld which hath noe other lovers. oh the ld God will plead with thee[,] thou deceiver of Nacions And betrayer of Soules[.] And whereas thou lyinge betrayinge Serpent did write to Francis Benson in thy [former?] letter that wee did denie the righteousnes of faith & in my letter I badd thee to prove it either by our words or writings[,] And that that thou proves it by is that wee deny Imputacion of faith[.] oh thou blind Hippocrite[,] dost thou know no difference betwixt the rightenes of faith & the Imputation of faith. the rightenes of faith Speaketh on this wise[:] the word is nigh in the heart, & this is the word that wee preach, and this thou denyes who houldes the imputation of faith, & by this eternall word which is nigh in the heart doe we deny thee & thy faith & thy righteousnes who is yet in thy sins, and thy imputation of faith wee doe deny, which doth not purify, and thy hope which doth not purify, we doe deny; and here we have prooved thee to be a lyar and of thy Father the devill[,] who was a lyar from the beginninge[,] & this god thou serves, & soe wee deny thy god. And now that thou might see, thy darknes, & Ignorance of god & if it were possible we have againe prooved thee accordinge to thy owne Charge first to be a pleader for sin, & against perfection. & Secondly to be an enemy of god & of all truth & of the righteousnes of Jesus which purges & washes, & Thirdly to be an enemy to the light which is the first principle which leads into the eternall truth, And Fourthly to be antichrist & a denyer of Christ come in the flesh; And Fifthly to be a devourer of widdowes houses & for the Church of Corin[th]; let them alone[;] thou knowes nothing of their Apearing for thou hath not yet appeared nether to purgation nor Justification nor sanctification[,] and thy clothing is filthy[,] polluted & uncleane[,] & when thou art found you will be found nacked but the Apostle groned being burdined[;] not that hee would have been unclothed but clothed upon[.] now if you be not blind[,] thou may read the Apostle heare and then thou may know what wee hould[,] and till then you shall never know & thy apeareing & acounpt [account] is yet behind[.] therefor stand still and see where thou art[.] thou art the painted beast[;] therefor wait to see thy selfe soe but in these things thou hast curruped [corrupted] thy selfe and thy paint and coler [color] rubes [rubs] off and thy nackednes apeares & thou art mad[e] manifest[,] and Francis hath fulfiled thy desire in sending thy page to the author of the other Letter which is and shalbe as gale [gall] and worme wood to thee[.] read thy porshon in the 8 of Jerimiah the 12 13 14 [Jer. 8:12–14.]

M F

The following is written just below George Fox's endorsement, in a different hand: "And the people called quakers their testimony is proved to be atrue proficie in that they tould thee and others that god would confound them & cast thee and them out of place[,] which now is fulfilled upon them because you preacht against the light." C. Horle *notes: "This was apparently added after August 1662 when Camelford and others were ejected by the Act of Uniformity" ("Index," p. 68).*

Spence 3/127, 136. Endorsed: "M F to prst Camulford [George Fox]"; "M F to Camelford 1653".

44 To Philip Bennett, a Minister 1655?

"And thou & Cammelford hath done
more service for the truth by your writings
then ever you can doe hurt by all your lyinge preachings."

Philip Bennett (?–1689) was a curate at Cartmel, one of the ministers who "joined together . . . against the Truth," according to George Fox (Nickalls, p. 122). At one time he was a curate at Ulverston and was ejected from the parish, thus being one of many ministers who lost their positions because of being Independent. After the Restoration in 1660 when the Anglican church was re-established, Bennett conformed and was given another parish (Nightingale, Ejected, *p. 813).*

Bennett published one tract listed in Smith's Bibliotheca Anti-Quakeriana, *called* A Paper directed to Richard Roper, and his Quaking Friend, with Twenty queries *(p. 70). Edward Burrough, one of the staunchest and most brilliant of young Quakers, answered this tract with his* Answers to several Queries Put forth to the despised People called Quakers, by Philip Bennett. *Perhaps because Edward Burrough published this paper, Margaret's answer to Bennett was never printed. The manuscript is incomplete, ending in the middle of a sentence; it may be a draft.*

The letter is a lengthy answer to Bennett's claim that the Quakers refused to answer him, and she in turn claims that he is "guilty of what the Queries mention." She addresses several issues that were of importance to Quakers in their relations with authorities of church and state.

She accuses him and Gabriel Camelford of promoting violence and using "Carnall weapons" against Quakers. Quakers generally use the term carnal *to refer, not to sensual matters, but to temporal, human, and worldly rather than spiritual means. Furthermore, he is defended by the "popish law," whereas the Friends' "freedome & liberty & preservation & Safty is in the Lord our God."*

*Bennett had referred to a "declaration," which was probably the proclamation of February 1655 issued by Cromwell in order to curb the Quakers's disturbances of Meetings or church services. The right of a person to speak or preach after a Meeting or church service was protected by law, but he or she could not interfere with the service itself. Quakers were sometimes, though rarely, guilty of this. Clergy often transgressed by refusing permission to speak and even inciting violence against the speaker (*BQ, *pp. 180–181, 434–435).*

The Oath of Abjuration was one of several Elizabethan laws designed to punish Roman Catholic recusants who refused to attend Church of England services. The law was invoked against Quakers and other dissidents "in some confusion as to the terms 'recusant' and 'popish recusant'" (Horle, Q.&EngLegalSys, *p. 48) Margaret rejects Bennett's claim that they are of the same "Judgment" in understanding the Apostles and the Light. He does not understand that "our libertie is that which thou nor none of thy Generation shall ever hinder or Stopp . . . nor all the rigour of thy Law shall ever touch or hinder our libertye."*

Bennett had questioned the Quaker refusal to take oaths and asked if that "be not a peece of leven [leaven] sent from Roome [Rome]." Margaret quotes Matthew and

James to prove Jesus's insistence on "Swear not at all; neither by heaven . . . nor by earth." She rejects the notion that Quakers have anything to do with Roman Catholics, with Jesuits in particular, or with infallibility. This charge, though unfounded, caused many people to fear the Quakers, that they would lead England into a Catholic nation's power.

She turns the concept of abjuration around to say that Bennett "hast abjured thyself from the Doctrine of Christ & of the Apostles." Bennett had said that the Quakers exaggerated their persecution, and Margaret responds, "I doe beleeve that the persecution that we receive is lookt upon to be very little with thy mind which thirsteth for blood."

A few words in reply to thy ramblinge Confused answearcs which hath made it manifest that thou art guilty of what the Queries mentions, and that in thy Conscience answeares the same & stopps thy mouth that thou cannot tell how to answeare, but by thy sylence makes it manifest. that thou art guilty.

And first to thy words where thou saith that wee have lately written that we will not answeare thee with which lye thou concludes thy paper; for that is false & it wee doe deny for there is noe such word Spoken or written by us: For there is nothinge that thou, nor any of thy Generation writes but we are ready to give an answeare. And as we said before (upon which thou builds thy lye) our end is not for Satisfying thee nor none of you who write, but for the Simple ones sake which is betrayed by you, and for the lying you open to them. And thou & Cammelford hath done more service for the truth by your writings then ever you can doe hurt by all your lyinge preachings: which by you have bene made manifest to poore Ignorant people who was betrayed by you; and thou makest this lye because thou art afrayd of an answeare.

First whereas thou saith that your Doctrine flyes not to man, nor mans Law for refuge though you doe & wee alsoe.

Reply[:] Here let all who reads these words & thyne & thy practice read thee to be a Lyur: Let any of thy hearers beare witnesse against thee what thou hast to defend thee with, or the Doctrine that thou preaches or what thou hast opened thy mouth to defend thee against those that speake against thee, but the Carnall weapons, or the lyinge on of mens hands to take them away. Now let all thy hearers beare witnes against thee of thy Lyes, when did ever thou or Cammelford Stand, but run your wayes, and let others laye violent hands on them, & hayle them to stockes, or violently beate them, & shamfully entreated them as you all can beare witnes[,] to that in your consciences we appeale[,] and wheras thou saith, and wee alsoe. In that againe stopp thy mouth thou Impudent lyur, and let all thy owne Congregation beare witnes against thee whether we fly to any Law of man for refuge for all your abusinge. oh that ever thou shouldest be ledd with the Devill in Lyinge Soe impudently that all may beare witnes against thee.

And wheras thou saith that that Law is taken from the Romish magisterates & put into better hands, which hath given new life to it for your peace in your publique worshipp.

Reply[:] Here thou hast given it under thy hand, & is a witnesse against thySelfe that the popish Law which was once Dead & out of use; hath now a new life given to it for your peace in your publique wor[ship] Soe heare be a witnesse against thy Selfe that thy defence & peace in thy worshipp is by thy popish law which hath the new life given to it. Oh blush & be ashamed of this beasticall worshipp which the peace & the Defence of it is the popish Law: God abhorres thee & thy worshipp, and all who is of him, And wheras thou saith that the Liberty & peace that we enjoye in our publique meetings is upheld by the very Same Law. Here in this stopp thy mouth, thou Lyinge Spirit, for the liberty & peace which wee enjoye in our meetings; thou nor none of thy Generation shall ever know nor none who is preserved by that Law. And by that Eternall Spirit of life by which wee have libertie and peace in our meetinges doe wee deny thee & the popish Law that guards thee and thy Libertie and peace that thou hast in it. And our freedome & liberty & preservation & Safty is in the Lord our God which thou art an enemy to[,] who flyes to the popish law for refuge.

[The following lines are crossed out but readable.]

And wheras thou sayth, it is through the Courtesie of the Law, & the Lawmakers of the Land; & Saith that God hath put it into the Magistrates to Send out a Declaration Conserninge our Disturbance

Reply[:]. In that thou art a Lyar and the magistrates will witnes against thee, as the Declaration hath made it appeare there is not one word in it Concerninge us. oh thou abominable Lyer[,] that ever thou shouldst have thy mouth opened to utter forth soe many lyes as thou hast done: Nay it is such filthy Baalams Priests as thou, who hath nothing to uphould you and your Doctrine with but popish Lawes, or any colleur that you can gett from the Law of man to shelter yourSelves under, but the Lord God of power is made manifest, which pulls of[f] your covers and

[End of crossed out section.]

and all your lawes and false covers will not suerve you for that is made manifest which unmaskes you, and lyes you open. And for the Oath of abjuration there is not one word ______ concerning us in it. And thou Speakes of the Apostles, and thou speakes of professors, oh thou filthy beast, wouldest thou have the Apostle a professor, who was a possessor and enjoyer of the Eternall truth and a witnesse against Such filthy Diceivers as thou ar[t] who takes his worde for a cloake for thy persecution & tyranny; and wheras thou saith thou hath beene longe of our Judgment in the word for many yeares; in that thou art a Lyer, & a Blaspheamer against the truth of God, for in the Eternall light we Dwell which is the worlds condemnation, and thou nor never any of the world was of our Judgment. And in that thou speakes of many yeares thou canst not instance any, Since the Apostles of Jesus Christs tyme who dwells in the light which comes from Jesus and none is of our Judgment but who dwells in the light, which thou who art a Child of darknes & a minister of Darknes, art an enemie too, and denyes the Eternall light which is and ever was the Saints teacher, & all who is of God is taught by the Eternall light which comes from God who is the father of light which thou who art an enemy of all truth denyes, and all thy generation, who are for condemnation with the light which never Changes.

And thou saith that they were not visible while the rigour of the Law was executed against Schismatickes; but now of late when the shade of liberty is Soe largly extended you are growne up under it very hygh [high] & that on a Suddaine.

Reply[:]. Thy torment is but begininge and that sun=shyne is risen in which thou and all thy deceiptfull merchandize shall wither & fall before, & is curst, and our Libertie is that which thou nor none of thy Generation Shall ever hinder or Stopp; nor all the rigour of thy Law Shall ever touch or hinder our libertye, for it is hid from thy eyes & all eyes livinge; & Thou that writes for the fallinge of that which is Eternall by that shalt thou fall, for thou art nigh unto Cursinge whose end is to be burnt:

And wheras thou saith for the Oath of abjuration wee are Ignorant of it, but thou couldst tell us: but that wee seeme to be ______[;] and thou saith that the people Challengeth a Supreame power over all causes & persons in Church & Commonwealth, & that he hath Authority to set up & cast downe as he pleaseth

Reply[:] Wee do deny, & scorne, & abhorre thy teachinge who art for Condemnation with the light which is Eternall which is our teacher, & in it, & with it we doe trye thee, & know thee that if thou were where the pope Challengeth Supreamacie he might change thee and aulter thee as he would: for thou & thy Doctrine will change as the Law changes, and thou wilbe Set up & Cast Downe as the powers of the Earth Standes or falles, for thou & thy Doctrines hanges on nothinge but the outward Lawes of men: for if thou & thy Generation had not carnall lawes to uphould you, you would quickly be overturned & confounded. But glory & prayse be to the livinge God for ever, that stone is risen and made manifest which yee have refused, but is now become the head of the Corner [Matt. 21:42] glory for evermore, and the rocke upon which the whole Church is built is made manifest which you & all your Doctrine Shall be Splitt in peeces, & the stone which grindes to powder [Matt. 21:44] shall fall upon you & this thou shalt Eternally witnesse, though thou may slight it, & looke over it, but one Day when the booke of Conscience is opened then Shalt thou say that I Spoke truth when it will be too late for thee to repent.

And thou saith that it were worth the enquiringe wheither our uncivill Carrigdes towards Magistrates and refusinge to take an oath though never soe lawfully tendered be not a peece of leven sent from Roome [Rome]:

Reply[:]. Here let all people take notice of thy blaspheamy & lyinge who saith that not to Sweare is a peece of leven sent from Roome, which is the Doctrine which Christ Jesus preached who said Sweare not at all, neither by heaven for it is gods throne, neither by the Earth for it is his footstoole, neither shalt thou Sweare by thy head because thou canst not make one haire white or blacke, but let your Comunication be yea, yea, nay, nay, for whatsoever is more then this Cometh of evill [Matt. 5:34–37]; And thou saith this is a peece of leven come from Roome, oh thou abominable Blaspheamer. And the Apostle James saith above all things my Bretheren Sweare not at all[,] nether by heaven nor by Earth[,] neither by any other Oath[,] but let your yea, be yea, & your nay, nay, lest you fall into Condemnation [James 5:12] and thou saith that an oath is lawfull, Contrary, to Christs & the Apostles Doctrine, & saith that this Doctrine is a peece of leven come from Rome, oh that ever poore people should be soe blinde as to follow such a Blaspheamous Darke Ignorant beast as thou art. And by this Doctrine of Christ & the Apostle (which thou calls Leven Come from Rome) by this shall all the nations & Kingdomes of the world be Levened & shall become the Kingdomes of the lord & of his Christ which Shalbe for the Downe fall of thee & of thy Kingdome of Antichrist and for [thy?] destruction & torment forevermore.

And [whereas?] thou sayth whether wee or you deserve to be ranked with Jesuits[;] let your practice speake

1: Thou saith that the Jesuits say there is free will in every man, & free power to Act in Spirituals[,] to repent & turne to God of himselfe & thou saith Doe not wee say soe?

2: Thou saith that the Jesuits maintaine that they are perfectly Sanctified And thou saith doe not some of you say soe?

(3) thou saith the Jesuits hould that they fulfill the law in every poynt, & transgresse in none, and thou saith further

(4) that the Jesuits say the workes of misticall Christ or such as are wrought by Christ in his saints & by his saints are meritorious & thou asketh if wee doe not say soe?

(5:) thou saith that the Jesuits pleads infallibility of Judgment & that the Pope cannot erre: and doe not some of you say Soe of yourselves

(6) Angaine [again] thou saith the Jesuits affirme a man may be in the State of grace, & yet fall finally away, and of a Child of God become a Child of the Divill

(7) thou saith the Jesuits refuse to Sweare obeydience to the magistrates & lawes of this land; & doe not you soe

Reply / To the first, nay we doe not say Soe[.] thou art a Lyar (as no other can come out of thy mouth) who art of thy father the Devill who was a Lyar from the begininge for wee know that in thee nor in none of thy Generation is any power or free will to act in Spiritualls, for that which acts for God is of another power then thou art under and contrary to thy will & all the will of man: And thou who art in selfe & pleads for selfe can never repent nor turne to God and therfore stopp thy mouth who art here prooved a Lyar. And for thy (2) our answeare is Chr: Jesus[.] his doctrine saith be yee perfect as your heavenly father is perfect 5 Math:48: And he saith againe Math:19:21: to the younge man if thou wilt be perfect goe sell that thou hast, and thou saith the Jesuits Saith Soe. And the Apostle Saith, my Strength is made perfect in weaknes [2 Cor. 12:9], and againe he saith be yee perfect; be of good Comfort [2 Cor. 13:11], and the Apostle laboured to present every man perfect in Christ Jesus and because wee say the same that the Scriptures saith thou rankest us amonge the Jesuits. And to thy (3) Christ Jesus saith

thinke not that I am come to Destroye the Law or the prophetts, I am not come to Destroy, but to fulfill [Matt. 5:17], and here thou Blaspheamer Denyes the end of Chr: cominge, and saith the Jesuits Say Soe, and he saith againe that one title Shall in no wise passe from the law till all be fulfilled: But to thee this is a mistery who art alive without the law, and thou that sins without the Law Shall perish without the Law. And the Apostle saith god sent forth his sonne in the likeness of sinfull flesh, & for sin condemned Sin in the flesh, and that the righteousnes of the Law might be fulfilled in [us?] [Rom. 8:3–4] and thou Blasphemer Deneyes this the end of Gods Sendinge his sonne & saith the Jesuits saith Soe, and the Apostle was made free from the Law by the body of Christ, & he witnessed J[esus] though the Law am dead to the Law, & he saith Shall I make voyd the Law[,] god forbidd [Rom. 3:31], but this is a Sealed booke to thee who art a blinde Sottish beast. And for thy (4) where thou talkes of a misticall Christ and merritts and such like darke blacke Egiptian Language which we deny thee and the Jesuits and to thee & to all such Darke Beasts as thee Christ Jesus is a mistery which thou knowes nothinge of nor his workinge but art an enemy to him & to his truth & all righteousnes & what thou knowes thou knowes naturally as a bruit beast[.]
[The following line is written at the top of the page, upside down, before the remainder of this paper.]

This page is unconcluded whether to write or not[.]

And for thy (5) wheras thou speaketh of infallibility of Judgment: The Pope[,] not thou nor none of yor Generation[,] can plead for it, who are out of the Eternall light & life which is infallible, & eternall & thou & the popes Judgment is curst & Judged with the Spirit which is infalible and from that spirit which is infallible & eternall doe wee plead against thee & the Pope & all the powers of Darknes, and by the Eternall infallible spirit which is our teacher & leader & guide Shall thou & all the powers of hell & Death be confounded & Overturned eternally, and this thou shalt Eternally witnes to be from a Spirit which is infallible & eternall though thou may Slight it & make light of it, but upon thy head & necke it stands & thy power Eternally. And to thy (6) where thou Speaketh of a mans beinge in a State of grace, & fall finally away, & of a Child of God become a Child of the Devill here thou darke Blasphemer Speakes thou knowes not what[,] for thou wast never in the state of Grace, but thy state is sine [sin] & filthynes and

Corrupt as thou conffesseth, and thou that art a Child of the Devill shalt never be a Child of God, and soe there thou art: thou wast never a Child of God yet or a Child of Grace ____ _____ ______ _____ that nature thou art in, if thou be not blinde thou may read mee. and for thy (7) thou saith the Jesuites refuseth to Sweare but that I have answeared before. And soe let all people that reads thy particulers that thou hast layd downe, read thy Blaspheamy & Ignorance of God, & be a witnesse against thyselfe there under thy owne hand, & let the Scripture trye thee that the Jesuits walketh nearer the Scriptures then thou, as thou hast made it manifest by thy blacke confused ramblinge. And thou bidds us quitt our selves of these if wee cann for thou doth abjure them and lye them at our doore as thou sayes. Here be a witnesse against thy selfe that thou hast abjured thyself from the Doctrine of Christ & of the Apostles by the black Spirit of the pope & Antichrist, and we doe quit our Selves of the popes & the Jesuites doctrine, and of thee & of thy Doctrine who hath abjured thySelfe from Christ & the Apostles Doctrine, and in the Eternall liveing truth of Christ Jesus and the Apostles & their Doctrine doe we live, and in the name and power of the Lord Jesus Christ (at whose name every knee shall bow) doe we deny & abhorre thee & thy Doctrine, & all the pope & Jesuits in the world who stand abjured from the truth, against you doe we stand witnesses Eternally: for the livinge God doe wee witnesse agains all deceivers.

And wheras thou saith, it is well knowne that our Cominge into your meetinge places is to no other and but to carpe & Cavill, to distract; & Disturbe

Reply Such as thou art quickly disturbed, and for carpinge & cavillinge (as thou calls it) if we come for that we may catch Such a foole as thee oft enought, who art uttering forth thy folly, and getts a rod for thy owne backe, and a rod is for the backe of the foole and thy Doctrine & preachinge (as thou calls it) will bringe nothinge but sorrow and torment upon thee[,] for thou hast nothinge to defend ether thySelfe or it with, but as thou getts people to take them away by layinge violent hands on them, and if thou had not a law to protect thee with, thou wouldst quickly have the shame of thy stolne [stolen] stoff. Thou saith thou art not ashamed of thy Doctrine, but it is because thou hast no shame in thee, for Christ & all who are of him is ashamed of thee; and of thy Doctrine (as thou calls it). Thou saith that thou hast not heard of the tearinge & Devouringe & thou saith that we will call any thinge persecution. I doe beleeve that the persecution that we receive is lookt upon to be very litle with thy mind which thirsteth for blood, who hath given it under thy hand that thou wilt not beleeve that the same mind is in ______, as was in Christ Jesus except thou see him hange upon a tree[.] the Apostle exhorted those whom he spoke to to be of the same mind which was in Christ Jesus, he did not bid them hang on a [tree] as thou[,] bloody Cain[,] doth who saith thou cannot beleeve any to be of the same mind except thou see them hange on a tree[.] thou Devourer[,] the righteousse god will plead with thee. And thou acknowledgeth that thou art in the number of those that are in the fall, and thou that art in the fall art under the Curse, & driven out from God, & the flaming Sword is set against thee [Gen. 3:24], thou shalt never enter paradice. And thou saith thou beleeves in that God that Justifieth the ungodly[.] Here thou hast made manifest not only thySelfe, but thy God alsoe; and here thou hast layd it open that thy God is the God of the world & the prince of the Ayre which ruleth in the Children of Disobeydience. For David saith blessed is the man that walketh not in the Counsell of the ungodly [Ps. 1:1], and he saith the ungodly is like the Chaffe which the winde driveth away[.] The ungodly Cannot stand in Judgment [Ps. 1:2–5], but the way of the ungodly shall perish & there art thou and

Spence 3/140–141. Endorsed: "To priest Bennet"; "To the confounding of his folly".

45 TO JAMES CAVE, A MINISTER PROBABLY 1656

"And though thou dragon hath cast forth
thy flood after this booke, which was given forth
in love to the lost, yet thou Shalt not prevaile:
for Michall feights & his Angells."

James Cave (?–1694) and James Nayler (ca. 1618–1660) both served in Oliver Cromwell's army and then became preachers. While James Nayler became one of the leading Quakers, Cave became an Independent minister strongly opposed to them. From 1652 to 1660 he was the minister of Thornwaite in Cumberland, being ordained in 1656 by a combination of Presbyterians and Congregationalists. He was ejected from his position in 1660, and "he took the opportunity of King Charles's

Declaration in 1672, publickly to exercise his Ministry taking out a Licence" (Nightingale. Ejected, *pp. 660, 665).*

According to the endorsement of this letter Cave collected Quaker literature in order to prevent others from reading it. James Nayler wrote a tract called Love to the Lost, *which Cave criticized, and Margaret is here rebutting Cave's criticism. Margaret numbers eight statements of which seven are quotations, with small variations, from Nayler's tract. Caves's objection follows each statement, and then her counter-argument. In Nayler's* A Collection of Sundry Books, *his works published in 1716,* Love to the Lost, *which was first published in 1656, runs from page 253 to 360; the seven quotations are all from the first two sections "Concerning the Fall of Man" and "Concerning Light and Life." This "Answer to James Cave" is thus not a complete discussion of Nayler's work.*

The eight questions concern doctrines of the fall of man, the seed of god in man, the light, sin and righteousness, and others. She uses scriptural language, particularly paraphrasing John, "Doth not Jesus Christ say walke while yee have light, least darknes come. while ye have the light beleeve in the light, that yee may be the Children of the light."

She ends, as she begins, with the accusation that he is a serpent venting poison against a book given in Love to the Lost.

An Answer To James Cave priest in Cumberland
from M: F: 1655

To thee who art of the Same Serpent as ever was who goes aboute to Defile & to cast out thy flood of poyson & enmity against the truth; and the seed of the woman: whom the lord god is gathering in this his Day. Thou who art ventinge thy poyson against that booke which was given forth in love to the lost, which thou Serpent was the Cause of. And to thee, nor to thy seed it was never given, but for thy destruction. And therfore doth thy envie & bitternes risse against it. For to thee, (he who brings on earth peace & good will towards men) brings a Sword to thee, by which thou shalt be cast downe & utterly destroyed.

1 Concerninge the fall of man. The Tree of Life in the midst of the Garden & The Tree of Knowledge of good & evill [Gen. 2:9]. And both these were good in there place but the tree of knowledge was not good for food. Therfore did he that made it forewarne of it, as a thinge wherin death was placed [Gen. 2:17]; as in the other tree was life and herein was the blessinge, and the Cursse placed. The life & the Death, the obeydience & the Disobeydience, Election & Reprobation etc. [Nayler, p. 257].

[o]bject: This is utterly false; for election was an Act of God from Eternity before man or the tree had a beinge.

Answ: Thou Blaspheamous Beast, and denyer of the livinge God & his Truth. Hath not the Tree of life, a beinge in god, The tree of life Stands in the midst of the Paradice of god; and he that overcomes hath right to the tree of life. Hee that hath an eare may heare. But to thee Blaspheamer & murtherer of the Just this is a mistery [mystery] and therfore stopp thy mouth forever Speakinge of the livinge god or of the election or of the Tree of life. For thou art the Curssed tree whose end is to be burnt[,] which cannot bringe forth good fruite [Matt. 7:18–19]. Thy poyson & enmity (which is thy fruite) hath made thee manifest in this: and the livinge pure eternall truth thou cannot touch for it shall endure forever: but thy wickednesse Shall come to an end.

2 And Soe became bruitish in his understandinge [Prov. 30:2], and as to the things of God as the beast that perisheth, For the Seed he hath lost etc. [Nayler, p. 258].

[o]bject: 2: If man lost the seed of god by the fall, How Say you that every man hath the Seed in him?

Answ: That is false, we doe not say soe; for we know That though Israell be as the sand of the Sea, yet a remnant Shall be Saved [Rom. 9:27], and the promisse is in ISaacke. he that hath an eare may heare. But thou art the deafe adder who art the seed of the serpent And to thy seed he that is the Salvation of ISraell, is thy Condemnation & destruction to thee: and bruiseth thy head, & breakes thee to peeces. And he who is the seed (to which the promisse is) is the salvation of all that beleeves. But to thee Reprobate & all thy Generation; he is Condemnation. And soe stopp thy mouth from sayinge that we say every one hath a Seed in them. And yet we say Christ Jesus who is the seed to which the promisse is, is the light of the world and the Condemnation of thee and all that is in the world _____ _____ _____ ____ And every one hath this light by which you are condemned, & shall be Judged at the last day. And soe thy blacke filthy darke Spirit Cannot Comprehend this. But one day it shall finde thee out: and be an Eternall witnesse against thee.

3: And beinge falne [fallen] under the Earthly principle, he is Covered with thicke darknesse. Soe that the mind of god he knowes not etc. [Nayler, p. 259].

[o]bject 3. Then he hath noe light in him.

Answ: O thou Blaspheamer against Christ Jesus and his doctrine who hath said he doth enlighten every one that cometh into the world, and that he is the light of the world [John 1:9 and 8:12]. And yet he said if the light that is in thee be darknesse, how great is that darknesse, and here thou art in grosse darknes, which cannot Comprehend the light [John 1:5], & yet the light is thy Condemnation, because thou loves darknes rather then light. Soe now if the god of the world had not blinded thy eye thou might read here, but thy foolish hart is darkned, and the prince of Darknes is thy God. But he is rison who is his Judge; and where he is lifted up hee drawes all men after him: and this is thy Torment, and shall be for thy destruction for evermore

4: Healinge your Selves in false perswasions which will not stand instead in the evill day, nor reconcile to god to be accepted in anythinge yee doe: for this is but the first man with his riteiousnesse. But to that from which yee are falne [fallen] must you looke and returne into that from which you are gone out that by the light that is in the midst of all this darknese & death you may be ledd in againe by the blood of the Crosse etc. [Col. 1:20].

Objet:4: Pure nonsence & Contradictions.

Answ: To thee it must needs be soe, who art to be slaine, & crucifyed, thou who hath slaine the Just, thou must be putt of[f] who art the ould man, and all thy filthy affections, and lusts, And soe thou that art alive to Sinn, must needs be free from righteousness. And thou who art alive without the law, shall perish without the law. if thou be not blind thou may read. But thou art groapinge with thy blind darke mind, and art out of the light, & soe stumbles at noone [noon] day [Isa. 59:10]. And Soe that which is seene with the eternall eye (which the god of the world hath blinded in thee) it cannot but be confusion to thee, who art blind.

5: Nor he whose leader is any visible thinge; for by this Spirit from whome man is fallne & gone out: By the same must he be ledd in againe etc. [Nayler, p. 261].

object: 5: was not Christ & his ministers (that you speake of in the former page) visible things or persons? how then doe you here say our leader must be noe visible things.

Answ: Noe, To thee nor none of thy Generation was Christ nor none of his ministers; nor the Spirit that they spoke from, was never visible to Such Carnall filthy blacke deceiptfull spiritts as thyne. for if they had seene Christ, they had not Crucifyed him, or if they had seene the Apostles and their Doctrine, they had not persecuted them and slaine them. Thou has here manifested thy selfe, to be a Carnall beast indeed, Dost thou looke upon Christ and the Apostles to be such as thee? who spoke the wisdome of god in a Mistery, oh thou sottish beast; Nay thou art the visible leader, and all that thou hath to lead with may be seene with the Carnall eyes; and Soe thou art the blind leader of the blind into the pitt where thou art [Matt. 15:14]. But thou canst lead none but who is blind, and the eyes of the blind is openninge which doth see thee, and such blind watchmen as thou art: and therfore are yee diviners madd, because yee are taken in your sorcery Your day of howlinge & lamentation is cominge upon you, and your day of Gloominess and bitter lamentation hastens: and your torment is begunn but it shall never have end; and eternally thou & thy Generation Shall witnesse this.

6: God is the life of every Creature, though few there be that know it, for darknes sees him not, nor his life, though the Children of Darknes have gott words in the Scripture (which were given forth from the light) to talke of: yet God such knowes not present etc. [Nayler, p. 261].

object: 6 Then God is in every Creature. yea, in the Divells, for they are Creatures & doe live.

Answ: This Testimony thou may beare for they live in thee, and the Divell is thy God[.] But when Saw thou them that thou saith, they are Creatures or what shape have they? thou beares his Image & his marcke in thy fore=head, & thou shalt be sure to drinke of the wine of the wrath of god, which is powered [poured] out without mixture [Rev. 14:10–11].

7: And here the soule beinge in death, breathinge after the life, But Darknes gott above[.] in the Darknes is the Creature ledd into Sects & opinions [Nayler, p. 262]?

object:7: Can a dead Breathinge, breath after life?

Answer Thou art dead in Sin, and death raignes [reigns] in thee which hath passed over all men, and hell and the grave hath dominion over thee, and that which is in the grave which is held in captivity by thee, breathes for God who is the life. But thou enemie of God slayes the Just, and garnisheth his Sepulcher [Matt. 23:29], thou art the grave that men goes over, who art full of rottennes & Dead=mens bones Corrupt & filthy. But the Lord god will be avenged of thee who hath Slaine the prophett, and beaten his Son and would alsoe kill the heire [heir].

8: He hath soe left his dominion that he is brought to serve the Creature over which he was ruler. Hence it is that some become servants and are captivators object: If this be true how say you that man may, & should obey the light within him?

Answ: O thou darke ignorant Infidell, hath not God sent his only begotten sonne into the world, that whosoever beleeves in him should not perish but have everlastinge life [John 3:16], and is not the Gospell the power of god unto Salvation to all that beleeves[?] but how should thou know this who art a Child of Disobeydience in whom the prince of the Aire rules [Eph. 2:2] as thy owne words makes thee manifest, who neither knowes the light, nor the obeydience[.] Doth not Jesus Christ say walke while yee have light, least darknes come. for he that walkes in darknesse knoweth not whither he goes. while yee have the light beleeve in the light, that yee may be the Children of the light [John 12:35–36]. But thou Child of darknes whose message is for the prince of darknes, preaches another Gospell: and therfore all that are of god houlds thee acurssed. And though thou dragon hath cast forth thy flood after this booke, which was given forth in love to the Lost yet thou Shalt not prevaile: for Michaell feights & his Angells, and thou dragon the ould Serpent (which deceiveth the world) is to be cast out into the earth. And Salvation is come and the strength of the Kingdome of our god, and the power of his Christ, who shall raigne for evermore. By which thou and all thy power shall be bound & chayned & sealed into the pitt. Hee who is Kinge of Kings, & Lord of Lords raignes, the Lambe who hath the victory over the Beast & the false prophet to whom be dominion for evermore.

M F

Spence 3/142–143. Endorsed: "The Answer to one Cave in Cumberland or that aways"; "M F an anser to prest Cave [George Fox] by M: F: 1655" [another hand inserted "James" before Cave]; " priest's objections against a book of J. N.'s called love to the Lost. This priest Cave was an high Indepent priest at Keiswick [Keswick] in Cumberland who in his high notions some times preached in words some things according to the Truth. But when Truth appeared more clearly against it Then he went from that which he had holden forth: & preached against it & Laboured to hinder Truth from spreading, by gathering upp all Friends' books, that he Could gett: that people might not se [see] them, But the everlasting Truth prevailed, & spread and came over him. & he came under, for first he was a Capt in O.C. [Oliver Cromwell] army, & then after a priest, & in 60 fled away and left his flock, he being a hireling."

46 To a Professor 1655

"The Spirit of god is the same as it was to the Former profetts in Script[ure] and we beare testimony of the Same Spirit which never changeth, which is the same yesterday, today & forever."

"The Quakers of the 1650s seized every opportunity to debate their principles with parish ministers, and from the 1650s to the 1670s had taken part in heated pamphlet exchanges and public confrontations . . . " (Mortimer, p. 387). This was Margaret's response to a paper written by a professor, evidently in answer to a paper of his sons. The professor acknowledges that Jesus is the light but then goes on to say that the scriptures are the way. Margaret asserts that Jesus said, "I am the way, the truth, & the life," not that the scriptures are the way.

Her letter contains a series of the professor's statements and her rebuttal of each of them. The topics are the doctrinal issues that divided the newly evolving sect from other churches. They include, among others, discussions of the authority of scripture versus the authority of the spirit of God or the light of Christ as realized in contemporary life; the place of ordinances, like baptism; questions of sin and mercy; and the possibility of prophecy.

She stresses that it is not the writing down of the words of scripture that matter. She concludes: "Thou art but a talker of the Prophetts words, & the Apostles words . . . but thou wants the Spirit that he spoke from."

To a Professer from M: F: 1655

Friend in the beginnnge of thy paper thou Seemes to owne the light in thy Conscience which before the latters end thou denyes, & opposes Severall tymes[,] as I Shall proove, thou Speakes of a paper which came to thee which had noe name at all yet thou art perswaded it came from thy Sonne, & thou Saith therein thou finds nothinge disagreeinge to the pure light of Jesus xt [Christ] in thy owne Conscience and thou Saith further, I doe not in the least oppose my Selfe against what you (or Some [one? on] your behalfe) have written, beinge it doth not varie from the Sacred Scriptures. My answer is. Beinge that thou beares Such a testimony to the paper, as that it is agreeable to the light of Jesus xt in thy Conscience, & that it varyes not from the Sacred Script: It is good for thee to owne it, & to be Subject to the directions of it, which is to the pure light of xt in thee, & beinge that it varyes not from the Sacred Scriptures its one with them, & came from the Same Spirit as gave them forth, by thy owne testimony that thou gives of it.

But thou Saith further That the Scriptures together with the Spirit bearinge witnesse is the ready way to Salvation. Ans[wer]: How thou varyes from the light of christ in thy Conscience, & from the Scriptures, for Christ Jesus saith (who is the light) I am the way the truth, & the life, & there is none that comes to the Father but by mee [John 14:6]. Now he saith not that the Scriptures is the way, For thousands have the Scriptures which is out of the way but he speakes of a straight gate & narrow way that leads to life, & few there be that finde it [Matt. 7:14]. Now if the Scriptures were the way, it were a broud way for many hath the Scriptures. Yet the Scriptures wee owne, & beare testimony to the truth of them by the Same Spirit as he gave them forth, which they cannot doe which is out of the straite way. Christ Jesus the light who is the way & there is noe Salvation in any other[.] Soe if ever thou come to the way that leads to life & Salvation thou must turne thy mind to the light of christ in thy Conscience, & let that be thy guide[,] teacher & leader. Keepe thy mind subject to that, there is the path, the mind beinge guided by the pure light which shines in the Conscience. Soe as every ones mind is, Soe is the man: with the hart man beleeveth unto righteounes: with the mouth confession is made unto Salvation [Rom. 10:10]. If thy heart condemne thee, god is greater & knoweth all things. Soe flatter not thySelfe with vaine Imaginations, for these will not stand in the day of tryall, when the [search of hearts comes?] & Separation is betweene the pretious & the vile.

Thou saith thou hath beene a Sinner, & yet thou assurers thySelfe to attaine mercy,

Ans: Here againe thou art out from the light of xt in thy Conscience. For if thy mind were guided by that, thou would See that, that leads into noe Sin, nor doth not approve of any Sin, or evill: but reprooves, Judges, & condemnes all that is contrary to it: All unrighteousnes is Sin, & he that Sinnes is of the devill and he that breakes the least Comandement is guilty of all: Soe if thou were guided by the light of Christ, thou would read these things, & See them clearly as they are. All Siners Say they hope for mercy as thou doth: But where is there assurance[?] there assurance is that they have Sinned. But that hope will perish which is not founded upon the rocke [Matt. 7:25].

Thou Saith thou confesseth with the Apostle.

Ans[wer] nay, Thou art not with the Apostle, he was Servinge the law of god with his mind, and he delighted in the law of god accordinge to the Inner man, which thou art Ignorant of who art pleadinge for thy Sin: And thou confesseth if thou Sin after thou knowes the light, thou remaines noe more Sacrifice, minde that, For Christ wh[o is the] light, is the Sacrifice, and if thou sin against that, there is noe more thou wilt [paper torn] _______ _______ ___ it soe.

[Thou] saith thou strives to become a new creature [Gal. 6:15], I Say Strive to enter at [the st]raite gate [Matt. 7:13], else thy strivinge is in vaine, there is noe new creatures _____ _________ broad way that leads to destruction; The new creature passeth in the way that leads to life which is the light xt Jesus[,] the way the truth the life[.]

Thou Saith thou hath mused much to know whether god hath given us a spetiall revelation, or warninge as to the former profetts in Scripture. Ans[wer]: _______
The Spirit of god is the same as it was to the Former profetts in Script[ure] and we beare testimony of the Same Spirit which never changeth, which is the same yesterday, today & forever. And if thou mind the light of xt in thy Conscience therby to be guided taught, & ledd, thou will be Satisfyed, & know the testimony that wee beare against all sorts of people. But if thy mind be turned from the light of xt, thou art an alien from the know.[ledge] ______ of promise & this commonwealth of Israell [Eph. 2:12], and can never know us, nor our testimony, But thou saith further, & which allready have prooved contrary, the tyme beinge expired etc.

Answ: Here thou art in thy doubtfull disputations, and art of a doubtfull mind, & he that doubts is damned 14: Rom 23. And thou lookes at things outward through the blindnes of thy heart; but this I Say unto thee, who art guided by the Spirit of truth, Speakes the words of truth, which is the leader & guider of all the faithfull, & obeydient children of god, But the disobeydient & high flowen spiritts, which is not guided by the pure light & Spirit of God may erre in their minds, though they may professe the same truth in words as they doe who are guided, & Subject to it. But for such I doe not answerr and neither doe we owne, though they may professe truth in words, & seeme to owne us. But I charge thee to take heed how thou Judgeth the pure truth of god by such uncleane Spiritts, which erres from it, though they may professe it in words. Thou wants the tryer to trye the Spiritts whether they be of god[.] take heed how thou speakes evill of the things thou knowes not. For the Apostle saith, that they are as naturall bruite=beasts, that Speakes evill [of] the things they understand not, & Shall utterly perish in their owne Corup[ption] read 2Pet: 2:12: And thou saith you only beleeve Such prophecyes as in Scripture is Sett downe.

Answ: Nay, you doe not beleeve, the prophecyes in the Scriptures, who hath not the Spirit of prophecy which is the testimony of Jesus: For noe prophecy of old came by the will of man, but holy men spoke as they were mooved of the holy ghost. And you that knowes not the holy=ghost, doth not beleeve the prophecies of Scripture though yee have them to talke of, and professe which is but a Cloake for your Sin. And the Spirit of god which gave forth the Script[ures] was the same then as it is now. And holy men spoke as they were mooved then, as they doe now: And you that have not the same spirit beleeve not them, no more then yee doe them that Speakes by the Same Spirit now: though yee may Say yee doe in words, as all the dissemblers of old did.

Thou saith we have the pure light of Jesus xt. but we acknowledge our slipping by reason of the Tabernacle we carry about us. Answ: It is your corrupt uncleane hearts that causeth you to sin. Sin is conceived in the heart. If your eye were Single, your whole body would be full of light [Matt. 6:22]. It is not the outward tabernacle that causeth Sin: If the filth & Corrupti[on] were cleaned out that would be a Temple for god, Therfore doth the A[postle] Say[,] cleanse your hands yee sinners, & purify your hearts yee double [minded] [James 4:8] & you that sin[,] your Slippings is out of the light of Christ for the [light?] __________ is pure & leads in the pure path. he that walkes in the light stum[bleth not.] he that walkes in darknes Stumbles at noone day, Soe there is your slip____ [paper torn] _________ power of darknes, not the outward ________ ___________ the cause of your Slippinge. Thou saith we restraine our selves from liberty of sinning yet when wee resolve to doe well, we have our stronge temptations.

Answ: How thou art ramblinge in thy Imaginations, and art erringe, not knowinge the Script[ures]: For the Apostle Saith that xt Jesus which is the Light takes away Sin, & in him is noe sin[.] who walkes & dwells in the light of Jesus christ walkes in that where there is noe sin. For the Apostle Saith he that walkes in the Light, as he is in the light, the blood of Jesus Cleanseth from all Sin, and soe thou that art pleading for sin, & temptation art ramblinge in the power of darknes out of the light: And to confirme it thou brings a Scripture where christ saith it must needs be that offenses must come, and thou leaves out the latter part of the verse, where he saith, but woe be to them by whom it comes [Matt. 18:7] Here thou may take notice how thou goes about to wraist [wrest?] christs words as though he would Countenance Sin, but such a Cover will not hide thee in the day of the Lord when he comes to plead with all flesh[;] and thou bringes another Scripture where the Apostle Saith, blessed is the man whose Iniquityes are forgiven & Sins are covered [Rom. 4:7]. Answeare: who lives & walkes in the new Covent [covenant] & is guided by the Law written in the heart of the Spirit that is Cutt into the inward parts where this teaches & leads & guides, there Sins & Iniquityes are remembered noe more: And they are blessed & David who spoke those words was of the Seed which the blessinge is too, but this is nothinge to thee, nor none that lives in sin & wickednes; though many may plead the same words with thee; David walked in the Law of god, and kept it: it was his delight, it was a light unto his feet, & a lantherne to his pathes: but thou art out of this pathe stumbling in the Darke, and though thou be restraining & resolvinge, yet all that will avayle thee nothinge. And whereas thou saith the ordinances appoynted by Jesus christ, confirmed to us by his Apostles[,] we hould, & they as principle meanes of our Salvation which neglected is a contemninge of himselfe etc.

Answ: Here thou art denyinge the light of Jesus which I charged thee with in the begininge of thy paper, which thou their Seemed to owne, and now thou art talkinge of Ordinances which the Apostle saith was blotted out & Sayd why are yee subject to ordinances [Col. 2:20] which was a Carnall commandemt. contyned [contained] in ordinances. But thou who art Soe blinde & Ignorant of the light of truth that thou knowes not the Difference betweene carnall ordinances, & the power which is ordayned of god: & whosoever resisteth the power resisteth the ordinance of god: [Rom. 13:2] And the Apostle exorted them to keepe the ordinances & he delivered them to them & he saith that the head of every man is xt [1 Cor. 11:2–3]. this is the ordinance which is ordeyned of god for Salvation[,] xt the light the power of god unto Salvation to every one that beleeves[,] & he that resisteth this power resisteth the ordinance of god. This is the ordinance which the Apostle delivered unto them & bidd them keepe: But thou art talkinge of other ordinances, and art in the beggarly rudiments and are not dead with xt from the rudaments of the world, which the Apostle saith[,] touch not, tast[e] not, handle not, which all are to perish with the usinge of them after the Comandements & Doctrines of men 2:Coll:20: [Col. 2:20–22] And here art thou found. Againe thou Speakes as if Christ had prescribed a way ________ outward ordinances which is quite contrary to Christs own words. he said I will not drinke henceforth of this fruite of the vine until [that] day I drinke it new with you in my Fathers Kingdome 26 Math 29 ________ this outward: oh the blindnes that you are in, & againe Christ Saith[,] I will not any more eate thereof untill it be fulfilled in the Kingdome of God. I will not drinke of the fruite of the vine untill the Kingdome of god shall come 22:Luke 18 But thou & all such who art confessinge christ the light in words but in workes deny him, are farr from knowinge or seeinge of this Thou askes wt [what] the meaninge of the Apostle 1:Cor:11:23 & 6:Rom:13:

I Answere[,] The Apostle was Baptized into xt & Baptized into his death And the Apostle had reced. [received] of the Lord the Cupp of the New testament & he drunke of it & gave it unto the Church, and he meant as he spoke[;] and the the cupp that they Drunke of was new, & they drunke all into one spirit & they were all baptized by one spirit into one body, and this is out of all your Imitations, & Imaginations; who are under the power of darkenes shall never know the meaning of this.

And thou saith thou doth beleeve that any after prophecying to that in Scripture is and will proove false[.]

Answ: Here againe thou hath denyed the light which thou seemed to owne in the begininge of thy paper. Soe read thy dissemblinge & hyppocrisy who saith that any prophecy after the Scriptures will proove false. The Spirit of prophecy is the testimony of Jesus, who is the same yesterday, today, & for ever. And thou that saith the testimony of Jesus will proove falce, thou hath denyed the light which thou sayd before entered to within the vayle. And the same Spirit gave forth the Scriptures chang[eth] not, but is the same for ever where it is made manifest.

But thou saith further. Because both the old & new Testament are a way perfect, & ready, & Sufficient for our Salvation.

Answ: Here againe thou hath denyed the light of Jesus xt which is the way[,] the truth, & the life, & there is noe salvation in any other. And thou saith the Scriptures is the perfect & ready & sufficient way to salvation, and this is contrary to the scriptures[.] For the scripture saith xt is the way, & the Scripture saith, we are perfect and compleate in him, & the Scripture saith all our sufficiency is of him. now here read thy confusion & blindnes. And soe what thy confession of the light of xt is in words but thou hast made it manifest that in workes thou denyes him. And though thou & many in the world have Moses & the Prophetts words[,] yet yee cannot heare them, for yee are Deafe, & yet hath eares, & blind, & yet hath eyes: and the Spirit that they spoke from you are Ignorant of, as thou hast manifested in thy paper who doth not beleeve that any prophecy Since the Scripture will proove true. Soe thou art but a talker of the Prophetts words, & the Apostles words, as thou can take his words in the latter end of thy paper & write them downe in the Same forme in Imitation of him, but thou wants the Spirit that he spoke from. And its not writing of his words downe in a paper that will Justify thee, when thou art in blindnes & Ignorance of god & of his truth[.] consider while thou hast tyme, & mind that in thy conscience which Shewes thee the Deceipt of thy heart, that which tells thee thou should be, what thou seemes, God is Just, & the hippocrite & Dissembers [dissemblers] hath their portion unbeleevers. what will it avayle thee that thy deceiptfull heart, & ton[gue] Should Speake anothers words which another Spoke in the truth & purity & ________ of heart, from the Spirit of the livinge god (which thou art ignora[nt] & are not guided by) but thy foolish heart is darkened & thou speakes of ________ ________ god & art guided by the prince of darknes. while thou hast tyme prize it & ________ while it is called to day least it be to late & there be noe place of repentance found, remember that thou art warned in thy life tyme[.]

Spence 3/158–159. Endorsed: "M. F. paper to a Professer"; "1655".

47 An Epistle to Friends 1655

"So Read, and with the Eternal Light
Examine and Search, and try what it is that you thirst after."

This pastoral epistle to Friends is most effective if read aloud. The words are sonorous, and biblical phrases resonate as Margaret expounds her beliefs.

She reminds Friends of their privilege in receiving the message of the Light, "the Lord God of Life and Power hath visited you, and sent his Servants to awaken you." She warns them to beware how they spend their money and their time. It is "the Low, and the Meek, and Humble" that God will reward and not "the Proud, the High, and the Lofty." She emphasizes unity, that the "Living God . . . is one in all . . . [and] this gathers your Hearts together."

She writes "in love and tenderness" to their souls, telling them, "you can never fly [from] The Witness of God in your Consciences." She alternates comforting and challenging words, "For a sweet Savour we are unto God, both in them that are saved, and in them that perish."

Friends, whom the Lord God hath called unto the Light which is Eternal, which the Lord God hath sent, to bring his Seed out of Bondage, and out of the House of Darkness, from under Pharaoh, and his TaskMasters, which hath so long been held under the dark Power and Mystery of Iniquity. The Lord God of Life and Power hath visited you, and sent his Servants to awaken you, and to raise you from the Dead, that Christ might give you Life, who is now come, and coming to redeem Israel, and to divide the Red-Sea, and to overturn Pharaoh and his Host. Stand still (I say unto you) and see the Salvation of God; and in the fear of the living God wait low in your own measure of Grace, and hearken diligently unto that, that your Souls may live. And this you must do, if ever you witness the Living God: So in the Name and Power of the Lord Jesus Christ, at whose Name every knee shall bow, and every Tongue confess, beware how you spend your Money for that which is not Bread, and your Labour for that which perisheth; it is the diligent Hand that maketh Rich, but the Idle, Slothful and Negligent suffer want. And beware of going from your Guide, which keepeth you low and tender, and prize the Love of God that ever he should visit you; and beware that you do not requite him evil for good, for he is a jealous God, and will not clear the guilty; and it is the Low, and the Meek, and Humble that the Lord God teacheth, and it is the broken and contrite Spirit, that God will not despise [Ps. 51:17]. And he, who is the High and Lofty one, that Inhabiteth Eternity, dwelleth in the Hearts of the Humble.

But all who are got up in their Imaginations, the Lord God will scatter, and the Proud, the High, and the Lofty, the Lord doth resist; and this you shall witness; and the Lord feeds the Hungry, but the Rich is sent empty away [Luke 1:53]: And they who thirst and breath after Righteousness, such the Lord satisfieth [Matt. 5:6]. So Read, and with the Eternal Light Examine and Search, and try what it is that you thirst after; whether it be Righteouness, Purity, and Holiness, for these will the Lord satisfie; and whoever is not thus seeking, shall never receive satisfaction from the Lord God; but Wrath, and Terror, and Horror shall fall upon that which is contrary to this. So, as you love your Eternal Peace, and the Redemption of your Souls, keep low in your measures of the Living Testimony which cometh from the Living God, which is one in all; in its measure, and there is no Division, nor no Rent, but all one; and this gathers your Hearts together, and this knits and unites unto the Body, where the Unity is; and who gathers not here, scatters abroad; and he that is not with us here, is against us. So Examine now, and try whether you are gathering now, or scattering abroad, with the Light which is Eternal, which is one in all. Examine and try your own selves, I Charge you, as you will answer it before the Lord God; come down and stoop to the Yoak of Christ, which is easie, and take his Yoak upon you, and his burthen, which is light [Matt. 11:30]; and beware of starting from under the Yoak of Obedience, or pulling away the Shoulder; for the Lord God required not only Sacrifice, but Obedience, which is better. And that Mind that looks outward, from the measure enjoyed, and joins to anything without, contrary to the freedom of the Spirit within, that Mind is for Judgment, and the Eternal Spirit of God is one in all. And that which divides one from another, is for Judgment; for where division is, that is of the Kingdom that cannot stand: so Read where you are, for if you are in that which is divided, you cannot stand [Mark 3:24]. So in Love and Tenderness to your Souls, I Warn and Charge you from the Lord, keep in the Light, which is one, in the Power, which is one, in the measure of Life made manifest in you, which is one: And here is no Division, nor Separation, but a gathering and a knitting. And if you love the Light, then you come to the Light to be proved, and tried, whether your Works be wrought in God. But that which hates the Light, turns from the Light, and that shall be condemned by the Light forever. And though you may turn from the Light, where the Unity is, and you may turn from the Eternal Truth: But from it the Witness of God in your Consciences, (which he hath placed in you, which beareth witness for the Living God) you can never fly; and that shall pursue you where-ever you go. And they who turn out from the Light, their Resurrection is to Condemnation, and on the Left Hand they are put, among the Goats, and shall have their Portion with Hypocrites and Unbelievers; and this shall be witnessed forever.

And this I was moved of the Lord to write to you, in Love and Tenderness to the Measure of God in you, with which I have Unity, which will witness for me for ever; and this is in Love to your Souls. So the Lord God of Life and Power keep you alive in that, which he hath placed in you, to his Everlasting Glory: For a sweet Savour we are unto God, both in them that are saved, and in them that perish. And beware how you draw back from the Everlasting Truth, that the Lord God hath tender'd to you, which you shall eternally witness to be of God: *For he that draweth back, my Soul hath no pleasure in him,* said God [Heb. 10:38]; *And that which we have heard, and have seen, and felt, and our hands have handled, even the Word of Life* [1 John 1:1] *which hath been declared unto you.*

From one who desires the Good of all Souls.

M. F.

Works, *pp.* 70–73.

48 To Samuel Fisher March 17, 1656

"It hath bene In mee a prety while to ly before thee for the seeds sake A Booke of myne, to translate into Ebrue [Hebrew] . . . for the Jues [Jews]."

*Samuel Fisher (1604–1665) was a learned man and a distinguished writer on theology and religion who was trained at Oxford. He received Presbyterian ordination and had a well paid position, which he renounced when he came to believe, with the Baptists, that preaching for hire was wrong. He then supported himself by farming and continued to preach as a Baptist. When he was asked to talk to Luke Howard, a young Quaker, about the appropriateness of singing psalms, instead of convincing Howard, Fisher was persuaded of the Quaker view. He became a Quaker about 1655 and spent the rest of his life in the ministry, writing, and teaching. Christopher Hill praises his scholarship and his style of writing and adds: "Fisher deserves greater recognition as a precursor of the English enlightenment than he has yet received (*World, *p. 215). He was highly regarded among Friends. He traveled on the Continent, as far as Venice and Rome, and then returned to London. He spent several years in various prisons and died of the plague in 1665 (Greaves, 1:285–286).*

At the time of this letter Margaret Fell had not met Fisher but had probably read some of his work, and she had heard about him from George Fox, Will Caton, and John Stubbs. She was eager to have her book, For Manesseh Ben Israel, The Call of the Jewes, *translated into Hebrew, and she hoped Fisher would do this. He was not able to, but he did translate another of her books,* The Second Call to the Seed of Israel, *into Latin in 1657.*

Swarthmore 17th of the 1st month (1656)
S:F:

Deare Brother, in the purest love which Indureth for ever doe I writt unto thee, that unto my owne I may Reach which is one in all, the same forever more: who is mannefested In his eternall Spirit, the first fruits and the first borne Amongst many Bretheren, who is gathering in his Elected seed In to his fould [fold,] which is the seed of the Promis[e,] Children not of the bond woman but of the free [Gal. 4:31], who abides in the faith, who Seeketh after Righteousnes[,] Looketh unto the Roke [rock] forom whence they were hewn[;] they who seeketh the Lord looketh onto Abraham theire Father, who was Called out of his own Contery[,] And unto Sarah who hath cast out the bond woman and her Sonn [Gen. 21:10], (and Abraham obeidd). I have Called him alone saith the Lord[,] and Blessed him and Increased him, the Lord is coming to comfort Sion, And will make here [her] willderness like Edene [Isa. 51:2–3], hee hath brought his Righteousnes and salvation neare; and his Judgment A Light for his People to walke by, glowry unto him for Ever more, (oh my Deare;) hee hath Called thee and chosen thee for his worke and sarvise [service], to Beare his name, and his testemony, give up Freely to his will from whom thou hast Receved freely, Abraham was a freind of god [James 2:23]; and the Lord saide unto Abraham[,] Shall I hide from Abraham [Gen. 18:17], that which is in my hart, and xt [Christ] Jesus saith[,] who according to the flesh is the Sonn of Abraham, hence forth I Calle yee no more servants[,] but friends, for the sarvant knoweth not what his Lord doth [John 15:15] yee are my freinds when you doe what soe ever I command you, soe deare hart, here is the knowlidg of the lord manifested, where the Command is kept; & where the faith is dwelt in, I have finnished my Corse, I have kept the Faith [2 Tim. 4:7] saith the Apostell, & all who are of faith are of Abraham, and where the puer [pure] Commandement & the faith is cept [kept], there is nothing hidd; which shall not be made manifest[,] nor nothing covered but it shall be seene [Luke 12:2], and who knowes the sonn knowes the father allsoe; and hee that loves him that begott, loves him that is begotten of him, Deare hart[,] in much tenderness, and bowels of dearest Everlasting Love, have I wretten unto thee, not knowing thee after the flesh, but knowing thee to bee a member of the body, And a chosen vessell for my fathers worke, in the Eternell Spirit and power I have writen unto thee, it hath bene In mee a prety while to ly before thee for the seeds sake A Booke of myne, to translaite into Ebrue [Hebrew], which the Lord moved for the Jues [Jews], and alsoe another booke which was given forth sencc [since] which may be sarvasable; if it were translaited into Latten ore Greeke; as you see it fitt in the Lord; my deare Brother, in what thou doth in this thou dothe it to the lord whose everlasting love is to the seed & the word given forth for the seeds sacke [sake], and soe the Eternell god of power and of wisdom make thee obedient and willing in this day of his power.

Spence 3/37. Also in Works, *pp. 99–100. Endorsed: "M. F. to S. Fisher [George Fox]"; "1656"; "A copy of a letter which M. F. sent to Sammul Fisher".*

49 TO JAMES NAYLER OCTOBER 15, 1556

"I could ly downe at thy feete that thou might trample upon mee for thy good[,] & soe I know would hee whom thou hath resisted."

Of all the heroic figures that appeared in this turbulent age, James Nayler is one of the most tragic. He was a leader and spokesperson of the Quakers, like George Fox, and the two were often linked together. For example, a letter in December 1653 was addressed "To my dear friends George Fox and James Nayler, or to either of them" (Bittle, p. 59). Nayler was an effective writer and answered many of the anti-Quaker pamphlets. He had been a friend of both Margaret and Thomas Fell since 1652 (Letter 7). After working in the North for several years Nayler began preaching in London and was one of the most popular Friends, attracting many followers.

In 1656 Margaret received many letters telling her of the unseemly behavior of some of Nayler's friends, which included breaking up Quaker Meetings with loud speaking and singing. In regard to Nayler himself his followers expressed admiration, even adoration, comparing him to Jesus Christ. Quaker leaders, like Edward Burrough and Francis Howgill, were concerned about Nayler's willingness to accept these followers and their behavior. George Fox also received news of the troubles in London, but he was in prison at Launceston from December 1655 to September 13, 1656.

At the time of this letter Fox had been released and visited Nayler who was imprisoned at Exeter. Fox was rebuffed by Nayler's friends, and the two men had an ugly encounter. Fox feared for the future of the movement. The Ranterish behavior of some of Nayler's followers brought Quakers into disrepute and increased persecution. There are various accounts of Nayler's and Fox's relations during the latter part of 1656. It seems that George Fox was proud and unbending, and James Nayler was weak with fasting and under the influence of his adoring friends.

In this letter of October 15 Margaret expresses her support of George Fox's position and begs Nayler to change his course. She refers to a time when Nayler "would not bend nor bow nor Joyne" with Fox in prayer. In a stern and emotional appeal, she writes that he is causing "the seed" and "the truth," the body of Friends, to suffer. The entire series of events was painful for Quakers, particularly those who were trying to keep the movement together.

On October 24 Nayler and his friends entered Bristol, Nayler riding on a horse, with men and women chanting, "Holy, holy, holy, Lord God of Israel." The extravagant behavior resulted in his being arrested for blasphemy, and the authorities used the incident as a way to attempt to break the Quaker movement. Nayler was tried before Parliament, the trial lasting three weeks in December. Nayler was sentenced to be branded on the forehead with the letter "B," to be whipped through London at the cart-tail, to be imprisoned, whipped again at Bristol, to have his tongue bored, and imprisoned again. He survived these terrible punishments, became reconciled with Friends, and wrote some of the most beautiful prose of spiritual literature before his death in 1660 (Ross, pp. 98–114, Greaves, Bittle, Ingle, pp. 144–150).

Swarthmore, 15th of the 8th month (56)
Deare Brother

I have received thy Letter and it was gladness to mee; when I received it[,] and I Could receive and beare what thou had written in it if thou had kept in Subjection love and unity[,] as thou did express in thy Letter; But since, I have heard that thou would not bee subjecte to him to whom all Nations shall bow [Gen. 27:29]; it hath greeved my Spiritt; Thou hath confessed him to bee thy Father And thy Life bound up in him[,] and when hee sent for thee and thou would not come to him where was thy life then; was thou not then banished from the Fathers House[,] as thou knowes thou hath writt to mee; And that which shewed thee this which was to come I owne; but that which banished thee I must deny[;] and when hee bended his Knees to the most high god for the seeds sake and thou would not bend nor bow nor Joyne with him; How wilt thou answer this to him who hath given him a name Better then every name[,] to which every knee must bow[.] This is contrary to what thou writt to mee; where thou saith hee is buring [burying] thy name that hee may raise his owne[;] but it was thy name that stood against him then[.] And thou wrett to mee the truth should never suffer by thee[,] for where the seed Suffers The truth Suffers[.] doth not the seed and all the body suffer by that spiritt that houlds not the head But rebels against him; oh consider what thou art doing[.] I ame sure the lambe in his suffering is in subjection[,] not resisting nor exalting; but in the time of his Suffering hee is servant to all the seed[,] and if Thou stood in the suffering for the seed thou had not resisted him who is the promise of the Father to the seed[,] who hath said blessed are they that are not offend[ed] in mee [Matt.11:6] oh deare heart[,] mind while it is called today what thou art doeing[,] Least thou walke naked and be astombling [a stumbling] blocke to the simple; & bee tender of the truth which thou hath served before and suffered for[,] which draws thyne eare from uncleane spiritts[,] which is like Froggs which cometh out of the Mouth of the dragon[,] the Beast[,] and the False profitt [prophet.] these was seene when the sixt Angell pouered [poured] out his viall upon the great river Euphratus [Rev. 16:12–13] read & understand & returne to thy first husband; my deare Brother I cann beare all that hath beene past[,] if thou will be subject to the will of the Father[;] and he who doeth the will hath Learned obedience & is subject; & I could ly downe at thy feete that thou might trample upon mee for thy good[,] & soe I know would hee whom thou hath resisted[;] though to that spiritt that rebels it cannot bee[,] for that is not one with the father[.] soe in dearness & tenderness have I wretten to thee[,] my Father shall beare mee witness[;] and I warne thee from The Lord god that thou beware of siding with uncleane spirits Least thou bee cutt of[f] for ever[.] Lett mee heare from thee as shortly as thou cann after the receit of this

Thy deare Sister in the
Eternall love
M.F.

I wrett to thee after I had received thy Letter which may bee may come to thee after this but then I did not know of this

my husband tooke some Letters from the foote post which was to mee which menshoned the differance betwene G and thee and hee red them

Spence 3/38–39. Also in Ross, pp. 396–397 and BQ, pp. 249–250. Addressed: "For James Nailer, prisoner of the Lord at Exeter, these with care dd." Endorsed: "J. Nayler to [by George Fox, but crossed out by him]"; "M. F. to J. Naler [George Fox]"; "1656".

50 To Jeffrey Elletson, with a postscript by John Clayton 1656

"Thou must first know thy selfe to be
A theife in stealeing of these words which thou hast heard
without thee before thou know the beloved."

Margaret wrote this letter at the request of John Clayton (see the endorsement and the postscript). Clayton had been in the army with Elletson, and they had exchanged correspondence on the subject of Quakerism. Clayton evidently felt the need for a stronger voice to answer Elletson's challenges, and Margaret is replying for him.

Elletson had called the Quakers "deluded" and expressed sorrow that Clayton had joined them. Margaret turns the word back on him, "Who can be worse deluded then thee that is yet in sin and ignorance." She urges him to listen to "Christ Jesus within thee" and not to the "Gospell ministers." Elletson had called himself "A poore silly sinfull ignorant creature," and she agrees with this assessment. However, truth has been revealed, and if he will listen to the light within, it will lead him out of sin and "into purite up to god."

Friend thou sayest in thy letter that my letter was welcome to thee in reguard of the love that thou beares mee, which love is changeable and will not abide in the time of tryal which is when iniquitie doth abound[.] then thy love will waxe cold for it is feigned love, and not the same love which Chr: Jesus loved his withall. therefore it will not stand; though thou saith my letter was welcome to thee[,] that in thy conscience will tell thee thou lyes, for that in thy conscience would have received it, but thou that writes the letter cannot for it is the savour of death unto thee, but unto the life it is the savour of life; and thou art for death and destruction. And thou speakes not the truth but dessembles, and saith that, which that in thy conscience tells thee it is not soe, soe that in thy conscience will condemne thee eternally and wittness for mee for to that I speake, but thee I deny; And whereas thou saieth thou art sary [sorry] to see mee turne aside with these deluded people Let thy sorrow turne backe for thy selfe, & not sory [sorrow] for mee, for thy sorrow and thy love is fained, and true sorrow thou dost not know but talkes of it with the light mind which is for sorrow and distruction; and thou sayest I am turned aside with these poore deluded people which turneing I wittnes in my measure to be the knowing of the true god, and the unknowne god to thee, which thou and all the world worshipes ignorantly [Acts 17:23]. And if ever thou knows god thou must turne to us, for as yet thou art ignorant of him & knowe him not (but by hearsay) if thou did thou would know us, whom thou calls A deluded people, but it is that which ever they did who professed god in words[,] as thou dost[,] but art ignorant of him in life & power[;] for they called Christ A devill & Belzabube but who professed the scriptures as thou dost for thou art A stranger to the eternall life of god, that in thy conscience will tell thee soe. Though thou sayest thou can thinke no better of them, and hopes that some of them will be saved though by fire. And here thou makes it manifest, that thou speakes evill of that thou knowe not, which knowe nothing but by thinking[,] for he that thinkes he knowes any thing knowes nothing as he ought to know[;] and there thou art[,] and thy thoughts are vaine, and thou that thinke, knowe not god, and soe thou thinkes evill of god because thou knowes him not, but wee know thee and thy thinking to be for Condemnation[.] by the eternall spirit doe wee see thee & judge thee infallablely and all who thinkes as thou dost[.] for thy thinkeing wee deny & thy hope we deny[,] for it is the hope of the hypocrite, which shall perish & not the hope that purifies[.] to that in thy conscience I speake which will wittnesse for me and against thee, and against thy dissembling and hypocrisie; thou sayest wee shall be saved though by fire, Silence flesh for there is no safety for thee, for thou art for condemnation & distruction by the fire, and the fire thou knowe not nor cannot wittnesse, but thou shalt know it to the destruction of that, which speakes in thee bee fore [before] ever thou know the liveing god[;] for he dwells in the everlasting burneing[.] he that can receive it let him, but thou cannot nor knowes it not; And thou sayest that thou art A poore silly sinfull ignorant creature, Here thou hast laid thy selfe open to the vew [view] of all the children of light[,] thy speech betrayes thee. thy language is of Egipt[,] A child of darkenesse thou art, thy faith is vaine who is yet in thy sin & ignorance[;] and who can be worse deluded then thee that is yet in sin & ignorance. & see what it is that thou sees us deluded with, that art yet in thy sin & ignorance[.] O thou blasphemeous beast, For there thou must see thy selfe to bee, who blasphemes god & his temple whom thou knowes not, For here thou confesses thou knowes not god[,] for thou that sines is of the devill and never knew god. and yet thou takes upon thee to judge the saints conditions & calls it delution [delusion.] O thou enemie of god[,] how darest thou speake of god & christ & confesses thou art yet in sin & ignorance, who art of purer eys [eyes] then to behold iniquity, oh blush & be ashamed before the liveing god, who sees thy hypocrisie & dissimulation, & thy deceitfull hart which thou sees not, but art an enemie to god[,] Though thou sayeth thou hast hope in an another[,] the Lord Jesus, who dyed for thee, yea rather is rissen, O thou dessembler where had thou this? examine thy conscience & see where thou had it, had thou it not in the Letter[?] to that in thy conscience I speake, dost thou know Chr: dead & rissen if thou had not seen the letter[,] that in thy conscience will tell thee that thou had it but by hearsay because thou reeds [reads] of it without thee, but Christ Jesus within thee thou art ignorant of, that in thy conscience will tell thee soe, And he is the mistery and the true hope & he that hath this hope purefies himselfe even as he is pure, which thou art ignorant of[,] as thou thy selfe confesses, & soe thy hope is for distruction. And thou sayest he sitts at the right hand of the Father pleading his righteousnesse for thee, there againe thou hast stolne [stolen] these words out of the Letter, And had not thou seen the Letter thou could not have spoken these words[.] For the right hand of god thou knowes not but art ignorant of as thou confesses who art yet in thy Sin & ignorance, & the pleading of Chr: righteousnesse is for thy distruction[,] thou man of sin. For his righeousnesse is to be reveailed in flames of fire upon all that know him not, that is scripture [2 Thess. 1:8] read it and the wrath of god upon all the children of disobence [disobedience] & see if thou be not there[.] out of thy own mouth thou art judged; thou sayeth through the grace of god thou art accepted in the beloved _______ grace hath appeared unto all men and teacheth us to deny ungodlyness and worldly lusts, & all such as thou art turnes it into wantonness and lives in ungodlynesse & pride & coveteousnesse[;] and thou wilt see thy selfe an enemie to them that deny ungodlynesse[.] that in thy conscience will tell thee soe, and calls us A deluded people because we turne from such wayes as thou lives in; that in thy conscience will tell thee soe, Thou confesses that thou art in thy sin & ignorance, & he that sines is of the devill, and the beloved thou knowes not, Thou must first know thy selfe to be A theife in stealeing of these words which thou hast heard without thee before thou know the beloved and thou art not beloved nor accepted but to be condemned eternally & if thou harken to that in thy conscience it will condemne thee with mee, for that I have united with, but thee I deny for thou art for the fire, and thou sayest whosoever wrote these reasons why we deny the priests of the world which thou calls ministers of England, which thou sayest preaches the gospell, and say they are written from and by the spirit of the Lord, I must needs tell you yee blasphemee of the spirit of the lord[,] which if ever the spirit enlighten you to see, you will see cause to repent of, & to thee I Answer[,] the ministers of England preacheth thy Gospell who hath bene A follower of them ______ _______ and yet thou art in thy sin & ignorance as thou confesses, and that in thy Conscience will let thee see that for all their ans [answers] thy Gospell thou knowes not god, and the glad tydings of the everlasting Gospell of peace thou knowes not, neither did they ever preach the everlasting Gospell, and to thee who art in thy sin there is no peace to the wicked, And Jesus xt comes not to send peace to such as thou art, but A sword [Matt. 10:34], for where Jesus xt is made manifest, he destroyes the workes of the devill, which is sin, which thou confesses thou art in, and the spirit of god thou knowes not, but calls it blasphemie as they ever did who was in the profession of the outward Letter[,] as thou art, which knowes no spirit of god, but what thou hast found in the Letter[.] that in thy conscience if thou harken to it, will tell thee soe, therefore let thy mouth be stopt and be silent[,] for by the eternall spirit of the liveing god thou art seen & knowne to be without god in the world, & all thy Gospell ministers[,] as thou calls them[,] to be Antichrist, & in the steps of these that ever denyed Christ where he was made manifest, and these are them that keep people in their sins as thou thy selfe confesses/ ____ ______ ______ _____ _____ _____ _____ ______ ____ & yet thou art but A poor silly ignorant sinfull Creature, alacke for thee[,] what was thou before thou went after them, and yet thou art talkeing of the spirit of the lord, O thou ignorant [Sott crossed out] man, the spirit of god where it is made manifest sanctifieth and cleanseth from sin, & ye are sanctified there on the obeydience of the spirit, And thou that confesses thou art in thy sin, dare judge this spirit to speak blasphemey[.] oh woefull and miserable is thy _______ _______ Therefore repent & turne to the Lord for A day of Lamentation

& howleing & woe and misery is comeing upon thee, & all thy Gospell ministers as thou calls them, and all thy profession cannot cover thee in the day of the Lords fearce [fierce] wrath, thy Covering will be to narrow, & thy vaile [veil] of profession of god and christ without the possession of him will be pulled of[f], and then thy filthynesse & thy sinfullnesse & thy ignorance which thou speakes of will be seen and all thy prayers and all thy preachings, and all thy ordinances as thou calls them, and all thy fasting & dayes of humilyation & all that ever thou hast done evill be spread as dung upon thy face, and are as fillthy rags before the lord, & the woe is to thee that is covered & not with the spirit of the liveing God, for it is all Caines sacrifice & is abomination to the lord[,] who art in thy first nature & in thy sin & ignorance, but he that is borne of god sinneth not for the seed of god remaines in him[,] and he cannot sin because hee is borne of god. And the Gospell ministery thou speakes of[,] the decree of the lord is gone forth against them for the confounding & overturneing their very foundation, For they are built upon the sand [Matt. 7:26], & they & thou & with all their profession is comeing to be tryed by the touchstone cutt out of the mountain without hands, which strikes at the foott of the Image which hath bene soe long set up [Dan. 2:45], Therefore harken to the Light of God in thy conscience for by that thou must be judged and tryed when the booke of conscience is opened, and then that wilt witt[nes] us to speake the Truth, & will let thee see thy deceivers & deluders, which hath soe long deluded thy Soull, who art yet in thy sines, soe if thou love thy owne soull[,] harken to the light in thy conscience, which shewes thee thy sin & condemnes thee when thou hast sinned; and that will lead thee out of thy sin if thou harken to it[.]

If thou love it, thou loves Christ[.] if thou hate that thou hates christ, and talkes of him with that which is an enemie to him, and soe farre as thou loves & obeys, the light in thee, it will lead thee out of thy sin, & it will lead thee into puritie up to god, And it will let thee see all thy Gospell teachers not to be built upon the rocke which is christ the Light, which hath enlightened everyone that comes into the world, but are talkeing of A Christ without them, and soe thou & they are yet in your sines, And thou shalt never know the liveing god in that way & condition thou art in, but Jesus xt is rissen & revealed and made manifest in these, whom thou & thy Gospell ministers calls deluded people, glory & prayses be to the gloryous god for ever, who hath hid these things from generation ages past but hath revealed them to us[,]

A despised people, and all your false accusations & lyes & scandells is trampled upon and are under our feett for they are without us, and our testimony is within, which testifies for us and wittnesseth the liveing god to be true and all men to be Lyars and there is our union & fellowship in that which all the world & the ministers of the world knowes not, And take heed how thou speakes of the saints condition (the Scriptures) for they are Anothers & are not thine (for they were spoken forth from the life & power which life & power wee wittnesse, made manifest in us,) and if thou know them thou would know us, for Christ is the same to day yesturday & for ever, & the eternall spirit is one, which cannot be limmitted by no carnall fleshly minds, but limmitts & Comprehends all the creation, Therefore take heed how thou speakes evill of things thou knowes not[,] least the woe be pronounced against thee which the scripture speakes of; Soe I turne thee to the light of Christ in thy conscience which if thou obey it, it will let thee see the truth of these things & if thou hate it it will be thy eternall condemnation, And that will let thee see the deceitefullnesse of thy hart [heart], and that thou art not what thou seems to bee, but speakes feained colloured words, which thou hast not cleare testimony for, soe harken to that, & see if thou can be deluded by that for that is the saints Teacher & that teacheth us to deny ungodlynesse & worldly lusts & to that in thee have I cleared my conscience & that will wittness mee & Condemne thee eternally if thou dost not obey it

M F

[different hand, at bottom of page]

writen from the moving of the spirit of the lord in one of them whom thou cales [calls] deluded[,] in love to thy soull; this is the word of the lord to thee[.] doe not then cale this railling for if thou doast; in soe doing thou heapes coalls of fier [fire] upon thy owne head;

John Clayton

Spence 3/153–154. Endorsed: "M F to Jeffre eleson [George Fox] 1656"; "This [Letter crossed out] paper is an Answer to one that Jeffrey Eletson writt to Jo Clayton who was a souldier with him in the Army in Scotland who came to be Convinced of the Truth, & Eletson hearing of it writt a letter to him, & Jo Clayton brought it to M F to Answer."

51 TO JOHN STUBBS 1656

"My Deare Brother, I haveing an Intrust [trust] in thee, that thou will gett theis things Carfully, & truly don."

John Stubbs (ca. 1618–1674) was born in Ulverston (Margaret Fell's town), was skilled in languages, served in Cromwell's army, became a Quaker in 1652, and spent the rest of his life as an itinerant minister and writer. He traveled widely, to America, to Amsterdam, and to Rome with Samuel Fisher. He shared many of George Fox's journeys and imprisonments.

Stubbs and his wife, Elizabeth, were trusted friends of Margaret's, and in this letter she is asking Stubbs to do various errands for her regarding her books. He was on his way to London and then to Holland, and she gives directions on how the books are to be printed and distributed. It is not clear to which of her titles she is referring, but A Testimony of the Touchstone for all Professions *was published by Thomas Simmonds in 1656 and a translation into Dutch was published the next year.*

Several of her writings were being distributed in England and on the Continent, and several translations were under way. Kunze untangles the confusion about the various titles as much as is possible. Both she and Ross have valuable accounts of Margaret's work in relation to Jews, and Kunze particularly relates the passion of the Quakers to convert the Jews (Ross, pp. 89–97; Kunze, pp. 211–228).

The second page of this letter is a series of twenty queries addressed to Jewish teachers and rabbis that aim to demonstrate to Jews that portions of the Hebrew Bible, the Old Testament, lead toward the theology of the Quakers. Her queries all refer to Old Testament passages and do not mention Jesus Christ, which seems a sensitive approach.

She mentions Thomas Simmonds (1623/24–1665), a printer in London who produced over three hundred Quaker works (EQW, pp. 609–610). His wife, Martha Simmonds, was one of James Nayler's enthusiastic followers.

Elizabeth Stubbs, John's wife, was also an active Friend who had much of the duty of raising their daughters while John traveled in the ministry. She lived in Ulverston most of the time, and Margaret helped her. Elizabeth later wrote, "I consider thy great care and unchangeable love & bountiful goodness to me and my children" (Ross, p. 245; Mack, p. 217).

Margaret also requested that Stubbs deliver a letter to Oliver Cromwell by giving it to a Friend in the Cromwell household. Since mail service at that time was highly irregular, many letters and packages were carried by individuals who hap-

pened to be traveling. It is amazing how much communcation there was among Quakers in this era when transportation was by foot, horse, carriage, or boat.

My dearly Beloved Brother in the lord; my dare and tender love is Dearly Remembered unto thee[,] not in words only, but in that Truth that Enduers for Ever; I have receved thy Letter, & glad I am to here from thee; Dear hart, thou knows thy wife anxsious, lett her Stay bee as litle as Can bee; & for the Booke & the Epistle they may be put together, as they are, & as shortly as thou Can lett them be gott into the Sarvice, if thou se [see] any Sarvice for the Einlish [English] Coppy which thou tooke with thee from Hence, Thou may take it along with thee; But if thou Intend not to tak[e] it along with thee; leave it with Thomas Simmands, & lett him keep it carfully till hee here [hear] from mee, And for the other in Hebrew, if hee Cann gett it Don befor thou goes to take a long with you, it would be well, My Deare Brother, here is Another; that I desire thee to take Kare of, to put it to Thomas Simmands, and see it truly Sett in the Presse, & after it is don to Correct what is amis in it, its the Lords provedance, that I Should have this oportunity to Send it & likwise thee to looke to it, they may goe forth amongst frends as the Rist [rest] of Books doeth, the Same Quantety to Every place, & as they are Called for[,] Soe they may bee prented, in Quantety, I would have, A pretty Quantety Sent into other Nations, as oportunity is offered; I would have thee to take som alonge with thee, and gett Summ in to Holland; tho they be in English, they may be Servisable, Mebe [maybe] Summ [some one] may tranclaite them[.] it is only what is Contained in the ould Testement, Lett it be don as shortly as Can bee, & lett only the two letters Stand for the Name [i.e. MF's initials.] here is likewise a letter, to Oliver [Cromwell], which I would have thee gitt carfully Conveaied to him, ther is Sarvants in his house that is freinds, if it can be safly gotten to any of them and laid upon them to deliver it, its like they will gett it to him, Soe my Deare Brother, I having an Intrust [trust] in thee, that thou will gett theis things Carfully, & truly don, I leave them with thee; & Commits thee & all thy undertakings, to the Strength & power of the allmighty, which is able to Cary thee on & to uphould thee, & give thee domminyon, Soe god almighty be with thee, hasten Sam: to gett that other don, Thy wife, if you see it fitt, may Com alonge with the Caryer, safly; if you observe the day hee Comes forth

Thy Dear Sister in the Eternall Life M: F:

Certain Que. [Queries] To the Teachers & Rabbis
Amongst the Jewes//

1 What the way of holynes is, & where it is, where the unclean cannot passe. Isa. 35 [:8]

2 What the voice of him is that cryeth in the wildernes, Prepare yee the way of the lord, make streight in the desart a high way for our god; & what this way is. Isa. 40 [:3]

3 What the way in the wildernes is, & the rivers in the desert. Isa. 43 [:19]

4 What the word is which is heard behinde, saying, This is the way, walk in it. Isa. 30 [:21]

5 What the tongue of the learned is, that speakes a word in season to him that is weary. Isa. 50 [:4]

6 What that Wisdome is which cryes, & understanding that puts forth her voice, to the sons of men. Prov. 8 [:1]

7 What that was in Salomon which was set up from everlasting, from the beginning, or ever the earth was. [Prov. 8:23]

8 What that was in Salomon which said, By mee kings rule, & princes decrees Justice & nobles, overall the Judges of the earth. [Prov. 8:15–16]

9 What was that in Job, which said, I will teach you by the hand of god, that which is with the Almighty will I not conceall. Job. 27 [:11]

10 What the path is, which Job speakes of, & where is the place of that wisdome, that is hid from all eyes living. Job. 28 [:20–21]

11 What the fountain of Jacob is, which moses [Moses] spoke of. Deut. 33 [:28]

12 What that fountain is, which shall come forth of the house of the lord, & Joel 3 [:18]

13 What that fountain is which is opened to the house of David, & to the inhabitants of Jerusalem. & Zach. 13 [:1]

14 What the living waters is that shall go from Jerusalem. Zach. 14 [:8]

15 What those rivers & fountaines are, which the lord will open in the high places, & in the midst of the valleyes, when hee makes the wildernes a poole & dry land springs of waters. Isa. 52 [Isa. 41:18]

16 How it is, & by what, that water is drawne out of the wells of salvation. Isa.12 [:3]

17 What that fountain of gardens, & well of living waters, & streams from Lebanon is, which Salomon speakes of. Cant.4 [Song 4:15]

18 Where doth the Ancient of dayes sit when he comes, when Judgment is given to the saints of the most high, & Dan 7 [:22]

19 What the kingdome & dominion, which is given to the saints of the most high is, whose kingdome is an everlasting kingdome, & all dominions shall serv and obey him.ver.27 [Dan. 7:27]
20 What was that in David which said, yet have I set my king upon my holy hill of Zion. The lord hath said unto mee, Thou art my son, this day have I begotten thee. [Ps. 2:6]

Answer these [Queries, according to the Law and Prophets. First Printed, in the Year 1657. (per *Works*, p. 191)]

Spence 3/40. Queries only in Works, *pp. 190–191. Endorsed: "MF To Jo Stubs 1656"; "concern[ing] a book of MF's".*

52 To Humphrey Norton 1656

"Thy false accusation concerning lightnesse, this is it which lyes upon mee, and really in this accusation thou hath stricken at my life."

*Humphrey Norton wrote to George Fox and complained that at a Meeting at Swarthmoor Hall there had been unsuitable "lightness" and improper singing and many prayers (*CJ*, 1:245–246). Word of this complaint had just reached Margaret Fell, and she takes Norton to task for not speaking at the time but rather that he did "backbite & smite in secrett."*

Humphrey Norton (fl. 1655–1660 DNB*) was an active Friend and an early supporter of George Fox. The letter that mentions Swarthmoor Hall is primarily about Norton's love and admiration for George Fox and his willingness to take Fox's place in Doomsdale prison, "body for body." Norton's offer was made to Oliver Cromwell, who refused it. Norton traveled to Ireland and to New England and suffered many severe punishments. He left the movement about 1660.*

Margaret ends her letter by passing on news, which would indicate that she continued to regard him as a Friend, even if misguided.

William Ames (d. 1662 EQW*) was an important missionary in Holland and active in distributing Margaret's writings.*

Edward Burrough (1632–1663) was a brilliant young Quaker preacher and writer who died in Newgate prison (Greaves, 1:107–108).

H.N. Deare Brother[,] my deare love in the lord Jesus Chr: is to thee, who is the righteous Judge, & Judgeth righteously, whose Judgement is one with the father, who hath commited all Judgment to the sonn, and that which Judges and is not the son is Judged by the son, yesterday I heard of thy Information to G: F: [George Fox] & J. N. [James Nayler] Concerning our meeting, but in that thou might have spared thy paines, for they doe know us and see us and feele us[,] in that which thou wanted to Judge with them[;] and they neither of them neither spoke nor writt anything concerning that, yet I have had severall Letters from them both since[,] for I know they tried and saw, both us and thy Judgement what it was, yet the lord in his pruidence [prudence] ordered it soe that I came to know of it, there was that spoken to thee then in the meeting, which might have stoped thy mouth[,] which thou shall Eternally wittness to be truth, that there is the true groanes and sighs of the spirit which cannot be uttered, and there is false groanes, & there is true mourning in sion [Sion], & there is Esah weeping for his birthright [Gen. 27:38] & there is true promisse which the ransomed gives when hee returnes to Sion, with the song of deliverance upon his head, & there is false singing, & this I know eternaly, thou was not able to distinguish and Judge of at that time & therefore thy Judgement was before the time, which was by outward apearance, & not righteous Judgement, & the beame not being cast out [Matt. 7:5] & the state which thou Judged thou never came to, Eternally thou shall wittnesse mee, & the Just & righteous wittnesse of god in thee, shall answer to this, that thou never came to know nor wittnessd that condition, which thou then Judged[;] and whether then thou did not Judge befor thy time, let that in thy Conscience speake[;] yet I passed by it, and spoke little of it to any, though I saw through thee & Comprehended thee, neither should I, (I beleeve) have menshoned [mentioned] this that thou hast said to them, to thee, But that thou hast said that which I know in the presence of god is false, and that is that thou saw Lightnesse amongst us, this I doe utterly deny[;] & thou art A false wittnesse for god if thou did see this & did not reprove it[;] for the true & faithfull wittnesse, reproves in the gate and doth not goe to smite in secrett, as thou did to severall which I now perseve [perceive;] for something was write in a Letter by E: B: [Edward Burrough] which was sumthing strange to mee when I received it, but now I see the ground of that hath beene thy false accusation concerning lightnesse, this is it which lyes upon mee, and really in this accusation thou hath stricken at my life, which is my kroun [crown] (And here I must deale plainly with thee) thou hast mannifested thyselfe to bee one of the false Bretheren, (which the Apostell saith hee was in peralls [peril] of) [2 Cor. 11:26] in that thou did not speake to mee one word concerning these things, but what thou spoke in the meeting in opposition, the Eternall suffered by thee, (then) and the Enemy and Accuser of the Bretheren was strengthened by thee, And yet this was borne without any surmizing behind thy backe, But thou was not sattisfied here, But would have rendered us odious in there [their] eyes who knowes us better than thou doth, for thou put[?] us & them of Kendal to go ther[,] which made thy spirit clearly mannifest by which thou Judges And soe when thou Judgeth againe, know thy ground from whence thou speaks and what thou speaks to, ore else be silent[;] Least the shame of this nakednesse doe appeare, & them that thou thus Judges doth Comprehend thee far, in the Eternall living truth as it is in ge: [Genesis?] I know it Eternally, & this I speake without boasting of them, ore any Contempt of thee, (god is my wittnesse) for I love & honhour in my soule the least appearance of truth, And is willing to ly down down my life, and to bee servant to all, & to wash any of the least of the dissiples [disciples] feete, & this I beare not wittnesse of my selfe, but my heavenly father beareth wittnesse of mee, Soe when thou writes let mee know thy ground of the word Lightnesse, and who it was that thou saw it in, & let the light Judge & Condemne that which did not reprove it then, but did backbite & smite in secrett, this is Condemend with the light forever.

If thou bee about watterford [Waterford] ore cann send to Freinds there[,] let them know that I have received a letter from Holland, From Will: Aimes Hee is well & the truth prospers there.

Spence 3/41. Addressed several times: "For Humphry Norton in Ireland this with Care and Speed". Endorsed: "MF to humfrey norton 1656 this is read [George Fox]"; "Sarah Fell"' written several times]".

53 To Colonel William West 1656

"Our marriages which is in the Light,
whom the Lord Joynes together no man can putt assunder."

Colonel William West (see Letters 4, 54, 132), a member of Parliament and friend of the Fells, found it difficult to accept the Quakers' position on marriage. Their refusal to follow usual procedures and their insistence on conducting weddings in their own Meetings, without clergy, put them at odds with the legal system. Horle writes: "Potentially the Quaker crime with the most serious ramifications was their marriage within their own Meeting. Canon law stressed that marriages were legal only if they took place in the parish church or chapel before a minister. . . . If Quaker marriages were illegal, the children of such unions were illegitimate, and technically could be challenged over inheritances" (Horle, Q.&EngLegalSys, p. 234).

In this letter, Margaret does not deal with legal consequences, although she did at another time. She is attempting instead to express the theological defense of the Quaker position: "the children of Light is not of this world . . . And this redeemes from under the worlds ways and Customes." If disobeying a law caused suffering to Friends, they were willing to endure it. Jesus Christ "is our beloved, and we have found him whom our soull loveth, and with him wee are willing to goe through good report, & evill report, not only to beleeve on him but also to suffer for his sake."

Dear hart

I have received thine, wherein I see A trouble upon thee as Concerning our friends, in that wee cannot Consent to submitt to your Law to Come under it. Concerning which I shall endeaver[,] if the Lord please[,] to Informe thy mind, as concerning us in that particular, which from the world wee shutt, with that which shutts & none opens[,] and are willing to suffer by them, till the winepresse be broken by him who treades it alone[.]

And first, the Light of Jesus who is your head & Captaine, is our Teacher & our leader[,] our way[,] our Truth[,] & our life, & here is our unity, & our Joyneing & marriage is in the Light and in that Law which moses [Moses] gives[,] which bringes the seed out of bondage, which is according to that in every mans Conscience, which lyes hold upon the transgressor & executes the sword upon the offender where ever it is, as well in the Inward man as in the outward, this cutts downe & passeth true Judgemt upon the offender, and this is added because of transgression, and this comes from our Lawgiver, who is the Judge of the world, who Judges in righteousnes & equity, And to this are we subject & by this are wee guided, And against those who are guided by this & bring forth the fruite of the spirit the Apostle saith[,] their is no Law [Gal. 5:22–23] And soe under the Lawes of man, which is made in the will of man, wee cannot Come, nor stoop to that Law which is made by the Carnall mind, which the Apostle saith is not subject to the Law of god[,] neither indeed can bee, neither can wee, who are guided by the Law of god, & subject to it, wee cannot be subject to that which is contrary to this Law, & acts contrary and transgresseth against this Law, which this Law which wee are guided by lyes hold upon, & wittnesses against. this wee cannot come under, for if wee doe we come under the curse, for our Law saith[,] cursed be the man that maketh any graven or molten Image, which is abomination to the Lord, And whether this Law bee, not an Image, which hath bene set up and acted out of the Light, & out of the Truth of god[,] I appeale to that in thy Conscience, which cannot bear false wittnes, but is A swift wittnesse against the Idollator & false swearer[;] & this wittnes wittnesseth against this Law, which is acted Contrary to scripture, & Contrary to all that ever was or is taught of god, And whosoever is taught of the Liveing god can never be subject to this Law, And if wee suffer by this Law, it is nothing to us, soe Long as wee keep in that where the blessing is, from under the Curse, though our enemyes Come in one way[,] they shall goe out seaven [seven] wayes, & our enemyes shall be smitten before our face, and this wee know for our god is A faithfull god, And I apeale to that in thy Conscience, if it bee not with them who made this Law, as it was with those whom Jerim= [Jeremiah] speakes of, Jer:2.8. The preists said not where is the Lord, and they that handled the Law know mee not[,] saith the Lord, And whether these be not sure[,] let that of god Judge, And Moses[,] who brings the seed out of Egipt, who gives the righteous Law of god because of transgresion, cannot be subject to pharoh [Pharaoh] & his Lawes[,] which keepes the seed in bondage, & brings the wrath and the plagues of god upon him; And soe now here I have clearly laid before thee, why wee cannot Come under the Law which is made in the house of darknes & bondage, of oppression of Pharoh, for if wee doe wee come under the plagues and Judgement and wrath of god[,] which wee are redeemed from, and the clear & the pure way is set before us which wee walke in, which leades us into the pure & parfect Law of Lyberty, glory, and prayses bee to our pure & faithfull god, who is our light & our life, & our lawgiver[,] & wee are his people[;] read the 7 of Deutronomy; And the children of this world marry & are given in marriage, & ever did before the flood, there they were found, & before the comeing of the son of man their they are found; but the children of Light is not of this world[,] for the Light is the Condemnation of the world; and beares witness against the world that the deeds thereof are evill, And this redeemes from under the worlds wayes and Customes: and the Apostles doctrine is to the saints, be not Conformable to the world but be yee transformed and renewed in your mindes [Rom.12:2], And this is that which wee owne, & this will carry us above and thorow all suffering, For they that went before us rejoyced that they were Countted worthy to suffer for his name[.] read the 8 of the Romans from the 14: to 30: Our marriages which is in the Light, whom the Lord Joynes together no man can putt assunder, and he alone treades the winepresse without the City [Rev. 14:20], and hee hath left us an example that wee should follow his stepes, who is made parfect thorrow suffering; soe let not that trouble thee, for there I must stand for ever, For hee who is the Author is the finisher of our faith, and if wee suffer with him, wee shall reign with him; but if wee deny him hee will deny us, but hee is our beloved, and we have found him whom our soull loveth, and with him wee are willing, to goe through good report, & evill report, not only to beleeve on him but also to suffer for his sake, And soe the Lord god of power & life enlighten thy understanding, that thou may Clearly see, the ground and rocke on which wee stand, and then hee will not be an offense, nor cause of stumbleing, who walkes in the Light, there is no occassion of stumbling, but who turnes from the Light stumbles at none day [noon day], and this is from A Friend of thy soull who desires thy eternall good & peace with god[,] which is better then all the treasures of Egipt

M.F.

Spence 3/43–44. Addressed: "To Collonell West, these". Endorsed: "M F to w: west [George Fox]"; "1656"; "Concerning not marring with the world but keeping to the law of god".

54 To Judge Thomas Fell and Colonel William West from Margaret Fell, Jr. 1656

"Would thou have, thy children to forsake xt [Christ] Jesus, the husband of his church, and chosen ones, for a husband of the world?"

A letter of Margaret Fell, Jr.'s should not be in this collection, but it suggests so much that an exception to the rule seems justified. (See also Letter 126.) It gives a glimpse of the fervor of a Fell daughter's devotion to Quakerism; it indicates Judge Fell's wish to have Margaret, Jr. make a good marriage within the gentry class; and it illustrates the kind of discussion that probably took place in many Quaker households as their new beliefs affected their lives.

In 1656 Col. William West proposed marriage to Margaret Fell, Jr. He was forty-four and she was twenty-three. He was a respected friend of her father, but evidently Margaret, Jr. was unwilling.

There is no indication that any Fell daughter was forced or even strongly urged to marry for a social position, as was the usual custom, particularly in families of some wealth. Each daughter eventually married a Quaker of her own choice. We can only speculate on discussions that Col. West's proposal may have initiated (Kunze, pp. 35–36).

In that patriarchal age it was unusual for young women to have as much independence as the Fell daughters had. After their father's death in 1658 they each "had their own legacies and their own expense accounts deriving from their father's estate. Thomas Fell left each of his daughters an equal share of the residual of his personal and real property" (Kunze, p. 43). It is an indication of his attitude toward women and of his trust in his daughters.

The first part of the letter seems to be addressed to Judge Fell and the second to Col. West. It is a passionate defense of the importance of obeying biblical commands against "marriages with the heathen." Although Col. West was sympathetic to Friends and helped them in innumerable ways, he did not subscribe to their tenets. We would like to know more of what each of the parties involved thought and felt, but twenty-first-century frankness was not a part of that era.

Why will not thou trust god who hath been good and gracios unto thee, and tenderly, and faithfully preserved thee from many dangers, whose long suffering & patience, is exercised every day, towards thee, though thou goe on in transgresion and rebelion against him, it is his mercy that preserves or els the transgressor would bee consumed[;] but his compassion failes not, & why will not thou stand in his will who will nothing but the good of all[,] his who taketh care to provide for his children, who is the father of all the faithfull. would thou have, thy children to forsake xt [Christ] Jesus, the husband of his church, and chosen ones, for a husband of the world, in this his day, wn [when] many that hath husbands is made to deny theire will for xt who hath said[,] he that will not forsake wife or husband or father and mother for me is not worthy of mee, and what is it that thy children doe, that thou saith they kill thy heart any more[,] but forsa[ke] the world for xt sake, which all must doe that will have him, and they that have christ for there husband[,] have they not enough, but with this thou art not content, soe thou cannot receive him upon his owne tearmes[.] who is not willing to waite upon him, until hee give them husbands in Christ, where the blesing of the lord they may receive, and if they should continue, all there dayes, chast to the lord[,] what reason had thou to murmer at this condition, the apostle gives his testimony of it to bee the best, but not to chuse but what the lord chuseth, with whom there is noe want, who giveth librererly [liberally] and obradeth [upbraideth] not [James 1:5].

For Collonell West

they that will owne us, must first owne god, to bee theire guide and teacher, and come into the unyty of the spirit[,] where the marriage of the lamb is, for wee cannot transgres against the command of the lord, who did command his not to make marrages with the heathen[.] deutrimeny 7[:] 3 and 4[,] Josua 23 the 12 and 13[.] this was that, that brought the flood and caused the lord to complean, who said my spirit shall not alwayes strive with man which is but flesh. it was this that caused the wrath of the lord to fal upon the children of Israell when they Joyned themselves to the heathen. And the apostle[,] when he spake as unto his children[,] saith be not unequally yoked together with unbeleevers[.] Cor 6:14:15:16: [2 Cor. 6:14–16] and truth and peace is more to us then all the tresures [treasures] in egipt [Egypt], and if wee should sell the truth of god, which Indures forever[,] for a fadeing inheritance, which will perish as, the gras that withers, by this wee should hould that peace which the whole world could not purchase for us. soe with xt jesus, wee are satisfied, who is our beloved, whom wee have found, who will Give husbands in his time[,] who created the male and female in his owne Image, which is undefiled.

M: F:

Spence 3/42. Addressed: "This is to My Father and Coll West by M: F: [The word "junior" is written below.] Endorsed: "to Col. West on marrage"; "M: F: to t.fell & wilam west [George Fox]" this has been altered by a different hand to "M: F: younger to her father & wilam west"; "The tryall of M F & her Children Concerning her childrens marrying with the world 1656".

55 To Friends, an Epistle on Marriage 1656

"As they are moved of the lord, by his power & in his fear, they may take each other [in marriage] in the meeting, & speak what the unlimitted power & spirit gives utterance."

This epistle on marriage shows Margaret Fell, the clear-headed, well-organized woman who understands the necessity to satisfy legal and social requirements for a valid marriage. She first lays out the steps necessary to meet the Friends concept of marriage, that it is the two individuals speaking their vows to each other after due clearance by their Meeting. No clergyman is necessary.

The couple should initially declare their intentions before the Meeting; she uses the word "church," which to Quakers meant the people in the Meeting, not a building or an institution. There should then be a space of time for Friends to consider "in the light" any possible objections. If there are none the marriage may then take place. At that time men who are present should sign their names to a "note" testifying to the time of the marriage. The couple should take that note to the nearest justice of the peace the next day or as soon as convenient.

This last step "was an important innovation in the 'regularizing' of marriage among Quakers, and it was Fell who was the first to call for an obligatory civil recording of Quaker marriages" (Kunze, p. 158). Margaret here demonstrates her knowledge of legal practice, which often made her adept at dealing with legal problems faced by Quakers. It seems likely that she had many discussions with Judge Fell about the law.

Friends in the truth, who in the light seeth a joining together in marriage, let it be done in order as followeth.

In the name & power of the lord, & in his fear, wisdome & counsell let it be tryed & weighed in the light in the particular, And so in the fear of the lord, & in his wisdome & counsell, declare it to the other party to bee tryed, & weighed in the light, that each may have a sure testimony in the light, & life, which cannot bee blotted out, And so having unity in the light & life, & a clear sight of being joined in the lord, then declare it to the church, to be tryed in the light, which is one in all, that so the church may have unity with it in the same light & life. A[nd] let there bee a space after the first declaration to the meeting, that if any have any thing to object against the things, they may have time to speak in the fear of the lord, what they see in it, (in the meeting) that so freinds in the eternall truth, may try & weigh the objection, in the light, & if it be found contrary to the truth, let it be condemned with the light; And likewise if freinds in the meeting who dwells in the eternall light & life, which is the true touchstone & tryer finde the thing mencioned by the partyes, to bee out of the light, & out of the unity, let it be condemned with the light. But those who in the fear of the lord, & in his wisdome & counsell are carryed on in that action, & comes to the light to be proved & tryed, & feelt in the unity as before mencioned, Then as they are moved of the lord, by his power & in his fear, they may take each other in the meeting, & speak what the unlimitted power & spirit gives utterance. And after the meeting, freinds may draw a litle note, concerning that action of the day, which they were witnesses of. And as many freinds, who are men, as are free may set their hands to it. So that nothing bee acted among freinds in the dark, & so come under reproach, but that truth may be clear of all scandalls, & stand over all the powers of darkness.

This of the lord I was moved to give forth for the Truthes sake.

M. F.

Let the litle Note bee as followeth.

Wee whose names are under written do bear testimony in the presence of the lord of the two persons (naming the partyes) being joined together in marriage according to church order this day (naming the day of the month)

1 Cor.7. 17,22,38. 1 Tim. 5. 14.

So when the hands are set to these words, Let the partyes marryed carry the note to the next Justice of peace so called, the next day, or within some convenient time.

Let this be copyed over
& sent among freinds.

Swarthmore MSS v. 8. Endorsed: "Epesell to Frends of mareges by M F [George Fox] 1656".

56 TO A CIVIL MAGISTRATE 1656

"If thou obey it [conscience] in thy own particular[,] in thy measure, it will lead thee out of all changable things, and . . . bring thee into the entrence of the Inheritance which never fades awaye."

This kind, pastoral letter was written to a civil magistrate (name unknown) who was sympathetic to Friends but thought they were in error. Margaret felt a need to explain the truth of Quakerism to him, "to inform his mind." A number of themes that appear regularly in her writings occur here.

The idea of "conscience" is central. It is the "pure light of god in [the] conscience" which will let him see the truth. He needs to be guided by the light within him "which is eternally of god & the same today[,] yesterday & for ever, and changes not."

The phrases "in thy measure" and "in thy owne particular" appear often. Different individuals may be called to different duties. Her emphasis of this point may help to explain the strong influence that she had. It made her understanding of individuals and their needs and capabilities.

She speaks of the magistrate's "high wisdome, & apprehention & comprehention" as a barrier, because it prevents him from being humble enough to "enter into the Kingdome." That requires the simplicity of a child and a willingness to listen to the inner voice.

She warns against looking to outward knowledge but urges "dear hart as thou loves thy own soull, doe not Adulterate from that which is of god in thee."

Friend[,] since I parted with thee, there is something that hath laine upon mee to speake to that in thy conscience & to informe thy mind[.] alible [a libel], which I see is high and abo [above] the pure, & is led much forth out of thy owne particular, to observe things without thee, & to comprehend in thy wisdome the wisdome of god, and doth Comprehend and weigh that in thy wisdome which comes from an eternall fountaine, which is the life of god, which is in his saints, to which all the world is strangers, & all the wisdome of the world is foolishnesse with god, & is shutt out forever from knowing the mistery of the kingdome, Thou saist that thou hast observed the severall formes that hath rissen in these late times, & how they have exceeded one another[,] & now wee that the world calls quakers, thou confesses exceeds them all, & yet thou lookes for Another that will exceed us, and this is that which lay upon mee, to informe thy mind to see that that in thy conscience may arise in thee which is the light of Christ, which will let thee see thy darke mind rulling [ruling] in thee now, & soe art ignorant of the doctrine of Christ, and art not guided by the light in thee which is eternall[y] of god & the same today[,] yesterday & for ever [Heb. 13:8], and changes not, And all the formes which thou speakes of & profession that was before, was profession without them[,] of a Christ which was not possessed within, but knowne by the Letter without them, and all the formes in the world & the highest profession knowes him no otherwise, but as they hear of him without them, & by the declaration of him, which was spoken from the life & possession of him, which all who are in formes are ignorant of, for where he is made manifest he is without forme, And the mistery which is Christ within, which is our hope of glory[,] they shall never know, which lookes for it without them, therefore to that in thy conscience I speak[,] which is of god in thee, which never changes, and that is it if thou obey it in thy owne particular[,] in thy measure, it will lead thee out of all changable things, and give thee an Intrest & bring thee into the entrence of the Inheritance which never fades awaye, & if thou stand & continue in the obeydience to it, it will open to thee the mistery of god, & bring thee into the eternall onenesse, which is where the Lord is one & his name one eternally, and the remaneing of these things that are shaken, as of things that are made, is that these things that cannot be shaken may remaine[;] and if thou wilt mind that of god in thy conscience & be led & guided by it, and keep in the obeydience of it, thou wilt see & wittnesse, that, that in thy owne particular never changes, but stands pure & leads to purity & is alwayes present to checke for sin & all uncleannesse, if thou would harken to it, but the disobeydient part starts backe from it, & the high nature gets above, & if thou doe mind the light of god & come downe to it in thee, it will be A bitt to stay thee and turne thee about into obeydience to the Lord, as the Apostle James speakes of [James 3:3], For thou must come downe to the pure light of god in thy conscience if ever thou know god[,] and thou must let that be thy guide & teacher[,] and all the high wisdome, & aprehention & comprehention in the notion, & the light mind[,] which is above[,] is all fuell for the fire, & the light as it arises in thee, it will discover all that to be shutt out of the kingdome & shall never enter[.] For Chr: Jesus saith[,] as thou may reed in the Letter [,] whosoever enters into the Kingdome must be as A little child [Matt. 18:3] and as A fooll, & this condition thou must wittnesse if ever thou know the true & liveing god; And I see plainly that this is thy great & bitter enemie, thy high wisdome & comprehention, which is for the fire, for it is that which is cursed from god, which keepes thee from the obeydience of that which is eternall, & soe thou feeds upon the huske, & upon the tree of knowledge which is forbidden, which brought the curse upon all mankind, and as long as thou lookes forth without thee, thou shalt never know the hidden manna which feeds the invissible, which comes from the Invissible god[,] which no mortall eye can behold, therefore dear hart [heart] as thou loves thy own soull, doe not Adulterate from that which is pure of god in thee, nor committ fornication with other lovers, for Christ Jesus is the husband of that & that is his spaues [spouse], which is eternall, and never changes, & if thou did abide in that, thou would not looke for any other[,] but it is that mind that changeth & perishes that lookes after changeable things, read the 5 Ephe: from the 3. to the 18th. And take heed how thou saith, thou can doe nothing, for Chr: Jesus is now visitting his owne in thee[,] & take heed that his owne receive him not, but to as many as receives him[,] to them he gives power to become the sons of god, and when light shines in darkenesse, darkenesse cannot comprehend it, therefore waite to be comprehended in the light, & then thou wilt see clearly that which is spoken from the light & have unitie with it, & that will shutt out all this wisdome & reason & method & sense which thou soe much speakes of, And would have it satisifed, if thou wilt see the things of god can never be made out to that which is naturall, because they are spiritually discerned[,] & there is an utter enmity betwixt that which is naturall & carnall & that which is spirituall & eternall, soe if thou wilt know the mistery of god, thou must mind that of god in thee, which opens & none shutts, & shutts & none opens [Rev. 3:7]. and I charge thee in the presence of the Lord[,] beware that thou shutt not thy soull out of the Inheritance which never fades away, by thy slighting of the mercyes & the love of god to thy soull, & lookeing lightly over the obeydience of the lord, for he is terrible to the disobeydient, & A jelous [jealous] god visitting for sin & transgression. Thou was saying that thou would have had nothing done against them that persecuted friends, I know thou spoke it in love & tendernes to friends, but yet mind that in thy conscience, of god[,] & it will let thee see that there is A necessity laid upon you[,] who is the sivill [civil] magistrates[,] to execute the Law upon the transgressor, for the law was added because of transgression, & is to be excecuted upon them that transgresse the Law, and there you are the ministers of god in your place, for Justice & equity is to punish the disobeydient & evill doers, that way & freedome may be made for the just to reign & rull [rule], & this I was moved of the Lord for the good of thy soull to write to thee, & beware of the deceite of thy hart, for that lyes near[.] And the Lord god Almighty of heaven & earth guid[,] direct & lead thee, & bring thee downe, that thou may cast all thy crownes at the feet of Jesus

M F

Spence 3/45. Endorsed: "M: F: Epistle to one who looked for a discovery beyond the Quakers 1656".

57 Concerning a Dispute at Manchester 1656

"Therfore all people who desire to know the livinge God . . . turne your mindes to within to the light . . . this will ripp you up and lye you open and makes all things manifest."

The first part of this document is missing. It is a polemical, theological tract written to counter arguments given at "a dispute at Manchester" between Quakers and "Independents, Baptists, and Fifth Monarch Men," according to the endorsement.

The first section is a mocking comment on those who are "lookinge for a Christ cominge in the Clouds of the Sky," but it soon becomes an earnest call to know the Christ within. She says that the leaders of the other sects are in "contention, and striving about the body of Jesus" instead of teaching people to know the light that is available to all and to realize that "Jesus Christ is come in the flesh" and is available now.

She quotes scripture, but her most eloquent argument is a description of the effect of allowing the light to shine on one's life. This is not an easy thing to bear. Rather it "shews you sin & evill, and Checkes you when you doe amisse . . . this will ripp you up and lye you open." She seems to be describing something that happened to her when she first heard this doctrine and it changed her life: "this will let you see the mistery [mystery] which is christ within."

She refers to five men who argued against the Quakers at Manchester and who "were at variance amonst themselves." They could not keep control of the Meeting though they had set it up, "all was on an uproare." These men were highly regarded by their own congregations though the Quakers considered them "hireling priests" who led people astray. Samuel Eaton (ca. 1596–1665) was a Puritan minister and colonizer who was ejected from several churches and imprisoned several times. He wrote The Quakers Confuted *in 1659 (Greaves, 1:243–244). John Wigan (d. 1665) was a Baptist and Fifth Monarchist who had bitter arguments with Quakers, including one with George Fox in 1664 when they were both imprisoned in Lancaster Castle (Greaves, 3:320–321; CJ, 2:394–395). Richard Hollingworth (d. ca. 1660) wrote, "the religion of Quakers is 'a mixture of Popery with other errors.'" Nightingale refers to him as one of "many stars of the greatest magnitude" (Nightingale,* Ejected, *pp. 949, 1024).*

. . . .Scriptures to be your rule soe the fruites of your profession and of your ministry which you run after, Some for the presbiterians and some for the Independants, Some lookinge for a Christ cominge in the Clouds of the Sky and in their minds Imagines a personall raigne and thus you are confused and Divided in your vaine thoughts & Imaginations, which makes you manifest that you know him not come at all nor cannot confesse him come in the flesh[,] and soe you are prooved by the scripture to be the Antichrists which John speakes of [1 John 4:2–3] which shall be in the last tymes where the Apostle saith[,] litle Children it is the last tyme, and as yee have heard the Antichrist shall come, even now are there many Antichrists wherby we know that is the last tyme. 1 John 2:18. And the Apostle saith further hereby know yee the spirit of God, Every Spirit that confesseth that Jesus Christ is come in the flesh is of god: and every spirit that confesseth not that Jesus Christ is come in the flesh is not of god. And this is that Spirit of Antichrist wherof you have heard that it should come, and even now allready is it in the world 1 John:4:2:3: Now all people try your teachers by the scriptures, & their practice, and let their owne words try them, who lookes for a Christ yet to come, as some of them said[,] what will you Quakers doe who saith Christ within you, when Christ comes in the Clouds. Here now all people doe but honestly examine & see whether these spirits confesse Christ come who lookes for him yet to come, and let the light of Christ Jesus in your Conscience examine[,] search you, & try you, whether you Dare Say the Apostle spoke truth who said every spirit who doth not confesse him come in the flesh is not of god; or those Deceivers who lookes for him yet to come. And thus you are Divided; some for a personall raigne, and some for the Indipendant way & some for the Presbiterian way, and some of you utterly denyes the Scripture as William Barret did who denyed that any should witnesse the receivinge the end of their faith the salvation of their soules as it is in the 1 Pet:1:9: and others denyed that Christs body is Spirituall as Richard Herrick lately did at Manchester, and soe thus you are in your contention, and striving about the body of Jesus, as the Divell did about the body of moses [Moses], which makes you clearly manifest to all who hath their eyes opened in the least measure to be those filthy dreamers which defile the flesh, which Jude speakes of [Jude 1:8–9], And yee are plainly manifested, that yee are they that eateth & drinketh unworthyly and soe eateth and drinketh your owne Damnation, not discerninge the lords body [1 Cor. 11:29]. And heare let all poore people about Manchester who are betrayed, & deceived with you[,] Seriously consider what you are leading them into who knowes not the body yet wherof Christ Jesus is the head, but are at variance about the body of Christ, therfore consider of what body yee are members seeinge your leaders knowes not the body of Christ and beware of deceivinge your owne soules, & beinge betrayed by those deceivers who lead you in the Darke; and soe is the blind leaders of the blind, and soe both falls into the pitt [Matt. 15:14]; for they can lead none but who is blind, for any who hath their minds turned in the least measure to the light Sees them, & Discernes them to be ministers of Antichrist and the Deceivers and false prophetts which John speakes of which are gone out into the world from the light which is the worlds condemnation and denyes the light, by which the lord God teacheth his people, as some of them have said, that the scripture is a more lively orackle then the light, when as Christ Jesus saith the light of the body is the eye, and if the eye be single the whole body is full of light [Matt. 6:22]. And soe these Deceivers that denyes the light of the body were not like to know the body, but makes Images in their Darke vaine minds, and Imagininge one way, and another, And soe betrayes poore people, & keepes their soules in death: But the Lord god is risen who is the Father of light, and he who is the light of the whole body is redeeminge his people from under the Devourers mouthes Therfore all people who desire to know the livinge God and the lords body turne your mindes to within to the light which shines in your Consciences which shewes you sin & evill, and Checkes you when you doe amisse, and letts you see your vaine thoughts, and your Deceiptfull hearts, this will ripp you up and lye you open, and makes all things manifest. This convinceth of sin and brings all things to remembrance, which all the Doctrine that ever your hyrelings preached never did. Therfore give over goinge after them, and search into the scriptures, and you will see them the Deceivers of your soules[.] the scriptures wittnesses against them & their practices, even in their manner of there worshipp, for nothinge that they Act in that which they call their worshipp, is accordinge to the scriptures. And all the sts. [saints] in light which gave forth the scriptures witnessed against those practices they live in[.] doe but honestly consider, and you will see that all them that were at variance amongst themselves as wiggin, & Eaton, and Herricke & Barret and Hollingsworth, all these agree together in opposinge, & persecutinge the truth, And although that some of them were the men that appoynted the meetinge yet had they not soe much power over the people, as to have the meeting kept peacable, but all was on an uproare. Soe let all people see what order, & goverment is in these Churches, & severall opinions, which makes them manifest, they who are soe devided amongst themselves, are all devided from the livinge god, and from the livinge truth; from Christ Jesus who is the way the truth & the life, and this is but one. Therfore all people a warninge from the lord god to you, as you will answeare it before him who is a consuminge fire to the wicked, turne to the light of Jesus Christ which will examine and search & trye you, and bringe you to know Christ within you, and soe bringe you out of the reprobate faith. This will let you see the mistery [mystery] which is Christ within; and this will bringe you to know him come in the flesh: and it will let you see those Antichrists who are in the world Strivinge amongst their many opinions; and therfore are they condemned with the light which is the worlds condemnation. For the light is the condemnation of the world, and all the Antichrists, that are in the world. And soe now see whether you will turne to the light of Jesus Christ who is the way the truth & the life, which is but one, or you will continue amongst them who are of the many opinions, who denyes the light, & Christ come in the flesh, and soe is found to be the Antichrists, & deceivers of your soules. and soe here is life & death set before you, light & Darknes, truth, & errour, the straite way & the broad way, there is but these two. Soe now see what way yee will take and this yee shall Eternally wittnesse to be truth[,] whether yee will heare or forbeare.

M: F:

Spence 3/160. Endorsed: "This was given forth after a dispute at Manchester with Independents, Baptists and [Fifth] Monarchy Men about 1656; is on that profession".

58 To George Braithwaite 1656

"Therfore now prize thy time, & let the time past of thy life suffice that thou hast spent in blindness & ignorance of god."

George Braithwaite had argued that Quakers have a religion of works, not faith, a theological issue of importance to Puritans. Margaret Fell quotes scripture to prove his error. Her argument is that if he would examine his conscience he would see that that is his "own stand." His worship is based on "outward occasions" and "sets times & dayes apart," rather than the Quaker position that all days and times are holy.

He has been led astray by Gabriel Camelford (Letters 20 and 43) and has not listened to those who have tried to show him the right way. She writes about the necessity for obedience. If he will only cease rebelling and "bee willing & obedient . . . [he] shall eat the good of the land." The letter seems to be a last attempt to persuade him.

A few words to thee[,] George Braythwait[,] who sayest thou canst not be perswaded but that our religion stands in works, To the light in thy conscience do I speak, which light is not of the world but comes from Christ Jesus whose kingdome is not of this world[.] this light is the condemnation of the world, & the condemnation of all the works that are wrought by the world, therefore to this light in thee do I speak, that with it thou mayest see thy blindness & ignorance of god, who sayest that our religion stands in works, & dost not see thy own stand there, but the scripture is fullfilled upon thee, the god of the world hath blinded thy eyes, for let any honest or wise hearted judge whether you bee not in the covenant of works & selfe actings & selfrighteousnes, who sets times & dayes apart & takes such a place of scripture according to your own will, & sings such a psalme as you like to take, & then when you have done begin to pray at such a time as you please, & pray as long as you will & as litle as you will as your outward occasions give you leave. Now to let that of god in thy conscience examine & try whether you do not thus, & if so, let all that have but a principle of honesty judge how blinde thou art, who sayest that that is acted by others who do not act it, & dost not see it in thy selfe where it is acted[.] And againe mark thy ignorance of the scripture, who sayest wee are in the covenant of works because wee teach obedience to the light, wheras the Apostle saith in his epistle which hee wrote to the Romuns[,] who was an Apostle separated unto the gospell of god Jesus and whom hee declared to bee the son of god according to the spirit of holyness[,] by whom wee have received grace and Apostleship for obedience to the faith & this thou callest workes [Rom. 1:4–5]. And againe the Apostle saith Rom.5:19 for as by one mans disobedience many were made sinners, so by the obedience of one many shall bee made righteous[.] And againe, the [Rom.] 6:16. know yee not that to whom yee yield yourselves servants to obey, his servants yee are to whom yee obey[,] whether of sin unto death or of obedience unto righteousnes & the Apostle Peter when hee wrote to the sts [saints] elect according to the foreknowledge of god, through the sanctification of the spirit unto obedience[,] & those that do obey the measure of the holy spirit according to its moving this thou callest the covenant of works and yet dost not see thy own blind zealle to bee there, which makes thee manifest that thou dost not know the teaching of the spirit of god at all[,] not in the least measure, for thy minde is turned from the eye which is the light of the body, & its not thy prayers with thy minde turned from the light that will open the blinde eye, nor its not running after Priest Camilford & there with thy outward ear hear a blinde guide, this will not unstop thy deafe eare though thou run after them all thy dayes to their preaching & their prayers, & their expounding. thou shalt never bee satisfyed here, eternally thou shalt witness mee, for they are without god, & knowes him no more than thou nor none that they speak to, but they know god as much as they for they deny the light by which god is known, which many of their own hearers can witness against them that they have that which they deny, & yet are blinded by them,

Therfore now prize thy time, & let the time past of thy life suffice that thou hast spent in blindness & ignorance of god, who hast been a fighter against god, & an enemy to his truth, who hath waited to bee gracious unto thee, & hath tendered thee his love & free grace many a time as that in thy conscience can witness, & still thou hast rebelled against the witness in thy selfe & others, & rebellion is as the sin of witchcraft and stubborness as iniquity & idolatry; & if thou dost reject the word of the lord, hee will also reject thee, read 1 Sam.15 chapt & Deut.4:13 when thou art in tribulation & all these things are come upon thee, even in the latter dayes[,] if thou turn to the lord thy god & bee obedient to his voice, then shalt thou have the covenant[;] & Isay [Isaiah] saith, if you bee willing & obedient yee shall eat the good of the land, but if yee refuse & rebell yee shall be devoured with the sword, for the mouth of the lord hath spoken it Is.1.19,20. Now see where thou art whether thou be obedient to the holy spirit according to the scriptures, or thou art in thy blinde zeale, offering Cains sacrifice, which is abomination to the lord, an enemy to the truth of god, in the steps of the scribes & pharisees, making clean the outside of the cup, but within is rottenness & dead mens bones [Matt. 23:25–27], making long prayers in that nature which knowes not christ when hee comes & thinkes to bee heard for thy much babling & so goest on in blindness under the wo [woe], shutting the kingdome of heaven against men, neither going in thy self, nor wilt suffer others, here thou art, read thy portion, & stay thy hand & beware what thou doest. its hard for thee to kick against the pricks [Acts 9:5]. kiss the son least hee bee angry, remember that thou art called & warned in thy life time & if thou go on in thy disobedience & rebellion, when the day of thy calamity comes thou wilt remember mee, & witness this to bee love to thy soule, & att that day will Camilford & all thy other companions have enough to answer for their own sins. So if thou wilt not come down, & minde & hearken to that of god in thy conscience, thy blood bee upon thy own head, for the lord is clear of thee, who hath often sent to thee his servants & prophets.

M. F:

Spence 3/151–152. Endorsed: "A paper from M F: to Gor: Brathweth 1656"; "a professer".

59 To William Knipe 1656

"Where Christ sayd be wyse as serpents . . . that was not to hinder [his disciples] of there messuage & testimony that they were to beare of him."

William Knipe is described as a "gentleman" and a "professor" in the endorsement, and Nightingale refers to him as one of several "gentlemen Patrons" (Ejected, *p. 940). In 1664 Knipe was an informer against George Fox. Fox noted in his* Journal *with some relish "Will Knipe the witness against me soon after died" (Nickalls, p. 505).*

At the time of this letter Margaret still had hope of convincing Knipe of the necessity for Quakers to publish their message. Knipe was urging Friends to stop preaching and to stop annoying authorities, and he quoted "Be wise as serpents and harmless as doves" to prove his point. Her answer is to relate a series of actions of Jesus' disciples as shown in Matthew and Acts that prove the necessity to continue preaching in spite of persecution.

Willyem Cnipe a few words unto thee which may be Answer of what thou and I was spekeing of when wee were Last together[.] thou said where was any of the aposiles sent to any that was not Converted[.] I answer Christ Jesus when hee sent forth his aposiles matthe 10 said go not into the way of the gentiles and in to the sittie [city] of the samaritanes Enter yee not but goe yee unto the Loste shiepe [sheep] of the house of Israell [Matt. 10:5–6] and was not the scribes and farisies [Pharisees] of the house of Israell [?] Ried [Read] mathew the 23 wher for I send unto you profitts [prophets] and wise men and som of them you shall kill and crusifi [crucify] and som of them you shall scourg in your sinagogues and persecute them from sitti to sitti and did not Christ say unto them[,] where unto shall wee Licken [liken] this generation[,] saying wee have pipeed [piped] unto you and yee have not danced wee have mourned unto you and yee have not Lamented[.] for John came nether eating nor drinking and they say hee hath a divel[.] the son of man came eating and drinking and they say behould a man Glutnous[,] a winebiber[,] a frid [friend] of puplikines [Publicans] and sinners [Matt. 11:17–19] and did not they say when Christ wrought meracales [miracles] and cast out divles that hee cast them out by belsebub [Beelzebub; Matt. 12:24] and did not Christ say hee could not do mighty workes and marveles beCues [because] of ther unbylife [unbelief]. Marke the 6 Chap [Mark 6:6] againe did not Christ say when the sonn of man cometh shall hee find faith upon earth Luke the 18 [Luke 18:8] and Pieter and John who went together in to the tempell and as they wer going healeed the man that was Lame from his mothers wome [womb] and Testified of the lord Jesus that thorough faith in his name the man was mad[e] strong[.] ye [yea] saith the aposieles[,] the faith which is by him hath givne him this perfect soundnes in the presence of you all[,] acts the 3 [Acts 3:1–3, 16] in which temple the aposeles preached Largely, and as they spake the priest and the capten of the tempil lead [laid] handes of them and put them in hould[,] acts the 4[,] and Chargeed them that they should speke no more in his name[.] not with standing peter and Gohn [John] bore a nouble [noble] Testimony as you may read the 4 and 5 of the acts and after wardes when the Lord sent his Engles [angels] to deliver the aposiles out of prison the Capten of the Temple and the priest said[,] Did wee not streitly [straightly] charge you that you should speak nomore in his name and when the aposiles weare more bould in ther testimony they weare cut to the hart and Tooke Counsell to slay them [Acts 5:33] with the 5 [?] allso the aposil stiven [Stephen] who was ful of fith [faith] and powre [power] when they Lookeed on his face his face was Like the face of a Engel and when hee bore his Testimony for the Lord Gesus [Jesus] when they heard him they were cut to the hart and gnashed on him with there Tithe [teeth] but steven being full of the holy goste Lookeed steadfastly up to heven[,] who seaeled his Testimony with hi[s] blud [blood,] acts the 6 & 7[;] & how they goe with paule when hee preached Christ att Damascus and perceveed that hee was the very Christ[.] after that hee had Continueed many dayes they tooke Consell to kill him[.] acts the 6[.] and what did they doe unto paule at antioch when hee went intoo the sinnogogue of the sabeth day and preached unto them the Law & the prophit & the ministriasion of John and allsoe of Christ death & his resurection & of Those that heard him Contredickted him & blasfeameed and sterod [stirred] up the people to persicuision [persecution] against paule & barnebas & expelled them out of there Coste [coast] acts the 13[.] when they had healed the Impotent man at Lystra the people stoneed paule & druehim [drew him] out of the sitty sepposein [supposing] hee had beene dead acts the 14 [Acts 14:19] & allso of masadony [Macedonia], where Paule & Silas preached serten dayes the multytude Rose up againste them, & the magistrate Rent of[f] there Close [clothes] & commanded them to bee beatten & when they had leyd many stripes upon them they Cast them into prison[,] acts 16[,] & how the aposieles were abuesed & ther Doctrine & gospell which they preached was derided mocked & skofed at & villyfied all which may bee Red at large[,] acts the 17. by this time I desire thee to bee war [beware] of aposeing [opposing] & sleighting the Lords Truth Least itt meet with thee in Judgement[.] if thou tourne away from it while thou hast a day it will meet with thee in the end[.] its time for thy greheres [gray hairs] to tourn to the Lords truth in thy hart & that would tri [try] thy Reanes [reins] & search thy hart which is desetfull [deceitful] that the Lord may give thee a new hart for according to that must thou Reseve [receive] thy Reward [Jer. 17:9–10]

And wheras thou broughtest that scripture where Christ sayd be wyse as serpents [Matt. 10:16], that was when Christ sent forth his discipls as lambs amongt [amongst] the woolfesh natures of men[,] as thou may see in the next vers[,] beware of men[,] but that was not to hinder them of there messuage & testimony that they were to beare of him for he tould them that they should be brought before Governors for his names sake And for A testimony against them[,] as thou may read Mathew 10:18: and whereas thou sayes when they was persecuted in one Citty he bad them fly to Another[.] read 23 verse if it be not as I said unto thee where Christ said for verily I say unto you[,] yee shall not have gone over the Cittiys of Israell till the sonn of man come [Matt. 10:23] & therfore hath hastened them to go on with theire testimony, that they might finish it upon the Citties before he suffered; not that he would have had them to _________ their testimony for fear of persecution, as the deceitfull minde would Read it, & so get strength to fly in time of persecution,

M. Fell

Spence 3/149–150. Endorsed: "M F To William Knipe 1656"; "Called a gentleman a professer, who was once partly Convinced of the Truth 1656"; "These are all Answers to Priests & Proffessers by M F".

60 TO FRIENDS, BRETHREN AND SISTERS 1656

"Dearly beloved brethren consider what you are called to, & what you are made partakers of, even of a living & pure & holy preisthood, a peculiar people you are."

This epistle was probably read at Meetings according to the direction of the postscript, "Let this be copied & sent abroad amongst all friends." Margaret is informing Friends of Quaker practices, encouraging them to experience the Light, to walk and dwell in it. They will be "living stones" on which the true church is built. The terms "light," "living god," and "Melchisedeck" are used and sometimes interchanged to teach the concept of Friends as a priesthood, as people "called out of the world," as a "peculiar people," with no distinction in status between laymen and priests.

She emphasizes the need for cleansing oneself from sin in order to be able to experience the "everlasting promise of God." The sign of true disciples is that they love one another. "To the pure eternal principle of God, all turne, & keep your mindes unto this." She adds, "my joy & life is that you would take heed to your owne measure received . . . [then they will be] plants in the garden of the Lord."

Dear Friends brethren & sisters in the eternall Light by which we are gathered which is our teacher & leader, which Light comes from our Lord Jesus Christ the Captaine of our Salvation in whom is life & this life is the Light of men, which life he hath laid down for his sheep, & who gives unto his sheep eternall life, & this life is in the son, & your righteousnese is of me, saith the Lord, & this is the heritage of the saints, & this you are partakers of, who walkes in the Light, & dwells in the Light, shall have the Light of life, & come to know the onely true God & Jesus Christ whom he hath sent, who is come a Light into the world, he that believes in him shall not walke in darknese nor shall not perish but have everlasting life, & this is the fathers fre[e] Love to send his onely begotten into the world, who is hated & rejected of men, but chosen of God & pretious, who is becom'd the head of our corner, glory eternall be to the Liveing God on him are we built, on him are we rooted & grounded, he is our foundation & root on whom we stand fast unremoveable[.] this is the corner stone which all builders refuses & rejects, but on this rocke is the whole Church built which is made of living stones elect & pretious [1 Pet. 2:4,6–7], the spirituall temple whose builder & maker is God, & we now having an high preist over the house of God Let us draw near with a true heart in full assurance of faith, having our hearts sprinkled from an evill conscience, & our bodies washed with pure water, wherefore returne to the sheappard of your soules & unchangable preist which is made with an oath for ever after the order of Melchisedeck, who is made surety of a better testement, who needeth not allwayes to offer sacrifice, but he hath offered one sacrifice for sinne & for ever is set down at the right hand of God from henceforth expectinge till his enimies be made his foot stoole, for by this one offering hath he for ever perfected them that are sanctified, & of this is the holy Ghost a witness to us in the fulfilling of the everlasting promisse of God, who hath said I will put my law in their hearts, & in their mindes will I write them [Heb. 10:16], now dear brethre[n] of this you are witnesses, & of the truth & faithfullnese of God you may set to your seales all who abides in the Light[,] who departs from iniquity[,] who names his name which is better then other names[,] to which every knee must bow, & every tongue confess, & now that you are made partakers of a living pure eternall immortall principle which come[s] from the living God, by which you may enter into the holiest by the blood of Jesus, by this [new and?] living way which he hath consecrated for us & through the vaile[,] that is to [say?] his flesh, therefore hold fast the profession of your faith without wavering[;] for faithfull is he that hath promised, & in the strait & n[a]rrow way that leads To life pass on, that through the strait gate ye may enter, which few there be that findes, & in the eternall Light which is one in all, which leads up to the father of Light, & in the measure of life received from the father & fountaine of Light & life all wait, & all dwell, & to the life raised by the immortall word of life joyne your mindes & pass from the death to the life, that so you may come to know & witness the true love that is to the brethren where the unitye is, whereby yee may all know that you are true disciples in that ye love one another & here you fulfill the whole Law & keepe the new commandements which the Lord & Maister hath commanded who dwells in Love, therfore dearly beloved brethren consider what you are called to, & what you are made partakers of, even of a living & pure & holy preisthood, a peculiar people you are, & of the holy nation [1 Pet. 2:9], & of the royall seed, now with the Light which is eternall which searches & tryes, & examines & weighes & makes all things manifest of what sort it is, let this search & trye you how you grow up in the eternall & immortall birth, & do not deceive yourselves for eternally except you be borne againe by the water & the spirit yee cannot enter, now se [see] wheither you can read this in the eternall & wheither you know & se & witness this in your owne particulars yea or nay, & se wheither you be not like Nichodemus, who said how can these things be [John 3:9], & wheither you be not ignorant of this, therefore all come down to the witness of God & deale plainly with your soules, & let the judge which stands at the doore pass upon you, let the time past suffice that you have hidd your talent in the earth which you have received from the Lord to profit withall, & now let the earth give up her dead, & the sea give up her dead, & hell give up her dead, & let all come to judgment, & let death & hell be cast into the Lake & freely offer that which is for the sword to the sword & that which is for the fire to the fire, that so the dead may rise for what availes it else, for you to make a profession & forme of the Living truth if the dead rise not[?] you are yet in your sins & your faith is vaine [1 Cor. 15:14], therfore se what you are doing, for it is not the sayer but he that doth the will of my father, & many shall be called & few chosen & now se with the Light which is eternall that ye be not onely of the many which is called but of the few which is chosen, & give all diligence not to make only your calling but your election sure, & friends, your day of calling is come, ye are called out of the world, & separated from the world by the call of the Living God the Light which calls out of Sodom & Egypt[;] but this is but of the many, this is not of the few, ye may looke upon this scripture to be spoken to the world but the world is not called yet, therfore do not deceive yourselves, for yee are the many that are called, & ye are made partakers of that which calles continualy, the voice behinde which cryes this is the way[.] walke in it[.] why will you die now[?] consider how you hearken to this holy call, & how you are obedient to it, & how you are subject, & how you are taught & guided by the measure of God, for all the children of the Lord are taught of the Lord & in righteousness are they established, now search with the Light which is eternall whether ye be established in righteousness & purity, if ye be not yee denye the teaching of the Lord, for he that walkes in the Light[,] as he is in the Light[,] the blood of Jesus cleanseth from all sinn [1 John 1:7], now examine whether yee be cleansed, whether ye be purged[,] whether ye be washed, for ye walk in the Light[;] there yee witness cleansing & washing, & bew[are] of betraying of the just & innocent in you, I warn you & charge you, as you will answere it with a forme & profession of truth without the life & so betrayes your own soules, but to the pure eternall principle of God, all turne, & keep your mindes unto this, which is given you for the redeming & ransoming of your soules from the captivity & bondage of sinn & corruption & hearken, diligently to that of God, that your soules may live & that you may se your saviour who saves his people from their sines[,] And so come to witness the salvation of your soules, Ye are made partakers of the free grace of God which brings salvation, so let it be your teacher & leader

& beware of turning his grace into wantonness which is able to save your soules, but receive with meekness the ingrafted word [James 1:21], that the milke thereof you may witness, & as new borne babes desire that you may grow thereby, & se the word that is nigh in the heart which is the word of faith which we preach, which word was in the begining, by which word the heavens & the earth were made, which we have heard[,] which we have seen, which our hands have handled [1 John 1:1], this we declare unto you, & to the measure of this in you am I made manifest, & my joy & life is, that you would take heed to your owne measure received, & be true & faithfull to that which is able to save your soules, that eternall pure redemption you may come to witness & the unity of the faith, & so joyning to the head which holds the body, from which the living vertue is received, that so you may grow apace, living plants in the garden of the Lord which now he is dressing & watering & pruning that to him fruit may be brought forth[,] who is the Lord of the vineyard, & the husbandman which purgeth every plant which beareth fruit, that it may bring forth more fruit, & every branch which beareth not fruit he taketh away, now see with the eternall Light, whether yee bring forth fruit unto God, for every tre [tree] is known by its fruit, & every branch which the Lord plants brings forth fruit, not leaves but fruit[.] now search wheither ye bring forth fruit or leaves, for that tree which is in the garden of God & brings forth nothing but leaves, is cut downe, now friends deale plainly with yourselves, & let the eternall Light search you & trye you for the good of your soules, for this will deale plainly with you, it will rip you up & lye you open, & make all manifest which lodgeth in you, the secret subtilty of the enimie of your soules, this eternall searcher & tryer will make manifest, therefore all to this come & by this be searched & judged & led & guided, for to this must you stand or fall & if you turne from this, this is the swift witness against the adulterer, & sorcerer, & from this you cannot flye, & to this I have cleared my conscience, & for the good of your soules I have written this who desires that you may be where I am that so we might all be one, & so the Lord God of life & power keep you in his fear that the Lord God you may serve & honour, that your hearts may be kept clean & the secrets of the Lord you may come to know, which none shall ever know but those that fear him, & this you shall all eternally witness, & therfore I say againe[,] fear the Lord God, & so the pure wisdome you may come to learne[,] for dreadfull & teribile is the Lord God, & the day of vengeance of our God is come in which he renders to every one according to their deeds, & the backslider & revolter & the disobedient ones, and the careless & the sloathfull, & those whose mindes is at lyberty, & will not abide in the cross of Christ[,] all these shall receive according to their deeds, therfore dear friends abide in the Cross & keep your mindes to that which is pure, that so you may come to witness the enmity slain & the hand writing of ordinances blotted out & nailed to his cross, & you cruscified to the world & the world to you, & consider one another & provoke one another to love & good workes[,] not forsaking the assembling of yourselves but exhorting one another & so much the more as you see the day approaching, & dwell in love & unity in the pure eternall Light, there is the fellowshipp[,] there is the cleansing & washing, & here is the mistery to all the disobedient ones, & the everlasting God of everlasting Light & everlasting life & power keep you all here faithfull to your own measures, & so the resurrection of life you may witness, & the living bread you may feed on, which whosoever eats shall never die, so God Almighty be with you & preserve you all faithfull in Christ Jesus.

From your dear Sister in the
eternall unchangable Love
who desires the good of
all your soules.
Margret Fell

Let this be copied & sent abroad
amongst all friends where it Comes

Caton MSS 1:60–66, n.d.; In Works, *pp. 91–97, 1656; according to Ross this was also in Miller MSS 65 of which only a brief summary exists.*

61 To Friends and Brethren 1656

"O dear hearts put your hands in this worke,
& be not slak [slack] . . . offer freely to his service,
that in the freeness & willingnesse of your spirits,
the brethren may be refreshed."

In this letter addressed to northern Friends, Margaret pleads for aid to those working in the ministry. She emphasizes the unity of all Friends, those traveling and those at home "for they that are joyned unto the Lord are one spirit, one heart one soule." At that time Friends had already traveled to "Holland, Barbados, Ireland, Scotland, Flanders, Denmarke, & Germany."

She invokes the suffering of those who experienced "tryalls, buffetings, whippings, scoffings, imprisonings," and is certain that God "shall have the victory." She quotes Revelation with its strong images of destruction and the end of the world and then uses the image of "the flying angel" to shift toward the "seed," those who hear the message of God's love. She ends with a plea for funds, "he that soweth bountifully shall reap bountifully," and she adds the practical direction of where to send the money.

Friends & brethren

In the eternall Light, life & power of the eternall spirit, where our unity stands [I] send greeting, grace & peace be multiplyed amongst you that in the unity of the spirit you all may dwell, for they that are joyned unto the Lord are one spirit, one heart one soule; My dearly beloved in the nakedness of your spirits, & in the innocency of the Love keep your station & habitation, there will you come to read your peace[,] there will you come to know your life & stren[g]th to come from the head, which dwells in the fulness bodily, in whom is hid all the treasures & riches, in the pure measures which holds the head all dwell, that you may receive of his fulness grace for grace[,] that you may be like minded, having the same Love, being of one accord & of one minde[,] that you may know the mistery of fellowshipp & be in the unity of the brethren[,] that you may be one with them in their sufferings, & in their travells [travails], tryalls, buffetings, whippings, scoffings, imprisonings, beatings in the Sinogoges, halings before Majestrates, who is sent as Lambes amongst wolves, amongst whom their is no mercy, but the innocency of the Lambe preserves, upon whom the everlasting seale is set, that he shall have the victory, who is king of kings & Lord of Lords[,] who is blessed for evermore, who is cloathed in a vesture dipt in blood, his name is called the word of God & the armies which are in Heaven follow him upon white horses, cloathed in the Living white & cleane, & out of his mouth cometh a sharpe two edged sword [Rev. 1:16], & with it he smites the nations, & he rules it with his iron rod & he treadeth the winepress of his feirsness, & wrath of the Almighty God, & this is he who shakes the nations, & therefore they are angry, all is on a fire & on a flame, Mistery[,] Babilon, & mother of Harlots her abominations [Rev. 17:5] is come up into the remembrance of the Allmighty, & he is giving her double, & his everlasting word is sounding forth through the nations in this his day[.] the flying Angell is gone forth who hath the everlasting Gospell to preach unto them that dwell on the earth, unto every nation & kindred & tongue, & people calling for the fear of God & his worshipp, who hath made Heaven & earth, so dearly beloved[,] if there be any bowells of mercy toward the seed which lyes yet buried in the graves where death hath passed over, let bowells of pitty reach unto the seed which the everlasting love of God is too, which lyes in the open feild, which no eye pittieth but the Lord whose time is a time of Love, which now he is visiting in an acceptable time & sending forth his Messengers & Ministers, to call in the outcasts of Israell & the dispersed of Juda: & to gather in his Elect from the fower [four] winds of the Heavens [Matt. 24:31,] O dear hearts put your hands in this worke, & be not slake [slack], but up & be doing in the name & power of Jesus and in the fear of the Lord, offer freely to his service, that in the freeness & willingnesse of your spirits, the brethren may be refreshed, in & by your freness in your spirets unto the Lord, who beare the heat of the day, who is a Butt for all the powers of Hell & death to shut [shoot?] at, friends[,] the worke & service of the Lord requires of you in the freeness of your spirits, to gather, collect, & contribute in your severall meetings for providing, & maintaning of your brethren what [?] nescessaries, whom the Lord hath called out of Late, & is calling out into severall nations, As Holland, Barbados, Ireland, Scotland, Flanders, Denmarke & Germany, all these within this month & a great part of North country friends, so the Lord God open your hearts[.] the Apostle thought it necessary to exhort the brethren that they would goe before, & make up before hand their bounty; that it might be ready as a matter of bounty & not of covetousness, for this I say[,] he that soweth sparingly shall reap also sparingly, & he that soweth bountifully shall reap bountifully, for every man as he purposeth in his heart, so let him give, not grudgingly nor of necessity for the Lord loves a chearfull giver, read the 2. Coren: the 9 [2 Cor. 9:5–7.] so the Lord, God of power open your hearts by his eternall spirit, & enlighten your understandings, that you may know the Love, of God which passeth knowledge[,] that as you have received freely you may give, so God Almighty of Life, & power preserve you in his fear & obedience of his grace.

Your dear sister in the Life of truth

Margret Fell

That which you gather at your severall meetings
Let it be sent to George Tayler & Thomas Willand at Kendal, to be dispersed for the service of the truth.
Let this pass amongst friends in Lanckeshire[,] Westmerland & Cumberland Bishobrickshire & Yorkeshire

Caton MSS 1:82–84 n.d.; in Works, *pp. 97–99, 1656.*

62 TO JOHN HALL APRIL 16, 1657

"It is the enimie of thy Soule that tels thee
Thou must not goe to meetings except thou be moved."

A serious problem for some Quakers was discerning the boundary between following one's own internal spirit and listening to the wisdom of the group, and how to discern the difference between "empty forms" and those forms of worship that upheld the presence of God. Since Quakers rejected traditional church rituals and practices in order to be more attuned to obedience to the Light they were receiving, how could they preserve discipline and unity? It brought conflict to some Friends and the groups they were in during this period of development. The dilemna confronted George Fox and the Quakers many times in different ways.

John Hall had questioned the need to attend Meetings of silent worship if he was not "moved" to do so. It was an impractical position, and Margaret had no doubt that it was necessary to attend Meeting. She tells him that it is there "where thou might finde comfort & refreshment to thy soule; where the presence of the Lord is." She is convinced of the existence of evil, that it can lead him astray, but equally convinced that light will prevail. The word "light" appears more often than "darkness" in this and other letters. She quotes Jeremiah who wrote, "But fear thee not thou, O my servant Jacob, and be not dismayed, O Israel: for, behold, I will save thee from afar off" [Jer. 46:27].

Besse's Sufferings *lists several Quakers named John Hall who were fined or imprisoned at various times. This "John Hall who lives in Cheshire" may be one of these.*

Frend

Thou are turned out of the pure Light of christ which is the rocke onn which the church is built, and thy mind is turned unto the Imaginations[;] & this arery [airy] spirit leads thee under the power of darkness; where thou hast left thy pure guide & art as a blind man groping & stumbling & would find ease in making application of the Letter without thee[;] but hear [here] thou seekes the liveing amongst the dead [Luke 24:5]. This increaseth thy trouble & leads thee further in the darke; & hee that walkes in darkness knoweth not whither hee goeth[;] & thou that art in the power of darkness Lyes open to the temptation of the enimie, & hee leads thee captive at his will[.] it is the enimie of thy Soule that tels thee Thou must not goe to meetings except thou be moved; The Moveing of the Lord is in light & in the power of the Lord & not in the power of darkness; Soe while thou harkens to this[,] thou harkens to the enemie[,] who knowes where hee hath thee[,] soe long as thou yeelds to him in this; And the Moveing of the Lord[,] under the power of darkness[,] Thou shalt never know eternally[.] Thou shalt witness mee Theirfore in the fear of the Lord come down to the Light of Jesus which convinceth thee of sinne & evill[,] which showes thee the thoughts of thy heart & the outgoeings of Thy minde[,] which maketh thee change thy wayes[.] That which cals [calls] thy mind in[,] which chekes [checks] thee[,] & approves thee when thou turnes to the right hand or to the Left that is Light[.] And if Thou would harken and abid in this[,] it would stay thy mind and setle thee upon the rocke where Thou could not bee moved; and if Thou would keepe thy mind staid and dwell in the Light[,] hear [here] would the power of the Lord attend thee[,] which would raise the seed out of the grane [grain] and bringe it foorth of the house of bondage[,] from under the power of Pharah[,] which houlds the seed in captivitie [Jer. 46:27] soe hear [here] is Thy way[,] Joyning thy minde to the Light[,] being guided by the light[.] soe thou will come to have union with the Children of Light & will come to see thy enimie[,] which would not have thee to goe to their meetings[,] where thou might finde comfort & refreshment to thy soule; where the presence of the Lord is[.] soe beeware of that temptation for thou knows not, what the lord might manifest to thee, the wind bloweth where it listeth [John 3:8], the power of the lord is unlimited, soe waite in the light, & beleeve in the light, for Xt [Christ] Jesus is come A light into the world[,] that all men theron him might beeleeve, soe continue & abide in the light, & doe not forsake the Assembly of the saintes

from A Friend of thy soule
who desires the resurrection of the lord
Margrett Fell

Spence 3/52. Endorsed: "M F to john hall in Chesher [George Fox] 1657"; "M: F: Letters to particular Friends"; "This is to John Hall who lives in Cheshire given forth by M: Fell the 16th day of the 2d month 1657".

63 To William Caton May 10, 1657

"I thinke longe that I doe not heare from thee nor noe answer of my last letter; My love is deare unto thee[,] and the deare love of this Family is dearely Remembered unto Thee."

Will Caton (1636–1665) entered the household at Swarthmoor Hall when he was about fourteen years of age to study with son George Fell, who was two years younger than Caton. The following quotations are from Caton's Journal *as printed in* The Rise of Quakerism in Amsterdam 1655–1665.

After he arrived at Swarthmoor Hall he was soon "promoted to be a Companion night & day to the Judge's Son, and did eat as he did eat, and lodged as he lodged, and went to the same pleasure which he went unto, as to Fishing, Hunting, Shooting, etc . . . Forasmuch as Providence had cast me into such a Noble Family, where there were such sweet Children, . . . in much pleasure, ease, and fulness I lived with them as my heart could well desire" (Hull, p. 90).

Will went away to school with George Fell, and they returned to Swarthmoor Hall together. In June 1652 when Will was seventeen a momentous event occurred: "that faithful Messenger and Servant of the Most High (by Name George Fox) cast among us, who declared unto us the way of Life and Peace. And among the rest in that Family that believed his Report, I was one, who came finally to be affected with his Doctrin, tho at the first did as much admire at his Non conformity to our . . . Customs as Strangers at this day admire at our Nonconformity unto them, yet behold something in me did love him, and own his Testimony . . .

"And then I had not left the School, but did go along with Judge Fell's son . . . And in the process of time my Study became my burden . . . neither could I well give unto the Master [of the school] the trivial Complement of the Hat, for I was Convinced in my Conscience of the vanity of it. And my special Friend Margaret Fell (the Judge's wife) taking notice of my condition . . . caused me to stay at home to teach her Children, and to go along with her when she went abroad, and to write for her, etc., which was a happy time for me" (Hull, p. 92).

By the time he was eighteen Will frequently accompanied "dear George Fox, who as a tender-hearted Father . . . sought to nurture me up in all Wisdom, Faithfulness, and Righteousness . . . And on the other hand was I cherished, and encouraged in the way of Life, by my entirely beloved Friend Margaret Fell, who as a tender-hearted Nursing Mother cared for me, and was as tender of me, as if I had been one of her own Children" (Hull, p. 94).

By 1655 Will was traveling in the ministry himself, preaching, getting arrested, annoying some, and convincing others. His companion on some journeys was John Stubbs, an older, experienced Friend (Letter 51). Together they convinced Samuel Fisher (Letter 48) and many others. Will went to the continent, particularly to Holland, where he spent most of the rest of his short life. He learned Dutch, married a Dutch woman, and worked with the small Quaker community in Holland. He wrote many tracts in English and in Dutch.

Will returned to England numerous times, always visiting Swarthmoor Hall, even when it meant walking across England to get there (Hull, p. 102). On one visit he began editing and transcribing Friends' correspondence (Greaves, 1:129–130). His wife also visited Swarthmoor Hall.

At the time of this letter Will was still learning Dutch and using interpreters. Margaret is concerned about getting her books published and distributed. In a letter of June 1657 Will writes to her, "Of thine [the pamphlet] to the Jews there hath bene seven or eight score of them delivered to them at their synagouge, some to the Rabbyes and some to the Doctors, and I cannot understand that they have anything against it, but only they apprehend that the Authour doth judge that the Mesias is come already and they look for him yet to come" (Hull, p. 118).

Margaret mentions looking for a companion for William Ames who is about to return to Holland. The rapid expansion of Quakerism occurred because of the coordination of those Friends who went to various cities and countries, usually traveling in pairs. In the first years of the movement a significant amount of the planning was done at Swarthmoor Hall.

William Ames (?–1662) began a career in the army of Charles I, then became a marine soldier on Prince Rupert's ship, then joined the parliamentary army in Ireland. He was a Baptist but became a Quaker about 1655. He knew Dutch, and along with John Stubbs and Will Caton, was responsible for the founding of Quakerism in Holland and in Germany. He was a prolific writer in both English and Dutch (Greaves, 1:14–15).

Margaret expresses her understanding of Will's wishing to come to England, and it is her desire too. She was capable of warm affection for many men, women, and children; but her love for Will Caton was particularly strong.

Swarthmore 10th of the 3 month 1657

My deare Lambe[,] my deare love and life and bowels flowes freely unto Thee who art a true vessall fitted for the Masters use; And babe of the Immortall Seed & of the Royall Preest Hoode: and of the true Tabernacle[,] which the lord Hath piched [pitched] and not man [Heb. 8:2]; In thy owne portion & Inheritance[,] which is given unto Thee[,] dwell continualy[,] that a dayly renewing and an Increase of his goverment thou may feele and agrowing from glory to Glory, from one stature unto an other[,] unto the perfitt [perfect] man in Christ; The everlasting god[,] the father of our Lord Jesus Christ; bee with thee & carry thee & preserve thee and lead and guide thee In his Counsell And wisedome; It is long Since I heard from Thee[.] I have written to thee And to: J:S: [John Stubbs] 2 or 3 Month agoe Concerning severall particulars which thou menshoned [mentioned] in the last that I had from Thee, one thinge was conserning My Booke, what Landgue [language] it might be printed in, My answer was[:] I would have had it Translated into Hebrew and Dutch both[,] & if the Charges had beene greater[,] Wee should have borne most of it heare in England; I perceive by Will Ames that Thou was unsatisfied of Some Thing conserning the booke (but Hee could not tell wher in) at which I much wonder[;] for Jo: Stubes knew of the book before hee went out of England what was Intended conserning it; And How I would have had him gotten it printed And have taken Some of Them alonge with him; And that hee should cause the other Booke to bee translated[,] which was conserning the Law; And neglect the other which was Intitled a Salutation to the Seed of Israell; I Perceive Thou hath a desire to Come for England which I should bee glad of; & I have accquainted George [Fox]; And alsoe have Desired him to get some to goe alonge with William [Ames] for Holland[.] Soe when the Lord make way for thee & Thou see freedom in him; that in the Same Thou may returne in which thou went[.] Then will thy blessing and thy Peace bee[.] I would have thee to take care that these Bookes bee done and printed[,] if it cann bee done conveniently before thou come; I thinke longe that I doe not heare from thee nor noe answer of my last letter; My love is deare unto thee[,] and the deare love of this Family is dearely Remembered unto Thee; Soe the God of love and life bee with thee And Keepe Thee in his arme of love

Thy Deare Sister in the Life
Margret Fell

Spence 3/46. Also a brief section in Works, *pp. 194–195. Addressed: "For Will Caton at Amsterdam in Holland". Endorsed: "M F to W Caton [all but the W is by George Fox]"; "1657".*

64 TO FRANCIS HOWGILL AND THOMAS ROBERTSON JUNE 21, 1657

"Wee have heard of your Imprisonment, and of your reLeasing, the god of Infinet power preserve you, from the hands of unreasonable men for the seeds sake."

Francis Howgill and Thomas Robertson were among the "First Publishers of Truth" who devoted their adult lives to preaching, writing, and traveling to spread the gospel. (For Francis Howgill see Letters 7 and 32.)

Thomas Robertson (?–1695) was a Westmorland man and lived at Grayrigg, like Francis Howgill. He suffered imprisonments many times in his life (Besse, 1:55; 2:10; 2:22) and was prosecuted for not paying tithes (Besse, 2:8).

Margaret writes to them to encourage them in their work. She replies to something that Francis Howgill wrote by saying, "I shall say little to [that] at present." She was usually cautious in her remarks about personal matters and was presumably waiting until she could speak to him directly.

F:H: T:R: Deare bretheren

In the bowels of dearest Love doe I dearely salute you. And in that doe I write which is not soone angry, nor soone shaken, But in that, which beares all things, Indureth al things, and hopeth all things, which suffereth Long, which vaunteth not it selfe [1 Cor. 13:4], but in the one Accord; in the one spirit I am one with you, in my Fathers worke, & service, My soule & bowels reacheth unto you, I cannot forgett you, yee are Fresh before mee, the record of life, & the worke and servise that yee are in, my soule longs after, your publishing the glad tideings to the poore, Liberty to the Captive, that the prisoner might have his Liberty [Isa. 61:1], For which the Earnest expectation of the Creature waiteth, even for the manifestation of the sones [sons] of god [Rom. 8:19], which the opressor, & the keeper in captivity cannot Indure to heare of, oh my dearely beloved bretheren, my soule is even melted, to beehold the gloryous Liberty of the Children of god, And the miserable bondage of the Captivated seed, For which my soule travailes, and waites For the deliveranse of, Soe deare ones[,] as you have received freely, freely give, the Infinet fountaine of free Love is set open to you, that yee may freely call, every one that thirsteth[,] come and buy, wine, and milke[,] without money, You neede not bee ashamed of the gospell, of xt [Christ]. For it is the power of god unto salvation, unto every one that beleeveth, And you that are made partakers, of this free gospell of Jesus, and that you are made ministers of the word, of his power and reconsilliation, you are debters, both to the Greekes, and to the Barbarians, both to the wise, and to the unwise [Rom. 1:14–16], soe preach the gospell freely to every Creature, & soe you will bee free from the blood of all men, soe god almighty be your strength, wisedome, and Counseler, and cloth you with his armor of light;

F: H: I received A letter from thee, which I shall say litle to at present[,] onely [only] this I know, that noe man speakeing by the spirit of god calleth Jesus accused, wee have heard of your Imprisonment, and of your reLeasing, the god of Infinet power preserve you, from the hands of unreasonable men for the seeds sake; let us heare from you how it is with you, and how the worke of the lord prospers,

Your deare sister
M:F:

Swarthmore the 21 of the 4th month (1657)

Spence 3/48. Also in Works, *pp. 195–196 and* Webb, *p. 90. Addressed: "This is to Fran [the word Fran is crossed out] F: H: and T. Robertson given forth by M: F:". Endorsed: "M F to f hougell [George Fox] 1657".*

65 To Oliver Cromwell September 16, 1657

"Soe the god of power and life enlighten thy understanding That in his light thou mayest see which is the place of Justice . . . which will bee health And comfort to thy soule."

This short pastoral letter warns Oliver Cromwell to use his power for the benefit of the oppressed. Margaret prays for his understanding of justice and equity, which will also benefit his soul.

Now in the feare of the lord, as thou desires the good of thy soule, & thy eternall peace and as thou desires to Continue, and prosper in those things that thou Hast undertaken, Consider seriousely of these Things, for god is Just, And hee will not bee Mocked, and the cry of the oppression of the Innocent reacheth him, hee heares these cry, And knowes their sorrowes, hee onely is their Deliverer and pleader of there cause, and their Sufferings doth treasure wrath, against the day of Wrath, for the oppressors, and all the wickednesse of The wicked will come to an end, and the Just shall Bee established, And all outward pompe and glory Will come to an end, and all outward honhour & exaltation Must bee throwne in the dust, and the day is come That hee that rules in righteousnesse, and humbles Himselfe, must bee exalted[,] whos throwne [throne] Is established for ever and ever[;] and to him all earthly powers Shall bow, and all earthly crownes bee cast downe at His feete, and blessed and happy is hee that receives His testimony, hee cann set to his seale that god is true,

Soe the god of power and life enlighten thy understanding That in his light thou mayest see which is the place Of Justice, by which thou mayest see thy place and Calling, and what thou hast undertaken, soe in truth Justice And equity, thou mayst discharge it, which will bee health And comfort to thy soule

From A true Lover of those that executes
Justice, and true Judgement and rules
in righteousnesse, who desires the good
of thy soule.

M: F:

Swarthemore the 16th day of the 7th month
in the yeare of the worlds accounpt (1657)

Spence 3/92. Summary in Works, *pp. 16–17. Addressed: "To O.C. given forth by M:F:". Endorsed: "To O:C: given forth by M.F., 1657 written & compared".*

66 To William Caton and John Stubbs September 1657

"Oh my Deare Babes & lambes, sent forth of my heavenly Father, though yee be younge & tender,

> yet will he make your foot as the prancinge of horses to tread Downe, and trample Downe all his Enemyes."

This letter is a part of the continuing correspondence between Margaret Fell and Will Caton (Letter 63). According to Ross, "Caton, together with John Stubbs (Letter 51), sailed for Holland in September. Owing to delays, the two men were forced to come as far north as Sunderland to get passage, and while waiting there for a ship, Caton could not resist walking across England—a matter of over a hundred miles, over the Pennines—to see his friends at Swarthmoor again. 'Oh, the refreshmnent which we had at our meeting,' he wrote in his Journal . . . *After a short stay, Caton recrossed England, met Stubbs again, and the two men sailed for Holland" (p. 70). The lengthy address continues the story.*

Margaret expresses her enthusiasm for their mission and assures them of her love and unity with them, "Yee are presnt with mee, you in mee, and I in you[,] never to be separated." The biblical phrases vividly express her love for them. The strong emotion may also reflect Margaret's knowledge that she may not see them again. Traveling was dangerous in general, and carrying the Quaker message was dangerous in particular. In a few years, Caton would be dead; and by the 1670s many of the men and women who were the early ministers were dead, having been worn out through travel, imprisonment, and mistreatment.

My Deare Bretheren

Whoe are the Dearly beloved of my father, Elected before the foundation of the world was, and now are chosen & called for to be faithfull to the Lambe, who is now at warr, & Shall have the victory, in whose Battle yee are now engaged to fight under his Banner & to follow the Lambe where Ever he goes. oh my Deare ones who are the Dearly beloved of my Soule, unto you my life & strength reacheth[;] yea, yee are present with mee, you in mee, and I in you[,] never to be separated, Earth nor Sin, Death nor hell cannot Seperate, that which God hath joyned together, oh my Deare ones keepe neare unto mee, and there shall my soule be powered [poured] into your bosomes, and there shall yee receive Strength & power, life, & virtue, from the livinge Ocean, yea the Lord God of life is your Sword & buckler, your shield & speare & rocke of Defence, his word is your Sword, by which all shall fall before you, noe weapon Shall prosper in your Enimys hand. oh my Deare Babes & lambes, sent forth of my heavenly Father, though yee be younge & tender, yet will he make your foot as the prancinge of horses to tread Downe, and trample Downe all his Enemyes, oh my Deare ones[,] in the Dreadfull power & Authority of the livinge God where the wine presse of the wrath of God is troden alone without the Citty [Rev. 14:19–20], even thither are yee going from Edom with your garments Dyed read [red] [Isa. 63:1], & there doe you witnesse the beloved who is white & ready, the cheifest amonge ten thousand [Song 5:10]: oh my Deare ones[,] here yee come to be washed & changed in the blood of the Lambe; yea cast all Crownes at his feet and be faithfull unto the Death that the Crowne Imortall yee may wittnesse[.] The breathings of my Soule into the Everlasting ocean is for you which is Streaming & Shedding abroad in this day of grace & glory. The infinite everlastinge God of life & power Strength & wisdome glory & riches be with you and carry you in his Arme of power, & bosome of love to his Everlasting prayse & glory for Evermore. Let me heare from you as you can conveniently.

I have rece[ived] one of yours
Your Deare Sister in the Immortall
M: F:

Swarthmore MSS v. 8. Addressed: "Take care that this bee conveyed to John Stubbs or William Caton at Sunderland or NewCastle or if they have taken shippinge with the first messenger let this be sent to Holland". Endorsed: "MF to Wilan Caton [George Fox] 1657".

67 To Daniel Davis 1657?

"Let the wise in hart Judge if thou be not drounke with Envy Against the trouth of god, and soe thy Efinity [affinity] is with the Devell who art in the power of darknes."

This paper is a lengthy screed against Daniel Davis, who had charged Quakers with being Roman Catholics under the domination of the pope. Margaret repeats his charges and answers each one, using biblical language and imagery, particularly from the Book of Revelation. The paper is a sample of a seventeenth-century technique of argument, not necessarily persuasive today.

The charge of "Popery" in the seventeenth century was akin to that of "Communist" in the 1950s and 1960s in the United States. It had no basis in fact, but it had potentially lethal consequences. The Quakers therefore took particular care to refute such charges.

The charges that Davis made are:

1. The pope declares himself infallible, and so do the Quakers.

2. The pope declares himself to be Christ, and so do the Quakers.

3. The pope declares himself to be spotless, sinless, and perfect, and so do the Quakers.

4. The pope wants to be lord and master over all men's faith, and so do the Quakers.

5. The pope condemns all who do not have the mark of the beast on their foreheads, and so do the Quakers.

6. The pope does not reverence any power under heaven, and neither do the Quakers.

7. The pope sends his priests throughout the world to convert to his religion, and so do the Quakers.

The paper is incomplete and partially illegible. I have been unable to transcribe the last page. Margaret has included biblical citations for many of her statements, some of them within the text and some in the margins. The latter are obscured by tape.

Daniell Davis: thou hast oppened thy mouth as blasphemy against the lambe & his folowers: which is a trew marke of the Beast. which is in thy forhead And the wine of the wrath of god shall thou drinke which is pouered [poured] out without mixteuer into the copp of his indignation, Revelations 14:10: and thou that art in the worship of the beast and his image, thy great swelling words, cannot move them that are Roted [rooted] & grounded, upon the cheefe cornerstone xt [Christ] Jesus[,] The Light[,] Rock and foundation on which all the Prophetts & appostels were bult [built.] the Light maks thee manifest where thou art & where thy foundation is Bult upon the sand[.] the storme and the tempest is coming upon thee & thou cannot stand[.] thy house will fall and great will be the fall of it[.] its not thy envy against the trouth of god, and thy Ery [airy] immagenations that cann tuch [touch] the trouth, the Trouth of god is clear and proven[,] and its not thy filth cast upon it that can defiell it[.] in this thou doth but uter [utter] forth thy owne shame: glowrying in thy owne destruction For that which that thou contends against shall Indeuer [endure] forever, and thou & all thy pouer [power] Doth he tread under his feet[;] for they shall have noe Rest day nor night who worship the beast & his Image & who

Receves the marke of his name; and in these [followinge?] ________ thou hast manifested thy Ignorance of god & the scripttuers[.] Thy Envy is soe great to those thou cauls Quakers that thou hast [found?] out thy owne shame and set the Pope [nearer?] the trouth then thou art thyselfe[.] surly thy owne Jeneration [generation] will be asshamed of thee, and for thy particelers [particulars] we shall answer them by scripteuer, and then let the wise in hart Judge if thou be not drounke with Envy Against the trouth of god, and soe thy Efinity [affinity] is with the Devell who art in the power of darknes:

1. And Ferst thou saith the Pop[e] declares himselfe that hee is infalaubell; soe doth the Quakers

Answere; Heare [here] in the very first of thy particolers thou art a lyer: for if the Pope decla[res] him selfe to be infalabell the Quakers doe not soe; I charg thee to prove where Ever thou did here [hear] a Quaker say that himselfe was infalabell, ether prove this or confes thyselfe to be a lier[,] for this the Quakers doe deny. And the pope (and his and thy Lying spirit wee doe deny) who cannot speake trouth because yee knowe it not[,] and thou that art not guided by the Etarnall Infalabell spirit which Judges and condemnes selfe, thou art guided by a lying spirit which is one with the pop[e.] And by the Etarnall spirit which finds and leads those whom thou calls Quakers art thy spirit & the pope spirit Judged to be a lying spirit which is of the divell[.] And in this thou hast uttered forth thy Poason [poison] and Enmety against the spirit of god and hath clearly manifested thyselfe to have none of his spirit[;] for the spirit of god is an Itarnell [eternal] Infalibell spirit, & not a falibell Lying spirit, such as thine and the Pops [pope's], [in margin: John 13:] the Etarnall spirit whose Judgment shall stand condems thee and the pop[e] together who hath shut thyselfe out from the spirit of truth And the Record of god thou knowest not, who knowest not his spirit Jn 14:17, hereby knowe that wee dwell in him and hee in us becaues hee hath given of his spirit & this[,] thou enemy of god[,] thou knowes not, wee are of god. hee that knoweth god hereth us, hee that is not of god hereth not us, hereby know wee the spirit of truth & the spirit of Errer ferst of Johne 4:6: [1 John 4:6] here thou may say the appostle had Efinity [affinity] with the pope Because hee had the spirit of god: which is Etarnell and Infalibell.

2. Thou saith the Pope declares him selfe to be xt and soe doth the Quakers.

Answer Heare thou hast manifested thyselfe to be ________ & that anti-christ indeed _____ ______ ________with the pope who art abselutely against xt Jesus, his comming _____ _____ ________ manifestation and Reagening [reigning] in his saints. thou Enemy of christ dost thou profes christ and would not have him to Reagne. thou must be Brought before him and slaine & bound and cast in to uter darkness (This is thy porshon;) thou art the Antichrist indeed, and one of the many decevers [deceivers] that art entered into the world, who confess not that Jesus xt is com in the flesh. This is A decever and an antichrist 2 John:7: and Every spirit that confesses not that Jesus Christ is com in the flesh is not of god, and this is the spirit of antechrist John ______ and here thou art who saith to confess christ is one with the pope[.] do not say they ar of Christ but they confess christ come in the flesh _____ ____ ______

3ly [thirdly] thou saith the Pope declares him selfe to be spotles sinneless perfect; soe doth the Quakers

answer: Heare thou hast manifested thy selfe to stand more for the Devels Kingd[om] of sinne then the Pope; the appostell saith he that sinns is of the Divell; in thyne thou saith christ Jesus hath affinity with the Pop[e]; who saith be yee perfecte as your hevenly Father is Parfecte Mathew:5:48: and the appostell saith & who soe keepeth his word in him varily is the Love of god perfected[.] hereby know that wee are in him John:1:2:5: [1 John 2:5] but this thou knoweth not who art not in him, but art in thy sinne and in thy filth, hee that saith hee abideth in him ought to walke even as hee walked, and the Appostell spoke wisdom amonst them that were perfect, and he bad them bee perfectt[,] be of good comphort, 2 Cor.13:11: be of one mind, live in peace, but this was the appostels Bretheren[.] this was not such as thee, who pleads for the devils kingdom of sinn[.] thou art contrary to that doctren of the appostels; ther desier [desire] was that they might be perfect & every man perfect in christ Jesus. & that they might stand perfect and compleat [Col. 4:12]; and that They might perfect that which was lacking in there faith, for when christ which is perfect is com then that which is imperfect shall bee don away (first Cor:15:10) [?] and the appostel James saith, let patience have his perfect worke that yee may bee perfect and wanting nothing [James 1:4] & hee saith that every good and perfict gift is from above: & that the law of god is perfict, and the appostels said[,] let us goe unto perfection and this wee wish[,] even your perfection [2 Cor. 13:9]. Let ous clons [cleanse] ourselves from all filthines of the Flesh & of the spirit perfict in holynes in the feare of the lord [2 Cor. 7:1], and the gifts we are given for the perfictting of the saints, for the worke of the ministry, but these gifts thou enemy of all Righteousnes who art pleading for sinne art Ignorant of, thou hast shut thy selfe out from Receiving any gift from god. thou hast set thy selfe behind the Pope, soe there thou may stand, for if the pope declare himselfe to be sinneless, and spotles as thou saith; hee is a greater enemy to sinne then thou[;] for ______ _____ displeased that all are not sinners, and thou that sinns is of the Divell[.] soe there thou art

4ly thou saith The Poape would be Lord and Master over all mens fiath [faith] soe would the Q[uakers]

Anser: The poape may be lord and Master over thy faith for thou art A Reprobeat as consarning the faith; for thy faith art kaines [Cain's] who art yet in thy sinns, & if christ be not Resen [risen], then is our preaching vaine and your faith is alsoe vaine, first Cor:15:14: for if the dead Rise not then is not christ Resed [raised] and if christ be not resed youre faith is vaine[.] yee are yett in your sinns [1 Cor. 15:16–17] here thou art, if thou be not Blind thou may reed thy faith here and here thou who art in this faith[.] the Pop[e] is thy lord and Mr [master] who houlds thy faith with Respect of persons, this is none of the saints faith, thou & the Pop[e] is both shut out from that faith which is houlden in a pouer [pure] conscience[.] this is a mistery to thee, the faith that works by love thou knows not, for faith where it is if it be as a graine of mostard [mustard] seed Removes the mountane [Matt. 17:20], but thy mountans and sinns is standing, soe never mention the saints Faith for there [their] faith purifyes the harte: Now the end of the commandement is Charity out of a peuer [pure] hart and of a good conscience, and of faith unfained, ferst of Tim:1:5: [1 Tim. 1:5] this is not thy Faith, this is the saints faith, & over this faith the Pope nor thou nor the Divell himselfe shall never Lord over, for by this faith the Just lives; & the harts is purified by this faith, and this gives the victory over the world [1 John 5:4] & of this Faith was the appostell mad [made] a minnister and was sent unto the gentiles to oppen the eyes, & to tern [turn] them from the Darknes to the light and from the power of satten [Satan] unto god which thou art yet in and under, and soe under the poopes dominyone.

5ly thou saith the pope questions all & condemnes all for all Corsed [cursed] heretiques [heretics,] vipers, & Devils which have not his marke in ther forheads[.] soe doth the Quakers.

anser/ the Pope need not Condemne thee for thou art one of his linnes [lineage?] and hath his imag [image] and his marke in thy forhead, and the Qu: [Quakers] condemne the Pope and thee, and your way is the broade way, which leadeth to distruction, and the streat [straight] and narrow way which Leadeth unto life yee know not: for yee are all gone out of this way, yee are all corropt[,] yee are all filthy[.] thers none that doth good[,] noe not one.

I am com a light into the world that whosoeever beleeveth on mee shall not abide in darnes [darkness], saith christ Jesus who is the way, the truth and the life [John 14:6], and thou that walks not in the light are in the Pop[e]s way, and thou that art in thy sinnes[,] thy way is not in the light, and the light condemnes thee and thy way, and the light condemnes the Pope and his way, and this is the way the Quakers walks in, the light xt Jesus[,] The one way[,] the one truth and the one life, and thers none that coms to the father but by him, nor noe other way nor [none] under heven, by which any shallbe saved, Thou that art not turned from the darkness to the light art ought [out] of this way, and the light of Jesus which is this way, condemns thee and the Pope, & all that is out of this Way, for this is the way of holines where the uncleane cannot pas [pass] & this is the Condemnation of the whole world that light is com and men love darnes [darkness], Rather then Light Becase [because] there deeds as evell [John 3:19], & there thou art found./

6ly thou saith the Pope will not Reverrence any pouer under heaven[,] like wise the Quakers will not/

answer: the Quaker is subject to the higher power; which is ordered of god, the gospell which is the power of god unto salvation: for god who commanded the light too shine out of darkness, hath shined in oure harts, and hath given ous the light of the knolige [knowledge]; of the glory of god in the face of Jesus 2Cor 4:6, and this is the power which wee reverence, and To him all power in heven and Earth is committed & this is hee that binds & cleans the Popes power and thy power; and all the power of darknes[.] this power Cleans the draggen[,] the ould serpent which is caled [called] the Divell, & in this power of Jesus xt wee are mor then quonkerers [conquerors], and tryomphs over all the powers of hell

7ly thou saith the Pope sends up and downe the world his preists and friers to Convart to his Religion/. soe doth the Quakers. send up and downe to convart to there Religions.

answer the Pope neede not send thee, for thou art already in the world deceving the nations By thy sorserys [sorceries]. But the lord god is Resen in his power for the gathering of the Nations, & the mountaine of the lords house is to be astablished in the tope [top] of mountains, and all Nations shall flow unto it, and hee is Resen whoe shalt Reuell [rule] the Nations with his Rode [rod] of Irone; which shall breake to peeces, all his enemis [enemies], and hath taken to him his great power and doth Reagne [Rev. 2:26–27]: and therfor The Nations is angery, & thy wrath is com, and the tyme of the dead that they Should be Judged, & that thou shoulds Give Reward unto thy servants the profets, and to the saints, and them that feare thy name[,] smale and great, and shoulds Destroy them that destroy the earth; this is that that raseth [raiseth] thee to Rage; & many more of the Marchants of Babylone, which hath made the Nations dronk with the Cupe of your abomination, But the voyce cryeth [now?] Com out of her my people[,] that yee be not partacare [partaker] of ther sinns, and that yee Receve not of her plags [plagues,] for her sinns have Reached unto heaven, God hath remembered her InIquities; _____ ________ her Marchants ________ Be Rewarded dobbell [double]; as you have filled unto her; the Copp of fornication, soe much torment, and sorro shall you Receve; according to your works in the Copp which shee hath filled fill [sic] her dobbell: Revelations 18: [Rev. 18:3–7] there you may Reed the fall of thy sitty [city], which thou art a marchant of; whose foundati[on] now shaks [shakes;] its the sharpe edged sword which proseeds out of the lams [lambs] mouth with which hee smits the nations, which torments thee [and] thousands more, in this day of hi[s] power, for power it Receved from above, & the Commition is gone forth to goe Teach all Nations, and the desier of all Nations is Com[,] glory And prayses for Ever, the gospell must be published among all nations, & this Torments thee, and this is but the begining of sorows, & the scripteure is fulfilled, ye shall deliver you up to be afflickted, & shall kill you, and yee shall be heated [hated] of all Nations for my nams sake; & then many shall bee offended And shall Betray one another and hate one another, if thou were not blynde thou might see this fullfilled, yet the gospell of the kingdom shall be preached in all the world, for a witnes, then shall the End Com Mathew:24:14: [Another page with queries 8–10 is mostly illegible. The paper is incomplete, ending in the middle of a sentence.]

Spence 3/163–164.

68 To Gerrard Roberts October 21, 1657

"There is a booke which I sent to J: Stubbs . . .
let it Com forth Speedely and Bee Sent Abroade,
before my Husband Com up to London, lest hee light
of it and prevent the Sarvice of it."

Gerrard Roberts (ca. 1621–1703) was a wine-cooper living at the Sign of the Fleur-de-Lys in London, and his home was a Meeting place for Quakers (CJ, 1:434). He was a successful merchant and assisted Friends in many business matters. At the time of Margaret's letter they were not personally acquainted, but they became lifelong friends. He attended Margaret's wedding to George Fox in 1669 (Fox.Short, p. 337).

Her letter gives an indication of the role that Roberts played in transmitting information among widely dispersed Friends. She asks him to convey letters to Will Caton (Letter 63) and John Stubbs (Letter 51) as he had done previously. She asks him to urge Thomas Simmonds, the printer (Letter 51), to print and distribute copies of a book, before her husband (Letter 5) "Com up to London." Kunze writes, "The particular book of October 1657 was not published at this time, which suggests Judge Fell may have stopped its publication" (p. 35).

Margaret also asks Roberts to question a servant in Oliver Cromwell's household about whether Cromwell received a letter that was to be delivered to him. She then in turn passes on information to Roberts about George Fox's whereabouts in Scotland and what Friends are doing there.

Swarthmoore the 21st of the 8th month, (57)
G:R:

Deere Brother; my deere unfained love is to thee, and tho I never saw thy face; yeet thy Spirit I know; and feell, and there Doe I Desire to be red [read] and knowne, where noe onclene Can come, I Have receved som letters this week, from William Caton and John Stubbs; which Requirs an answer Speedely, Soe I desier thee to take Care that theis bee safly Convaied to them. I wret to them In the 6th month, which was Sent up to thee, John Stobbs did Receeve His[,] but W:C: had unRecved his In the 11th of the 7th month[,] & he were of Concernement; I desire thee to Inquire after them, There is a booke which I sent to J: Stubbs, to be putt in the priss [press]; I desire thee ask Thomas Simmonds of it; & let it Com forth Speedely and Bee Sent Abrode, before my Husband Com up to London, lest hee light of it and prevent the Sarvice of it; I would Have a Quantety of them Sent into

Holland and to John Stubbs and Will: Caton to dispers amongst they [the] Jues [Jews] there, And Likewis Sum to the Barbadus [Barbados] to be given to they Jues Theire, as Shortly as you can convaniently, and the rest may goe throrow the Nation, amongst Freinds. Likwise there was a note which was to be given to Olliver Cromwell, I would know whether it was delivered or noe, That Friend that is the Sarveant in the Hous its like may tell, Soe knowing thy faithfulnes In the Truthe, I was free to ly [lay] these things upon thee; for Passages her [here] is little, only this day Here is one Com out of Scotland from G:F: [George Fox] which Hath been with him Ever Sence hee went in, hee Saith, the Truth is well sounded thorow that nation, In So much that they are at a ____ ________ Surpriseth them, the Truth hath Bene Preached thorow their Sitys [cities], Towns, Markets, Steeplehowses, Hallhowses, its Soe Sounded in there Eares that they are goeIng [going] about to beat it out of theire Nation, But it hath overgon them, they all wais [always] Com behind, the Day before hee cam from G:F: there cam a Sommance [summons] for G:F: to appere before the privy Councell at Edenbrough, which hee was Redy to doe, but the Issu is not yet knowne; persecution is there plot[.] But the lord is the pleader of the Caues of his Innosent; Soe with my Deare love Remembred to all faithfull Freinds.

M: Fell

Spence 3/49. Addressed: "This for Gerrard Robberts at the Signe of the Flour Deluse [fleur-de-lys] of Thomas [Apostles] [George Fox]". Endorsed; "M.F. To G.Robards [George Fox]"; "1657"; "A letter in which M.F. fears her husband J[udge] Fell shd [should] hear of her writing" [written in pencil in a modern hand, at the bottom of the letter].

69 To John Wilkinson 1657

"Let the light of Christ in thy Conscience Examine thee, and see that thou be taught thy selfe, before thou teach others."

John Wilkinson (?–1675) was pastor of a church at Brigham in Cumberland. George Fox writes "I was moved to . . . appoint a meetinge att one Jo: Wilkinsons steeplehouse whoe had three parishes under him: & was a preist in great repute and esteeme" (CJ,

1:109). This event occurred in 1653, and in the next few years frequent visits and preaching by Fox and other Quaker ministers caused Wilkinson's congregations to diminish and to migrate to the Friends. By 1657 he had only a few followers left and was then himself finally convinced by Fox, who writes that Wilkinson "became an able minister & freely preacht the gospell & . . . hee continued many yeares in the free ministry & preachinge of the gospell & dyed in the truth" (CJ, 1:292).

In this letter Margaret acknowledges that Wilkinson has begun to see the error of his previous beliefs. She urges him to be "obedient to the light" and examine his own actions. Only then will he be capable of teaching others, so that he will no longer be betraying "poore people, and deceiv[ing] their soules."

Another John Wilkinson (?–1683), of Westmorland, was part of the Separatist movement with John Story in the 1670s (CJ, 1:417).

To thee John Wilkinson am I mooved of the Lord to Speake to the Light of Christ Jesus in thy Conscience, which convinced thee of the evill of thy Actions[,] which formerly thou wast acted in. The same light (if thou turne thy mind to it) will show thee thy Deceipt that lodgeth in thy heart[,] which Deceipt thou does not yet see, thy mind being turned from the light, by which the lord god teacheth his people, All the Children of the lord is taught of the lord, who is the Father of light, & in whom is no darknesse at all. which light shines in the Consciences of men (for in him is life[,] & this life is the light of men) and this light shines in Darknes, but the Darknes Comprehends it not [John 1:5]. But this light makes manifest Darknes, and beares witnesse against the deeds of darknes. Therefore a warninge from the lord god to thee (who is a consuminge fire to the wicked) that thou turne thy mind to the light, which shewes thee thy evill deeds, and the filthy Deceipt, which thou lives in who betrayes poore people, and deceives their soules and causes them to looke after thee for teachinge, when thou thyselfe is not yet taught; in the first principle of the orackles of God [Heb. 5:12] Eternally thou shalt witnesse mee; that this is truth, that I Speake[;] for thou, that is not obeydient to the light; but actes contrary to the light: thou art an enemie of god, and of his truth, and the light is thy Condemnation. And never any people shall come to know the livinge God by following of thee (where thou art) And this both thou, & they shall Eternally witnesse. Therefore give over Deceivinge, & betrayinge of the soules of the poore people. I warne thee, and charge thee as thou will answeare it in the presence of the livinge God, before whom thou must give an accot. [account,] who rendders to every one accordinge to their deeds: lest the blood of their soules be required of thee; and thou be found guilty of keeping their soules in Death, & in bondage, and in captivity, in this day of the lords free grace[,] which hath appred [appeared] to all men: and which teacheth all that is taught of god to deny all ungodlynes and worldly lusts, by this free grace is he callinge in this his day; and turning from the Darknes to the light: and from the power of Sathan unto God And thou[,] blind watchman[,] keepes them from the measure of grace reced [received] from the livinge god[,] which measure of grace would lead them & guide them up to the livinge God. And heare [here] thou art found to be a murtherer & a betrayer of the Innocent: for which the lord god will plead with thee[,] who can by noe meanes cleare the guilty, but renders unto every one accordinge to their deeds. Therefore as thou loves thy soule, & thy Eternall peace; let the light of Christ in thy Conscience Examine thee, and see that thou be taught thy selfe, before thou teach others, least both they and thou goe into the pitt together. And soe I have cleared my Conscience, in obeydience to the lord[,] in givinge thee a warning, that soe thou may repent & turne to the lord while thou hast tyme[,] least it be to [too] late, & thou seeke thy birth Right with teares (as Esau did [Gen. 27:34]) and cannot have it. and this thou shall Eternally witnesse to be love to thy soule, & for thy Eternall good. From one who desires the deliverance of the seed & the bring[ing] backe of the Captivity from under the mouthes of the destroyers

M: F:

Spence 3/50. Endorsed: "M F to j wilkeson [George Fox] of Cumberland 1657".

70 To Friends Concerning the Kendal Fund 1657

"All these things being Considered[,] you may all in the Etternall light see it Convenient, Just, & Equall, that their be some generall helpe made for them."

This is one of Margaret's fundraising letters. Four or five Friends were going to "New: England, a place soe farr Remote." Each passage would cost £5, which is the equivalent of $500. She points out that Friends in London have already paid for others, and

so it is only "Convenient, Just, & Equall" that those in the North should help to support those who are willing to risk their lives. The money is to be sent to Thomas Willan of Kendal.

It is a short letter intended to be read at Meetings in Westmorland, Cumberland, and Lancashire. The phrasing is felicitous, and it was successful in its goal.

Friends

It is ordered by the providence of the Lord, & by his power, to move in the hearts of some Friends that are poore in the outward to goe for New: England, A place soe farr Remote as that their passage will come to A great sume of money, they being 4:or 5: or more, which will cost when they come at London for their passage in the shipp. 5£: A peice [piece], And the Friends at London has paid for the passage of many, & severall, and some who have gone out of the north, they have paid for, which they thought something hard; All these things being Considered[,] you may all in the Etternall light see it Convenient, Just, & Equall, that their be some generall helpe made for them, heare Amongst Friends in the North, what as it pleases the Lord to open their hearts, to doe for them, by way of Contribution to their Necessities & the present occation, who is willing to offer up their bodies, & their lives, for the service, & will of the Lord, and to Answer his Motion in their hearts, without which they cannot have peace with God, nor to have peace to follow their lawfull Callings, & Imployments heare [here], who has beene taken of their callings, with dread & feare, of the Lord, therron the weight of this service, & soe Friends who is sensible of the Motion of the Lord, & of his worke & service, & of obedience of his will, and alsoe knowes the reward of disobedience & is not Ignorant of these things; And soe the God of power and Life Inlarge your hearts Toward God, his worke & service.

M.F.

What you doe Contribute send it with all speed to Tho: Willan in Kendal; The Friends that goes are of Bootle Meeting, & one from Hawshead [Hawkshead] Meeting; For Friends in Cumberland, Westmorland and the upper part of Lancashire to be read in their Meetings.

Spence 3/10. Endorsed: "M. F. To Frends [George Fox]"; "1657".

71 To Brethren and Sisters 1657

"This is Narrow and deepe to descarne [discern] betwext him that Sheweth himself of god, and is not, and him that is the trew Image."

In a general pastoral letter Margaret reminds Friends of their rich "Herritage" and their "unity of the Spirite and Bond of pease." She is concerned that the gospel be given to the poor and the oppressed. Quakers were working for radical change, and she speaks of the quickening spirit in the land and then makes the transition to Friends being "Quickened out of the Sleepe & death of Corruption." She discusses the difficulty of discerning between a good and an evil spirit, quoting some of the Apostle Paul's words, and the necessity to appreciate each person's gifts.

The version of this letter in the Works *is basically the same though it deletes some lines that refer to Quaker ministers, "Servants of the Lord," who had evidently not been well received.*

Deere Bretheren & Sisters, which be gathered in the Light of Christ Jesus, the Fountaine of all lite & life, From whence Light coms, from whence Life coms, from whence power Coms, which redeems Oute of Nations, out of kindreds, Peoples and Tongues, to be kings and Preests unto god, and to Reagne with him upon the Earth [Rev. 5:10]. This is the Herritage of the Saints, who Dwels in the Light, that Leads them into the Life, and fountaine from whence it coms. Here is the unity of the Spirite and Bond of pease [Eph. 4:3] which never can be broken, here the puer [pure] languidge, & the worship of the Lord is, with one hart and one Concenet [consent] [Zeph. 3:9], and the one Soule, where there is noe Devition, but the puer path of Life is knowne[,] the way of holyness, whence the uncleane Cannot pass [Isa. 35:8], whence the presence of the lord is which is fulness of Joy, and pleaseurs for Ever more, Now that Every one may reed his Name heare, in the unchaingable Life (is this wreten,) that the puer in all may haive [have] its Liberty, and That the poore may Receive the Gospell which is glad tydings of great Joy to the oppressed, to the weary and heavyloaden, which grons under the Bondage of Corruption [Rom. 8:21], and Crys for deliverance, the Crye whereof is entered Into the Eares of the Lord of the Sabbath[;] and hee hath determened in the Thoughts of his harte, that the deliverer Shall Come from Sion, and the Captivity of his people will hee bringe Bake [back] and The Salvation will Come unto Israell,

Soe that Jacobe Shall Rejoyce and Israell Shall be gladd [Ps. 14:7], Glory everlasting glory, be unto his everlasting Arme for ever; by which he gits himselfe a nam [name] and a victory, Even to the Astonishment of the Heathen, and to the Confounding of his ennemys, And to the Recovering, raisinge and quickning of his owne, which bears witness and testemony for him who hath Longe bene Slaine, in the Streets of Thy greate City, and hee a god unknowne, who hath made Darkness his pavillion [Ps. 18:11] Thike waters have bene Round aboute him But now is hee resen in his bright Shining Light, which Shineth in the Conscience; and hee hath comanded it to Shine, Theron the Darkness and hath Shined in the harte, who gives the Light of the Knowledge of the glory of god in the face of Jesus Xt: [Christ] his express Immage; And Now unto Theme [them] who hath Longe Satue [sat] in darkness and under the Saddow [shadow] of death, even unto them hath this Light Shined, who were Sume Tymes [sometimes] Darkness but now are the Lyght in the Lord, who weare [were] dead in Trispasses and Sins; Even them hath hee Quickened togethere with Christ, glory and praysess be unto him for ever, Now Deere Friends, in This Quickning Spirit, where with you are Quickned out of the Sleepe & death of Corruption, where xt [Christ] hath given you Light, walke in him, Larne [learn] of him who is Lowly, who is meeke, and be Swift to heare, Slow to Speake, and Slow to wrath [James 1:19], and keep downe and bake [back] that part which Receivess a prjewdess [prejudice], Search Narrowly, and beware that you Receive it not from a wrong Spirit, for that will wrong the Innosent, The Simplisity both in yourselvess & others, its hard to know the Spirituall wickedness in high placess; & it is the Spirituall Weapon, of the living god That Cann wrastle [wrestle] with the Prensepallitys [principalities] and poweres of the spirituall wikedness, And it is the brightness of his comeing and Spirit of his Mouth that Cann revill [reveal] the man of Sinn, the Sonn of perdition, that siteth in the Temple of god, Exalted, above all that is Called god, Showing himselfe as god, This is Narrow and deepe to descarne [discern] betwext him that Sheweth himself of god, and is not, and him that is the trew Image indeed, Deere Friends [,] This I write unto you in tender and deere Love to the sed [seed] of god in you all for which my Soule Travals [travails], & knowing and being Acquainted with the danger of this Spirit which measures it selfe by its selfe [,] which the Apostle said was not wise; for Such will boste [boast] of things with out there measure; and will boste of other mens Lyns [lines] [2 Cor. 10:15–16], Now that you may know and feele, the life and the power of Every spirit, knowing the puer Light in your selves, you will com to Saver [savour] the Life in others and that that savors of the Deth, will be deth to the Life, In the feare of the Lord god beware of Strangling the puer berth [birth] of god In you, and of wronging the puer Innocent seed in you, which god is Coming to plead the Cause of Xt with all Flesh in This his day, & beware that you joyn [join] not with gods Enemy nether in your selfes nor others; but Joyn with gods puer witness and testemony, & there will be your pease & here you will know him who is the Life and the Reserection, & hee that beleevs on him tho hee were dedd yett Should hee live [John 11:25], and there is noe other name under heaven by which any Shall be saved, then By that name which is beter then every Name; to which every knee shall Bow and every Tonge confess [Rom. 14:11], but therss [there is] none that knows this Name but hee that hath it, the whit [white] stone [Rev. 2:17] Reed [read] & understand; You have laid Burthens of Sume [some] of the Servants of the Lord which hath com among you, being moved of the Lord, & for the good of your Souls, have thought there [their] Lives not to [too] deere unto them whom god hath Justifyed in soe doeing for Ever, and will Seall to there [their] testemony, which Sum of you hath Sleighted[;] but Lord[,] that it be not Laid to your Charge.

From a trew freind of the Seed of god
for all Nations who knows the weight and
burthen that it lise [lies] under, and
who waits for the freedom and deliverance of it.

Spence 3/11–12. Also in Works, *pp. 192–194. Endorsed: "mf to frends [George Fox]"; "1657".*

72 To John Moore 1657

"While thou hath the light[,]
beeleeve in the light, that thou may bee
A Child of light, and here will bee thy peace."

The recipient of this short pastoral letter is apparently John Moore, though the name has been written and crossed out in two places but allowed to remain in the address. John Moore was a common name. The most likely candidate is the John Moore of Eldroth in northwest York. He traveled with George Fox in 1663; set aside a portion of his land as a Quaker burial ground in 1662 (Boulton, pp. 35–36); in 1669 Sarah and Susannah Fell met George Fox at Eldroth (Nickalls, p. 534). The postscript implies an acquaintainship with the family.

John Moore

In the name and power, of our lord Jesus Christ, have faith in god, And stand up in the light, And Judge out the enemy of the soule, which would draw thee downe into the death[,] to under the power of darkenesse, where thou knowes not wither thou goes. But dwell in the light, in the feare of the lord, there is noe cause of stumbleing, the Cause of stumbleing is Acted out of the light, soe as thou loves thy soule, come into the light, and lett the light Judge out all Actions Acted out of the light[,] which causes stumbleing, And lett the light search in thee, and try that which is pure as Refinners fire [Mal. 3:2], A swift wittnesse Against the forserer [forswearer] and Adulterer, which comes neare in Judgement, soe here dwell & live in the pure Judgement which Judgeth downe, and Casteth out the uncleane, and Lend not thy eare to the temptations but Judge them out with the light, and dwell in the pure light that showes them in the pure beeleefe [belief], while thou hath the light[,] beeleeve in the light, that thou may bee A Child of light, and here will bee thy peace, Faith as A graine of Musterdseed will remove the mountain [Matt. 17:20] the Eternall god bee thy strength, and uphold thee, by the word of his power, and guide thy feete from falling,

Thy Friend in the lord,

M:F:

Lett my deare love bee remembered to thy wife and family,

Spence 3/51. Endorsed: "M: F to jhon more [George Fox] 1657" (jhon more is crossed out and changed to "a friend" and the date may be 1658). Addressed: "This is to John Moore given forth by M. F."

73 To Colonel William Osburne 1657

"And soe my dear hart, low, low, to thy owne measure keepe, that the pure plant may arise, where the unity is, which my heavenly Father planteth."

Lieutenant-Colonel William Osburne's home was the first meeting place, in 1653, of Friends in Edinburgh (CJ, 1:451). Colonel Osburne became a "zealous minister," and he guided George Fox through Scotland in 1657. In November 1660 he was committed to prison in the Edinburgh Tolbooth (Greaves, Deliver, *p. 46).*

Margaret writes encouragingly. Twice she indicates that biblical words must be interpreted by the same spirit that inspired the original writer, "this thou must read within" and "this thou must read in thy owne bossome." It is the Quaker principle that every person has access to the divine.

Willm Osborne

My dear love is to thee, dear hart, waite & be faithfull to thy measure of the good word of god, which thou hast received, that with it thou may see, that which is Contrary cutt downe, and the Axe that is laid to the roott of the tree [Luke 3:9] keep it there, that the fruites may bee brought forth[,] meett for repentance, And let the voyce [voice] cry thorrow [through] the wildernesse, that every tree that growes there may be cut downe[,] that the way may be prepared for him, & the pathes made stright[,] & every mountaine & hill laid low, & the rough wayes made smooth [Luke 3:5] this thou must read within, for this is the messenger that goes beefore him, to prepare the way for him, that baptizes with fire & the holy ghost, & Soe keep low at the bottome, that the tree which cannot bring forth evill fruite, may take roott downeward & upward, that soe thy growth may be true, rootted & grounded into the rocke, unmoveable, that the stormes & tempests cannot beate downe, that when troubles & tryalls & afflictions comes, thou may know A sure habitation, & portion, & liveing strength in the Lord[,] & A pure peace which cannot be taken from thee, Soe my dear hart, low in the fear of the Lord waite, & keep the fast to the Lord, that the heavy burden may be undone, & the bonds of wickednesse undone, & the oppressed may have freedome, & the hungry may have bread, & the soull that thirst may be satisfied, & this thou must read in thy owne bossome, & soe make sure & cleane thy owne house, for he that rulls [rules] his owne house well is worthy of double honour, & soe the Candle that is lighted, put it not under A bed nor under A bushell but on A Candlesticke[,] that all may be seen that is in the house, that the enemyes there may be kept downe & Under [Mark 4:21] For tow [two] nations thou wilt see in thee, & the elder must serve the younger; Soe keep in the pure Judgement, that the first man may be kept A servant, & the earth helpe the woman; And soe my dear hart, low, low, to thy owne measure keepe, that the pure plant may arise, where the unity is, which my heavenly Father planteth, And every plant that he planteth not, let it bee cutt downe, & every plant that he planteth he purgeth it, and cleanseth it, & soe in the Light dwell & walke, where the purgeing is, where the blood cleanseth & washeth, here is our fellowshipe & unity, & Soe the Lord god of life & power, keep thee faithfull & obeydient, low in his fear to waite, in the pure beleefe, which makes not hayt [hate,] but stands still where the strength is, & this is that, that overcomes, the eternall god of power keep thee faithfull, that A pure growing up in the eternall thou may wittnes, that soe an Instuement for his glory thou may bee[.]

Spence 3/47. Addressed: "To Will Osborne". Endorsed: "M. F. to W. Osborn [George Fox]"; "M.F. to Will Osborn, 1657."

74 To Jeffrey Elletson 1657

"Oh deare heart Consider, thy former love and zeal and desires after god, when thou went seekeing for him From mountaine to hill."

This fourth letter to Jeffrey Elletson (see Letters 18, 19, 50) reproaches him for turning away from "Communion with god." It suggests he could not endure the hardships that being a Quaker presented. She contrasts the present "liveing word" with "dead workes," the previous offerings that prefigured the truth of Jesus Christ's offering with the current reality that Friends were experiencing.

Margaret paraphrases Psalm 139, "If I take the wings of the morning, and dwell in the uttermost parts of the sea" to again urge him to listen to his conscience.

Jeafrey Elletson

in dear and tender love, & in the bowels and compassion of my soule doe I write unto thee, and not for any end or relation as unto men outwardly, (god is my wittness,) but in deare & tender love to thy soule, and for the seeds sake, for which I suffer, and am sencible of the heavy burden, greavous too bee borne to which the seed and the promisse is, is pressed as a cart with sheaves, and this thou shalt Eternally wittnesse to bee true, when thou turnes thy mind to my wittness, which will wittness with mee, who beares thy Inniquity, oh deare heart Consider, thy former love and zeal and desires after god, when thou went seekeing for him From mountaine to hill, in the cloudy & darke day[,] seekeing for rest but finding none[,] then thou left thy outward habitation and dwelling, for haveing a further Communion with god, and wilt thou now that hee cals unto thee, and stretcheth out his hand of love unto thee, wilt thou now runn away from him and turne from him, and pull away thy shoulder, because that his name & truth goeth under reproache, (as it ever did) soe if ever thou cann find that the truth of god was ever received by the world, but was ever persecuted and reproached by the world, The spirit of truth the world cannot receive, oh consider who thou Jogues [jogs] with in this day of the lambs war in which hee is rissen in his light in the Conscience of men, which manifests the darknes and deceptfullnes of there hearts, which light and manifestation, as it is minded & waited in, and as it rises it destroyes the worke of the divell in man, and as the light is walked in & dwelt in, the life comes to bee knowne and wittnessed And the blood of Jesus which cleanseth from all sinn, & here your fellowshipp is the cleanseing, washing, and purging, & wee have noe fellowshipp but in that liveing word which maks [makes] clean[,] sanctifieth & purifieth, and that purgeth the Conscience from dead workes [Heb. 9:14], doth not the apostle say that the offering which was a [figure] of the true, did not make the comers there unto perfect as pertaining to the Conscience [Heb. 9:9], And now that hee is rissen, who is the substance of the figar [figure], the unchangable preist, the one everlasting offering, which is offered up thorrow the Eternall spirit without spot to God, will you then not now turne to him that hee may purge thy Conscienc from dead workes, will you stay in the pharisees way[,] onely searching of the scriptures which testifies of him, and will thou not come unto him that thou may have life, who is the way the truth & the life, And theres none comes to the father but by him [John 14:6] and Eternally if ever thou know the father, or hee who is the [sonn?] to him thou must ________ to the light in thy Conscience [,] or reproach I was come in thy mind, soe that I might gaine ______ ______ that thou might partake with mee of the living grace, and living [god] of life and workes, & of which flowes from the living god, for __________ ________ I have a deare love to thee (the lord is my wittnes,) and my fat[her] hath a seede in thee, & if thou turne thy mind into the light xt [Christ] Jesus who is the promise of the father, hee will come to take upon him the seede[.] he who is made of a woman made under the law, who _______ thorrow the law [?] _________ fulfils the law, that the righteousnes of the law, may be fulfilled[;] but to thee this is a mistery who art in the trasgression of the law, and acts contrary to that [in] thy conscience, which is the Judge in the righteous law, And soe Long as thou acts and walks contrary to that in thy Conscience, thou art under Judement and Condemnation with that in thy Conscience, and from this Judge thou shalt never fly god where thou will, Eternally thou shalt wittness mee[.] when thou comes neere this wittnes hee cove[rs] thee[.] if thou goe into hell hee is there, or if thou goe into heaven hee is there[.] if thou take the wings of a dove and fly into the uttermost part of the earth hee is there alsoe [Ps. 139:8–9], soe whether thou heare, or forbeare, I have cleared my Conscience of thee, and the lord is cleare of thy blood for this is the 3d time that I have written to thee in obeydience to the moving of the spirit of the lord whos[e] spirit will not alwayes strive with man, but whose long suffering is great, who waites to bee gracious for the seeds sake which hee hath loved with an everlasting lov soe now if thou love thy soule & thy eternall pea[ce] hearken to the voice that cal[l]s thee[.] this is the way[,] walk in it, with ____ _______ secret which brings all things to thy rememberance[.] the god of power & life give thee hart to understand, that thou may know the things that belong to thy peace, that they may not bee hid from thine ey[es] and see there bee none to deliver thee, this shalbe a true testimony for the living god for ever, and soe remember that thou art warned in thy lifetime

from a true lover of thy soulle and thy eternall good, who cannot flatt[er]

M: F:

Spence 3/157. Endorsed: "m F to Jeffry elletson 1657"; "m f to jefery eletson".

75 To George Fell 1657

"My deare one[,] I Cannot forgit thee[,] my Cryes to my heavenly father is for thee that thou may be kept and that the measure of him in thee may be presarved."

George Fell (1638–October 1670), Margaret's only son, was brought up as was suitable for a seventeenth-century gentleman. He was educated primarily at home by tutors and went to London in 1653, when he was fifteen, to study law at Gray's Inn, as his father had done. He had been attracted to George Fox and Quakerism at first but, unlike his sisters, he did not remain with it.

Margaret expresses her concern for him and urges him not to "depart from the feare of the lord." His sisters send their love to him, and they have received his letters. It sounds like a typical letter from a mother to a son who has gone far from home. A Puritan mother of the same period, Lady Brilliana Harley, wrote a similar letter to her son at Oxford, "My dear Ned, keep always a watch over your precious soul . . . " (Eales, p. 52).

George married Hannah Potter in 1660, and they had four children, two of whom died in infancy. They lived in London until 1664 and then moved north and lived at Marsh Grange, Margaret Fell's birthplace, near Swarthmoor Hall. While he was in London George kept in touch with the family, and numerous Quakers visited him.

In later years there was growing estrangement between George and the rest of the Fell family. Kunze writes: "It appears that George Fell probably was embarrassed by his mother's radical sectarianism and her marriage to Fox" (p. 53). George Fell may have wished to live the life that would have been expected of the son of Judge Thomas Fell with its high social position, rather than that of the son of a mother who had taken up a despised religion.

In the late 1660s there were bitter battles among the family concerning Swarthmoor Hall and other property, and there was even the suggestion that George Fell was responsible for Margaret's spending a second period in prison in 1670 (Kunze, p. 51). He died early, in October 1670, and the relations between George's widow and the rest of the Fell family continued to be strained.

George

my deare lo[ve] take heede of wildenes lightnes and vanyty and take heed of pride giting hould of thee; my deare hart keepe in the feare of the lord thy Creator who hath Created thee and brought thee forth and presarved and kept thee all thy life time untill nowe; nowe beeweare that thou requit him not evell For good, in sining against hime and transgressing against that in thy Conscience which tels thee thou shouldst not doe evell nor wickedly; and soe sinn against god[,] my deare beabe[,] if thou mind the lord and feare him thou will bee with mee as presant, and there thou will bee kept safe from all daingers, if thou keepe in the feare of the lord thou will bee kept from all temtatons, and bee delivered from all evell, but if thou depart from the feare of the lord[,] then thou lies open to the temtations and will be drane [drawn] awaie with the enemies of thy soule[.] my deare love[,] all the wayes of the wicked will com to nought and parish[,] tho never soe delyghtfull for the present[.] yeet [yet] woe and misary will be the end of all sinn and wickednes; therefore my dear love[,] turne From evell and sinn and take and tak [sic] heed of rishnesse [rashness] and forrardnes and headines[.] keepe these downe and strive for patiance and thou will see the blessing of god will bee upon thee. my deare one[,] I Cannot forgit thee[,] my Cryes to my heavenly father is for thee that thou may be kept and that the mesure of him in thee may be presarved/ soe my deare lov[,] the lord god of powre bee with thee and kepe thee in his feare[.] read this often and as often as thou read it thou will bee with mee/ Thy Sisters which is att home is all [well?] and remembers there dear love to thee[;] and let ous heare heare [sic] from the as often as thou cann[.] we receved thiene.

M:F:

Spence 3/60. Also in Crosfield pp. 35–36. Endorsed: "mf to her son G F [George Fox] 1657".

76 TO JUSTICE ANTHONY PEARSON EARLY MARCH 1658

"If you See it good that a collection may bee gathered thorouout your County for the Supply of the ould stock at Kendal which hath been out alonge time and they out of purse[;] yett it could not bee helped."

This short business note to Justice Anthony Pearson (Letters 6, 22) of county Durham gives directions about various funds used to support Quakers: the money used for those going to Scotland to be sent to London; an account should be drawn up of borrowed funds and sent to Kendal; a collection to restock the Kendal fund should be gathered in his county, "If you See it good;" some funds were spent for a Friend whose house was burnt.

Deare freinde

it is desired that the charge of Scotlands voiadge may bee cleared out of the generall collection which is now latly gathered in these three Countyes which is yett at Kendal [,] and then it may bee returned upon accompt to london with the rest of the mony that remaines[;] and this will bee the clearest way[,] being it is the service for another nation[.] lett it lay upon the Generall as was Intended; besides their is severall Sommes which was disbursed to freinds before they went & while they were their [there] that went from Kendal [.] Soe I desire thee to lett a particular [account] bee drawn of that which is behind [left over] whether borrowed of freinds or other ways [otherwise] and lett it bee sent to Kendal that Soe the mony may be returned with speed[.] And then if you See it good that a collection may bee gathered thorouout your County for the Supply of the ould stock at Kendal which hath been out alonge time and they out of purse[;] yett it could not bee helped because this was to goe amongst freinds & alsoe another collection for a freind in comberland which had his house burnt soe that freinds heare [here] awayes hath borne much of late[;] and this I was pressed in spirit to lay before thee[.] my deare love is remembered to thee and to thy wife and familie

M F

Swarthmore MSS 1:308. Endorsed: "m f to antane person 1657 read over [George Fox]"; A Coppie of what was Sent to Anth: Pearson."

Part II

Margaret Fell During the Restoration, 1659–1668

A LOVING

SALUTATION

To the Seed of

ABRAHAM

Among the *Jewes*, where ever they are ſcattered up and down upon the face of the Earth: And to the Seed of *Abraham* among all people upon the face of the Earth; which are all out of the way: wandring up and down from Mountain to Hill, ſeeking reſt, and finding none.

And the way of Truth opened to them, which is the way of holineſs, which all that comes to be made alive unto God muſt walk in, where the unclean cannot paſs, but is for the ranſomed and redeemed to return to *Zion*.

Thus ſaith the Lord, thy Redeemer, the holy One of Iſrael, *I am the Lord thy God, which teacheth thee to profit, which leadeth thee by the way that thou ſhouldeſt go,* Iſai. 48. 17.

As many as were aſtoniſhed at thee, his Viſage was ſo marred more than any man, and his form more than the Sons of men; ſo ſhall he ſprinkle many Nations. The Kings ſhall ſhut their Mouths at him: for that which had not been told them they ſhall ſee, and that which they had not heard ſhall they conſider, Iſai. 52. 14, 15.

In the laſt dayes it ſhall come to paſſe, that the Mountain of the Lords houſe ſhall be eſtabliſhed in the top of the Mountains, and it ſhall be exalted above the Hills, and the People ſhall flow unto it: And many Nations ſhall ſay, Come, let us go up to the Mountain of the Lord, and to the houſe of the God of Jacob, *and he will teach us of his wayes, and we will walk in his pathes; for the Law ſhall go forth of* Zion, *and the word of the Lord from* Jeruſalem. Micha. 4. and Iſai 2.

By *Margaret Fell.*

London, Printed for *Robert Willſon* at the ſigne of the *Black-Spread-Eagle* and *Wind-mill* in *Martins Le Grand*, 1660.

שאלת שלום באהבה

אל זרע אברהם בין היהודים באשר הם נפוצים בנשא או בשפל על כל פני האדמה ואל כל זרע אברהם אשר בתוך כל עמי הארץ אשר הם סרים מן הדרך ותעים בהר ובשפלה מהר אל גבעה מנוחה מבקשים ואינם מוצאים:

ונם דרך האמת הנגלית אליהם אשר היא דרך הקודש אשר ישלכל הבאים אל יהוה ויחיו ללכת בה ובאשר הטמא לא יעבור אבל היא לפדויים ולנאולים לשוב ציונה:

כה אמר יי נאלך קדוש ישראל אני יהוה אלהיך מלמדך להועיל מדריכך בדרך תלך: היעשי ו׳׳י ח׳׳מ

כאשר שממו עליך רבים כן משחת מאיש מראהו ותארו מבני אדם כן יזה גוים רבים עליו יקפצו מלכים פיהם בי אשר לא ספר להם ראו ואשר לא שמעו התבוננו: ישעיה נ׳׳ב יד׳׳ טו׳

והיה באחרית הימים נכון יהיה הר בית יהוה בראש ההרים ונשא מגבעות ונהרו אליו כל הגוים והלכו עמים רבים ואמרו לכו ונעלה אל הר יהוה אל בית אלהי יעקב ויורנו מדרכיו ונלכה בארחתיו כי מציון תצא תורה ודבר יהוה מירושלם: מיכה׳ ד׳ ישעיה ב׳׳

ממרגריטא פאל

LONDON,

Printed in the Year, 1660.

Title Page of A Loving Salutation To the Seed of Abraham, *one of the five tracts Margaret Fell wrote to the Jews.* *(Reproduced with permission of the Religious Society of Friends in Britain.)*

Chronology 1659–1668

July 1659	Margaret Fell and daughters' signatures lead a petition of 7,000 Quaker women presented to Parliament protesting the tithe
April 1660	Declaration of Breda
May 1660	Restoration of Charles II
May 1660	Arrest of George Fox at Swarthmoor and imprisonment in Lancaster Castle until September
June 1660–Sept 1661	Margaret Fell's first visit to London with Margaret Fell, Jr.
June 1660	Margaret Fell's declaration against violence and war
1660	Margaret Fell writes *This was given to Major Generall Harrison* (the Regicide)
Dec 1660	Marriage of George Fell and Hannah Potter
Jan 1661	Rising of Fifth Monarchy Men Nationwide persecution of Friends
Sept 1661	Margaret Fell and Margaret, Jr. return to Swarthmoor Hall
Jan 1662	Marriage of Margaret Fell, Jr. to John Rous
Mar 1662	Marriage of Bridget Fell to John Draper
May 1662	Quaker Act passed
May–Sept 1662	Margaret Fell's second visit to London
Aug 1662	Quakers freed from prison
Winter 1662–1663	Margaret Fell goes to be with Bridget Draper at Headlam, Durham
Mar 1663	Death of Bridget Draper and her baby, Isaac
May–Aug 1663	One thousand-mile journey through England—Margaret, Sarah, and Mary Fell, with Leonard Fell, Thomas Salthouse, and Will Caton. George Fox and Thomas Lower with them in the Southwest
Aug 1663	Kaber Rigg Plot in the North Renewed persecution of Quakers
Winter 1664	George Fox, at Swarthmoor, arrested; examination of George Fox and Margaret Fell
Feb 1664	Margaret Fell arrested and imprisoned at Lancaster
Mar 1664	Trial and imprisonment of both George Fox and Margaret Fell
July 1664	Marriage of Isabel Fell to William Yeamans
July 1664	First Conventicle Act

Aug 1664–June 1668	Margaret Fell praemunired and imprisoned at Lancaster Castle
1664	Margaret Fell writes *A call to the Universal Seed of God*
Nov 1664	Mary Fell ill, probably of plague, in London
Jan 1664	Swarthmoor estate of Margaret Fell granted to George Fell by King Charles II
Mar 1665–Sept 1666	George Fox praemunired, imprisoned at Scarborough Castle
April 1665	John and Margaret Rous, Mary Fell return to Swarthmoor
1665	Plague in London
Nov 1665	Death of Will Caton in Holland
Sept 1666	The Great Fire in London
1666	Margaret Fell writes *Womens Speaking Justified* and *The Standard of the Lord Revealed*
1667	Margaret Fell writes *A Touch-stone, or, a Perfect Tryal*
	William Penn and Robert Barclay join the Quakers
1668	Margaret Fell writes *A Call unto the Seed of Israel*
June 1668	Margaret Fell released from Lancaster Castle
Aug 1668	Marriage of Mary Fell to Thomas Lower
	Margaret Fell travels in north and western England with Rachel, and to Bristol, Devon, and Somerset
Winter 1668–1669	Margaret Fell's third visit to London, with Rachel

The Restoration and the Declaration of Breda

Charles II, the king after his father's execution in 1649, went into exile to the Continent until 1660, living primarily in France with his Catholic mother, and in Protestant Holland. He was surrounded by a small number of loyal followers who continued to plan and plot for the restoration of the monarchy throughout the Cromwell era. Charles made several attempts in the 1650s to raise a strong enough army to gain control of England but was unsuccessful.

In the uncertain period after Cromwell's death the two major political powers that sought to control the country were the Army and Parliament. The Royalists gained support as the Protectorate weakened. The turning point came in 1660 when General George Monck, who had been commander-in-chief in Scotland under Cromwell, marched his army from Scotland to London and joined the Royalist cause. Through astute political maneuvering he gained control of both the Army and Parliament, and King Charles II was invited to return to England.

Monck was a Presbyterian who had had many years of service to King Charles I before the Civil Wars. He is credited with urging Charles II to issue the Declaration of Breda (*DNB*). This important document, written by Charles and his advisors while he was in exile, was designed to assure the people of England that he would address important economic issues and that he would seek the approval of Parliament. The most important provision of the Declaration to Quakers was a statement of religious tolerance, of liberty of conscience. The Declaration of Breda gave some hope to nonconformists of the King's intentions, but the Parliament would have to agree. Charles signed the document on April 4, 1660, at Breda in Holland, and on May 24 he landed at Dover. He made a triumphal progress to London where he was greeted with great joy and celebration.

Charles II promoted tolerance to a degree because he wished to aid Roman Catholics. Quakers were fearful that the return of the monarchy meant more persecution, which indeed occurred. Margaret Fell and other Friends attempted to make the new government understand their peaceful intentions. Treatment of Quakers and other dissenters varied at different times in the 1660s, but the Parliament passed harsh laws which resulted in many heavy fines and imprisonments, as Margaret's letters illustrate.

One promoter of persecution was Sir Daniel Fleming, who took pride in sending Quakers to prison and even to death. He was much involved in Margaret Fell's imprisonment. He wrote to Sir Joseph Williamson in 1663, " . . . I then secured about twenty persons, who had been Captaines or other officers against his Majesty, ejected Ministers, leading Quakers, or other disaffected and suspicious persons . . . Though at present these persons [i.e., Quakers] are not much regarded, yet I am confident the first reall danger wee shall see will bee from them . . . they are such that will do mischief the most resolute of any" (Nightingale, *Ejected of* 1662 pp. 114–115).

BRIEF BIOGRAPHY AND IMPRISONMENT 1660–1668

The years 1660–1668 brought great activity, traveling, and persecution to Margaret Fell. As a widow she was no longer protected by her husband. But as a widow responsible for her own estate she also had more freedom to act on her religious beliefs. Though she still had the Swarthmoor estate to maintain, her daughters were growing and able to take increasing responsibility. Four daughters married Quaker men, and her son also married. One daughter, Bridget, died in childbirth. Some members of the family scattered in this period, but the warm connections continued.

George Fox was charged with plotting against the king, arrested, and imprisoned in Lancaster Castle from June to September 1660, shortly after the Restoration. Margaret went to London for two reasons: to work for George Fox's release and to explain the principles of Friends to the king and the new government. It was important they understand that Quaker beliefs did not permit the use of force, and thus they were no danger to the government. Because Margaret was the widow of Judge Thomas Fell, she had access to King Charles II and the court and was courteously received. She wrote many letters to the king and delivered most of them herself.

She and her daughter, Margaret, Jr., were planning to return to Swarthmoor Hall when an uprising by a sect called the Fifth Monarchy Men, in January 1661 kept them in London. In the following weeks, 4,230 Quakers were arrested. Margaret remained in London until September 1661, a total of sixteen months, until most prisoners were released (Ross, p. 139).

In 1664 Margaret was arrested and charged with a violation of the Conventicle Act, which stipulated that no more than five persons outside of the household could have a Meeting; the government feared conspiracy. Her trial was dramatic, with many in attendance. The judge offered to release Margaret if she would promise to hold no more Meetings at Swarthmoor Hall, but her conscience did not permit this. She refused and was found guilty.

She was then tendered the Oath of Allegiance, which she also refused. It was a Quaker testimony that the biblical injunction, "But I say unto you, Swear not at all" (Matt. 5:35) must be observed literally. Friends believed that since truth should always be spoken there is no need for oaths. Requiring a Quaker to take an oath was a method that judges and magistrates used to put the person in prison. "The determined refusal of the early Quakers to take an oath brought suffering and loss upon them when all other measures failed, for this refusal was often construed into disloyalty to the government, despite their strong assertions of willingness to conform to all law which did not violate their individual sense of right and wrong" (*CJ*, 2:483).

Margaret Fell was then praemunired, a sentence "which placed the offender outside the king's protection and involved forfeiture of goods and chattels, loss of all income from real property, and imprisonment for life or at the king's pleasure" (Horle, *Q.&EngLegSys*, p. 49). The sentence was so severe because the Oath of Allegiance was basically a loyalty oath. Margaret spent four years, from 1664 to 1668, in prison in Lancaster Castle.

Margaret Fell's Published Writings

Margaret Fell wrote and published twenty-four pamphlets and books in her lifetime. She wrote extensively during the years in prison. Most authors in the seventeenth century were men, but more than three hundred women published pamphlets, books, and broadsides. Of these "the Quakers produced the single largest group of women who published their writings, both during the Commonwealth and afterward" (Ezell, pp. 83, 93). Margaret was one of the most prolific.

One of her most important writings was *A Declaration and an Information from us the People of God called QUAKERS, to the present Government, the King and both Houses of Parliament*. It was subscribed by thirteen men, including George Fox, Richard Hubberthorne, Samuel Fisher, William Caton, and John Stubbs. She "delivered [it] into the King's hand, the 22nd day of the Fourth month [i.e., June]." The timing is remarkable. King Charles II had been in the country less than a month. It shows the concern that Quakers felt about the importance of clearly expressing their principles. It also illustrates Margaret Fell's position as the one to best articulate these principles and to be able to deliver it personally to the king.

She wrote theological works, like *The Standard of the Lord Revealed* (1667) and *A Touch-stone, or, a Perfect Tryal by the Scripture* (1667).

Her most famous pamphlet is *Womens Speaking Justified by the Scriptures* (1666; 2nd ed. 1667), which is still in print. Belief in the spiritual equality of all men and women was not unique to Quakers in the seventeenth century, but Quakers more readily accepted women ministers. The pamphlet is a carefully reasoned discussion of women's ministry, with references to the Old and New Testaments and answers to possible biblical objections.

Margaret had a deep concern for the Jews, who had been excluded from England since 1290 and were admitted by an edict of Cromwell only in 1656. She thought they, as another persecuted people, would welcome the Quaker message. She wrote five tracts addressed to them, the first in 1656, *For Manasseh Ben Israel, The Call of the Jewes*, and the last in 1677, *The Daughter of Sion Awakened*. In her frequent scriptural references, she tactfully stays with the Old Testament.

A few years after her death, a memorial volume of over five hundred pages was published, entitled *A Brief Collection of Remarkable Passages and Occurrences Relating to the Birth, Education, Life . . .* (1710, usually referred to as her *Works*). It contains a number of her pamphlets and books, broadsides, numerous epistles, a memoir, and a brief biography.

In 1992 T. H. S. Wallace published *A Sincere and Constant Love, An Introduction to the Work of Margaret Fell*, which includes several of her writings, with introductions, in a modernized form.

MARGARET FELL'S LETTERS

Margaret Fell's letters of this period include many to her children, "Deare Lambes and Babes," during her journeys to London and during the years in prison. Even while she was in Lancaster Castle she wrote comforting letters to her family and to other prisoners.

The extensive lobbying that Margaret Fell did with her writing was of major importance in informing authorities of Quaker principles and in convincing them of their peaceful intentions. The letters to King Charles II and other officials had two purposes. The first was the immediate cause of a particular letter: to gain the release of a prisoner; to protest some instance of persecution; or to promote or protest a particular law. The second aim was to help people gain a basic understanding of the Quaker message. Quakers were convinced of the truth of their beliefs, rejoiced in it, and wanted to share it.

LIST OF LETTERS 77–132, 1658–1668 PAGE

77 TO BRETHREN AND SISTERS 1658

"The word is veary nigh in your hearts . . .
Friends, cleave to this word, keep close to it . . .
this is not a dead word, this is quicke and powerfull,
and a liveing word . . . by this word you stand and
are preserved in tyme of tryal and temptations."

Margaret eloquently describes the Light and how it may work in a person's life, but she does not shy away from mentioning hardships that may come. She emphasizes the love of God and man Friends may experience if they remain faithful and steadfast to the teaching. As usual the epistle is full of biblical phrases and references, a natural part of her language and thought. She gives an interpretation of the place of the law among Gentiles and Jews and in the heart.

My dearly beloved bretheren and sisters, friends of god who are in the unity of the faith, and in the spirit of grace, grace and peace bee multiplyed amongst you, in the bowells of everlasting Love I write unto you, and in the name and power of Jesus christ I exhort you, that as you have Received christ Jesus, soe walke in him, as you have received the truth, soe abide in the truth, that the truth may make you free, as you have received the light from christ Jesus, the fountaine and fullnesse of all light and life, soe abide in the light, dwell in the light, walke in the light, have your being and habitation in the light: life and immortality moves in the light, soe waite every one in your measure for the manifestation of god, his will is revealed in the light, his workes wrought in the light, the power is one with the light, and works in the light. here is the vineyard of God, here the Lord planteth, and here he watereth in the light, and here hee gains the increase, I am the vine, saith christ Jesus, the true light and life of men, and my father is the husbandman[.] every branch in mee that beareth not fruite, hee taketh away [John 15:1–2], Marke this, you that owne the light for your leader, and doe not abide in it & beare fruite, bee ware that you bee not taken away, for christ Jesus saith (whoe is the vine) if a man abide not in mee, hee is cast forth as a branch that is withered, and men gather them and cast them into the fire, and they are burned [John 15:6], consider this, you that are sloathfull servants, yee that are negligent in the lords Worke, you that are unstable, and unconstant to your measures, which would have your minds at liberty, you that will not come downe to the yoake of christ and take it upon you, that you may find rest to your souls, you that would bee exalted above the seed of god, which humbled himselfe, yee that will not waite Low in the pure feare of the Lord, and waite upon him, and learn of him that is Lowly and meeke. I say read this in the feare of the Lord, and understand: hee is the same too day[,] yesterday, and forever, who changes not. who saith againe, and every branch that beareth fruite, hee purgeth, that it may bring forth more fruite, now you are clean through the word [John 15:3] that I have spoken unto you, saith christ the light, whoe was dead but is alive, whose name is called the word of god, this yee are all witnesses of, the light is risen in your consciences, the word is veary nigh in your hearts, which is the word of faith which wee preach; Friends, cleave to this word, keep close to it, mind the work and opperation of this word in you, this is not a dead word, this is quicke and powerfull, and a liveing word, this is able to save your souls, by this word you stand and are preserved in tyme of tryal and temptations, when the stormes and tempests beates, then doth he uphold you, whoe upholds all things by this word of his power; My deare hearts[,] looke not out, nor bee not troubled, nor thinke it not strange concerning the firy tryalls; to the word of patience keep in the light[,] waiteing, as new borne babes desire the sensere [sincere] milke of the word, that yee may grow thereby, that soe you may come to tast[e] how good and gratious the Lord is, to whom yee may come, as to a liveing stone, disalowed indeed of men, but chosen of god and pretious, that upon him you may all bee built up[,] a spirituall house of liveing stones, and that you may bee a holy priesthood, to offer up spirituall sacrifice, this is acceptable unto god [1 Pet. 2:5]: oh my dearely beloved, wait Lowe in the feare of the Lord, in his light, where the unity of the spirit is, where there is no rent nor division, nor exaltation, nor strife for mastery, but each esteeming other better then themselves, in lowlinesse and meeknesse of the spirit [Phil. 2:3], in love[,] peace[,] longsuffering[,] goodnesse[,] faith, against this there is noe law; But where there is rashnesse, that is judged by the Law; where there is hastinesse, frowardnesse, that is judged, where there is an exalted spirit, that will not bee guided by the feare of the Lord, which would utter wordes before the Lord, that is in the transgression, against this the Law is. soe deare freinds[,] read, and understand, search and examine in every perticuler, with the Candle of the Lord, which is lighted in you, which makes all manifest of what sort it is: soe that this spirit bee not found in you and amongst you[,] against which the Law is, which the light hath not unity with, nor cannot approve of this, the light condemnes it, and that which the light Condemnes is in the transgression, and that the Law was added for: And soe all waite in your measures of the pure light, that there you may passe through the Law, and soe come to know what it is to bee dead to the Law, and when you are dead to the Law, yee are dead to sin, then yee Can live noe longer therein, then yee will bee made free from the Law by the body of christ, for christ is the end of the Law[,] for righteousness to every one that believeth. soe read and examine by the light of Jesus in every perticuler, how you stand in the presence of God concerning these things, and bee not deceived yourselves, nor betraye your soules, & how you Can beare witnesse in your measures to the truth of these things, for not one jot nor tittle of the Law shall passe away till all bee fullfilled [Matt. 5:18], this is the Covenant of god, and his promise, hee writess the Law in there [their] hearts, and puts his spirit in there inward parts, not with paper and inke, but with the spirit of the Liveing god, by this the hand writeing is taken away, the Law of commandements contayned in Ordinances, which was outward; and this was the Pertition wall which stood betwixt the jewes and the Gentiles, but this hee hath taken away, nailing it to his Crosse, glory and praises to him, soe that now Jewe and Gentile that comes to the light of christ, where the Law is written in the heart, this is the Crosse of christ, by this come to the father, even through him, whoe is the light, for when the fullnesse of the time was come, god sent forth his sone, made of a woman, made under the Law, to redeeme them that were under the Law, that wee might receive the adoption of Sonns, god hath sent forth the spirit of his sone into your hearts[,] Cryinge abba father; soe friends[,] here is your way, by which this you must you enter, even by the spirit of god in your hearts, this is hee that workes the worke of god in you, god is a spirit, and it is truth in the Inward parts that hee lookes at, and it is the Law written in there hearts that is his Covenant, and it is Circumcission that is of the heart, that worships god in spirit, which is the seal of this Covenant, to which the promise of god remaines, to Abraham and to his seed for ever. know ye therefore that they that are of the faith, the same are the Children of Abraham, and they which bee of faith are blessed with faithfull Abraham. Abraham was the friend of God [James

2:23], and yee are my freinds[,] saith christ, if you doe whatsoever I command you [John 15:14], soe dwelling in the light, there is the Commaund of the Lord received, there is the will of the Lord done, and his worke wrought, abideing in the light[,] there is the unity of the faith, which worketh by love, by which the just lives, thou standest by faith[,] saith the Apostle, bee not high minded but fear, and by faith yee stand, soe in the faith continue firme and steadfast, and bee not tossed too and froe, neither wandering, but in the unity of the Faith of gods elect all stand, and all waite[,] building up one another in your most holy faith, for the Lord preserveth the faithfull[,] mine eyes shall bee upon the faithfull [Ps. 101:6] saith the Lord. So the Lord God of life and power keep you firme and constant every one to your measures of him[,] whoe is gathering you in his everlasting love, with which hee hath loved you, and that you bee not soone shaken in this tyme of tempest, but that upon the rocke of Ages you may stand rooted and grounded upon him, unmoveable, whose faithfulnesse endures forever, whoe waites to bee gratious to you, whoe saith[,] If any man thirst let him come to mee and drinke, whoe is the liveing fountaine which is set open, this is the River, the streams where of doth make glad the Citty of god, the holy place of the tabernacle of the most high [Ps. 46:4] this is the fountaine of gardines[,] a well of liveing water, and streams from Lebanon [Song 4:15]. soe the Lord God Allmighty of power and life and wisdom, keep you and preserve you all[,] waiting upon him, that you may bee aboundantly refreshed in him, whoe is full of grace, of truth, that of his truth you may receive grace for grace, to whom bee glory and Dominion for ever. And that you may abide in him, and his word abide in you, that you may bring forth much fruite, if you keep my Commandements, yee shall abide in my love[,] saith christ, and this is my Commandement[,] that you love one another. Soe in this love, the Eternal God preserve you all, for this love is the fullfilling of the Law, and stand firm for your freedom in the truth[,] which is of great price, which is not purchased with Corruptable things, but by the blood of the sone of god, which blood[,] if you walk in the light, and dwell in the light[,] will cleanse you from all sin, and soe you will dwell in fellowship one with another, soe here abide continually, and hold fast that which you have, let none take your Crowne from you, and the god of power and life keep you and preserve you by his power to stand fast in the liberty wherewith hee hath made you free.

Written in love to the seed, that the lambs may bee fead [fed], and the plants watered, and the babes nourished; whoe desires the preservation of the whole body.

Margret Fell

Markey MSS, pp. 140–143, FHL Box C41/1. Also in Works, *pp. 196–201.*

78 To William Dewsbury May 8, 1659

"Not knowing whether thy wife be yett in the Earthly Tabernacle; but a member of the boddy of Christ I know she is."

Margaret evidently wrote very few letters in the year 1658; only the two preceding ones still exist. Judge Fell died in October of that year. She wrote of her husband many years later: "He lived about six years after I was convinced, in which time it pleased the Lord to visit him with sickness, wherein he became more than usually loving and kind to Friends. He was a merciful man to God's people" (Webb, p. 121).

Her attitude to death was accepting: the Lord gives and the Lord takes away, and it is necessary to accept this without complaint. She writes little of losses that she suffered. The mortality rate, particularly for children, was high in the seventeenth century. Quakers, with their willingness to endure imprisonment, also suffered many deaths. This short letter to William Dewsbury (Letter 41) early in 1659 expresses her sympathy for him as he was facing his wife Ann's illness and death.

My deare Brother, in the Bowels of deare love doe I remember thee and wright unto thee in the life etarnell as A testemony of my deare Love and unyty with the same Life in thee, which chaingheth not but indureth for ever, not knowing whether thy wife be yett in the Earthly Tabernacle; but a member of the boddy of Christ I know she is, which boddy is made perfect Throrow Tryels and Sufferings, and he a man A Sorows for the boddys sake, who is blessed for ever, Soe my deare brother, my deere love in the Lord is to thee and Remaines with thee,

Thy sister in the
Life etarnall, m: F:

The 8th of the 3d month /(59).

York 25. Also in JFHS Suppl. 22, *p. 53. Address: "For My Deere Brother William Dewsbery This is."*

79 To Justice Anthony Pearson 1659

"This is love to thy soule, & thy etternall good, And the everlastinge god of life & power preserve the liveinge principle in thee, & strengthen & refresh & nourish the tender plant in thee."

Anthony Pearson (Letters 6, 22, 76), the longtime friend of Margaret and Thomas Fell, had indicated that he wished her to write to him. She had hoped to see him "outwardly," in person, but is writing instead. Judge Pearson was a strong support to Quakers but evidently had doubts.

The words "judge" and judgement" are used fourteen times to remind him that Christ is the one true judge, and Pearson needs to beware of how he judges. He needs to distinguish between the "precious & the vile." She laments the loss of power among Friends. Her letter is an attempt to explain a mystery he does not understand.

Deare bro[ther]:

In the etternall liveinge truth of the Liveing god my love is to thee, whome the Lord hath made serviceable for the truth; when thou was Called to itt by the power of the Lord; I received a Note from thee wherein thou did hint that you desired that I should write to thee, I did expect to have seene thee here before this; And truely itt hath beene much in mee to write to thee severall times, Butt that I waited to have seene thee outwardly; for in that which is Invisible and eternall I have seene thee; and my life doth breath for the good of thy soule, which is eternall[.] And deare heart beware of the betrayer which lyes neare thee, the same Judas as ever was which betrayes the Just one into the hand of sinners; In the feare of the lord god stand & waite least thou run before thy guide, And soe bee overtaken with the enemy of thy soule, Butt in the pure etternall measure of the pure god, which Ministers Condemnation upon the head of the wicked, in this abide, & in this dwell: I Charge thee lest thou betray thy soule, that through the pure Judgment thou may wittness the doore of mercy, & peace, & reconciliation with the pure god. which thou shall never obtaine butt through the Judgement & this thou shalt etternally wittness, Therefore in the feare, & name & power of the Lord Jesus, att whose name every knee shall bow; see that thou make cleane first the Inside of thy owne house & dwellinge, Which if thou Come to the light, & lett itt bee sett upon the Candlesticke, where all may bee seene that is in the house, then thou will see much fillthyness & uncleanenesse unpurged out yett, And hither thou must Come, to bee tryed & searched with the light whether thy workes bee wrought in god. for the worke that god workes itt is in the light, & that which is nott wrought in the light, is that which is evell: & is for Condemnation, & this thou may read in the Invisible, Therefore in that which cleanses, & purges out the old leaven & fitts the vessell for the Lord, in that abide where thou wittnesses Cleansinge & purgeing & washinge with cleare water; that soe thou may come to wittness the record which is on earth; the spiritt the water & the blood: which to thee is yett a Mistery: god can dwell with noe uncleane thinge, holynesse becomes the house of god; Soe if thou come to wittness to rule thy owne house well; then thou will bee worthy of double honour; And then thou will know how to rule thy family: & as a pattern walke before them & keepe downe & under. the deceipt which rules & raignes Amongst them: by which I feele the Just suffer in you all: Therefore deare heart come home to thy owne measure to the Judgement seate of Christ, where the Judge sitts as a refiners fire, which will nott bee Quenched if thou abide there, till the Judgement bee brought forth into victory, And then itt will bee sett in the earth: & till then thou art noe pure Judge, For all Judgement is Committed to the sonn, & whatsoever Judges which is nott the sonn is for Judgement with the son, Therefore beware, of Judgeinge[,] thou & all freinds[,] lest yee Judge before the time by outward appeareance, & soe nott righteous Judgment[.] For whosoever thou art that Judges another, & dost the same thinge thou shalt nott escape the Judgment of god: & hee that Judges his brother, except the beame bee Cast out is the hypocrite & the woe from the Lord Jesus is to him: Therefore I warne you all to beware how yee Judge the unlimited power & workinge of the lord, which in itts operations are various; which all the wisdome of Mann Cannott Comprehend, Butt lett itt have itts worke & force upon the deceipt, & lett itt worke itt downe before whome noe deceipt cann stand, for I know the Just hath suffered in Many & the deceipt & the tempter is strengthened by the serpents wisdome Judgeinge the power, which from god is Curst Insoemuch that the power in most of freinds that hath beene long Convinced is quite lost. And the liberty of the flesh lived in, & the forme of the truth taken upp. & the pure etternall buryed in the earth, & the wicked nature gott the name of truth; Butt all this from god is shutt, & with the Liveinge etternall word (which is the sword of the Liveinge god) is this Cutt asunder & devided from the Liveinge god, Therefore to the Measure of the pure etternall turne; & in itt waite, to have the pure discerninge betwixt the precious & the vile in thee [Jer. 15:19], for Noething will stand before the Righteous pure god, butt that which is pure, And as that moves, & leades & guides, bee obedient to itt, & bee subject, & learne of itt which makes manifest the will of god, that which is low, & meeke in thee, And bee nott negligent nor bee not sloathfull nor Careless of the worke of the lord, in thy owne particular, nor anywhere els [else] where thou may bee serviceable[.] I warne thee & charge thee as thou will Answer itt before the lord; Before whome thou must come to give an account of all thy actions, sooner, or latter; Therefore as thou loves thy soule hast [haste] to meete the lord, & to the touchstone come to bee tryed, & give up frely to the death that which is for the sword to the sword, that which is for the fire to the fire, & that which is for the famin to the famin, that soe thou may witnese the flameinge fire of the lords righteousness reveallled, & all the Chaff burnt with unquenchable fire; And this I was moved of the lord to write to thee, And if thou bee obedient to the Measure of the liveing god in thee, which answers for mee, with which I have unity that will wittness this is love to thy soule, & thy etternall good, And the everlastinge god of life & power preserve the liveinge principle in thee, & strengthen & refresh & nourish the tender plant in thee which the devourer would devoure, & the wild beare & the beasts of the forrest would destroy[.] My deare love to thy wife, & to that of god in her which is kept in bondage & Captivity doth my love reach, And the desire of my soule is that by the etternall power Redemption shee may wittness; And the etternall god of power keepe you faithfull to your Measures in his feare to waite in the Cross to the carnall & to the flesh: And to all the wisdome of man, which from god is shutt, to which wisedom the Cross is foolishness, butt by itt & noe other way is the enmyty slaine and this thou shalt etternally wittness; Therefore as thou loves thy soule bee obedient to the death of the Cross: so there I leave thee to bee Nayled

Thy Deare sister made manifest in the
etternall principle where the unity is,

M:F:

Consider, & with the light which is the eye see, what the Appostle saith when hee saith know yee nott that they which run in a race, runneth: Butt one receiveth the price [prize], Soe runn that yee may obtaine; And agayne hee said yee did runn well[.] who did hinder you that yee should nott obay the truth: Therefore Beware, that thou run nott as uncertainly & soe feight as one that beateth the ayre [air], Butt keepe under thy body, & bring itt into subjection lest by any mean[s] when thou hast preached to others thou thy selfe shall bee a Castaway; [1 Cor. 9:24–27]/

Spence 3/54–55. Endorsed: "M:F: to antane Parson, 1659 [George Fox]"; "Anthony Pearsons letter".

80 To the Saints, Brethren and Sisters 1659

"The desier of my Soul is that yee would Com in puer [pure] Singlness, to that which Convinsed you in the begininge[.]"

In this pastoral letter, Margaret Fell laments that Friends are straying from the truth of the Quaker message. She fears that "another Sperit is gott up amongst you." It is a "Greefe" to her soul, and she pleads with them to "Come into the Innocent life."

She does not explain exactly who is involved or what they have done. There are references to jealousy and envy and "Ministers that would Side and draw into parties" within the Quaker community. Margaret is usually so confident in her letters, whether she is praising, exhorting, or blaming, that the discouragement she expresses is notable: "my Soule Even morns, for the Sepereation from the Seed in others."

This is to they Saints

Bretheren and Sisters in our Lord & Saviour Jesus Christ. The Everlasting Covenant, and Shiloe which is come to whom the gathering is, [Gen. 49:10] A lamb without Spot or blemish in life in Natur in Image. The Second Addam, the lord from Heaven, whose power is now Resen, and whose Light is now Shininge in the Consciences of men, but Especelly in his Saints, in whom he is to be Glorified, and Admired, as his name and Nature Ariseth and growes in them, and as his Image is Renewed, Soe there light Shines forth amongst men, Soe there Father is Glorified which is in Heaven, and there good works are Seene, as they live in the Etarnell[.] The Image of the Invisable god growes [Col. 1:15] in them, Soe they are the Salte of the Earth & the light of the world, and A Citty Set in a hill [Matt. 5:13–14], which judgeth the World yea Angels, but This is hee that triumphs in victory, over Principallitys and powers, and over Speritual wickedness in high places [Eph. 6:12], and this is hee that is lowly and meeke, who Saith Learne of mee; & this is he that is Come to Save mens lives, and not to destrow them and this is hee that Saith love your Enemies, and this is hee that hath laid downe his life for his Enemiess, and this is he that Saith, Judgement, for with what Judgment yee Judge yee Shall be Judged, and this he that is maid of a Quicke understanding in the feare of the lord, and he Judgeth not after the Sight of his Eye; Nether Reproveth After the Hearing of the Eare, But with Righteousness doth hee Judge; & Reprove with Equity. for the meeke of the Earth, and this is the Image and the Spirit that the father is Seeking to rease [raise] in this his day[.]

But oh Frends, to the Greefe of my Soule & burthening of my Spirit I feele another Sperit is gott up amongst you which hath ever Spred amongst Freinds even as A gangering [gangrene], over the Nations (to witt) England[,] Scotland and Ireland, and I am assured as the Lord lives that wher it is lodging and Remaining, it will Even eat as A Cancere [cancer]. oh how is this degenerat Plant gott into your harts, that Even Beareth Sower graps [sour grapes], to the greeving and Sadening the Harts of the Righteous, and to the opressing and Sufferinge of the Seed within you, oh how you __________ precious/

The puer [pure] Seed of god in you, oh how you Robb the puer Seed of god in you of the Marcie of god the ________ Marcies of Davide, and oh how low you Sett the right of the Puer Imortall Birth of god in you, while you are Surmizing in your minds, while you are prayinge and Serchinge; and Watchinge with an Evell Eye, what you Can Catch or get against others ________ ___ _____ might Sleight them, & looke upon them to be worse then yourSelves that you Might have more Ease in yourSelves, in takinge of Libertie, and Soe Set yourSelves above others in your minds, and others below you, and how you Sat at Ease exalted[,] but know this that though this be as high as Lusifer it must condemne as low as hell, And oh that you did but know the wrath and Justice that is [due to?] this _______ _____ _______ ________ it would Even Stricke dread and Terror into your Harts, and Con[science?] this Cannot Escape the Justice of god, for this is Even the Catterpillar that would Eat upe the green in All.

oh how hath this Invious [envious] man gotten in amonge you, Suerly he hath Comm in the Night, when men was ASleepe: & hath Sown Tears [tares] Amonge the wheate, which when the Reapers coms must be bound in bondals and Cast into the fier, for I know that there was good Seed Sown amongst you at the first, which when it found good ground, would Have brought forth good fruite, but sence there hath com mixed Seedsmen amonge you [Matt. 13:25–26] & Some hath Preached Christ of Envie and Some of good will, & it was Easy to beget that Image in you, you havinge a ground in yourSelves & was one with it, & Soe it was Easy to Ster [stir] upe Jelesy in you, you having the ground of Jelesie in yourSelves which is as Stronge as Death[.]

And trewly Friends[,] in the Presence of the Almighty god, who Searcheth Every Hart, _________ you Recevd [?] that this is the vary ground Causs, of your being Erred from the Spirit of the Lambe of god in you, Even by Ministers that would Side and draw into parties, and _________ would gather togather & draw to themSelves, and under_________ others, & Soe Sow prejudice & Secret Surmizinges and Soe begett Jelesiese in you, you having a ground of all those things in yourSelves, & Soe you are led into the wilderness, And you know few or none in the life as you ought to know them, but you are Even Jeless of all, and redy to Question all, and dare hardly Joy [?] to any, except it be these that are one with the Spirit that is head in you, and Soe yee be come one for Paule and one for Apallow [Apollo], & one for Cephes [1 Cor. 1:12], But oh frends this must downe; this is for utter rewin [ruin] and distruction, els it would destroy the Lamb of god, for it is but Carnall. Christ is not devided[;] the Puer [pure] Sperit of the Lamb is one in all, and the Same for Ever: oh behould the Lamb of god that takes away this Sinn, & Com into the Innocent life; which is harmless and undefiled, and Separate from Sinne, which Thinks noe Evill, nor watcheth not for evill, but waiteth to be gracious, and would have all men to be Saved and Come to the knowledge of the Truth, and would even that all the lords peeple were Prophets, oh this Seed is blessed for Ever. This, Saith why Seest thou the mote in thy Brothers Eye and not the beame in thy owne [Matt. 7:3], (Friends read this neare). and why dost thou Judg thy Brother, and why dost thou Set at Nought thy brother; oh frends is not this the Sperit yee should be seeking after, and why are yee Erred from that that wisheth well to all, and desireth good of all People & loves that which is good in all, who is in the Everlasting Covenant, where Sinn and Iniquity is blotted out, & not Remembred, the Speritt of the Saints in light savors, the etarnal life in all, and loves it in all, and Seese and feels it in all, according to its measure, and houlds it in the unity of the Sperit, but who turns into that which [sees?] into this, and Heads Turns into the Carnall, turnes into that which remembers Sin & iniquity, & Sets up the Sin of god. people, as god hath Said[,] ye Eate up the Sin of my people, but read there portion that did soe[.] Jlosaye [jealousy] & every Sin that a man doth is without the body: But

Now there is Another Path [?] which my Soule desireth to draw into, Even the New Covenant of the Everlasting god, the law wretten in the hart, and the Truth in the Inward, and the washing and The Cleansing of the Inside; where the knowledg of the Etarnall god is, and where god Retained in the knowlidge for that which Can be knowne of god[,] you must looke for it in you, and where god is worshiped as god, who is A Sperit, & who is worshiped in Sperit and in tru[th] and that in the Inward, Suer [sure] Frends, you are not looking for the knowlege of god, when you are looking at others without you, yea and it may be at the outside of others, what doth ____________ differ from the Pharesies of ould, have you not got a better Tryer & Tuchston [touchstone] yett then th[at] to Judge by outward apearance; this is A Shame to the profession, how Soon may you get a li[ttle?] of the Pride of the outside Strept [stripped] of you, which is but the lust of the Eye, and get into A form, or garb in Imitation of others; to be as they are, of the outsid, & Judgeth all, that are not as you are, Pharasy Like ______ within you there be rottenness, & dead mens Bones and Sepulchers that the prophet is, ______ _________ in, & ye are garnishing the outside like the Prophets, and that [Nature?] within alive, which Slew them, Judging of others by the outside: who are [Clered?] from that filth that liveth in you, doe you think that this will Stand in the day of the lord, when he Coms to Looke for Fruite, and to reward Every one According to there works, I tell you Nay, therefore beware of the love of the Phariseess for they are Hipocrits, and let it be purdged out of you, & I Assure you their leven _____ _________ Som of you, therefor I Say againe beware of it; and Watch against it, that you may beCom a newling and be gathered into the unity with the Saints in Light, where there is noe devition [division] nor noe Strife, Noe Contention, nor noe lording over one Another, as the Gentils did, but where you may be one in christ Jesus in unity of the faith, where you may Edify Another [Rom. 14:19], and _________ upon another in love: and in your most holly faith, that faith[,] hope and Charity may rema[ine] amongst you, that the Cheefest of These which is Charety [1 Cor. 13:13] ye may know, which yet yee are [unlearned?] in, yea really Freinds[,] I doe afferme it, in the presence of the Almighty god, that manny amonge you know and practice litle Charity, and what will it availe you, if you have not Charity, [Charity] Suffereth long & is kind[,] Charity invieth [envieth] not, Charity vanteth [vaunteth] not itSelfe, is not puffed up, Looketh not her own, thinketh noe Evell nor repayeth Not Iniquity, but rejoyceth in the Truth, beareth all things, beleeveth all things & hopes all things, Indures all things, Charity Never faileth [1 Cor. 13:4–8]/

Now I appeale to the Testemonny of Jesus in you, how much of this ___________ you reed ____ you, Nay let every on[e] lay there hand upon there mouth, and with the witness of the living god which Cannot lie[,] Search and try, and you shall find Quite the Contrary, under the [burden?] of which Sperit, my Soule hath Suffered with the Seed of god in all, and for the Seeds Sa[ke] have I wretten this, and in obaidence to the motion of my Heavenly Father, and for noe other End, but that the Seed may be recovered, into the unity of the life, and fellowship with the father, and Son, for Trewly my Soule Even morns, for the Sepereation from the Seed in others, and that vaile [veil] that I feel _______ which keeps away the good things, but for the renting of the vaile my Soule wats [waits], and there for in obaidience to the lord have I wretten this, and in his nam and power, have given you a Cleare Testemony, of these things which yee shall etarnally wittness to be Trew, and I know the faithfull and Trew witness in you all that deals plainly and trewly with you, Answers and Seals to the truth of This, and the desier of my Soul is that yee would Com in puer [pure] Singlness, to that which Convinsed you in the begininge[.] Frends[,] This is the Same for Ever, and the highest measure hath unity with this, for he that Contenews [continues] in the Annoynting, which he hath receved from the begining, and that Annointing abiding in him, then hath he fellowship with the Son & with the father, and this is the ould Comandement, and the New which the Apostle wret unto the bretheren who said[,] Bretheren[,] I wright no New Comandement unto you, but an ould Comandement which yee hav had from the begining, that ould Comandement is the word, which yee have had from the begin[ning], again a New Comandement I wright unto you, which Thing is Trew in him and in you, because the darkness is past and the Trew light now shineth [1 John 2:7–8] (Marke) here is the word which was in the begining, by which all things weare maide And Created, & her [here] is the light[,] christ Jesus[,] the New Covenent, who raiseth and Redeems out of the ould and out of the Darkness which is past in to the Trew light which now shineth, here the Apostle bring[s] them in to one, and Shewes them that the word was in the begining, and the Trew light, which Now Shineth, and the Anointing which they had Receved, they might abide in, and Soe here is the resting Place, that you must all meet in where the true fellowshipe is on[e] with another, which all the Saints in Light was gathered into, Sence the begining, and all meets here, from Etarnity to Etarnity, & he that Saith that he is in the light, and hats [hates] his Brother, he is in Darkness, he that loveth his Brother is in the Light, & there is noe Accation [occasion] of Stumbling in him[.] he that hateth his Brother is in the darkness, and walketh in darkness, and knoweth not whether he goeth, beCause darkness hath blinded his Eyes. ______ ______ ______ ______ ______ ______ ______ ______ ______ Soe the Etarnal god open your harts, and your understandings, that you may reed and understand, and walke in the light as he is in the light, where the blood of Jesus xt [Christ] Clenseth from all Sin & where the fellowship is felt on[e] with another, which is out of all Jelesies and dowbt[full] Disputations, for that drawes A vaile, and the Apostle Saith he that doubts is damned, [that Every] puer light prove and Try Every Sperit, whether he be of god or noe, for this Can pas trew Judgment, which will Stand and let the mouth of Jelesy whispering and Questioning be Stopped. & let not the good be Evill Spooken of[,] but follow often those things that makes for peace, where in you may Edify on[e] another & the god of love keep you and gather you into this love[.]

From a Trew lover of Peace unity
and Fellowshipp with the father
and the Son and one with another

M: F:

Spence 3/13–14. Endorsed: "M F to Frends [George Fox]"; "1659".

81 An Epistle to Friends 1659

"To the Word of his Eternal Power
I commit you, and commend you to his Eternal Arm."

This brief epistle in the Works *is a benediction—no controversy, no admonitions. Is it complete?*

My dearly beloved Brethren and Sisters, in the everlasting Truth, and eternal Love, and Power of an endless Life, into which we were begotten, and have been nursed up, and kept in, as living Stones growing up in the Temple of the living God; the same Power and Arm is present with you, and owns you: Therefore keep in it, and let your Faith stand in the Power and Life of God in every particular; and in that Book of Life will you read me near, as if present, in the everlasting Covenant and Bond of Peace, which is never to be broken; and in that Love of Jesus Christ, which none can separate us from, Height nor Depth, Life nor Death. The Eternal God keep you, who brought again our Lord Jesus Christ from the Dead, through the Blood of the Everlasting Covenant; and by his Blood wash you, and cleanse you from all Sin, and all that would separate from God; that you may have Fellowship one with another in the Eternal Light and Life, and there I leave you: And to the Word of his Eternal Power I commit you, and commend you to his Eternal Arm, which is able to save your Souls, and to keep you up to himself.

M. F.

Works, *p. 201.*

82 To Margaret Fell, Jr. May 8, 1660

"I Cannot limit thee, thou thyselfe may See
and feel, the god of power guide thee and Direct thee."

Margaret had great trust in her daughters' ability to manage business affairs. Early in 1660 Margaret Fell, Jr. (ca. 1633–1706) was staying in London for some months to get medical treatment for her knee. Margaret, Jr. (Letter 54) had been a convinced

Quaker since 1652. She had visited Friends in prison, one of whom wrote: "My soul was refreshed when she came this away, truly she is glorious comely and beautiful, in that which is eternal and never fades away" (Ross, pp. 24–25, 126).

In 1661 she married John Rous, a Quaker from Barbados. They had twelve children, four dying in infancy. Their home at Kingston upon Thames, near London, became the place where George Fox lodged during the periods that he lived in London (CJ, 2:421).

The letter refers to "the man," never named, "whose heart is only to get Mony." Margaret was loath to use names in correspondence, particularly if there was a negative connotation.

Richard Davies (1635–1708) was a Welsh Quaker who was responsible for converting many in Wales. Davies preached and traveled and spent periods in prison. Unlike some of the other Quaker ministers he "always spoke with so much courtesy that he generally parted on friendly terms with the preachers he interrupted, and many of his closest friends were ministers whom he opposed" (DNB).

Thomas Coulton was a trusted servant of the Swarthmoor household who conducted business for the family. He was one of two executors of Judge Fell's will (Ross p. 398). Margaret mentions that daughter Sarah may travel to London with him and Gerrard Roberts (Letter 68). Coulton was carrying letters and documents from Swarthmoor Hall to London.

Margaret also encourages Margaret, Jr. to spend time with her brother George (Letter 75) so that he will "be not too much amonge profane Company."

the 8th of 3d month, 60
M. F.

Dear and Eternally beloved[,] In the dear Immortall life of the living god which Makes & keeps alive [?] up to him, doe I dearly remember thee, & to this commit, I received thine, In which thou mencions thou desire an Answer from me Concerning the man. I Expect that thou hast had an answer ear [ere] this by R: D: [Richard Davies] Sence I have spoke to G: F: [George Fox] who seth [saith] he sed [said] litle to thee but thou might doe if thou wilt. I Expect litle Cure from that man whose heart is only to get Mony, yet I would have thee fully Satisfyed Conserning him, that if hee Could Ether make thee An Instrument, or any other thing upon reasonable tearms, thou may make use in him, but no other wise not to Satisfy his wicked minde, I Cannot limit thee, thou thyselfe may See and feel, the god of power guide thee and Direct thee. I intend for anything I know that Sarah may Com along with G.R. [Gerrard Roberts] and T. C. [Thomas Coulton]. G. F. is here[.] we are all well in the lord[,] blessed be his holly Name, take care that this be gotten Speedly to thy brother, be with him as much as thou can and have a care of him, that he be not too much amonge profane Company

thy mother
M. F.

put T: C: upon doing these things mentioned
in the Inclosed, & get the monny for the Robes
before he returne, I expct [expect] 20£
for them & I know the worth [?] of mine to them[.]
what he gott for them[,] let him pay it to thee &
Sarah

Spence 3/68, partially in Crosfield p. 62–63. Addressed: "For Margrett Fell at her lodging in Well Ally in Wappinge, deliver, London." Endorsed: "M.F. to M.F., her daughter, 3d m.,60".

83 To the Magistrates Late May or early June 1660

"I am conserned in the thing, in as much as he was apprehended in my house, and if he be guilty, I am soe too."

In late May or early June while George Fox was at Swarthmoor Hall, four constables came with a search warrant and arrested him. In his words: "I was in the pearlour att Swarthmoore & Rich: Richardson was with mee: & Margarett Fell unto whome some of her servants brought her worde that some was come to search for armes" (CJ, 1:358). The warrant to apprehend Fox was initiated by Justice Henry Porter (1613–1666), mayor of Lancaster in 1659 and 1661 and constable of Lancaster Castle in 1660 (CJ, 1:463).

Margaret addresses this letter to magistrates to protest the illegal entry to her home and the arrest of an innocent person. Fox was taken to Justice Porter. Fox offered bail, which was his right, but Porter refused it, contrary to law. Fox was imprisoned at Lancaster Castle. He asked to see the mittimus, the warrant of committal, which was his right, but this was refused. It was read aloud to him, and Margaret asserts that all the charges are false. She asks the magistrates to investigate the injustice done to Fox and to herself.

There are two contemporary copies of this letter, Spence 3:105 verso and Ms. Vol.

101/43. I have used the Ms. Vol. version because it has George Fox's endorsement. The two copies have identical words; the only differences are spelling, punctuation, and capitalization. This is an instance that seems to confirm the accuracy of contemporary copies.

A declaration of M: F: to all magistrates concerninge the wrong takeinge upp & Imprisoninge of G.F. at [Lancaster]

I doe Informe the Governours of this Nation that Henry Porter[,] Mayer of Lancaster[,] sent a Warrant with foure Constables to my house[,] for which he had noe Authority nor order, And they searched my house and apprehended a Man [George Fox] in it, which was not giulty of the breach of any Law nor giulty of any offense to any in the Nation, and after they had apprehended him and brought him before Porter there was baile offered, what he would demand for his appearance to what could be laid to his charge, but he contrary to Law, (if he had taken him lawfully) denyed any bayle & clapt him up in close prison; After he was in prison, a coppy of his Mittimus was demanded, which ought not to bee denyed to any prisoner, nor noe lawfull Magistrate will[,] that soe hee may see what is laid to his charge, but it was denyed him, a coppy of it he could not have, only they were suffered to read it over[;] and every word that was there charged against him, was utterly false, & he was not giulty of any one charge in it. this will be proved & Manifested to the Nation. soe lett the Governours consider of it[.] I am conserned in the thing, in as much as he was apprehended in my house, and if he be guilty, I am soe too. soe I desire to have this searched out.

Margaret Fell

FHL MsVol 101/43 and Spence 3:105 verso. Also in Webb, p. 138 and Nickalls, p. 382. Endorsed: "M F of G F conserning porter when gf was in preson A lankaster 1660 to the govers [George Fox]".

84 To King Charles II Probably May 1660

"The love of god . . . hath now brought you into this Nation in much peace & comfort: oh that you would See his goodnes, & walke worthy of his love[,] that you might ever have a rich portion Suitable to your Birth & degree, of this infinite love."

The first of many letters to King Charles II (1630–1685) was written shortly after his accession to the throne in May 1660. His father, King Charles I, had been beheaded in 1649. The young prince, nineteen at the time, escaped to the Continent. He spent the next eleven years in France, Germany, and the Netherlands trying to raise sufficient support to defeat Cromwell and the republican government. He and his followers made many attempts to enter England but with no success until Oliver Cromwell's death and the ensuing confusion over who would govern the country.

Parliament and the powerful generals invited Charles to return, and on May 8, 1660, King Charles II was solemnly proclaimed in Westminster Hall. He landed at Dover and made a splendid progress with celebrations and multitudes dancing in the streets and arrived in London on May 30.

His character was very different from his uncompromising father. He was charming, courageous, and, most important, pragmatic; he understood that he had to get along with Parliament. Religion was not a passion for him. He was most sympathetic to Catholicism but knew that he must support the Anglican Church if he wished to rule England. He was tolerant of nonconformists, perhaps because he hoped that in giving them more freedom, Catholics would also benefit.

The significant act that reconciled Quakers and other nonconformists to the Restoration of the monarchy was Charles's signing of the Declaration of Breda. This momentous document signed on April 4, 1660, promised religious toleration and liberty to tender consciences.

Margaret wrote to remind Charles II that it is the love of God that preserved him through "troubles, sorrowes & afflictions and hath now brought you into this Nation in much peace & comfort." She speaks of the "new Covenant," of "the liveing god, & the eternall truth," and of her desire that he will taste "lardgly of the love of god." She is introducing him to the Quaker understanding of the Gospel.

Deare Friend Consider the mighty god of heaven & earth Creator of all things, Orderer and governour of all things by whom all things consist. It is he that that hath preserved & kept you[,] who upholds all things by the word of his power, who is the Lord of all principalityes and powers, thrones, & dominions to whom every knee must bow, and every tongue conffesse; Therefore feare before him to whom all Nations is as the droppe of a buckett, or as the Small dust of the Ballance [Isa. 40:15]; who hath the breath of all men, & people in his hand and can turne them as the Rivers of water[.] There is a measure of this pure eternall god of life in thee, whose Imortallity dwells in the light. And who lookes for the life & Imortallity to be brought to light through the Gospell [,] must looke unto Jesus xt [Christ] who is the true light that lighteth everyone that cometh into the world[,] in whom is life, & this life is the light of men, which light dwells in the heart of every man & woman[;] & heare must every one looke for their teacher, & leader that leads to god who is the Father of lights, with whom there is noe variablnes, nor shaddow of turninge [James 1:17] whosoever is by his Spirit in the heart & his word is nigh in the heart, & he writes his law in the heart & putts his Spirit in the Inward parts. And this is the new Covenant which the Lord hath made with the house of Iasraell, & with the house of Judah [Jer. 31:31; Heb. 8:8], when the sin of the Iniquityes Shall be remembered noe more. And soe if thou desire to know the livinge god, & the eternall truth, as it is in Jesus xt[,] thou must turne thy minde unto this pure light of xt Jesus in the heart which manifests all sin, & all evill; and all transgression. This will manifest wrath, & envy, strife, & mallice & emulation & whatsoever is evill and this will lead up unto god the Father of Spiritts, and redeemes the minde out of the vissible things: and if thou be guided by this pure light of Jesus christ in thee[,] thou wilt then answer to the love of god which hath beene great unto thee & thy Bretheren & Fathers house, who hath persecuted you, & kept you in the midst of troubles, sorrowes & afflictions, & hath now brought you into this Nation in much peace & comfort: oh that you would See his goodnes, & walke worthy of his love[,] that you might ever have a rich portion Suitable to your Birth & degree, of this infinite love, & life of goodnes & mercy & grace, & [virtue?] that he is Sheddinge abroad in and amonge & upon his people in this Nation: oh infinite is the goodnes & love of god that is felt with many[;] that which eye hath not seene, nor eare heard, nor hath it entered into the heart of man to conceive that infinite love of god which many are partakers of in this nation: and that you might even partake with us, & tast [taste] lardgly of the love of god is the desire of my soule. my love is deare unto you all & not for any outward end (the lord knowes) but it hath pleased the lord to make it soe unto me. the Lord grant that he may have glory thereby[.] Soe I have set before you the way to eternall life, and there is noe other way nor name under heaven given by which any shall be saved but by Jesus Christ in whom is life, & his life is the light of men which hath lighted every one that cometh into the world.

From one who truly desires the peace & welfare of you all

Margt. Fell

Spence 3/109. Endorsed: "M F to the king [George Fox]".

85 To King Charles II 1660?

"Beware of sideing or joyning with any particuler interest which is to advance & exalt an end, for that will cause the Just to suffer & limitt others."

*As soon as King Charles II arrived in England many parties and interests sought his favor. Parliament was heavily weighted toward Anglican and Presbyterian landowners who feared or distained the nonconformists. The Restoration Parliament saw religious and political radicalism as inseparable. Christopher Hill writes, "M.P.s were anxious to finish once and for all with the policy of religious toleration which, in their view, had been the bane of England for a decade" (*World*, p. 200). Hill is writing of the Nayler affair of 1656, but the conservative elements of Parliament were even stronger in 1660. Charles II's attempts to promote toleration were thwarted.*

Quakers visited him and other influential members of the court when they could gain entrance, and they wrote to him. Margaret's letter warns against Presbyterians and "their sinister ends." She brings in the image of the king as "head of these Nations" and protector of the people "as a family, the poore as well as the rich." By allowing liberty of conscience he will avoid injustice, oppression, and thus tyranny.

King Charles The Almighty God hath sett thee over these Nations a free man and hath brought thee in by his owne Free will[,] Arme, & power and thou stand free from any Engagement to any Man, as to restoreing thee to thy power the Lord hath donne it without any mans life or shedding any blood, and the Lord made thyne Enimies instrumentall for this worke, who never intended it for thee, but for the Presbiterian, & Priests interest, which have allwayes been thyne Enimies, the which Gods Arme is against, therefore beware how thou joynes with them or harkens to them, who would bind and limitt thee, & the whole Nation to their sinister ends under pretence & colleur of a Law which was made not for the Just & righteous but for the Transgressor, and this they would pervert & corrupt to lay it upon the Innocent, and soe by it limmitt the Just & holy one as the Jewes did, And they goe about to limmitt thee to their will (under pretence of a Law) to hinder thee thereby from releiveing the Innocent & oppressed, which lawes were made for the limitting of Tyrants & such as ruled over people in Tyranny[,] which if thou doe not but rule in righteousnes[,] Justice & Equitie, this is not against the Law but for it & answers to the end of the Law, but oh Consider[,] thou art deeply engaged to the Lord, who hath sett thee head of these Nations[,] & the people thereof is as thy family & thou art to provide for them & protect them as a family, the poore as well as the rich, & That every one may enjoy their particuler rights and proprietyes as subjects & the liberty of their Conscience towards God & men & take of[f] oppression & undoe the heavy burdens, & in soe doeing thou rules for God & answers his end in bringing thee in & restoreing thee to thy place, but beware of sideing or joyning with any particuler interest which is to advance & exalt an end, for that will cause the Just to suffer & limitt others, & this is that which produceth Tyranny[,] but to the Lord thou art engaged to stand for all, & the good of all, & soe to keep all in order & in peace, that every one may have & enjoy their Just right & not to limmit tender Consciences, for the Lords hand is against this, & his Arme is stretched forth to undoe this & he is bringing his people from under the bondage of Taskmasters that they may serve him in freenes of spirit, he hath heard the cry of the oppressed & his Eare is open to the groanes of the Innocent, & it will be good for thee that thy Eare bee not shutt, for if it bee[,] thy heart will grow hard, thou hast apeople to rule over, such as noe man upon the face of the Earth hath, which is soe deare to the Lord, that he will owne them, & plead their cause, as he will for these, therefore beware how thou deales with them[,] for it will bee for thy owne Everlasting peace & safety not to slite [slight] nor to looke highly Over what they say unto thee[,] for they have a Testimony from the Lord, & he will beare them witnes when he comes to make inquisition for blood/

from a true freind & lover of thy peace & good:

M: F:

Spence 3/98. Also Works, *p. 19. Endorsed: "M F to the king [George Fox]".*

86 To King Charles II 1660

"This wee declare, That it is our principle[,] life & practice to live peaceably with all men, And not to act . . . by . . . carnall weapons."

The preceding letter (Letter 85) seems to be a quickly written personal one, whereas this is a carefully worded document to express the Quaker policy on the use of force and on other issues that might be misunderstood by the authorities.

In the 1650s there were many expressions by Friends, including George Fox and Margaret Fell, of their opposition to the use of "carnall weapons" and that they were a "harmless people." The new royal government, struggling to establish itself, was justifiably alarmed by refusals to obey established laws and customs. They had enemies, and there were conspiracies. The fact that some Quakers had served in Cromwell's army was troubling to them. Margaret wrote this very clear statement: "This wee declare, That it is our principle [,] life & practice to live peaceably with all men." It was based on their most fundamental beliefs. The letter was also signed by a number of other Friends.

Margaret explains that Quakers cannot take oaths, for conscience sake, but that they are loyal subjects. She stresses their obedience to all "just & lawful Commands." Nor can they take off hats in the presence of magistrates, since all men are worthy of respect. Eighty-nine people were in prison for these two offenses, and she asks for their freedom. She also asks the king to instruct local justices of the peace not to require oaths or to forcefully break up Meetings, for Friends were "haled out, & beat & bruised & thrown into waters, & stampt upon till the blood hath gushed out."

This may Certifie that whereas wee have the promise & word of a King in severall Declarations for the Liberty of tender Consciences, that noe man shall be disquieted or called in question for differences of opinions in matters of Religion which doe not disturb the peace of the Kingdome

This wee declare, That it is our principle[,] life & practice to live peaceably with all men, And not to act any thing against the King nor the peace of the Nation, by any plotts, contrivances, insurrections, or carnall weapons to hurt or destroy either him or the Nation thereby, but to be obedient unto all just & lawfull Commands.

And whereas for Conscience sake we cannot sweare at all, nether for nor against any, But have under the late powers suffered imprisonment & spoiling of our goods, because we would not sweare against the King, and now also we suffer imprisonment & spoiling of our goods because we could not sweare the Oath of Allegeance for him, to the number of seventy one persons which are now in prison in severall Goales [jails] in England[,] onely upon that account which is a matter of Religion to us; And because we could not putt off our hatts to Magistrates & soe respect mens persons, which the Apostle saith is Sinne, are eighteene persons imprisoned.

Therefore if this testimony of our obedience to the present Government may be received[,] instead of an Oath, which wee doe intend in the Lords power to performe, then we desire to receive an answere, whereby all our friends now in prison may be set free, & all future imprisonment and suffering upon that account prevented

And wee have been persecuted & suffered in all these changes bacause we could not sweare, & take an Oath, but kept to Yea and Nay according to Christs Doctrine, & therefore we would have you, that have been sufferers, to minde it that it is for Conscience sake that we doe not sweare now, And that you would consider, & give forth something to the Justices that they might not impose an Oath on us, and if wee be not faithfull to you in our yea & nay, let us suffer by you as much as for breaking an Oath.

And though the King hath given forth a Declaration (which is lately renewed) that tender Consciences should not be disturbed, & they that doe soe have noe Direction from him, and yet our Meetings are dayly broken up & friends haled out, & beat & bruised & thrown into waters, & stampt upon till the blood hath gushed out, & can hardly passe in the streetes, And armed men come with swords[,] clubbs & staves, & forbids us to meete in our owne houses, & wee are threatened & indited because we will not come to the publique place of worship, and this practice is in diverse places of the Nation which are too many to relate.

Witnesses of the truth of this
who are lovers of your soules
& your eternall peace
M: F:

Spence 3/117. Endorsed: "M F & others [George Fox]".

87 TO KING CHARLES II; JAMES, DUKE OF YORK; AND HENRY, DUKE OF GLOUCESTER JUNE 1660

"You have been sufferrers while you have been out of this Nation, now you are come into a Nation, where God hath a suffering people, which he hath owned & will owne."

Margaret writes to the king and his two younger brothers, James, Duke of York, and Henry, Duke of Gloucester, congratulating them on their survival of the years of exile. She tells them that it is by the goodness of God that this was achieved "without the shedding of any blood." They now have the opportunity to show mercy to "a suffering people."

Margaret delivered this letter to the king herself in June 1660. She had traveled to London on horseback with a member of her household, Mary Askew. Roads were poor, and travel by horse or carriage was strenuous. She was determined to do all she could to obtain George Fox's release from Lancaster Castle, as well as to plead for the numerous other Friends in prison.

It was easier to get access to the king at that time, and it was her position as widow of Judge Thomas Fell that gave her that privilege. Alexander Parker described the interview in a letter to George Fox: "[She] had a full and large time to lay all things before him, of Friends' sufferings. He was very moderate and promised fair things, if he perform them it will be good for him; he also desires a particular account of all friends that are present sufferers here, and the cause of their sufferings and the names of the magistrates who sent them to prison."

On June 22 Margaret delivered a document to the king that was the first printed, clear exposition of the Quaker position on peace. This paper, "A Declaration and an Information from us the People of God called Quakers, to the present Governors, the King and both Houses of Parliament, and all whom it may concern," was written by Margaret Fell and signed by thirteen men (Ross, pp. 126–128).

Kunze writes about Margaret in this crucial period: "Fell's statements in this period express not only a sense of the immediacy of the religious and political fervor that was abroad but also they address specific political issues" (p. 135).

O King & you the two Dukes, childeren of the late King deceased. there is something upon my spirit towards you, & in deare & tender bowelles of Love doe I write unto you, not in feignednes or dissembling for an end, but in sincerity of heart, & true Love to you[,] the Lord knowes that searches the secrets of all heartes, & I know & can beare my testimony, that the Love of God is towards you, and moved towards you at present, slight not his tenders of Love, least you be hardned, oh consider the goodnes of an Infinite God, that hath preserved you & kept you, & delivered you from all your Enimies, which were many & great[,] & he hath visitted you in Love, & mercy in all your troubles & Tryalls & sufferings, & hath brought you thorow them, & hath now given you what your hearts can desire as to the outward man, & hath sett you upon your Fathers throan, & brought you to your Native being, oh consider who hath donne this, hath not the Lord by whom Kings reign and Princes decree Justice, look not at Man in this thing, least you take glory from the Lord, for what is man to be accounted of, who is less than nothing, & vanity without the Lord, yett an Instrument in the hand of the Lord as he is pleased, to make use of him, heere you may look uppon man, but lett the Lord have the glory, that is due unto him for it is he alone that hath done it; thousands of Mens lives could not purchase it for your Father, yett hath the Lord brought you to this without the shedding of any blood[.] of his owne good will & pleasure hath he done this, yett none must say why hast thou donne it, you have been sufferrers while you have been out of this Nation, now you are come into a Nation, where God hath a suffering people, which he hath owned & will owne, & he hath reproved, & rebuked & overturned the powers of this Nation for their sake, & all Nations shall see that they are the seed which God hath blessed, Now God hath brought you to the Throane to try you, what you will doe for his people, & he hath put an opportunity into your hands, wherein you may answer his deare & tender Love to you, in the time of your need & nessessity; oh forgett not his benefitts, & mercy towards you; if you be a blessing to this Nation, blessed will you bee, and for what you doe for the People of God, yee shall never be ashamed, it is our desire that your hands may be kept out of blood, & persecution that God may blesse & prosper you, And as you rule for God, & for his Truth, soe you will have our prayers, for we have accesse to the God of heaven, who is king of Kings & Lord of Lords, who hath heard us[,] doth heare us[,] & will heare us, & when the Innocent is wronged & persecuted, he is engaged to plead for them, & to stand for them, soe this in deare love, I was moved of the Lord, to write to you before hand, that you might not be found actors against God, & his people, and I am to warne you to beware, & take heed who you lett come neere you, & about you[,] least you be betrayed, for there is a deceitfull dissembling Murtherous spirit, in this Nation, amongst those people, which may seeme to be your friends, the same as took away your Fathers life, which have turned to every power for their owne ends, beware of these & trust them not

From a true Lover of your soules & your Eternall good

Margaret: Fell:

Spence 3/99 and Spence 3/105 (probably an earlier version). Also in Works, *pp. 17–18 dated June 1660. Endorsed: "M F to the King [George Fox]".*

88 To George Fox July 17, 1660

"Wee was with the King this day about it and . . . the prisbiterion party is exceeding Mad that hee should admitt us soe to come to him and in any measure hearken to us."

As Friends tried to gain King Charles II's influence to release George Fox from prison, one effective spokesperson was Anne Curtis (ca. 1631–?). She was the daughter of Robert Yeamans, who had been sheriff of Bristol, hanged in 1643 while defending the cause of King Charles I and the Royalists. Anne and her husband, Thomas Curtis, were staunch friends of George Fox; he stayed in their house in Reading for ten weeks in 1659 while he was ill (Ross, p. 129).

At the interview Margaret describes, Anne offers to take George Fox's place in prison. If that offer is not accepted she asks that the king have George Fox brought to London so that he (the king) may hear the case. The king's staff did not permit this but invoked a portion of law that only would allow George Fox to be brought to London to be heard by judges. Margaret comments on the king's position, that he is "Moderate" but concerned for his own safety, and "hee is darke and ignorant of god."

Margaret adds news of several others in London. Elizabeth Trott (ca. 1628–1668) was a wealthy widow with a large house in London where Friends, including Margaret, often stayed. She visited America in 1662 (Tolles, p. 38) and held Meetings at her home until her death (CJ, 1:466).

Thomas Salthouse (1630–January 29, 1691) was a member of the Swarthmoor household, Judge Fell's land steward, when he was convinced by George Fox at his first visit in 1652. Salthouse was an eloquent preacher, traveled widely for many years, and "the spread and consolidation of Quakerism in the west of England were in large measure the result of his efforts" (Greaves, 3:135). He spent numerous periods in prison, and he wrote tracts and an autobiography (DNB).

My deare love and life everlasting, the last 7 day Ann Curtiss came Hither Aboute the 11 houre and I went with her to White Hall and Brought her to the King[,] And shee made known to him whose Daughter shee was & how that her Father was executed for him or in his Fathers cause where upon hee showed much love to her, And shee said shee had now arequest to Him, hee axed her what it was, shee said shee had a deare freind in Lancaster Castle whom shee had been to see and shee desired her persone Might bee accepted for his or else that hee might bee Brought up with his accusers to before him, and hee might be Judg in the cause, and hee gave command to his Secretary to Issue forth an order to that purposs, but the Subtilty of the Secretary gave out order to the Judge to bee brought up by Horposs scorpions [habeas corpus] and to apeare before the Judges, soe that shee was disapointed of her request to him and of what hee had granted, if the Secretary had proseede according to order, wee Might have had it to have sent downe this day but being it was contrary wee could not send it[.] wee was with the King this day about it and hee appointed us to come to Morrow soe what the effecte will bee wee know not, the prisbiterion party is exceeding Mad that hee should admitt us soe to come to him and in any measure hearken to us, and I doe beleeve doth insence him that if hee answer our desires the whole Nation will be against him, but the Man is Moderate & I doe beleeve hath an intent in his mind and a desire to doe for freinds if he knew how & not to indanger his own safty, hee is darke and Ignorant of god & soe any thing feares him but wee have gotten aplace in his heart that hee doth beleeve wee will bee true to him and soe doth many of his own party, and truly the power is exceedingly over them and over the citty meetings ar all quiet & peacable and many saith they never saw them soe full, J N [James Nayler, Letter 49] had a Meeting the first day in the strand[.] the most part of them had beene seldom at meetings[.] freinds their abouts were drawn out to E T [Elizabeth Trott] in the pellmell [Pall Mall,] where their was a Meeting that day which was the first that was there, & its like to bee be agreat Meeting, T S [Thomas Salthouse] is heare[,] whose love is dearly to thee, and severall freinds in the Ministrey[,] and all very well [.] my returne to me is yett unsertaine, How thou may com up wee know not, whether they will give us way to bring thee up or they will send for thee up by order[,] but wee shall not neglect any thing, they that have to doe with these people must be contended to waite, my deare love eternall is to thee and freinds.

Margrett [Fell, Jr.'s] deere love is to thee;

M F

the 17 of the 5 Month. 1660

Ann Curtiss is heare yett and alsoe her Husband is come up who remembers his deare love to thee[.]

Spence 1:171. Also in CJ, 1:372–373. Endorsed: "M F to G F at Lankster in preson 1660 17 day 5 mo:"; "For G.F.".

89 TO ALEXANDER PARKER AND GEORGE WHITEHEAD JULY 24, 1660

"It is like to be A sad time of tryall to many, who are not very well prepared for sufferinge; Coll. [Francis] Hacker is like to suffer deeply[,] he with many more are in the Tower."

Alexander Parker and George Whitehead were in Newgate prison, and Margaret tells them of her visits to King Charles and of other political events. She describes her own work: "I have laboured five or six weekes hereabout these great ones . . . "

Alexander Parker (1628–1689) was one of George Fox's close friends and traveling companions. Greaves writes: "His affectionate letters to Margaret Fell illustrate the depth of sympathy between men and women which was one of Quakerism's most remarkable features." He played a major part in the growth and organization of the Quaker movement. He was well educated and an effective mediator in dealing with Quakers and with outside forces (Greaves, 3:7).

George Whitehead (1636–1723), also an important figure in the development of Quakerism, traveled in the ministry, wrote over one hundred tracts, and spent lengthy periods in prison, during which time he studied legal procedures to help himself and others to assert their rights. After Fox's death in 1691 he became the foremost leader of the Quakers (Greaves, 3:314).

Colonel Francis Hacker (?–October 19, 1660) was commander of the guard and signed the order for the execution of King Charles I in 1649. The Act of Indemnity at the Restoration pardoned all those who had fought against the monarchy except the few men who had signed the death warrant or were immediately responsible for

Charles I's death. In 1660 Col. Hacker was locked in the Tower, tried with the Regicides, and executed (Greaves, 2:36–37).

Margaret's sympathy reaches out to Col. Hacker at this time, even though he was generally ill-disposed to nonconformists; he had arrested George Fox in 1654. She was against violent deaths and the suffering of prisoners and was concerned that those in the Tower were not prepared to endure this. She wrote and published a letter to Major-General Harrison, another of the Regicides: "This was given to Major Generall Harrison and the rest. Read this in the Fear of the Lord, and in the moderation of Your Spirits, without prejudice."

*Among the courtiers who did not want the king to release George Fox was General George Monck, later Duke of Albemarle (1608–1670). He had served in the armies of Charles I and of Oliver Cromwell. After the demise of the Commonwealth he favored the monarchy and, with his army, was of major importance in the return of Charles II to England (*DNB*).*

*John Swinton (1621?–1679) was a Scottish politician, served in both the Scottish and English parliaments, and held numerous high offices under Cromwell. He became a Quaker in 1657. "On July 20, 1660 he was arrested in London in the house of a quaker," and he spent several years in prison, probably for political rather than religious causes (*DNB*).*

Lond: the 24 of the 5th Mo: 60

A.P. and W.G.

With all the rest of my dear bretheren Sufferers for the testymony of Jesus; my dear Love in the everlasting Fountaine of all Love is unto you all, And though I have bene silent in not writeing unto you, by reason of my service here, and heavy burthens and travells [travails] that I have bene exersised in[,] yet I have not bene unmindfull of you, nor unsensible of your sufferinges but it is faith and patience that most [must] cary through, For whenever the Lord suffers his enemyes to exercise their Cruelty upon his Children & servents it is for the Accomplishing of his owne will & pleasure, which is for his owne service; And therefore dear harts be not weary, for when the Lords end and time is come then will deliverance come, For in vaine is it looked for, from the hills and from the Mountaines but from the Lord alone in whom is everlasting strength.

I have Laboured this five or six weekes hereabout these great ones that are in power to Informe them, and hath made knowne unto them, the sufferinges of all Friends in the Nation, And the King hath promised much often and severall times he hath said it should bee helped and hee would looke to it, And that wee should not be abussed nor suffer for our Religion; There hath not bene A weeke since I first spoke with him, but I have bene with him twice or thrice, And both hee & many about him carryes faire and very Loveing towardes us[.] Soe I beleeve if our prisoneres were forth, it would be pritty well with the Truth at present, but I see after people bee cast into prison it is hard to recover them out againe, though wicked bloody mindes even make light of it to take more Lybertyes from them. When the King should come to doe any thing, they will not suffer him, but what as they will have him to doe; Hee had once given order to bring G.F. from Lancaster to be tryed here, but Monke and the rest that were about him would not suffer it; soe now he hath nothing to say when I goe to him, but that he will give the Judges orders that they shall hear Friendes and set them free, but what they will doe the Lord only knowes.

I was with him the last seventh day, And when I spoke to him, they that were about him gave Answer and they are very fearfull least he should speake any thing that they would not have him; they would[,] if they could[,] make him act contrary to what he hath spoken concerning Lyberty of conscience, but the Lordes determined will will be brought forth; And therefore all in patience waite untill the chang [change] come.

Friends and the Truth hereaway are very well, And meetting[s] very quiet and full, And many desires to hear the Truth; the power is over all, which cheines & bindes downe the unrully[,] though there bee A great enmity and envy in many[,] yet it is kept under by the secrett Arme of the Almighty, glory & prayses be unto him for ever; I am not yet clear of this place, but at present am set forth here, And my returne as yet I doe not see, but to the lord I am Committed who is my all in all[.] It is like to be A sad time of tryall to many, who are not very well prepared for sufferinge; Coll. [Francis] Hacker is like to suffer deeply[.] he with many more are in the Tower, And certainely Gods hand of Justice, they doe and must tast [taste] of, John Swinton was Apprehended the last sixt day, their wrath & violence is much against him. but the man is pritty sensible and low, And I beleeve will patiently endure what they are suffered to Act against him; The God of power keep all his in that testimony which shall never dye but hath power and victory over death & hell; My Love is dear unto you all[.] farewell And the god of power [preserve &] keep you all in his owne name.

Your dear friend in the Truth

M.F.

Spence 3/56. Endorsed: "M.F. to A. Parker and G. Whighed, 1660, read over, G.F. in Lankester, prsener, 31 [appears to be in George Fox's hand]".

90 To her Children, with a postscript by Will Caton July 24, 1660

"The last week wee received A Letter which made mention of Bridg: [Bridget Fell] not being well; I would have her to drinke at least twenty days of her Janesse drinke."

While Margaret was in London with her eldest daughter, Margaret, Jr., Bridget Fell (1635?–1663), then twenty-six years old, was left in charge of the younger children and the management of the Swarthmoor household. Margaret recommends two herbal drinks to Bridget: Janesse, *a jaundice drink made from barberry; and* Alice, *from sweet alyssum (Ross, p. 133). She had heavy responsibilities, including business matters and dealing with "rude fellows" who interrupted the Meetings that they continued to hold at Swarthmoor Hall (Crosfield, p. 93).*

Bridget married John Draper of Headlam, County Durham, on March 22, 1662. In 1663 she had a son, Isaac, and both mother and child died. Margaret was with her at that time. Bridget is seldom mentioned thereafter, but two of her sisters, Margaret and Mary, named daughters Bridget (Ross, pp. 149–150).

Walter Miers (1633?–1723/24) was one of the many members of the Swarthmoor Meeting who traveled as missionaries. He settled in London by 1665 and remained a prominent London Friend (CJ, 2:475).

The pardon that son George Fell needed was the result of his anxiety about having been authorized by Richard Cromwell's government to raise troops for the Parliamentary cause. He was also concerned that his father, Judge Fell, had been a supporter of Oliver Cromwell. The pardon was granted on June 22, 1660 (Ross, p. 179).

Will Caton (Letters 63, 66), who wrote this letter for Margaret, adds a postscript of his own.

London the 24 of the 5th mo: 60

My dear Lambes and babes of God[,] the Father of you all, my dear Love flowes freely unto you, in the bowells of endlesse Love be yee Refreshed and nourished forever; And there doe you drinke freely and eate abundantly and be satisfied; Dear harts my way and time of Returne is not yet manifested to mee, but here I am set fast, the will of the Lord to fulfill every jot and tittle, which is the desire of my soul, And therein shall I be satisfied; The last weeke wee received A Letter which made mention of Bridg: [Bridget Fell] not being well; I would have her to drinke at least twenty days of her Janesse drinke, and I would have her take A Quantytie of Alice three mornings together, and keep warm & to [drink?] warm broath [broth], I am told this is good for her disease; let this be done shortly after the receipt of this[.] may bee wee may send her some pills by water [Walter] Mires when hee comes, let us hear from you as often as you can; And as Concerning the Karter I can say little, for my testimony in that thing standes to mee, And I cannot goe against it, but let the Lord doe what he will in it; The other hath not much ground more than hee had, as farre as I doe understand he hath only A promise of the renewing of his patten [patent?], which I beleeve is not yet done, If the little fellow be willing to Continue he may, if not he may doe as hee will, But let him not goe out upon the others words except that he have some Lawfull Authoritie to put him out by[.] Your bro: [brother, George Fell] is well[.] hee was here yesterday & sealed the Lease to his sister, but he hath not gott his pardon sealed yet, but hee doth not fear but get it done. Keep all in the fear of the Lord god, and there you will be preserved in his Counsell and wisedome, the Arme of the Almighty reach over you, And his blessing rest upon you for ever; My dear Love to all Friendes.

I have writt every weeke since you
went, but wee have received few from you
Your dear Mother in the eternall life of Truth

Margrett Fell

Dear ones, the dearest love of my Soul reacheth unto you, who are often in my Remembrance, and indeed my hart and soul is affected [with?] your love and and life which I am very sensible of, even as if I were with you; For behold wee are as A Famelly here, now our dear bro: T. S. [Thomas Salthouse] being with us, whose Love _____ ______ ______ is very dear unto you, And we are all very well in the Lord, whom our soules blesseth for this pretious oportunity which wee have through the mercy of god, which doth indeed tend to the Refreshing of our soules & to the Renewing of our strength in the Inward man; your Sister [Margaret Fell, Jr.] Salutes you dearly; Salute us to M. A. [Mary

Askew] J. P. [James Parke] to J. E. [John Edge?] to L. F. [Leonard Fell] Rob: Salt. [Robert Salthouse] and to any other who may enquire after us, & be desirous to hear of our welfarre;

W. C. [Will Caton]

Bridgett my dear love[,] keep in the patience and be Subject to the will of the Lord[.] My dear love to little Rachell and all the rest

M.F.

Spence 3/70. Also Crosfield, pp. 72–73 and Ross, p. 133. Addressed: "For the handes of Bridg. Fell at Swarthmore, in Lancashire". Endorsed: "M.F. to her children 5m., 60".

91 To George Fox July 24, 1660

"Hee [King Charles II] promissed mee that the Judges should take order concerning friends . . . but being that he is prevented of doeing that he promised, he shames & will not stay, when one speakes to him."

On the same day as the previous two letters Margaret writes to George Fox to relate their progress in getting his release. She has come to the conclusion that it is counter-productive to speak to the king when he is surrounded by those opposed to Quakers, because he feels ashamed that his power is limited and that he cannot do as he wishes. Laws then, as now, were myriad and complex, and provisions could be interpreted and executed with greater or lesser severity.

In addition to the concern for Quaker prisoners, Margaret is aware of scaffolds being built for Col. Hacker and the Regicides.

London the 24 of the 5th Mo. (60.

My dear eternall Love and Life: I gave thee an accountt the last weeke, how farre An [Anne] Curtes [Letter 88] had gone in the buissines concerning thee, And according as I wrote we went the next morning, but before they would suffer us to goe in to speake to him [i.e. to King Charles], Generall Monke [Letter 90] did come I beleeve on purposse to prevent us, And we were with him A pritty while before wee were called in; And wee were called in while hee was there, and while wee spoke to him, he stood by, and before wee could get any thing spoke to him to any purposse, they tooke him away from us, and the most that hee said to us was that hee would speake to the Judges And they should set Friendes at Lyberty; And he said they told him, that he could not send A perticular order from himselfe, And I perceive by severall, both Friendes and others that saith, by their Law he cannot send for any prisoner any otherwayes then by A habeas Corpus, but because that thou wrote that wee should speake to him of that thing, wee were willing to desire it of him, but it had bene better wee had not, being hee could not doe it. Thou mentioned in thy Letter that I should get porter [Henry Porter, see Letter 83] before him; how should I doe that, when hee can doe nothing but by their order, And I have nothing to ingage them to such A thing; I was with three parliament men & did desire to have him before them, And they told mee they had noe Authoritie to call him before them; for any thing that I can see or perceive, there can be nothing done before the Sisses [Assizes]; For the more that wee stirre in it the greater they looke upon the Crime to bee, And if it had not bene soe much mentioned and turned over Amongst them, it is like it might have bene better.

The last seventh day after An was gone I was with the King in his bed chamber and spoke to him about the oath which Friends could not take, And spoke to him about all the prisoners; And hee promissed mee that the Judges should take order concerning friends, And that he had given them order to that purposse, but being that he is prevented of doeing that he promised, he shames & will not stay, when one speakes to him; They apprehended John Swinton [Letter 89] the last sixt day, their enmitie & envy is very great towards him, I felt their spirits were stired up & exasperated; Collo: Hacker [Letter 89] is in the Tower in A sad condition & is like to suffer sadly, It is A sad day of suffering with many of them; It is said that they are makeing Scaffolds & thinges to take away mens lives, but there is A hand that stayes them, which they are ignorant of; I am yet stayed here, but how long it may be, it is not yet clear unto mee, my Love is unto all Friends; Truth here hath A powerfull dominion & Authoritie over all; Meettinges never quieter; then of late they have bene; This day there came A contentious preist to the Meeting at Palluce yard, but his folly appeared to all sober people, and he fled, and the meetting was kept in pritty good order:

M. F.

Spence 1:172. Also CJ, 1:373–375. Endorsed: "MF to GF 1660 at Lankester presen 24:day 5 mo:"; "For G.F. this".

92 To George Fox July 31, 1660

"I spoke to him [King Charles II] concerning the oath that Friends could not take."

Margaret summarizes her recent activities, since George Fox had also complained about not hearing from her. She describes her various visits to King Charles.

Taking oaths was one source of difficulties for Quakers. People were required to take an oath in a court proceeding or to hold office, and Quakers refused, taking literally Jesus's injunction to "Swear not at all" [Matt. 5:34]. Holding to this principle caused many Friends to be imprisoned or fined. The king evidently was somewhat sympathetic but not able to respond favorably to Margaret's appeal. She knew that under these circumstances "we could not expect any thing but to suffer."

She gave the king a "paper" of her own. A companion distributed three copies of a book at the court. This was A Battle-Door for Teachers and Professors to Learn Singular and Plural, *a book that Fox wrote with John Stubbs and Benjamin Furley. Larry Ingle describes this as "one of Fox's oddest works, a linguistic survey and defense of the use of 'thee' and 'thou'" (p. 333). Margaret also mentions several contentious pamphlets then being circulated. One was the* Phanatic History, *an attack on James Nayler (Letters 7, 49) to which he had replied, and another some "quiries" put forth by Jesuites," also being answered by Nayler (Ross, p. 131).*

London, 31 of 5th mo: 1660.

My dear and eternally beloved, Thine I received, wherein thou mentions thou had noe letter that weeke, which is strainge to me, for I have not missed a weeke since I came hither of writting, but that weeke especially I gave A particular accountt, how that I carried An Curtis [Letter 88] to the King, and what she said to him & hee to her, concerning thy being brought up to London, to be examined, which he himselfe did consent too, and gave order to issue out an order to that purposse, but the Secretary, who was to write the order, would not write it as from him in particular but by way of A habeus corpus, and soe after the thing came into question and dispute Generale Monk [Letter 89] and severall others would not consent that the King should or could send any particular order, but just as were according to Law; the next day I was with the King againe, and he promised mee that he would give special order to the Judges to release Friends[,] but what hee would doe[,] he cannot, I spoke to him concerning the oath that Friends could not take, and told him that there would be exaction [i.e., the action of demanding "excessive payment, extortionate" *OED*] at the Assizes, for it would be offerdd to Friends who were to doe service for their Country, which requires swearing according to their Law, And I gave him friends answer to the oath, and told him if that would serve[,] there should be some manifestation from him that he was satisfied with that, And if he was not, then we could not expect any thing but to suffer, And it put him to stand, And he said he knew not what to doe in it, And they that were about him gave answer and said the King could doe nothing but according to Law, And if wee would not be subject to the Laws of the Nation, then wee might suffer by them, And soe at that time they took him away from mee,

The last first day I was at Whitehall, and gave the King a paper which I was moved to write to him, And there was one with mee that had some bookes, three of the Battle-doore were deliveredd, one to the Kings bedchamberman, and another to the Dean of the Chapell, and another to a great man of the court; there were likewise some answers given to the phanatick history[,] which thou spoke of in thy last letter, there are likewise now some quiries put forth by Jesuites or some papists to Friends, which J. N. [James Nayler] is now answering[.]

I doe not know but there may be way made for my return ere it be long, but I doe not see, that it will be before the Sissis [Assizes], let me hear from thee by the next, and weigh the thing, for I am given up to the will and service of the Lord:

All is very well here, And all Meettings full and quiet[,] and the power restrains and binds and chaines; Let enquiry be made at the post-house what became of the letters, there were some to the children, that I would not have lost. G. F. was put on the backside [outside of the letters] and it may be that was the cause [that they were not delivered]: our dear everlasting love is unto you,

M. F.

FHL Port. 23:37. Also Cash Collection, Temp. MSS 747:6. Addressed: "For G.F." Endorsed: "M.F. to G F at lankester presen consaring [concerning] the kings saiings 31 day 6 mo 1660 [Should be 5th mo.]"; "Copied from the original by P.____ 2 mo: 20th 1846.".

93 To King Charles II August ? 1660

"These that have been guilty of thy fathers blood, oh that thou wouldst shew mercy unto them."

During July and August much of Parliament's energies were spent in debating the provisions of the Bill of Indemnity and Oblivion. This was King Charles II's "great gesture to reunite the country" by pardoning all those who had acted against the monarchy in the preceding decade, excepting only seven men who had actively participated in his father's death. Members of Parliament were less merciful and added more than fifty names to the list. The two Houses could not agree on specific individuals, and when the king finally signed the act on August 29, thirty-three men were named. The trials took place in October, and only ten men were actually executed (Hutton, pp. 132–134).

Margaret writes an earnest letter to the king, asking that he show mercy. She writes of the spirit of love, that God is love, and that vengeance belongs to God alone. She quotes Daniel, that it is "the most high that rules in the Kingdomes of men," Daniel's message to King Nebuchadnezzar that he rules only with the will of God. Margaret points to the advantage for Charles "to be cleere in the sight of God & all men" and urges him to use his power with "wisdome & an understanding heart."

She writes of the connection between liberty of conscience and a populace that will not plot or conspire against the king. In a more Puritan mode, she also asks for restraints on "Ballad singing[,] stage plays[,] with other such like vaine things."

A Loveing salutation with advise & Counsell which will be found soe, if it bee received in the Love

That thou may continue in Long and happy dayes[,] oh King[,] & Answere the goodnes of the gracious God, whose Love hath exceedingly extended towards thee and to thy Fathers house & Family, though he seemed to frowne; & to hide his face from you for a Moment[.] yett in Everlasting kindnes is he now visitting you in this your day, and goeing about to gather you into his Bowells of Love & restore unto you your formes[,] rights & privilledges as men, (which others have withholden from you, not without the permission of the Lord, soe they had their day & will receive their reward), and this he hath donne for you not by the strength of Man nor arme of flesh, nor by the violence of the sword[,] but by his owne power & Arme, & not only soe, but by this power & Arme doth he bow mens heartes unto you, & under you, and even strangely changed their minds towards you, that have beene in Rebellion & bitter Envy against you formerly[,] allthough there is a spirit of the same Nature, remaining amongst them which lusteth unto Envy for blood and Murther secretly, yett it is wonderfully calmed & quenched generally amongst the people[,] soe that if heeere be wise ordering & governing & dealing with them in meeknes & Love & patience[,] it will even over power their heartes and change their minds, & will lay downe the high & lofty rebellious spt [spirit] & cause them to bee subject[.] I shall not Limmitt nor Lay any bound, but in deare Love & tendernes exhort in the spt of Meeknes according to what the spt of Grace & Love hath revealed in me & unto me, which I know is the mind of his Eternall spirit, for God is Love, & he that dwells in God dwells in Love[,] & love is the fullfilling of the Law[,] & Love thinketh noe Evill nor doeth noe Evill, but overcometh Evill with good[,] & they that are endowed with this spirit of Love, are blessed of God, soe now consider it is the Lord that hath donne this great & wonnderfull worke, and it is he that hath the heartes of all men in his hands & turnes them as the Riverse of water [Prov. 21:1] and it is him by whom Kings rule & princes decree Justice, [Prov. 8:15] and it is the most high that rules in the Kingdomes of men [Dan. 4:17,25,32] & vengeance belongs unto him who will repay it, according to the good pleasure of his will who is infinite in wisdome, rich in Mercy[,] abundant in Loveing kindnes & Truth[,] full of Long suffering which is salvation unto many[;] for if he should take vengeance & execute his wrath upon them suddainly, which is provoked every moment[,] many thousands might fall into the pitt, but oh the goodnes & the patience & the long suffering & Mercy of an Infinite God who desires not the death of sinners, but rather that they might turne from their wickednes & live.

Now lett this sink into thy heart o King[,] & consider the place where this God hath sett thee over many sortes of peple of severall opinions as concerning the worship of God, which is a weighty and a great thing on which the salvation of their Immortall soules depends[;] and therefore it will be good for thee to be cleere of all their bloods to lett them every one enjoy the liberty of their owne Consciences to that worshipp which they dare trust their soules under, & dare answer to a just & righteous god, & heere thou wilt be cleere in the sight of God & all men, God hath alsoe given thee, power over many thousand peoples lives & estates, oh that thou wouldst be even as sollomon [Solomon] that thou wouldst ask of him wisdome & an understanding heart, that in the wisdome of god, thou might order & govern these Nations & people, to his glory & thy Everlasting peace & Comfort[.] soe would thy dayes bee prolonged & thy yeares continued, the God of Mercy & Love hath brought thee into this Nation in Love & Mercy without the shedding of any blood or revenging of the blood that hath been shedd, oh that thou wouldst but consider this & commit thy Cause unto him who hath said[,] Vengeance is mine & I will repay it[,] & these that have been guilty of thy fathers blood, oh that thou wouldst shew mercy unto them, & forgive thy Enimies[;] soe wouldst thou engage the god of heaven & all good people to Love thee, thou cann never suffer[,] neither from God nor Man by shewing of Mercy, for the Lord hath said[,] to the Mercifull I will shew my selfe mercifull, to the froward I will shew my selfe froward[,] & to doe Justly & love mercy & to walk humbly with the Lord is that which he requires [Mic. 6:8], and though the Lord God hath said, he that shedds mans blood, by man shall his blood be shedd, yett christ Jesus who is the end of the Law for righteousnes & hath fullfilled every jot & tittle of the Law by his owne blood[,] he saith[,] Love your Enimies[,] blesse them that curse you[,] pray for them that dispitefully use you & persecute you, that you may be the Children of your Father which is in heaven [Matt. 5:44–45], this is christs doctrine, & Command who hath given the power & committed into thy hands thy Enimies to doe with them according to the Minafestation of his will in thy owne heart, Now if thou would mind this of God in thy owne particular[,] by which measure of himselfe, God teaches his people & doth manifest himselfe unto them, and if thou be guided by this Manifestation & not look out at others that may insence [incense] thee & provoke thee to revenge[,] which is not the will of God nor his way[;] for Man is not to revenge[,] nor that will not be good for thee, nor for thy prosperity, thy only way is to shew mercy & forgivenes unto them, that all the Nations can beare witnes of [words missing] have been thyne & thy Fathers Enimies, & Committ thy cause to the god of heaven. This will be of good savor & of good report & would bring Everlasting peace & Comfort to thee[,] & thou will never receive any thing but love & mercy from the Lord in shewing & manifesting [forgiveness?] & would gaine peoples heartes, & the blessing of the Lord would be upon them in soe doeing[,] & though thy Enimies doe plott & hatch up in the dark & invent wickednes against thee whom god hath sett up by his power, Justice unto them[,] if thou keep thy heart inclineing unto Love & Mercy & give liberty unto the Consciences of people where Gods throan [throne] is & where he sways his scepter in righteousness, & where the antient of dayes sitts[,] which is as the refiners fire & as fullers soap[,] whose fann is in his hand, now I say if thou give people the liberty of their Consciences to worship him[,] in this thou rules for god[,] and then all the plotts & Inventions and secret conspiracies of men shall never [prevail?] against thee[,] but they shall be confounded & frustrated in all their devices, & if thou wouldst but suppresse wickednes[,] oathes and drunkennes, lightnes, & vanities that is gott up in people some what more then hath been formerly[,] which doth open the Mouthes of many which are Enimies to this present goverment, which formerly did not appeare in the Nation, as bonfires[,] may poles[,] Ballad singing[,] stage plays[,] with other such like vaine things which was restrained[,] though they were hard hearted & Carnell, yett they were strick [strict] in these things, to which now there is more liberty, which opens the mouths of people, & setts their heartes more against this present government[.] the Proclamation against drinking helthes & other debauchdnes was of exceeding service to the Nation and did much quell & terrify debauched persons & gave satisfaction to sober minded people & put them even to a stand[;] & truly I hope none can Judg this _______ _______ _______ any thing but true Love unto you all, which is upon me from the Lord to lay before thee, the same god of power who hath the heartes of all men in his Hand[,] yea[,] Kings alsoe[,] make it effectuall unto thee & give thee to consider that it neerely [nearly] concernes thee, to ask Councell & wisdome of God[,] that thou may doe his will, & answer to his Love[,] which he hath manifested to thee, who is king of kings & Lord of Lords.

Spence 3/104. Summary in Works, *pp. 19–21. Endorsed: "M F to the king 60"; "M: F: To the King 60".*

94 TO HER CHILDREN, WITH A POSTSCRIPT BY MARGARET FELL, JR. AUGUST 1, 1660

"They are now begining to stir[.] And its like as if they would proceed towards the tryall . . . I doe not see but that these things will be accation [occasion] to stay me some what longer."

Margaret and Margaret, Jr. send their "deare love" to the children at Swarthmoor but are too much engaged in events in London to consider returning. Margaret writes that Walter Miers will carry some pills for Bridget (Letter 90). Margaret, Jr. mentions two members of the Swarthmoor household, Mary Askew and James Parke.

Mary Askew, a servant and friend, was given twenty pounds in Judge Thomas Fell's will; she traveled with Margaret to London in 1660; and she is frequently mentioned in family correspondence (Ross, pp. 12, 126, 399).

The DNB *refers to James Parke (1636–1696) as "apparently one of the band of preachers in the north of England sent out from Swarthmore Hall." He was an active traveler in the ministry and wrote many religious and controversial works. He and Margaret together wrote* Two General Epistles to the Flock of God, *published in 1664. George Fox visited him in 1685 and 1686, and Parke spoke at Fox's funeral in 1691 (Greaves, 3:6).*

Margaret was particularly concerned for three of the men who were tried under the Act of Indemnity (Letter 93). They were Major-General John Lambert, Sir Henry Vane, and Sir Arthur Haselrig. Each of them was an influential radical during the English Revolution and the Commonwealth, holding high offices.

Sir Henry Vane (1613–June 14, 1662) was for a short time governor of Massachusetts Bay where he supported Anne Hutchinson when she was tried for heresy. He is the only one of the three who was executed, although, like the other two, he had no part in the death of Charles I. His life was spared by King Charles II in 1660, but in 1661 Parliament renewed the charge against him. He was executed in 1662. He was considered too dangerous to live due to both his political and his religious ideas (Greaves, 3:262–263; Enc. Brit.*).*

Sir Arthur Haselrig (1601–1661) also played a major role in the various Parliaments and in the military, and he was a leader of the war party in the 1640s, along with Cromwell and Sir Henry Vane. He had a strong concern for religion and supported the Independents against both the Church of England and the Presbyterians. Anthony Pearson, a Quaker, was Haselrig's agent in the 1650s (Greaves, 3:15–16). Haselrig was named as one of King Charles I's judges in 1649 but refused to attend the trial. Because of this, Charles II pardoned him. He died naturally in 1661 (Greaves, 2:69–71).

Major-General John Lambert (1619–1684) was an army officer and parliamentary radical. He ruled Scotland from December 1651 to March 1652 with George Monck, and later he was considered by some to be Cromwell's successor. He was tolerant in religion and defended James Nayler during his trial. Lambert was exempted from the trials of 1660, but the Parliament of 1662 charged him with high treason. He was sentenced to death, but the sentence was commuted to imprisonment. He spent the rest of his life in Guernsey and Plymouth (Greaves, 2:167–170; Enc. Brit.*).*

Dearely beloved in the lord Jesus Christ[,] the Fountaine of all our love and life[,] my deare love runs forth freely unto you all in that one love & Spiritt of life which is but one in us all and which fils and feeds all that lives in it[,] and Drinkes of this fountaine where I desire you may eat and drinke abundantly and be satisfied, wee are well in the lord in his worke and service[.] the time of my Returne I doe not yett see, they are now begining to stir[.] And its like as if they would proceed towards the tryall of them that hath been acting aboute the Kings life[.] And there is other five which they intend to try for there lifes, Lamber [Major-General John Lambert], vaine [Sir Henry Vane] and Haslerig [Sir Arthur Haselrig] are three of them[.] I doe not see but that these things will be accation [occasion] to stay mee some what longer; till I see some end of these things, Hower [however] my Deare Lambe[,] dwell in the faith of gods elect which will work theron all these things and their you will bee one with mee and Dwell in love and unity and peace one with another and in that patience posses your selves[.] And doe not desire my returne till the lord that brought me Hither give mee bake [back] againe[,] to whose will I stand commited if I had a thousand lifes[.] And I doubt not but his Arme and power will be over you and his sweet love and presence will be with you[,] who is your father and Head of that family who careth for you and knoweth what you have need of[,] unto whose Arme & bosome alone I committ you[.]

Bri [Bridget,] my deare love[,] have a care to take such things as will doe thee good[.] wee shall send by Walt Mires [Walter Miers] some piles [pills], keep in the faith and in the patience which worketh by love[,] all of you[.] And the lord will Bless you[,] the Arme of the eternall god compass you aboute and preserve you

Your Deare Mo: [Mother]

M F

Pellmell; the 1 of the 6 Month 60

my deare love is deare unto all freinds

My der sisters[,] my true unfained love is derly to you all in the bowels of endlese love, the lord keep us in his holy feare in obedience to the Spiritt of truth that hee alone may be exalted[.] my Bro: [Brother George Fell] is well[.] hee comes heare sometimes; I know his love is to you; My dearest love is to my sweet Rach: [Rachel Fell] and Dr [dear] Mary [Fell] and Susans [Susannah Fell]; and to Deare M A [Mary Askew] and J P [James Parke] with the rest of friends I ame in hast;

Your truly loveing
Sister M F [Margaret Fell, Jr.]

Spence 3/71. Also Crosfield pp. 73–75. Addressed: "For Bridgett Fell at Swarthmore, these". Endorsed: "MF to her Children 6 mo.1660".

95 To her Children, with a postscript by Henry Fell August 21, 1660

"I am in hast & Soe I cannot enlarge."

When George Fox was arrested at Swarthmoor Hall in late May or early June (Letter 83) he was locked up for a night at nearby Ulverston and the next day taken to Lancaster prison with an escort of thirty soldiers. Margaret went to London, and she and others worked for his release. Ingle writes: "An intensive lobbying operation to convince the king to free Fox was launched immediately." The king was not able to free Fox but after five months, in September, "an order to Lancaster that the prisoner be freed on a writ of habeas corpus" was received. The Lancaster officials could not decide who should pay the expense of escorting him, so he was released on his own promise to appear in London by a certain day. He took three weeks, visiting Friends and holding Meetings on the way" (Ingle, pp. 187, 191).

Margaret adds the news that Colonel Daniel Axtell (?–1660), one of the Regicides, as well as Francis Hacker and seven of Charles I's judges, were to be condemned as exceptions to the Act of Indemnity. Axtell had served in Cromwell's army and as governor of Kilkenny in Ireland, and he had commanded the soldiers at the trial and execution of Charles I. Axtell was executed on October 15, 1660, and his head displayed at Westminster Hall (Greaves, 1:30).

Anne Downer (1624–July 27, 1686) was a Quaker preacher, active in London. She spent twelve weeks in a "house of correction" for "some expressions" against a preacher, and in 1656 went to Cornwall to take food to George Fox and other prisoners there. She wrote "An Epistle for True Love, Unity, and Order in the Church" (1680) and was highly regarded for her work with the sick and poor, as well as for her ministry (Greaves, 1:232).

Gobart Sykes (or Sikes), a Friend, held Meetings at his home in Hackney, Middlesex. In 1663 or 1664 he was "convicted in order to Banishment," along with 218 persons at Bristol; only three were actually transported abroad, not including Sykes (Besse, 2:638, 1:51).

*Henry Fell (ca. 1630–ca. 1678), not related to Judge Fell, traveled in the Quaker ministry in England, Barbados, Holland, Germany, and as far as Egypt, where he was turned back by the English consul. "His few and brief writings show him to have received an education above the average; their style is good, and the language well chosen" (*DNB*). He served as amanuensis for Margaret in writing this letter and adds the brief postscript.*

London the 21th of the 6:mo: 1660

Deare & eternally beloved Lambes & babes of God[,] my deare love in the everlastinge fountaine flowes forth freely unto you who are deare & neare unto me, even as my owne life; never to be forgotten in that everlastinge bond of love & unity. my deare loves[,] dwell & keepe where our life is hidd with xt {Christ] in god. the God of love be your everlastinge Strength for ever. I am in hast & Soe I cannot enlarge. I expect that G:F: [George Fox] Should be heare Some tyme the next weeke; but yet I have not heard how they have proceeded as in order to his bringing up hither. the Act of indemnity is not yet perfectly past [passed]; but this day the two houses hath satt in a grand Committee & it is sayd that Coll: Hacker [Letter 89] & Coll: Axtell is left out of the Act as intendes to Suffer, besides :7: of the Kings Judges that is the most _____ [.] your Brother [George Fell] is in health, he was here with us this day[.] An Downer, & Mary Sanders is this day sett forwards towards the North with G: Robts. [Gerrard Roberts, Letter 68] & Gobart Sykes[,] which two doth intend to returne with G F [George Fox] if he come for London[.] Thus in short I rest with my deare love in the Lord to all Friends

Your deare mother

M: F:

My deare love is dearly remembered
to you all & to Friends:

H: F: [Henry Fell]

Spence 3/72.

96 To King Charles II Mid-September 1660

"I have beene heare a Quarter of a yeare, and have layd many things before thee; and thou hast given me many good words."

In mid-September Margaret wrote to King Charles summarizing the matters that concerned Quakers. She had spoken to him in person and had written to him. It is difficult to estimate her influence; but it is clear that at this time Quakers were a factor in the political scene, admired by some and considered a disturbance by others. Earlier historians quite often did not mention Margaret Fell, but the work of such writers as Christopher Hill, Richard Greaves, Bonnelyn Young Kunze, Phyllis Mack, and most recently, Rosemary Moore, has changed that. Ronald Hutton writes: "In Furness in late 1663 resided two of the most distinguished Quaker leaders, George Fox and Margaret Fell, who were noted not only for their influence within the movement but for the favour they had obtained from the King in 1660–1661, and who had accordingly escaped molestation" (Restoration, *p. 207).*

Margaret writes eloquently of the Quakers' nonviolence and the hardships it imposes on them. She makes it clear that if Friends are guilty of breaking any "Just law of the Nation" they should then rightfully be punished. She asks the king's help to relieve them of suffering but also has concern for the state of his "honour, & peace."

Good Counsell To the King From M. F.

Oh that the Lord would give thee to See how nearly it concernes thee (to watch over us for good) whom god hath called, & Sett the head Ruler over the Nation over the unruly, and prophane which is to be ruled by Law, & Comand, It is thy duty to the Lord to See us live peacably under thy Goverment, Seeing that for Conscience Sake we cannot defend ourSelves by violence; neither by resistinge with carnall weapons, nor takinge of Suite [suit] on law to right ourSelves: but we doe appeale unto thee, and lay our wronges, and Sufferings before thee who doe not wronge, nor Injure any man; but desires to live at peace with all men. It is for thy owne Safty, and prosperity and will be for thy Eternall peace to doe us Justice, & to right us, in what lyes in thy power. One word from thee would keepe the Multitude from persecutinge of us, and Imprisoninge without cause. I have tould thee often that noe man in the Nation would doe us right, or ease us of our Burdens exceptinge thee: and if thou alsoe deny to stand up to right us (who are Innocent of wronginge any man) we must be contented to

Suffer, as have done under those that went before untill the Lord plead our cause. which we know he will doe when he hath tryed men; and Sees that they fayle.

The desire of my heart is; that thou might be Servicable for the Lord in thy place: who hath by his owne power, & Arme brought thee, and Sett thee to try thee, who hath tryed others before. It will be good for thee to performe, as neare as thou canst, what thou Speakes in words: and that is honourable and of a good Report. I have beene heare a Quarter of a yeare, and have layd many things before thee; and thou hast given me many good words, and promissed me as faire as I could desire. Now it will be for thy honour, & peace that thy actions answere unto thy words. And if thou wouldst not have us to be troublsome to thee; in cominge to lay our Sufferings before thee: Doe but Signifie (if it were but one lyne to the Nation) that thou wouldst not have us soe abused, & Imprisoned, & evill Intreated; without we gave Just cause of offense. For we desire noe other, But if that we be guilty of the breach of any Just law of the Nation or of wronginge of any mans person, or estate, that then by the Law of the Nation we might Suffer.

And I beleeve this privilege we might have under any Goverment being true, & faithfull, & Loyall Subjects.

The Judges have done litle or nothinge for us, neither will they, nor can they doe anythinge for us. It must be thy owne particular act, or else we must Suffer under many hands in the Nation. which if any thinge preceede from thee (who art the head) it would bynde all others. Soe these things I am conStrayned to lay before thee; the lord is my witnesse; that thou may not be Ignorant but doe that which is Just & reasonable as the cheife [chief] magistrate of the nation and that will Satisfy us who are at present a sufferinge people and truly this I say unto thee which thou wilt finde to be truth[,] if thou doe not doe somthinge to ease the Innocent from sufferinge; thou wilt suffer by it from the Lord[.]

They are castinge into prison dayly & if thou Suffer them to goe on; both they & thee will be hardened in persecutinge, & then you will see what will follow. you have many Enemyes in the Nation which waites for an oportunity to manifest themselves but we are thy Friends[,] the Lord knowes[,] & tells thee the truth: and though we suffer much hardshipp yet by the power & strength of the Lord we Shall be kept cleare from doinge you any wronge or injury[,] the day will manifest all things, & the Lord god give thee to consider in tyme.

Spence 3/108. Also summarized in Works, *pp. 26–27.*

97 To King Charles II and James, Duke of York Late-September 1660

"That now in the tyme of your Joy hath turned it into mourning."

Margaret wrote two short letters to King Charles and James, duke of York, shortly after the sudden death of their younger brother, Henry, the duke of Gloucester, who had died of the small pox on September 13, 1660. "The Duke was only twenty. He had had no time to make his mark on history, but all contemporaries spoke of his bright promise, and his death was sincerely lamented. King Charles was deeply distressed; he had been devoted to his young brother, and for several days he refused to see anybody" (Morrah, p. 177).

Margaret refers to Lamentations 5:15–16: "The joy of our heart is ceased; our dance is turned into mourning, The crown is fallen from our head: woe unto us that we have sinned." She urges them to make God their "only Jewell" and "satisfaction." They must expect "tryalls, and Crosses" for god "Chasteneth every one whom he loveth."

[To King Charles]

The Lord is come very neare thee. oh that thou wouldst consider and See his hand; that therby thou might learne rightousnes and to doe Justice, & love mercy, and walke humbly with the Lord [Mic. 6:8] That soe thy Throne may be established. And that thou would See the Lord, testifyinge that he doth not love pride, vanity, & vaine glory; that now in the tyme of your Joy hath turned it into mourning [Lam. 5:15]. The god of power give thee to understand his will, & minde: and that thou may make him thy only Jewell; who hath the Life & breath of all men in his hand[;] and this is not come to passe without his determination[,] though there hath beene Instruments to helpe it forwards[.] Satisfy thySelfe in the Lord, who is fulnesse of Satisfaction to all that trust in him.

[To James, Duke of York]

Deare heart[,] the good and gratious God hath beene mercyfull to you in preservinge of you, and keepinge of you in many dangers and tryalls. And now hath brought you into this Land of your nativity. Oh that yee would feare before him and See his hand that hath Smitten and come neare you least he strike againe. Consider in tyme; God hath prooved & tryed you, and you have had a small tyme in this Nation which you have Spent in wildnes, in wantonnes, in vanity, Sporting yourSelves in the Day=tyme: and now your joy is turned into mourning. Oh that you would see in tyme that you did not provoake the Lord, But that you might Raigne and prosper is the Desire of my heart. God is rissen in this Nation[,] Quicke, & powerfull; and it is Dangerous sleighting of his word, and gaine=sayinge of his truth: and I doe warne you to beware of hearkeninge to the Counsell of the Priests of the Nations: of what sort Soe ever: For god is departed from them. And his Cursse will be in their undertakings, & Counsells, whether you can beleeve it or noe. And them that the Lord doth permitt to live upon the earth will see it[.] This I was mooved of the Lord to write to thee in particuler[,] and I desire the Kinge may see it alsoe. My Soules desire is that you may be preserved; in the midst, & through the firy tryalls that is cominge upon all Flesh. And you must expect tryalls, and Crosses; for god is cominge to plead with all flesh, by sword, & by fire [Isa. 66:16]. Truly I stand admireinge to see the Infinite goodnes of God unto you, how he deales with you[,] even as if he intended to doe you good: For he Chasteneth every one whom he loveth [Heb. 12:6]; and the way to him is through tryalls and tribulations: the Lord grant this may not be in vaine to you

From one that cannot flatter, that is a
true lover of your Soules, &
your eternall good
Margret Fell

Spence 3/103. Also in part in Ross, pp. 136–137 and Works, *pp. 22–23. Endorsed: "M F to the king & the duke of Yorke [George Fox]".*

98 TO HER CHILDREN, WITH A POSTSCRIPT BY HENRY FELL SEPTEMBER 25, 1660

"I am waitinge Still for my liberty to come home;
Not knowinge but the Lord will give me liberty ere longe."

There is a tone of homesickness and a longing to hear more from her children in this letter. It also indicates conflict between her desire to return to Swarthmoor and the importance of the work that kept her in London. The second half of the letter deals with business matters. She was scrupulous in accounting for funds, a characteristic of Quakers that helped them to be successful in business in later years.

Richard Hubberthorne (1628–1662) had conversations with King Charles II and was a persuasive advocate of the Quaker cause (Greaves, 2:118–119). Margaret mentions Gerrard Roberts (Letter 68) and Henry Ward's daughter. She was Rebecca Ward, who preached in London and was sent to Bridewell prison. She was one of the seven thousand "Hand-maids and daughters of the Lord" who filed a petition to Parliament in 1659 against persecution for non-payment of tithes. Margaret Fell and her seven daughters headed the list of signatures (Ross, p. 42).

*Thomas Turner, Lancelot Wardell, and Robert Dring were all Quakers. Turner is described as a "shopkeeper, upon the bridge at Newcastle" (Nuttall, p. 74). Wardell, of Sunderland, preached in Ireland in 1655. In 1661 he and others "were taken at Meeting . . . and cast into nasty Holes" at Timothy Castle (Besse, 1:175). Robert Dring's and his brother Simon's homes in London were the first sites of London Meetings (*FPT*, p. 163).*

Roger Harper, whom Margaret says is "dead worse then nothinge," assisted William Ames in his preparations for going to Holland in 1656 (Hull, Rise, *pp. 22–23).*

Margaret voices concern for her son, George, and she and Henry Fell (Letter 95) both send remembrances from Ann Clayton who was in London at that time. Ann Clayton had been a member of the Swarthmoor household in 1652, was convinced by George Fox, and became a minister, traveling, preaching, and suffering various imprisonments. Ross says of her, "She was a woman of intrepid courage." She went to Barbados, Boston, and Rhode Island, and she married successively two governors of Rhode Island, the Quakers Nicholas Easton and Henry Bull (Ross, p. 68, 12; Natl Cycl Am Biog*).*

Pell=mell the 25th of the 7th Month 1660

My dearly beloved Children & Babes of God, begotten by the Imortall words of life. My dear love in the Over=flowinge Fountaine, Runns forth freely unto you; and my desire is to see you when the Lord is pleased to give me my Freedom, & Liberty in himselfe: that I may come to you in everlastinge Dominion, & peace, which my life, & soule waites for[.] And untill then I am content to stand Rendered up to his blessed holy will, & pleasure: G: F: [George Fox] is not yet come up; neither doe we know what they intend to doe concerning him. There is other things besides that which lyes upon me; which yet I am not cleared, nor freed of; which I waite to see the end of; if it please the Lord to worke. A litle tyme may bringe things to passe whereby the Lord might sett me free[.] My deare Lambs[,] it is the Lord his worke & Service that houlds mee heare. Soe be content & satisfyed in the Lords love unto you & presence with you. We are none of our owne, we are bought with a price[.] I desire to heare from you. The last weeke I had none from you, only one from G: F: & another from R: H: [Richard Hubberthorne] have a care of my three litle ones which is my Chardge: but especially one my litle Rachell [age 7, Susannah 10, and Mary 13]. The god of everlastinge infinite love preserve, & keepe you, and watch over you all. I am waitinge Still for my liberty to come home; Not knowinge but the Lord will give me liberty ere longe[.] And I doe beleeve that if G: F: come I shall have liberty in a short tyme after; But I doe not See att present that this place I can leave[,] except hee were heare. I would heare how things are with you every way.

you must procure some money, for we have had 20£ of Gerrard [Roberts] Since yee went away besides the Ten pounds which was taken out of the 50£ before yee went: and your Brother had taken 20£ on him before we came to London which I knew not of, till after the Lease was Sealed: Soe that there is 50£ owinge to Gerrard, which must be returned to Kendal; and payd to Hen: wards [Henry Ward's] Daughter that came from London: and Gerrard is to receive it of hers here. Make it ready as Soone as yee can, & let us know, when it is ready and I Shall get a dischardge from Gerrard. Yee must write to Newcastle with all speed to Thomas Turner, & Lanct. wardell [Lancelot Wardell] that they doe returne the money hither to London with Speed for Robert Dringe [Dring.] we heare that Roger Harp [Harper] is dead worse then nothinge, Soe it is good to get it out of their hands. I am in hopes to get your Brother downe into the Country; for he had need of; for he hath beene more Idle this tyme then ever he was: But the Lord is my strength & trust concerninge him, whom I beleeve will prevent his wickednes & preserve him

your deare Mother

M: F:

[Postscript by Henry Fell:] Margret your Sister is well[,] whose deare love is to you all: Alsoe A. Cleaton [Ann Clayton] is here at present whose love is to you all remembered. My love is alsoe dearly remembered to you all & Friends in the Familly & elswhere[.]

H F

[Postscript by Margaret:] A C: [Ann Clayton] desires you to Remember love to her Mother & Brother & Friends.

Spence 3/73 and Crosfield, pp. 76–77. Endorsed: "M.F. to her cheldern [George Fox]".

99 To King Charles II from Margaret Fell and Samuel Fisher Between April 25 and October 25, 1660

"Let Three men come before you . . .
Soe that they may be fairly heard with Moderation."

Margaret and Samuel Fisher (Letter 48) wrote this proposal to the king asking that he would listen to a debate between three Quakers and three bishops or ministers in order for him to judge the rightness of the Quakers' religious principles. Theological argumentation of this nature was not unusual at the time. The Works *comments that: "the King consented at the first . . . when he had read the said Letter, before he spoke with the Bishops; and he appointed a day in which they should meet. And our Friends concern'd went at the day appointed, and . . . after they had waited some time, one of the King's Servants came to them, and said they were not ready, and so the Appointment was put by . . . some of the Bishops perswading the King against it" (p. 22). The meeting was never held.*

In the last paragraph Margaret refers to the Declaration of Worcester of October 25, 1660, which outlined the nation's policy on religion and reflected the uneasy reconciliation of the episcopal form of church government with the Presbyterian model. "Charles generally pursued a policy of toleration based on his perceived rights of dispensation and suspension . . . Although toleration for Catholics was probably his long-term goal, dissenters, including Quakers, would also benefit. But this policy was unpopular both with his supporters and with the conservative Presbyterians" (Horle, Q.&EngLegalSys, *p. 73).*

Wee doe Humbly and heartily Desire oh King! That some of us might be brought before you to be proved, & tryed whether we bee of God. This is accordinge to the Scripture; That we may be first tryed before we be Judged. And that yee may not be Ignorant of us and our principles, and desires after peace with all men: and holynesse towards God.

And accordinge to thy propoundinge, let Three men come before you; and deale with them as yee see good, and most for your owne advantage. Soe that they may be fairly heard with Moderation. That thou thy Selfe, may throughly be informed; and thereby able to Judge with Truth, and Equitie of things. For we doe know that thou art of the most temperate, Milde, Meeke spirit, & reasonable and fitt, and able to be Judge in this Matter of any one amongst them. For we doe know, and feele mens Spirritts (Though the world cannot beleeve it) And for thee to be by, and to heare what is spoken for us, and against us; Is but Reasonable, Just, and Equall. Wee beinge True, and Faithfull, and Loyall Subjects to thee: Which none of you Shall ever finde, nor know any other by us.

And we desire that this may be done before That Declaration be given forth which is mentioned in the Chancellors Speech. & let us know the tyme when thou wilt be pleased to heare us in these things: that it may not be deferred as it hath beene before.

M F & Samuell Fisher

Spence 3/97, mentioned in Works, *p. 22. Endorsed: "M. F. and Samuell Fisher [George Fox]".*

100 TO HER CHILDREN OCTOBER 8, 1660

"I expect to gett your Bro. [brother] home with us."

When Margaret was preparing to return home she still hoped that her son, George (Letter 75), would go with her to Swarthmoor Hall and be reconciled to the Quaker way of life. However, he remained in London. In December 1660 he married Hannah Potter (Kunze, p. 39).

The only reference to a Thomas Petty in Quaker sources is that in 1682 he was sent to prison for refusing to take the Oath of Allegiance (Besse, 2:150–151).

My dearely beloved Lambes and babes of god, my everlasting infinat love is unto you dearely[,] & my life & bowels reacheth unto to you & often asendeth up unto the Thron of grace for you that yee may be kept and preserved by the arme of his power and the deare love & life and unity of the eternall spirit into which yee are baptized[,] that their you may put on Jesuschrist the Righteousness and live in him and unto him & unto his praise for ever[,] whose goodness reacheth unto you and shineth upon you as the Morning light[.] the god of life & glory bless[,] preserve and keepe you[,] and his blessing rest upon you[,] & the light of his Countenance shine upon you for ever.

I am waiting for an opportunitie and freedome from the lord to returne unto you[,] but clearness I doe not see nor doth not expect till G.F. [George Fox] be heare[,] that we see how things is ordered of the lord; in the meane time rest in the patience in Subjection to the lord[,] freely given up to his will & in his love and blessing to receive _______[.] their shall you and I have ever lasting _________ and comfort in the Lord, This day I received yours wherein you menshon steares [steers or oxen] you may doe as you see convenient[,] onely the money I spoke of in my last must be paid at Kendal; and for the Joyners [carpenters] lett them have what was bargened for and lett the overplus remaine till my comeing[.] I have paid 5 Markes heare for the poole [poll] money and your sister hath paid hers [Margaret Fell, Jr.,] lett them know that they may gather none of yours for us. I have lett west [Col. William West] know the same who is one of the commishoners and he hath sent him the originall of this; I expect to gett your Bro: [brother George Fell] hom with us[.] we are well, blessed be the lord[.] my deare love to my dear little ones and especially my deare R [Rachell.] we gave Tho Petty order to bring our things from Warington [Warrington.] their is a chair for Rachell[.] if it doe not com[,] send for it[.] your sister [Margaret Fell, Jr.] dearely salutes you all

Yor deare Mo: [Mother]
M Fell

Pell Mell the 8 of 8 Month 1660
G F [George Fox] is not heare till the next week

Spence 3/75. Addressed: "For Bridgett Fell at Swarthmore, these; leave this with Tho[mas] Willan in Kendal to be send as above said, Westmerland". Endorsed: "M.F. to her childern [George Fox] London 1660 8 mo 8 day".

101 To her Children October 25, 1660

"G. F. [George Fox] is now freed, blessed be the Lord god whose arme & power alone has donne it[.]"

Margaret writes to her children to give them the good news that George Fox has been freed and to give them an account of the proceedings that were required to accomplish this. He had to appear before the Lord Chief Justice, Sir Robert Foster (1589–1663), who was harsh and arbitrary in dealing with political prisoners, particularly Quakers (DNB, Campbell 2:156–157). Then George Fox appeared before the judges at the King's Bench and was finally freed, although the king had earlier sent an order to accomplish exactly that.

Margaret briefly mentions the death of James Nayler (Letter 49). Whenever she speaks of death, it is always in a very matter of fact tone, not dwelling on its sadness. In the seventeenth century death was close to all families. Infants frequently died; women died in childbirth; and disease and epidemics carried off adults. Margaret accepted literally the principle that God's will will prevail.

She then turns to a matter of business. It concerns rents due to the Fells from a purchase that Judge Fell had made many years before. Thomas Coulton, their servant (Letter 82), can help them to find the various documents, "quittance" and "Acquitance," to substantiate that appropriate payments were made before the purchase.

My dearely beloved Lambs & babes & Immortall seed of gods covenant of love & life, in this same unction of the holy one my love is to you all[.] my prayers to the Lord is for you all that in his Arme & power you may be kept up to him in the bosome of his love[.] there to be nursed & nourished up to Eternall life where the true record, & knowledge of the Lord is.

G. F. [George Fox] is now freed, blessed be the Lord god whose arme & power alone has donne it[.] after he had appeared before the Judg which sent for him up[,] then he appeared before the Lord cheefe Justice of England in his chamber, & the next day he appeared before them all in open court in the Kings bench[;] & all this after the king had granted out an order to sett him free[.] but they would not sett him free till he had appeared in all those places to see if anything would come against him. It was of great service for the Truth. I cannot write at present punctually[,] nor the tyme of my returne, for I do feel that yett I am no[t free] of this place, but still doe waite for the Lords w[ill and] pleasure & his tyme to be manifested to me, and __________ you rest satisfyed in that[,] for there is Everlasting ___________ & there you will enjoy me, I doe not know how suddainly the Lord may please to give me my freedome to come home & when it is I shall embrace it loveingly, lett me heare of my litle ones how it is with them all, you mention litle of them when you write, & my desire is to heare of you all and of your well being in the Lord, It may be you have heard ere this how J N [James Nayler] hath finished his Naturall life, & hath laid downe his body of Earth about 3 score miles of London[.]

you mentioned in your last concerning the payment of the rent for the mills, with the last quittance lett Coulton [Thomas Colton] search for the last Accquittance, but yee must withall lett them understand that your father purchased them soe many yeares since, & paid the Parliament [timely?] for them, & after that purcase [purchase] there was no acquittance, the writing that belonged to it you must look for it amongst the writings[.] it is a particular thing of it selfe, & __________ only the mills & the __________ of ___________ as I remember[.] lett Colton look for it, & if there be an acquittance that yee can find[,] yee may show it, and alsoe lett them understand that for the remainder of the yeares the rents was purchased[.] and if yee find not the last acquittance before the purchase[,] show none at all but lett them understand that they have been purchased so many yeares[,] which I beleve is about 9 [?] yeares & that remaining the ________ & Armes [?] lett nothing be paid concerning me but lett them doe what they will, And lett Colton be careful that he be not too hagly [haggling] in yeelding to them[.]

concerning your brother [George Fell] I have not spoke with him since your letter came[.] I know not what he will do in it, soe no more but my love in the Lord Jesus is with you & as soon as the Lord gives me leave I shall returne[.] the Eternall Arme of the Almighty be with you

M. F.

25th 8th Mo
London 1660

Gibson MSS 4:43. Also Barclay, J. pp. 88–90. Endorsed: "M F [George Fox] to her children 8 mo 1660".

102 To King Charles II October ? 1660

[Do not] "offend the Lord whose mercy endureth forever And who delighteth in mercy[,] who hath said to the Mercyfull hee will Shew mercy."

Margaret felt great sympathy for the Regicides and was much disturbed by their plight. She felt that the general atmosphere of blood and revenge that affected the nation during the trials and executions was harmful to all. This, in addition to her concern for Quakers in prison, kept her in London trying to influence the king and the court.

The letter is an eloquent plea for mercy and forgiveness and the hope that the king "might turn this Streame and Tarant [torrent] into another Chanell." She had also written and published a pamphlet addressed to one of the Regicides, Major General Thomas Harrison (1606–October 13, 1660), in the spirit of urging repentance and emphasizing the mercy of God. The pamphlet is headed This was given to Major Generall Harrison and the rest. Read this in the Fear of the Lord, and in the moderation of Your spirits, without prejudice.

To the King From M F

Triumpe in mercy; And now Lett this bloody Issue bee Stopt that hath rune [run] Twelve yeares. And forgive thine enimies and Lett them have there lives for prayer[?] that Soe they may have time to Repent of their wickedness, soe wilt thou bee Cleare before the Lord of their Blood, And this will Stop the fury and rage of thire Enimies which is Great, And heareby thou wilt receive mercy and forgiveness From the Lord, as thou forgiveth others that Trespass against thee[.] And now this man haveing Suffered which is in gods Justice and Righteousness, this will Stop all objections and accusations that can bee laid against thee Conserning thy Fathers death; And Dear Heart[,] consider that it is much more Safe for thee and For thy Soules peace and comfort that Thou offend these Spirits that thursts for blood in Shewing of mercy then it is to Answer their desires and soe to offend the Lord whose mercy endureth for ever And who delighteth in mercy[,] who hath said to the Mercyfull hee will Shew mercy; There is a hott and Rageing spiritt got up in People[,] and much is in their Hearts of great Bloodshed and of much Cruelty that will bee acted by you, oh that the Lord would give thee a heart and Bowels of mercy that thou might turne this Streame and Tarant [torrent] into another Chanell[,] that they might bee confounded in their devices, For I doe beleeve they doe Feare and forethinke of much more cruelty then is in your Hearts to doe. the Lord give you power and strength to turne their Surmissings and disapoint them of their expectations[.] this would be good for you & it would shame and Confound them; there can bee noe danger in beareing and forebearing[.] the Lord is at Hand, whose hand will establish if thou shew mercy And forgiveness; But if there be much Blood shed it will bee dangerous; for god is a god of Love & mercy and forgivness;

M.F.

Spence 3/110. Also Works, *p. 27. Endorsed: "M.F. to the King, 1660 [George Fox]".*

103 TO KING CHARLES II AFTER DEATH OF REGICIDES 1660

"Wherein have wee offended any man any otherwise then in that wee worshipp God in the Spirit . . . and for this must wee be made the object of merciles mens Cruelty."

The Quaker position of nonviolence was not well understood, and their actions in not observing the norms of conventional behavior were found offensive and even threatening. Preaching in the streets, successfully holding large Meetings, and slighting some forms of polite discourse aroused anger. Margaret mentions one hundred Friends recently put in prison and asks the king's help.

MF To the King

If it may please the King to suffer and admitt of Consideration in his heart according unto reason Righteousnes and Equitie concerning us[,] a People under his Government and in his dominions[,] our just liberties and rights to maintayne. who is engaged to the Lord[,] in his power to protecke us from wrongs and injuryes and violence donne unto us by Millitary and merciles men, who are a People fearing the Lord, and dare not to wrong injure or hurt any man upon the face of the Earth and who are a People that has been subject and alsoe very willing[,] ready and free to serve him in all his Civill demands, and whatsoever has been imposed upon us tributary or volluntary wee freely answered his demands to our utmost powers, and been more ready and willing than any other people in the Nation[;] and for this wee shall appeale to all the Magistrates of the kingdome in their severall Countyes for them to testifie, and now what have wee donne or wherein have wee offended any man any otherwise then in that wee worshipp God in the Spirit and are subject to Christ Jesus and his Comands, and for this must wee be made the object of merciles mens Cruelty whom you know has had their hands in blood before, and must wee be the very front of such mens actions, oh farr be it from the King to suffer such things or soe to requite the Lord whose love & Fatherly tendernes brought him in and sett him upon his throan & has thus farr prospered & preserved him[,] not that he should turne or banish the Lords people out of his dominions[,] but that they might be a blessing unto the King & he unto them & soe the Lord give the King to Consider and to see and understand these things in time, least there be a hand lifted up which Cannot be resisted, I desire to have the kings answer to these things[.]

M F

for wee lye every day liable to suffer great persecution[,] even in danger of our lives[;] for since the King went from London they have putt a 100 of our friends in prison[.]

Spence 3/111–112. Partially in Works, *p. 28. Endorsed: "MF to the king [George Fox]".*

104 To her Children, with a postscript by Margaret Fell, Jr. November 12, 1660

"The last 7 day [Saturday] I was with the Qeene [Henrietta Maria] and had time to discharge what I had to her."

In a short letter to her daughters Margaret gives them her love and a bit of news: she met with Henrietta Maria, the Queen Mother (see Letter 105). Margaret, Jr.'s postscript tells of other matters that occupied them, namely the purchase of a petticoat for Bridget, black cloth (very expensive), and other articles.

Pell Mell, the 12 of the 9 month, 1660

My dear loves and lambes of god, and plants which his owne Right Hand hath planted[,] who hath loved you with an everlasting love and with his gracious mercy and love hath visited you and begoten you by his owne power and imortall word into his owne Image[,] and being with himselfe where you may rest in his bosom, and sitt downe under his shadow and feed of his pleasant fruite[,] in this my salutation is unto you and my der love and life remains with you forever[.] Wee received yours this day and wee are glad to heare that you are well in the Lord every way[,] all glory and Honour be unto the Most High for ever And ever, who is the fountaine of all our mercy And comforts and the rock of our inheritance and consolation for ever; wee are all well heare in the Lord[,] your Bro: [brother George Fell] is well[.] he was heare this day; The last 7 day [Saturday] I was with the Qeene [Henrietta Maria] and had time to discharge what I had to her. I know nothing but that the Lord may make way for us to returne ere it be long; and may come by coach[,] but wee may stay some time before all things will be ready; So, with my unchangeable love I remaine

your deare Mo: [mother]

M F

Sister B [Bridget] as tuchinge a peticoate[,] before our Things went Downe I bought a peece of one and sent it amonst them[.] Blackes are very deare[;] they are so much worn[.] I could wish you would lett me know if all the thinge came home, 2 Trunkes, 1 box, 1 hatt case with severall little things in it, 1 fraile [basket] with 3 deskes and other things[.] my deare love to all my sisters and friends in the family.

M.F. [Jr.]

Spence 3/82 and Crosfield, pp. 79–80. Addressed: "For Bridgett Fell at Swarthmore these". Endorsed: "M.F. to Briget Fell [by George Fox; Bridget Fell is crossed out and changed to:] her children, 1660".

105 To Henrietta Maria, Queen Mother November 1660

"Our desire is that all people might come to this light & Spirit of God, which is in them, . . . then they would . . . partake with us of the Lord."

Henrietta Maria (1609–1669), queen of Charles I and mother of Charles II, was the daughter of the French King Henry IV. She was a fervent Catholic. In the early years of her marriage she took no part in politics, but as troubles gathered about her husband she worked actively to raise money and armies for him, appealing to the pope and the French king. She always labored for the benefit of Catholics and thus was unpopular with the English public. She spent the years of Charles II's exile in France, but after the Restoration she was in England for several years (DNB).

It was then that Margaret visited her and gave her several books and this letter (Works, pp. 33–34). Margaret explains some of the basic principles of the Quakers, that the Light is in every heart and that the same spirit that descended on the Apostles is available today. The letter contains a large number of scriptural references, which she annotated in the margins.

Margaret also speaks of the persecution suffered by Quakers "not for any evill or wrong that we have done . . . but for exercising a good conscience." Henrietta Maria had little power to influence events in England, but Margaret was ready to try to convince any and all to understand Quakerism.

For Queen Mary
Frend

Thou art come into a Nation, where God is Risen in Life & power in his people, which are the Light of the World, & the salt of the Earth[,] who is to let their Light shine forth before men, that they may see their good workes & Glorify their father which is in heaven [Matt. 5:16], & in this Light are we to bear our testimony to all people, & nations, & kindreds upon the Earth; for this is the Covenant of Light, not only to raise up the tribes unto Jacob, & to restore again the preserved of Israell, but also he is given a Light to the Gentiles, & to be the salvation to the ends of the Earth [Isa. 49:6], & this is he that John bare witnes to Joh:1. who said in him is Life & this Life is the Light of men, he was in the world, & the world was made by him, and the world knew him not, the Light [John 1:10] shined in Darknes, & the darknes comprehended it not, he came to his owne, & his owne Received him not, & but soe many as received him to them he gave power to become the Sons of God [John 1:11–12], John [the Baptist] Saith he was not that Light, but was sent to bear witnes of the Light, that was the true Light that Lighteth every man that cometh into the world [John 1:8–9], & this is that which we turne every one to, the light they are Enlightened with all (which thou hast a measure of, which lets thee see thy heart, & the secret intents of it) this light as the minde is turned to it, lets everyone see their Evill thoughts, & what proceeds out of the heart, which Jeremiah Saith is deceitfull above all things [Jer. 17:9], who knows it? & the answer is, this Light that shines in the heart, knows the heart and the secrets of it, & searcheth the heart & tryes the Reines [Ps. 7:9], & by this[,] God teacheth his people, & leads them & guides them in all their waies [ways], that they may walke in his pathes, for this Light is of God & comes from God the father of Lights, & leads up to God from whence it comes, for God is light, & in him is noe darknes at all, & the workes that he worke are in the Light, & the law that he writes in the heart, & the spirit that he puts in the Inward parts is Light, & this is the new and Everlasting Covenant that he makes with his people, And by this doth he gather his seed to himselfe wherever it is scattered upon the face of the Earth, & all the nations that are saved must walke in this Light of the Lambe, & noe other way or name under heaven can any one be saved but by Jesus Christ [Acts 4:12] who is the true and Everlasting Light, that Lighteth every man that cometh into the world [John 1:9], and as all people are guided & taught by this, soe they come into the unity of this Eternall Spirit, which is the bond of Peace, all that walked in the Light & Life of it, the blood of Jesus Christ cleanseth them from all sin, & here is the fellowship one with another [1 John 1:7], & our desire is that all people might come to this light & Spirit of God, which is in them, therby to be guided & taught, & then they would have unity with us, & partake with us of the Lord, and of the mercy, & of the virtue which we received from the fountain of all Life, which is set open, who hath said if any man thirst let him come unto me & drinke [John 7:37], & this he spoake of the Spirit, which now he is pouring upon all flesh, soe that sons & daughters doe prophesy [Joel 2:28], & this the Apostles witnessed, came upon them in their day, & the same spirit and not another [Acts 2:17–18] we doe witnes discending upon us, & manifesting himselfe in us & through us, & this is our testimony, the word of faith which we preach, which is nigh in the heart & in the mouth, which preacheth Righteousnes, and saith neither ascend nor descend[,] but the word is very nigh to hear it & doe it [Rom. 10:6–8]. And onto this Immortall & engrafted worde[,] Life, which is able to save thy soule I commit thee, And for this testimony we are & alwais have been in suffering since we were a people, by every change of Government, & every power that hath ruled in these nations, which hath been severall in these last few years[,] have we suffered under, for speaking the truth in plainnes, & for exercising a good conscience in the fear of God towards God & towards man, & not for any evill or wrong that we have done to any man upon the Earth, for we desire to owe nothing to any man but love[,] even to our Enimies, & those that persecute us & dispitefully use us we can pray for, & desires that all may be saved & come to the knowledge of the truth of God, as it is in Jesus, which is a great mistery, & for the publishing & declaring this hath our sufferings been, not only from the Rude and prophane but from the highest professors & gathered Congregations in the nations whose glorey God hath stained, & overturned, as he is engaged so to doe unto all that persecutes & hurts his little ones, which is unto him as the Apple of his Eye, & soe unto him we commit and hath committed our cause, who hath said vengeance is mine & I will repay it, who pleads the cause of the Innocent, who was before all things & by him all things consist, who hath created all things in heaven & in earth, whether they be thrones or dominions principalities, or powers[,] all things created by him & for him [Col. 1:16] to whom Eternall glory & honour for evermore

From a true Lover of thy Soule
& thy Eternall peace & Comfort
Margaret Fell

Spence 3/101. Partially in Works, *pp. 33–34. Endorsed: "M F to quene mare [George Fox] This is written".*

106 To King Charles II and the privy council
Late 1660

"And this we doe certainly know: if we doe Suffer under this presure of injustice . . . that then we have not our Civill rights, and privilidges as Subjects."

Margaret reminds the king and privy council that their power is delegated to many others, local constables and judges, who may be guilty of cruelty. "And yee are to have Speciall care, that yee comitt not the Sword of Justice Into Such mens hands."

The Quakers's refusal to take oaths was used as a weapon to punish them, and she asks the king and council to "mittigate theise heavy Burthens." Margaret rightly points out that the oaths of allegiance and supremacy were intended for those in high offices or "suspicious persons, including Catholics, and those who refused to be disarmed" (Greaves, Enemies, *p. 43). She assures the king of Quaker loyalty and willingness to pay taxes and "whatsoever is demannded in a civill way." King Charles actually freed "approximately 700" Quakers in 1660 (Greaves,* Deliver, *p. 26).*

*She refers particularly to two Friends who in October 1660 were praemunired for refusing to take an oath by the judge, Sir William Waller. She describes this severe sentence which includes being "out of the Kings Protection . . . all your lands, goods . . . are forfeited . . . and . . . to remaine in prison." Sir William Waller (1597?–1668) had been an eminent parliamentary general, a political leader of the Presbyterian party, and "a zealous puritan." He later turned against Cromwell, and he supported the Restoration (*DNB*).*

There is an incident mentioned in Besse that shows how Waller regarded Quakers: "Likewise Ellis Hookes, going to visit his Mother, then residing at the House of Sir William Waller at Stauton-Harcout, because he did not pay the Knight & his Lady the Hat-honour & customary Compliments, was by them, & their Servants, beaten & abused: And by their Influence, his own father was so incensed against him, that he turned him out of doors" (Besse, 1:564).

To the Kinge and his privy Counsell:

Friends You are highly engaged to the Lord God of power of Heaven & Earth whose Arme hath preserved, & delivered you from your hardshipps, & tryalls, and hath made way for you, and brought you, and now set you Rulers over theise Nations. And you are nearly concerned to take care; and beware least you Act anythinge against this hand in which the Inocent are. It concernes your peace, and prosperity

& Establishment to be tender of those; whom God is tender of: and for whose sake he is engaged to reproove Kings. Take heed & beware that yee lift not your hand against the Lord, and his people; in Sufferings, or making any Lawes that may tende to the oppressinge of the Innocent[,] thereby to persecute[.] And yee are to have Speciall care, that yee comitt not the Sword of Justice Into Such mens hands as make noe Conscience of Justice, & Equity: but exercise their owne wills & Envy, against the Innocent in your names; and as your Servants (which you doe not know of) whereby the Innocent Servants of the Lord may Suffer much, and you ignorant of it. But of you the Lord will require it who are the head Rulers whom he hath Intrusted with theise Nations at thy tyme outwardly to Rule & Governe:

And that yee would observe, & take notice of the unjust dealinges of severall Justices of the peace in these Nations; In the tenderinge of the oathes of Alleagance & Supremacy upon every occasion that any of us are brought before. Notwithstandinge they know us to be an Innocent, and harmlesse people: not doeinge, or offeringe any wronge to any man (much lesse to the Kinge) yet because they know we cannot Sweare any Oath at all for Conscience sake obeyinge Christs command: therefore on purpose they tender us the Oath that thereby they might cast us into prison. And Severall in this Nation there now in prison, for this very thinge; which accordinge to Justice, Law, & Equity (yee all know) they ought not to doe. For it is but upon Speciall occasion, & upon Speciall offices, and upon Speciall men (that are Suspitious) that the Oathes of Supremacy & Alleagance is to be tendered.

Now if these Nations be a body Civill, and the Kinge the head; it cannot be Supposed that every ordnary man, & member Should be an enemy to their head. And this we doe certainly know: if we doe Suffer under this presure of injustice (which we are in noe wise capable of by any just Law of the Nation) that then we have not our Civill rights, and privilidges as Subjects. If that upon every denyall and tender of this Oath, we must be cast into prison; because for conScience Sake we cannot take it in the Forme. Though we cannot but be true and Faithfull to the Kinge.

And Seeinge that we are willinge to pay Assessments, Taxes, Polemoney, & whatsoever is demannded in a civill way. Givinge unto Caesar the thinges that are Caesars; and beinge his true, & faithfull Subjects in every just, and lawfull Demand to the Kinge. And alsoe we have his promise Severall tymes that we Shall not Suffer for our Religion and that we Shall have the Liberty of our Consciences to worshippe God as it is Revealed in us[.] Yet we are pulled, and hayled out of our Meetings by violence, beaten, & Abused & Severall cast into prison upon no other account but for meetinge together in the feare of the Lord. And that we should have the Oathes of Allegance & Supremacy Soe frequently tendered to us, upon every Small occasion which is Certainly knowne throughout the Nation (even by them that tenders the Oathes to us) that we are noe such people, as it ought to be tendered to. Neither ought it to be tendered to any people upon every Slight occasion, as they tender it to us, Seeinge they Say there is Such a paenulty [penalty] for the not takinge of it, as that which was passed upon two of our Friends lately at Oxford viz. that you are out of the Kings Protection; and all your lands, goods, & chattells are forfeited, and to be Ceised [seized] on for the use of the Kinge; and you are to remaine in prison duringe the Kings pleasure. And one of our Friends Asked the Judge of the court (called Sir William Waller) if he gave order to the Jaylor to put Irons upon him (which was on when he was brought before them, & when he was brought ferst [first] into prison. He answered[,] The Jaylor might doe what he would with him (or words to this purpose) for he was out of the Kings protection. Now let any honest, Just, reasonable men Judge, whether this is fitt to be to an Innocent, harmlesse people upon theise accounts who are willinge to doe all dutyes, Services, & homage in a Civill way to the Kinge, which doth not Intrench upon their Consciences, Neither can be unfaithfull, or untrue to the Kinge, nor any man upon the face of the Earth. Now theise things we could not but lay before you[,] beinge that we suffer Soe deeply, and are like to doe under theise things. That Soe yee might for your owne peace & Safety take of [off], and mittigate theise heavy Burthens.

M: F:

Spence 3/107. Partially in Works, *pp. 24–25. Endorsed: "M: F: & Henry Fell [George Fox]"; Henry Fell crossed out.*

107 To King Charles II November or December 1660

"You cannot expect that the takeing of these oathes do alter their minds, or principals, being they are Imposed upon them by force."

Margaret asks the king to fulfill the promise of liberty of conscience, a promise that was made by the Declaration of Breda in April 1660. In addition, in October another declaration, the Declaration Concerning Ecclesiasticl Affairs mentioned a proclamation that would allow religious Meetings (Horle, p. 62).

Margaret argues that oaths imposed by force will not produce good actions, for those disloyal to the king " did not take it [i.e., an oath] because they did intend to performe it, but because they would not Suffer for the not takeing of it." Quakers, who were loyal to the king, could not take an oath for religious reasons, even if they had to suffer for it.

King Charles

The God of heaven and Earth who is king of kings, by whose Arme and power, thou stands, who hath been good unto thee: in all that thy heart can desire, and hast restored unto thee, that which thou looked upon to bee thy right, thy Crown and Scepter, whereby thou mightest rule these Nations as Chiefe Magistrate as amongst men, and Now let him have his right, and prerogative, whose throne and Scepter, is in the hearts, and Consciences of his people, and performe thy promise with God and men unto tender Consciences, which was promised first at Breday [Breda]; and agn. [again] in a Speech before both houses of the last Parliament which was to hasten the act of Indemnity, in which there was a full promiss, of giving liberty to tender Consciences.

And againe in the Declaration concerning Ecclesiastiall affaires, all which hath been printed and published to the Nations, and in particular there was a promiss made unto us that we should have a proclamation by which we should enjoy our meetings, and not be Constrained to any publique worshipp, Since which tyme wee have sufferd sore and have burdens, and opressions, and Imprisonments even to the death of many: not withstanding, that we have been cleare and Innocent before the lord and all men of Transgressing against any power, or person whatsoever, nor have wee in the least forfeited our liberties, which before was granted to us; Now to performe these things is required of

God and men; And liberty of Conscience wilbee a maine pillar that must preserve your standing, which you will find otherwise if to the Contrary you act, and so let us enjoye our liberty, and meetings in peace and quietness[,] that wee may worship the lord our God, without disturbance, and this will be for your pease and Comfort & Safety.

Concerning Oaths[,] it cannot be Expected by any of you that those that take these oathes that are tendered to them[,] whom you look upon to be an adverss and Contrary partie, _____ _____ you cannot expect that the takeing of these oathes do alter their minds, or princi-pals, being they are Imposed upon them by force, for they would not take them, if they could have their liberty, if they did not take them, and no reasonable man can think, that those oathes that they take by force will any way Compell them to act Contrary to their own inten-tions, but whensoever they have an opportunity, the oath is nothing to them, for they did not take it because they did intend to performe it, but because they would not Suffer for the not takeing of it.

Now if the kings Safety lye in Impositions of Oathes and swearing it will be very weake, for first of all[,] by this Christs Commands is broken who saith sweare not at all neither by heaven nor by earth nor by any oath. But this you look upon to be litle, but you may read the truth of it by the Consequence and by the fruits and effects; that hath ensued after the Imposition of so many oathes as hath been Imposed upon these Nations, what profit hath it brought upon them, that did Impose them, or what efforts, hath it wrought upon the people[?] have they not turned every way notwithstanding these oathes; but the onely way, that might appeare to be Safe for the king, and his Government will be to lay pennalties and establish them by law upon such and such offenders according to the nature of every offense given as it is in it selfe more or less, those that doe Transgress against the kings power or his Government in Civill things or his person, let the pennalty be thereafter what sort of people soever they be, This would be to some purpose, and this would somewhat terrify the people and keep them off, of offenses which the breaking of Christs Commands, and Trans-gressing both against god and man cannot do.

M F

Spence 3/113–114. Summary in Works, *pp. 18–19. Endorsed:* "M F *to the kinge [George Fox]*".

108 To Mary, Princess of Orange? or to King Charles II? 1660

"My love is and hath beene much unto thee[;] and I knowe the lords love hath beene the same, o that thou had a heart and a mind and a Courage to Answere his love."

This letter is headed and endorsed by George Fox to the prince or princess of Orange, the sister of King Charles II, who was in England from September 23, 1660 until her death on December 24, 1660 (Horle, p. 062). The Works *states that Margaret gave a letter "unto the Princess, in her Presence-Chamber at White-Hall," but it must have been a different letter. The contents of this are clearly addressed to someone who had more power than the princess. Margaret writes: God "hath brought thee onto the land of thy Nativity, & set thee here to prove thee . . . & alsoe to try thee . . . Never a man upon earth hath seen a People to rule over as thou hast."*

It is a pastoral letter, emphasizing God's love for the king and also for his people, and Charles II's responsibility for the people. These letters to members of the royal family reflect the breadth and depth of the Quaker lobbying effort for both Friends imprisoned and for Friends' faith.

M F To the Prince of Noridge
Deare Heart

Let thy mind be turned unto the measure of christ Jesus which is in thee, with which he hath enlightned every man that commeth into the world, that with it thou may see the hand of the lord, and his dealeings with thee, & his preserving of thee, & keeping of thee in former times through many dangers, Travels & hardshipps, & hath brought thee onto the land of thy Nativity, & set thee here to prove thee and to try thee what thou wilt doe for him, & how thou wilt answere his love & Mercy to thee, & alsoe to try thee, how thou wilt deal with his People, that is as tender to him as the apple of his owne eye. And as I have said before unto thee, Never a man upon the earth hath seen a People to rule over as thou hast, that the Lord will owne them & their cause as he will doe this People that is in thy Dominion; Therefore it nearly concernes thee to beware howe thou deales with this People & how thou suffers them to be dealt withall, for the mighty God by whom kings rule takes it as done unto himselfe[,] soe as thou desires that he should prosper thee and preserve thee, & establish thee, soe must thou doe with his People, & not suffer them to be oppressed and wronged and persecuted without any cause but for exercise of our pure conscience towards God and men, who are an Innocent harmelesse People, & desires the Good of all People upon earth and who hath been deare and tender towards thee, & desires thy Good and the Salvation of thy Soule as their owne, & that peace & truth might rule within thy Borders, and that thou might be established in truth & Righteousnesse, & yet do they greivously Suffer under thy power, in thy Dominions in thy Name[,] at which God is angry: Therefore as thou loves thy eternall comfort and peace, take heed betime, & take off the yoke of oppression speedyly, that lyes upon the Innocent, which God is Engaged to plead the cause of, & with the light of christ Jesus in thy conscience eye the dealeings of the lord with thee, & mind that hee takes Notice of thee, and see his love to thee that hee should Smite thee on the right hand & on the left, that thereby thou might see his mind and his will, & what he will exalt and what he will cast downe[,] and yet to spare thee and to try thee if it be possible to gaine thee[,] who hath been tender over thee, & his People hath beene tender over thee, oh sleight not his love, nor neglect the day of visitation, nor let the day passe that God hath given thee, and put into thy hand to doe good for him & for his People, lest he take it from thee and give it to another.

These things laid up [upon] me to mind thee of, for my love is and hath beene much unto thee[;] and I knowe the lords love hath beene the same, o that thou had a heart and a mind and a Courage to Answere his love that therby thou might be blessed forever, & that the hand of his judgments might be turned away from thee.

Because of Oaths the land mournes, The Innocent suffers, & swearing & foreswearing, hath beene the destruction & ruine of many, and this is contrary to Gods will & Christ Commands; And therefore Beware & take heed of laying & Imposing of this upon the Innocent, who cannot for conscience sake obey mens Commands Contrary to Christs.

M F

Spence 3/115. See Works, *p. 23 and Ross, p. 135. Endorsed: "M F to prinss of morig [George Fox] norigg 1660".*

109 TO HER CHILDREN DECEMBER 18, 1660

"I would have you to keepe the two Bay horses . . .
and lett Thomas ride on the one of them:
and get the other carryed alonge with him as farr as Coventry."

Margaret wrote a long letter, primarily about business, to Bridget in preparation for leaving London. She has bought "a litle coach" and hired a man and horses to travel with her. She gives directions for Thomas Coulton (Letter 82) from Swarthmoor Hall to travel to London carrying numerous documents concerning rents, accounts, and deeds. Some of the deeds concern rents that Judge Fell had conveyed to the children, which the Fells are having difficulty collecting because of Colonel Birch.

Colonel John Birch (1615–1691), an army officer and a parliamentary radical, came from a Puritan gentry family. He was much admired as an army officer in the parliamentary forces in the 1640s, but his career had many vicissitudes. He was a shrewd and successful businessman, profiting from the Cromwell era's confiscation of royalist and church properties. He was in partnership with Thomas Fell in some of these dealings, but after Judge Fell's death, Margaret had difficulty collecting the funds that were due. With the help of Col. William West and Sir John Otway, she was pursuing legal means to force Col. Birch to account. He had a long career in Parliament, and he defended dissenters and Quakers in support of toleration in the 1660s and as late as 1688. "An unfriendly witness called him 'a very nimble gentleman, who neglected no opportunity of providing for himself.' The judgement is accurate, but incomplete . . . Birch was a staunch supporter of parliamentary privilege and an opponent of arbitrary government" (Greaves, 1:64–66).

Margaret brushes aside "a report in the Country concerninge my Stay." Her unusual behavior of staying so long in London aroused gossip.

Henry Fell (Letter 95), in a postscript, stresses the importance of copying two documents that Margaret is including with this letter. They are papers from the king and council concerning the treatment of Quakers and are to be forwarded to Friends Anthony Pearson (Letter 6) and James Taylor (Letter 8).

John Simpson, a Friend, was one of eight men who signed a paper entitled "A Testimony of some of the souldiers: that were turned out of the army whoe owned them selves to bee quakers, 1657" (CJ, 1:454).

Sir John Otway of Ingmire Hall, Yorkshire, (ca. 1620–1693) was vice-chancellor of the Duchy of Lancaster from 1660 to 1687, an office earlier held by Judge Thomas Fell. Although Otway was a royalist, serving in the army in the first Civil War and later in Parliament, he was sympathetic to Quakers and assisted them (Henning, p. 188–189).

James Fell was not of the immediate family of Thomas Fell.

London the 18th of the 10th Month 1660
Bridget & the rest

My deare loves, & Babes in xt [Christ] Jesus[,] my deare love in the Lord is deare unto you all, gladd would I be if the Lord give me freedome & liberty to be with you, & returne unto you[,] which I hope and waite for. We reced [received] yours wherin yee mentioned that there is a report in the Country concerninge my Stay; which is litle to me; I am well used to them I know how to beare them, but the Lord of heaven & earth knowes, that if his hand had not houlden me heare [here,] I had beene with you ere now: But to that Arme in which I stand and am preserved must I be subject. What is allready done by the Kinge & the Counsell I have Sent you here inclosed[.] And we have bought a litle Coach, and hyred a man & two horses to come ether all or a part of the way with us: and we want yet a horse which would putt us to a great Chardge to buy one[;] & likewise we want the deeds concerninge the Rents[.]

Soe I thinke it will be the most convenient for us that Thomas Coulton Should come up and bringe all the coppyes of the deeds concerninge the Rents betweene Collo: Birch & us or any other Rents[.] But I perceive that these deeds that are here are of those Rents that my husband bought in his owne name, here is none of those which belonges to Collo: Birch[.] here he must alsoe bringe that deed by which your Father conveyed the Rents to you Children, not that which concernes the Mills, but the Rents that it may be Related in the petition[,] how it was the Childrens portions. Let Thomas take a coppy of the deed which concernes your portions to leave behinde when he bringes the other up. He must alsoe bringe a perfect coppy of the accots [accounts] betwixt Birch & us, & leave another of the Same in the Country. And I could have him as he comes to Speake with Rich: Kinge at Preston & advise with him whether we may not exhibitt a Bill, to call Birch to an acct from the first tyme, Seeinge that my husband payd him Forty pounds every yeare; and when we came to the Division it did appeare that it was not due to him; nor he had none the last yeare. yee may likewise advise with Jo: Simpson about it, for he knowes of it: and likewise he beeinge an 100£ in arreare I would desire Rich: Kinge that he would avise [advise] us what to doe with him in this case. I have beene with Oataway [Sir John Otway] the vice=Chancellor; and he Saith it is Just that he Should be called to an accot. and we cannot force him noe other way then by Bill. Take these last words out concerninge the accounts and let him Show them to Rich: Kinge. I would have Thomas likewise w[hen] he comes up to goe to Collo: Birch & Speake with him, for I gott Collo: west [Col. William West] to write to him to let him know that we intended to call him to an acct. and in his letter to Collonell west he promisseth that he will doe us noe wronge. But we know his performance. He hath gotten an Order for the Receivinge the last yeares Rents; let Thomas know of him whether it will extend to us that we may receive ours by the same; if not; let him aske him what way we must proceed to gett an order for the receipt of ours: if he would be soe kinde to us as he pretends in his letter, he might have let our rents have beene Included in his Order[,] Seeing they were purchased both in a deed together. Let Thom[as] alsoe know of him what he will doe concerninge of the purchase _____ _____ _____ he will come up & Joyne with us: or we must doe the best we can for ourSelves. Let Thomas Bringe a perfect acct what our last yeares Rents are in every place, both them which are purchased in our owne name, & them in Collo Birches[,] that we may know what the demand of them. Here is a note come from John Simpson[.] we know not what to make of it; nor what our part is; nor it never mentions those Rents which James Fell used to gather, nor those in Furness[.] Soe let him bringe a Certaine acct. of them all.

I would have you to keepe the two Bay horses which the Carter had very well, and lett Thomas ride on the one of them; and get the other carryed alonge with him as farr as Coventry by Some meanes as yee can conveniently to hire one or otherwise[.] And lett him there be left at Coventry at Jo: Morducks[,] a Baker[,] accordinge to this litle note within here Inclosed to Badgley [Baddesley]. For we doe not know that we shall take the Coach=man and his horses any further then Coventry though we have it in our Bargaine with him to goe through with us if we please[.] Let all these particular things be observed punctually for they are of great weight & concernment to us. It is strange that Thomas Coulton could not write one word to me never Since he went from this place; let him be Sent away as Shortly as you can get the horses Ready & these things done in their Order. I doe expect that within a weeke or ten dayes after the Recept of this Thomas may be Sett forward on his Jorney.

Let my dearest love be remembred to my deare Rachell & all the rest; and be yee all patient, & waite in the Fear of the Lord that you may receive me, & I you in his owne name, & power, in the dominion of the goverment of his will that he in all things may be glorified. fayle not to let me heare from you of the receipt of this. the last weeke we omitted writinge to you[,] which we never did before Since I came here, but we writt twice the weeke before. G: F: [George Fox] & we are all well here in the Lord[,] blessed be the Lord god; and that which yee writt concerninge the other G F: it was nothinge but rumours, & lyes that was raysed concerninge a letter which he writt to the Kinge. Soe my love which is everlastinge is remembered to you all & reacheth unto you all

Your deare Mother
M: F:

Yee are to Send a Coppy of these two papers Inclosed (vizt. the Kings Order & the other) to Kendal with all convenient Speed for them to Send them to Anthony person [Pearson] & Friends in Bishoppricke, to Show the Justices where Friends meetings are broken up; And yee are to send coppyes of them to Carmell [Cartmel] to James Taylor[,] Seeing their meetings is threatened; and yee are to keepe coppyes of them both yourselves.

My deare Love in the Lord doth Salute you all my deare Friends whom my Soule loves unfaynedly. I doe not know but that I may See you ere longe if the Lord permitt

Soe I bidd yee all Farwell in the Lord

H: F: [Henry Fell]

now but lately to London out of Norffolke & Suffolke

Spence 3/78–79. Also Crosfield, pp. 81–83. Addressed: "This for Bridget Fell at Swarthmore in Furnesse. Leave this with Thomas Willan at Kendal to be Sent as above directed with Speed, Kendal in Westmorland". Endorsed: "M: F: to her childeren [George Fox]".

110 TO KING CHARLES II AFTER JANUARY 6, 1661

"Who doe they thinke we would have to rull over us, the pope or the Turk or the man that we know God hath brought in by his power?"

On January 6, 1661, Thomas Venner led a group of about fifty men through the London streets to overthrow the monarchy and bring about the millennium. He was a leader of the Fifth Monarchists, the most violent of the sects. They preached against the evil world, primogeniture, capital punishment, and monarchy; and they preached for democratic government and the rule of King Jesus. Troops were quickly raised against them; there was panic in the streets; and the rebels were soon subdued. "The number of rebels proved to be small, but the rising confirmed the suspicions of conservatives who viewed sectarian congregations as nurseries of sedition" (Greaves, Deliver, *pp. 49–57).*

Suspicion also focused on the Quakers, for it was difficult for them to convince the authorities that they would not use violence. Hundreds were put in prison in London and all around the country, for fears were high.

In this letter Margaret scornfully derides the reasoning of those who do not understand that Quakers are no threat to the nation and that they have suffered equally under "the Monarchy, the presbyterian, the Independant & Baptist." The Quakers know that "the Lord hath given [King Charles] A hart & nature inclining to doe good to this Nation." They are "true & faithfull, Loyall and obeydient subjects," though they are despised like the "worme Jacob," an allusion to the Israelites in the Babylonian exile. She also warns against the effects of cruelty.

To the King from M F

This is A sad day, that we should have the word of A King, for the Lyberty of our conscience and yet be hailed out of our Meettings and had to prison[,] as fifteen were at Shearborn [Sherborne] in Dorsetshire, six of them were bayled and nine of them yet remaines in prison; And likewise at Northhampton the last first day, they had their Meettinge broken up, and the man of the house and Another friend were hailed to prison. And it is alsoe very hard that above A hundred should lye in prison, because they cannot pay Tithes against their conscience, nor owne that ministry that is upheld and maintained by them.

It is likewise strange that the men of this Nation should cast us into prison for not takeing the forme of the oath of Allegance, being they know that we have suffered imprisonment for not takeing an oath upon any Account, which is noe other but for Conscience sake, that wee cannot take the oath in their forme and way, though wee cannot but fullfill and Answer every tittle of that oath as it is intended; That is to be true & faithfull, Loyall and obeydient subjects to the King, which we cannot but performe; For the same conscience that binds us not to swear at all, binds us to be true & faithfull to the King and to all men, And if the same penalty were inflicted upon us for being true and faithfull to the king, to cause us to take up Armes against him, or any other disloyalty whatsoever, we should undergoe the same sufferinge for the one as for the other. For the same christ that commands us not to swear at all, did alsoe command us to let our yea, be yea, and our nay, nay, for whatsoever is more than this comes of evill.

Now how unjustly are we dealt withall, being we have the promise of the Lyberty of our conscience[,] let but the honest-harted judge, being that wee have suffered under every power for this same thing ever since we were A people; And whether this be not the same old secrett envy and enmity, that ever did appear against us in Magistrates to take every occation whereby they might insnare us, that thereby they might persecute us and cast us into prison: They might wel keepe us out of prison till they did see that we did opposse or gainesay our Allegance, being that it is for conscience sake that we cannot take that oath noe more than any other, but it is truly fulfilled upon us[.] they have hated us without A cause; and indeed they doe not deale with us according to reason, For if they did but come to sound reason & there judge of us, they would see it is not like that we should be disobeydient to the king; For what man can they thinke that we would have to rul over us, have we not had the Monarchy, the presbyterian, the Independant & Baptist[,] and have we not suffered sadly & deeply under their cruelty? have we not suffered greiviously under the professors in New England, even to the looseing of Lives? And have we not found all profession cruelty? who doe they thinke we would have to rull over us, the pope or the Turk or the man that we know God hath brought in by his power & hath set him over this nation to Scourge his enemies, and to try him, what he would doe for the Lord and for his people, And as he doth for them[,] soe will he prosper; and as he stoppeth persecution of the Innocent and harmeless people of god, soe will the blessing of the Lord be upon him. And we know that the Lord hath given him A hart & nature Inclineing to doe good to this Nation, and God hath put power into his hand to doe good, and if he doe not give his power out of his hand[,] he may doe much good in the Nation[,] for the Lord & for his people, but if he give his power out of his hand[,] or suffer cruell men to use their power under him in his name to exersise their cruelty,] he may suffer from the Lord for this; And whosoever draweth him into cruelty and persecution and oppression draweth him unto his owne Ruein [ruin]; And it will be good for all the Nation that he doe good, for to them that doth good, good cometh upon them, and them that doth evll, evill is unto them.

And though we be contemned and dispissed of all people & trod upon as the worme Jacob [Isa. 41:14]; yet I say it will be good for you all that you carry towards us and deale with us soe, as yee may have our prayers, For we have free Accesse to the God of Heaven and he heareth us, and we are your friends whatever you thinke of us, and we desire your good that you may partake with us; And if you doe cause us to suffer as others have done, the same reproufe you will receive for our sakes

M F

Spence 3/106. Partially in Works, *pp. 21–22. Endorsed: "M. F. to the king [George Fox]"; "This 5th letter is written".*

111 TO BRIDGET FELL, WITH POSTSCRIPTS BY HENRY FELL AND MARGARET FELL, JR. FEBRUARY 27, 1661

"I desire that you would be content,
& doe what you can well without much trouble
to yourselves, and leave all things to the Lord."

A letter filled with instructions concerning the legality of a marriage. The unorthodox marriages of Quakers, their not going to a church or having a pastor, caused difficulties with inheritance and ownership of land. In the 1650s and 1660s Friends had yet to develop a standard approach to meet the minimum requirement of the law for proof of marriage. With her usual reticence Margaret does not name the couple who must present acceptable proof of marriage at the next assize.

It was Isabel Fell (ca. 1637–1704), the third eldest daughter, age twenty-four, who was to take care of the rather complicated legal matter. She later became an

*active preacher, and in 1677 she traveled on the Continent for several months with George Fox, William Penn, and Robert Barclay. She was married twice, to William Yeamans from 1664–1674, and to Abraham Morrice in 1689. She had four children who died young (*CJ, 2:492; PWP, 1:132 n. 20*).*

Margaret directs Isabel to seek advice from Richard Kinge (Letter 109) and her uncle Matthew Richardson on how to present matters at the assize. Isabel is also to try to get a copy of any certificate that exists. In London, Margaret has arranged for three lawyers who will be present at the assize, and Colonel Richard Kirkby, a neighboring justice, has been helpful to her. In later years he was not so helpful, in fact, becoming one of their chief persecutors (Letters 122, 123). Margaret returns to the topic in a postscript with the suggestion that they try to get affidavits or witnesses, with the hope that these witnesses will not deny their knowledge.

She speaks of Quakers who were in prison, a part of the great roundup after Venner's Rebellion. In addition to 4,230 Quakers, there were over 400 Baptists, and numerous other dissenters. Most of them were released in the following months as the crisis passed, but others remained in prison for many months (Greaves, Deliver, *p. 58).*

A postscript by Margaret, Jr. reiterates Margaret's assurance that they understand the burdens of those remaining in Lancashire and that they will return "according as the Lord orders and gives freedom."

"Fairkilling" may be the name of a particular field. Farmers used to name their fields, and the reference may be to the particular field of grass to cut for hay (S. V. Hartshorne, letter of 11 August 1997).

Matthew Richardson was Margaret's brother-in-law, an attorney and a justice. He was not a Quaker (Kunze, p. 111).

There was evidently a resolution to the question of rents since Bridget would be able to get the money from John Simpson (Letter 109).

London the 27th of the 12th month 1660

My dearly Beloved in the everlastinge fountaine of deare love doe I dearly Remember you, and let it never enter into your hearts that I Should stay here upon any acct. [account] or concernninge any outward things, but upon the Lords acct & the truthe; the Lord of heaven & earth knowes that searcheth all hearts, whose habitation is with me, that if I were cleare in his presence and free before him, noe outward thinge should have stayed me from you, therefore have noe Such beleefe of me. we recd [received] three letters from you lately[,] one that was directed to Gerrard [Roberts] and two besides wherein you mention Somethinge concernninge ISabell. I writt the last weeke by Thomas

Corker concernninge it; but may bee this may come to your hands before it. I would have you to enquire of Myles Fell what parish in Chester it was that they Should have beene marryed in and send a carefull messenger to gett the Regester of that parish Searched; and if it be not there let them bringe a Certificate that it is not there which may doe some service. It is but now three weekes to the Assize therefore yee must doe it speedily; if yee thinke yee could trust Thomas Corker, he were the likest to get it done. It was the same yeare the ladd was borne soe yee may know by his age what yeare[.] I have entertayned here three lawyers that will be for it at Lancaster and I shall likewise write to Richard Kinge; and yee must be with him the First day of the Assize to take his directions about it; yee may enquire about it, whether they have a Certificate of their marriage or noe; & if it were convenient Isabell might goe her selfe, and take Thomas Corker with her; and Speake with Richard Kinge by the way and take his direction; for if it be not recorded in the Regester, I perceive it will doe litle service for them[.] Concernninge Fairkilling you may let it alone if there can be grasse gotten in another place, for I never intended it Should be taken for one yeare. I desire that you would be content, & doe what you can well without much trouble to yourselves, and leave all things to the Lord in whom we must all stand, and be preserved by him. I have written every weeke to you but one but whether they come to you or noe I know not.

It is expected that Friends will be sett free at the Assizes at the Furthest. however, be all Subject to the will of the lord. The Sufferings of Friends [in] most part in the Nation is gott into the Counsill [;] in Number above Foure Thousand; and we waite for an answer.

You may send to John Sympson to pay you that money that is in his hands of the arreares of that Rents; we have gotten an Order for the receivinge thereof From Lord Seymore [Seymour, per CH], we Should have sent you a coppy of it; but it is now with the Audittor Sir Ralph, but I doe not Question but John Sympson will beleeve us, you may give him a Receipt under your hand for the receipt of it. The gettinge of it one way & other will cost us neare 5£ & we are like to loose the knowing [?]

I have writt in my letter to Rich: Kinge to lett yee know what yee Shall doe concerning your search & the Certificate at Chester. I writt to Isabell in my last to goe to her uncle Mathew [Richardson] to desire him to be for her; ________ when she may aske him this Question alsoe ________ ______ that if she could get a Certificate from the prist [priest], where they say they were marry[ed] that they are not regestered, whether this will not be servicable to her or noe, & Soe that she may be informed before she goes; & if he Say it will; then let her goe Imediatly; In your next let us heare what Successe[.] Collo: Kirkby; he was very free, & willinge to doe more than I could desire him. This is all at present From yor deare Mother

M: F:

And Bridget must have that paper at the Assize which she had the last Assize about the Information of the Judges.

[Postscript]

my deare love in the Lord is dearly remembered to you all; I received a letter the last weeke from our deare Brother W: C: [Will Caton] whose love is dearely remembered to you all[.] Soe I bid you all farwell in the Lord

H: F: [Henry Fell]

[2nd postscript]

Deare Sisters,

My deare intire [entire] Love is to you all unexpressibly[,] and truly deare loves though I be separated from you outwardly yett I cann truly say I am partaker with you in your sufferings and am sensible of your great weights and burdens and that Cheefly in regard of my Mo: [mother's] Long absence, and truly to her and my selfe it is noe smalle tryall; but to the lord god of all our comforts that wee Injoy [enjoy] both outward and inward wee must all laboure to be content and given up to his will [,] wholy to be subjected in all things[,] that in him wee may have peace and satisfaction that none cann deprive us of, which in measure wee are witnesses of[.] glory glory to his holy name fore ever; and as for the time of our coming I am not able to give you any accounpt for in this thing wee are not at our owne dispossing, but according as the Lord orders and gives freedom whose wee all are and not our owne, I know noe time will be deferred in coming to you but as way is made ____________ for her returne she will with all speed answer you in this thing and therefore my deare loves in the holy power of the lord which orders all things and by which all things are accomplished and brought to pass according to his good will and pleasure; lett us all keepe that therein wee may be found answering his blessed will in which I rest with you and I ame your truly Loving Sister

M. F [Margaret Fell, jr.]

give my dearest Love to M A [Mary Askew] and to the rest of friends in the family.

[The following is on the address portion of the letter and is in a different hand.]

Whether that if any of the person which was Sett down in the Certificatt that the woman Brought doe deny that they know anything of it, as Pack the Minister did when he was Examined within a few years after that he should admit it[,] if they, anny of those persons Can be found & they be caried befor som Majestrat there & make affedes [affidavits] befor them of what they know will not be as good as if they [are] present at Lanc[aster].

Spence 3/87. Also in Crosfield, pp. 90–92. Addressed: "For Bridget Fell at Swarthmore these with care in Lancashire". Endorsed: "28 M.F. to her children, 1660".

112 TO FRIENDS IN PRISON, WITH A POSTSCRIPT BY HENRY FELL MARCH 5, 1661

"Keepe the just, & the pure in your conscien[ces]
at li[ber]ty which witnesseth for the living God.
And all outward prisons will be litle."

This pastoral epistle was written for circulation to Friends in prison. The theme is the paradox of physical confinement but spiritual freedom. Margaret likens the prisoners to the priests of the order of Melchizedek who are under God's protection. "He [God] is engaged unto his owne Seed, he is a God that keepeth covenant with his people."

The numerous biblical words and phrases would resonate with her hearers. The images of God the father, God the son, and the Shepherd who cares for the sheep shift and merge into each other to convey the strength of their support. Margaret urges the Friends to "let patience possesse your soules that thereby you may run." God can move mountains as the prophet Zechariah wrote, "Who art thou, O great mountain? before Zerabbabel [a governor of Judah] thou shalt become a plain." She acknowledges the prisoners' suffering, but they are helping to bring about "the everlasting Gospell of peace & glad tidings."

Henry Fell, the scribe, adds a postscript with a greeting from Richard Hubberthorne. (Letter 98)

London 5th day 1st month 1661

Friends of the living God & witnesses of his living truth, and sufferers for him, who are made partakers, of the heavenly & rich treasures, of everlasting life, everlasting power strength & vertue is your portion, & inheritance, as you abyde, & are kept in his owne name, & hand, which none can plucke you out of[,] My deare Lambes, the great shepheard of the sheepe, (whose owne the sheepe are) hath layd downe his life for you & doth give unto you, eternall life, in that living record of his owne eternall spirit (which he hath given you) of his only begotten Sonne, in whom he is well pleased, thorow his obedience, who is made perfect thorow sufferings, who hath offered up strong cryes, And by that one offering, doth perfect for ever all those that are sanctifyed thorow the obedience of his spirit, And washed & bathed in his owne blood, o stand fast in that liberty, wherwith Christ Jesus (the sonne of the living) God, hath made you free by his owne free spirit, which is the covering of all the righteous, & where this covering of the spirit of the Lord is, there is pure liberty, for the Lord is that spirit & by this spirit doth he conquer, & tread downe principalityes, & powers & thrones & dominions, under his feete, And will have all Government to himselfe whose right it is, this is the name, to which evrie [every] knee shall bowe, & every tongue confesse to God by this spirit & power, must all the mountaines be removed, yea even, them that stands before Zorababel [Zerubbabel] must be as a playne [Zech. 4:6–7], O let patience possesse your soules that therby you may run, the race that is set before you, throrow the faith of Gods elect before the world began, this obtaynes the promise, & the price of the marke, of the high calling, though thorow much suffering, tryalls & afflictions, which for the present may not seeme joyous but grievous, but they doe afterwards receive a reward of righteousnesse, Let faith, hope, & charity, which remaynes [1 Cor. 13:13] bee your crowne, & desyre of your soules, which suffereth all things, beareth all things, & hopeth all things, & endureth all things [1 Cor. 13:7], This will preserve you indeed, this will keepe you low & sensible, & seasoned, and will sanctify your hearts, & purify your minds, soe that you will not vallue nor care, what man can doe unto you, who is but as a vapour, but the everlasting kingdom, the everlasting inheritance, which is not of this world, you will come to receive, for it is your fathers good pleasure, to give you a kingdome, & this is the tyme, that he is agayne restoring, the kingdome unto Israell, And blessed & happy are all they, that first seekes the kingdome of God, all other things will be given unto them [Matt. 6:33], And who are faithfull unto the death, a crowne of life & immortality is reserved in the bosome of the father unto such who are truly, & faithfully, & singly given up to his will, And to his worke, & to his service, or to suffer for his names sake, Such are writ upon the palmes of his hands, though a woman forgot, the sucking child of her wombe, yet cannot he forget such, Therfore my deare brethren & sisters, be bould & of good courage, & keepe not backe, or bee not weary nor thinke not long, for he that shall come, will come, who hath sayd, I will not leave thee nor forsake thee, he is engaged unto his owne Seed, he is a God that keepeth covenant with his people, he hath bound himselfe, with an oath, in that he could sweare by no greater, he hath sworne by himself & Thou art a priest for ever after the order of Melchisedec, who is without father, or without mother[,] without descent, or begining or end of dayes, who remaynes a priest continually [Heb. 7:3, 17], And this is he for whom you suffer, who hath redeemed you out of all oathes, & swearing, & hath put an end to all strife, & to all priests, temple & tythes, offerings, washings, & circumcisions, which were but all a figure of this good thing which is now come, which fullfills the Lawe & the righteousnesse therof, who is the end of the Law & the prophets & the full substance of life, light, & immortality, & the everlasting Gospell of peace & glad tidings of great joy, And this gospell you can witnesse, not to you lost, nor to you hide [hidden], but to them that perish, but to them that believe in the Gospell of our Lord Jesus Christ, it is the wisdome of God, & the power of God, And this is that that gives you pure freedome, from the entanglements of this world, from the engagements of the earth, from outward preferment or advantages, which are but all the snares of Sathan, Therfore my deare hearts, keepe cleare, keepe your consciences cleane, keepe out of transgressing in any kind against the liberty & the freedome of your consciences, keepe the just, & the pure in your conscien[ces] at li[ber]ty which witnesseth for the living God. And all outward prisons will be litle, But if you imbondage or imprison, or in any measure, cause Gods testimony to suffer in you, than all outward liberty would be litle to you, Soe my deare frends, seale this upon your hearts, that you keepe cleare your consciences in the sight of God in every thing, now that he hath called you for witnesses for him, And now that you are engaged, & have taken upon you to stand witnesses, for the living God be ye living witnesses indeed, & let not the enemy have any cause, to say that ye shrinke & draw backe, in the tyme of sufferings, & tryalls, but that they may be convinced, in the[ir] owne hearts & minds, that God is among you of a truth, And this will be for the honour & for the glory, of yoar Lord & master, for whom & for whose sake, you suffer, And this will be everlasting peace, & comfort unto you, & everlasting salvation to your soules And soe the eternall & Almighty, & infinite God, preserve & keepe you, in his owne name & in his own Arme, & power to stand, there to quench all the fiery darts of the divell

From your deare freind that is one
with you in all your sufferings
M:F

Let this be coppyed & sent to
prison to be read to all freinds
Send a Coppy of this to yorke [York] if
ye can conveniently, & another
to Swarthmoore
Rich. Hubberthornes deare love
is remembered to you all & myne

H:F: [Henry Fell]

Hist. Soc. of PA, Etting Papers; Early Quakers, *p. 46. Also in* Works, *pp. 271–274.*

113 To King Charles II
Late April or early May 1661

"It is laid upon me from the Lord God,
that I should not let another first day [Sunday] passe,
untill I had acquainted the King with it."

This passionate letter to the king vividly describes the actions of soldiers in breaking into Meetings. Judges and other authorities were guilty of instigating and perpetrating such violence. Margaret reminds King Charles that God has been good to him and that it is incumbent on him to stop the persecution.

Her strong sense of responsibility was the result of her conviction that it was her task to inform the king of what was happening to Quakers. She was equally sure that in the end, God's will would be done. The Works *states: "This I gave into his own Hand at Hampton-Court, and shortly after he set our Friends at Liberty; but their Liberty did not long continue" (p. 38). A memoir of Edward Burrough notes of a set of prisoners, "They were all released in consequence of a second proclamation of the king, obtained by the efforts of Margaret Fell, who represented to him the grievous sufferings his first proclamation had occasioned" (p. 199). For many years imprisonments and releases continued, alternating according to political shifts and events.*

King Charles I [*beseech* crossed out] desire thee read this over for it neerly Concernes thee to search into these things.

It hath been the desire of our hearts (the searcher of all hearts knowes) who are people of God (called Quakers) that yee might walke before the Lord & towards us[,] soe as the Lord might prosper & establish you, that your hands might be kept of[f] persecution & cruelty, for certainly the same measure that everyone measureth it must be mett to them again at sometime; And the truth of this hath been fulfilled in our age: And now doe but soberly & seriously consider, what reward & recompence; such things as here followeth will bring upon the Rulers & Governours of this kingdom; vizt:

When cruell men, who are already guilty of shedding much innocent blood & is yet blood thirsty, that these should be put in Authority & power, to send rude souldiers with naked swords, speares & halberts, & muskets cock't amongst an innocent people, that never did you wrong, nor never desired your hurt, but their desire hath been (the God of heaven knows, that searcheth all hearts) that the goodnes of the Lord might extend unto you, & that you might be preserved soe as his hand might not be turned against you; And when they have been mett together in the fear of the Lord, to worship the Lord in spirit & truth, & for noe other end (the Lord God is our witnes) & that even then souldiers breake in upon them, with that violence & cruelty, as if they were an enimie they had besieged, beat them with their naked swords, knock them with the but=end of their muskets, & beat them with their halberts & pikes, untill some were wounded with their swords, & others run in with their halberts, & this man that sets these souldiers thus to worke, & soe comes to be the executioner of this wrong to them, & he comes into the court & there sits to accuse them, & also sits as one of the judges over them, & when they Come to speake of the injustice they have suffered by him, then the officers fals [falls] a beating them with spears & halberts openly in the face of the Court, to the terrifying of hundreds, & many cried out, Murder, Murder, & this the fruits of such unjust action from such bloody men.

And we have noe pleader in the Earth, it is the Lord that must plead our cause for us, if men will not[.] he is engaged in our cause, for it is for his sake, & because of his command (the Righteous God knows) that we cannot sweare at all, & for noe other cause nor end, but because he hath commanded it (the Lord of heaven & earth knows) & if we must suffer the forfeiture of our estates to the King, & the Loss of our liberty all our Daies, & be out of his protection & the laws, the will of the Lord be done, it is for him & his sake, & blessed be his name who hath called us to it, & our Estates & liberty will adde little to the King, nor is it our desire that the King should ever buy poor mens estates soe dear, for we desire his good (the Lord of heaven knows) but as soon as the sentence of premunire was pronounced, officers were soon in poor mens houses, to Rifle them & take away their goods for the King.

And now it concernes the King to search into these matters, & see if they are not true, & also consider, that the Lord God who hath set King Charles to rule this nation, the head ruler of men in this nation, he will look for an account of his people from him, for he & the Laws of the land ought to protect them from violent & blood=thirsty men, they not any way wronging or injuring him, nor any man in the realme, but are true & faithfull, & loyall subjects to him in every lawfull demand, that doth not infringe the liberty of their Consciences, which the Lord of heaven knows & soe doth the King, that he is engaged to give them that liberty; However the will of the Lord be done; if we cannot have our liberty, we can suffer for our liberty.

It is laid upon me from the Lord God, that I should not let another first day [Sunday] passe, untill I had acquainted the King with it, least that innocent blood should be shed; & now remember you know these things, & are warned, & as everyone in the street can say & are ready to say, now it is in the Kings power to stop all these things with a word: And now consider what have we done, & what are we guilty of, & are we used as one Christian ought to use another, make not slaves of us before you have cause; must we pay taxes & assesments, pole=mony [poll money] & chimney=mony, & benevolence=mony, & all this to pay souldiers to fall violently upon us in our own houses, it would be very good for you in time to Consider these things, before the fury of the Lord be Kindled, who is a just & a righteous God, & can by noe meanes clear the guilty, And now people Casts it upon us, & say, you may see what the word of a King comes to, & all is fair promises.

And now these things are laid before you, let the King doe what it pleaseth the Lord to put into his heart.

M F

Spence 3/118–119. Also in Works, *pp. 36–37. Addressed: "For the King". Endorsed: "MF to the King [George Fox]"; "These are Ingrossed".*

114 TO THE MAYOR OF LONDON AND JUSTICES 1661

"Is it just, or equall that people be pulled, or hayled from the worshipp of the Lord god violently by Souldiers, with drawne Swords, and musquetts?"

Margaret wrote to the mayor of London and the judges about the abuses suffered by Friends. She emphasizes the Quakers' innocence and harmlessness, and the consequent brutishness of the conduct of the soldiers and also of the authorities who allow it. She asks, "Is this justice?" and writes disdainfully, "yee need not bringe Swords, and musketts amongst us," and "its below the parts of a man to exceede his power."

To the Mayor of London & the rest of the
Justices on the Bench

Let your Moderation appeare unto all men. Yee professe Christ, and your selves to be Christians; wee are soe indeed, and in Truth as well as you. It is now your day, It hath beene others before you, and it will be others when your day is past away. The god of Heaven lookes over you; and sees your usuage of his Servants, who are harmlesse, and Innocent, who gives noe Just cause of offense. But its Evident, that the worrshipp of god is an offense to you who have an Act which ought not to be executed but in a Civill Legall way: But you have violated it, by acting without the Rule of it, and contrary, and against it. Is it just, or equall that people be pulled, or hayled from the worshipp of the Lord god violently by Souldiers, with drawne Swords, and musquetts? Doth your Act prescribe you this way? Or is it violence, or cruelty of men?

Our Kingdome is not of this world, neither can the Subjects of it feight. yee need not bringe Swords, and musketts amongst us. It is Severe enough for men of Justice to proceed accordinge to their Law, and Rule they have to Act by. And its below the parts of a man to exceede his power, and Loyall Authority over a people. Consider if yee would be Soe delt with yourSelves, if it were your owne case. What evill have we done? Or whom have we wronged, That we should be taken by a Company of Souldiers and had to a Goale [jail], and never See the face of a magistrate? Is this Justice? Is it not tyme for the Lord to arrise Since that yee have made voyd his Law? to Thrust poore Innocent people into Goales on heapes, even till Sicknes, & Death overtake them. The Lord open your eyes to see these things in tyme before it be too Late.

M: F:

Spence 3/122 and 3/128, two copies, same words, different hands. Also in Works, *p. 31. Endorsed: "mf to the mare of london [George Fox]".*

115 To Elizabeth, Queen of Bohemia Between May and September 1661

"It is upon me . . . to speke unto thee who art a native plant of this nation, & which is now returned againe after many trialls & hard sufferings."

*Elizabeth, Queen of Bohemia (1596–1662), was the daughter of James I and the aunt of Charles II. She was married, with much pomp, to Frederick V, Elector Palatine, in 1613. In 1618 Frederick, as a leading Protestant prince, was offered the throne of the Bohemians; but by the end of 1620 he was defeated in battle by a Catholic army and deposed. Elizabeth, sometimes called the Winter Queen, spent the remainder of her life at various courts on the Continent and returned to England only in May 1661. She had thirteen children and was the grandmother of George I, the first of the Hanoverian kings of England (*DNB*).*

*Elizabeth was a firm Protestant, and in this pastoral letter Margaret explains something of Quaker beliefs. She denies any "evill doeing" committed by persons claiming to be Quakers. Margaret expresses her desire that Elizabeth would "partake with us . . . to the Liveing word of God in the heart." Margaret presented the letter to the Queen and it was read to her and "several more with her" (*Works, *p. 35).*

To the qeene of Bohemia

The God of heaven & earth who is the most high that dwells in the kingdomes of men[,] he is rissen in this nation in power & in Life & Light & in glory in his saints in a people dispised & hated of all or the most of men, not for any evill deeds nor any transgressions but for their seperation from the rest of the people of the nations, & for Liveing unto God in Righteousnes & true holiness, & soe the scripture is fulfilled, they that depart from Iniquity become a prey, & Christs words is fullfilld who sayd, they should be persecuted & hated for his names sake [John 15:20–21] & for no other cause[,] but for Christ & his names sake hath our sufferings ben great & grevious[,] but thorough faith & patience & obedience we have obtained a good report, & bin carryed thorough our sufferings thus farr & none is able to lay any thing to the charge of any of us that shalbe owned to be of us, for God doth Justifie us, but there may be many particular persons which may goe under the name, & soe shelter themselves in ther evill doeing[;] but such we doe deny who are not faithfull to the Lord, & his truth, for it allwayes was in the Apostles time & saints of old that there was severall persons that did that which was not Conveniuent, for it is Impossible that such a number of people professing one thing should all be kept faithfull to the Lord[;] but If there be some dry branches that must be cutt of[f] from the vine[,] the whole body of the vine must not be Judged by that; It is upon me from the Lord of heaven & earth to speke unto thee who art a native plant of this nation, & which is now returned againe after many trialls & hard sufferings into this nation which is thy native country, that thou wouldst a littell minde & take notice, there is a measure of the same guift of God in thee, by which thou may come to know God as he is a spirit & whose worship is in the spirit & in truth, & who puts the spirit in the inward parte & wrights his Law in the harte of people, which is his new Covenant with his people[,] which is everlasting, thou hast read in the scriptures that they should be all taught of God, & that there teacher should be never more removed into a Corner & there eyes should see there teacher & they should heare a word saying[,] this is the way walke in it [Isa. 30:21]; now this word is in thy heart, & it is this word in our hearts that hath taught us & tould us all that ever we did[,] & this is the word which was in the beginning with God, by which the worlds were made. which preacheth the Righteousnes of faith, & the word is very nigh in the heart & in the mouth[,] as thou may read in the 10 ch of the Romans [Rom. 10:8], now Christs name is called the word of God, he had his vesture dipt in blood, & his name is called the word of God, now this word is become flesh & dwells among us, & we behold his glory[,] of the glory of the onely begotten son of God, & the desire of my soule is that thou might come & partake with us, & if thou come to that Liveing word of God in thy heart, which is one with the same in us, then thou wilt receive the Same life & of the same power & of the same vertue, & be begot by it into life & Immortallitie, for God is Light & in him is noe darkness at all[,] as in the first epistle of John [1 John 1:5] & this word is Light which shines in thy heart, & it let thee see the thoughts & intent of thy heart, & it checks & reproves when there is any evill thoughts or any evill words or any evill actions[.] this Light that shines in the heart makes it manifest, & the apostle saith, whatsoever makes manifest is Light, & soe if thou turne thy minde to within[,] to this Light[,] thou wilt see from whence ariseth envie & strife & evill surmising, theft & murder & all that can be called evil proceeds out of the heart of men & women, now this spirit of the lord being put to this Light[,] this cleanseth & purgeth, & washeth the Inward parts, so here is the teacher of all people upon the face of the earth, that ever comes to be taught of God[,] & there is noe other way nor name under heaven by which any shalbe saved but by the Light of Jesus Christ that hath Lighted everyman that cometh into the world, & he that walks in the Light, as he is in the Light[,] the blood of Jesus Christ cleanseth, from all sin, & here is the fellowship of the saints one with another in the Light[,] as in the first epistle of John, & soe Loveing the Light it is here teacher & holding the Light it is here condemnation, Light is come into the world[,] but now foul darkness rather then Light[,] because there deeds be evill.

a true Lover of the soules of all people
Margaret Fell

Spence 3/102, partially in Works, *pp. 34–35. Endorsed: "M.F. to the Quen of Beheme [George Fox]".*

116 To Bridget Fell and Children, with a postscript by Henry Fell Before September 29, 1661

"Keepe in love, & peace, & unity one with another that yee may be a good Savour, & a good example to others that behould your order."

The term "your order" in this short note means "condition." A steady supply of money must have been required to enable Margaret and her daughter to stay in London, thus Henry Fell's postscript about rents (Letters 82, 109). This is the last letter to her children from Margaret's first visit to London. She returned to Swarthmoor Hall in September 1661, having been away fifteen months.

Leonard Fell (1624–ca. 1700) was a retainer at Swarthmoor Hall until 1665, not related to Thomas Fell. He was convinced to Quakerism by George Fox in 1652 and spent nearly fifty years as an active minister. He was imprisoned and fined numerous times. He was twice imprisoned for non-payment of tithes and then released because his prosecutor died. "His preaching is said to have been of an earnest and loving character rather than argumentative or doctrinal" (DNB).

For Major-General Lambert and Sir Henry Vane see Letters 93 and 94.

Bridget with the rest of my deare Lambs, my deare Everlastinge love is to you, and in that doe I behould you and see your Order; my deare Lambs; keepe in the unity of the Spiritt of life by which yee are made partakers of a devine nature; that into that Image Immortall yee may grow in grace, continually, and in your knowledge of the Lord Jesus xt [Christ] in whom is hidd all the treasures of wisdome and knowledge which toucheth all things and gives power, and wisdome to order all things[;] to whose Arme & power and eternall word I comitt you and be low; & humble & learne of him that is lowly; & keepe in love, & peace, & unity one with another that yee may be a good Savour, & a good example to others that behould your order; I reced [received] noe letter from you the last weeke, only one from L. Fell [Leonard Fell] from Lancaster: passages here is little this weeke; only Lambert [Major-General John Lambert] & vane [Sir Henry Vane] is like to come upon tryall: things are not yet come to noe Issue; Soe here I do waite for the Lords will & power to release me[,] to whom I am wholly comitted. Your Sisters [Margaret Fell, jr.] dear love is remembered to you all, And for the Carter, if he putt him out by any Order from Authority that he shews, let him not resist that but alsoe let him keepe in[.]

Your deare
Mother M: F:

my deare love is dearly remembered to you all & to the rest of Friends[.] Let Tho: Coulton search the notes whether there bee any Rents due to be payd before next Michaellmas [September 29th], Either by John Simpson or any others, and let them be called for & gathered up:

H: F: [Henry Fell]

Spence 3/88. Addressed: "For Bridgett Fell at Swarthmore this". Endorsed: "MF to briget F. [George Fox]".

117 To William and John Edmondson November 25, 1661

"Be faithfull & bould & trew to your maker & he will be a husband unto you & sett your feete upon the Rock Moste sure."

The ringing, encouraging phrases of this epistle were intended to be read aloud. The themes are love, suffering, and the ultimate victory of the Lamb, or Christ, and God's people. It is a fine example of the seventeenth-century Quaker style, which Jackson Cope called the "incantatory style." Its characteristics are "incredible repetition, a combining and recombining of a cluster of words and phrases drawn from scripture" (p. 733). Terry Wallace points to "the use of parallel structuring in sentences—that love of building one's thoughts through a torrent of similarly structured grammatical phrases" (pp. vi–vii).

The letter was sent to William Edmondson (1627–1712), the founder of Irish Quakerism, and his brother, John. William Edmondson had served in Cromwell's army and was converted to Quakerism in 1653 by James Nayler. He traveled widely in Ireland as a minister and also went to America three times. He wrote six tracts and a Journal *(DNB). The latter mentions three visits to Swarthmoor Hall, in 1655, 1691, and 1701. Of that last visit he writes: "Next day we rode to Swarthmore to see Margaret Fox, who was then weak in Body" (p. 230).*

Swarthmore the 25th Day of the 9th month 1661
Deare W.E. & J:E with all the rest of frends in that nation

My deare Love in the Lord god allmightie is unto you all, which never changeth but Indures for evermore which Love, as it is Lived in, preserves & keeps us to the Lord god & keeps his Comandments[,] Lawes & Statuts [;] which Love is the fulfilling of the whole Law of god & answers to all his Righteous Comands, in thought[,] word, and action[;] this keeps Clean, Low, and Inocent and moulds us into its own frame & temper and so brings to be a New Lumpe [1 Cor. 5:7], leavined into the bowills [bowels] of everlasting Love which reacheth unto all & Extends unto all [,] Even unto Enemies. oh blessed and happy are all they that are comet into this sweet beeing of unevarsall Love[,] which would have all to be Saved & Come to the knowledge of the Truth. this is the Image and nature of the blessed god, that houlds forth his tender hand & sweet bowels of everlasting Love unto all people Nations Languadges Kindreds & tongues; who is noe Respecter of persons[;] but every nation that feares & worketh righteousness is Accepted of him [Acts 10: 34–35] whose Calle is to every one that thirsteth[.] Come & whosoever is athirst lett him Come & drink of the watter of Life freely [Rev. 21:6] oh the Infinite Love & bowels of everlasting Life & fullnes that dwells in his blessed bosom, Righteousness & peace is the habitation of his throne [Ps. 97:2] oh my deare Lambs lett the Issewes [issues] of Life be keept oppen, that issueth forth into your Soules from this blessed fountaine that you may feele it alwayes open unto you & you open unto it, that you may feele it alwayes fresh and new floweing into your soules. So will you feele the word of the Lord god sweeter unto you then the honey or the honey-Combe [Ps. 19:10] & so will you Come truly to know that man Liveth not by bread alone but by every word that proceedeth from the Lord god [Matt. 4:4]. heere stands the Life that is eternall & soe to doe the will of the Lord god: will be Meate & Drinke unto you & will be More delitfull then your ordinary food [,] & then will not sufferings, tryalls & Hardship be strange unto you[,] knowing that the Capton of your salvation, which is gone before you[,] is maid perfect through sufferings [Heb. 2:10] who in the days of his flesh when he had offer[ed] up prayers & suplications with stronge Cryes & Tears unto him that was able to save _____ _____ _____ _____ sonn, yett Learned he obedience by the things that he suffered and so must all that follow his stepps; the servants is not greater then there Lord [John 13:16] and blessed & happe are all they that learne this

Lesson in the power of Mighty god[,] not only to beleve on him but also to suffer for his sake [1 Pet. 3:14] they Reaigne with him when they suffer[;] they reign over there enemies with him; & in his power they will subdue & Conquer at the Last[.] for the Lambe Must have the victory; it is decreed & determined [,] & his armies that followes him sitts opon white horses & is Clothed with fine Linen white & Cleane [Rev. 19:14]; & so my dearly beloved[,] be strong in the Lord and in the power of his might & be faithfull & bould & trew to your maker & he will be a husband unto you & sett your feete upon the Rock Moste sure [Ps. 40:2] that if the storms beate & the tempest blow yett you will not be shaken[,] through him that keepeth you that is greater then all, & none is able to pluck you oute of my fathers hand[,] into whose arme & power I Comite [commit] you Everlastingly to dwell & abide with the Lord god, with whome all things is possible[.] the god of Love whose mercyes fails not preserve & keepe you all, and Nurse you up in his owne bosom to his owne prayse & glory that you may be a people saved by the Lord.

From your Deare Frend And sister,

M F

Lett this be Copied over &
Redd in your meetings in the fere of the Lord

Spence 3/19–20. Also in Works, *pp. 274–276. Endorsed: "A epesell of* M F *to frends in ierland [George Fox]"; "Examined by mee SF [Sarah Fell]".*

118 To King Charles II and his Council Late 1661 or early 1662

"This slighting of the command of the King in his letter to them, by acting contrary to it as they have done . . . is a great dishonour to the King."

The Quakers in New England received harsher treatment from the Puritan authorities than those in England. A Calvinistic theocracy with no tolerance for dissent ruled in the Massachusetts Bay Colony. When Governor John Endecott died in 1665 an admirer wrote in his diary: "Our honored Governor, Mr. John Endecott, departed this life . . . he had faithfully endeavored the suppression of a pestilent generation, the troublers of our peace, civil and ecelesiastical, called Quakers" (Mayo, p. 284).

In Boston, Quaker books were burned and, when that proved ineffective, four Quakers were hanged: William Robinson and Marmaduke Stephenson in 1659, Mary Dyer in 1660, and William Ledra in 1661 (BQ, p. 404). Many others were imprisoned, whipped, banished, or otherwise punished because they refused to accept the Bay Colony's laws against their preaching. As continuing complaints reached King Charles, he sent an order, dated September 9, 1661, against such extreme measures. It reached Boston in November 1661 (Mayo, p. 253).

John Leverett (1616–1679), later governor of Massachusetts, was the London agent for the Massachusetts Bay Colony at this time. He kept Governor Endecott informed of the king's position as favor toward the Quakers waxed and waned (DAB).

"Captain Oliver" is referred to several times in the Records of the Governor and Company of the Massachusetts Bay in New England but with no mention of Quakers.

Margaret relates several incidents of persecution and emphasizes the disrespectfull attitude of New England magistrates toward the king's command. She mentions two women. One of them was Anne Coleman, who with two other women were sentenced to be made "fast to the Cart's Tail, & driving your several Towns, to whip them on their Backs, not exceeding 10 Stripes . . . till they come out of this Jurisdiction." This was done in three towns until one constable was "moved with Compassion & set them at Liberty" (Besse, 2:227–228).

Elizabeth Hooton (ca. 1600–1672) was in a sense the first Quaker. She was a respected Baptist preacher, and her separatist group called themselves "Friends" before she met George Fox in 1646 and became his faithful follower and a highly regarded Quaker minister. She went to Boston in 1661 and was briefly imprisoned, flogged, and taken to the border of the colony in the wilderness and abandoned there. She returned to England and procured a license from King Charles to build a Meetinghouse in Boston, but the license was not honored. She actively preached during the reminder of her life and wrote one tract (Greaves, 2:112; Barbour, The Quakers, *p. 233).*

Nicholas Upshall of Boston was one of a number of people who became Quakers because they were outraged by the grossly unjust treatment they witnessed. In 1656 two women, Mary Fisher and Ann Austin, went to Boston, were imprisoned and kept with no food. Upshall, an elderly man, bribed a jailor to allow him to provide food. After five weeks the women were put on board a ship and returned to England. Nicholas Upshall was fined and banished. He then went to Rhode Island, which allowed freedom of religion (Besse, 2:178–181).

To the King & his Counsell

Being a short Relation of some of the sad sufferings of our freinds in New England called Quakers, since they received the kings letter that they should not inflict any Corporall punishment upon them.

They have stokt [put in the stocks], & whipt an inhabitant of Boston having a wife & 5 children & fined freinds for praying & speaking in their meetings, & also have banished Anne Coleman out of the Country, & Configned an old man[,] one Nicholas Upshall[,] to prison as long as he shall live, & through the abuse they have done to one prisoner in Boston, they have put him out of his sences, & then sent severall letters with lies in them to vilifie him; that he should speake blasphemy; And to cover over this prisoning, whiping, fining, banishing & stocking, they spread it abroad to incense the people, that we forged the kings letter ourselves, & counterfeited the kings seale[,] how untrue which thing is the king himselfe knows. And we having several letters of the cruell usage of our freinds in New England, & what a pittifull rage they are in against them, that they are not suffered to live quietly upon the Earth; some friends here in London went with the letters to one Broadstreet[,] one of the New England Magistrates, to let him see what was done in New England Notwithstanding to [the] kings letter, & had some discourse with him; he said unto them, they at first understood by the kings letter, that it was his minde they should wholy refraine inflicting any corporall punishment upon freinds, but since they were informed by John Leveret (their Agent) that the King did never intend that they should wholy refrain inflicting Corporall punishment upon them, but only death; And that the king did not rebuke them for putting freinds to death, & that the king was noe freind to the Quakers, & that the King intended to make sharp laws against them here to punish them with, & that the Kings minde was not understood by them, but that they might goe on to inflict corporall punishments upon freinds in New England, though his letter to them signifies the contrary, upon which they are in a mighty rage, & fall on stocking, whiping, banishing, & imprisoning for tearme [term] of life, & one Captaine Oliver said to a freind, that for all the kings letter (to the Contrary) yet they would persecute freinds, & another said in the Governours [John Endecott] house, that he Could take delight in following a freind to execution; And when the aforementioned Magistrate was asked whether any punishment should be inflicted upon freinds for matters of religion[,] but if they were manslayers, whoremongers, Adulteres & that the civill law was against them if they were such, but he could not tax them with any such practice, but he said if all our freinds had been as sober there as they are here, they should not have suffered such punishments as they did; soe here are three at London who had suffered at new England, one of which was sentenced to die, & the other two had one of their ears cut at Boston, & when he was demanded, what he had against them or any of the others that were put to death, he could prove nothing against them, but said they were justly put to death according to their law: we told him that before we laid these things before the King & his Counsell, as men we came to let him see what sufferings they had inflicted upon our freinds in New England, contrary to any Just law, & the minde of the King in his letter to them; And one Elizabeth Hooten an Antient [ancient] woman being at Boston two nights could not get a bed to lie in, under 20 shillings a night (they having made a law that whosoever entertaines a Quaker should pay 20 shillings) was moved of the Lord for the sake of divers freinds that came thither from other parts to proffer money for a house & land, the house to entaine [entertain] strangers in, & the ground to bury the dead in, whom the New England Magestrates by their unjust laws put to death, that soe they might not be buried under their gallowes in an oppen feild, which did somewhat strike them with shame:

And now these things are laid before you to Consider of, for though these men may come before the King with many fair words, & make a show unto him, as if they were his faithfull & loyall subiects, yet it is not soe with them in reallity, for besides these words of Major Denison concerning the changing of the Goverment of England, with which baying the King hath been already acquainted, & this slighting of the command of the King in his letter to them, by acting contrary to it as they have done, which is a great dishonour to the King, & an ill president to other Collonies; upon a report that went thither of the Kings intent to send over a new Governour, which being spread there, the Jaylour came to a freind then in prison at Boston, & said, that he heard the King intended to send over a new Governour, but they intended[,] if he did[,] to stand upon their guard & oppose his coming by force of armes, these things and diverse others to effect _____ _____ _____ _____ of them which being Considered & well & truly weighed it plainly appeares that it is not what the King doth, but what he doth to please them that they wilbe subject to him in; & for Confirmation of the truth of what is before related, which of late they have done to our freinds in New England Contrary to the Kings Command, there are severall freinds that are come over that can testifie of the same also: from them that desire your Eternall Good & welfare & that in the wisdome of God you may be guided, that you may be a terrour unto evill doers & a praise to them that doe well, for which you will have a reward from the Lord.

M F

Spence 3/116 and summary in Works, *pp. 32–33. Endorsed: "MF to the king & officers [George Fox]".*

119 To King Charles II After May 2, 1662

"Wee perceive that you have made an Act against us, for what cause and Reason the Lord in heaven knowes."

The 1662 Quaker Act was directed against those who attended Quaker Meetings, "illegal assemblies," and who refused to swear an oath in court. The first two offenses were punished with a fine or imprisonment, and the third with transportation. Trial by jury was permitted only with the third offense. The Act was passed by a Parliament that had many Royalists and Presbyterians who, in spite of many differences in other matters, shared a deep hostility to Quakers. The act was administered with greater or lesser severity according to local conditions and the politics and good will of local justices and people (Horle, Q.&EngLegalSys, *pp.* 50, 16, 259).

King Charles

Often hath the desire of my heart been to the God of heaven for thee that thou might bee preserved out of persecution of the Saints and People of God, who are deare unto him as the Apple of his Eye [Deut. 32:10] as you will find, how ever you may beleive otherwise[,] through which you might have been preserved soe the Lord might have prospered you, as you know the Lord has been good and gratious and long suffering unto you, this time that you rulled while moderation has in some measure been kept to tender Consciences. And certainly that promise that thou made in true simplicitie and according I doe beleive as it was then in thy heart, that thou wouldst give libertie to tender Consciences, I am assured it is upon Record in the sight of the Lord God, and thou art bound unto him in thy Conscience to performe with him, and therefore is my heart affected with the danger that thou runns, seing that I see merciles men sett a worke to come into the Meetings of Gods People with swords and Pistolls and Musketts as if it were against a Theife, or against the openst profest Enimies that the heart of Man could imagine, even as if they would drive and turne the Lord and his People out of the Nation, surely the Lord is engaged to stand upp for himselfe, since that heaven is his throan and Earth is his Footstoole[.] soe it is stongly upon my heart once more to give thee warning and to desire thee to take care of these things and take a little veiw of them betimes before it bee too late, Wee perceive that you have made an Act against us, for what cause and Reason the Lord in heaven knowes, for of all people in the Nation, wee have been the most harmless and Innocent, and I am sure the most tender towards you, yett our sufferings have been great and it is but righteous & just that wee should have our libertie as well as others[;] but now that you have made a law it is unreasonable and unequitable that you proceed according to the direction of it, for it is below a man of Justice to exceed his power that the law gives him by which he acts by, soe these things with many more, is laid upon me from the Lord to lay before thee. who hath putt power in thy hand to see Righteous[ness] and equitie acted in the Kingdom [The last three lines are torn & illegible.]

Faithfull lover of thy soule
M. F.

Spence 3/123. Also in Works, *pp. 35–36. Endorsed: "m f to the king [George Fox]".*

120 TO WILLIAM CATON MAY 8, 1663

"Soe my Deare heart; I desire thee to let Benjamin See this, if thou be free in thy selfe."

Margaret writes to her dear friend, Will Caton (Letters 63, 66) in Amsterdam, primarily about Benjamin Furley's errors of spiritual and intellectual pride. Furley (1636–1714) was a brilliant young man, a prosperous merchant and a scholar, who went to

Holland in 1658 and with Caton and a few others built up Dutch Quakerism. He wrote tracts in English, Dutch, and French and had a library of 4,400 volumes. Later in life he advised William Penn as the colony of Pennsylvania was being developed, and he was a friend of John Locke (Greaves, 1:307–308).

Furley had written a letter to Humphrey Norton (Letter 52) concerning the "Lordly spiritt" which Margaret found highly offensive, for it "tends to divition, & friends were grievd at it." She speaks of her love and pity for Furley but is sad that he has become puffed with pride and "as they were who became vaine in their owne Immagginations"; for that leads to "strife & Contention, & for Mastery." He is wise in the "wisdome of man" but a child in the "things of God." Margaret asks Will to show Benjamin her letter.

Swarthmore the 8th of the 3d month 1663
W:C:

My Deare & faithfull & everlastingly Beloved Friend, & Brother; In the Lord and in his Truth which makes free, & keepes cleare, & cleane and pure, and spotles in his sight; therrow the Immortall word, that purifies the heart & washes the secrett & Inward parts; where deceite & Deceiveablenesse Lodges in all Such as is not begotten & borne of the Immortall seed; not Corruptable, but Incorruptable which is of the will of God, and doth his will, in that body that is prepared, & in that volume of the Booke where its written, thou shalt worshipp the Lord thy God, & him onely shall thou serve, & who is out of the unity of the Eternall Spiritt, where God is worshipped, & felt & witnessed & knowne, who is A Spiritt, though they may professe him in words, or Appeare, in A Mind puffed up with Knowledge (and there hearts unsanctified to the Lord, and unseasoned, by his grace, and uncleansed by his word into which all that is of the Seed Immortall are begotten into); all their high Swelling words of vanity, and their Immaginations with the serpentine wisdome vainely puffed up; This will not profitt nor this will not stand; But will wither & vanish & come to noething; as all the Children of the Light, shall see who waites & abides with the Lord, whose Immortallity dwels in the Light; and soe My Dearely Beloved brother waite thou heare, and Abide heare in Gods Light and C[om]andment & thou shall see all these, money Changers buyers, & sellers of Immaginations, in Changable things; whipp't out; and the Dreadfull power of the Almighty God, and his standard that never Changes shall remaine; and I would desire that thou would remember me if thou seest fitt & Convenient, to B: Furley: and tell him, that I heare of A Letter that he hath sent to H: N: [Humphrey Norton] to Durham; which mentiond keepeing out the Lords or Lordly spiritt; which I perceive tends to divition; & friends were grievd at it, and truely my Love is soe much to him that I pitty him, for his proceeding in those things; for though he doth Looke upon himselfe, (and I beleeve he is soe); A wise man, as A man in the wisdome of man; But as to the things of God & to the powerfull workeing, & opperation of the Immortal word, I know he is A Child in these things; whatever he may thinke of himselfe, or what any other may Looke upon him to be, who are as Ignorant of their owne state & Condition as he; Conceits will nott change any ones Nature & Image; it is the Lords word & worke must doe it; they may say that they know soe, but I know they cannot say in the Lords presence, and in his Truth, that they are changed from what they were formerly; though they may professe & pretend Another thing, with the same mind & nature; But that is not the worke nor the thing it selfe; Therefore it had beene Safe & good for them to have beene Cautious of strikeing in with a false uncleane spriritt, which they & all that ever Lives upon the Earth shall see, will never worke for God nor for his truth; Butt workes for strife & Contention, & for Mastery; and if they had kept out the Lordly spiritt, they should have kept it out, But all that ever are betrayed, & ever was betrayed by the serpent, was under A pretence, of Another thing then it was; for the old Serpent that abode not in the truth said they should be as Gods [Gen. 3:4–5]; and soe they Entered into his Temptations, & became as devils; & the Same Serpentes alive still, and is tempting the Innocent, where he can gett hold or who will enter with him into this Temptation; & They that are weake, in the Lords truth, he getts hold on & the false prophett must needs be painted, which he would deceive if it were possible the very elect, but the Elect he cannott deceive nor lye anything to his charge, Since the Liveing God doth Justify, who binds And Chaines the serpent; & he is the same Ever, that was from the beginning, that saith, they who are in the Lords truth are Lords, or of A Lordly Spiritt; for their Innocency & humility shall plead for them in the hearts & Consciences of all, & they will bee A Good Savour unto God, both in them that beleeve & in them perish _____ and them that doth not beleeve in the Ld [Lord] Jesus Christ must perish, unto wm [whom] our Gospell is hid even unto Such as are Lost, & Scattered from it & have taken up another thing, & would have another Gospell, & Indeed another God, Such (must be, and) is his Accursed, & truely this is sad & sorrowfull to my heart that gods pure & liveing, precious truth should be turned from; and fables ___ _____ be beleeved in; But woe wilbe, & is to that old enemy that was the first founder of these things, & gods truth is noe Lording spiritt, for that is the spiritt, of the gambler & of the heathen; & he that Exalts himselfe must be brought downe & humbled; which the Lds truth shall never be; nor xt [Christ] Je[sus]: the Author of our Eternall Salvation who hath humbled himselfe, to the death of the cross & he is & shalbe Exalted forever, over all the powers of darknes, & he binds & chaines that old serpent which is called the divill & Satan, his place must be in the Lake; & there is but these: & its Good to draw near unto God & to beware of meddleing with the Subtilty of the Serpent that Appeares Good but hath his sting in his taile: My Soule is ever sad for the seed of God that suffers under the treachery of the enemy, thorrow the darknes that is entered, as they were who became vaine in their owne Immagginations, & soe their foolish hearts came to be darkened; this came upon Such as professed themselves wise; and Soe this is my Love, the Lord is my witness, however it be taken, and Soe my Deare heart; I desire thee to let Benjamin See this, if thou be free in thy selfe, doe not _____ what I may obtaine by it, for I am A witnes for the Lord & his truth, & the wickedness that we have to warr with is spirituall; & his Letter was conveyed secretly in the North, & I am something Condemed & lett me receive what the Lord pleases, and my Testimony I must beare for him;

My Love is deare & Everlasting to thy wife & her Sister & to all faithfull friends, & the God of power & love, keepe you all in the Spirituall discerning, & in that word that is quicke & powerfull, & discernes betwixt that Spiritt that serves the Liveing God & him that serves him not, & he that will not serve & keepe to the Liveing God wn he is come; nor abide in his truth, he will not abide in another wn [when] he comes, But the pur [pure] truth of the Ld was Long Looked for before it came, and now he is come[.] They that Looked for another way Looke Longe; it had beene good for them if they had abodd [abode] in that they had received, for all their Expectations will come to noething; Soe dwell thou in Eternity and that will remaine;

Thy Deare & faithfull friend

M:F:

Spence 3/57–58. Addressed: "For My Deare Friend Willm Caton at Amsterdam these with Care in Holland". Endorsed: "M: F to Wilem Caton 1663 read over".

121 To the Judges at Lancaster August 29, 1663

"This I write unto you to prevent all false accusations: which might be otherwise Cast upon us: who are an inocent & an harmlesse people."

In the summer of 1663 rumours of a new plot against the government spread from the North to London. A group of Puritans planned to overturn the monarchy, starting in the town of Kaber Rigg. The date of the uprising was to be October 12, but "already in July the authorities were on the alert, & . . . directed to prevent and punish unlawful meetings and to secure dangerous persons" (Braithwaite, p. 30).

Margaret reminds the judges that George Fox was released by order of the king three years earlier, after being "wrongfully . . . Committed prisoner by henry Porter," justice and mayor of Lancaster (Letter 83). She anticipates actions against Quakers and insists on their peaceful and nonviolent stance. A number of eminent Quakers had been in Cromwell's New Model Army, which aroused doubt about their peaceful intentions. By 1663 Quakers rejected the use of violence, but there were some former Quakers who were involved in the Kaber Rigg Plot.

To the Judges at Lancaster from M F 1653 [should be 1663]

This is to Certifie the Justices of peace in this Countie or any other whom it may Conserne to prevent Jealousies: thoughts doubts: or misapprehansions of any; as also to take away misinformation or accusations: from others Consearning G F: [George Fox] who was apprehended in this Countie wrongfully; & unrighteously: & Comitted prisoner by henry Porter: 3 years since as it did appeare when he came upon his tryall: at the kings bench: where he was Cleared by the kings Judges; & set at Liberty by the kings particuler order. & ever since hath: & doth: & ever will remaine a peaceable man suffering by many but not wronging or injuring any man,—This is to acquaint you that he is now at my house a sojourner & so you may be satisfied hereby: that you shall never know any thing by us the people of God Called Quakers: but lovers of peace, Truth: & Righteousnesse, how ever wee Come to suffer, it is for the Lords sake, & his Truth sake, & as Christians; & not as evill doers—

we Came thorow the Countreys & all was peaceable & quiet: till we Came in Yorkeshire Bishoprick, & westmorland, & in all these places we heard of a Rumor & speaking of a plot; but what it is wee know not;

but Certainely there is wickednesse in the hearts of some, but those that feares the lord & workes Righteousness wilbe preserved out of all wickednesse & the power that acts it, which is the power of darknesse[,] which our Testimony is against; which we utterly deny & abhor; such designs: & manslayers & plotters: which Christ Jesus denies who Came not to destroy mens lives but to save: whose kingdom is not of this world and therefore his servants Cannot fight[,] for fighters fight for the world & the earth which we deny, & declare against for ever:—And this I write unto you to prevent all false accusations: which might be otherwise Cast upon us: who are an inocent & an harmlesse people, & ye shall ever finde us true & faithfull

Margaret: Fell

Swarthmore the 29th of 6th month
Called August 1663

Spence 3/132–133. Endorsed: "M F her laters [letters, George Fox]"; "3 m.f. to the Judges at Lancer 63".

122 To Colonel Richard Kirkby Late 1663

"Truely we have often many of us,
stood Amazed, to see your proceedings,
that you should in the first place fall upon us,
who will never doe you hurt nor wronge."

Colonel Richard Kirkby (ca. 1625–1681) of Furness, near Marsh Grange, Margaret's birthplace, was with Sir Daniel Fleming one of the chief persecutors of Quakers in Lancashire and the North. He represented one of the leading families in the area and held various offices. He was a firm royalist and opposed to Quakers and other dissenters (CJ, 2:390–391).

While Judge Thomas Fell was alive Kirkby did not actively act against the Fell family, but in 1661 while Margaret was in London, he tried to prevent Meetings from being held at Swarthmoor Hall. Daughter Bridget Fell wrote that Kirkby "is sumtymes very moderate but often very high and much against Friends" (Spence 3/89).

In 1663, because of the Kaber Rigg Plot (Letter 121), there was widespread persecution which included the forcible breaking up of Meetings, imposing fines, and imprisoning Friends, particularly poor families. Margaret wrote to Col. Kirkby to

plead their case, though probably not with much hope. She repeats King Charles's words to her and emphasizes that they want only "to worship & serve the liveing god." Her letter did not change Col. Kirkby's views. In 1666 Ellis Hookes wrote to Margaret: "I received thy letter wherein I perceive thee art troubled at my short writeing; but it was because I was afraid to write much of it least it should come to Kirkby & soe the business [of releasing George Fox from prison] should be hindred" (CJ, 2:102).

The endorsement on the letter says "1665," but 1663 is more likely. Margaret says that she has not written to Kirkby before, and there is another letter dated January 20, 1664 (Letter 123). Also, her statement that "there may be some which may be Called of us, that are not of us" is a reference to the Kaber Rigg Plot of 1663.

Coll: Kirkby

I have never before this time presumed to write unto thee upon this Acctt [account] haveing had the benefitt of thy [levety?]. Although upon the truthes Account, I have writt to many of the heads of this nation and now haveing this occation, that thou hast sent A warrant with the Constables into our Meeting I Could not but sertify unto thee, our Innocency and clearenesse upon any Account of giveing any Just Accation [occasion] thereof (God is o.r [our] witnesse), and I know thou with many more of you are not Ignorant, that we are not such people as are any way ill Affected to Either to the King, State, or Government or to any man or person upon the Earth, but we desire the good & the peace of all men, and that under this government, we might Live A Godly & A peaceable Life, and the K: [King] & many more about him, are absolutely persuaded that we will never wrong nor Injure him & I am certaine, & dare Ingage [engage], both body, life & Estate, that you shall never find otherwise by us, nor by any that shalbe [shall be] owned to be of us. I do not deny, but there may be some which may be Called of us, that are not of us, but my word goes for those, that we owne to be of us, the last time, that I spoke with the K: he said these words to me

I will not hinder you of your religion, keepe it in your owne house, God forbid that I should hinder you, now you _____ very well know that if you send off warrants to take up meetings, in A generall way, you will find few Escape us, & us you wilbe [will be] Sure to find, but truely we have often many of us, stood Amazed, to see your proceedings, that you should in the first place fall upon us, who will never doe you hurt nor wronge, & by that meanes your Enemies, that waites for an opportunity goes free, and shelters under our sufferings but certainely these things are hid from your eys [eyes], or else you would see this, and that the Lords Righteous hand Cannott Escape such things, that the Innocent should suffer and the guilty is pased by; my desire at this time to thee, is that thou would be as favourable to these poore men, that has families to maintaine, and is Innocent before God & all men, as thou can well[.] and now we heare that thou art agoeing out of the Country, & it wilbe good, & for thy peace & Comfort, to leave A good example, and as I have sd [said] to severall before, you shall never be Ashamed, of showeing favor unto us for you shall never take us in that action, which shall Justly Incur any mans displeasure, but to worship & serve the liveing god, we are bound in our Con: [conscience] to dare, & whereever we suffer for the Lds [Lord's] sake, the Ld in his time will plead our Case and cleare our Innocency; and soe the God of power Direct thy heart to doe in this thing, as thou wouldst be done unto;

from A true and faithful Lover of thee & all men;

M.F.

Spence 3/6. Also in Ross pp. 164–165. Endorsed: "5, M.F. to Cornall Carbe, 1665 [George Fox]".

123 To Colonel Richard Kirkby
January 20, 1664

"When I spooke to him after the sescions, hee [William Kirkby] threatened mee that this was but a begining of what I should find, soe I persaive [perceive] that their is great Intencions against mee and us."

The years 1662 to 1672 were filled with persecution of Quakers. It began with the Quaker Act of 1662, two provisions of which made it unlawful firstly, to refuse to take an oath, and secondly, for more than five people to assemble, which was considered a "conventicle." The punishments for the first and second offense were fines or imprisonments; the third conviction resulted in "transportation to any of His Majesty's plantations beyound the seas" (Braithwaite, p. 23).

In London, Meetings were brutally raided. Samuel Pepys, the seventeenth-century diarist, is quoted: "I saw several poor creatures carried by, by constables, for being at a conventicle. They go like lambs, without any resistance. I would to God they would either conform, or be more wise, and not be catched!" (Braithwaite, p. 22).

In the North, Col. Richard Kirkby (Letter 122) detested the Quakers but did not express his true feelings to George Fox in the incident that Margaret refers to in this letter. Fox wrote in his Journal: *"They tolde mee that Coll. Kirby had sent his leifetenant there to search for mee who had searched both boxes & trunkes . . . I was moved of the Lord God to goe the next day to Coll: Kirbeys house . . . & when I came there was the Flemmings & severall of the gentry . . . And after a little time Coll: Kirby came in & soe I tolde him I came to visitt him understanding that hee would have seene me: & to know what hee had to say to mee or whether he had anythinge against mee: & he saide before all . . . that as hee was a gentleman hee had nothing against mee: but saide that* M: *Fell must not keepe great meetings att her house"* (CJ, *2:37–38).*

Margaret addresses Col. Kirkby as a neighbor who has hypocritcally spoken kindly to her face but acted treacherously behind her back. His brother, William Kirkby, went into a Meeting and became a witness against Friends, causing them to be fined. She stresses the hardship that fines impose on poor people. William Kirkby also threatened her outrightly.

Colonel Roger Sawrey was "an old Cromwellian soldier," and his residence, Broughton Tower in Lancashire, "served as a shelter for the outed Ministers in the time of storm." In 1664 he was "bound over to good behaviour to keep from Conventicles and to appear when required" (Nightingale, Ejected, *p. 124, 691).*

The Public Record Office (PRO) copy of this letter is one of the few original letters of Margaret Fell. It is part of a collection documenting the government's fears of nonconformists and containing numerous intercepted letters. The copy in the Spence Manuscript seems to be a draft. It is basically the same with minor differences of words and spelling. The PRO copy has one addition of five lines beginning with "It hath formerly bein the Honner of Magstrats."

Swarth more the 20th of 11th mo caled Jenauary

Coll: Kirby, the lord Requires of thee and all men, to love mercy [Mic. 6:8] and to doe Justis, And to walke humbly with the lord &c: this is Comly in A Magestrate in the sight of god and all men; And the law which god gave unto his people is first to love god, And secondly their neighbor, And the last time thou was in this Contry there was a show and an apearance Made of love unto mee and my famally, And when George fox Came to thee, thou said thou had noe thing Against him and said if hee stayed at this house none should medll with him, with many other faire Speeches, but at the Sescions before, I psave [perceive] there was then Intentions in thy minde, for I heard that thou

Said when you weare about to Indite Roger Soray [Sawrey], that you should allsoe have had mee, but it seems that was passed by or forgotten, And our friends Inquiered after and severall fined. And pore people had theire goods distreaned [distrained] trible [treble] the value of their fines. And since that thy Brother Came into our Meeting & became a witnes against our friends and hath Caused severall pore men to bee fined some in five Marks and some in five noubles [noble was a gold coin], And some they have fined that is porer then many that begs. And here is the Charraty [charity] and the love that your pore Nighbors Receives from you. It hath formerly bein the Honnor of Magstrats to take Care of their Nighbors & to doe what good ofice they Could for them, And Rether show Mercy then Severety; for the Rock of Isrerall hath said that hee that Ruls amongst men must be Just Ruling in the feare of god [2 Sam. 23:3]. But Contrary to this it seems there was a letter sent from thee which Came to the bench in the Sescions which is looked upon to be the Cause of soe many pore people Suffering Such fines and Imprisonments, and this is not of good Report nor a good Savor that any man should have a mind to doe his Nighbors harme at Such A distance, it had beine enough for thee to have laid thy Rod upon us when thee was amongst us, & not to have Incoriged [encouraged] others in thy absense. It was but a meane ofis [office] for thy brother to be a wittnes against an Inosent people for punishing them for serveing and worshiping the lord, And when I spoke to him after the sescions, hee threatened mee that this was but a begining of what I should find, soe I persaive [perceive] that their is great Intencions against mee and us but wee are willing to give up to the will of the lord, And to give our backs to the smiter [Isa. 50:6], knowing that the lord in his due time will visit for these things.

And what ever the Spoyler doe unto us, the lord taks [takes] Notice of it for his Eyes beholds the Children of men, And I am suer [sure] its without Cause given by mee or any that ever belounged to mee, to thee or any of your family. And one of the Justises of the bench tould mee that my house had not beine trubled but for thee, soe I see And find that A profesed Enemie is a better friend then A profesed friend and a secret Enemie. This is noe good Carrecter [character] Nether is it a great Conquest to get eight Inosent [innocent] men into prison by a snare. And to fine a Company of pore people for worshiping the lord but all these things is Commited to the Righteous Judge that Judgeth Righteously unto whom every man must give an account of his works and must Receive his Reward accordingly and there is many of the people Caled quakers in other parts of the nation, that is not soe hevely delt with by theire Neighbors, But wee Can say unto thee and unto you all, for all that you doe unto us the lord for give you: & you shall never have any Just Cause against us for what you doe against us it shall be against the Inosent and that Cause ther lord will plead, unto whom wee Commit it.

From thy Reall and
Truly Loving Friend
Margrett Fell

Postscript:
The InClosed peper is Georg Foxs is Testimony
that hee gave to the Justices of the bench. Vale.
[along the margin] I beleve never man soffer for such a testimony Among Christians Magasters.

PRO SP 29/91, Spence 3/134, and Extracts from State Papers pp. 187–188. Public Record Office copy addressed: "To Coll: Kirby att His Lodging These present in London." Spence copy endorsed: "M F to Carbe 1663 read over [George Fox]".

124 Excerpts from Trials at Lancaster and Letter to the Magistrates and People of England June 7, 1664

"Oh take up a Lamentation for England [!] surely there is some heavy sad greivous Judgment waiting over her."

At the time of this letter, Margaret had been in prison for three months, since February 18, 1664, due primarily to the zealousness of Sir Daniel Fleming (1633–1701). A powerful landowner and the sheriff of Cumberland, he was in frequent correspondence with Secretary of State Joseph Williamson at Whitehall in London (DNB). The excerpts below, still retained in the Public Record Office, show his wish to extirpate Quakerism and to punish Margaret Fell. They also show the difficulty he had persuading other justices and judges to proceed against Friends.

"Jan.16. 63/64.
Sir,

At the Quarter Sessions holden at Lancaster upon Tuesday last, wee proceeded . . . smartly against the Quakers; Wee Praemunired one, committed to close Gaol [jail] George Fox & halfe a score more, for refusineing of the Oath of Allegiance, & wee fined near three score upon the new Act for unlawfull meetings, not withstanding Mrs. Fell (Oliver's Judge Fel's widdow) [reference to Oliver Cromwell] used her utmost endeavors with many of the Justices to prevent it . . . I doubt not but this proceeding aginst them here will break their meetings. . . . if they procure not somewhat by way of favour from you at Whitehall" (Extracts, SP, p. 186).

"Jan.28.63/64.
Sir

I gave you an account in my last of our proceedings against the Quakers at Lancaster & Kendal, & not withstanding the same, Mrs. Fell (Oliver's Judge Fell's widdow, & now wife or I know not what to Geo. Fox) had a greater meeting of them at her house then ever, the very next Sunday after the Sessions, on purpose as 'tis generally thought to affront our authority. . . . If wee receive any encouragement from you herein, wee'l tender her the oath, & so praemunire her . . . which will bee the onely way to take effectuall course with her, who is the cheife maintainer of the party in this Countrey, I find a coolness in severall honest Justices to act against them . . . " (Extracts, SP, pp. 188–189).

"19 Feb. 1663/4.
Sir

Haveing received yours by the last Post,

I mett yesterday at Ulverstone the Sherif & some Justices of the Peace for Lancashire, where . . . I press'd the Justices there to send for Mrs Fell . . . if she would not assure us to have no more [meetings], that wee might then . . . proceed against her . . . To which manner of proceeding some of my Fellows were a little backward, untill I communicated your letter unto them . . . wee tendered her the Oath of Allegiance which shee refused to take, whereupon wee committed her unto the Common Gaol at Lancaster, there to be kept, without Bail or Mainprise, untill the next Assizes, when wee hope the Judges will tender her it againe that so she may be Praemunired; which will (I am confident) much abate the interrest of that Faction . . . " (Extracts, SP, p. 189).

"March 21 1664
Sir

Having received yours of the 1st instant, I went the 10th unto Lancaster Assizes there to justify the committing of George Fox & Mrs. Fell unto prison, & to acquaint the Judges with the state of the County . . . meeting also with some whispers that the Judges would not proceede against any of the Quakers . . . wee resolved to wait that afternoon upon Judge Twisden." (Extracts, SP, p. 191).

Having been persuaded by Fleming, Judge Sir Thomas Twisden presided over the first of the two trials of Margaret Fell, though he was clearly reluctant to do so. Judge Twisden treated Margaret kindly at first but gradually became impatient as she skillfully argued her case, refusing to admit any illegal activities. An almost verbatim account of this trial of March 14 to 16 is included in her Works. *The following excerpts give a glimpse of Margaret's skill in debate and her refusal to compromise her principles. The courtroom scene was high drama, with the judge and his advisors, and Margaret and her supporters, and with a life sentence hanging in the balance.*

"First: She was called to the Bar, and when she was at the Bar, Order was given to the Gaoler by the Judge, to set a Stool, and a Cushion for her to sit upon:—And she had four of her Daughters with her at the Bar, And the Judge said, Let not Mrs. Fell's Daughters stand at the Bar, but let them come up hither, they shall not stand at the Bar: So they plucked them up, and set them near where the Judge sate.—Then after a while, the Mittimus was Read, and the Judge spoke to her, and she stood up to the Bar, and he began to speak to her as followeth.

Judge: He said, Mrs. Fell, you are Committed by the Justices of Peace for Refusing to take the Oath of Obedience: and I am commanded, and set by the King, to tender it to any that shall refuse it.

M. Fell: I was sent for from my own House, and Family, but for what Cause or Transgression I do not know.

Judge: I am Informed by the Justices of Peace in this County, that you keep multitudes of People at Your House, in pretence to worship God; and it may be you worship him in part, but we are not to dispute that.

M. F.: I have the King's word from his own Mouth, that he would not hinder me of my Religion. *God forbid* (said he) *that I should hinder you of your Religion, you may keep it in your own House,* And I Appeal to all the Country, whether those People that meet at my House, be not a Peaceable, a Quiet and a Godly Honest People? And whether there hath been any just occasion of offense given by the Meeting that was kept in my House.

Judge: If you will give Security that you will have no more Meetings, I will not tender the Oath to you:—You think if there be no Fighting nor Quarrelling amongst you, that you keep the Peace, and break no Law; but I tell you, that you are a Breaker of the Law, by keeping of unlawful Meetings: And again, you break the Law, in that you will not take the Oath of Allegiance.

M. F.: I desire that I may have Liberty to Answer to those two Things which are Charged against me. And First, for that which is looked upon to be matter of Fact, which is, concerning our Meetings: There are several of my Neighbours, that are of the same Faith, Principle, and Spirit and Judgment that I am of, and these are they that meet at my House, and I cannot shut my Doors against them.

Judge: Mrs. you begin at the wrong end, for the first is the Oath.

M. F.: I suppose, that the first Occasion of tendering me the Oath, was because of Meeting: but as for that, if I have begun at the wrong end, I shall begin at the other. And first then, as to the Oath, the substance of which, is Allegiance to the King: And this I shall say, as for my Allegiance, I Love, Own, and Honour the King, and desire his Peace, and Welfare: and that we may live a Peaceable, a Quiet and a Godly Life under his Government, according to the Scriptures; and this is my Allegiance to the King. And as for the Oath it self, Christ Jesus, the King of Kings, hath Commanded me not to Swear at all, neither by Heaven, nor by Earth, nor by any other Oath.

Judge: Then he called for the Statute-Book, and the Grand-Jury to be present,—Then one of the Justices that Committed her, said, Mrs. Fell, You know, that before the Oath was tendred to you, we offered, that if you would put in Security to have no more Meetings at your House, we would not tender you the Oath.

M. F.: I shall not deny that.

Judge: If you will put in Security, that you will have no more Meetings, I will not tender the Oath to you.

M. F.: I speak to the Judge, and the Court, and the rest of the People:

You all here profess to be Christians, and likewise you profess the Scriptures to be your Rule; so in Answer to those things that are laid against me: . . . . I, and these that meet at my House, do meet, and Worship God, in obedience to Christ's Doctrine and Commands. . . . Secondly, The same Christ Jesus, hath Commanded in plain words, *That I should not Swear at all,* Mat.5 and for obedience to Christs's Doctrine am I here Arraigned this day . . . .

Judge: You are not here, for Obedience to Christs's Commands, but for keeping of unlawful Meetings. And you think, that if you do not Fight and Quarrel, or break the Peace, that you break no Law; but there is a Law against unlawful Meetings.

M. F.: What Law have I broken, for Worshipping God in my own House?

Judge: The Common Law.

M. F.: I thought you had proceeded by a Statute:

(Then the Sheriff whispered to him, and mention'd the Statute of the 35th of Elizabeth.)

Judge: I could tell you of a Law, but it is too Penal for you, for it might cost you your Life.

M. F.: I must offer and tender my Life, and all, for my Testimony, if it be required of me . . . .

Judge: And then the Judge inform'd the Jury, and the Prisoner, concerning the Penalty of the Statute, upon Refusal: for it would be to the Forfeiture of all her Estate, Real, and Personal, and Imprisonment during Life.

M. F.: I am a Widow, and my Estate is a Dowry, and I have Five Children unprefer'd [unmarried], and if the King's Pleasure be to take my Estate from me, upon the account of my Conscience, and not for any Evil or Wrong done, let him do as he pleaseth. And further, I desire that I may speak to the Jury . . .

Judge: The Jury is to hear nothing but me, to tender you the Oath, and you to refuse it, or take[.]

M. F.: You will let me have the Liberty that other Prisoners have.— And then she turn'd to the Jury, and said: Friends, I am here this day upon the Account of my Conscience, and not for any Evil, or wrong done to any Man, but for obeying Christ's Doctrine and Commands . . . am I here Arraigned this day. Now you profess your selves to be Christians, and you own the Scriptures to be true . . . So I now Appeal to the witness of God in all your Consciences, to judge of me according to that . . .

Then the Judge seem'd to be Angry, and said, she was not there upon the account of her Conscience; and said, she had an everlasting Tongue, you draw the whole Court after you; and she continued speaking on, and he still crying, will you take the Oath or no? . . . .

M. F.: I say I owe Obedience and Allegiance unto Christ Jesus, who Commands me not to Swear at all.

Judge: I say unto you, that is no Answer, will you take it, or will you not take it? . . . .

Justice: Then one of the Justices that Committed her, said, Mistress Fell, you may with a good Conscience (if you cannot take the Oath) put in Security, that you will have no more Meetings at your House?

M. F.: Wilt thou make it good, that I may with a safe Conscience make an Engagement to forbear Meetings, for fear of losing my Liberty, and Estate? wilt not thou, and all you here judge of me, that it was for saving of my Estate, and Liberty, that did it? And should not I in this deny my Testimony, and would not this defile my Conscience?

Judge: This is no Answer, will you take the Oath? we must not spend time.

M. F.: I never took Oath in my Life; I have spent my days thus far, and I never took an Oath; I own Allegiance to the King, as he is King of England, but Christ Jesus is King of my Conscience.

Clerk: Then the Clerk held out the Book, and bid her pull off her Glove, and lay her Hand on the Book . . . .

Then they asked her, if she would have the Oath read? She answered, I do not care if I never hear an Oath read, for the Land mourns because of Oaths.

Judge: Then the Judge cryed, Take her away, and asked her, If she would give Security, that she would have no more Meetings?

M. F.: Nay, I can give no such Security; I have spoken enough for that—And so they took her civilly away" (*Works*, pp. 276–282).

Margaret was then returned to prison until the next trial to be held at the Assizes in August. She wrote the following letter to the Magistrates and the People of England in June. It is not a plea for mercy for herself, but rather a lament for the nation's loss of greatness, a country that had been "a garden and a Nursary of christianity and Religion" and the home of "free-born Englishmen and women." She warns against the judgement that will fall upon "Lawmakers of England, that hath hardened their hearts" and have passed laws against people who never broke a law until one was specifically passed against them.

What is the mater [matter] with the christians of our age and of our English Nation[,] that hath been looked upon to be a garden and a Nursary of christianity and Religion, beyond all other nations[,] that hath made soe great profesion of God and Christ and of the scriptures and are they now turned persecutors and law-makers against christianity and against those that are in the same spirit and power and fellowship As they were in that gave forth the scriptures[,] which they themselves profess[?] and is these now become the greatest enemyes that England hath, and for noe other cause but because they worship god and obey Christs Command and abides in his doctrine and beares the same testimony of the truth and Resurrection of the Lord Jesus Christ as the Apostles did[?] and all that they doe[,] act and speake and suffer for it's according to the scriptures. is these things become a crime in England[?] and is this the greatest offense that England hath taken with the people of god even because they believe in the Lord Jesus Christ and obeyes his doctrine,

oh take up a Lamentation for England[!] surely there is some heavy sad greivous Judgment waiting over her. and is not heardnes of heart and a reprobate mind and a seared conscience one of the greatest Judgements that can befall a people; and is not this already seazed [seized] upon the Lawmakers of England, that hath hardened their hearts against the Lord and his people[,] as if they had noe other enemyes but they who never did them wrong, nor hurt, nor never desired or intended Any hurt against them, But have ever desired their good, and peace and welfare, and that they might come to the true knowledge of the Lord, and to the true knowledge of his truth, as it is in Jesus[,] which they clearly manifest they are ignorant of; By their making of lawes against those; Amongst them that feares god and worships him, and gives glory to his Name, though they be free-born Englishmen and women[,] nor hath not transgresed any Just law of England[,] untill they were forced to make one, to make them transgressors which though they be of the same religion that they themselves professe; they profess Christ and the scriptures in words, But those that comes to the workes of righteouness and to believe in the Lord Jesus Christ which is the worke of god such they persecute and make Lawes against: soe that England appears now as if it would shut Christianity out of its dominions, And what will they bring in and set up next[?] seeing they Banish out Christ and his members; and servants and Saints who hath been a Blessing unto them, and to the Land wherein they lived, and no hurt to them; and if they had given them Liberty of their Consciences to have served the lord god they might have partaken of the Blessing with them; But being that they have turned their hand against the lord and turned their sword backwards against the Righteous; surely the Lord will plead for this, and surely there will a Recompence Come, for it is hard to strive against the lord and to touch his Anointed and doe his prophets any harme[.] when they were but few in number he reproved kings for their sake and he is the same; he changes not, and his power and Arme is the same[,] and his Righeousness is the same, which is to be revealed upon the heads of the wicked[;] and he is ingaged to plead the cause of the innocent who hath noe pleader in the Earth, and his eye sees, and beholds all the Actions of the children of men, and those that Acts against him and his servants he takes special notice of[;] and he saw the Aflictions of his people formerly, when they were afflicted in Egipt, and heard their Cryes, and knowes their sufferings[,] and surely he is the same now as he was then; And as he hath said himselfe[:] inasmuch as you do it to my litle ones you doe it unto mee [Matt. 25:40] this he said when he knew his next appearance should bee in his saints; And certainly those that persecute his saints even without a law when they had none; and contrary to severall laws of England[,] as severall of the servants of the lord hath suffered[.] by those that were in power formerly hath Christs servants been persecuted[,] and they that did this and they that makes new lawes; now certainly if christ and the Apostles had been and were upon the earth they would have done the same unto them. But all these things the Lord hath taken notice of, and they are written downe where they cannot bee blotted out[.] and all the Righteous Blood that hath been shed since Abel [,] and all the saints sufferings in all ages[,] the Lord hath taken notice off; and all ___ _______ Christians that hath suffered amongst those that hath called themselves Christians in these latter times[,] where several hath been imprisoned to death for the Christian faith; all this the lord hath in everlasting remembrance[,] and when he comes to make Inquisition of blood of his servants, it will bee a hard and a sad day for the Acters and fighters against god./

And soe all ye Christian magistrates, beware what ye do and keep your hands out of blood and persecution of the Innocent[,] and let that which is past suffice[,] for you will find it heavye enough, and for the time to come, dread and fear the lord god of heaven and earth; that hath all your lifes and breath in his hand to give and take away at his pleasure[;] do not that which may Incurre the lords displeasure[.] it is better for you to offend man then god and soe indanger your owne soules[,] soe mind that which concerns your eternal peace. And this I am moved of the lord to forewarne you of, least you bring woe and misery upon yourselves, and A general Judgement upon the whole land[,] and remember that you are warned.

M: F:

From A prisoner of the Lord in Lancaster Castle
The 7th of the 4th month: 1664

FHL MS Box P2/18 pp. 73–80, also in Works, *pp. 290–293. For trials see* Works, *pp. 276–290.*

125 AN EPISTLE TO FRIENDS JUNE 7, 1664

"This is Precious indeed. And what if this be obtained through some Sufferings, and Hardships, and Tryals? how should it be otherwise?"

This epistle to the "Flock of God" was written the same day as the preceding letter. It is a tender and loving call to bear any suffering that may come, with certainty that liberty of spirit far outweighs "Oppression and corruption": "It is but for an Hour, stand it out." The emphasis is on liberty and "Spiritual Freedom," for "the Faith which is tried is much more Precious than gold that perisheth."

Margaret had been in prison three months and was preparing for another trial, with the strong possibility of remaining in prison for years. Such an epistle of comfort is impressive from someone in such a situation. She was able to use the years in prison to do her most extensive writing.

An Epistle to the Flock of God, where-ever they are dispersed upon the Earth, where this may come, who are Called, and Gathered, and Separated from the World, and their Ways and Worships, to bear Testimony for the Lord God, against their Deceit and Deceiveableness, which all the Worships of the World hath lain in, in the dark Night of Apostacy.

My Dearly-Beloved Friends and Brethren, in the Everlasting Unity and Fellowship of the Gospel of Peace, which is Glad-Tidings unto all that shall receive it, and which hath been Glad-Tidings unto you, who have received it; of which Gospel none need be ashamed, for it is the Power of God unto Salvation unto every one that believes. And in the Unity of this Faith, and Fellowship of this Gospel, do I write unto you, as unto dear and near Members of this Body, the Church, whereof Christ Jesus is the Head, and hath given himself for it, that he might make it a Glorious Church, without Spot or Wrinkle [Eph. 5:27], who is ascended far above all Heavens, and was glorified with the Father before the World began, and hath all Power in Heaven and Earth committed unto him, and who hath trodden down Principalities and Powers; and Angels and Authorities are subject unto him; so that none of you need to fear what Man can do, who receives his Breath and Being from the Lord of Heaven and Earth, who hath all their Hearts in his Hand, and can turn them at his pleasure.

Oh my dearly-beloved Friends, stand fast in the Liberty wherewith Christ Jesus hath made you free; and beware of being intangled again into Bondage! Oh! it is not Liberty unto you, to be from under the Yoke of the Oppressors, and to be from having your Consciences bound, under the Wills of Men, and to be freed from having your Consciences subject to the Beggarly Rudiments and Carnal Ordinances, set up by Men, and established by Men's Laws, contrary to the Law of God, and contrary unto Christ, and his Apostles, witnessing forth in the Scriptures; and also contrary to the Light of Christ, the Witness of God in your own Consciences. Oh! prize this Liberty, which the Lord Jesus Christ hath manifested unto you; and prize the blessed Visitation of the Lord's Love, in making known unto you his Way and Truth, and opening unto you that which hath been shut in the Night of Apostacy, the Revelation of Jesus Christ being made manifest in your Consciences, and the Law of the New Covenant being written in your Hearts, which you have read in; which Law, and Testimony, and Book, hath been sealed in the Night of Apostacy, and hath been hid from Generations past, but hath been revealed unto you by his Spirit: Glory to the Lord for ever! Oh prize this Matchless Love, which is precious Liberty indeed.

The whole Creation hath long groaned under the Burthen of Oppression and Corruption; the Redemption out of which, is thorough Christ Jesus, by the Operation of his Spirit; and they who are guided by his Spirit, are his Sons: And the Redemption of the Body is through waiting in the Spirit of Adoption, whereby every Member may call God Father: For the Church is in God, and he is the Father of it. And so you that abide in the Spirit, and are gather'd in the Spirit, and drink together into the Spirit, and are baptized into it; here you are in the precious Liberty of the Children of God, and are taught of him, and established in his Truth and Righteousness; and the Lord is your Shepherd, and Christ Jesus is your everlasting High Priest of your Profession, and the Bishop of your Souls; and so becomes your Leader, and your Guider and Ruler: And so the Lord is your King, and your Lawgiver, and your Judge. And so here is Glorious and Precious Liberty, you that come hither to be ordered and governed, under the Power and Dominion of Christ, and to be translated into the Kingdom of the Lord Jesus Christ, from under the Power and Dominion of Antichrist: This is Precious indeed. And what if this be obtained through some Sufferings, and Hardships, and Tryals? how should it be othewise? since the Gentiles exercise Lordship one over another, how should Babylon part with her Children quietly? It is not like but there should be Opposition and Wars betwixt those two Kingdoms; the Kingdom of Antichrist, and Darkness, and Oppression, and Tyranny; and the Kingdom of Christ, which is in the Light, Power, Righteousness and Peace, Freedom and Liberty.

Oh! Consider him that hath gone before you, who thought it no Robbery to be equal with God; yet he made himself of no Reputation, and took upon him the form of a Servant, and in that he humbled himself to the Death of the Cross; for which Cause God hath given him a Name above every Name, to which every Knee must bow, and every Tongue confess unto this Name. And so now as you are gathered into this Name, bow unto this Name, and confess unto this Name; but bow to no other, nor confess to any other before Men, lest Christ Jesus deny you before his Father which is in Heaven, and you be found Transgressors against him; then will your Condition be sad, and your Reward be heavy, and your Spirits will come into Bondage again, which you will find more grievous, than any outward Persecution or Suffering can be; for the very Life of the Righteous stands in the Spiritual Freedom and Dominion: For to keep out of Disobedience and Transgression, and keeping the Conscience clear, there is the Spirit free; and there is Dominion and Power in the Truth of the Lord Jesus Christ, over all the Powers of Darkness: For as you abide and continue in the Truth, it will make you free, and whom the Son makes free, they are perfectly free indeed, though there my be outward Bonds, or outward Laws executed upon them; yet in the Lord they are free, and have Peace and Dominion in him.

And so dear Friends above all mind your Spiritual Freedom, and your Spiritual Reward, which will be sure to be received, according to every one's Deeds done in the Body; he that doth good Deeds in the Body, will receive good; He that doth Evil Deeds in the Body, he shall receive his Reward accordingly. And so it nearly concerns all you that have given up your Names unto the Lord, and are engaged in the Lamb's Spiritual War, to be Faithful unto him; for if you be not, you will turn Enemies to your own Souls, and his Hand, and Arm, and Power will turn against you, and then, whether can you fly from his Presence? Therefore keep Faithful to the Lord God, and his Truth, and make War in Righteousness, and give your Backs to the Smiter, and your Cheeks to them that pull off the Hair [Isa. 50:6]; it is but for an Hour, stand it out, the Lamb shall have the Victory. And mind the Glory and the Honour of Christ Jesus your Lord and Master, more than your outward Privileges, and follow him, whethersoever he goeth, follow him through the Regeneration, and Washing, where you will come to be cleansed, and made clean through Tribulations, your Garments will be made White through the Blood of the Lamb; Christ Jesus was made Perfect through Sufferings, and who comes to Perfection it must be through the Sufferings by that which is Imperfect, which will be done away, and have an end; but that which is Perfect, will endure and remain for ever.

And so prize this precious Pearl, and sell it not, but rather sell all for it, and keep it as your chiefest Treasury [Matt. 13:46]; Your Redemption and Perfection hath been purchased at a dear Rate; no corruptible Perishing Thing could purchase it; but the precious Blood of Christ Jesus, who hath given himself a Ransom for you: Let this precious Redemption, be precious unto you, and value not the Sufferings of this present time with it; for they are not worthy to be compared to it. And now seeing that the Lord Jesus Christ is come, that you might have Life, and that you might have it more abundantly: Oh! keep unto him, and to the Testimony of him in you, that he hath written in your Hearts, and abide there with him; for you are near unto him, and have cost him dear: For he hath not left you Comfortless, but he is come to you in his Spirit, believe in him, and ask of him the Living Water which he gives, and it will be in you a Well springing up to Eternal Life; so that out of your Bellies will flow Rivers of Living Water [John 7:38]: Here is the true Treasure, here is the desirable durable Riches, far surpassing all created Things.

And so my dearly beloved Friends, in the Bowels of tender and hearty Love, do I desire and beseech you, to be true and faithful to the Lord God, and to his Truth, and to your own Souls in this his Day, which may be a Day of Tryal; for Satan desires to winnow and sift you; but blessed are you, whose Faith fails not, but abides the fiery Tryal, which is to try every one's Faith; and the Faith which is tried, is much more Precious than Gold that perisheth.

So the God of Power, of Strength, and of Wisdom, whose Arm is the Strength, and the Deliverer, and the Preserver of his People, keep you all, who will be sure to be Faithful, and Dear, and Tender to all those that are True and Faithful unto him. And Blessed and Happy are all you that sit down in the Power of the Lord God, and choose the better Part; that so the Elect Seed may obtain its Inheritance, even the Immortal Crown of Life and Righteousness, and in that you may all have Dominion, being nothing terrified by your Adversaries. And as the Apostle saith, it is a faithful Saying, and worthy of all Acceptation, *If we suffer with him, we shall also Reign with him; If we deny him, he also will deny us, if we believe in him, he is Faithful and Just, and cannot deny himself* [2 Tim. 2:12].

From your Friend and Sister in the Lord,

M. F.

Lancaster-Castle the 7th of the 4th Month, 1664.

Works, *pp.* 293–298.

126 TO MARGARET FELL FROM MARY FELL JUNE 24, 1664

"He [King Charles] was then vary loving to mee
and as thow [though] he pited [pitied] mee
and sayd he would tack it into considereashon,
and sayd[,] they shall not have her esteate from her."

While Margaret was in prison her friends and family in London were writing and calling on officials to gain her release. Here, her daughter Mary writes of one visit to King Charles. Mary was then seventeen and was with her older sister, Margaret Rous. They asked the king to write to the judges to release Margaret before the next assizes. He clearly felt sympathy for them and treated them kindly, but political necessities took precedent. The reference to replevin is in anticipation of the sentence of praemunire being imposed on Margaret and all of her property taken.

Mary Fell (1647–1720) was Margaret's third youngest daughter. She married Thomas Lower in 1668. He was a noted physician and trusted friend and later literary executor of George Fox. The Lowers made their home partly at Marsh Grange, Margaret's birthplace, and partly in London. They had ten children, but only five lived to adulthood. Mary had the heavy responsibilities of caring for her family during the periods when Thomas Lower was in jail or traveling with George Fox (Ross).

Indeared and tender harted Mother,

My deuty and vary dear love is freely given and Remembered unto thee, as all so my very deare love is to deare G. F. [George Fox]

this is chefly to lett thee understand that yisterday sis: [sister, Margaret Rous] and I was at whit hole [Whitehall,] whear wee spocke [spoke] with the king and tould him that if he would pleas to signifye samthing to the Judgis befor they went thear sirket [circuit,] to releas you[,] otherwis it would be past For the time dreu vary near of the asises [assizes.] he sayd he would releas you if wee would promies you would not goe to meetings—Sister sayd wee kould mack [make] no such ingaidgements[,] for the meting it hath ben kepe [kept] many years and never hath donn any harm[.] he sayd[,] cannot your mother kepe with in her own Famely[,] and she may have 5 more[,] but she must have such teumultes [tumultuous] metings[.] we sayd[,] she hath no such metings[;] they are onely her nebors [neighbors] that koumes [come.] the king sayd theare was soum quakers in the last plot [Kaber Rigg Plot]. Sister sayd that kould not be proved[.] he sayd he had letters of it and ther names.—So Chifines [the King's page] bid ous koum of the 4 [4th] day; so we doe intend to goe to-morow[.] I was theare about a week sens [since] and tould the king that now the asises drew vary near and sayd if he did not doe sumthing For thee[,] they would roun [ruin] thee into apriminiere [a praemunire] and get thy esteate from thee and thy children and desiered him to tack [take] it into considerashon[.] he was then vary loving to mee and as thow [though] he pited [pitied] mee and sayd he would tack it into considereashon, and sayd[,] they shall not have her esteate from her[.] he tock [took] me by the hand as son [soon] as he keme [came] neare mee[.] and I spocke to prins Ruperd [Prince Rupert, cousin of the King, and son of Queen Elizabeth of Bohemia and Frederick V, Elector Palatine] and desiered him to put the King in mind of it[,] and he sayd he would doe what he kould in it[,] and went then to the King and spocke to him[.] prins Rupert hath all ways ben vary loving to Friends and hath often spock to the King about you[.]

Sister gives the Renoued [renewed] Rememberens of her intyer [entire] love to thee & deare G F [George Fox] as all so doth my brother [George Fell.] dear Mother[.] sens I have ben hear I have bene prity much troubeled with stopidges [OED: " obstructed condition of a bodily organ"] which doth soum what macke me as Jenessed [jaundiced] to bee thou [though] as yeat [yet] not near so il[.] sister & I was with dockter Trige [?] & he gave me soum thing that he sayd would doe me good[.] I have tacken twis [twice] of it[.] the nex[t] wek [week] thou may expekt to know how I am—I have not writen to non[e] of my sisters this weke. I would vary gladly that sisters Susana & Rachell might have this sent to them, I sopos [suppose] sisters Iss[abel] & Sarah will be gone[.] so deare Mother[,] not more of mateariell to [write?]

I am thy deuty Full & obediant daughter

Mary Fell

Remember me to sisters Susanna and Rachell [.]

when we was with Dobson last, he tould ous that it would be the best way For thee to remove all things from Swarthmor to soum plas [place] then they be ours, for they say theare is no repleaving [replevin, i.e., recovery of goods] against the King.

Mary Halford Remembers her dear love to thee & to dear G F & my sisters

Gibson MSS, 5:55 Addressed: "For the hands of my very dear Mother Margrett Fell at Lankaster Leave this with Thomas Gren Grosyer at his shope in Lankaster to be conveyed Lancaster". Endorsed: "Mary Fell to MF of paseges to the king 1664".

127 TO THE JUDGES AT LANCASTER AUGUST 1664

"The prisons that they keep us in: is not fit for people to lye in; for it Raines into them . . . & is so wett: that in the winter time it is not fitt, for neither beasts nor doges to lye in."

After six months in prison Margaret wrote to the judges in Lancaster detailing injustices that had been committed against her, her family, and other Quakers. These included: firstly, prison conditions; secondly, that neither she nor George Fox were permitted to leave the prison although they had entered their traverse, i.e., denied the allegations in the indictment; thirdly, that they had broken no law when they were arrested; fourthly, Colonel Richard Kirkby and his cousin, Sir Daniel Fleming, were disturbing and threatening her children; fifthly, other Friends were being illegally punished twice for the same offense. She asks the judges to restrain justices "whose Cruelty exceeds their power." She ends with "I am freely given up to [the Lord's] will & pleasure . . . In which doing I shall rest Content; whether it be Mercy or Cruelty."

An Information to the Judges at Lancaster Concerning
G F: & M Fs Imprisonment these 1663 [i.e. 1664]

This is to Acquaint the Judges—that George Fox: & Margaret Fell: hath laid here the one of us above 7 monthes: & the other six; & the prisons that they keep us in: is not fit for people to lye in; for it Raines into them; especially the one Raines in so; & is so wett: that in the winter time it is not fitt, for neither beasts nor doges to lye in: & since the last assizes that we entered our travise [traverse]: they would hardly ever suffer G F: to goe out of the Libertie of the Castle: without a keeper, nor would suffer me to goe home to se [see] my children & family above this six monthes: which severall looked upon to be unjust: being that wee had entred our travise to our inditements: & when they did apprehend us; there was noe ground nor cause, of any law broken: nor Transgression: for we were neither taken in any meeting; nor on noe meeting day: for they took G: F: one morning from my house; & me also they fetched out of my own house & family; under a false pretence of another thing, & so when they had us before them: they tendered us the oath: haveing noe other snare: to lay hold of us by,—

They took me by Order from Cornell Kirbie [Richard Kirkby, Letter 122], to his Brother [William Kirkby]; & his Cozen Fleming [Daniel Fleming, Letter 124] out of my own house & family: he haveing envie & prejudice against mee, not for any just Cause that ever I gave him in all my life; the Lord knowes—& since they have brought me to prison they have Continually disturbed my Children: & family: hurrying them to the sessions: & threatining them with Imprisonment; which is Contrary to Law: for if I suffer upon the Account of my Conscience, the Law allowes my Children & family should Live peaceably; And this is very hard: that we should be thus persecuted, & Troubled & Contrary to Law: & that for noe other Cause but that we Cannot Contrary to our Conscience take an oath, when we se many that are breakers of the law: goes unpunished.

And this may also acquaint the Judges that William Kirbie hath Acted Contrary to law: with severall of his neighbours: who were indited, & fined upon the old Act against Conventicles: & they were to appeare the next Quarter sessions & now since they have taken them againe, & hath brought ten of them to prison: & hath put them in a Roum; where they have neither beds nor straw; & hath Comitted them for two monthes; & hath fined them againe & threatens: that they will take their fines; notwithstanding they have put them in prison; which in two particulars; is Contrary to the expresse words of the Act; which saith, A man shall not be punished for the same offense by the vertue of any other Act: & Likewise if he be brought to prison the Act saith unlesse such offenders pay downe the said sum of money The Justices shall not both Imprison: & fine; & so here the Judges may se what Justices wee have to prosecute these Lawes; whose Cruelty exceeds their power; & here poor men are abused, & run upon; & so wee desire you to take it into your Considerations these our sufferings: for if you doe not: when you are gone: they will say as they have done formerly; you ordered them to doe what they doe: & so wee desire you: to let your lawes be Justly executed upon us; if wee must suffer let us not suffer Contrary to law—And you all know that my estate is but a widdowes estate, & it would not be very much advantage to my neighbors if they had it; & I have four daughters unpreferred [i.e., unmarried], & what I suffer for: it is upon the account of my Conscience, & for the Lords sake, & I am freely given up to his will & pleasure; what he permits & suffers to bee done unto mee: In which doing I shall rest Content; whether it be Mercy or Cruelty

Margaret Fell

Spence 3/132–133. Summary in Ross, p. 177.

The second portion of the trial took place before Judge Turner, baron of the Exchequer. Margaret had counsel with her who pointed out errors in the indictment, and she again defended herself vigorously. Col. Kirkby was present and whispered to the judge, which Margaret protested. In the end the sentence of praemunire was pronounced against her. This meant being out of the king's protection, loss of estates, and imprisonment for life.

At the same sessions, George Fox was released because of errors in his indictment, though he was soon tried again and imprisoned. During this period Judge Turner also conducted the trial of Francis Howgill at Appleby. Howgill was praemunired and imprisoned for five years until he died (Ross, pp. 174–5). Margaret summarized this portion of the trial and its results as follows:

> The next Assizes we came to Tryal, and G. Fox's Indictment was found to be dated wrong . . . so that his Indictment was quash'd, but mine they would not allow the Errors that were found in it, to make it void, altho' there were several; so they passed Sentence of Praemunire upon me . . . But the great God of Heaven and Earth supported my Spirit under this severe Sentence, that I was not terrified; but gave this Answer to Judge Turner, who gave the Sentence, *Although I am out of the King's Protection, yet I am not out of the Protection of the Almighty God,* so there I remained in Prison Twenty Months, before I could get so much Favour of the Sheriff, as to go to my own House; which then I did for a little time, and returned to Prison again. And when I had been a Prisoner about Four Years, I was set at Liberty by an order from the King and Council in 1668

Works, *pp.* 7–8.

128 TO JOHN AND MARGARET FELL ROUS OCTOBER 1, 1664

"It has pleased the Lord, to Devide us Equaly,
that if you be together there, and we be together here,
it is well, and Blessed be his holy name."

From prison Margaret writes to her daughter and son-in-law, Margaret and John Rous, in London concerning Mary Fell's illness. Margaret Rous was evidently blaming herself for not giving sufficient care to Mary, who probably had an early case of the plague which devastated London the following year. Margaret assures her daughter that she is confident that Mary is receiving the best possible care.

Mary did recover, but Margaret did not know that when she wrote this letter. It shows her attitude toward death which is accepting of God's will: "and soe in the name of the Lord Jesus Christ, be all Satisfied, & content, with the will of the Lord, and Lett neither Murmerring nor Repining enter none of your minds."

B. Kunze writes: "This seeming cavalier attitude toward death is somewhat unnerving to the modern reader . . . But the stoic attitude expressed here by Margaret as well as the total silence in the family record about Bridget's death one year earlier is not due to lack of emotional bonding with the family. Quaker sensibilities reacted against all outward forms as seen in the absence of gravestones in their burial grounds. To express grief meant to be weak in the faith that promised eternal life" (p. 48).

Paul S. Seaver comments in Wallington's World, *a study of seventeenth-century Puritans, "The relations that are the most opaque [to us] are those that were most intimate—those between husband and wife and between parents and children," . . . and "Wallington cared greatly for his wife and children, and the death of the young children overwhelmed him. His wife was better able to handle the grief than he," . . . and "Yet if Nehemiah [Wallington] never really learned the lesson of that first death [his daughter Elizabeth], it is perhaps not to be wondered at, for Grace's [his wife] patient acceptance is surely harder for us to comprehend than Nehemiah's nervous anxiety" (pp. 85, 87, 88).*

Margaret ends the letter with several businesslike notes concerning her son George, George Fox, and Col. Kirkby's continuing persecution.

A postscript refers to George Whitehead (Letter 89) and and Gilbert Latey who were at the royal court attempting to free Margaret and George Fox from prison. Gilbert Latey (1626–1705) was a tailor, apprenticed in Cornwall, who moved to London in 1648. He became a popular court tailor until his conscience prevented him from supplying lace and other superfluous ornaments to his customers (CJ, 2:401). During the terrible plague year of 1665 both Whitehead and Latey assisted and visited Friends who were ill, "especially for poor people confined to their own houses, many of whom had running sores upon them." Latey caught the plague, but he survived. He lived as a respected and influential Friend (Braithwaite, pp. 47–48).

Lancaster Castle, 1st 8th mo. 1664.

My Deare Sonn and Daughter[,] in the deare and Infinite bowells of tender compassion, of Everlasting Love, & in the Everlasting life, which never has end, doe I write unto you, in which eternal life, and power of the Godhead doe I injoy and possesse[.] My Deare Mary, her spiritt neare and Deare, & present with mee, whether in the Body or out, with the Lord and to the Lord of Heaven and Earth, she is given freely, and his heavenly and holy will, I freely submitt too, that every Jott and title thereof may be fulfilled, to the Glory & praise of his great & holy name, and my Deare Daughter[,] In the name and power of the Lord Jesus, (who has all power in heaven and Earth in his hand, who gives the life & breath of all his Creaters [creatures], and takes away at his pleasure;) Keepe over all visibles, and in the Invisible holy life, of the holy God, which thou art made partaker of, and has a rich portion in, solace thy soule in that, and in the life & power of Almighty God, which thou Injoyes, rest satisfied & be Content. And as I have said often to thee, give up to be Crosed, and that is the way to please the Lord, and to follow him, in his owne way & will, whose way is the best, and all these things are well, and blessed and happy are all they, that is well with the Lord, And in his arme and bosome theres An Endureing & Eternall Inheritance, where there will never be more Change, and Lett nothing Enter thy mind, Concerning any thing, for I am very well Contented, with the handy=worke of the Lord, and I know your care and Tenderness was not Awanting to her, and soe be all Satisfied in the will of the Lord God, I hope in the Lord that you are all together, ere this come to you, and soe in the name of the Lord Jesus Christ, be all Satisfied, & content, with the will of the Lord, and Lett neither Murmerring nor Repining enter none of your minds; nor let not sorrow fill your hearts, for we have all cause to rejoice, in the Lord evermore, and I most of all, that bought her Deare, and brought her up for the Lord, whom I am sure is the true owner of her [1 Cor. 6:19–20], and therein is my Joy, and blessed be his holy name, who has given me her to that End, that he might take her away at his pleasure; All your 3 sisters was here with me when we Received the Letters, and it was well, it was soe, & I Intend they shall stay 2 or 3 dayes more till the sessions be over, and soe it has pleased the Lord, to Devide us Equaly, that if you be together there, and we be together here, it is well, and Blessed be his holy name.—I writt the last weeke Concerning thy Brother Fell, [George Fell, Letter 75], what my mind is, and I would desire to know his mind and Intention, what he Intends to doe, as shortly as may be, for we Intend to make A sale, of some part of the Goods however, but if he doe Intend to come & live in the Country, and take things into his hand, we should make A sale of all, & he shall have what as he sees fitting for him. I would have you to perswade him to come into the Country as shortly as may be, as for passages heres litle but as has beene;

Your sisters Sarah, Susan and Rachell, who are all here, remember their Deare Love to you and to their Brother Fell, and their [brother] & sister yeamuns [Isabel and William Yeamans]—No more but rests

your Deare Mother
Margt Fell.

It is very much satisfaction to me [that] you let me know all alonge how twas with her, and it was very well done of you.

Coll. Kirkby [Letter 122, 123] causes our bonds to be renewed, and straightened more and more, and they Locke G. F. [George Fox] under pretence of An order [that] should come from London; get this Inclosed Letter of G.F.s sent to Gilbert Laty, that G: whitehead [George Whitehead] & they may draw out what as they see Convenient; The Inclosed to Bro. Fell deliver it to him thyselfe.

Swarthmore MSS 1:101, also in Crosfield, pp. 119–121 and Ross, pp. 187–189. Addressed: "To John Rous Mercht at the Beare and Fountaine in Leathbury these deliver with care in London". Endorsed: "MF when she was a prisoner sent this to her Sonn John Rous 1664".

129 TO ALL PRISONERS, FROM LANCASTER PRISON JANUARY 11, 1665

"With their Lawes & threats of banishment . . .
they canot banish you from the coasts
and sanctuary of the liveing god."

In 1664 the Conventicle Act was passed, which forbade a Meeting of more than five persons. It fell most heavily on Quakers, though it also affected other nonconformists. In London, for example, there were over 2,100 imprisonments for attendance at Meetings within a year (Braithwaite, p. 42). Many of the sentences were light, but some resulted in years of imprisonment and banishment.

In this epistle to prisoners Margaret condemns the officials who "forbids to meet and worship in the name and power of our lord Jesus Christ" and warns that they will be broken "like a potters Vessell." She expresses her love and pride in those who suffer and who are faithful. They are the true church, like all the saints of old. It is an epistle full of biblical words and phrases used, not to explicate scripture, but to comfort and strengthen the prisoners. She praises their endurance; they "stand for the contention [i.e., the active striving, OED*] for the faith."*

My dearly beloved brethren and sisters in the Lord Jesus Christ which are become sufferers for the lords truth and for the testimony of his name, which the princes of this world never knew in times nor ages past but forbad to speake and preach in that name upon paine of penalties and sufferings, and soe they crucifyed the lord of glory, And soe this generation now forbids to meet and worship in the name and power of our lord Jesus Christ, to which name every knee must bowe, and confesse to him, though they now strive and contend against his word and worke, which hee is working and bringing to passe in this his day, but they know not what they doe [Luke 23:34] for persecution was allwayes blinde[,] being sett against that which should open their eye of their minds and understandings, by which they might come to see the Lord and his precious truth, and his great worke that hee is working, who is building up the Ruines of Sion and the walls [Ps. 51:18] of Jerusalem and Raising up the Tabernacle of David and makeing up the breaches thereof [Amos 9:11] and bringing his church forth of the wildernes [Acts 7:38] which was a place prepared for her, for one thousand two hundred and threescore days, And now her manchild that was caught up unto god, is coming to rule all nations with his rod of Iron [Rev. 12:5–6] and to break to peeces his Enemies[,] like a potters Vessell [Ps. 2:9], in which hee will make them all to know that the most high rules in the kingdoms of men, soe that he is Lord of heaven and also of earth, and is comenge [coming] to fulfill and performe his noble decrees[,] soe that his will may be done in earth as it is in heaven [Matt. 6:10] according to the petition that he taught his disciples, and his great and mighty worke is hee comeing to worke in the earth soe that blessed & happy are all they that keeps the word of god & the Testimony of Jesus and follows the Lamb continually[,] who sitts upon the white horse [Rev. 6:1–2] and in righteousnes doth he make warre [Rev. 19:11], oh my dearly beloved in the lord, my love is very dearly and everlastingly in the fountaine of life Rememberd unto you, and wee are rejoyced and can prayse the lord for your valiant sufferings, that yee stand for the contention of the faith which was once deliverd to the saints, by which all the elders before you obtained a good Report, theron which you may all know, that the worlds were made [Heb. 1:2] by the word of god, which word is your Testimony, in which you may stand surely and perfectly in the Invisible word which made those things which doe visibly apeare[;] on this foundation you are sure[,] beinge rooted and grounded on him by which all things was made and created whose name is called the word of god, you may be assured that he hath power over his owne handy works as the potter hath power over his clay [Rom. 9:21], Therfore feare not man who hath received life & breath from the Lord, whome he orders of his will [,] not a sparrow falls to the ground, concerning without the Lord, and you are of m[ore] value than many sparrowes [Matt. 10:31], and though the vessells of wrath [Rom. 9:22] and pottsheards of the earth [Isa. 45:9] cumber themselves and take counsell together against the Lord and his anoynted[,] he that sitts in heaven, even laughs. the Lord hath them in derision. hee will speake to them in his wrath and vexe them in his sore displeasure and sett his kinge upon his holy hill of Sion that he may aske the heathen for his inheritance, and the utermost parts of the earth for his possession [Ps. 2:2–8] And soe my dearely beloved in our lord & saviour Jesus Christ, stand still rooted and grounded in him, for yee have his light to Enlighten you with, and you have his arme and power to uphold you & to strenthen you in the greatest time of tryall [,] and you have his holy spirit to leade you and to guide you into all truth [John 16:13], which receives of his, and gives unto you, and you have the faith of the son of god by which the apostles and all the saints Lived, and fought the good fight [2 Tim. 4:7] & obtained the victory, the same by which Abell offered an offering which was accepted [,] and by which faith Enoch was translated [Heb. 11:4–5], by which faith moses [Moses] forsooke the pleasures of Egypt & chused rather to suffer persecution with the people of god [Heb. 11:24–25], through which faith the saints in former dayes subdued Kingdomes[,] Quenched the violence of fire, stopped the mouths of Lyons[,] put to flight the armies of the aliens [Heb. 11:33–34], thorough which faith you have accesse unto the god of heaven[,] who bindes kings in chaines and nobles in fetters of Iron [Ps. 149:8]. soe here is the armor and shield of the saints [;] and the weapons of their warfare are spirituall & not carnall, and so in this power & spirit[,] my dearly beloved in the lord [,] you being all found faithfull unto his great name & majesty & true subjects of his kingdome, which is not of this world, you will find that he is made higher than the kings of the earth, who is the king Immortall who is now reveiled [revealed] unto us to be the onely [only] Potentate, who is Immortality & dwels in the light [1Tim. 6:15–16], into which he gathers all his saints[,] servants & children into unity and fellowship one with another where they all sitt downe together in peace & quietenesse in the heavenly places in christ Jesus where none can make them affraid[,] And soe here is his glorious & pure church and house of Jacob, which is his building[,] over which he raignes [reigns] for ever, for the father is your husbandman, and you are his husbandry, soe that we have a citty whose builder and maker is god [Heb. 11:10] and soe yee are gods building, which is made of Living stones [1 Pet. 2:4], where he takes delight to dwell and where his presence shines for ever[,] who hath given himselfe for his church that he might make it a pure and a holy church[,] not haveing spott or wrinkle nor any such thing [Eph. 5:27], soe dear harts yee are purged, yee are washed and cleansed & purifyed thorow sufferings, for in that hee was a sonne yet learnd he obedience by the things that hee suffered, and being made perfect he became the author of Eternall salvation unto all them that obey him [Heb. 5:9] & follow his stepps, And soe thinke it not strange concerning the firey tryall that is to try you[,] but rejoyce in as much as yee are made partakers of christs sufferings, and if you be reproached for the name of christ[,] happy are yee for therein the spirit of glory and of power resteth upon you, and in this ye have a cloud of witnesses [Heb. 12:1] and therin hath unity with all the saints in Light and with christ Jesus your lord and master, wherfore gird up the loynes of your minds, and hope unto the end [1 Pet. 1:13] for hee that called you is holy and pure, and true & faithfull is hee that hath promised, and soe cast your care upon the Lord of heaven and earth for he careth for you, give up freely unto his good will and pleasure, for we have not such an high priest as cannot be touched with the sufferinse & infirmityes [Heb. 4:15] of his people, but hath freely declared that what they doe unto his litle ones they doe unto him, soe hee haveing taken part of the same with you, you may all be strong in his power and might and couragious for him in this day and hower [hour] of suffering, thorow [through] which you will obtaine the crowne of righteousnes [2 Tim. 4:8] and soe in this my deare love is freely given unto you all, who hath had a perfect sense of your sufferings, and my life and bowels is freely powered [poured] forth unto the lord for the preservation and keeping of you all, in his owne name and in his owne light and Life and power where his presence and life may rest upon you for Ever.

From your deare freind and sister in the Lord

Margret Fell

This for all the prisoners of the Lord
in London & Bristoll or elsewhere
where this may come

My dearly Beloved in the entyrest [entire-est] love, be stronge in the mighty god and nothing terifyed with your adversaryes[,] which to them is condemnation but to you comfort[,] nor with their Lawes & threats of banishment[,] for they canot banish you from the coasts and sanctuary of the liveing god[,] as you abide in gods covenent of Light and life and power and in the unity of the eternall spirit which Joynes all his saints and members unto the Lord, here you are within the measuring line that measures the temple and the altar, and they that worship therin [Rev. 11:1] soe that the destroyer canot come here to tread[;] soe heare you are safe in a quiet habitation [Isa. 33:20] where the presence of the lord god is, and his covenant reaches, and his salvatio[n] to the ends of the earth and he sees the Intentions of his enemeys[.] their violence and cruelty he records in everlasting remembrance, yet they must not passe beyond the bounds and limitts which he setts, for he stops them and stayes them att his pleasure.

Lancaster Castle the 11th of the 11th month 1664.

Spence 3/21–22. Also in Works, *pp. 299–303. Endorsed: "M: F: to Friends at London & Bristoll 1664, An Epistle".*

130 TO KING CHARLES II AUGUST 6, 1666

"When you first entered into this kingdome, I was sent of the lord to you to informe you truly of the state & condition of our people."

After more than two years in prison Margaret wrote to King Charles to tell him of the conditions under which she was kept and to remind him of the promises that he had made about freedom of religion. She asks: "for which of these things hast thou kept me in prison 3 long winters, in A place not fitt for people to lye in, sometime for wind & storme & rains & sometime for smoke?"

She reviews the things she had told him about the Quakers, their beliefs, their nonviolence, and also about the oppression that they suffer. She speaks of God's judgement on the kingdom as shown by "pestilence & sword," the plague of 1665, and the Great Fire of 1666. She also warns him against listening to the counsel of the intolerant bishops.

During the four years she was in prison Margaret had many visitors. For a short time in 1665 she was allowed to return to Swarthmoor Hall (Ross, p. 191). She wrote and received many letters, and she wrote five books. They are:

A Call to the Universal Seed of God Throughout the whole World, to come up to the spiritual Worship, etc., *addressed to Jews and Gentiles, written in November 1664, printed in 1665, and in* Works, *pp. 304–324;*

Womens Speaking Justified, Proved, and Allowed of by the Scriptures, all such as speak by the spirit and power of the Lord Jesus, *a plea for spiritual equality between men and women, her most important book to today's readers. It was published in 1666, reprinted in 1667 with "A Further Addition," and translated into Dutch in 1668. In* Works, *pp. 331–350;*

The Standard of the Lord Revealed, *an abstract of the Bible, printed in 1667, 132 pages, not included in the* Works. *The manuscript was sent to "London shortly before the Great Fire in September 1666, and was saved from destruction by Ellis Hookes who later saw to its publication" (Ross, p. 202);*

A Touch-Stone, or, a Perfect Tryal by the Scriptures, of all the Priests, Bishops and Ministers, *a study of the errors of both catholic and protestant clergy, printed in 1667, in* Works, *pp. 351–466;*

A Call unto the Seed of Israel, *printed ca. 1668 and in* Works, *pp. 467–492.*

The Spence Manuscript copy of this letter seems to be a draft and has numerous crossed out words and blots and tears. The version published in her Works *has an additional salutation and several lengthy additions; these are indicated by italics.*

King Charles, *I desire thee, to Read this over, which may be for thy Salvation and Profit.*

For the feare of the lord god stand still & consider what thou & yours hath beene doeing these six yeares since the lord brought you peaceably into this realm & made you rulers over this people, the righteous eye of the Almightie hath beene over you & seene all your doings & actions: what laws have you made or changed save such as hath laid oppression & bondage on the Consciences of gods people[,] & ______ noe lesse penaltie then banishment out of their native country ______

____ the greatest crime that you could find with the people of god was that they obeyed & [worshipped] christ Jesus, soe that the greatest stroke that hath appeared of your justice hath beene upon such as you counted offenders for worshiping of god; in soe much [insomuch] that severall of your judges of the land hath severall times said in open courte to any that did confesse that they mett to worship the lord god, that that was crime enough whereby they could proceed to banishment, & when it was asked in open courte whether it was now become A transgression or A crime in Ingland to worship god, he that was then the cheife justice of England, answered yeas, yeas; oh wonderfull; let this be cronickled in Ingland for after ages that all majestrates may dread & feare soe to afraite the almightie, except they dare say they are stronger than he; And all this hath beene without any just cause given, at any time by that people which was the object of this law, soe that men that had but the least measure of righteousnes & equitie could never have proceeded or to have inflicted such punishment without some just ground, & all that ever was pretended was but suspition, which never can be paraled [paralleled] to be prosecuted to such A height of suffering without A just ground given; Although occasion hath beene continualy sought & watched for but never found[;] but the lord hath preserved his people inocent & harmlesse, & therefore is he ingadged [engaged] to plead there cause, into whose hand it is wholy given & committed[.] I desire thee also to consider seriously in the feare of the lord, what efects & fruits these things hath brought forth, first I beleeve It hath brought hundreds of gods people to their graves, it hath also rendered this Realm & the governors of it cruell in the eyes of people both within its owne body & in other nations, besides the guilt of inocent blood lyes upon this kingdome, since which time the lord in his judgment hath taken many thousands of its people away by his two judgments[,] pestilence & sword. And before any of this was, when you first entered into this kingdome, I was sent of the lord to you to informe you truly of the state & condition of our people[,] when I came before thee[,] oh king, I tould thee I was come to thee in the behalfe of an inocent, harmless, peacable people, which words I would then & ever since & should at this day seale with my blood, if I were put to it. And thy answer was to me (if they be peacable they shall be protected), I also writt to thee several times concerning our faith & principls, how that we could not sweare for conscience sake, neither could we take up armes nor plott, nor contrive to doe any man wrong nor injury, much lesse the king, I also tould you that we must worship god, for god requires it of us,

We did likewise give you many of our Books, which contained our Faith, and Principles, and Doctrine, that thereby we might be tryed by the Scriptures of Truth (which all of you do profess) whether our Principles were erroneous or no; and to that purpose we gave our Books to the King and Parliament, and to the Bishops and Ministers, both Ecclesiastical and Civil.

Our Books were sold openly amongst all People; and our Principles declared in a Declaration, and freely holden forth to the whole World.

We also desired that we might have a Meeting of the Bishops or Ministers of the Land, and that our Friends would freely and willingly give them a Meeting, that thereby they and we might be tryed by the Scriptures, which of us was in the error;—whereupon thou wast pleased to grant us our Requests, and promised us that we should have a Meeting, which was but reasonable; but the Bishops, and those that were concerned, they turned if off, when our Friends were ready, and would not give us a Meeting; this Action of theirs, did cleary manifest them to be out of the Life and Power of the Scriptures; For Christ Jesus said to those that he sent forth, that they should not be afraid, for he would give them a Mouth and Wisdom, that all their Adversaires should not be able to gainsay nor resist; and likewise the Apostle when he wrote to his Son Timothy, in 2 Tim. 2.24, 25, 26. And the Servant of the Lord (saith he) must not strive, but be gentle unto all Men, apt to teach, patient, in meekness instucting those that oppose themselves, if God peradventure will give them Repentance, and come to the acknowledging of the Truth, &c.

If they had been the Ministers of Christ, and in the Apostles Doctrine, they would have taken this way with us; they would have endeavoured to have convinced us by sound Doctrine, or at least have try'd us this way, before they had agreed with the Civil Magistrates to make Laws against us; but this manifested their Spirits and Principle; for they rather chose to deliver us up to you, that had the Whip and the Scourge in your hands, and that which they could not do by sound Doctrine, they agreed with others to do it for them by Compulsion.

But the All-seeing God, hath seen all this.

& all this was that you should not be ignorant what we could doe & what we could not doe, I tould you also that wee could give unto Cesar the things that was Cesars & we might give unto god also the things that was gods[.] & this is A wittnes for the lord in this day that he pleads, that you were not ignorant, I also writt to thee to beware how thou ruled in this nation, for the people of this nation was A britle people generaly, & besides them the lord hath A people here that is deare unto him, And I desired thee not to touch them nor hurt them, I also desired thee to beware of the counsell of the bishops, for if thou harkened to their counsell they would be thy ruine, for it was their counsell was the ruine of thy father, for their counsell is the same that Rehebohams [Rehoboam's] young men was, read what the lord did with that king, in the 1 of kings C 12 [1 Kings 12]: Thou knows this is true, their counsell is to make the burden heavier, as theirs was. All this with much more I writt to thee & warned thee of, I can truly say in the feare of the lord, in much love & tendernes to thee, & now I may say unto thee, for which of these things hast thou kept me in prison 3 long winters, in A place not fitt for people to lye in, some time for wind & storme & rains & sometime for smoke, soe that it is much that I am alive but that the power & goodnes of god hath beene with me, I was kept A yeare & 7 months in this prison before I was suffered to see the house that was mine, or children or family except they came to me over two dangerous sandes in the could winter, when they came with much danger of their lives, but since the last Assissis I have had A litle more respect from this sheriffe then formerly from others, And all this I am very well satisfied in & prayses the lord who counts me worthy to suffer for his sake, for I never did thee nor any other man in the nation any wrong, & soe I may say for many more of our friends that hath suffered even till death, & all that we could writte or speake, we were not beleeved, & all the warnings that we gave of judgments & tould you plainly we had done soe with other governors before you, & how the lord had overthrowne them, & desired you many times to beware least the lords judgments came over you also, but all was to noe purpose, for as long as there was peace in the land the maine bussines of the parliament was to invent laws to punish & persecute Quakers, but to make laws to punish vice, sin, & wickednes & lacivioussnes, we heard but A litle of such laws, And now after all my sufferings in the same love that I visited thee in the begining, I desire thee once more to feare the lord god by whom kings rule & princes decree justice, who sets up and pulls downe another at his pleasure

And let not the Guilt of the Burthen of the Breach of that Word that passed from thee at Breda lie upon thy Conscience, but as thou promised when thou wast in distress, and also renewed it many times since, that thou would'st give Liberty to tender Consciences: In the Fear of the Lord perform

it, and purge thy Conscience of it; and hearken not to wicked Councellors, that have stopped it in thee all this time; for they will bear none of thy Burthen for thee, when the Lord pleads for Breach of Covenant with him and his People; I know it hath been often in thy Heart to perform it, and thou hast seen what Fruit the want of it hath brought forth.

So if thou lovest thy Eternal Peace and Comfort with the Lord, try what the performance of it will bring forth, who wilt thereby see thou hast hearkned to wrong Councellors.

& every mortall man hath but A moment in this life either to serve, feare, & honour the lord & therein to receive mercy from him, or els to transgresse, sin, disobey & dishonour him, & soe receive the judgment of eternall misery[.] soe never A one of you knows how long or how short your day may be, therefore feare not man that can kill the body but feare the lord who when he hath killed the body can cast the soul into hell, yea I say unto you[,] feare him[.]

From A true lover of all your soules[,] though A sufferer by you, And the desire of my harte is that you may take these things into consideration betime, before it be too late, & sett open the prison doors & let the inocent goe Free, & that will take parte of the burden & guilt of you, least the doore of mercy be shutt to you,

Margret Fell

from my prison at lancaster castell,
the 6th day of the 6th month 1666

Spence 3/120–121 and Works, *pp. 325–330. Endorsed: "M F to the king 1666 [George Fox]".*

131 TO THE JUSTICES AT LANCASTER FROM SEVEN PRISONERS, INCLUDING MARGARET FELL, IN LANCASTER CASTLE JANUARY 1668

"We have suffered patiently and peaceably have undergone whatever hath been afflicted upon us."

This joint letter from seven prisoners in Lancaster Castle refers to papers delivered to the "Kinge and Councell." Many Friends in London were taking up the cause of freeing prisoners, as well as their non-Quaker friends, such as court physician Dr.

Richard Lower. He was the brother of Thomas Lower who later married Mary Fell, Margaret's daughter (Ross, p. 203).

The Conventicle Act of 1664 had expired in 1667, and the majority of members in the House of Commons were eager to pass an even harsher law. The king and his council were more tolerant, and the proposed new Commons bill did not become law. So in 1668 there was a release of many prisoners, including Margaret Fell. Sir Daniel Fleming complained, "her discharge from her easy imprisonment doth not a little encourage that rabble of fanatics and discourage all magistrates from acting against them" (Braithwaite, p. 37). She was able to return to Swarthmoor Hall and resume her life there.

January 1667–8

Wee doe hereby Acquainte the Justices of the Bench That we have received Intelligence from our friends att London who were Interceded for our freends in Prison; and Delivered our papers to the Kinge and Councell whoe Received our papers att theire Hands and did discourse with them aboute our frends in prison (And the next day did reporte our Grievances to the Kinge and Councill) by whom wee are Certainly Informed That the Kinge with many of his Councill were Inclyned to Sett our freinds att Liberty forthwith. But being perswaded by some of his Councill to send an order or a Letter To the Justices of peace at the Quarter Sessions By whose procurement it was That these words were put in the order vizt [videlicet: i.e., namely] Rngleaders of faction in Contempt of the Lawes Concerninge which wee Canne speak unto the whole world To that which is Righteous Juste and true, in every hearte And perticularly wee Appeale unto you upon the Bench what you have knowne of us Concerninge anie faction or anie disturbance of the peace or Goverment or anie Contempt of anie Lawes Though they were never so Contrary to our Libertys, yea, and many of our Lyfes[,] yeat we have suffered patiently and peaceably have undergone whatever hath been afflicted upon us by them, For it is contrary to our principles to be factious or Turbulent or Contemners of Lawes And it is Contrary to our Lord & Maisters Commande whoe came not to destroy the Lawe but to fulfill it whose Doctrine is not to Resist Evill. But that if any one smite us on the one Cheeke to turn the other And so all faction and contention and contemners of Lawes wee doe deny; And our practice and peacable life has shewed the same and ever shall: And so to the Righteous and just principle of God in all your Hearts wee doe speake to Returne us as that Judge of us

John Townson	John White	
Rich Walker	Geo Benson	Prisoners
Margt Fell	Robt Widder	
Tho Green		

County Record Office, Preston (Checked by Susan V. Hartshorne); and Nightingale, Early Stages of the Quaker Movement in Lancashire.

132 TO COLONEL WILLIAM WEST MARCH 5, 1668

"Wee have beene & are like to bee very troublesome to thee, but it is soe, as wee cannott helpe it."

This letter concerns one action in a lengthy lawsuit between Margaret Fell and Thomas Rawlinson (?–1689). He had been the steward of Force Forge, an enterprise owned by the Fell women from 1658 to 1681. Margaret accused him of defrauding her, and he defended himself vigorously. A notable fact from the Quaker perspective is that Friends were not supposed to use legal means to correct wrongs within the Quaker community; they were to use mediation. Rawlinson was equally a devoted Quaker. An early letter of his, dated May 11, 1659, addresses Margaret as "Dear Heart" and ends "Thy dear brother in the Truth of God." (Friends' Library, 11:345) B.Y. Kunze has an entire chapter on the dispute. Her summing up is that Margaret may have been mistaken in accusing Rawlinson of fraud but that the evidence is not conclusive.

Colonel William West was a friend and colleague of Judge Thomas Fell who had served with Judge Fell when he was on the bench (Letters 53, 54). Matthew Richardson (–1677) was Margaret's brother-in-law, an attorney, and an investor in Force Forge (Kunze, pp. 111–112, 263).

Deare Friende,

This is to Lett thee know, that wee have Recd [received] A New Commission out of the Dutchy Court; wherein Rawlinson hath prevailed to gett 2: Commissioners to sitt with you; & our Wittnesses that was Examined before is to here [hear] ther former depositions reade over & then they stande good by order of Court; Hee hath Chosen Stephen Husbande, & John Gardner of Kendal; & our Councell prevailed soe farr; as to gett you 2: to stande on for us; my Brother [Matthew Richardson] hath sent out your warrt [warrant], & wee have given Tho: Rawlinson sommons, & wee have summoned some of our Wittnesses, to sitt in the Assize weeke, & afterwarde to Adjourne as you see meett; My Bro: [brother] & wee have Appointed Monday, in the Assize weeke, because wee hope that that day, thou will have the best time; Hee desired us to write to thee to bringe the depositions with thee, thither in Readinesse, & what else, as thou hath, that Concerns that Business; wee have Appointed Alice weareings [Waring's?] house in Lancaster; to Sitt at; Wee have beene & are like to bee very troublesome to thee, but it is soe, as wee cannott helpe it, & I hope you will see, it wilbee for good in the End; And soe noe more but my deare Love is unto thee; & that I Remaine

Thy obliged Friende
Margarett Fell

Swarthmore the 5th:
of 1st: moth: 1667/8

U. Texas, Ransome. Addressed: "To My Esteemed Friende William West Esqr. These deliver with speed. Leave this at the shippe to be delivered as above. in Lancaster".

Part III

Marriage to George Fox and Later Life, 1669–1702

Dungeons, Lancaster Castle, Shire Hall, where Margaret Fell, George Fox, and many other Quakers were imprisoned. Lancashire County Council. Used by permission.

Chronology 1669–1702

Spring–Summer 1669	Margaret Fell and Rachel visit Friends in Kent and London
Oct 1669	Marriage of Margaret Fell to George Fox at Bristol George Fox travels in the South and Midlands Margaret Fell returns to Swarthmoor.
Dec 1669	George Fell scheming in London to get his mother's estate and Swarthmoor; Susannah and Rachel Fell at Swarthmoor; Sarah Fell in London; Thomas and Mary Lower and John and Margaret Rous living in London
April 1670	Margaret Fell's second imprisonment, Lancaster
May 1670	Second Conventicle Act
Summer 1670	Sarah Fell returns home
Oct 1670	Death of George Fell
Sept 1670–Spring 1671	George Fox very ill in London, nursed by Margaret Rous
April 1671	Margaret Fell released by discharge under the Broad Seal
May–Aug 1671	Margaret Fell's fourth visit to London
Aug 1671–1673	George Fox in America
Oct 1671	Swarthmoor Women's Monthly Meeting formed at Swarthmoor, the first continuous Women's Meeting outside London
1672	Declaration of Indulgence
April 1672	Margaret Fell and Rachel travel in Yorkshire
June 1673	Margaret Fell, with Sarah and Rachel Fell, and Thomas Lower go to Bristol to meet George Fox on his return from America. Margaret's fifth visit to London
1673	Test Act
1673–1685	Continuous and severe persecution of Quakers
Dec 1673–Feb 1675	George Fox arrested and imprisoned at Worcester
Oct 1674	Margaret Fell's sixth visit to London, interviews king
June 1675–Mar 1677	George Fox, Margaret and Susannah Fell return to Swarthmoor; George Fox stays at Swarthmoor twenty-one months
April 1675	William Penn at Swarthmoor
1678	Thomas and Mary Lower move to Marsh Grange

Sept 1678–Mar 1680	George Fox at Swarthmoor (last visit)
1681–1691	George Fox in or near London
June 1681	Marriage of Sarah Fell to William Meade
May–July 1681	Margaret Fell's seventh visit to London
1682	William Penn founds Pennsylvania
1683–1686	Thomas Lower in prison at Launceston, Cornwall
Mar 1683	Marriage of Rachel Fell to Daniel Abraham
Sept 1683	Margaret Fell, Rachel and Daniel Abraham arrested and tried by Roger and William Kirkby in Lancaster
June 1684	These three fined heavily and imprisoned
Nov 1684–Mar 1685	Margaret Fell's eighth visit to London, with Mary Lower, Susannah Fell, and Leonard Fell
Feb 1685	Death of King Charles II; Margaret Fell interviews King James II
1685	Robert Barclay visits Swarthmoor
Mar 1686	King James II's General Pardon and Royal Warrant releases Friends from prison
1687	Declaration of Indulgence for all nonconformists
1688	Swarthmoor Meetinghouse given by George Fox
1689	Fall of James II; Accession of William and Mary Toleration Act gives limited religious freedom
1690	Marriage of Isabel Yeamans to Abraham Morrice
Apr–June 1690	Margaret Fell's ninth visit to London
1690	Margaret Fell writes *A Relation of Margaret Fell, Her Birth, Life, Testimony and Sufferings*
Jan 1691	Death of George Fox in London
1691	Marriage of Susannah Fell to William Ingram
1694	Margaret Fell writes *The Testimony of Margaret Fell concerning her late husband*
Mar 1696	Death of John Rous at sea, on returning from Barbados
1697–1698	Margaret Fell, now eighty-three years old, makes her tenth and last visit to London
June 1698	Margaret Fell writes to King William III
April 1700	Margaret Fell's second epistle against regimentation
Nov 1701	Margaret Fell's last Testimony
Mar 1702	Death of William III; Accession of Anne
April 1702	Death of Margaret Fell, aged nearly eighty-eight at Swarthmoor Hall

1710 Margaret Fell's *Works* published under the title, *A Brief Collection of Remarkable Passages and Occurrances Relating to the Birth, Education, Life, Conversation, Travels, Services and Deep Sufferings of that ancient Eminent and Faithful Servant of the Lord, Margaret Fell, but by her Second Marriage M. Fox*

PERSECUTION AND TOLERANCE

Craig Horle writes, "The harshest period of prosecution was restricted generally to the period 1660–1689" and "Yet the Quakers—highly visible, socially aberrant and abrasive, but personally nonviolent—were ideal targets, not only for harassment, but also for physical abuse" (Horle, *Q.& EngLegalSys*, pp. xi, 127). Margaret Fell was imprisoned again for one year in 1670–1671.

Charles II, king from 1660–1685, having no legitimate children as heirs, was succeeded by his brother, James II. King Charles had a preference for Catholicism, and James II was a professed Catholic, which greatly disturbed their subjects. They feared it betokened a return to Rome and subservience to the French King, Louis XIV, who gave subsidies to both Charles and James. The two kings both favored toleration of dissenters, primarily because it might include Catholics, but they were inconsistent in promoting it. As toleration was opposed by Parliament, the Presbyterians, and the increasingly powerful Anglican Church, dissenters were persecuted.

The following list of laws used to prosecute Quakers gives a glimpse of the process:

1662 Quaker Act
1664 First Conventicle Act
1666 Five Mile Act
1670 Second Conventicle Act

The following were the Crown's offer of toleration:

1672 Declaration of Indulgence, issued and withdrawn
1687 Declaration of Indulgence for all Nonconformists
1688 Declaration of Indulgence reissued
1689 Toleration Act

When James II became king in 1685 he sent a mission to Rome, planned to pack Parliament, and prosecuted seven Anglican bishops. The disaffection of the English with James encouraged Prince William of Orange to invade England. He was James's nephew, and his wife, Mary, was James's daughter. James fled to France, and William and Mary were proclaimed king and queen in February 1689.

After 1660 most of the dissenting sects died out, except for the Quakers. Their numbers continued to increase, which made them the object of persecution until the late 1680s. By the time of the Toleration Act they were generally accepted as no danger to the state, and in the 1690s they had achieved most, if not all, rights of other Englishmen.

Brief Biography 1669–1702

In October 1669 Margaret Fell married George Fox, who had been her guide and warm friend since his first coming to Swarthmoor Hall in 1652. He was beloved by all of her children, and Swarthmoor Hall was always a place of refreshment for him, though he did not stay there long. Margaret adopted the religious principles he preached, shared his vision, and became an enthusiastic leader of the movement. The marriage of the two leaders was an important event, and they carefully followed procedures set up by Quakers. Her daughters and sons-in-law all approved of the marriage, though her son did not. He considered it a betrayal of their social class. George Fox gave up all rights to her estate, an unusual step.

Margaret was fifty-five at the time of their marriage, and George was ten years younger. They were married for twenty-two years until his death in 1691. They lived apart much of the time as they each continued their work. George traveled to America, to the Continent, and to all parts of England, strengthening Meetings and gradually setting up the system of monthly and quarterly Meetings, and a yearly Meeting, that would sustain the movement.

Margaret also traveled, making a total of ten trips to London in her lifetime and numerous other journeys to parts of England, visiting Meetings and Friends. She particularly encouraged the setting up of "Women's Meetings." Travel by horseback or in a carriage on primitive roads was physically taxing, but she continued to do it until her last few years.

Persecution of Quakers was heavy in the 1670s and into the 1680s, and Margaret continued her work of petitioning for Friends who were suffering and trying to achieve the liberty of conscience that had been promised. She spent another year in prison in 1670 and 1671 and also suffered loss of property.

In her last decade she was still the respected leader and an honored and loved mother and grandmother. Her daughter Rachel and her husband, Daniel Abraham, lived with Margaret at Swarthmoor Hall. She was active in local affairs but had less influence on the Quaker movement as its center had gradually moved from the north of England to London. Margaret's eyesight became poor, and she did less writing. Her letters demonstrate her continued clear thinking and a somewhat lesser but remaining willingness to engage in controversy. She died in 1702, almost eighty-eight years old, at home, and was buried close to Swarthmoor Hall at Sunbreck Quaker burial ground in an unmarked grave, as was the custom of the earliest Friends.

MARGARET FELL'S WORK AND WOMEN'S MEETINGS

Margaret Fell was one of the chief founders of what became the Society of Friends that still exists today. Her life work had three main focuses, pastoral, doctrinal, and organizational.

The pastoral work began in 1652 when she invited friends and neighbors to meet at Swarthmoor Hall, and Meetings were held there for thirty-eight years. In 1688, George Fox donated a nearby property for a Meetinghouse, where the Swarthmoor Meeting still meets. The encouragement and the hospitality she gave to Friends is warmly attested by many letters written to her. Her letters were a source of information and comfort for her correspondents. She made numerous long journeys visiting Meetings and Friends throughout her life.

She gave material aid personally, as well as setting up the Kendal Fund in 1654 to help itinerant ministers, prisoners, and their families. As Meetings became more formalized, the practice of Quakers helping others continued to be an important part of keeping the community together.

Margaret was well versed in the Bible and in theology before her conversion to Quakerism, and she was quickly able to understand and articulate the principles of the new doctrine. She did this through her letters, both personal and more formal epistles, and through her published writings.

The organization of Friends was another important concern of George Fox and the leaders of the movement. Margaret Fell had an important role in establishing the position of women and in the organization of Friends. A structure had to be created, and it was not to be centered in one person or one authoritarian body. Groups in the North were already holding "Meetings for Discipline" by 1654 for oversight, to help those being persecuted, and to regularize marriages. It was difficult to make the transition from informal groups of enthusiastic seekers who had found a religion that stressed a personal relationship with God, to an organized system with the authority to maintain important principles and discipline. Gradually a system of monthly Meetings (local), quarterly Meetings (regional), and eventually a yearly Meeting was set up. The itinerant Quakers who traveled all over England, Ireland, Scotland, and America, communicated via Swarthmoor Hall in the early years.

The setting up of Women's Meetings was an important chapter in the growth of the movement. There was no doubt among Quakers about women's equality in spiritual matters, but their having authority in business and other matters was not a part of seventeenth-century ethos in the wider community. An early Quaker Women's Meeting was the Box Meeting, set up in London in 1660. Money was collected in a box to disperse to the needy. Regular Women's Meetings with authority over general business and marriages developed gradually in some places in the 1660s.

Margaret Fell was released from a year in prison in April 1671. She went to London to be with George Fox and with Margaret and John Rous. In June 1671 George Fox issued a circular letter advocating the establishment of Women's Meetings. In August he went to America. In October 1671 a Women's Meeting was established at Swarthmoor. Margaret and her daughters were mainstays of this and other Meetings for many years. The purpose of Women's Meetings was to provide material help, spiritual discipline, education, and employment.

An issue that arose in the 1690s, after toleration, was the matter of conformity in dress and mixing with the "world." There began to be strictures about wearing bright colors and attending non-Friends gatherings. The group's turning inward was manifested in rules about marrying "out of Meeting" and about clothing. Margaret Fell wanted nothing to do with such petty things.

Margaret Fell's letters through the last three decades of her life show her continuing care for her family and friends. There are pastoral epistles to individuals and Meetings. She protested against persecution and explained Quaker principles, including one letter to King William III in 1698. It is appropriate that her last letter is a strongly worded warning to Friends to beware of excessive concern about dress, that it "is a poor silly gospel."

List of Letters 133–166, 1671–1700

133 To Sarah and Rachel Fell August 19, 1671

"Wee parted with your father [George Fox] and the rest of the Company and stayed on the shore till we saw them under saile and soe ever since they have had as fair an East wind for them as ever could blow."

There are no extant letters between 1668 and 1671. It was a busy time with many family events and a second period in prison for Margaret. After four years she had been released from Lancaster Castle in June 1668 to return to Swarthmoor Hall and her daughters, Sarah, Susannah, Mary, and Rachel. John and Margaret Rous had been living at Swarthmoor, where their first two children were born, but they left shortly before their mother's return. Thomas Lower had been courting Mary for several years, evidently against Margaret's wishes at first, but in August 1668 he and Mary were married (Ross, pp. 205–210).

Shortly thereafter Margaret set off on journeys throughout England, visiting Meetings and prisons. Rachel, then fifteen, accompanied her. Margaret spent about three months in London, staying with Margaret Rous. George Fox was also there at the time working to better establish the internal organization of Quaker Meetings. Margaret's journeys continued, and while she was in Bristol with her daughter Isabel Yeamans, we have her concise statement: "And then it was Eleven Years after my former Husband's decease; and G. Fox being then returned from visiting Friends in Ireland. At Bristol he declared his Intentions of Marrlage with me; and there was also our Marriage solemnized, in a publick Meeting of many Friends, who were our witnesses" (Works, *p. 8).*

The marriage of the two foremost leaders of the movement was a great event, conducted with due dignity. The couple appeared before three Meetings to publish their intention; George Fox requested the consent of all the daughters and sons-in-law; and at the wedding itself, on October 27, 1669, ninety-four Friends signed the marriage certificate. George Fox renounced all rights to Margaret Fell's property, an unusual step (Ross, pp. 214–219). Margaret was fifty-five at the time, and George was forty-five. There has been considerable speculation as to whether the marriage was symbolic and spiritual, but its intimate nature remains unknown. There was clearly great love, respect, and friendship between the two, though they spent little time together in the twenty-two years of their marriage.

Persecution of all nonconformists was heightened with the passage of the Second Conventicle Act of 1670. From April 1670 to April 1671 Margaret was again in prison, this time as a result of her son George's attempts to take over Swarthmoor Hall and Marsh Grange. He was strongly against Quakerism and, in particular, his mother's part in it. He sought the aid of Colonel Kirkby and other anti-Quaker officials to seize the property. He regarded his mother's marriage to Fox as a violation of class standards. Margaret was taken to the prison at Lancaster and kept there until George Fox and her daughters were able to get an order of discharge from King Charles. George Fell died while Margaret was in prison (Ross, pp. 220–225).

After this second release from prison Margaret continued her work, and George Fox was preparing for a voyage to America. In the following letter of August 1671 Margaret wrote to Sarah and Rachel at Swarthmoor of the beginning of this voyage. Margaret and a group of Friends traveled from London to Gravesend to see George Fox and twelve other Friends, two of them women, off on the ship, Industry. *The journey would take almost two years, and George Fox would visit Friends from Barbados, Jamaica, Maryland, all the way to Rhode Island. Margaret describes the auspicious beginning of the voyage, the winds were fair, and then continues with extensive news of Friends in London.*

She comments, "I have much to doe to get one to write for me now." Several of her faithful scribes sailed on the voyage, and Margaret's eyesight was weakening.

London the 19:6:mo:1671

My dear and blessed and Beloved Children

In the dear Everlasting love of God which is Everlasting and changes not, in this is my dear love remembered unto you, and by this you may know according as I writt in my last unto you, wee with many more went downe the last 7th Day with your father [George Fox] to the ship a litle below Gravesend, and there Susan [Susannah Fell] and I laid all night, and the next morning severall freinds came to the ship to us to goe along with us to the downes, and soe that day being the ferst day [Sunday] wee had a fair gale of wind, and a prosperous Journey unto the Downes, and about the 9th hour at night wee cast ancher, and that night your father with severall other freinds that were passengers came ashore with us unto Deal and there wee stayed all night[;] and the next day they tooke in Provisions and water for the ship, and then there was a fair wind to goe out of the Downes[;] and so about the 2nd hower [hour] wee parted with your father and the rest of the Company and stayed on the shore till we saw them under saile and soe ever since they have had as fair an East wind for them as ever could blow, and it is wonderfull remarkeable, and freinds takes great notice of it that the wind should turne every way according as they had occasion for one wind—caryed into the downes one day[,] another wind caryed out of the downes the next day[.] they were speaking of putting in at Plymouth and soe to send for your Brother and sister Lower, but it may be that this fair wind may hinder them least they should misse of their opportunity, but if they want any conveniences or find any fault in the ship, I beleive they will put in before they passe the lands end of Cornwall.

We came on the second day after wee had parted with them[,] a mater [matter] of 16 freinds that might to Canterbury by land, and go next day to Gravesend by land, and the fourth day to London by Water, where we met with your letter with the Inclosed, and soe according to thy desire I shall indeavour to make sure with Tho: Yoakely for the 100 £ against the time thou speakes of. And I have a bond from him and Wm. Willson for the 250 £ and the other 50 £ Walter Miers hath paid to Robert Eleston. I thinke it will be the best way to leave this Bond with Walter Miers to keepe till the time the mony be paid, but I shall speake with them all and Consider further of it. It is now fair weather and I would gladly be away, but I am not yet quite clear of the meetings, but I trust in the Lord that I shall get ready to set forward out of this City this day weeke. And soe I doe not know that I can write any more to you. soe if the Lord will wee may be at some meeting not far of London the next day[,] being the first day, and soe set forward on our Journey the second day towards warwicke and stafford, and soe home as the Lord makes way for us, wee doe not know of any Company but Leonard [Leonard Fell] and I [,] for Miles Hubertsey [Hubbersty] and his wife is not like to be ready. wee intend if the Lord please tomorrow to goe see Margrett Prestone who sets forward towards the north next 2.d day [Monday]. I had a letter yesterday from your sister [Mary] Lower And it seemes shee is very poor and weake[,] but there is some hopes of Recovery[.] your sister yeamonds [Isabel Yeamans] hath been very Ill ever since before the fair, and continues very poor and feeble still. I had a letter from her this weeke, in which shee does informe me every way how its with her and I have taken advise about it and intend to send downe the things by Susan. Susan cannot goe till next second day come a weeke for Thomas Yoakely and his wife and some other freinds intends to goe to Bristoll along with her and soe shee was willing to stay for their Company, And I hope Thomas Salthouse will stay on here to take her along to Cornwall. I have seen Thom: Greene once since he came to towne and it was in the street and I could say but litle to him. and John Lawson I have not seen at all, but I intend to send some things by them in the ship which thou writt for, Soe this is the most that I have at present[.] I have much to doe to get one to write for me now[,] John Salthouse having gone away, and Elise H. [?] has got a great fall from a horse as he was rideing to the Downes that he is not able to [set] up. I am now at Walter Meirs and intends in the streingth of the Lord and his power to be at Horsly downe tomorrow, and at Peele on the third day, and at Gratious street on the 4th day. and to goe to Kingstone on the 5th day and to come backe one the sixth day and to set forward if the Lord pleases on the 7th day. and to Visit Thomas Dry his wife as I goe along. And soe in the streingth and power of the Almighty God I bid you farewell.

From Your Dear Mother
In the Lord. M: F:

Haverford College Library (photocopy) and partially in Ross, pp. 237–238. Addressed: "Swartmore DD Leave this with John Higgin in Lancaster to be dd as above with care and speed Lancashire". Endorsed: "m f to her childeren 1671 Consarns gf parting beyond the seas read over 19:d 6 mo: [George Fox]".

134 To William Welch January 1674?

"I doe certify to thy satisfaction,
that I know noe such thinge."

This brief note to William Welch, which may be in Margaret's handwriting, is attached to a letter of John Rous's to her. William Welch's wife was "convinced" by George Fox in Edinburgh in 1657. In 1674 Welch's daughter, Sarah, was married to John Swinton, Jr., of Edinburgh (CJ, 1:297, 453). The cryptic mention of "John Swinton the younger" is typical of Margaret's reticence in speaking of personal matters. John Swinton, Jr., the son of an important Scottish politician (Letter 89) was in some financial difficulty. Quakers placed great importance on probity in fiscal affairs.

Willm Welch: Dr [dear] Frd [Friend] my dr Love in the Lord is unto thee; & to thy dr wife, thy daughter & family, & to all dr faithfull frinds with you; & I doe acknowledge your dr & tender love & kindenesse to us when wee were with you; I Recd [received] a letr [letter] from thee, wherein thou mentions somethinge Concerninge, Jn Swinton the younger in Answer to which I doe certify to thy satisfaction, that I know noe such thinge; Neither was there ever any such thinge propounded that ever I knew of; soe in this, thou may be satisfied; This is all at present from

Thy dere Friende
in the Lord M: F:

Spence 3/172–173.

135 TO WILLIAM PENN NOVEMBER 25, 1674

"Dear william lett mee know thy Answer by the next post."

This letter and the next to Heanage Finch, the lord-keeper, concern George Fox's imprisonment at Worcester from December 1673 to February 1675. The letter to the Lord-Keeper describes the circumstances of Fox's arrest. It was clearly illegal, but once in prison Fox was caught in a net of technicalities. Since he was innocent of law-breaking he refused to accept a pardon from the king, but that made it more difficult to help him. Margaret's phrase "stickes with the keeper" refers to the lord-keeper's refusal to honor an order from the king.

Many friends were using all possible means to effect Fox's release, and William Penn (1644–1718) was particularly active (PWP, 1:287). At thirty years of age he had become one of the most influential Quakers. He was famous for his writings, his many abilities, and his strong convictions. He was the son of Admiral Sir William Penn, the friend and associate of James, Duke of York, later James II, and of King Charles II. Admiral Penn deplored William's turning to Quakerism and tried unsuccessfully to dissuade him.

Penn had been expelled from Oxford University and in 1668 wrote The Sandy Foundation Shaken, *a book the Bishop of London found to be heretical. He had Penn put into the Tower of London. Penn was there for eight months, until he and his friends (including King Charles) were able to have him released (PWP, 1:86, 97; 5:100).*

In 1670 Penn was arrested for inciting to riot. He was preaching at a Meeting in the street at Gracechurch Street because soldiers had shut the Quakers out of their Meetinghouse. This incident resulted in a famous trial that established the right of a jury to be free of coercion by judges (PWP, 1:172–173).

In 1681 King Charles made Penn the proprietor of the colony of Pennsylvania as payment of a debt to his father. Penn had already proved himself capable of planning the development and governance of the New Jersey colony. He dreamed of a shelter for Quakers and others who longed for a land where people could live with toleration of religion and just laws, a "Holy Experiment." King Charles may also have been happy to be rid of some troublesome people (Greaves, 3:24–28).

Margaret and her family, including son-in-law Thomas Lower, exchanged visits and letters with the Penns. The only surviving letter of Gulielma Penn (William's wife) was written to Margaret. Kunze speculates that their social standing was a particular bond between Margaret and the Penns (pp. 169–170).

D [dear] william penn

If thou thinke that my Comeinge upp concerninge this busnesse [business] of my husbands that stickes with the keeper, If I could be any way serviceable In it, I am willinge to come upp: although I have stayed here soe longe: yett I am willinge to doe my utmost endeavore before I returne backe home if it bee thought Convenient & requisite: though I doe thinge [think] In my minde there might be an order obtayned from the kinge & Councell for the settinge of him at liberty: if it Cannott be gotten through this way: that thou hast already begunn: dear william lett mee know thy Answer by the next post: for if I come I woulde doe soe by the first opportunity: & soe with my deare eternall love to thee & thy deare wiffe & all deare & Faithfull Freindes: I remaine

Thy deare & truly loveinge
Freinde for the Lorde
M. F.

worester [Worcester] this 25th of the 9th moth 1674
My son Lower & daughter susans dear love is unto thee & thy wiffe:

FHL Ms. Box 7.1(3); HSP/Penn-Forbes 2:517. Endorsed: "G: Fox 9 mo 74".

136 TO HENEAGE FINCH, LORD KEEPER DECEMBER 25, 1674

"When they could find the breach of noe Law against him then they tendered him the Oath & he was sent for up to London."

George Fox's imprisonments and travels had seriously weakened his health. Margaret was particularly concerned about him at this time, as well as being outraged by the obvious unjustness of the legal maneuverings that kept Fox in prison. He was arrested in the parlor of John Halford's home, not at a Meeting. When the judges found that he had broken no law, he was tendered the oath; had several hearings; was transferred back and forth from Worcester to London; and was praemunired. At the time of this letter the king had issued a warrant for Fox's release which Heneage Finch, the lord-keeper, was refusing to honor by ruling that the matter must return to the court at Worcester. Finally Fox was freed on the basis of a legal technicality by the judges of the King's Bench at Westminster (PWP, 1:287; Ross, pp. 247–255).

Heneage Finch (1621–1682), first earl of Nottingham, was successively solicitor-general, lord-keeper, and lord chancellor. He was a strong supporter of King Charles except that he opposed the king's policy of toleration of dissent (DNB).

Henry Parker (1638–1713), Justice and Recorder of Evesham, was the most active agent in prosecuting Fox during this period (Henning, p. 206; CJ, 2:447; Ross, pp. 250–253).

For the Lord Keeper

Whom I desire to consider the long & sad Imprisonement of my deare husband who hath wanted his health a long time & hath not gone forth of his prison Chamber above 23 weekes but about 3 times[,] & it is 20 weekes since I & my sonne [Thomas Lower] & daughter left my family not knoweing that I should find him alive[,] & we have stayed ever since waiteing & expecteing that the kinge & his governours would have some pittey & some compassion upon him for to Sett him at Lyberty[,] he being an Innocent man & was never found in any thing that was evil or against the King or his government[,] & being that he & my sonne were taken up & apprehended contrary to all Law when we were travaileing on our Journey[,] not so much as under pretence of being in a meeteing but was in a frends private house when Justice parker [Henry Parker] & a preiste came & apprehended them[,] & so when he appeared before them at Sessions when they could find the breach of noe Law against him then they tendered him the Oath & he was sent for up to London by a Habeas Corpus & was remmitted by the Judges to the Kings bench & afterwards parker & the Rest moved the Judges againe And gott him backe to Worster & praemunired him[,] & thus hath he beene tossed to & froe without any Just ground[.] Now I beseech thee Consider of our Condition for I am now 200 myles from my owne house & hath beene from it ever since I came to Worster & I was yesterday with the King & he desired me to come to thee[.] I am informd that the King had Signed a warrant a pritey while Since[.] we heard before I came from worster that it was stoped by thee so I beseech thee & intreate thee let pittey & tendernes enter into thy hearte & consider that it is a Sad thing both to be sicke & in prison & let him have his Lyberty That we may returne home to our owne Countrey[;] for it is for the Lords Sake & his truths sake that we suffer & have suffered these many years & not for any evill[,] & so if thou doe good in thy place & office the Lord will reward thee

25:x mo: 1674 Margt: Fox

Spence 3/129. Also see Ross, pp. 254–255 and Crosfield p. 157. Endorsed: "m f to lord keeper [George Fox]"; "1674 Ingrossed".

137 TO WILLIAM PENN JUNE 25, 1675

"My Husband held out better then cold [could] bee Expected, & was better in his health, but very weary."

After George Fox's release from Worcester prison in February 1675, he and Margaret spent several months near London attending Meetings and consulting with Friends and then slowly made their way to Swarthmoor Hall. They visited numerous friends on the way, including the Penns, traveling by coach since George was not well enough to ride horseback.

Margaret and George were then together at Swarthmoor for two years, the longest period that they spent together. It was during this time that he dictated his Journal *to his son-in-law, Thomas Lower, and that he read and sorted through the massive Swarthmoor correspondence, making the "endorsements" noted on many letters (Ingle, p. 250).*

Morgan Watkins had been a Quaker since 1653, preaching and writing. In 1665 he spent six months in prison and on being released he wrote in a letter to Margaret: "But the two imprisonments in Newgate, and the one at Gatehouse (both in London) in which I had several battles with death, have much weakened my body" (Webb, pp. 202–203). The DNB *gives his dates as "fl. 1653–1670," but he lived at least until 1675.*

Swarthmore the 26th of the 4th mo: 1675
W:P: Deare Freinde.

In the Bond of truth, & unity of life, in which the Liveing God has Ingaged us, for his owne Service & honour, and for our Etternall Comfort, & Everlastinge Joy and peace & felicity, In this is my deare & Etternall love Remembred unto thee, & thy Dr [dear] wife, whom I love & Honour in the Lord, and my Ingagements being soe great unto you upon many Accounts, I cold [could] doe noe lesse then signify unto you of our welbeinge, & of our gratious & prosperous Journey, which the Lord vouchsafed us, Praised & honoured bee his name; Wee came to Lancaster in 8: dayes, where wee stayed 2: dayes, in Regard of the

Menn & Weomens Quarterly Meettinge, Beinge both there of one day, which wee cold not well passe till they were over, and soe yesternight wee came to Swarthmore, where wee found our Family well, & every way Comfortable, Praised & honoured bee the Lord; My Husband held out better then cold bee Expected, & was better in his health, but very weary: Wee mett with Morgan Watkins at Lancr [Lancaster] who hath done great service in these Northerne parts, & has had somethinge to doe with the 2: Jues [Justices] and is partly Confident, hee may bee a moderater in the case, but there is litle probability of it, for they have had A Meettinge last 4th day, & its as unlike as ever,—My Sonn Lower & daughter doe Remember there deare Love to thee & thy wife; as thou hast oppertunity, I shall bee glad to heare from thee;—This is all at present from.-

Thy Deare Friende in the Lord
MF:

My Husband Remembers his deare Love
to thee, & thy wife.-

H.S.P. Penn-Forbes Collection 2:56. Addressed: "To William Penn These Leave this with Phillip Forde at the signe of the hood & scarfe in Bowland neare Cheapside These in London".

138 TO WILLIAM PENN SEPTEMBER 13, 1675

"You have seene losseings & Changes but the foundation of God stands sure."

Deare W:P:

In the deare & pretious truth, which makes pretious, & makes pure & holy, in this is my deare & eternall love remembered unto thee & unto thy deare wife, both whom the Lord has made honourable, & whom may be glorious Instruments, in the hand of the Lord for his servise & honour, O my dearely beloved, keepe Close & neere to the pretious & to the pure & liveing testimony of the liveing God, in your owne hearte that never varyes nor Changes, you have seene losseings & Changes but the foundation of God stands sure, & the stone that is cut out of the Mountaine without hands, will breake to peices all Images though they be of gold or of silver [Dan. 2:45], beware of men, that said they were Gods but they shall die like men, this is a time of tryall, [with?] the True touchstone & perilous & the serpent is very Cunning & is close at worke & will appeare as an Angell of light [2 Cor. 11:14], keepe cleare & all is safe for the topstone is laid, which cannot be moved, & the Lord & his truth & the Lamb shall have the victory, & you will see that all things will worke together for good to those that love God, & soe the Lord God Almighty keepe & preserve all his pure & Cleane & undefiled in his sight, from your deare friend & sister in the Lord

Margret Fox

My son Lower & all my five daughters
which is now all with me, all their deare
loves is dearely remembered unto you.
Swarthmoore the 13th of the 7mo. 1675

HSP Penn-Forbes Collection 2:57. Addressed: These For William Penn with Care".

139 To Sarah and Susannah Fell March 31, 1677

"I was this Morninge with the Vice Chancelor att his house . . . and hee was very Loveing & Kind to us."

Margaret and George Fox, accompanied by daughter Rachel, visited several Meetings in the North before Margaret returned to Swarthmoor and George went on to London. Margaret was able to visit Sir John Otway, the vice-chancellor of Lancashire, concerning Sarah, who had been imprisoned for about one month in 1676. The reason for her arrest is unknown but probably was her refusal to pay tithes. Sarah had been released from prison, but the case was still pending (Ross, p. 280). The vice-chancellor had helped Margaret when she was in prison several years before, and he again agreed to assist them. His cousin and secretary, Thomas Heblethwaite, was charged with copying a warrant and carrying out various tasks. Margaret gave Sir John Otway a guinea and several shillings to Heblethwaite (JFHS, 2:21–23).

The letter is addressed to Sarah and Susannah Fell. Sarah (ca. 1642–1714) was the most intellectual and accomplished of Margaret's daughters. She served as clerk (chair) of Women's Meetings in Lancashire and London and was a gifted business-

woman, managing the Swarthmoor estates in her mother's absence and keeping account books that are basic information for seventeenth-century historians. She studied Hebrew and preached. In 1681 she married William Meade, who was the co-defendant in William Penn's trial of 1670. They had one son, Nathaniel (Greaves, 1:275).

John Blaykling (1625–1705) of Draw-well offered hospitality to George Fox many times. He was a Quaker who preached, suffered imprisonments, and he wrote one tract (EQW, pp. 584–585).

Richard Clayton, another Friend, was on the staff at Swarthmoor Hall. He had a small estate and traveled in the Quaker ministry (EQW, p. 588).

Draw-well the 31st of the 1st moth, 1677.

Deare Sarah & Susanna.

In the blessed Love & Life that remaines for Ever, in which our deare portion and Inheritance stands & consists: in this is your Father & My deare Love, remembered unto you, knowing that you have A portion and an Inheritance in this, with us: and that It may Increase & multiply, is the desire of OUR SOULES. And by this you may know, that wee are well gott hither, praised bee the Lord, and your Father Is not Altogether so weary as Hee was, but hee cannot endure to ryde but very little Journeys, & Lytes often; but hee is pretty well & harty, praised bee the Lord. I was this Morninge with the Vice Chancelor att his house, Jn [John] Blaykelinge went with mee: and hee was very Loveing & Kind to us, and I acknowledged his favour that Hee had done for us the last Assizes: and I also told him how they threatned the Bayliffe, to Indicte him, & gett him fined: and Hee said, lett him alone for that, hee would see to that; and then I spoke to Him Concerning the order that the Judge gave in open Court the last Assizes, and that it was quasht by the mans Oath, after it was given in open Court; and I desired him to acquaint the Judge with that order: and hee said, Hee would: And hee said, if there was not another order Recorded, to dissanull that former order (which gave thee thy Liberty), then they could doe well enought, but if there was another order, to Continue the Imprisonment, then there could bee nothing done; And hee sent for Tho: Heblethwaite and badd him looke out the Pleas, and hee said, Hee had them in his Poke-mantle at Kendal, and hee would looke them out at Lancaster. thy Father gave mee A Ginny [guinea] to give him & hee was mighty well pleased, and said, Hee Loved SARAH dearly, hee would doe what ever layd in his power for her: I gave Tho: Heblethwaite 5s. and desired him to bee carefull to looke about It, and told him Wee could none of us bee there, and therefore wee Committ it wholy to you: and hee bad mee write to Rich: Cleayton to putt them in minde of It, and to looke about It, and his Mr [Master—Sir John Otway] said soe too: and I give him the warrant, & hee called for Tho: Heblethwaite to take a Coppy of It: and after hee had written It, another young man & hee examined It, & gave mee It, and I saw hee looked for somthing more, and I had A shilling in my pockett, & I gave him Itt: and so they were mighty well pleased, and I beleive they will doe what they cann: and wee had a fine oppertunity with them; and It was somthing strange that wee should light soe, and never forcast for It: for hee has been but two nights at home: and I thinke hee goes away to morrow; For hee said hee thought the Judge would bee in to day. I have written to Rich: Cleayton as they ordered mee, and desired him [paper torn] the order of Henry Bodon: and also to looke about, to see if they did any thing Against Benson: and this Is all that wee cann doe at present. but Leaves It to the Lord. so Remember my dr [dear] & Etternall Love to Mary, & I hope in the Lord wee shall bee at home about this day weeke:

Your Mother In the Lord

M. F.

soe be cherfull in the seed of life which is over all in which you have satesfaction & life & you may anser in the next wee[k] for this i have writin to him to hould acoraspond[ence] with you[.] soe mi love to you & m l [Mary Lower] & frends

g F [George Fox]

the Indeared Salutashon of my love is un to you

R F. [Rachel Fell]

The salutation of m[y] [dea]r Love is to you all e: h:

FHL MSS vol. 101/38. Addressed: "To Sarah Fell att Swarthmoore These with care ddd in Lancashire." Endorsed: "m:F:& to S:F:& the 31, 1st moth 1677. Drawell these enclosed & Compared"; "My Dear & Honourd Grand Mothers Letter to my Dear Aunt Mead and Aunt Ingram before marridges—and a few lines in the Bottom of my Dear Grandfather Foxs and his own hand writing [John Abraham]."

140 TO WILLIAM PENN OCTOBER 1677

"Wee have also Received a very pretious paper of thine, Concerning the seperate meeting."

Margaret praises William Penn for his support of George Fox's position in an important dispute among Quakers, the Wilkinson-Story separation. The dispute is named after John Wilkinson and John Story, two Quakers in the North. The controversy threatened the unity of the movement that Fox, Penn, and others were seeking to achieve. The dispute had many facets, but the most basic issue was: should decisions be made by the individual's sense of God's will or with corporate spiritual guidance? George Fox had worked for years to ensure the continuance of Quakerism by setting up a loose form of governance of monthly and quarterly Meetings. The Wilkinson-Story party did not accept the authority of quarterly Meetings or yearly Meetings and particularly the setting up of Women's Meetings. The latter was not the major source of disagreement, but according to Ingle, gave "inchoate discontent an issue upon which to focus" (p. 252).

For several years there were meetings and debates, and many controversial letters and documents were written. In May 1675 the Wilkinson-Story party had set up their own business Meeting, separate from the Westmorland Quarterly Meeting (Braithwaite, p. 295). In 1677 "The Quarterly Meeting now decided to withdraw Meetings for worship from the houses of disaffected Friends, and thus itself took the step of bringing about a complete schism" (Braithwaite, p. 310). William Penn had sent a letter to Margaret from the Continent and a paper urging peaceful settlement of the dispute (PWP, 1:514). Margaret writes, "we waite in hope, for the Returne of such."

Thomas Langhorne (?–1687) is described in the First Publishers of Truth *as "Convinced 1653 . . . Nouble & Vallient in suffering both Imprisonment and spoileing of his goods to a great valliue . . . He stood as a firme pillar against that spt (spirit) of seperation, & was Instrumentall to preserve some out of that snare." He went to Pennsylvania in 1686 and died shortly thereafter (pp. 271–272).*

*James Fletcher (?–1697) began preaching in 1654 and, according to Nightingale, his "itinerant labours almost eclipsed those of Fox himself in the matter of extensiveness of area" (*Early*, p. 59).*

Richard Johnson (1630–1686) traveled in the ministry in England and Ireland. "He was a man comely both inwardly and outwardly of a cheerful Countenance" (CJ, 2:414).

Richard Ray of Edinburgh was a Scottish minister (PWP, 1:514).

John Wilkinson (?–ca. 1683), a farmer in Westmorland, was converted by Fox at

Firbank Fell in 1652, and he traveled in the Quaker ministry with John Story. He was a gentle person and at first encouraged Women's Meetings, but he later joined Story in opposing them and also the control of Meetings over Friends' lives. "He stressed the role of the Spirit within" (Greaves, 3:325–326).

W.P.

Dear & Faithfull: whom the Lord hath Chosen, & owned & honoured with his everlasting Truth, who hath manifested thy selfe to be a true follower of the Lamb, Blessed art thou for ever, that hath Chosen that Good part, that never shall be taken from thee, but in it thou wilt Live, & Grow, & thrive, & be Cloathed with beauty, Glory & majesty: my heart, & souls Love, is dearly Remembred unto thee & my spirit doth Rejoyce, in thy Faithfullness, & deligence, in the Lords work, & service, who art a Noble, & faithfull Instrument, in the hand of the Almighty: for the spreading abroad of his Truth, & for the exaltation of his Kingdome, O thy Name will be had in everlasting Remembrance, with all the Faithfull, as they Come into that same spirit of Grace, & Life, & power, by which thou art Acted, & Carryed & for the Good service that thou dost for the Lord, & for his Truth & the Gathering of his elect seed, he will Reward it a hundred fold into thy bosome, O: Beautifull is thy feet, that preaches Glad tideings to the poor, & Libertie to the Captives [Isa. 61:1–2] Children yet unborne will bless the Lord for thee,—I Received thy sweet, & blessed Letter, which was much Joy to mee, & many more, to hear of that Good service for the Lord, the day that it Came to my hand here was a meeting: & I was moved of the Lord, that it should be Read in the meeting & It was Great Comfort, & Joy, & Gladness to the hearts of Friends, to heare of thy Good service, & of the Truths prospering, Oh, blessed, & honoured by the holy Lord for ever, who is enlargeing the Borders of his sanctuary—& spreading abroad his Truth, & Blessed are the Publishers of it,—Wee have also Received, a very pretious paper of thine, Concerning the seperate meeting—& yester night we Received another from My Husband (writt from Amsterdam:) very pure & pretious, & to the same purpose; But we doe not know that either of them, will be gott Read amongst them, for Friends hath endeavoured to get thine to them, but they have not done it yet For they will not Receive any to Read them, themselves, & now Friends are seperated from them, & meets apart, & they by themselves so that they will hardly suffer any Friend to Come amongst them—(to Read a paper) for when they mett amongst Friends, they would hardly suffer any thing to be Read quietly, that they Looked upon was against themselves some of them growes more hard, & obstinate then ever; others that is more simple, is troubled, & Tormented, we waite in hope, for the Returne of such; Friends meetings more pretious, powerfull, fresh, & Lively since they went from them, then they have been many years before—

Tho Langhorne is now hear, who gives mee a very Good account of their perticuler meetings, & Generall meetings, & men, & womens meetings, all furnished, with the Lords power, & Liveing presence, praysed, & honoured be the powerfull God, so that (now) all is well, as our hearts Can desire: yet Friends is moved of the Lord to goe amongst them To bear their Testimony agst [against] them: James Fletcher & Richard Johnson is to be with them to morrow at John wilkinsons house & Rich: Ray a scotch Friend is to be with them on the first day he is moved to Goe amongst them, as to a priest in a steeplehouse (to deliver his Testimony: & so Come away.) Its to be feared, they will be very Rough, & boisterous with them but the Lords power is over them, which will bruise them, & break them—Dear w: Friends are very much Gladed, & Refresh'd in the Lord, hereaways on thy behalfe, for that thou hast had a tender Care over Friends, in this thy Great travells, & Journeys, but it is neither sea, nor Land, height nor depth, that Can seperate from the Love of God, which is in Christ Jesus our Lord, which he hath shedd abroad in the hearts of his people—Thy printed epistle was very serviceable, & very dearly Received amongst Friends—Remembr my very dear, & eternall Love, to thy dear wife whom I honour in the Lord for her Faithfulness, & Constancy, & Inocency The Arme of the Almighty preserve, & keep you (both) in that bond & Covenant of Love, & Life; that never Can be broken—My daugh[ters] Sarah[,] Susannah, & Rachells Love, is dearly, & Faithfully Remembered unto you both, & so I know it is with my sonn, & daughter Lower but they doe not know of my writeing now. Robt widd[ers] was here this day, whose dear Love is to thee,—And Tho Langho[rne] also Remembers his dear Love unto thee,—

And so dearly beloved this is all that I have at present but my ne[ver] dyeing Love Remaines with thee, & that I am thy

dear Friend & sister in the
Lord M F

I would desire a Coppy of thy Journall (at) this time for I would have it Recorded here.

The 8 moth 1677.

PWP, *1:512–514, also FHL Portfolio 36.*

141 To William Penn December 11, 1677

"I have been here with my daughter Lower, near a month, & the Lord hath been pleased to try her with a pretty Long & hard travell."

Thomas and Mary Lower were particular friends of William and Gulielma Penn. Here Margaret tells of Mary Lower's difficult labor. Mary had ten children in all, five of whom reached adulthood, and this child, named Loveday, was one of them. She was named for Thomas Lower's aunt, Loveday Hambly of Cornwall. It may be that Margaret's relief at the outcome influenced her view of the local Quaker state of affairs, "the Arme, & power of the Lord, is Gloriously manifested amongst Friends, & Truth prospers, & severall Comes in."

Marshgrange the 11th of 10th moth 1677
W.P.

Dear & Pretious, & Honoured in the Lord, & in his eternall Truth that never Changes, but endures forever, In this is my dear & eternall Love unto thee, & to thy dear wife, even to you both, whom the Lord hath Chosen, vessells for his honour, & service, Blessed & happy are yee, that hath Chosen to suffer with the People of God, The Immortall Riches, & Treasuries, attends the Faithfull, which noe vulterous eye nor venomous beast never knowes, but happy & blessed, are all those that Continues & endures to the end, & in the end those obtaines the Crowne,—Dear W: I Received an Acceptable Letter from thee, which gave mee notice of my dear Husbands safe arrivall in England, which was very gratefull, & delightfull to mee, & my heart is much engaged to thee for it, & though I did not write to thee since, yet thy dear Love, & Care hath been much in my minde, which by these Lines I doe signifie unto thee,—I have been here with my daughter Lower, near a month, & the Lord hath been pleased to try her with a pretty Long, & hard travell [travail, i.e. in labor], but blessed, & honoured bee his holy name, In the end his Arme, & power appeared for her, & brought her deliverance, when there was noe other to help, two days since, she was delivered of a daughter, a very bigg Large Child, which Caused her travell to be hard; & we hope in the Lord, she is upon Recovery—And so dear W: this I was willing to acquaint thee off [of], knowing thy dear & Faithfull Love, & so all things here are very well; & the Arme, & power of the Lord, is Gloriously manifested amongst Friends, & Truth prospers, & severall Comes in, & is Added dayly, & the uncleane spirit is tormented & vexes & frets, & Growes harder, & harder, & the Lord doth more, & more manifest it to the Simple, & it is driven into a Narrow Compass, & Growes weaker & weaker,—And so blessed are the Faithfull, that dwells in the Lords sanctuary, for they will dayly be enlarged, & things will Come to a period in time, & sinn will stay the wicked, but the Righteous, will Grow, & flourish, & shine as stars in the Firmament: And so the Lord God Almighty preserve & keep the simple, & Innocent hearts from the snares of the enemie, & the Lord keep all Dear Friends, Faithfull to the Lord, in whom is everlasting strength & safety And so in this pure & pretious eternall everlasting Truth Dear Friend I bid thee, & thy Dear wife farewell—

From thy Dear Friend
and sister in the Lord
M:F:

My son & daughter Lowers dear Love)
is dearly Remembred to thee, & thy wife:)

HSP Penn-Forbes Collection 2:58. Addressed: "To William Penn These ddd Leave this with Edward Mann Hosier next doore to the Golden Lyon within Bishoppsgate in London". Endorsed: "Marg Fox 11-10-77".

142 TO GEORGE FOX JULY 18, 1678

"Thy company would be more and better to us than all the world."

Only seven letters of Margaret to George Fox survive; undoubtedly there were many more. In this she expresses her longing to see him, but as always, "we must all submit to the Lord's will and time." After his two-year stay at Swarthmoor Hall, where he recovered his health, he was again on his travels to encourage Friends and their Meetings.

Leonard Fell had brought Margaret a gift from George. Other times he had sent her cloth, once scarlet and once Spanish black (Crosfield, p. 171). The Mary Fell mentioned here was probably Leonard Fell's wife (Ross, p. 319).

Margaret refers to "my daughter Rous. Poor woman!" because Margaret Rous had gone to Barbados with her husband and several children, a long and dangerous journey. Bethiah, their twelve-year-old daughter, stayed at Swarthmoor.

Swarthmoor, 18th of 5th mo., 1678

Dear Love,—Glad I am to hear that the Lord preserves thee in health and capacity to travel in His work and service, for which I praise His holy name. We hope and expect He will draw thee homewards in His blessed time. Thou art much expected and longed for here, but we must all submit to the Lord's will and time. I received thy kind token by Leonard, which I did not expect, but I know it is thy true love to remember us (thus). I thought to have sent something by Mary Fell to thee, but I (considered) thou would only buy something with it for me, as thou used to do, which caused me to omit it. I perceive thou has sent things to the children by Leonard, he hath not yet delivered them; but thy company would be more and better to us than all the world, or than all the earth can afford; but only for the Lord's Truth and service (are we willing to resign it), we would not exchange it for all beside.

This day Isabel set forward on her way to Scotland, Thomas and Mary Lower, Sarah, Susanna, and Rachel, with little Bethiah, their love and duty are dearly remembered unto thee, and gladly would they see thee here. I am glad to find thou hath writ to my daughter Rous. Poor woman! I am afraid she will have a heartless being there. The Lord uphold her over all her trials. We desire much to hear from thee, and what way thou passest. All things are well here with us. Praised and honoured be the Lord.

From thy endeared and loving wife.
M. F.

Thirnbeck MSS 16 (per JFHS *v. 9 [1912] pp. 134–140). Also Webb, pp. 258–59 and Crosfield, pp. 170–71. Endorsed: "M. F. to G. F., 5 mo., '78 [George Fox] and "My dear and honoured Grandmother's affectionate letter to my dear and honoured Grandfather Fox [John Abraham]" per Webb.*

143 TO KATHERINE EVANS AUGUST 3, 1678

"I have heard severall speake of that Ladyes desire, after the Lord, & his truth, for which my heart is glad."

Katherine Evans (?–1692) was an elderly Friend, like Margaret, who "lived to a great age" after an active and hazardous life (CJ, 2:375). Between 1658 and 1662 she and another woman spent four years as prisoners of the Inquisition in Malta and Rome. Henry Fell wrote in a letter to Gerrard Roberts in June 1661 from Spain: "I have this further to certify concerning the two women Friends, Catherine Evans and the other,—that they are prisoners in the Inquisition in Malta: for this morning we spoke with one Captain Harris . . . who was there, and endeavoured very much to have them released, but could not. . . . Captain Harris saith he himself did proffer to be bound in a £500 bond that the two Friends should not set foot upon the island again, if they would release them and send them aboard his ship; but they would not, except he would engage that they should never come within the Catholic dominions again. He made that offer unknown to the women—he was not given the liberty of seeing them, but the Consul . . . went in and saw them. They were knitting and he saw them have bread and water . . . they said they were pretty well and contented . . . "

The two women were finally released and wrote about it in a book, This is a Short Relation of some of the cruel sufferings of Katherine Evans and Sarah Chevers in the Inquisition in the Isle of Malta *(Ross, pp. 394–395).*

In the following Margaret is replying to a letter from Katherine Evans that was a request both for advice and for a servant for a "Lady." The lady was probably Lady Anne Conway known for her philosophical studies with Henry More. Lady Conway joined Quakers in 1677 and "in the last years of her life she lived at Ragley surrounded by Quakers" (Fraser, Weaker Vessell, *p. 350). She suffered debilitating headaches all of her life and for this reason she searched for Quaker servants: "for if they prove what they seeme to be, lovers of quiet and retirement, they will fitt the circumstances I am in (that cannot endure any noise) better then others." Lady Conway found that "my converse with them is . . . to receive health and refreshment from them." William Penn and George Fox had visited and corresponded with her. Priscilla Evans, the daughter of Katherine Evans, was in Lady Conway's service for a time, which explains Katherine Evans' interest (Nicolson,* Conway Letters, *pp. 421–422).*

To answer the request for guidance Margaret writes consolingly of her own trust in God, of "the safe harbor & rest, & habitaion, of all, that have been tossed too & fro." She sends Lady Conway her "deare Love" and prays that "the Lord God Almighty strengthen her faith . . . in her weake, and Antient dayes." Many people wrote to Margaret for help and advice.

Katherin Evans. Deare Friend

In the Blessed Everlasting truth of the pure God; My Love I dearly Remember unto thee; and to all Deare & Faithfull friends; that wished well into Sion, and its my continuall Labour & travell, & soules desire, to Almighty God, for the Enlargment & Prosperity, of his Everlasting truth, in the hearts of all, in whom hee hath, in any measure quickened and Enlightened, & raised A breathing desire after his truth, surely he will hold forth his hand of dear Love, & strength & Assistance unto such, whose soules breathes, & desires after him. I have heard severall speake of that Ladyes desire, after the Lord, & his truth, for which my heart is glad, that any lookes over the worlds Ambition, & height, which many Thousands & Millions are drowned in, but blessed & happy are all those, who looke after the Lord, that was before ever Sinn, Death, or Man, was, hee it is, that is the center and being of all the Faithfull, and the safe harber & rest, & habitation, of all, that have been tossed too & fro, when they come to him, hee is A Rocke of Safety, and A Rocke of Inheritance & rest forevermore; and the onely satisfier of the Immortall soule, that breathes continually after him, which all the visible universe cannot doe,—I would have thee to Remember my deare Love, unto the Lady, and its best for her, to settle, & fix, and fasten her minde upon the Lord, which will bee her onely repose, & comfort, & never matter nore minde outward things, but lett them hang of themselves, & come & goe, as the divine providence orders, for greatest concerne is peace with God, and that shee bee faithfull to his Light & spiritt, that God hath placed in her heart, & obeydient to the measure of grace, that will bring her salvation, and that which teaches, the denieing of all ungodlinesse & unrighteousness, & unhollynesse, & teaches to live Righteously, & holily, in this present evill world; and shee hath cause to blesse & Praise the Lord, that hath given her time &

oppertunity, to learne this Lesson, in her weake, and Antient dayes; The Lord God Almighty strengthen her faith and beliefe in Christ Jesus, who is come A Light into the world, that whosoever beleeve in him, should not perish, but have Everlasting life, there stands every ones life, & salvation, in the faith of Gods Elect, which is his light.—I Received thy Letter, but as to the substance of what thou writes, I cann say litle, for our parts, wee are bought with A price, & our service is wholly for the Lord, wee are none of our owne, nor cannott bee serv[an]ts unto Men [1 Cor 7:22–23]:—In these Northern parts, I doe not know of any friend, that would suite such A place, but I should thinke, if Enquiry were made in the South parts, there might bee Some found, that such A place might bee serviceable unto, that stood in need; for though they were but meane in the outward; if they bee Rich in God, & in his truth, that is the durable riches, that is worth looking after, And that is worthy to bee prised above all.—This is all that I cann say, onely I desire that my deare Love may bee Remembered in the Family, to Elizabeth Wingfeild & any other that feares the Lord; and my Soules desire is for their Prosperity, & growing up, in the Lords Etternall truth, and in his grace and in the knowledge of the Lord Jesus Christ, which is better, then A Thousand Worlds: Soe with my deare Love to thee, conclude am

Thy Deare Friend & sister
in the Lord
Margarett Fox:

Spence 3/Suppl. Folder. Endorsed: "A Copy of A Letter from M. F. to Katherine Evans the 3d of the 6 mo. 1678"; "The within Coppy is an Excellent Letter of my Dear and Honour'd Grandmother to that Excellent woman and Eminent Servant of the Lord Katherine Evans".

144 To Friendly Reader October 18, 1679

"So Reader[,] if you think that these following Answers be sharp, & Tart, Consider the time, & the height of bitterness that they were in."

In 1679 Margaret wrote this informal draft introduction to a collection of letters that she had written in the early days of the movement, in the 1650s and 1660s, ad-

dressed to "Priests & Professors." It is a charming, open recollection of her feelings and experiences of that time and includes: a description of George Fox's first appearance at Swarthmoor; the reaction of her pastor, William Lampitt, and some of her neighbors; and the importance of her husband Judge Fell's support. She describes her overwhelming conviction of the rightness of the new doctrine then and at present. The proposed volume was never published and only brief phrases of the introduction and letters appear in edited versions in the Works.

By 1679 her faith and beliefs were still as strong, but she was able to look back and see how immoderate her language had been, though it was suitable for those hard times. At the end of the document is a list of the biblical phrases that she and others used to debate theological issues.

*A quote from Christopher Story's memoir gives his response, repeated by many visitors, to a visit to Swarthmoor Hall in 1679. "Taking meetings in the way, I came to Swarthmore on the seventh-day [Saturday], and was at their meeting on the first-day [Sunday], where was George Fox, Margaret his wife, and four of her daughters, and all very loving and kind" (*Life of Christopher Story *in* Friends' Library *1:150).*

*"Priest Lampitt" was William Lampitt (?–1677), Oxford-educated minister of Ulverston, the Fell's parish church before Margaret became a Quaker. He was well respected, and the loss of all members but one (Judge Fell) of the most prominent family in the parish was understandably a cause of grievance to him. Nightingale writes of him: "William Lampit deserves to occupy a place of prominence among the illustrious men of the heroic age; but George Fox found in him one of his most powerful antagonists because he was much after his own type . . . He was ejected from his living . . . previous to his advent at Ulverston. At the latter place he was outed through the Uniformity Act." (*Early*, p. 21) Larry Ingle concludes: "The truth was that, just like Fox, Lampit was strongly attached to his own views." It was a clash of ideas and probably of personalities too (pp. 86–87).*

Frdly [Friendly] Reader

Here followeth some Letters, & Answers to Preists & Professors, which was written in the beginning att the first entrance of Truth amongst us; And I desire thee to Consider with mee a Little, the time, & the state, & Condition that we were in, when the blessed visitation of god Came first amongst us: we had not so much as heard of the people called quakers till wee heard of Geo: Fox Coming towards us. It may be when he was 20 miles off. And when he Came among us And opened us a book that we had never Read in, nor Indeed had never heard that it was our duty to Read in itt. to witt/ the Light of Christ in our Consciences[,] And our mindes never being turned towards itt before,

For my part when I heard him speak of it, & declare of itt, that itt was our Teacher, & that we should beleive in itt & turne our mindes to itt, & that the Letter killed, as the Apostle said. And that Christ, & the Apostles words was not ours but theirs that spoak them. when I heard him declare of these & many other things in the very first meeting in Ulverston steeplehouse where we were to have a Lecture sermon preached by preist Lampitt that very day. It pleased the Lord so to open my understanding Imediately in the time of G Fs [George Fox's] declaration. That I saw perfectly Just then that wee were all wrong, & that we were but Theives, that had stollen the scriptures. which caused mee to shed many tears. And I satt downe in my pew & wept all the while that the sd [said] Lampitt preacht, & I did not know what he said for I saw that all that we had done before was nothing worth And Lampit was willing that G F should speak in the steeplehouse before him, for he Lookt that G F would have been one with him for hee lookt upon himselfe to be one of the highest priests in that day—But when G F spoak, & opened things, & turned all their preachings together & manifested them all to be wrong that was out of the light and out of the doctrine of Christ & did not preach the Light, etc: But when he Came to touch them then they grew weary, & very Angry, & so sett the Churchwardens to haill G F out: But I stood up in my pew & lookt att the Churchwarden; & he stood behind G F : & lett him alon [alone] & G F spoak on a great while, till att Last they were so Angry, that one John Sawrah [John Sawrey, Letter 3] who was a Justice Caused G F to be hailld out: Many passages Could I declare of these things which I shall not trouble the Reader with at this time; however that sight, & Convincement that god had opened in mee, Continued with mee, & I grew in itt, & many more was Convinced besides mee, & a great Astonishment there was in the Country, but the Truth grew & encreased amongst us, & the Lords eternall power seared open many, & many was moved of the Lord to goe to the steeplehouses to Cry against the preists, so that it Raised such a Bitterness, & envy amongst the preists & professors, that all was on a fire, & being that they had never heard nor known of such things before, they all Concluded It was of the devill, & that it was sorcery & witchcraft, & that they gave us bottles to drink, & tyed strings about our armes, & fearfull lyes, & storyes, they Raised up against us; but the Lord preserved us, faithfull to him—And we kept our Integrity & mett together—At our house att Swarthmore with my Husbands Consent: And he being the Cheife magistrate in the Country, they Could not fall upon us in persecuting of us as their hearts desired. And so that Tormented them worst of all, because the Truth did spring & spread, & Increase, & they knew not how to gett itt supprest For all the great profession that was then in this nation of god, & xt, & ordinances: yet when Christ Jesus Came, & visited us in his power, & in the demonstration of his spirit, then they stood Against him, as bad as the Jewes in the days of his flesh, being that the Truth struck at all their profession, their foundation being false, standing not on Christ the Light—It was strange to think that all the ministers, that professed such high things should be all out of the doctrine of Christ; yet when we Come to witness, that the Light of Jesus which is the key that opens into the misteryes of gods kingdome & sees Christ the stone that is layd in sion [Sion] for a foundation, that all the prophets & apostles & saints of the Ld [Lord] is built upon, & they all denying this Light, & would not owne itt. Then we saw with the Light that they were all in the darkness, & turned out together, professors, & profaine, For if we doe but Consider how It was in the days that Christ in his flesh when he was upon earth, That then the pharises & scribes, & high preists that was the greatest professors, these were his greatest enemies, & Called him a devill, & Belzebub: & those were they that he pronounced the woe onto[;] but the publicans, & sinners; & the multitute that followed him, he had compassion on them, & wrought miricles for their sakes: And so it was in his spirituall Appearance, that the highest preists, & professors, was & is our greatest enemies. And so to Returne againe when the high preists of our times saw that the truth struck at their Foundation, & Root, & turned them out of their place of teaching, & brought the Light to be peoples teacher, that so there would be no need of them to teach & so manifested them not to be the ministers of Christ, but of Antichrist, & thereby turned them out of their maintenances & benefices. They seeing that the Truth struck at all this & that this would be the end if the Truth prospered. This made them all madd. so that they Joyned hand, in hand against the Truth, & they Petitioned the Parliament. & petitioned Crumwell [Oliver Cromwell], & Rich: Crumwell [Richard Cromwell], And the preists, & professors in our parts began to write against us: And G:F: being gone out of the Countrey First brought things to mee, & I answered them. And I was but Young in the truth yet I had a perfect & a pure Testimony of god in my heart, for god & his Truth. And I beleive I Could that day have Layd downe my Life for it. And I was very Zeallous in itt. And they were so wickedly bent against it That all the wicked names, & Calumnyes that their hearts Could Invent they Cast upon the Truth. And said It was of the devill, & satanicall, & Come from Rome with multitudes of such wicked Lyeing expressions:—

So Reader[,] if you think that these following Answers be sharpe, & Tart, Consider the time, & the height of bitterness that they were in against the Truth & its followers in Its Life & Infancy[;] And they were Resolved to the utmost of their power to subvert itt & bring it under; but the Lords power was over them & prevailled against them And our Answers layd so heavy, & hard upon them that very few of them ever Answered Againe, And now Reader[,] I have Informed thy minde & given thee to understand how things was with us at that time, which was much of it six or seven & twenty years since. And now let the witness of god in thy Conscience Judge what a dark time that was, & what an hard passage truth had past thorow such a body of darkness, when the beast, & false prophet stood up for their Lives, & maintenance, in warr with the Truth, & the followers of itt. And their Armaur & weapons was lyes, & slanders, & false accusations, & the Lords testimony in his servents saw them, & spoke to them as they were; & shutt them out with Judgement or else they would not have done with writing when they Called them Lyers, & beasts, & false prophets, as the scriptures Calls them; that made them say that Frds was Reillers [railers] because they gave them names as the scriptures give to such of them. when they Ly they tell them they Lye & when they Blaspheme against god & his Truth they tell them soe & this they account hard Language: And so Reader, the Lord open thy understanding that thou may Read with a single eye to the Lord & in itt Judge between Truth & error.

M: F:

Swarthmore the 18th of 8m 1679

Here followeth some scripture Language which sometimes we did give to the preists, & professors, in our words & writeings to them where att they were offended:

For David saith in psal: 58: the wicked are estranged from the wombe, & goe astray as soon as they are borne speaking Lyes; Their poysen is like the poysen of a serpent, they are like the deafe Adder that stoppeth her ear [Ps. 58:3–4]—And in psalm 140 they have sharpend their tongues like a serpent, Adders poysen is under their Lipps [Ps. 140:3]—And the prophet Isaiah saith, dust is the Serpents meat [Isa. 65:25] And in Isai:

27, The Great & stronge sword is drawne, which perisheth Leviathan, that peirceing serpent, even Leviathan that Crooked serpent.—[Isa. 27:1] And Christ saith in Math: 23: yee serpents, yee Generation of vipers; how Can yee escape the damnation of hell [Matt. 23:33]: with other such Language in that Chapt. And in Mark 12: Christ Jesus spoak to them that devoured widdowes houses & for a pretence make long prayers, these shall Receive greater damnation [Mark 12:40]. Mark 3:29: he that shall blaspheme against the holy ghost shall never be forgiven but is in danger of eternall damnation—John 6:70: Christ saith, have not I Chosen you 12, & one of you is a devill Acts 13:10 the Apostle said, O full of all subtilty, & all mischief, you Child of the devill, you enemy of Righteousness wilt you not Cease to pervert the Right wayes of the Lord John 8:44: ye are of your father the devill, & 1 John,3:8 he that Committeth sinn is of the devill, for the devill sinned from the beginning—1 Tim 3:6, not a novice, Least being Lifted upp with pride, he fall into Condemnation of the devill. -Rom.13:2 whosoever Resisteth power, Resisteth the ordinance of god, & they that Resist shall Receive to themselves damnation.—Mark 16:16 he that beleiveth not shall be damned—Rom:14:3 [Rom.14:23] he that doubts is damned—And 2: Thessa 2:12: that they all might be damned.—And 2 Thessa,1:8, when the Lord Jesus shall be Revealled from heaven in flames of fire taking vengeance on them that know not god, & that obey not the Gospell of our Lord Jesus Christ, who shall be punished with everlasting destruction, from the presence of the Lord, & from the Glory of his power—[2 Thess. 1:7–9] with many other scriptures of the like Language.

Spence 3/135, 124.

145 To John Abraham April 17, 1681

"I hope and Disier the lord may Lengthen thy Dayes . . . fore his glory yet Longer."

John Abraham (1629–1681) was the first Quaker in Manchester, active since the 1650s. He had been ill at the time of Margaret's letter. She was writing from London where she had accompanied daughter Sarah for her marriage to William Meade.

Besides Margaret and George Fox, two other sisters, Isabel Yeamans and Margaret Rous were present (Ross, pp. 314–315; JFHS, *9(1912) 139).*

Persecution against Quakers continued even into the 1680s, and Margaret and George were fighting a case in court involving tithes. William Meade was assisting them with legal advice (Ingle, pp. 276–277).

Ralph Ridgway was another Manchester Friend. He had "lost much blood" in an incident in 1659 and was in Lancaster prison in 1661 (Besse, 1:138, 309). In 1693 his house was "recorded For a Meeting place of Quakers" (Nightingale, Early, *p. 185).*

London the 17th of 2 mo. (81)
J: A:

Deare Frind; In The holy Preashas [precious] puer truth that Induers [endures] & Reamanes for Ever in this is my Deare and Eternall Love Remembred unto thee: and glade I am to heare of thy Recovery and I hope and Disier the lord may Lengthen thy Dayes & Prelong thy Life & presarve thee fore his honer and Sarvice: that thou may bee an Instrument in his hand fore his glory yet Longer: as thou hast beene fore meny yeares by past: and it is my Joy to heare that the Lords worke prospers amongest you: fore my Disiers is that his name may bee gloryes In the Earth: & that his Blesed truth may more & more Increses—

Wee ar all well thorow mercey: my Husbands Deare Love is unto thee[.] wee knowe not when wee may Returne home fore the Last terme ouer [our] Advarsaires did not apeare against us but the next terme which begines the next weeke wee Expect they will Prosecut against us Eader [either] fore bodyes or goods: but wee ar given up in the will of the Lord Beeleving all these things will worke together for good & knowing hee Sufereth nothing to befalle his Children but what Shall bee fore his honer & there Comfort[.] howe then cane these things Seeme hard[,] fore hee is on ouer Side & will pleade the Cause of his Innocent peoplle & will not Suffer allwayes the Roode [rod] of the wicked to Lye upon the Backes of the Rightuous—[Ps. 125:3]

As to what thee writes to have my Answere in and know what I cane object about the Consarne menshoned: things of that natuer is not Fitt to bee Committed to paper but to bee Discorsed of Face to Face: my Deare Love is to Ralfe Ridgway & his wife; I account my Selfe very much oblidged to them for Sparing there Daughter So Longe to accompany my Daughter Sus: [Susannah]

Frinds heare ar generally well & meetings peaceable at present but in likelyhood persecution is approaching[;] but the will of the Lord bee done Saith my Soulle: whoe cane turne the wrath of mane [man] to his glory & the Rest hee will Restrene—

this is the most at present but the Remembrance of my Daugters love to thee. I am in Some hast having other leters to writ So must Conclude

Thy Deare Frinde in the Holly truth
M: F:

Spence 3/180–181. Addressed: "To Ralph Ridgway, hosier, at his Shopp in Manchester these in Lancashier"; "Give this to John Abraham".

146 To George Fox Mid-1681

"It seems hee [John Abraham] very much Disiered that his Sonn might bee alitle whille with my Sonn Lower."

*The handwriting, spelling, and grammar of this letter are abominable. An editor comments: "Had we not been definitely informed (by an endorsement) that it was written by Rachel Fell, we should not have supposed it the work of any of the Swarthmore sisters" (*JFHS*, 9[1912] 138).*

Margaret writes to George Fox shortly after her return from London. She expresses the wish that he also would return to Swarthmoor: "I should bee glade if thou woueld Incline to come home;" and she gives him the news of events in the North. Persecution continued, and several Friends had died.

She writes particularly of John Abraham (Letter 145) and of his son, Daniel Abraham (1662–1731). The son was "much Dedgectt [dejected] & cast downe with his Father Death" and wished to stay with Mary and Thomas Lower at Marsh Grange. Thomas Lower was a trustee of John Abraham's considerable estate. Daniel Abraham's stay of several months with the Swarthmoor family evidently cheered him considerably, for in December upon returning to his home in Manchester, he wrote: "Dear Rachel, for to declare the nature and full extent of that centrinal, fixed and abiding love [etc.]" and they were married in 1683.

Rachel and Daniel Abraham had four children, only one of whom, John, survived childhood. Daniel bought Swarthmoor Hall, and he and his family lived there with Margaret. Rachel, the youngest daughter, was always particularly close to her

mother. Daniel was in prison in 1684, 1685, and from 1702 to 1704, primarily for refusal to pay tithes (Ross, pp. 315–317).

Deare Love

In the blesed holy Euenity [unity] of the Seed of Life that Indeureth & Remeneth for Ever in this is my Etarnell & Deare Love Remembred un to thee & by this thou may know that wee gott well to Lancaster In about tene dayes after wee left London[.] wee stayed some dayes in Chesher & Lancashier & had 2 meeting amongest them, & then came to ouer quarterly meeting which was the largest that wee have Ever had both for men & wemen & the lords powerfull precence was with us in a gloryes maner[,] prayses to his name fore Ever—there is noething done yett agenest the Friends only the adversaryes atorne [attorney] has Charged severall persons that is the Friends Creditorers not to Receve any of ther goods, hee makes greatt boasts whatt hee will doe againest them butt yett hee sath hee wants his atorety [authority?] which will com in a litle tim frome the King & Bishopes & then hee will Regaine his greatt Charges; it weare well if Inquiery weare made wheded [whether] ther is any such thing or noe: hee has brought a Reportt frome London that thou ofered to agree with him & sentt for an accouent of his Charges: but noe body beeleves his Lyes but those that ar like him Selfe: Friends ar Jenaraly well & truth prospers & getts grouend in these parts[,] blesed for Ever bee the Lords holy name;—will barnes of Sancke is ded[,] all so John Badally of Chesher: & John Abram: Roberd widers [Letter 8] wentt that way to see him butt hee was Departed some houer beefore hee gott theder but hee stayed his Funerall: hee has left a very Sweett Saver [savour] beehind him[,] both amongest the world & Friends[.] hee was A sarvsabell [serviceable] man in his life & his Death was very comfortabell to all that was with him & hee left a living testimony for the truth, Inded I was Refreshed to heare the accouent that Friends gave of him in the time of his siknes & at his Departuer; John hadacke and severabell [several] other minstering Friends was at his funerall & had greatt Service; ther being meny of the greatt ones of the Contry & towne[.] his sonn [Daniel Abraham] Came to the quarterly meeting to take Friends advice about his Father will. hee has left him & his mother Excecters & Tho: Ridgers & Rodger hadacke & my sone Lower Trustey: it seemes hee very much Disiered that his Sonn might bee alitle whille with my Sonn Lower & trully the younge mane is so much Dedgectt [dejected] & cast downe with his Father Death that I doe not see how wee cane Denie him; & hee has beene for many month prety much Exerciesed in his minde & having noe body to bee with at home but what is noe [not] Friends it is pretty harde & it beeing all so his Father['s] greatt Disier to hav him alitle time with my sone wee Disier to know what thy minde is consarning it[.] hee does Desier it but for alitle time for hee Intends to undertake partt of his father trade—I was yester day at march granges [Marsh Grange] to see my Daughter [Mary Lower] whoe is prety well & her Children[.] my Sonn & shee Remembred there Deare loves un to thee—I have spoken severall times to Leneard Fell [Letter 116] aboutt cominge to thee[,] but hee thinkes his bisnes will not admitt him to come this 2 month[,] which I am afread will bee too longe for thee to wantt one to bee constantly with thee. I Desier thee lett us heare from thee how thou artt in health & how every thing is with thee: I should bee glade if thou woueld Incline to come home, that thou might gett alitle Restt[.] mee thinkes its the most Comfortabell when one has a home to bee ther but the lord give us patience to beare all things[.] this is the most at presentt but my Deare Everlasting unallterabell love which thinkes noe Evell I am thy

Deare loving and Fathfull wife
M. F.

Susan & Rachell Remembers
there Dearest love & Duty un to thee.

Thirnbeck MSS 16 and JFHS, 9 *(1912) 138–140. Addressed: "To Issabell Yeamans leave this at Gorge Whitthead at the Sine of the wheatsheaf in Houndsdich—this in Lond."; "To Issabell Yeamans These D D to bee Left at George Whittheds at the Sine of Wheat." Endorsed: "A letter of my Dear Grandmothers to my Dear and Honourd GrandFather Fox writt by my Dear Mother when she was a Made [maid] where in there is an Account of my Dear Grandfathers Abraham's Sickness and Death with a Good Account of his excellent Life &c."*

147 To Thomas Lower September 28, 1683

"I know certainly, the Lord will never be wanting to you, as ye keep faithful and true, and single-hearted to him."

*Thomas Lower (Letter 126) was arrested in 1683 while he was in Cornwall, his former home, on business. He was praemunired and sentenced to prison for life, but was released by royal proclamation in 1686 (*DNB*). It seems unlikely that Margaret would write to her son-in-law without giving news of his wife and children at Marsh Grange; the letter in the* Works *is probably heavily edited.*

The years from 1680 to 1685 saw heavy persecution of dissenters, and Margaret was a particular target. In September 1683 she and her newly married daughter, Rachel, and her husband, Daniel Abraham, were fined and imprisoned for sixteen days (Ross, p. 319).

To Tho. Lower, and his Fellow-Sufferers for the Testimony of Jesus, when they were Praemunir'd and Prisoners in Lanceston-Goal.

Dear Son Lower, &c.

In the dear and precious Blessed Unity of the Eternal Spirit, and Fellowship of the Gospel of Peace, in this is my Heart and Soul's Love remembred unto thee, and to all thy dear Brethren and fellow-Prisoners with thee, that suffer for the Testimony of Jesus; my Soul's Desire is to the Powerful God for you all, That you may be more than Conquerors in Christ Jesus, who is the great King, and Lord over all, and hath all Power in Heaven and Earth in his Hands, and all the Inhabitants of the Earth are but as Grasshoppers before him [Isa. 40:22]; and therefore with Hearts and Courage may his Servants and Children suffer for him, without Fear or Fainting, under those that have but Power over the outward Man: The Lord preserve you in the Dominion over them all; and I am glad to hear in every Letter that comes from thee, that ye are well satisfy'd and content: And I know certainly, the Lord will never be wanting to you, as ye keep faithful and true, and single-hearted to him; his Eye beholds and sees all that his and your Enemies can do unto you, and a just and righteous Reward from him they will surely receive, &c.

And my dear Love is unto thee, in that which never changes, which gives Peace, and Content, and Faith to look over that which changes.

Thy dear Mother in the Lord,
M. F.

Swarthmore, the 28th of the 7th Month, 1683.

Works, *p.* 530.

148 To the Justices of the Sessions at Lancaster January 1684

"Wee are Informed [accused] by the Oath of two men, the One of them known to be a sheep staylor."

George Fox wrote: "My wife and I and several other Friends were sued in Cartmel-Wapentake Court in Lancashire for small tithes and we had demurred to the jurisdiction of the court" (Fox.Short, p. 315). Here Margaret is writing to the justices concerning several violations of the law in this case.

Firstly, she was fined twenty pounds, which was the fine for an unmarried woman, and she had been married to George Fox for fourteen years. The use of her earlier name was a challenge to the validity of Quaker marriages.

Secondly, she was protesting the use of unsavory informers whose word could not be trusted. The Conventicle Act of 1670 had a "provision that rewarded informants with a third of the fines" collected. There were many complaints about all aspects of the persecution of dissenters, but this proviso was a particular invitation for abuse of the legal system. Greaves writes: "Charles II's government was constantly faced with the necessity of monitoring radical activity and employing repressive measures" and thus "accusations from malicious informers, agents provocateurs, and enemies of nonconformity" were used (Greaves, Enemies, *pp. 154–155, 249).*

Thirdly, being fined and imprisoned for the same offense was illegal.

Justice Miles Dodding (?–1683) was an active Justice of the Peace in Lancashire and related to Sir Daniel Fleming and Colonel Richard Kirkby, the chief prosecutors of Margaret and other Quakers in the North (CJ, 1:463).

Jany. 1683–4.

To the Justises of the Sessions At Lancaster:

I Desire Justise of This Bench

You are the men the Law hath provided to determine Matters Concerning this Act[.] I desire you to take Notice Of the Abuse & rong [wrong] that is done to Mee:

I have been Marryed to my Husband this fourteen Years & the King & his Counsell have allowed our Mariage as I have It to shew in his pardon under the Broad Seal.

And the Act doth say Expressly that noe feme Covert, [under cover or protection of a husband] shall be fined above 10s [shillings] & Contrary to the words of the Act, They have fined Mee 20£ & did make distress of above 30£ worth of Goods & sold them the next day; & would not except of an appeall when It was desired, And This as wee are Informed by the Oath of two men, the One of them known to be a sheep staylor [stealer], & the Other kept Company with a Woman that was hanged within this twelv month: who confessed to Justiss Dodding that shee had stolen for him seven years;

Now I desire you to take these Things into your Consideration, why I may not have the Liberty of my Mariage as well as all our Friends in England beside; & that I must be made a Widow; that they may abuse Mee in my credit & reputation & allso be ruined in My Estate.

I & my poore Friends desires Justiss at Your hands for They prosecute us with two Acts at one Time; Contrary to the Express Words of the Act; & as I am Informed delivers out two warrants upon one day, for two severall Acts:

I doe not believe It is the Kings Mind to have his Subjects ruined.

Margret Fox

County Record Office at Preston: QSP 576/4. Also in Nightingale, Early, *pp. 155–156. Checked by Susan V. Hartshorne.*

149 To ? 1684

"The Mony is not disposed to the Poore or to the Kings use that wee can heare of."

A letter of George Fox to Margaret dated October 8, 1684, begins: "Dearly Beloved, There is a rumour here that one of the Justice Kirkbys . . . took one of our fat oxen and killed him for his own table in his own house, which was distrained and taken away from thee for your meeting at Swarthmoor." The news had reached London and George reports that "the Chief Justice showed his dislike to such doings" (Crosfield, p. 179).

Greaves writes of the Conventicle Act: "The Quakers generally followed their usual course of open defiance of the law of holding Meetings at their times and places, but they refused to pay fines and jail fees" (Enemies, *p. 157). Constables were then sent to distraine goods, and they usually took far more than the value of the fine. In this brief note Margaret points out the corrupt behavior of a justice who was taking the king's property and eating it!*

It was a policy of those who wished to stop nonconformists to ruin dissenters by the imposition of heavy fines. Margaret was concerned not only on her own behalf but also on account of many other families. In November of 1684 she went to London for the eighth time to appeal to King Charles II and to James, Duke of York, on behalf of those suffering for attending Meetings. She went to court, called on authorities, and wrote papers to describe injustices.

I was Encouraged by my Sonn Mead to lay my Grievances before Thee:

The Neighbouring Justises of the peac have fined Mee a hundred pound upon the Conventicle Act, viz 40£ for the house & three score pound for my speaking & praying in my own house, & they have taken four & twenty head of Cattle which was my husbands Goods under the Colour that I am a Widow, Allthough I showed them the Kings Warrant & Pardon, which Owneth Mee to be Margret Fox; One of the Cattle was a fat Ox, which was spent in the Justises one [own] house; as wee heare: The Mony is not disposed to the Poore or to the Kings use that wee can heare of.

Margret Fox

Spence 3/1. Brief quote in Ross, *p. 325.*

150 To King Charles II 1684

"I that am above seventy years of Age, am come up above Twohundred miles in this wett, cold winter."

*Margaret reminds King Charles of his promise to her twenty-four years before of "Liberty to Tender Consciences." She details the current sufferings of herself and others, fines of £140 and £220 worth of cattle, unjustly charged (*Works, *p. 11).*

Roger Kirkby, the son of Colonel Richard Kirkby (who was responsible for her praemunire in 1664), acting with his uncle, William Kirkby, sent constables to her home to take away the cattle. The constables did not carry warrants and also acted as informers. The Kirkbys illegally kept the monies gained by these fines and raids, and the king and the poor were not getting their rightful share of such monies. Margaret asks for the king's intercession.

Roger Kirkby (ca. 1649–1708) was governor of Chester in 1693 and high sheriff of Lancashire in 1708 (JFHS, *9(1912)144.*

King Charles
Whom God has preserved Chief Governour over this Nation to this Day.

Be pleased to Remember, that at Thy first Coming to Reign in this Kingdom, I was here to Inform Thee concerning the State and Condition of the Lord's people called Quakers; and at that time the King was pleased to promise Liberty to Tender Consciences, so long as they lived peaceably under his Government[.] And I then desired no more of the King, than that he would forbear persecuting of them, until he had Just Cause for their Disloyalty; which I believe and hope, that there is none that can Charge any of us, that shall be owned of us, found in any Disloyalty.

And yet we are now become very great Sufferers in this Nation, Insomuch that of all other people we are like to be Ruinated as to our outward Liberty and Estates, except the King will be pleased to put a stop to the Cruel proceedings, that are now against us.

I that am above Seventy years of Age, am come up above Twohundred miles in this wett, cold winter, to Lay before the King my Sufferings and some other poor people's, that meet with me in my own house and Country; and the King was pleased to say to me when I was with him at that time, when he first came to Reign in this Kingdom (which is now almost 24 years since) God forbid, that he should hinder me to worship God in my own house.

Its now above a year; Since we have been Continually pursued by Roger Kirkby and William Kirkby Justices; they fined my house four times, whereas the Act against Conventicles fines the house but once; one of which times they sent an High-Constable who drove away nine head of Cattel of mine, and sold them forthwith without giving me any Liberty for an Appeal: And also Charged him, as he Confessd, not to shew us his warrant, nor to give us a Copy of it: by which I was totally deprived of making my Defence within the time limited by the

Act; and now I have no outward Remedy left me, but to Complain to the King.

And when that High-Constables year was out, his brother was made High-Constable the next year in his place. And he that was in the year before, came with his brother, and drove away fifteen head of Cattel of mine more, and sold them; who then also denyed shewing the warrant, by which he Acted; and refused to give any Copy thereof, although often desired. And in the like manner drove many Cattel from several of my poor Friends almost all they had. So that they have taken from us above Twohundred & Twenty pounds worth of Cattel, &c.

They have since fined us seven score pounds more; and none of this that we can hear of, is Converted to the Uses that the Act directs: For they send the Constables and Church-wardens to our Meetings, and swear them, and make Informers of them; they knowing, they will not take that part allowed to Informers by the Act: So that the Informers part, the King's part and the poors part they keep themselves for anything we know. Thus we are sold for nought, and the King's Wealth is not Increased thereby. And those that were the first Informers before these, said the Justices never gave them anything, but the bare Charges they were put t[paper torn] that if this matter be not Amended, we shall be quickly Ruinated and spoiled. Some are almost Ruined already; and there is none that can help or Relieve us in this matter but the King.

And although they have taken 24 head of Cattel from me; that doth not suffice them; but they threaten to send the Officers to pull and hale me by force to prison: so that I was forced to come to Acquaint the King with these things.

Collonell Kirkby, who was Father to one of these Justices, and brother to the other of them, caused me to be Praemunired Twenty years since, and the King was pleased then to give my Estate to my Children, so that I might live peaceably and quietly with them. And I shewed them the King's Warrant for his Pardon under the broad seal, but they would take no notice of it. Thus have they used me, although I have always been their peaceable Neighbour, and never did any one Act to disoblidge them in all my life.

And now one of the said Justices and myself being in Town, I humbly desire the King would be pleased to cause the truth of this matter to be Examin'd face to face and afford us Relief according to the

Innocency of our Cause; we being a people that desire nothing but the Kings and all his peoples good & happiness in this World and that which is to come.

Margarett Fox, of Swarthmore in Lancashire.

Thirnbeck MSS 20. Also JFHS, *9(1912)143–145, which states: "This manuscript is a copy made by Mark Swanner, assistant to Richard Richardson, the Friends' Clerk."*

151 To Lord Ancram January 31, 1685

"I write this to thee for thy own Satisfaction which thou desired me Concerning my Relations and parents."

Charles Kerr, second earl of Ancram (1624–1690), was a supporter of the monarchy, active in Parliament, with a Scottish Presbyterian background. He was described by a political opponent as a man "of no principles either as to religion or virtue, but had studied the most in divinity of any man of quality I ever knew" (Henning, pp. 677–678). He was tolerant of nonconformists and assisted many Friends, for example, obtaining the release of Isaac Penington and Thomas Ellwood in 1666.

Lord Ancram was acquainted with George Fox and promised to help Margaret at this time (Fox.Short, pp. 348–349, 201). Her letter, a rare instance of autobiographical information, is in answer to his request for information about her family. Margaret briefly describes her father, John Askew; Thomas Fell, her first husband; and her eight children, "unpreferred", i.e., unmarried when she was widowed in 1658 but "preferred very well" by 1685.

31.11.1684/85

Lord Ancram,

I am very much engaged to thee for thy Christian kindness to me who am a Sufferer for the Lord of heavens Sake, and for Worshiping of him in his own Spirit and truth (as he hath left it upon record in John 4 to the woman of Samaria) [John 4:23–24], not for any Evill or wrong that I have done to any man but for the Lords Sake do I suffer, I write this to thee for thy own Satisfaction which thou desired me Concerning my Relations and parents, for my own self I have very few; my father was a Gentleman liveing in Furness behind the Sands[.] his name was Askew, and had a good Estate as it was Counted in his time, and he had Children only me and another daughter, and he left us as good as Six thousand pounds, when I was marryed to my First husband, who was a barrister at Law of Grayes Inn, and practised the Law many years, and was the vice-Chancellour of the County Pallatine of Lancaster, and in his own country a Justice of peace and Coraner, and in [the] Latter End of his dayes he was a Judge of Chester and Wales, he dyed above 26 years Since, and left me eight Children unpreferred, Seven daughters and one Son, but through the goodness of the Lord they are all (except one) preferred very well; and I am left to the Stroake of persecutours. Soe if thou canst make me any help that I may live peaceably at my own habitation[,] serving the Lord the rest of the time that he hath allotted me, I Shall acknowledge thy kindness very much, and I believe that the Lord will reward thee many fold into thy own bosom in such a Christian act of Charity, etc.

From her that desires thy happiness in this world and that which is to come.

Margret Fox

FHL MSS Vol 323:105 A.R.B. Mss, also Ross, p. 401. Endorsed: "To the Ld Ancram in London by Margarett Fox. the 31st 11 mo.(Jan.) 1684/85".

152 To Daniel and Rachel Fell Abraham February 7, 1685

"King Charles was taken Ill on 2nd day morning, and departed this life yesterday about Midday."

Margaret went to the court at Whitehall with Quaker George Whitehead and an influential lord to speak with King Charles, but he "was not well. Then we came forth into White-Hall-Court again; but all the Gates were shut, that we could not get forth. So we waited and walked up and down, and several came down from the King, and said, He could not stand; and others said, He could not speak. Then, after some Hours waiting; we got through Scotland-Yard, and came away." The king died six days later.

*Margaret had an interview with the new king, James II, two weeks later. He was not able to help her directly, but it seems that something was conveyed to the Lancashire justices, "a private Caution, for they troubled us no more" (*Works, *pp. 12–13).*

"Mary Woodburns busyness" was most likely part of the lawsuit that brought Margaret and George Fox to London. Mary Woodburn was a tithe farmer, someone who collects tithes or taxes for a commission (Nightingale, Early, *p. 56).*

Cousin Bethiah was Margaret Rous's daughter, about eighteen years old.

London 7 12th mo. 1684/5

Dear Son and Daughter Abraham, [Letter 146]

I received your letter and I praise the Lord for your preservation in the Truth and in your health as we are here all at this time, glory to the Lord for ever. our busyness at the L [Lawcourts] is not yet ended[,] but we hope in the Lord to get it ended this next week, here hath been a great and a Suddain [sudden] change. King Charles was taken Ill on 2nd day [Monday] morning, and departed this life yesterday about Mid-day, and in the afternoon Kings James the 2nd[,] Late Duke of York[,] was proclaimed, soe that this day the Judges have received Commission to Sit again (as we hear), We expecte your Sister Lower [Mary Lower] to be here the next week, for I writt to her to return as Shortly as She could because yee writt the Smallpox was Soe neare hand, which I confess I was affraid of, We doe not know how things will be as yet but we will wait upon the Lord to Manifest his will and pleasure[,] and for your Suffering you must be Content and in the Strength of the Lord give up to doe his will[;] and I hope in the Lord it will not be very long till we shall endeavour to return to you, My dear love and Constant prayer is to the Lord for you[,] that in his powerful arm and strength you may be preserved, My dear Love is to Leonard Fell and his wife and to all the Servants and friends, We Can give noe account of what will [become] of Mary Woodburns busyness till our Motion Comes on, Your Brother and Sister Mead [Sarah and William Meade] and Sister Susannah have their dear Loves remembered unto you, which is all at present,

From your dear Mother in the Lord

M. F.

Your Cussin Bethiah hath her
dear Love remembered unto you.

FHL Portfolio 41:83, also Ross, p. 327 and JFHS, *6:79–81. Addressed: "to Rachell Abraham at Swarthmore neare Lancaster These ddd in Lancashire". Endorsed: "My*

Dear & honoured Grand Moth letter to my Dear and Affectionate Father and Mother when she was at London. J. Abraham."

153 To John Rous April 3, 1687

"There must needs be some tenderness and mercy shewed towards her Eternal good, or how can shee be presarved."

John Rous (Letter 82), Margaret's son-in-law, wrote to her for advice on dealing with his daughter, Margaret. She was then twenty years old and was doing something of which her parents strongly disapproved. It probably related to her marrying a man named Manwaring and to his family. Margaret urges John Rous not to be "too sevare and hard with her . . . least she, despairing of your Favour, it may cause her to lean more upon them." Margaret also invokes Jesus's parable of the lost sheep to urge compassion.

Margaret Manwaring, Margaret's granddaughter, was not reconciled with her parents. In 1699 she was a widow with a child attending a Quaker school, but her mother Margaret Rous, considered her "wickedly bent and resolved in her mind" (Crosfield, p. 232).

Dear Sonn Rouse

Thyne of the 28th of last Month I this day received, and am glad to hear of all your health; praises be the Lord For itt—Thou desireth to hear From mee; and as I said before in my other Letter I desire the Lord to guide You and direct You how to doe, soe as to presarve your child to God, that shee be nott utterly cast away From the Lord and His truth; outward things are of little value, in comparison of that, For her preservation to the Lord and his truth is altogether in my Eye, and iff you be too sevare and hard with her; I am afraid, least she, despairing of your Favour, it may cause her to lean more upon them, and soe be further from recovering; there must needs be some tenderness and mercy shewed towards her Eternal good, or how can shee be presarved—I have writt and inclosed a Few lines, which I would have her to have if you think it convenient—We shall be very glad to see thee att Swarthmoore; wee Expect my Daughter Susan about Whitsuntide allsoe: Remembar my very dear Love to thy wife and all thy children; and I desire you to Use your Endeavour to gaine and recover what is lost, and remembar him that left the ninety and nine [Matt. 18:12] and went to seek that which was lost and brought it home and rejoiced more over it then over all the rest; and Consider though shee hath done Evill shee might have done worse: soe no more, but the Lords powerfull Arme guide you and direct you and lead you the way he would have you to goe[.] With my very dear Love to thy self, Rests

Thy Dear Mother

Margrett Fox.

Swarthmoore, The 3d of 2d month, 87.

Crosfield MSS, FHL MSS Vol. 329:1; also in Crosfield, pp. 210–211. Addressed: "To John Rouse These To be Left Att the Angell in Lambard=streett London DDD".

154 To Sarah Fell Meade December 10, 1688

"And after this, wee heard of his ill behaviour from London, and wee were cautioned at that time to carry wisely."

James Walvin, in The Quakers, Money and Morals, *describes the financial assistance that Friends provided for each other, which led to their survival and growing prosperity. The corollary was: "businessmen were under the permanent scrutiny of their immediate Meeting. Whenever a member was in financial trouble, when doubts or complaints surfaced about business practice, bad debts, poor judgment or, worst of all, insolvency, a deputation from the Meeting would examine the matter and question the people involved" (pp. 72–73).*

There are several records in the Friends House Library concerning John Scanfield and his problems. The transcript of the Morning Meeting Minutes 1673–1692 has this account: "J. Scanfield being here this day, & spoke to about his miscarriages & infamous behaviour; he promiseth to condemn them & endeavour to make satisfaction to his creditors; & in the meantime it is the advice of Friends; & their sense that he should not appear as a public Preacher, till he have given satisfaction to Friends, & they feel him in that he professeth" (p. 88).

Margaret was being questioned about Scanfield's actions in the North and whether she had encouraged his ministry. In this excerpt from a letter to her daughter Sarah she gives an account of her dealings with him.

An Accompt taken out of A Letter from Margarett Fox to Sarah Meade:— As Follows.—

Whereas thou desires me, to cleare my selfe, Concerninge Scamfielde, I am noe way guilty Concerning him, but that I cann cleare my selfe;— For hee had been both in Cumberland & Westmorland, before hee came to us, and I neither knew, nor had heard anythinge of him, till I saw him in the Meettinge, & hee did but dine with us, at that time, and soe went away.—

And after this, wee heard of his ill behaviour from London, and wee were cautioned at that time to carry wisely towards him, least hee should become an open Enemy to Truth:—After this hee came againe, And I tould him what I heard of him; somethings hee confessed and some things hee denied, Wee did see him, not to bee A seasoned man in the Truth; And I dealt very plainely with him, wherein I heard his Conversation was not Answerable thereto.—And Whereas hee hath told Friends, that I bade him, goe on with his Ministry; I am satisfied, I never said such A word to him, For hee had been thorough much of the North, before I saw him; wee were civill to him, beinge A Stranger; but hee had noe ground of support from mee, in anythinge, wherein hee doth not Accordinge to Truth.-

Swarthmore the 10th of 10th moth 1688.

FHL Port 15:137. Endorsed: "An abstract of A Letter from Margarett Fox about Jn. Scamfeilde".

155 TO DANIEL AND RACHEL FELL ABRAHAM MAY 25, 1690

"The letter which I am afraid you did not receive was the first Letter I writt from Gooses."

In April 1687 the Declaration of Indulgence was issued. A month before, King James had "announced his intention of granting a general liberty of conscience. It was rumored that William Penn had a large part in drafting it . . . Followed in 1689 by the Toleration Act [it] effectively ended the severer prosecutions of Quakers and other dissenters" (Horle, Q.&EngLegalSys, pp. 94–95). Margaret's ninth trip to London in

1690 was made solely for the purpose of visiting family and Friends and attending Meetings, and not with the need to go to court to plead against injustices.

Though they were now scattered in different parts of England, Margaret and her daughters continued to keep in close touch through correspondence and visits. Margaret stayed with Margaret and John Rous at Kingston near London and with Sarah and William Meade at Gooses in Essex, and she would return to the North with son-in-law Thomas Lower.

*George Fox's health was too poor for him to travel far, but he was still able to go to Meetings and to preach. He was lovingly cared for by his stepchildren. This visit was Margaret's last time to be with him, and later she wrote: "And the Lord hath given me Strength and Ability, that I have been at London to see my dear Husband and Children, and Relations and Friends there . . . And I was very well Satisfied, Refreshed, and Comforted in my Journey" (*Works, *p. 13).*

The receipt of mail was uncertain, and Margaret repeats some of what she had written in a previous letter. She gives directions about a carpenter, John Bell, building "a place" in the Swarthmoor Meetinghouse. George Fox had given three acres of land not far from Swarthmoor Hall, with house, barn, and stable for "the service of His sons and daughters and servants called Quakers" in 1687. Meetings were then held there, as they still are today. The "place" to be built was most likely the benches around the sides of the room, with wooden planking for a floor.

Kingston the 25 of the 3 moth 1690

Dear Son and Daughter

Wee have received your dear & Accepttable Letters & I am very glad & praise the Lord for your & the Childrens good health[,] and by this you may know that I & wee all hear [here] at kingston therou [through] the Lords goodness are all very well & in good health & your brother and sister Meade was here the last week to see us[.] I trust in the Lord ye are all well their [there] & your father [George Fox] is now att London[,] & I intend if the Lord will about a week hence to bee their ready to see freinds as they come to town, I received a letter from your brother Lower by which I perceive hee intends to bee att the Yearly Meetting & soe for the North with his famaly[;] but I perceive hee will bee a little stayed by the way by some buisiness for Widdow Rallison [Rawlinson] soe that he cannot reach Kingston till the very Latter end of the week so that I cannot [wait?] but I must bee at London before that[,] for I shall have a better time & Oppertunity to see freinds before the Meetting than I can have afterward, your Brother and

Sister Moris [Abraham and Isabel Morrice] wilbe there the next week, your Brother Lower desired mee in his Letter not to conclude of my going into the North till hee bee here[,] for hee saith hee hath some buisness which hee must doe after the Meetting in Susex[,] which hee hopes wilbe done in A weekes time but thats uncertain[.] hee desires that wee may return togather soe that I cannot give you noe certain notice of our return. I ever had and yet have An intention to bee at the Quarterly Meetting at Lancaster, if his buisiness doe not hinder mee; however, when wee know more I shall Lett you know, the Letter which I am afraid you did not receive was the first Letter I writt from Gooses in which I menshioned that you should gett John Bell to make us a place in the Meetting house[,] the Length of it should bee the half breadth of it and soe broad as it will hould A seat round about that one may sitt of both sides[.] plank itt and board it under foot and also A seat of the outside of it (this was writt in that Letter and some other things) thy sister very kindly receved thy Letter and she was very glad of it[.] Her husband and her dear Love is dearly remembred to you[,] and Bethiah and Anne [Margaret and John Rous and their children] Presents their Love and respects to their Unkle and Aunt, they are all very dear and tender to mee, I hear of your sister Lower and the Children and hope they are well. my dear Little John Abrahams is often in my remembrance[,] soe is Dear Little Thomas. Even the Lord god allmighty preserve them and bless them. Remember mee to all the famaly[,] and my dear and intire love is dearly Remembred to you.

so I remain
Your Dear Mother in the Lord
M F

I would thee to Enquire after the Maid at William Satterthais whether wee can have her or noe[.]

Abraham MSS 43, Crosfield, pp. 214–216, and Ross, pp. 402–403. Endorsed: "Margaret Fox to Daniel and Rachel Abraham. 25.iii.1690."

156 To Women's Meeting in London July 10, 1690

"And so, dear Friends, my Heart and Soul was so much Comforted and Refreshed, amongst you."

Upon her return to Swarthmoor from her ninth visit to London (Letter 155) Margaret wrote a letter of thanks to the Women's Meeting.

Dear Friends and Sisters,

In the Eternal Blessed Truth, into which we are begotten, and in which we stand, and are preserved, as we keep in it, and are guided by it: In this is my dear and unchangeable Love remember'd unto you all; acknowledging your dear, tender, and kind Love, when I was with you; in which my Heart was rejoyced, to feel the Ancient Love and Unity of the Eternal Spirit amongst you: And my Soul was, and is refresh'd in my Journey, in visiting of my dear Husband and Children, and you my dear Friends. And now I am returned to my own House and Family, where I find all well; Praised and Honoured be my Heavenly Father.

And, dear Friends, our Engagements are great unto the Lord, and he is Dear and Faithful unto us: And Blessed and Happy are all they, that are Dear and Faithful unto him. And those who keeps single and chaste unto him, they need not fear Evil Tidings, nor what Man can do; For he that hath all Power in Heaven and Earth in his Hand, he will surely keep his own Church and Family, those that worshippeth him, within the Measuring Line, that measures the Temple, and the Altar, and those that worships therein, they are kept safe, as in the Hallow of his Hand.

And so, dear Friends, my Heart and Soul was so much Comforted and Refreshed amongst you, that I could not but signifie the Remembrance of my dear Love unto you: And also my Acknowledgement of your dear Love and Tenderness to my dear Husband; for which, I doubt not, but the Lord doth and will Reward you: Into whose Hand and Arm and Power I commit you.

M.Fox

Swarthmore, the 10th of the 5th month, 1690.

Works, *pp. 13–14.*

157 TO FRIENDS AND SISTERS NOVEMBER 19, 1691

"And now hee is entered into his Celestiall Rest and Glory, where hee lives for evermore; and his Spiritt Lives with us."

George Fox died in London on January 13, 1691. He was surrounded by Friends, including William Penn, who immediately wrote to Margaret: "I am to be the teller to thee of sorrowful tydings . . . that thy dear husband and my beloved and dear friend, George Fox has finist his glorious testimony" (Kunze, p. 180).

There was heavy mourning among Friends, and as the leaders of the Quakers were preparing for the funeral the "session was interrupted by the tears and groans of men of the stature of Penn and Whitehead, people whose emotions were usually under tighter control." Over four thousand people attended the funeral service itself, and it took more than two hours for the funeral procession to walk the one mile to Bunhill Fields, the Quaker burial ground (Ingle, pp. 284–285).

Margaret's letter to friends/Friends in London demonstrates the close connections that bound together the women in the movement. Margaret expresses her thanks for their care of her husband and for their love and kindness to her, "my very deare and tender love in the Lord, is dearly Remembered unto you, as if I named you, one, by one."

Swarthmore the:16: of the 9th: moth. 1691:
Deare Friends & Sisters in the Lord.

In that which was in the Beginning, Now is; And shall bee Everlastingly for ever;—in the sences: Thereof doe I write these few Lines unto you; Acknowledging your tender love, & care to mee, and my dear Husband, when he was with you, in his service & Travells for the Lord;— And for your tender care and love unto him, you will have an Everlasting Reward:—And now hee is entered into his Celestiall Rest and Glory, where hee lives for evermore; and his Spiritt Lives with us.—And Deare Friends, as wee keep in his Etternall Testimony, that hee Published to the world; wee shall Live unto God,—And many Thousands are gathered to God by this Testimony, and shall bee to the end of the world,— I received your kinde & deare Letter, and am very much comforted, & satisfied with your love therein.- And I trust in the Almighty God, that as we keep in this same spiritt, life, & power, and abide in it, wee shall bee preserved, & kept unto God, to the End, and in the End.—And now my Deare Friends, my very deare and tender love in the Lord, is dearly Remembred unto you, as if I named you, one, by one, And your tender love, and kindeness, when I was with you, I cannott forgett;—And the Lord continue this Mutuall Love Amongst us, that not any of us ever wax cold; but that wee may live in the heat of the Sonn of Righteousness, and there shall wee grow, & bring forth fruite to God, and bee unto him Trees of Righteousness, the planting of the Lord, that hee may bee Glorified, in us, & thorrow us, & by us.—And Deare Friends, I am not uncensible; of your great Care, & service for the Lord, and his Etternall Truth; Therefore I Councell you, in the power of the Lord, to continue in it and to give upp freely to it, in the strength & wisdome of God; and you are sure to have comfort & satisfaction at the present, and in the End, an Everlasting & Etternall Reward.—And now I lett you know, that I am well in the Lord, every way, Praised & honnoured bee his holly name; And both my Sonn & Daughters, their children & Families are all well, And their deare love is Remembred dearly unto you all, and wee are all Engaged to you, for your deare Love, & kindness to us:—From

Your Deare Friende and sister in the Lord,
Margarett Fox.

FHL Box Meeting MSS 1671–1753:43.

158 TO SARAH FELL MEADE DECEMBER 11, 1693

"& soe Let all things Rest, for I beleeve there is noe ill intentions in any."

Susannah Fell Ingram (1650–ca. 1710), Margaret's sixth daughter, was also a minister, though she was not as active in Quaker affairs as some members of the family (Crosfield, p. 190). She had no children of her own, but there are numerous expressions of appreciation for her help to her sisters in caring for family members. In 1691 she married William Ingram, a widower with young children. He was a London merchant and a highly respected Friend. Before her marriage and after William Ingram's death in 1706 she lived for many years with Sarah and William Meade (Ross, pp. 334–341).

There was some matter of how Susannah "demeaned [conducted] herself that resulted in this letter where Margaret urges that "noe more troubles nor Rehearsings be About it." William Ingram's children were accepted as part of the Fell family, and Margaret refers to them as she does to all of her grandchildren.

The postscript to Nathaniel Meade (1684–1760), then nine years old, praises his ability to write and urges him to lead a virtuous life. She expresses the Quaker principle that he can know the right way "by the calling inn of thy minde to within thee." Nathaniel Meade became a successful barrister, was knighted, and died in 1760, "a gentleman universally respected." His cousin, Richard Lower, lived with the Meades at that time (Crosfield, pp. 219–220).

Swarthmore the 11th of the 10th month 1693
Dear daughter mead

I received thy dear & acceptable Letter, glad I am to hear of your well being in the Lord, I thought Long to hear from you, for it is great Joy & comfort to me & I am heartyly glad of what thou writes of thy sister Ingrim, that she demeanes & behaves her self according to truth & righteousness in that place where god has set her, my heart & soul praises the Lord for itt, & it is his doings & goodness that frames & fasions & moves into his owne Image & nature, for we are in his hands as the clay is in the hands of the potter [Jer. 18:6] & what is good in everyone he makes it[,] its of him, Courage must be upon him, to Receive & ask counsell & wisdom of him, & then we shall be furnished with grace, & wisdom to serve him & obey him in our severall places & conditions where he has sett us, that therein he may be gloryfied & honnoured, & his precious truth, which we are wittnesses of, may be verified,—& soe for my daughter Ingrims Lettr I am very well satisfied, in the Relation she gives, & I would have her to Lett it Rest, where it is & Let noe more troubles nor Rehearsings be About it, for in that there has been mistakes which makes things worse, that word growing old, gave an occation for the other word which she denies, for the truth never grows old, but is the same for ever, & those that Abides in it Lives unto god for ever, & soe Let all things Rest, for I beleeve there is noe ill intentions in any—& soe the Lord god Almighty, Keep us all in Love & unity with god, & with one Another, & then all will be well,—My Love is dearly Remembered, unto my son & daughtr Inggrim, & to there children, & they are as dear to me as ever, & my hearts desire & prayer to Eternall god is & shall be for them, as it is for my owne soulle & for all my dear Children & offspring, & soe in that Love that is everlasting I bid you all farewell -

and that I am yoaer Deare Mother
In the lord
M: Fox

Dear nathaniel mead

I Received thy dear Letter gladly, by which I perceive thou Learne very well, both to Read & to write for which I am very glad of, but dear child, I wod desire allso that thou would Learn to know god thy maker, & Jesus Christ thy Redeemer, whom to know is Eternall Life, & this thou must know by the calling inn of thy minde to within thee, & there thou will Remember thy Creator, & then he will bless thee & preserve thee, out of sin & Evill, & all Lightness & vanity, & soe thou will Learn to fear the Lord & to be Low in thy mind, & there thou will know thy duty to god, & thy parents, & this Lesson I desire allmighty god to Learne thee, & this is from thy Grandmother, & I desire thee to write this out with thy own hand & to keep it, & Remember my dear Love to thy Cousin Richard—& Let him write Another coppy for himselfe which thou has procured by thy diligence in writing to me.

Spence 3/194, partly in Crosfield, pp. 217–219 and Ross, p. 354.

159 To Thomas Lower December 24, 1694

"He hath had a concern upon his mind concerning the city of London this twelvemonth."

Margaret wrote to son-in-law Thomas Lower (Letters 126, 147) out of concern for Daniel Abraham, Rachel's husband (Letter 146). He was an extremely conscientious young man, sensitive to what he considered his mission, and went to London at this time out of a religious concern. There were no ill results on this occasion, but several years later he spent three years in prison for refusing to pay tithes (Ross, pp. 316–317).

James Dickerson (1658–1741), Abraham's traveling companion, was "a minister among Friends for 65 years" (note in Transcript).

Swarthmore, 24.10.1694.

Dear Son Lower,

I received thy letter and the account thou gave me of things was very satisfactory. I had writ to thee before this concerning my son Abraham journey to London, but waited for an account from him in his journey when he thought to be there which I have done this last post. It was two weeks since he went hence, and it pleased the Lord at the very time that he intended to go to send James Dickerson hither to be his companion. He hath had a concern upon his mind concerning the city of London this twelvemonth: how it will please the Lord to discharge him of it, we must commit it to him, for the exercise is very weighty and hard upon us all. It hath been much in my mind since he went if he could find liberty and freedom in himself to write what is upon him, and upon Friends' consideration and approbation it might be printed and dispersed in the City.

I desire much your kindness with respect to his present state and condition and also your advice and council as in the wisdom of God you see meet. For thou knows he is young and so easily hurt. I perceive he has a desire to lodge at thy house.

We are all well here through the Lord's great mercy and we hear nothing but that your concerns are in good order and well at Marsh Grange.

Our very dear and true loves is to thyself, wife and all thy dear children and I desire my dear love to all my other children [?]. We have little of passage only Ch of Barses Hall was buried last week, he died seventy.

FHL Transcript of Miller MSS 85. " M.F. to Thomas Lower 24.10.1694".

160 To Women's Yearly Meeting in London April 3, 1695

"Tho wee bee the weaker vessell, yet the Seed is one in male & Female."

Margaret emphasizes some of the main themes of her beliefs: the eternal church, the equality of the sexes, and the necessity for humility. The epistle to Women's Meetings has a valedictory tone: "the weary & heavy Laden will find Rest" and "when it pleaseth him to Call us to an account of our deeds done in the body."

Swarthmore the 3d of the 2d mo 1695
A Short Epistle to the Womens Yearly Meeting in London
And Else Where -

My Dearly beloved Friends & Sisters in the Lord the Salutation of my Deare Love in that Blessed ancient truth in which wee are & were begotten[,] the Antient of Days visiting us in an acceptable time & in a day of Salvation[,] which blesed Truth lives for Ever & waxes not old in this as in days past[,] I dearly greet you with hearty desires that you & wee all may Live in it & grow dayly in grace & in the Knowledge of the Lord Jesus Christ who is now at worke in this his Day[,] building up his Church & Rearing up the Tabernacle unto David that hath been fallen down & is makeing up the Breaches theirof [Amos 9:11]; the Blessed Seed of David with which his Covenant is; as with the Day & with the night, Soe is Gods Everlasting Covenant with David, & with his Seed For Evermore—Soe Dear friends & Sisters that wee may bee all found of this Seed & in this Covenant where God is ingaged to Bless us, & bee with us tho wee bee the weaker vessell [1 Pet. 3:7], yet the Seed is one in male & Female; for God is a Faithfull Keeper of his Covenant with his people; & Soe in humility & Lowlynesse of mind Let us all Keep, & their wee can learn of Christ who is meek & Lowly in heart, So their wee can take his Yoke upon us which is Easy & his burden which is Light, (when it is that his are given up to him it is Easy & Light) there the weary & heavy Laden will find Rest to Their Soules—

And So dear Friends the humble & the Lowly are Christ's Schollars & So keeping Chaste & Constant to his teachings their is our dayly Comfort, & their wee receive our dayly bread, & our dayly Strength in the Lord is Renewed, & here is our Chiefest portion & Inheritance that can never bee taken from us, glorious praises bee to the Eternall God who hath revealed his Son in us by which wee come to Inherit Eternall Life, In peace with the great God of Heaven & Earth; & this is more & better then all visibles in the universe;—

And So in the Sence & feelling of this great portion Let us all abide in thankfull Obedience, & faithfullnesse to him that hath bott [bought] us with his own blood; to him bee glory & honour for Ever; that so wee may appear before him when it pleaseth him to Call us to an account of our deeds done in the body; that soe wee may receive of him; well done good & faithfull Servant Enter into the Joy of thy Lord [Matt. 25:23], Soe the Lord God Almighty preserve us here unto the End & in the End

Margaret Fox

Let Coppies of this bee sent
into the Country Everywhere

Nottinghamshire Archives, NC/Q 315/5. Brief excerpts in Ross, p. 370.

161 To Friends January 11, 1698

"I perceive that some Friends' scruples to make use of these words, which the King and Parliament hath granted."

Margaret wrote to correct errors that had crept into Friends' beliefs. She was painfully aware that with the passage of time many Quakers did not know the struggles and suffering that George Fox and others had endured to win certain rights.

A crucial one was the right not to swear to an oath. An act passed by Parliament in 1696 finally granted this right. Some extremely scrupulous Friends felt that it was wrong to accept this concession, and Margaret urges them to accept "the mercy that God hath granted you for your ease and benefit."

At this time Margaret was in London visiting family and friends. She was there from late summer 1697 to June 1698, her tenth and last visit.

19.11.1697/8
Friends,

Here is something upon my mind and in my heart, to bear my testimony among my brethren, and also with my dear husband whom I know certainly had a great desire that Friends might obtain of the King and Government, words instead of an oath; which they have left upon record, which may be seen and read in a little book called "An Epistle from the Meeting for Sufferings to such Friends in England and Wales and elsewhere, as are or may be concerned, in the favour granted by the Government for the ease of Friends from the great oppression of oaths, etc." For want of which our Ancient Friends suffered great hardship in the beginning, and since the beginning, for want of answering, when they were sued for tithes, and for not swearing allegiance to the King; and several ways great sufferings, many praemunired their goods and their estates forfeited to the King, imprisonment for life, several lost their lives in prison. This is forgotten, now there is not such severity and hardship. The afflictions of Joseph they know not [Amos 6:6].

Now it hath pleased the Lord to remove those governors that were so cruel, and has placed those in their room that are more merciful, who are inclining to give more liberty to tender consciences, and have granted such a liberty as Friends desired instead of an oath.

Now here's some amongst Friends of a contrary mind against ancient Friends' testimonies and also the Scriptures, and hath brought in another thing, that we must not use the sacred name of God about outward things, and speaks of pawning our souls. I know no scripture that saith thus. The Papists indeed speak of sacraments, which there's no scripture for, and if we must not name God, nor say he is witness in outward things. This is a new doctrine, and another Gospel which the Apostle saith whosoever preacheth is accursed. Must we turn God out of the earth? Is he not the God of the whole earth? Did he not say by the Prophet Isaiah, before Christ came in the flesh, Heaven is my throne, and the earth is my footstool? Read the 50th Psalm. For every beast of the forest is mine, and the cattle upon a thousand hills are mine. The mighty God even the Lord hath spoken and called the Earth from the rising of the sun to the going down thereof and must he not be named in the Earth? And Christ Jesus saith without me you can do nothing. Must not we name him them? And when he teaches his disciples to pray, he teaches them to say—Thy will be done on earth as it is in Heaven. Can his will be done on earth, as it is in Heaven, if he must not be called upon, not named?

And again he saith, for this end was I born and for this cause did I come into the World, that I should bear witness to the Truth [John 18:37]. He saith himself that he is witness, and may not we say that he is witness and the Apostle Paul saith, Col.3.17, whatsoever ye do in word or deed, do all in the name of the Lord Jesus.

I am sorry that Friends should be so weak, and so childish in the Truth.

When Jesus spoke to his disciples, that they should not swear at all, he saith, let your communication be yea, yea, nay, nay, that is, be true and righteous in your communication. When you say yea, let it be yea in Truth, and when you say nay, let it be nay in Truth [Matt. 5:36–37]. So he would have Truth to rule them in all their communication. That was that, which he knew was beyond swearing. He did not say as some say now, that they might not mention the name of God about outward things. He put no such difficulty upon his words. Truth in all things was what he aimed at. These that speak as before, it is to darken and muddle people's minds. Whatsoever words are spoke in Truth and Verity, answers Christ's words in place of an oath. Read the 1st. of Timothy 2.7, where Paul saith, he is a teacher of the Gentiles in Faith and Verity. The Apostle saith to the Galations, I marvel that ye are so soon removed from him that called you into the grace of Christ, unto another Gospel: but there be some that trouble you and would pervert the Gospel of Christ, and he saith, I would that they were cut off that trouble you: (there were those that troubled the Church in the Apostles' days; and so there is now, many troublers as well as witnesses for the eternal Truth)

He also saith the cause of ground of an oath was to put an end to strife and they that are in strife, are not in the Truth. The peaceable spirit of Christ would have all to be in the Truth in their communication, where their yea is yea, and their nay is nay, more and better than an oath.

I write this because I perceive that some Friends' scruples to make use of these words, which the King and Parliament hath granted them instead of an oath, and so hinders themselves of the benefit and ease, it would bring Friends unto. When they had occasion formerly to prove wills or to put in answers, they were glad to see a clerk to put in Jurat. So that they can show how many Friends; names that have sworn, as they have recorded it. Are not these false, foul things? Whereas now they may go plainly before the face of all to speak their solemn Declaration.

So I desire Friends generally, let not this false blind doctrine pervail upon you, but make use of the mercy that God hath granted you for your ease and benefit. See what William Penn saith (in his answer to a letter in 1688) in vindication of K. James [King James II], that he never tempted him to be a Papist, which he affirms in these words; in the Presence of Almighty God I do declare, etc. Methinks that faithful, sensible Friends may easily see through these things. The rise and beginning of all this contest and difference was that Friends might not seek to this power and government for anything, which God hath now placed over the powers of Darkness, praises be to his Holy Name.

Margaret Fox

Gooses, the 19th of the 11th month 1697/8.

Miller MSS 89, Transcript. This manuscript was lost, but a partial transcription at FHL includes the above letter. It is prefaced with this note: "This is a copy of a paper by Margaret Fox to Friends. It was written at Gooseyes, 19.11.1697/98, when she was staying with Sarah and William Meade and is written in a clear good hand and has corrections in it made by Sarah. It looks as if it must have been dictated by Margaret and then gone through again with Sarah's help."

162 To Friends, Brethren and Sisters June 1698

"Its a Dangerous thing To Lead young Friends much into observation of outward things . . . for they can soon get into an outward garb, to be all alike outwardly."

In the last years of her life Margaret wrote two letters warning against the growing tendency of Quakers to pietism and conformity in manners and dress. She speaks for "the Gospell Leading & Guiding & Teaching which is a free spirit" and which is for essentials and not merely outward ceremonies. What came to be known as "Quaker gray" did not appeal to her. Her last letter, written two years later, (Letter 166), is even pithier.

Dear Friends, Brethren & Sisters

God the Father of our Blessed Lord & Saviour Jesus Christ, is an universall God, of Mercy and Love to all people; And in that Blessed Love, he vissitted us, in an acceptable time, and in a Day of Salvation; And hee that brought unto us the glad tidings of the Gospell of peace, hee Continued in the body amongst Gods plantation up & down Fourty yeares, And we had certaine directions & instructions, upon all accounts, & upon all occasions; hee has left us severall writings & Records, to be practised according to the Gospell which hee preached amongst us, And we have Lived under the Teaching of that blessed Eternall

Spirit of the Eternall God which hee directed us too, unto this Day: And now it is good for us all to go on & continue, hand in hand, in the unity & Fellowshipp of this eternall Spirit, in humillity & Lowliness of mind, Each esteeminge others better than our selves [Phil. 2:3]; And this is wellpleasing unto God: And Let us all take heed of touching any thing like the Ceremonies of the Jews, for that was hatefull unto Christ, for hee came to bear wittness against them, and Testified against their outside practises, who tould them of their Long Robes, and of their broad philacteries [Matt. 23:5], and against garnishing the Sepulchers of the prophets, and tould them, if the prophets had been there, they would have killed them, as their Fathers did [Matt. 23:29–30]; And when they found fault with him for Eating & drinking with publicans & Sinners, hee tould them, That publicans & sinners should enter into the Kingdom before them [Matt. 9:10–12]: so that wee may see how ill hee liked their outward Ceremonies; So Let us Keep to the Rule and Leading of the Eternall Spirit that God has given us to be our teacher, & Let that put on & off, as is meet & Servicable for every ones state & Condition: And Let us take heed of Limmitting that, neither practises is safe for us, wee are under the Gospell Leading & Guiding & Teaching which is a free spirit, which Leades into unity & Lowlyness of mind the Saints & servants of Christ, Desiring to be established in the free spirit, not bound nor limitted: Legall Ceremonies is far from Gospell Freedom: Let us beware of being guilty, or haveing a hand in ordering or contriving that which is Contrary to Gospell Freedom, for the Apostle would not have Dominion over their Faith, but to be helpers of their Faith: Its a Dangerous thing To Lead young Friends much into observation of outward things, for that will be Easily Done, for they can soon get into an outward garb, to be all alike outwardly, But this will not make them true Christians; its the spirit that gives life; I would be loath to have a hand in these things, the Lord preserves us That we do noe hurt to Gods work. But let him work, whose work it is, we have lived quietly, & peaceably thus farr; and its not for Gods Service to make breaches.

Swarthmore. 4.mo, 1698 — Margaret Fox.

Facsimile of manuscript, "Gift of Wm. Benson, Sydney, Australia, ALS," at Haverford College. Also in Works, *pp. 534–535.*

163 TO KING WILLIAM III JUNE 24, 1698

"I am not free and cleare to return to my Habitation, Untill I have cleared my selfe unto this Government."

William and Mary ascended the throne in 1689. Margaret wrote this letter to King William to tell him about Quakers, their past, and their appreciation of his "Gentle Government and Clemency, & Gratious Acts." Her conscience required her not to leave London until she had done this, just as she felt that she was required to explain the principles of Quakerism to Charles II in 1660. At the age of eighty-five, Margaret probably realized that this would be her last trip to London.

To the Kinge of Great Brittaine

It hath pleased Almighty God, to bring mee unto this place, Two hundred Miles from my outward Dwelling in my old Age (being entred into the 85th year of my Age) to bear my Testimony, for that Eternal Truth, which I and many more, are made Partakers of, praised bee the Lord;—and I am not free and cleare to return to my Habitation, Untill I have cleared my selfe unto this Government: I was Exercised in this manner, the first Year King Charles the Second came to the Crowne, and laboured Amongst them A whole Year; to Acquainte them and give them to Understand our Principles, in givinge Letters and Papers unto them for that End—And great opposition we had both from Church and State; yet it pleased God to cause them to give us some Liberty to worship him, though sometimes under great Sufferings;—And now I am to Acquaint King William, That we have been A People for about 46: Years, and have lived under several Reigns, and we have sufferred very much, as its well known to the Nation of England, even to the Death of several hundreds, by Imprisonments, and other hardships; And yet we were never found in Transgression of any Just or Righteous Law, but onely upon Account of our Consciences towards God, that was the cause of our Suffering; and not for Evill or Wrong done to any Man or Government;— For our Principle, which we Testifie of, is the Light of Jesus Christ, and his Etternal Spirit, which leads into all Truth and Righteousness, but not into any Untruth, or Evill Actions; And if any bearing the same Name amongst Us, have Transgressed against this pretious Truth and Royall Law of Liberty, wee doe with the same Spirit,

Judge and Condemne them, where ever they are found.- And we doe deny all Plotting and Contriveing against the Government, and all false and underhand Dealing; and wee live in that Principle, which is Righteous, Just and True; For God is a God of Truth, and blessed are all they that fear him, and walk in his Truth. And Now God has placed thee over us, in this Government, who hast been very Moderate and mercifull to us, and wee live very comfortably under thee and it, and doe Enjoy our Meettings Quietly, which formerly we were much disturbed in, which was A great Suffering unto us; and God has blessed thy Government, and Prospered thy Undertakings, for which the King, and we have cause to bless his holy name, who is A God of Peace, and his Son is Prince of Peace, who now has given us Peace and Tranquility; for which we Praise his holy Name:—and thy Gentle Government and Clemency, & Gratious Acts, God hath and will Reward thee for:—And as we abide in that Just & Righteous Principle of the Eternal God, by which we ought all to be Guided, I hope the Government shall never hear worse of us, but that we shall rather be A blessing then a Grievance to it and the Nation, For soe it will be, as we continue in the blessed Truth, in which I pray God for thy Preservation; who am his Servant, and thy Faithfull Subject,

Margarett Fox.

London, the 24th of the 4th Month,
called June, 1698:
Delivered to the King the 25th of the
4th Month, by Susan Ingram.

Port 41:84 FHL, also Works, *pp. 531–533, and summary* JFHS, 6:81. *Addressed: "To Kinge William the Third". Endorsed: "This is A Coppy of a paper, delivered to Kinge William the Third, at his Pallace at Kensington, the 25th of the 4th moth 1698:- by Susannah Ingram, sixth daughter of the above mentioned Margarett Fox [Sarah Fell Meade]."*

164 TO EDMUND WALLER JUNE 25, 1698

"I perceive by some Letters from thee . . .
that there is a Work of God begun in thy inward Man."

Edmund Waller was a young man who had recently joined the Quakers (Ross, p. 376). He was the son of Edmund Waller, the Cavalier poet, who wrote "Go, lovely Rose" and "On a Girdle."

Dear Friend,

I Should have been glad to have seen thee before I had returned to my outward Habitation, understanding that thou hast made Choice of that blessed Truth that we bear witness to, I cannot but say, It is well that thou hast chosen the better part, which, if thou abide in, and obey, it will never be taken from thee. I perceive by some Letters from thee, which I have heard read, that there is a Work of God begun in thy inward Man, where he works in his People, the new Creation in Christ Jesus, which is unto Righteousness, Holiness and Purity. The Apostles writ to the Saints, and deired that the Eyes of their Understandings might be opened [Eph. 1:18], and that they might be strengthned in the inward Man: Here is the Coming of Christ the Second time without Sin unto Salvation: This is the great Work that God is working in this his day in the Hearts of his People, as it was in the days of the Apostles; in which time there was some, though they professed all one thing, yet there was Divisions amongst them concerning some things, even betwixt Paul and Peter. And the Apostle writ to the Corinthians, though he had espoused them to one Husband, yet he was afraid of them, lest the Serpent should beguile them, through his Subtilty, as he did Eve, from the Simplicity which is in Christ [2 Cor. 11:2–3]. The Simplicity that is in Christ, is single, naked and innocent, without ends. Now the Subtilty of the Serpent is to draw aside for ends, and to appear another thing than it is in reality; the Subtilty hurts the Simplicity: But where Christ is the Leader and Guider, there will he bless and prosper; and he is an unchangeable God, and so ought all his Children and Servants to be.

So to this God, that is merciful, constant and faithful, I commit thee, to perfect his Work by his Word in thee, who is God over all, blessed for ever.

From thy Well-wishing Friend in the Truth,

Margaret Fox.

London, the 25th of the 4th Month, 1698.

Works, *pp. 532–533.*

165 To Bethiah [Rous] and David English November 17, 1699

"It is but a Chance that wee Cann get any thinge sent into your parts."

Mail had to go through London since there was no cross-country postal service from Swarthmoor Hall to Pontefract in Yorkshire. Margaret took advantage of a friend traveling to Pontefract to send a letter to her granddaughter, Bethiah, and her husband, David English.

Swarthmore the 17th of 9th mo 99

Dear Grand son and Grand Daughter English

In the deare and tender love and bowels of devine life I doe dearley remember you and write these few lines unto you as a testemony theof; desireing you to keepe Close to the Lords powe[r] love and life and theire you will grow and Abide neare the lord and he will bide neare to you as you abide Inwardly to him; dear Bethia[,] keepe up to the Lord[,] be Content with his will what ever it be for that is the best and the safest for thee; waite upon him in obediunce and that is the way for the Lord to give thee thy harts desire; it is longe sin[c]e I wrote to thee or heard from thee but I doe not forget thee[.] thou art often before me; I heard by two Friends that thou was at the Wells in Yorkeshire and was pretty well which I was glad of[.] I have not heard from thy Mother [Margaret Fell Rous] but once since shee Came From the Bath; but I hope shee is well; I have had two Letters From thy sister Dickes [Anne Rous Dykes or Dix] and one From hir Husband [Benjamin Dykes or Dix]; they are verry well and Lives very well and Comfortably; if thou would but write to thy Mother how it is with thee every way; and shee would Lett me know[.] I cann doe noe more but pray to almighty god for you all and I trust and hope the Lord his blessinge and grace may rest upon you[,] haveing this opertunity by this Friend I was willinge to write to you these few lines to let you know that the Lord has presaved [preserved] me in health ever since I came from London; I have writen to my Daughter Morris [Isabel Fell Yeamans Morrice,] and I desire thee to gett it to hir for I have not written to hir since I came From London[.] it is but a Chance that wee Cann get any thinge sent into your parts[.] My Daughter Abraham and hir Son [Rachel Fell Abraham and son John Abraham] has there deare Loves dearly Remembred unto you[.] hir husband [Daniel Abraham] is Now at London[,] presoner for tythe noe more[;] but my Love and prayers for you from your Deare Grand Mother

M: F:

Portfolio 31:108 FHL and JFHS, 1915:146–147. Addressed: "For David English att his house in Pomphrit Yorkeshire These".

166 To Friends, Brethren and Sisters April 1700

"But wee must bee all in one Dress, and one Collour; This is a silly poor Gospell."

It is appropriate that Margaret Fell's last letter is a strong affirmation of her commitment to Quakerism and of her willingness to speak clearly and plainly on tendencies of Friends in the 1690s that were not in keeping with basic tenets of Quakerism.

She finds the growth of rules and regulations about dress and association with people "of the world" limiting and leading "into things outwardly." God, the "holy one of Israel," is a sufficient teacher, and they do not need "outward things & Ceremonies," which is a "Narrowness & straitnes" and "Jewism" in the sense of emphasis on ritual.

She urges a common-sense practice of dealing with others: "If any of that beleive not, bidd you to a Feast, and you be disposed to goe, whatsoever is set before you, Eat." She writes eloquently, "Away with these whimsicall Narrow Imaginations." She cares about living "Righteously & Justly & hollyley" and not about petty rules.

Her statement, "This is not Delightful to mee, That I have this occasion to write to you" shows that she considered long and carefully before she wrote this letter to her Quaker community, but she felt compelled to do so. She ends with a particularly apt biblical quotation that could have been the motto for her own life, "I have set before you Life and Death, and Desires you to Chuse Life."

Friends, & Brethren, & Sisters

Wee are the people of the liveing God and God hath vissitted us, & brought us out in an acceptable Day of Salvation, a Gospell Day, in which the eternall God is Gathering his Elect, from the four winds of

Heaven and from the four Corners of the Earth [Mark 13:27]; And hee hath shined from the throne of his Glory, in our hearts; in his spirituall Light, and given us the true knowledg of himselfe, in the face & Image of Jesus Christ, hee hath made us partakers of his Divine Nature, And hee hath given us his good & holy Spirit to Lead us, and to guide us, into all truth, in all things.

Now Dear Friends, Brethren & Sisters, Let us all beware of Limitting the holy one of Israel or tampering with any thing Contrary to this holy spirit, for the Grace of God is Sufficient to Teach us, to Deny all ungodlyness & unrighteousness, & will teach us to live holily & Righteously, unto God & his Truth, in this present & evill world: And let us beware of medling with the things of God, otherwise than his Spirit Leads and guides: Now there is a spirit got up amongst Friends in some places, that would make & medle in their Imaginations, in leading of Friends into things outwardly, which our Lord Jesus Christ never comanded, for hee allways testified against the Jews manner of making & prescribing of things outwardly, for his Testimony is in every heart To work inwardly, & make them the inside, So let us beware of imitating & fashining after the Jewes manner in outward things & Ceremonies: For though it be said in Scripture, That his prophet should dwell alone, that was in that time under the Law when hee had chosen them out of all the famillies of the Earth, yet hee would punish them for their transgresion[.]

But now our Blessed Lord is come, & its but a small thing for him, to gather together the Tribes of Israell, & the Dispersed of Juda: hee is also given for a Light to the Gentiles & to be for Salvation to the end of the earth: hee would have all to be saved, and to come to the knowledge of his blessed Truth: And hee Testified against the phareses, that said, I am more holy than thee, Let us beware of this of separateing or looking upon our selves to be more holy, then in Deed & in truth we are; for what are we, but what we have received from God and God is all sufficient to bring in Thousands into the same Spirit & Light, to Lead & to Guide them, as he doth us: And let us frame & fashion our selves unto the Apostles Doctrine & practice, who was in a glorious shineing Light, Read 1.Cor.chap. 9:19,ver. & so to the end[.]

Now see how contrary our practice is to the Apostles, when wee must not goe to a Buriall of the people of the world, nor bidd them to any of our Burialls, or do that which is moderate and of a good report, as to meats or Drinks e[t]c. Again read 1.Cor.ch.10.ver.27 If any of them that beleive not, bidd you to a Feast, and you be disposed to goe, whatsoever is set before you, Eat, asking no question for conscience sake. This is more than a Birth or Buriall, which is needfull & necessary: Away with these whimsicall Narrow Imaginations, and let the Spirit of God which he hath given us, Lead us, & Guide us: And Let us stand fast in that liberty wherewith Christ hath made us free, and not be intangled againe into bondage in observing proscriptions, in outward things which will not profitt, nor cleanse the inward man. It is the work of Christ Jesus, in this his Day. And by this Let everyone do as they are perswaded in their own minds, for the Apostle saith, hee was not to Rule over any ones faith.

For its now gone 47. yeares since wee owned the Truth, And all things has gone well & peaceably till now of late, That this narrowness & straitness is entering in, That many cannot tell what to Do, or not Do:

Our Monthly & Quarterly Meetings, were set up for Reproveing, & looking into Superfluous or Disorderly walking, and such to be admonished & instructed in the Truth, And not private persons to take upon them to make orders, and say this must be done, and the other must not be done: And can Friends think, that those who are Taught & Guided of God can be subject & follow such low, mean orders: So its good for Friends of our County, to Leave these things to the Lord who is become our Leader, Teacher, & Guider, and not to goe abroad to Spread: for they will never do good, but hath done hurt allready: wee are now comeing into Jewism, into that which Christ Cried woe against[,] minding altogether outward things, neclecting the Inward work of Almighty God in our hearts; If wee can but frame according to outward prescriptions & orders, and deny eating & drinking with our neighbors, in so much that poor friends is mangled in their minds, that they know not what do doe: for one Friend sayes one way, and another, another, But Christ Jesus saith, that we must take no thought what wee shall eat, or what wee shall drink, or what we shall put on: but bidds us consider, the Lillies how they grow in more Royalty than Solomon [Matt. 6:28–31]: But Contrary to this wee must looke at no Collours, nor make any thing that is changable Collours as the hilles are, nor sell them, nor wear them. But wee must bee all in one Dress, and one Collour; This is a silly poor Gospell, It is more fitt for us, To be Covered with Gods Eternall Spirit, and Cloathed with his eternall Light which Leads us, & Guides us into Righteousness, and to live Righteously & Justly & hollyly in this profane evill world: This is the Cloathing that God putts upon us, and likes, & will bless, This will make our Light shine forth before men, that they may glorify our heavenly Father which is in heaven [Matt. 5:16], For we have God for our Teacher and wee have his promises and Doctrines, and wee have the Apostles practice in their Day and Generation: And wee have Gods holy Spirit, to Lead us & guide us, and wee have the blessed Truth, that wee are made partakers off [of], to be our practice, And why should wee turn to men & woman Teaching, which is contrary to Christ Jesus Comand and the Apostles practice, here is the __________ where those things beforementioned stands upon: where have wee had those whimses & Imaginations[.] Friends, wee have one God, & one mediator betwixt God & man, The man Christ Jesus[.] Let us keep to him, or wee are undone,/

This is not Delightfull to mee, That I have this occasion to write to you[,] for wherever I saw it appear, I have stud [stood] against it severall yeares, And now I dare neglect no longer, For I see, That our blessed precious holy Truth, That hath vissitted us from the begining is kept under, and these silly outside Imaginary practices is Coming up, & practised with great zeale, which hath often greived my heart:

Now, I have set before you Life and Death, and Desires you to Chuse Life [Deut. 30:19], and God and his Truth,

Margarett Fox./

the 2 mo. 1700.

Facsimile of manuscript at Haverford College; per Ross, p. 380, FHL Portfolio 25:66, "Gift of Wm Benson, Sydney, Australia, ALS."

Epilogue

Margaret Fell Fox was close to her eighty-eighth birthday when she died on April 23, 1702. Her mind was clear, and she was surrounded by children and grandchildren. She was buried within the walls of the Quaker burial ground at Sunbreck, not far from Swarthmoor Hall, next to Birkrigg Common. It is a lovely, lonely place, overlooking Morecambe Bay. In the Common there is a small circle of stones that probably dates to pre-Roman times, and sheep still graze there.

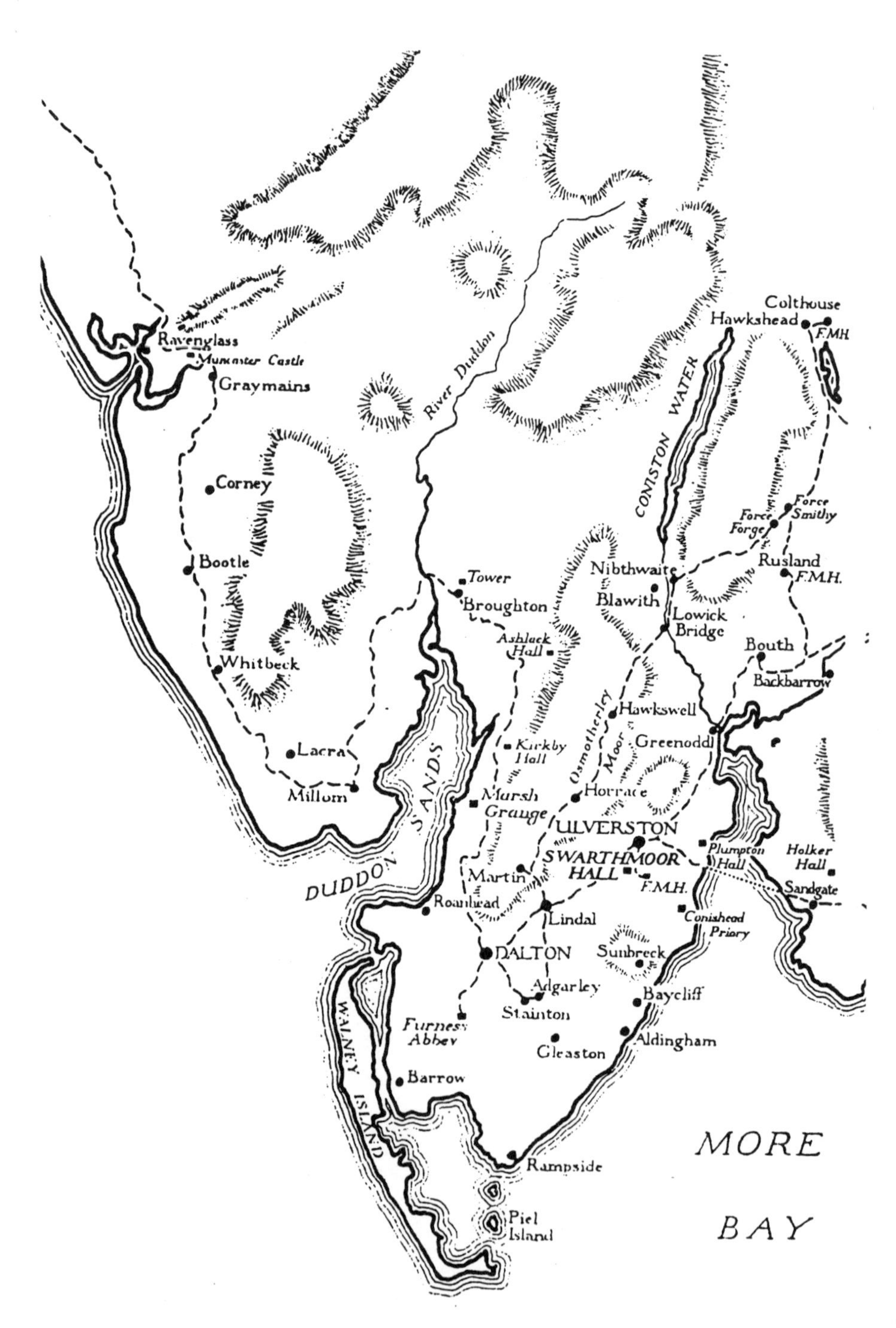

As reproduced in *Margaret Fell: Mother of Quakerism* by Isabel Ross (Sessions Book Trust 1996 Edition) by permission.

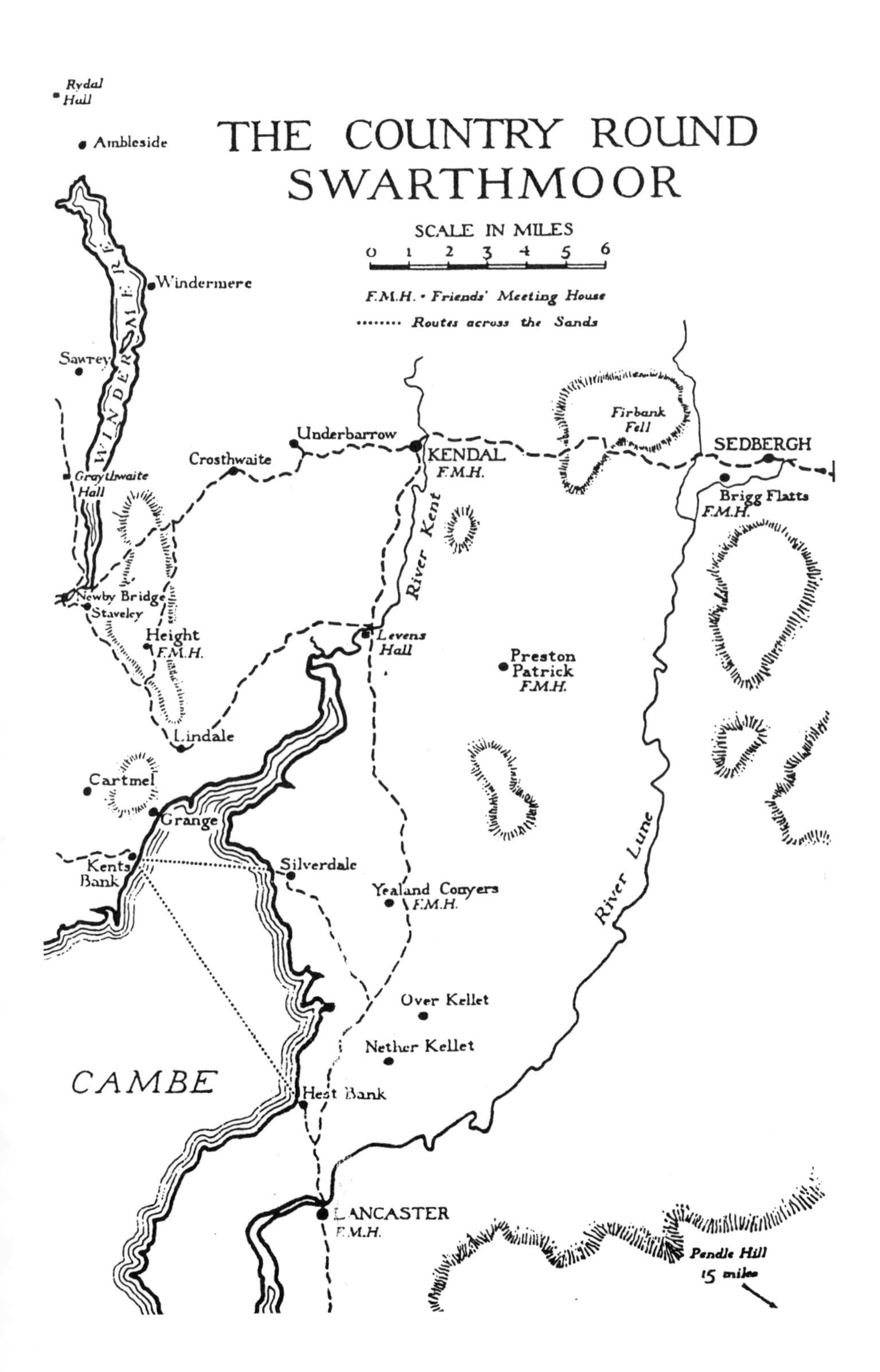
THE COUNTRY ROUND SWARTHMOOR
SCALE IN MILES
0 1 2 3 4 5 6
F.M.H. • Friends' Meeting House
.... Routes across the Sands
Rydal Hall
Ambleside
WINDERMERE
Windermere
Sawrey
Graythwaite Hall
Newby Bridge
Staveley
Height F.M.H.
Lindale
Cartmel
Grange
Kents Bank
Crosthwaite
Underbarrow
KENDAL F.M.H.
River Kent
Levens Hall
Firbank Fell
SEDBERGH
Brigg Flatts F.M.H.
Preston Patrick F.M.H.
Silverdale
Yealand Conyers F.M.H.
River Lune
Over Kellet
Nether Kellet
CAMBE
Hest Bank
LANCASTER F.M.H.
Pendle Hill 15 miles

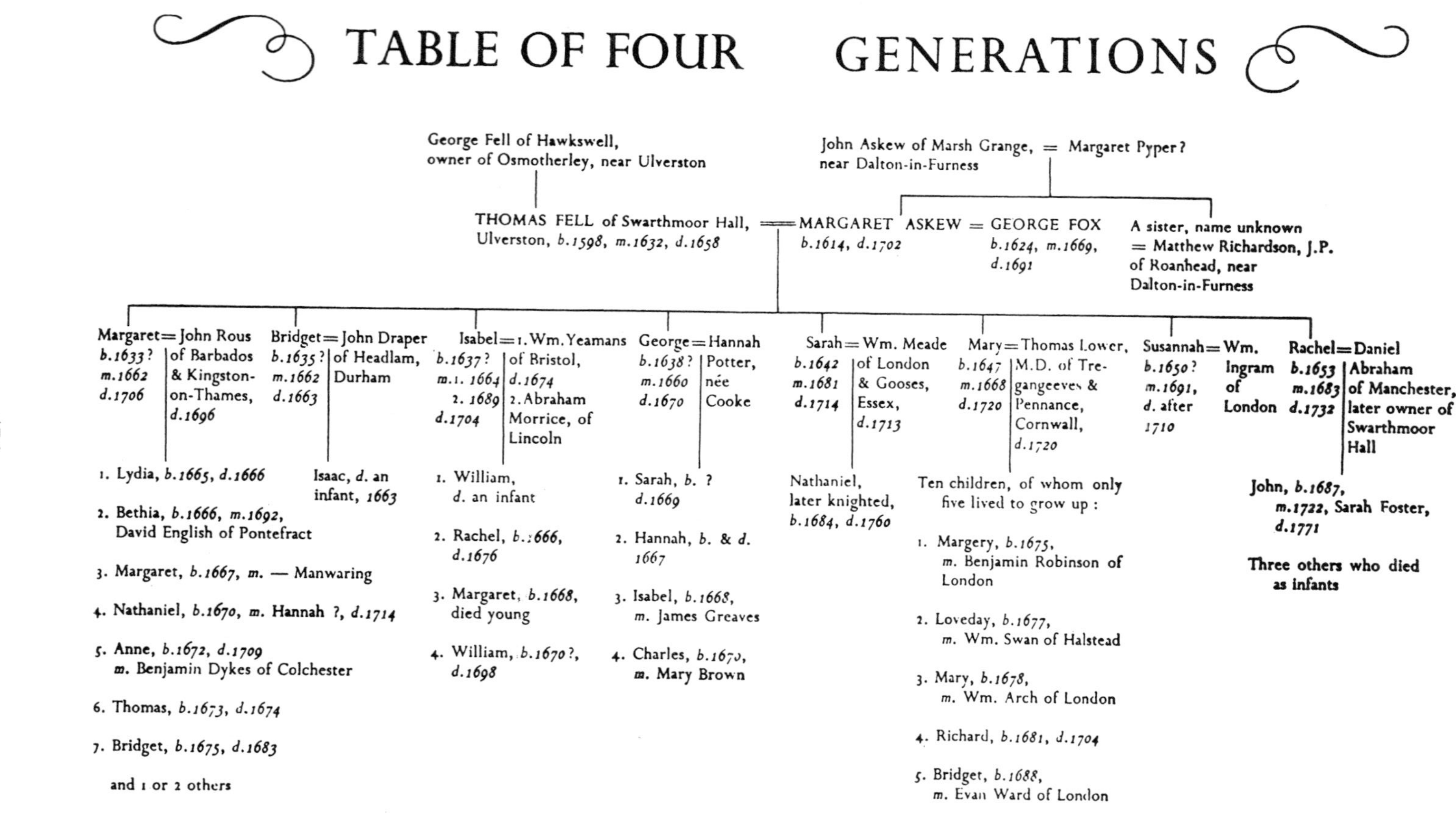
TABLE OF FOUR GENERATIONS
George Fell of Hawkswell, owner of Osmotherley, near Ulverston
John Askew of Marsh Grange, = Margaret Pyper? near Dalton-in-Furness
THOMAS FELL of Swarthmoor Hall, Ulverston, b.1598, m.1632, d.1658
= MARGARET ASKEW = GEORGE FOX
b.1614, d.1702
b.1624, m.1669, d.1691
A sister, name unknown = Matthew Richardson, J.P. of Roanhead, near Dalton-in-Furness
Margaret = John Rous
b.1633? m.1662 d.1706
of Barbados & Kingston-on-Thames, d.1696
Bridget = John Draper
b.1635? m.1662 d.1663
of Headlam, Durham
Isabel = 1. Wm. Yeamans
b.1637? m.1. 1664 2. 1689 d.1704
of Bristol, d.1674 2. Abraham Morrice, of Lincoln
George = Hannah
b.1638? m.1660 d.1670
Potter, née Cooke
Sarah = Wm. Meade
b.1642 m.1681 d.1714
of London & Gooses, Essex, d.1713
Mary = Thomas Lower,
b.1647 m.1668 d.1720
M.D. of Tregangeeves & Pennance, Cornwall, d.1720
Susannah = Wm. Ingram of London
b.1650? m.1691, d. after 1710
Rachel = Daniel Abraham
b.1653 m.1683 d.1732
of Manchester, later owner of Swarthmoor Hall
1. Lydia, b.1665, d.1666
2. Bethia, b.1666, m.1692, David English of Pontefract
3. Margaret, b.1667, m. — Manwaring
4. Nathaniel, b.1670, m. Hannah ?, d.1714
5. Anne, b.1672, d.1709 m. Benjamin Dykes of Colchester
6. Thomas, b.1673, d.1674
7. Bridget, b.1675, d.1683
and 1 or 2 others
Isaac, d. an infant, 1663
1. William, d. an infant
2. Rachel, b.1666, d.1676
3. Margaret, b.1668, died young
4. William, b.1670?, d.1698
1. Sarah, b. ? d.1669
2. Hannah, b. & d. 1667
3. Isabel, b.1668, m. James Greaves
4. Charles, b.1670, m. Mary Brown
Nathaniel, later knighted, b.1684, d.1760
Ten children, of whom only five lived to grow up:
1. Margery, b.1675, m. Benjamin Robinson of London
2. Loveday, b.1677, m. Wm. Swan of Halstead
3. Mary, b.1678, m. Wm. Arch of London
4. Richard, b.1681, d.1704
5. Bridget, b.1688, m. Evan Ward of London
John, b.1687, m.1722, Sarah Foster, d.1771
Three others who died as infants

As reproduced in *Margaret Fell: Mother of Quakerism* by Isabel Ross (Sessions Book Trust 1996 Edition) by permission.

Margaret Fell's Appearance

Lacking credible portraits or even sketches of Margaret Fell, we can only draw on styles of the period and scant information from letters for an idea of her appearance, including what she and her daughters wore. Amelia Mott Gummere gives her perspective in *The Quaker, a Study in Costume*:

> It would be very valuable to us to learn what was the exact costume worn by Margaret Fell (afterward Margaret Fox) and her talented and interesting daughters. We only know how her contemporaries dressed, and have a few details of the family wardrobe in those Swarthmoor account books which still exist. That they wore the popular style of dress, without adornments, is altogether likely, for she has left on record her disapproval of anything tending to uniformity among the Friends. We shall not be far wrong, I think, if we imagine George Fox's wife in a hood of black wadded silk, a short, full skirt, standing well out from the hips, and held in position by an array of petticoats (for she would never have worn the false hips then in vogue); a kerchief of muslin, over a low bodice, stiff and long in the waist, and laced with many eyelets, its cord of blue or white or black, depending upon whether her gown were red or blue; her shoes heavy, low and square-toed, with heels that may have been another color from the shoe itself, but not the fashionable red, and higher than we should now care to wear upon the street. Her cloak, whose color we dare not speculate upon, was of substantial cloth, with a hood for ornament when not in use, as it often was, particularly in her long journeys on horseback from county to county attending public Meetings. She may have called it a "capuchin," for that was the form of cloak then coming into wear. But we are not privileged to possess descriptions of her personal appearance nor of her style of dress, as is the case with both of her distinguished husbands. We learn from one or two references to old letters of ancient worthies, that she was fair and comely, and Maria Webb [The Fells of Swarthmoor Hall] says that she had a "beaming countenance," and a "most sweet, harmonious voice." . . .

A few items of clothing touched upon in the family letters give us our only clue to the style of dress worn by the women of the Swarthmoor circle. . . . Sarah (Fell) Meade wrote her sister, Rachel Abraham, from London, under date "The 19th. Of 10th. [December] 1683":

> I have endeavoured to fit my dear Mother with black cloth for a gown, which is very good and fine, and as much as Jno. Richards saith is enough to the full, 5 yards and half, and what materials as he thought was needful to send down, vizt. Silk, both sewing and stitching, gallowne ribbon, and laces. . . . (pp. 124–126)

This illustration of middle-class women's dress in the Commonwealth, 1651, hints at how Margaret Fell and her daughters might have dressed.

Portraits of Judge Fell and George Fox

Judge Thomas Fell (1598–1658)

Reproduction of a photograph from an oil painting. (Reproduced with permission of the Religious Society of Friends in Britain.)

George Fox (1624–1691)

Photograph of engraving taken from the Darton lithograph of a supposed portrait by Chinn, late eighteenth century. (Reproduced with permission of the Religious Society of Friends in Britain.)

Categories of Margaret Fell's Letters

Margaret Fell's letters may be grouped in four general categories. These are inexact, but they give an indication of the subjects and the tenor of particular letters.

LETTERS TO FAMILY AND FRIENDS

1, 4, 5, 6, 7, 8, 9, 22, 32, 41, 48, 49, 51, 52, 53, 54, 63, 64, 66, 68, 75, 76, 78, 79, 82, 88, 89, 90, 91, 92, 94, 95, 98, 100, 101, 104, 109, 111, 116, 120, 126, 128, 132, 133, 134, 135, 137, 138, 139, 140, 141, 142, 143, 145, 146, 147, 152, 153, 154, 155, 156, 157, 158, 159, 165.

PASTORAL LETTERS AND EPISTLES

4, 6, 9, 11, 16, 17, 18, 19, 25, 26, 27, 28, 29, 36, 37, 38, 47, 50, 55, 56, 61, 62, 69, 70, 71, 72, 73, 74, 77, 80, 81, 112, 117, 125, 129, 160, 161, 162, 164, 166.

PETITIONS TO THOSE IN AUTHORITY

11, 14, 15, 31, 33, 34, 42, 65, 83, 84, 85, 86, 87, 93, 96, 97, 99, 102, 103, 105, 106, 107, 108, 110, 113, 114, 115, 118, 119, 121, 122, 123, 124, 127, 130, 131, 136, 148, 149, 150, 151, 163.

POLEMICAL LETTERS/DOCTRINAL CONTROVERSY

20, 21, 23–24, 30, 35, 39, 40, 43, 44, 45, 46, 57, 58, 59, 67

Major Themes in Margaret Fell's Letters

While this is not an exhaustive list, it is representative of the major themes in the Fell letters. Numbers refer to the letters, not pages of this book.

CALL TO REPENTENCE

12, 15, 19, 21, 25, 30, 33, 35, 37, 69, 74

Glossary

Seventeenth-Century Usage

Binding over—"The act by which a court or magistrate requires a person to enter a recognizance or furnish bail to appear for trial, to keep the peace, to attend as a witness, etc." *Black's Law Dictionary.*

Bowels—"The seat of the tender and compassionate emotions" (*OED*).

Church—For Quakers, it is the community, "this body, the Church, whereof Christ Jesus is the Head" (Margaret Fell, Letter 125). It is not an institution or a building.

Color/Colour—"Figurative sense . . . that which serves to conceal or cloak the truth, or to give a show of justice to what is in itself unjustifiable" (*OED*).

Contention—"The act of straining or striving earnestly, earnest exertion, effort, endeavor" (*OED*).

Conventicle Act—Several Conventicle Acts were passed, in 1664, 1670, and 1674. They forbade any Meeting of more than five persons outside the household. They were intended to prevent conspiracy against the government and to discourage dissenters.

Exalted—"To assume superiority (*OED*). To Quakers, it had a negative connotation, meaning those with wild imagination.

Form—"A set method of outward behaviour or procedure in . . . etiquette, ritual, etc.; a ceremony or formality. (Often slightingly, as implying the absence of intrinsic meaning or reality)" (*OED*).

Hireling Priest—For Quakers, a derisive term for ministers or priests who preached for money, supported by mandatory tithes.

Informers—The Conventicle Act of 1674 particularly encouraged abuse, by rewarding informers with one-third of fines collected from persons convicted of violating the Act. Thousands of Quakers were fined.

Lamb's War—The Lamb of God may symbolize sacrifice and meekness. It sometimes refers to Jesus Christ, particularly in the Gospel of John and the Book of Revelation. The Lamb's War is a sign of victory over evil, despite weakness, a spiritual war. Quakers often used it in this sense.

Meetings—Early Quakers and other sects used the term *Meeting*, rather than *church*. Quaker Meetings were usually silent, with men or women speaking only when moved by a direct spiritual call. By the 1670s there were regular, organized monthly and quarterly Meetings, and a yearly Meeting. I have capitalized the word in my notes simply to indicate that a religious event or group is being referred to, and not a secular gathering.

Melchizedek—In Genesis, the name signifies a high priest; Melchizedek was a king and priest who blessed Abraham. In the epistle to the Hebrews, Jesus is considered a priest "after the order of Melchizedek."

Mittimus—A warrant of commitment to prison.

Perfection—Puritan doctrine emphasized the hopeless sinfulness of man, except for the elect. Quakers stressed the possibility of "labouring fervently ... that ye may stand perfect and complete in all the will of God" [Col. 4:12].

Praemunire—*Praemunire* was the severe sentence pronounced for an offense against the king and the government. It meant the loss of all property, imprisonment for life, and being "out of the king's protection."

Professor—Not an academic term, but, to Quakers, meaning a person who professed Christianity but did not understand or practice it.

Publishers of Truth—One of the terms used by Quakers for themselves. To "publish truth" was the goal of the itinerant ministers. Other sects have also used the term.

Ranters—Ranters were radical, religious individuals who believed in spiritual freedom and rejected all rules. "Ranters claimed to be morally liberated from outward 'legalisms' by the spirit of God within them and thus be justified in shouting, cursing, drunken behavior, and nudity" (Barbour, *Quakers*, p. 19). Quakers were sometimes accused of being Ranters, which they strenuously denied.

Saints—A term used by Quakers and other sects for their own members. Also used in the Bible.

Seed—*Seed* is a flexible term, frequently used in Quaker epistles. It could mean Jesus, or the people hearing the Quaker message, or the possibility of good arising through God's presence in the world.

Shepherd—The *shepherd*, a caring, unpaid pastor, was a term used to signify a Quaker minister, contrary to a hireling priest. As in biblical times, sheep were a living presence in Margaret Fell's Lancashire. Actually, they still are today.

Steeplehouse—A derisive Quaker term for a church building. The place where worshipers gathered was not important.

Tithe—The tax to support the established church, opposed by dissenters.

They did not wish to support a faith they did not accept. Also, tithing was a hardship on poor people.

Traverse—In law, it "signifies a denial. Thus, where a defendant denies any material allegation of fact in the plaintiff's declaration, he is said to traverse it" (*Black's Law Dictionary*).

Type—A theological term, "To prefigure or foreshadow as a type; to represent in prophetic similitude" (*OED*). To symbolize; a mental construct.

Unpreferred—Unmarried.

Bibliography

MANUSCRIPTS

Friends House Library, London
- Abraham Manuscript
- Box C14
- Box Meeting Manuscript
- Cash Collection
- Caton Manuscript
- Dix Z.1, MS Vol.294
- Gibson Manuscript
- Miller Manuscript (Transcript)
- MS Box 2, 7, 10
- MS Vol. 101, 323, 329
- Markey Manuscript, Box C41
- Morning Meeting Minutes 1673–1692. Transcript
- Portfolio 15, 23, 25, 31, 33, 36, 41
- Spence Manuscript, Volume 3
- Swarthmore Manuscripts, Volume 1, 3, 8
- Tapper Manuscript
- Thirnbeck Manuscript
- York Manuscript

Haverford College Library, Haverford, Pennsylvania
- Facsimiles (Letter 162, 166)
- Photocopy (Letter 133)

Historical Society of Pennsylvania, Philadelphia
- Etting Papers
- Penn-Forbes Collection

Lancashire County Record Office, Preston
- QSP 576/4

Nottinghamshire Archives, Nottingham
Manuscript NC/Q

Public Record Office, London
PRO SP 29/91

Swarthmore College Library, Swarthmore, Pennsylvania
Manuscript, Letter to John Ravell

University of Texas at Austin, Harry Ransom Humanities Research Center
Pforzheimer Collection

PUBLISHED BOOKS AND ARTICLES—WORKS CITED

Barbour, Hugh and Arthur Roberts, eds. *Early Quaker Writings, 1650–1700.* Grand Rapids, Mich.: William B. Eerdmans, 1973.

Barbour, Hugh, and J. William Frost. *The Quakers.* New York: Greenwood Press, 1988.

Barclay, John, ed. *Letters, etc. of Early Friends.* London: Harvey and Barton, 1841.

Bauman, Richard. *Let Your Words Be Few, Symbolism of Speaking and Silence Among Seventeenth-Century Quakers.* Cambridge: Cambridge University Press, 1983.

Besse, Joseph. *A Collection of the Sufferings of the People Called Quakers . . . from 1650–1689.* 2 vols. London: Luke Hinde, 1753.

Bittle, William G. *James Nayler, 1618–1660, the Quaker Indicted by Parliament.* York: William Sessions, 1986.

Black's Law Dictionary. Rev. 4th ed. St. Paul: West Publishing Co., 1968.

Boulton, David and Anthea. *In Fox's Footsteps, a Journey Through Three Centuries.* Dent, Cumbria: Dales Historical Monographs, 1998.

Braithwaite, William C. *The Beginnings of Quakerism (to 1660)* 2nd ed. rev. by Henry J. Cadbury. York: William Sessions, 1981.

Braithwaite, William C. *The Second Period of Quakerism.* 2nd ed. prepared by Henry J. Cadbury. York: William Sessions, 1979.

Burrough, Edward. *A Memoir of the Life and Religious Labors of Edward Burrough; an Eminent Servant of Christ and Minnister of the Gospel in the Society of Friends.* Philadelphia: Friends' Book Store, 1890.

Cadbury, Henry J., ed. *Annual Catalogue of George Fox's Papers, Compiled in 1694–1697.* London: Friends Book Centre, 1939.

Campbell, John. *The Lives of the Chief Justices of England,* 4 vols. New York: James Cockcroft & Co., 1873.

Clark, Alice. *The Working Life of Women in the 17th Century.* New York: Harcourt, Brace & Howe, 1920.

Cope, Jackson I. "Seventeenth Century Quaker Style." PMLA 71 (1956): 725–754.

Crosfield, Helen G. *Margaret Fox of Swarthmoor Hall.* London: Headley Brothers, 1913.

Davies, Horton. *Worship and Theology in England [v.2] From Andrews to Baxter and Fox, 1603–1690.* Princeton: Princeton University Press, 1975.

Dictionary of American Biography. 11 vols. New York: Charles Scribner's Sons, reprint 1957–1958.

Dictionary of National Biography. 22 vols. Oxford: Oxford University Press, reprint 1960.

Eales, Jacqueline. *Puritans and Roundheads, the Harleys of Brampton Bryan and the Outbreak of the English Civil War.* Cambridge: Cambridge University Press, 1990.

Edmundson, William. *A Journal of the Life, Travels, Sufferings and Labour of Love in the Work of the Ministry.* 2nd ed. London: Mary Hinde, 1774.

Ezell, Margaret M. *The Patriarch's Wife, Literary Evidence and the History of the Family.* Chapel Hill: University of North Carolina, 1987.

Fell, Margaret. *(Works) A Brief Collection of Remarkable Passages and Occurrences Relating to the Birth, Education, Life, Conversion, Travels, Services and Deep Sufferings of that Ancient and Faithful Servant of the Lord, Margaret Fell, but by her Second Marriage, M. Fox.* London: J. Sowle, 1710.

Fox, George. *The Journal of George Fox,* ed. by Norman Penney. 2 vols. Cambridge: Cambridge University Press, 1911.

Fox, George. *The Journal of George Fox,* rev. ed. by John L. Nickalls. London: Religious Society of Friends, 1975.

Fox, George. *The Short Journal and Itinerary Journals of George Fox, in Commemoration of the Tercentenary of his Birth (1624–1924).* ed. by Norman Penney. Cambridge: Cambridge University Press, 1925.

Fraser, Antonia. *The Weaker Vessel.* New York: Knopf, 1984.

The Friends' Library, Comprising Journals, Doctrinal Treatises, and other Writings of Members of the Religious Society of Friends. ed. by William and Thomas Evans. Philadelphia: Printed by Joseph Rakestraw, 1847.

Greaves, Richard L. *Deliver Us from Evil, the Radical Underground in Britain, 1660–1663*. New York: Oxford University Press, 1986.

Greaves, Richard L. *Enemies Under his Feet: Radicals and Nonconformists in Britain, 1664–1672*. Stanford: Stanford University Press, 1990.

Greaves, Richard L., and Robert Zaller, eds. *Biographical Dictionary of British Radicals in the 17th Century*. 3 vols. Brighton: Harvester Press, 1982–1984.

Gummere, Amelia Mott. *The Quaker, a Study in Costume*. Philadelphia: Ferris & Leach, 1901.

Hayes, Will. *Gray Ridge, the Book of Francis Howgill*. Meopham Green, Kent: Order of the Great Companions, 1942.

Henning, Basil Duke. *The House of Commons, 1660–1690*. 3 vols. London: Secker & Weidenfield, 1983.

Hill, Christopher. *Liberty Against the Law, Some Seventeenth-Century Controversies*. London: Penguin, 1996.

Hill, Christopher. *The World Turned Upside Down; Radical Ideas During the English Revolution*. London: Temple Smith, 1972; London, New York: Penguin Books, 1975.

Hobby, Elaine. *Virtue of Necessity, English Women's Writing, 1649–1688*. Ann Arbor: University of Michigan Press, 1989.

Horle, Craig. "Index to Spence MSS. vol. 3" (unpublished typescript). London: Friends House Library.

Horle, Craig. *The Quakers and the English Legal System, 1660–1688*. Philadelphia: University of Pennsylvania Press, 1988.

Horle, Craig, ed. *Records of the Courts of Sussex County of Delaware, 1677–1710*. Philadelphia: University of Pennsylvania Press, 1991.

Hull, William I. *The Rise of Quakerism in Amsterdam, 1655–1665*. Swarthmore College Monographs on Quaker History, no. 4, 1938.

Hutton, Ronald. *The Restoration: A Political and Religious History of England and Wales, 1658–1667*. Oxford: Clarendon Press, 1985.

Ingle, H. Larry. *First Among Friends, George Fox and the Creation of Quakerism*. New York: Oxford University Press, 1994.

Journal of the Friends Historical Society, London.

Kunze, Bonnelyn Young. *Margaret Fell and the Rise of Quakerism*. Stanford: Stanford University Press, 1994.

Mack, Phyllis. *Visionary Women, Ecstatic Prophecy in Seventeenth-Century England*. Berkeley: University of California Press, 1992.

Mack, Phyllis. "Women as Prophets During the English Civil War." In *The Origins of Anglo-American Radicalism*, ed. by Margaret and James Jacob. London: G. Allen & Unwin, 1984.

Mayo, Lawrence Shaw. *John Endecott, a Biography*. Cambridge: Harvard University Press, 1936.

Mendelson, Sara Heller. *The Mental World of Stuart Women*. Amherst: University of Massachusetts, 1987.

Moore, Rosemary. *The Light in Their Consciences: Early Quakers in Britain, 1646–1666*. University Park, Pennsylvania: University of Pennsylvania Press, 2000.

Morrah, Patrick. *1660, the Year of Restoration*. London: Chatto & Windus, 1960.

Mortimer, Russell. "Quakerism in Seventeenth-Century Bristol" (unpublished Bristol M.A. thesis), 1946.

National Cyclopedia of American Biography . . . 63 vols. New York: J. T. White, 1891–1984. Partially reprint.

Nayler, James. A *Collection of Sundry Books, Epistles and Papers*. London, J. Sowle, 1716.

Nicolson, Marjorie Hope. *Conway Letters, the Correspondence of Anne, Viscountess Conway, Henry More, and Their Friends, 1642–1684*. London: Oxford University Press, 1930.

Nightingale, Benjamin. *Early Stages of the Quaker Movement in Lancashire*. London: Congregational Union of England &Wales, 1921.

Nightingale, Benjamin. *The Ejected of 1662, in Cumberland and Westmorland, Their Predecessors and Successors*. 2 vols. Manchester: University Press, 1911.

Nuttall, Geoffrey F., Early Quaker Letters from the Swarthmore MSS. to 1660, Calendared, Indexed and Annotated (Typed manuscript.) London: The Library, Friends House, 1952.

Ormsby-Lennon, Hugh. "From Shibboleth to Apocalypse: Quaker Speechways During the Puritan Revolution" in *Language, Self, and Society, a Social History of Language*, ed. by Peter Burke and Roy Porter. Cambridge: Polity Press, 1991.

The Oxford Companion to the Bible. ed. by Bruce M. Metzger and Michael D. Coogan. New York: Oxford University Press, 1993.

Oxford English Dictionary, Compact Edition, Complete text. Oxford: Oxford University Press, 1971.

Penn, William. *The Papers of William Penn*, ed. by Mary Dunn and Richard S. Dunn (and others). 5 vols. Philadelphia: University of Pennsylvania Press, 1981–1986.

Penney, Norman, ed. "Extracts From State Papers Relating to Friends, 1654–1672." *JFHS* Supplement 8–11; London: Headley Brothers, 1913.

Penney, Norman, ed. *The First Publishers of Truth, Being Early Records (now first printed) of the Introduction of Quakerism into the Counties of England and Wales.* London: Headley Brothers, 1907.

Prior, Mary, ed. *Women in English Society, 1500–1800.* London: Methuen, 1985.

Quaker History, The Bulletin of the Friends Historical Association. Haverford, Pennsylvania.

Ross, Isabel. *Margaret Fell, Mother of Quakerism.* 2nd ed. York: William Sessions Book Trust, 1984.

Ruether, Rosemary Radford. "Prophets and Unmanists: Types of Religious Feminism in Stuart England" in *Journal of Religion* 70:1–18 (1990).

Seaver, Paul S. *Wallington's World, a Puritan Artisan in Seventeenth-Century London.* London: Methuen, 1985.

Smith, Hilda L. *Reason's Disciples, Seventeenth-Century English Feminists.* Urbana: University of Illinois, 1982.

Smith, Joseph. *Bibliotheca Anti-Quakeriana; or A Catalogue of Books Adverse to the Society of Friends.* London: Joseph Smith, 1873; New York: Kraus Reprint Co., 1968.

Story, Christopher. "Life of Christopher Story." In *Friends' Library* 1:150.

Tayler, Edward. *Upon the Types of the Old Testament.* 2 vols. Lincoln: University of Nebraska, 1989.

Tolles, Frederick B. *The Atlantic Community of the Early Friends.* London: JFHS Suppl. 24, 1952.

Wallace, T. H. S. *A Sincere and Constant Love: An Introduction to the Work of Margaret Fell.* Richmond, Ind.: Friends United Press, 1992.

Walvin, James. *The Quakers, Money and Morals.* London: John Murray, 1997.

Webb, Maria. *The Fells of Swarthmoor Hall and their Friends.* 2nd ed. London: F. Bowyer Kitto, 1867.

Scriptural References

The Old Testament

THE NEW TESTAMENT

Subject Index

(Numbers in bold indicate pages with identifications. Numbers in italics refer to illustrations in the text. See Appendix E for major themes in M.F.'s letters.)

ROSEMARY MOORE is an independent scholar who lives in England. She is the author of *The Light in Their Consciences: Early Quakers in Britain, 1646-1666* (University of Pennsylvania Press, 2000. Rosemary Moore is a member of the Executive Committee and is president of the Friends Historical Society (London).

Related Books from Friends United Press

A Living Faith: An Historical and Comparative Study of Quaker Beliefs (Cooper)
George Fox and the Quakers (Sharman)
George Fox's 'Book of Miracles'
Journal of George Fox (ed. Jones)
The Power of the Lord is Over All: The Pastoral Letters of George Fox (ed. Jones)
Reasons for Hope: The Faith and Future and the Friends Church (Punshon)